THE WORKS OF JOHN DRYDEN

General Editor

H. T. SWEDENBERG, JR.

Associate General Editors

GEORGE R. GUFFEY

ALAN ROPER

Textual Editor

VINTON A. DEARING

BAYES EXPLAINING THAT HE WROTE THE PART OF
"ARMARILLIS" FOR HIS MISTRESS:
ACT I, SCENE I, *The Rehearsal*
FROM *The Works of Buckingham* (1715), II

VOLUME XI

The Works
of John Dryden

Plays

THE CONQUEST OF GRANADA
MARRIAGE A-LA-MODE
THE ASSIGNATION

University of California Press

Berkeley   Los Angeles   London

1978

UNIVERSITY OF CALIFORNIA PRESS
Berkeley and Los Angeles, California

UNIVERSITY OF CALIFORNIA PRESS, LTD.
London, England

*The copy texts of this edition have been drawn in the
main from the Dryden Collection of the
William Andrews Clark Memorial Library*

Midwest out., 1979

*With Especial Gratitude for Their
Timely Efforts and Assistance
and for Their
Continuing Support of This Edition
the Editors Dedicate This Volume to
Charles E. Young
Chancellor, the University of California, Los Angeles,
and to
Robert Vosper
Director, the William Andrews Clark Memorial Library,
U C L A*

The preparation of this volume of the California edition of The Works of John Dryden *has been made possible by a grant from the Editing Program of the National Endowment for the Humanities and by a matching grant from the UCLA Foundation.*

Preface

The plays in this volume were first performed and published within thirty months. But those thirty months—from late December 1670 to early June 1673—were so crucial in Dryden's theatrical career, their story so complicated, that an adequate commentary demanded the research and knowledge of more than one scholar. The editors divided their labors in this way: David Stuart Rodes wrote the commentary to Marriage A-la-Mode, *and is grateful to Dr. Jane L. Curry and Professor Robert D. Hume for reading a draft of it and suggesting improvements; Rodes also prepared the section on actors and actresses; George R. Guffey supplied the annotations to* The Assignation, *and John Loftis wrote the headnote, with Alan Roper contributing its concluding discussion of the play's first publication and dedication. H. T. Swedenberg, Jr., and Roper assisted the other editors in putting their commentaries into final form and contributed the commentary upon* The Conquest of Granada, *with Swedenberg writing the annotations to the play and postscript, Roper the annotations to the dedication and preface; Roper wrote the headnote, with Swedenberg researching and drafting the section on sources. Vinton A. Dearing provided the text for this volume.*

The editors are indebted to the following student assistants of the UCLA Department of English for helping to gather and verify materials used in the commentary and for assistance in preparing and proofreading the text: Jane Abelson, Laurence Behrens, Lynda Boose, Judith Carnes, Sandra Fischer, Susan Grayson, Faye Joseph, David Latt, Janette Lewis, Sharon McMurray, Christine Metteer, Susan Nierengarten, Frances Reed, Diana Van Zile and Robert Hunt.

The editors are grateful to Mrs. Geneva Phillips and Mrs. Grace Stimson for preparing the manuscript so carefully for the printer, and to the former for coordinating the work of editors and research assistants. Work on this volume, like work on previously published volumes in this edition, called for and received the generous assistance of the staff of the William Andrews Clark Memorial Library.

The production of such a volume in such an edition is inevitably expensive, and, in addition to the grants separately ac-

knowledged on a previous page, the editors received and are grateful for financial support from the UCLA Committee on Research. The editors are also grateful to Chancellor Charles E. Young of UCLA for sabbatical leaves during the period when they were preparing this volume.

A. R.

Contents

Illustrations

THE CONQUEST OF GRANADA

BY THE SPANIARDS

THE FIRST PART

The Conqueſt

OF

GRANADA

BY THE

SPANIARDS:

In Two Parts.

Aɖed at the *Theater-Royall*.

Written by *JOHN DRYDEN* Servant
to His Majeſty.

—————*Major rerum mihi naſcitur Ordo;
Majus Opus moveo.* Virg: Æneid: 7.

In the *SAVOY*,
Printed by *T. N.* for *Henry Herringman*, and are to
be ſold at the *Anchor* in the Lower Walk
of the *New Exchange.* 1672.

To *His ROYAL HIGHNESS*
The DUKE.

SIR,

HEROIQUE Poesie has alwayes been sacred to Princes and to Heroes. Thus *Virgil* inscrib'd his *Æneids* to *Augustus Cæsar*; and, of latter Ages, *Tasso* and *Ariosto* dedicated their Poems to the house of *Est*. 'Tis, indeed, but justice, that the most excellent and most profitable kind of writing, should be addressed by Poets to such persons whose Characters have, for the most part, been the guides and patterns of their imitation. And Poets, while they imitate, instruct. The feign'd Heroe in-
10 flames the true: and the dead vertue animates the living. Since, therefore, the World is govern'd by precept and Example; and both these can onely have influence from those persons who are above us, that kind of Poesy which excites to vertue the greatest men, is of greatest use to humane kind.

'Tis from this consideration, that I have presum'd to dedicate to your Royal Highness these faint representations of your own worth and valour in Heroique Poetry: or, to speak more properly, not to dedicate, but to restore to you those Ideas, which, in the more perfect part of my characters, I have taken from you.
20 Heroes may lawfully be delighted with their own praises, both as they are farther incitements to their vertue, and as they are the highest returns which mankind can make them for it.

And certainly, if ever Nation were oblig'd either by the conduct, the personal valour, or the good fortune of a Leader, the *English* are acknowledging, in all of them, to your Royal Highness. Your whole life has been a continu'd Series of Heroique Actions: which you began so early that you were no sooner nam'd in the world, but it was with praise and Admiration. Even the first blossomes of your youth paid us all that could be ex-
30 pected from a ripening manhood. While you practis'd but the rudiments of War you out-went all other Captains: and have

---

2 Heroes] F, D; *Heroes* Q1–5. [These and other sigla are identified in the Textual Notes.]

since found none to surpass, but your self alone. The opening
of your glory was like that of light: you shone to us from afar;
and disclos'd your first beams on distant Nations: yet so, that
the lustre of them was spred abroad, and reflected brightly on
your native Country. You were then an honour to it, when it
was a reproach to it self: and, when the fortunate Usurper sent
his arms to *Flanders,* many of the adverse party were vanquish'd
by your fame, e're they try'd your valour. The report of it drew
over to your Ensigns whole Troops and Companies of converted
Rebels: and made them forsake successfull wickedness to follow
an oppress'd and exil'd vertue. Your reputation wag'd war with
the Enemies of your royal family, even within their trenches;
and the more obstinate, or more guilty of them, were forc'd to
be spyes over those whom they commanded: lest the name of
YORK should disband that Army in whose fate it was to defeat
the *Spaniards,* and force *Dunkirk* to surrender. Yet, those victorious forces of the Rebells were not able to sustain your arms:
where you charg'd in person you were a Conqueror: 'tis true
they afterwards recover'd Courage; and wrested that Victory
from others which they had lost to you. And it was a greater
action for them to rally than it was to overcome. Thus, by the
presence of your Royal Highness, the *English* on both sides remain'd victorious: and that Army, which was broken by your
valour, became a terror to those for whom they conquer'd. Then
it was that at the cost of other Nations you inform'd and culti-
vated that Valour which was to defend your native Country, and
to vindicate its honour from the insolence of our incroaching
Neighbours. When the *Hollanders,* not contented to withdraw
themselves from the obedience which they ow'd their lawful
Sovereign, affronted those by whose Charity they were first protected: and, (being swell'd up to a preheminence of Trade, by
a supine negligence on our side, and a sordid parsimony on their
own,) dar'd to dispute the Soveraignty of the Seas; the eyes of
three Nations were then cast on you: and, by the joynt suffrage
of King and People, you were chosen to revenge their common

---

injuries; to which, though you had an undoubted title by your birth, you had yet a greater by your courage. Neither did the success deceive our hopes and expectations: the most glorious victory which was gain'd by our Navy in that war, was in that first engagement: wherein, even by the confession of our enemies, who ever palliate their own losses, and diminish our advantages, your absolute triumph was acknowledg'd: you conquer'd at the *Hague* as intirely as at *London*; and the return of a shatter'd Fleet, without an Admiral, left not the most impudent among

10 them the least pretence for a false bon-fire, or a dissembled day of publick Thanks-giving. All our atchievements against them afterwards, though we sometimes conquer'd and were never overcome, were but a copy of that victory: and they still fell short of their original: somewhat of fortune was ever wanting, to fill up the title of so absolute a defeat. Or, perhaps, the Guardian Angel of our Nation was not enough concern'd when you were absent: and would not employ his utmost vigour for a less important stake than the life and honor of a Royal Admiral.

And, if since that memorable day, you have had leisure to

20 enjoy in peace the fruits of so glorious a reputation, 'twas occasion onely has been wanting to your courage; for, that can never be wanting to occasion. The same ardor still incites you to Heroique actions: and the same concernment for all the interests of your King and Brother, continue to give you restless nights, and a generous emulation for your own glory. You are still meditating on new labours for your self, and new triumphs for the Nation; and when our former enemies again provoke us, you will again solicite fate to provide you another Navy to overcome, and another Admiral to be slain. You will, then, lead

30 forth a Nation eager to revenge their past injuries: and, like the *Romans*, inexorable to Peace, till they have fully vanquish'd. Let our Enemies make their boast of a surprise; as the *Samnites* did of a successful stratagem: but the *Furcæ Caudinæ* will never be forgiv'n till they are reveng'd. I have alwaies observ'd in your

1   injuries;] Q2–5, F, D; ~. Q1.

7   acknowledg'd:] Q2–5, F, D; ~. Q1.

14 original:] Q2–5, F; ~. Q1; ~; D.

22 The] Q3–5, F, D; the Q1–2.

27 Nation;] Q2–5, F, D; ~. Q1.

3   expectations:] Q2–5, F, D; ~. Q1.

8   *London;*] Q2–5, F, D; ~. Q1.

15 Or] Q2–5, D; or Q1.

25 You] Q2–5, F, D; you Q1.

Royal Highness an extream concernment for the honour of your Country: 'tis a passion common to you with a Brother, the most excellent of Kings: and in your two persons, are eminent the Characters which *Homer* has given us of Heroique vertue: the commanding part in *Agamemnon*, and the executive in *Achilles*. And I doubt not, from both your actions, but to have abundant matter to fill the Annals of a glorious Reign: and to perform the part of a just Historian to my Royal Master, without inter-mixing with it any thing of the Poet.

In the mean time, while your Royal Highness is preparing fresh employments for our pens: I have been examining my own forces, and making tryal of my self how I shall be able to trans-mit you to Posterity. I have form'd a Heroe, I confess, not abso-lutely perfect, but of an excessive and overboyling courage: but *Homer* and *Tasso* are my precedents. Both the *Greek* and the *Italian* Poet had well consider'd that a tame Heroe who never transgresses the bounds of moral vertue, would shine but dimly in an Epick poem; the strictness of those Rules might well give precepts to the Reader, but would administer little of occasion to the writer. But a character of an excentrique vertue is the more exact Image of humane life, because he is not wholy ex-empted from its frailties. Such a person is *Almanzor:* whom I present, with all humility, to the Patronage of your Royal High-ness. I design'd in him a roughness of Character, impatient of injuries; and a confidence of himself, almost approaching to an arrogance. But these errors are incident only to great spirits; they are moles and dimples which hinder not a face from being beautifull; though that beauty be not regular; they are of the number of those amiable imperfections which we see in Mis-trisses: and which we pass over, without a strict examination, when they are accompanied with greater graces. And such, in *Almanzor*, are a frank and noble openness of Nature: an easiness

2 Country:] Q2–5, F; ~∧ Q1; ~; D.   3 and] Q2–5, F, D; aud Q1.

14 perfect,] Q2–5, F, D; ~: Q1.   14 courage:] Q2–5, F; ~. Q1; ~; D.

15 Both] Q2–5, F, D; both Q1.   15 *Greek*] Q5, F, D; Greek Q1–4.

16 *Italian*] Q5, F, D; Italian Q1–4.   18 poem;] Q2–5, F, D; ~. Q1.

21 he is] Q3–5, F, D; he Q1–2.   22 Such] F; such Q1–5, D.

26 But] Q2–5, F, D; but Q1.   26 spirits;] Q2–5, F, D; ~. Q1.

28 regular;] Q2–5, F, D; ~. Q1.

to forgive his conquer'd enemies; and to protect them in distress; and above all, an inviolable faith in his affection. This, Sir, I have briefly shaddow'd to your Royal Highness, that you may not be asham'd of that Heroe whose protection you undertake. Neither would I dedicate him to so illustrious a name, if I were conscious to my self that he did or said any thing, which was wholy unworthy of it. However, since it is not just that your Royal Highness shou'd defend or own, what, possibly, may be my errour, I bring before you this accus'd *Almanzor*, in the

10 nature of a suspected Criminal. By the suffrage of the most and best he already is acquitted; and by the sentence of some, condemn'd. But, as I have no reason to stand to the award of my Enemies, so neither dare I trust the partiality of my friends. I make my last appeal to your Royal Highness, as to a Soveraign Tribunal. Heroes shou'd onely be judg'd by Heroes; because they onely are capable of measuring great and Heroick actions by the rule and standard of their own. If *Almanzor* has fail'd in any point of Honor, I must therein acknowledge that he deviates from your Royal Highness, who are the patern of it. But, if

20 at any time he fulfils the parts of personal Vallour and of conduct, of a Souldier, and of a General; or, if I could yet give him a Character more advantagious than what he has; of the most unshaken friend, the greatest of Subjects, and the best of Masters, I shou'd then draw to all the world, a true resemblance of your worth and vertues; at least as farr as they are capable of being copied, by the mean abilities of

Sir,

Your Royal Highnesse's
Most humble and most
obedient Servant

J. DRYDEN.

OF HEROIQUE PLAYES.

An Essay.

WHETHER Heroique verse ought to be admitted into serious Playes, is not now to be disputed: 'tis already in possession of the Stage: and I dare confidently affirm, that very few Tragedies, in this Age, shall be receiv'd without it. All the arguments, which are form'd against it, can amount to no more than this, that it is not so near conversation as Prose; and therefore not so natural. But it is very clear to all, who understand Poetry, that serious Playes ought not to imitate Conversation too nearly. If nothing were to be rais'd above that level, the foundation of Poetry would be destroy'd. And, if you once admit of a Latitude, that thoughts may be exalted, and that Images and Actions may be rais'd above the life, and describ'd in measure without Rhyme, that leads you insensibly, from your own Principles to mine: You are already so far onward of your way, that you have forsaken the imitation of ordinary converse. You are gone beyond it; and, to continue where you are, is to lodge in the open field, betwixt two Inns. You have lost that which you call natural, and have not acquir'd the last perfection of Art. But it was onely custome which cozen'd us so long: we thought, because *Shakespear* and *Fletcher* went no farther, that there the Pillars of Poetry were to be erected: That, because they excellently describ'd Passion without Rhyme, therefore Rhyme was not capable of describing it. But time has now convinc'd most men of that Error. 'Tis indeed, so difficult to write verse, that the Adversaries of it have a good plea against many who undertake that task, without being form'd by Art or Nature for it. Yet, even they who have written worst in it, would have written worse without it. They have cozen'd many with their

---

10   And] Q2–5, F, D; *and* Q1.   17   You] Q2–5, F, D; *Yon* Q1.
21   erected:] ~. Q1–5, F, D.   23   But] Q2–5, F, D; *but* Q1.
28   They] Q2–5, F, D; *they* Q1.

sound, who never took the pains to examine their sence. In fine, they have succeeded: though 'tis true they have more dishonour'd Rhyme by their good Success than they could have done by their ill. But I am willing to let fall this argument: 'tis free for every man to write, or not to write, in verse, as he judges it to be, or not to be his Tallent; or as he imagines the Audience will receive it.

For Heroick Plays, (in which onely I have us'd it without the mixture of Prose) the first light we had of them on the *English* Theatre was from the late Sir *William D'Avenant:* It being forbidden him in the Rebellious times to act Tragedies and Comedies, because they contain'd some matter of Scandal to those good people, who could more easily dispossess their lawful Sovereign than endure a wanton jeast; he was forc'd to turn his thoughts another way: and to introduce the examples of moral vertue, writ in verse, and perform'd in Recitative Musique. The Original of this musick and of the Scenes which adorn'd his work, he had from the *Italian* Opera's: but he heightn'd his Characters (as I may probably imagine) from the example of *Corneille* and some *French* Poets. In this Condition did this part of Poetry remain at his Majesties return: When growing bolder, as being now own'd by a publick Authority, he review'd his *Siege of Rhodes,* and caus'd it to be acted as a just Drama; but as few men have the happiness to begin and finish any new project, so neither did he live to make his design perfect: There wanted the fulness of a Plot, and the variety of Characters to form it as it ought: and, perhaps, something might have been added to the beauty of the stile: All which he would have perform'd with more exactness had he pleas'd to have given us another work of the same nature. For my self and others, who come after him, we are bound, with all veneration to his memory, to acknowledge what advantage we receiv'd from that excellent

---

9–10   *English* Theatre] English Theatre Q1–5, F, D.
16   in Recitative Musique] *in* Recitative Musique Q1–5, F, D.
18   *Italian* Opera's] Italian Opera's Q1–5, F, D.
20   *French* Poets] F; French Poets Q1–5, D.
21   return:] ∼. Q1–5, F, D (*recurn* Q1).
23   just Drama] *just* Drama Q1–5, F, D.
28   stile:] ∼. Q1–5, F, D.

ground-work which he laid: and, since it is an easy thing to add to what already is invented, we ought all of us, without envy to him, or partiality to our selves, to yield him the precedence in it.

Having done him this justice, as my guide; I may do my self so much, as to give an account of what I have perform'd after him. I observ'd then, as I said, what was wanting to the perfection of his *Siege of Rhodes:* which was design, and variety of Characters. And in the midst of this consideration, by meer accident, I open'd the next Book that lay by me, which was an *Ariosto* in *Italian;* and the very first two lines of that Poem gave me light to all I could desire.

> *Le Donne, I Cavalier, L'arme, gli amori,*
> *Le Cortesie, l'audaci imprese jo canto,* &c.

for the very next reflection which I made was this, That an Heroick Play ought to be an imitation, in little of an Heroick Poem: and, consequently, that Love and Valour ought to be the Subject of it. Both these, Sir *William D'Avenant* had begun to shadow: but it was so, as first Discoverers draw their Maps, with headlands, and Promontories, and some few out-lines of somewhat taken at a distance, and which the designer saw not clearly. The common Drama oblig'd him to a Plot well-form'd and pleasant, or, as the Antients call'd it, one entire and great Action: but this he afforded not himself in a story, which he neither fill'd with Persons, nor beautified with Characters, nor varied with Accidents. The Laws of an Heroick Poem did not dispence with those of the other, but rais'd them to a greater height: and indulg'd him a farther liberty of Fancy, and of drawing all things as far above the ordinary proportion of the Stage, as that is beyond the common words and actions of humane life: and therefore, in the scanting of his Images, and design, he comply'd not enough with the greatness and Majesty of an Heroick Poem.

I am sorry I cannot discover my opinion of this kind of writing, without dissenting much from his, whose memory I love and honour. But I will do it with the same respect to him as if

---

13   *audaci*] Q2–5, F, D; audace Q1.
21   common Drama] *common* Drama Q1–5, F, D.

he were now alive, and overlooking my Paper while I write. His judgment of an Heroick Poem was this, *That it ought to be dress'd in a more familiar and easy shape: more fitted to the common actions and passions of humane life: and, in short, more like a glass of Nature, showing us our selves in our ordinary habits: and figuring a more practicable vertue to us, then was done by the Antients or Moderns:* thus he takes the Image of an Heroick Poem from the Drama, or stage Poetry: and accordingly, intended to divide it into five Books, representing the same num-
10 ber of Acts; and every Book into several Canto's, imitating the Scenes which compose our Acts.

But this, I think, is rather a Play in Narration (as I may call it) than an Heroick Poem: If at least you will not prefer the opinion of a single man to the practice of the most excellent Authors both of Antient and latter ages. I am no admirer of Quotations; but you shall hear, if you please, one of the Ancients delivering his judgment on this question: 'tis *Petronius Arbiter,* the most elegant; and one of the most judicious Authors of the *Latine* tongue: who, after he had given many admirable rules, for the
20 structure, and beauties of an Epick Poem, concludes all in these following words:

Non enim res gestæ versibus comprehendendæ sunt; quod longè melius Historici faciunt: sed, per ambages, Deorumque ministeria, præcipitandus est liber Spiritus, ut potius furentis animi vaticinatio appareat, quam religiosæ orationis, sub testibus, fides.

In which sentence, and in his own Essay of a Poem, which immediately he gives you, it is thought he taxes *Lucan;* who follow'd too much the truth of history, crowded Sentences together,
30 was too full of points, and too often offer'd at somewhat which had more of the sting of an Epigram, than of the dignity and state of an Heroick Poem. *Lucan* us'd not much the help of his heathen Deities, there was neither the ministry of the Gods, nor

---

1   write. His] F, D; *write. his* Q1; *write, his* Q2–5.
8   the Drama] *the* Drama Q1–5, F, D.
10   several Canto's] *several* Canto's Q1–5, F, D.
13   Poem:] ∼. Q1–5, D; ∼; F.
18   the *Latine*] Q2–5, F, D; *the Latine* Q1.
22   *comprehendendæ*] Q2–5, F, D; comprehendæ Q1.

the precipitation of the Soul, nor the fury of a Prophet, (of which my Author speaks) in his *Pharsalia:* he treats you more like a Philosopher, than a Poet: and instructs you, in verse, with what he had been taught by his Uncle *Seneca,* in Prose. In one word, he walks soberly, a foot, when he might fly. Yet *Lucan* is not al-wayes this Religious historian. The Oracle of *Appius,* and the witchcraft of *Erictho* will somewhat attone for him, who was, indeed, bound up by an ill-chosen, and known argument, to fol-low truth, with great exactness. For my part, I am of opinion,
10 that neither *Homer, Virgil, Statius, Ariosto, Tasso,* nor our *English Spencer* could have form'd their Poems half so beautiful, without those Gods and Spirits, and those Enthusiastick parts of Poetry, which compose the most noble parts of all their writ-ings. And I will ask any man who loves Heroick Poetry, (for I will not dispute their tastes who do not) if the Ghost of *Poly-dorus* in *Virgil,* the Enchanted wood in *Tasso,* and the Bower of bliss, in *Spencer* (which he borrows from that admirable *Italian*) could have been omitted without taking from their works some of the greatest beauties in them. And if any man object the im-
20 probabilities of a spirit appearing, or of a Palace rais'd by Mag-ick, I boldly answer him, that an Heroick Poet is not ty'd to a bare representation of what is true, or exceeding probable: but that he may let himself loose to visionary objects, and to the representation of such things, as depending not on sence, and therefore not to be comprehended by knowledge, may give him a freer scope for imagination. 'Tis enough that in all ages and Religions, the greatest part of mankind have believ'd the power of Magick, and that there are Spirits, or Spectres, which have appear'd. This I say is foundation enough for Poetry: and I dare
30 farther affirm that the whole Doctrine of separated beings, whether those Spirits are incorporeal substances, (which Mr. *Hobbs,* with some reason thinks to imply a contradiction,) or that they are a thinner and more Aerial sort of bodies (as some of the Fathers have conjectur'd) may better be explicated by Poets, than by Philosophers or Divines. For their speculations on this subject are wholy Poetical; they have only their fancy

---

6   The] Q2–5, F, D; *the* Q1.   14   And] Q2–5, F, D; *and* Q1.
19   And] Q2–5, F, D; *and* Q1.

for their guide, and that, being sharper in an excellent Poet, than it is likely it should in a phlegmatick, heavy gown-man, will see farther, in its own Empire, and produce more satisfactory notions on those dark and doubtful Problems.

Some men think they have rais'd a great argument against the use of Spectres and Magique in Heroique Poetry, by saying, They are unnatural: but, whether they or I believe there are such things, is not material, 'tis enough that, for ought we know, they may be in Nature: and what ever is or may be, is not, prop-
10 erly, unnatural. Neither am I much concern'd at Mr. *Cowleys* verses before *Gondibert;* (though his authority is almost sacred to me:) 'Tis true, he has resembled the old Epique Poetry to a fantastique fayery-land: but he has contradicted himself by his own Example. For, he has himself made use of Angels, and Visions in his *Davideis,* as well as *Tasso* in his *Godfrey.*

What I have written on this Subject will not be thought digression by the Reader, if he please to remember what I said in the beginning of this Essay, that I have modell'd my Heroique Playes, by the Rules of an Heroique Poem. And, if that be the
20 most noble, the most pleasant and the most instructive way of writing in verse, and, withall, the highest patern of humane life, as all Poets have agreed, I shall need no other Argument to justifie my choice in this imitation. One advantage the Drama has above the other, namely, that it represents to view, what the Poem onely does relate, and, *Segnius irritant animum demissa per aures, Quam quæ sunt oculis subjecta fidelibus,* as *Horace* tells us.

To those who object my frequent use of Drums and Trumpets; and my representations of Battels, I answer, I introduc'd them
30 not on the *English* Stage, *Shakespear* us'd them frequently: and, though *Jonson* shows no Battel in his *Catiline,* yet you hear from behind the Scenes, the sounding of Trumpets, and the shouts of fighting Armies. But, I add farther; that these warlike Instruments, and, even the representations of fighting on the Stage,

12 old Epique] Q3–5, F, D; *old* Epique Q1–2.
13 fayery-land] Q2–5, F, D; *fayery land* Q1.
23 the Drama] *the* Drama Q1–5, F, D.
30 the *English*] F, D; *the English* Q1–5.

are no more than necessary to produce the effects of an Heroick Play; that is, to raise the imagination of the Audience, and to perswade them, for the time, that what they behold on the Theater is really perform'd. The Poet is, then, to endeavour an absolute dominion over the minds of the Spectators: for, though our fancy will contribute to its own deceipt, yet a Writer ought to help its operation. And that the *Red Bull* has formerly done the same, is no more an Argument against our practice, than it would be for a Physician to forbear an approv'd medicine because a Mountebank has us'd it with success.

Thus I have given a short account of Heroick Plays. I might now, with the usual eagerness of an Author, make a particular defence of this. But the common opinion (how unjust soever,) has been so much to my advantage, that I have reason to be satis-fi'd: and to suffer, with patience, all that can be urg'd against it.

For, otherwise, what can be more easy for me, than to defend the character of *Almanzor*, which is one great exception that is made against the Play? 'Tis said that *Almanzor* is no perfect pat-tern of Heroick vertue: that he is a contemner of Kings; and that he is made to perform impossibilities.

I must therefore, avow, in the first place, from whence I took the Character. The first Image I had of him was from the *Achilles* of *Homer,* the next from *Tasso's Rinaldo,* (who was a copy of the former:) and the third from the *Artaban* of *Monsieur Cal-prenede:* (who has imitated both.) The original of these, (*Achil-les*) is taken by *Homer* for his Heroe: and is described by him as one, who in strength and courage surpass'd the rest of the *Gre-cian* Army: but, withall, of so fiery a temper, so impatient of an injury, even from his King, and General, that, when his Mistress was to be forc'd from him by the command of *Agamemnon,* he not onely disobey'd it; but return'd him an answer full of con-tumely; and in the most opprobrious terms he could imagine.

---

2   Play;] Q2–5, F, D; ~. Q1.

3–4   the Theater] *the* Theater Q1–5, F, D.

7   And] Q2–5, F, D; *and* Q1.

13   But] Q3–5, F, D; *but* Q1–2.

22   The first] Q2–5, F, D; *the first* Q1.

25   The] Q3–5, F, D; *the* Q1–2.

32   opprobrious] Q2, Q4–5, F, D; *approbrious* Q1, Q3.

They are *Homers* words which follow, and I have cited but some few amongst a multitude.

Οἰνοβαρὲς κυνὸς ὄμματ᾽ ἔχων, κραδίην δ᾽ ἐλάφοιο. *Il. α. v. 225.*

Δημοβόρος βασιλεύς, *&c. Il. α. v. 321.*

Nay, he proceeded so far in his insolence, as to draw out his sword, with intention to kill him.

Ἕλκετο δ᾽ ἐκ κολεοῖο μέγα ξίφος. *Il. α. v. 194.*

And, if *Minerva* had not appear'd, and held his hand, he had executed his design; and 'twas all she could do to diswade him
10 from it: the event was that he left the army; and would fight no more. *Agamemnon* gives his character thus to *Nestor*.

Ἀλλ᾽ ὅδ᾽ ἀνὴρ ἐθέλει περὶ πάντων ἔμμεναι ἄλλων,
Πάντων μὲν κρατέειν ἐθέλει, πάντεσσι δ᾽ ἀνάσσειν. *Il. α. v. 287, 288.*

And *Horace* gives the same description of him in his *Art of Poetry*.

————*Honoratum, si forte reponis Achillem,*
Impiger, iracundus, inexorabilis, Acer,
Jura neget sibi nata, nihil non arroget armis.

Tasso's chief Character, *Rinaldo*, was a man of the same tem-
20 per: for, when he had slain *Gernando*, in his heat of passion, he

---

1 They] *they* Q1–5, F, D.
3 Οἰνοβαρὲς] Οἰνοβαρὲ Q1–2; Οἰνοβαρὸς Q3–5, F, D.
3 ἐλάφοιο. *Il. α. v. 225.*] Q3–5, F, D; ἐλάφοιο : Q1–2.
4 βασιλεύς] D; βασιλεὺς Q1–2; βασιλεῦς Q3–5, F.
4 *&c. Il. α. v. 321.*] Q3–4; &c. Q1–2; Il. α. v. 321. Q5, F, D.
5 draw] Q2–5, F, D; ∼, Q1.
7 Ἕλκετο] D; Ἕλκετο Q1–5, F.
7 ξίφος. *Il. α. v. 194.*] Q3–5, F, D; ξίφος. Q1–2.
8 And, if] F; *and, if* Q1–5, D.
12 Ἀλλ᾽] D; Ἄλλ᾽ Q1–5; Ἄλλ᾽ F.
12 ὅδ᾽] Q3–5, F, D; ὁδ᾽ Q1; ὁδ᾽ Q2.
12 πάντων] Q3–5, F, D; ∼. Q1–2.
12 ἔμμεναι] Q3–5, F, D; ἐμμέναι Q1; ἐμμέναι Q2.
13 πάντεσσι] Q3–5, D; πάντεσσι Q1–2; παντέσσι F.
13 ἀνάσσειν. *Il. α. v. 287, 288.*] Q3–5, F, D (287. Q3–4; *between ll. 12 and 13 in Q3, on l. 12 in Q4–5, F, below l. 13 in D*); ἀνάσσειν. Q1–2.
14 And] F; *and* Q1–5, D.
14–15 his *Art of Poetry*] his *Art of Poetry* Q1–5, F, D.

not onely refus'd to be judg'd by *Godfrey,* his General, but threat-
n'd, that if he came to seize him, he would right himself by arms
upon him: witness these following lines of *Tasso.*

> *Venga egli, o mandi, jo terro fermo il piede;*
> *Giudici fian tra noi la sorte e l'arme:*
> *Fera tragedia vuol che s'appresenti*
> *Per lor diporto alle Nemiche genti.*

You see how little these great Authors did esteem the point of
Honour, so much magnified by the *French,* and so ridiculously
10 ap'd by us. They made their Hero's men of honour; but so, as
not to divest them quite of humane passions, and frailties. They
contented themselves to show you, what men of great spirits
would certainly do, when they were provok'd, not what they were
oblig'd to do by the strict rules of moral vertue. For my own
part, I declare my self for *Homer* and *Tasso;* and am more in
love with *Achilles* and *Rinaldo,* than with *Cyrus* and *Oroondates.* I shall never subject my characters to the *French* standard;
where Love and Honour are to be weigh'd by drams and scruples.
Yet, where I have design'd the patterns of exact vertue, such as
20 in this Play are the Parts of *Almahide,* of *Ozmyn,* and *Benzayda,*
I may safely challenge the best of theirs.

But *Almanzor* is tax'd with changing sides: And what tye has
he on him to the contrary? he is not born their Subject whom he
serves: and he is injur'd by them to a very high degree. He threatens them, and speaks insolently of Sovereign Power: but so do
Achilles and *Rinaldo;* who were Subjects and Soldiers to *Agamemnon* and *Godfrey* of *Bulloign.* He talks extravagantly in his
Passion: but, if I would take the pains to quote an hundred
passages of *Ben. Johnson's Cethegus,* I could easily shew you that
30 the Rhodomontades of *Almanzor* are neither so irrational as his,

---

2   him] Q2–5, F, D; *bim* Q1.   5   *e l'*] e' l' Q1; e'l' Q2–5, F; e'l D.
7   *diporto alle*] diporti a le Q1–5, F, D.
10   their Hero's] D; *their* Hero's Q1–5, F.
11   They] F; *they* Q1–5, D.   14   For] *for* Q1–5, F, D.
19   Yet] *yet* Q1–5, F, D.
24–25   He threatens] Q3–5, D; *he threatens* Q1–2.
27   He] F, D; *he* Q1–5.
30   the Rhodomontades] *the* Rhodomontades Q1–5, F, D.

nor so impossible to be put in execution. For *Cethegus* threatens to destroy Nature, and to raise a new one out of it: to kill all the Senate for his part of the action; to look *Cato* dead; and a thousand other things as extravagant, he sayes, but performs not one Action in the Play.

But none of the former calumnies will stick: and, therefore, 'tis at last charg'd upon me that *Almanzor* does all things: or if you will have an absurd Accusation, in their non-sence who make it, that he performs impossibilities. They say, that being a strang-
10 er he appeases two fighting factions, when the Authority of their Lawful Sovereign could not. This is, indeed, the most improbable of all his actions: but, 'tis far from being impossible. Their King had made himself contemptible to his people, as the History of *Granada* tells us. And *Almanzor*, though a stranger, yet, was already known to them, by his gallantry in the *Juego de toros,* his engagement on the weaker side, and, more especially, by the character of his person, and brave actions, given by *Abdalla* just before. And, after all, the greatness of the enterprize consisted onely in the daring: for, he had the Kings guards to second him.
20 But we have read both of *Cæsar,* and many other Generals, who have not onely calm'd a Mutiny with a word, but have presented themselves single before an Army of their enemies; which, upon sight of them, has revolted from their own Leaders, and come over to their trenches. In the rest of *Almanzors* actions, you see him for the most part victorious: but, the same fortune has constantly attended many Heroes who were not imaginary. Yet, you see it no Inheritance to him. For, in the first Part, he is made a Prisoner: and, in the last, defeated; and not able to preserve the City from being taken. If the History of the late Duke of *Guise*
30 be true, he hazarded more and perform'd not less in *Naples,* than *Almanzor* is feign'd to have done in *Granada.*

I have been too tedious in this Apology; but to make some satisfaction, I will leave the rest of my Play, expos'd to the Criticks, without defence.

1　For] F; *for* Q1–5, D.　　　　　9　They] F; *they* Q1–5, D.
11　Sovereign] Q4–5, F, D; *Soverign* Q1; *Soveraign* Q2–3.
11　This] F, D; *this* Q1–5.　　　　14　And] *and* Q1–5, F, D.
18　And] *and* Q1–5, F, D.　　　　20　But] F, D; *but* Q1–5.
27　For] F; *for* Q1–5, D.

The concernment of it is wholly past from me, and ought to be in them, who have been favorable to it, and are somewhat oblig'd to defend their own opinions. That there are errors in it, I deny not:

Ast opere in tanto fas est obrepere Somnum.

But I have already swept the stakes; and with the common good fortune of prosperous Gamesters, can be content to sit quietly; to hear my fortune curst by some, and my faults arraign'd by others, and to suffer both without reply.

PROLOGUE to the First Part.

Spoken by Mris. *Ellen Guyn* in a broad-brim'd hat, and wastbelt.

THIS jeast was first of t'other houses making,
And, five times try'd, has never fail'd of taking.
For 'twere a shame a Poet shoud be kill'd
Under the shelter of so broad a shield.
This is that hat whose very sight did win yee
To laugh and clap, as though the Devil were in yee.
As then, for Nokes, *so now, I hope, you'l be*
So dull, to laugh, once more, for love of me.
I'll write a Play, sayes one, for I have got
10   *A broad-brim'd hat, and wastbelt tow'rds a Plot.*
Sayes t'other, I have one more large than that.
Thus they out-write each other with a hat.
The brims still grew with every Play they writ;
And grew so large, they cover'd all the wit.
Hat was the Play: 'twas language, wit and tale:
Like them that find, Meat, drink, and cloth, in Ale.
What dulness do these Mungrill-wits confess
When all their hope is acting of a dress!
Thus two, the best Comedians of the Age
20   *Must be worn out, with being blocks o' th' Stage.*
Like a young Girl, who better things has known,
Beneath their Poets Impotence they groan.
See now, what Charity it was to save!
They thought you lik'd, what onely you forgave:
And brought you more dull sence, dull sence much worse
Than brisk, gay Non-sence; and the heavyer Curse.
They bring old Ir'n, and glass upon the Stage,
To barter with the Indians *of our Age.*

---

11   *that.*] Q3–5, F, D; ∼: Q1–2.
25   *sence, dull sence*] Q3–5, F, D; *sence. -dull sence*, Q1; *sence, dull sence*, Q2.
28   Indians] Q5, F, D; *Indians* Q1–4.

Still they write on; and like great Authors show: ⎞
30 *But 'tis as Rowlers in wet gardens grow;* ⎬
Heavy with dirt, and gath'ring as they goe. ⎠
May none who have so little understood
To like such trash, presume to praise what's good!
And may those drudges of the Stage, whose fate
Is, damn'd dull farce more dully to translate,
Fall under that excise the State thinks fit
To set on all French *wares, whose worst, is wit.*
French *farce worn out at home, is sent abroad;*
And, patch'd up here, is made our English *mode.*
40 *Hence forth, let Poets, 'ere allow'd to write,*
Be search'd, like Duellists, before they fight,
For wheel-broad hats, dull humour, all that chaffe,
Which makes you mourn, and makes the Vulgar *laugh.*
For these, in Playes, are as unlawful Arms,
As, in a Combat, Coats of Mayle, and Charms.

---

37   French] Q5, F, D; *French* Q1–4.   38   French] Q5, F, D; *French* Q1–4.
39   English] Q5, F, D; *English* Q1–4.

Persons Represented.

MEN.

By

Mahomet Boabdelin, the last King of *Granada*. Mr. *Kynaston*.

Prince *Abdalla*, his Brother. ───────────Mr. *Lydall*.

Abdelmelech, chief of the *Abencerrages*. ────Mr. *Mohun*.

Zulema, chief of the *Zegrys*. ──────────Mr. *Harris*.

Abenamar, an old *Abencerrago*. ─────────Mr. *Cartwright*.

Selin, an old *Zegry*. ────────────────Mr. *Wintershall*.

Ozmyn, a brave young *Abencerrago*, son
   to *Abenamar*. ─────────────────} Mr. *Beeston*.

Hamet, brother to *Zulema*, a *Zegry*. ─────Mr. *Watson*.

Gomel, a *Zegry*. ──────────────────Mr. *Powell*.

Almanzor. ────────────────────Mr. *Hart*.

Ferdinand, King of *Spain*. ────────────Mr. *Littlewood*.

Duke of *Arcos*, his General. ──────────Mr. *Bell*.

Don Alonzo d'Aguilar, a *Spanish* Captain.

─────────

Abencerrages] D; Abencerrages Q1–5, F.
Zegrys] D; Zegrys Q1–5, F (*and similarly below with Zegry*).
Abencerrago] D; Abencerago Q1–2; Abencerrago Q3–5, F (*and similarly below*).
Ozmyn,] Q2–5, F, D; ~ₐ Q1.
Abenamar.] Q2–5, F, D; ~ₐ Q1.
Spain] Q2–5, F, D; Spain Q1.
Alonzo d'Aguilar,] Q3–5 (~~;), F, D; *Alonzo*, d'Aguilar; Q1–2.
Spanish] D; Spanish Q1–5, F.

WOMEN.

By

Almahide, Queen of *Granada.* ————————Mrs. *Ellen Guyn.*
Lyndaraxa, Sister to *Zulema*; a *Zegry* Lady. ——Mrs. *Marshall.*
Benzayda, daughter to *Selin.* ————————Mrs. *Bowtell.*
Esperanza, slave to the Queen. ——————Mrs. *Reeve.*
Halyma, slave to *Lyndaraxa.* ——————Mrs. *Eastland.*
Isabel, Queen of *Spain.* ————————Mrs. *James.*

Messengers, Guards, Attendants, Men and Women.

The SCENE, in *Granada*, and the Christian Camp besieging it.

Granada . . . Ellen] Q2–5, F, D; Granada . . . ~. Q1.
Esperanza,] Q2–5, F, D; ~ₐ Q1.
Isabel] Isabella Q1–5, F, D.
James] Q2–5, F, D; *Jeames* Q1.

ALMANZOR AND ALMAHIDE,

OR, THE

CONQUEST OF GRANADA.

The First Part.

Boabdelin, Abenamar, Abdelmelech, *Guards.*

Boab. Thus, in the Triumphs of soft Peace I reign;
And, from my Walls, defy the Powr's of *Spain*:
With pomp and Sports my Love I celebrate,
While they keep distance; and attend my State.
Parent to her whose eyes my Soul inthrall;   [*To* Aben.
Whom I, in hope, already Father call;
Abenamar, thy Youth these sports has known,
Of which thy age is now Spectator grown:
Judge-like thou sitst, to praise, or to arraign
10 The flying skirmish of the darted Cane:
But, when fierce Bulls run loose upon the Place,
And our bold *Moors* their Loves with danger grace,
Then, heat new bends thy slacken'd Nerves again,
And a short youth runs warm through every Vein.
   Aben. I must confess th' Encounters of this day
Warm'd me indeed, but quite another way:
Not with the fire of Youth; but gen'rous rage
To see the glories of my Youthful age
So far outdone.

---

s.d. Boabdelin, Abenamar, Abdelmelech,] Q5, F, D; *Boabdelin, Abenamar, Abdel-*
melech. Q1–4 (*Abdelmelech*, Q3–4).
4   and] Q2–5, F, D; & Q1.
5   *s.d.* Aben.] Q2–3, Q5, F, D; *Aben.* Q1, Q4.

20   *Abdel. Castile* could never boast, in all its pride,
     A pomp so splendid; when the lists set wide,
     Gave room to the fierce Bulls, which wildly ran
     In *Sierra Ronda,* 'ere the War began:
     Who, with high Nostrils, Snuffing up the Wind,
     Now stood, the Champions of the Salvage kind.
     Just opposite, within the circled place,
     Ten of our bold *Abencerrages* race
     (Each brandishing his Bull-spear in his hand,)
     Did their proud Ginnets gracefully command.
30   On their steel'd heads their demy-Lances wore
     Small pennons, which their Ladies colours bore.
     Before this Troop did Warlike *Ozmyn* goe;
     Each Lady as he rode, saluting low;
     At the chief stands, with reverence more profound,
     His well-taught Courser, kneeling, touch'd the ground;
     Thence rais'd, he sidelong bore his Rider on,
     Still facing, till he out of sight was gone.
         Boab. You praise him like a friend, and I confess
     His brave deportment merited no less.
40   *Abdelm.* Nine Bulls were launch'd by his victorious arm,
     Whose wary Ginnet, shunning still the harm,
     Seem'd to attend the shock; and then leap'd wide:
     Mean while, his dext'rous Rider, when he spy'd
     The beast just stooping; 'twixt the neck and head
     His Lance, with never erring fury, sped.
         Aben. My Son did well; and so did *Hamet* too;
     Yet did no more then we were wont to do;
     But what the stranger did, was more then man.
         Abdel. He finish'd all those Triumphs we began.
50   One Bull, with curld black head beyond the rest,
     And dew-laps hanging from his brawny chest,
     With nodding front awhile did daring stand,
     And with his jetty hoof spurn'd back the sand:
     Then, leaping forth, he bellow'd out aloud:
     Th' amaz'd assistants back each other crowd,

---

48   man.] Q3, D;∼: Q1–2, Q4–5, F.
55   crowd] crow'd Q1; croud Q2–5, F, D.

While, Monarch-like he rang'd the listed field:
Some toss'd, some goar'd, some, trampling down, he kill'd.
Th' ignobler *Moors*, from far, his rage provoke,
With woods of darts, which from his sides he shooke.
60 Mean time, your valiant Son who had before
Gain'd fame, rode round to every *Mirador*,
Beneath each Ladies stand, a stop he made;
And, bowing, took th' applauses, which they paid.
Just in that point of time, the brave unknown,
Approach'd the Lists.
    Boab. ——————I mark'd him, when alone
(Observ'd by all, himself observing none)
He enter'd first; and with a graceful pride
His fiery Arab, dextrously did guide:
Who, while his Rider every stand survay'd,
70 Sprung loose, and flew, into an Escapade:
Not moving forward, yet, with every bound,
Pressing, and seeming still to quit his ground.
What after pass'd——
Was far from the *Ventanna* where I sate,   [*To* Abdel.
But you were near; and can the truth relate.
    Abdel. Thus, while he stood, the Bull who saw this foe,
His easier Conquests proudly did forego:
And, making at him, with a furious bound,
From his bent forehead aim'd a double wound.
80 A rising Murmure, ran through all the field,
And every Ladies blood with fear was chill'd.
Some schriek'd, while others, with more helpful care,
Cry'd out aloud, Beware, brave youth, beware!
At this he turn'd, and, as the Bull drew near,
Shun'd, and receiv'd him on his pointed Spear.
The Lance broke short: the beast then bellow'd lowd,
And his strong neck to a new onset bow'd.
Th' undaunted youth——————

56 Monarch-like] Q2–5, F, D; Monach-like Q1.
58 *Moors*] Q2–3, D; Moors Q1, Q4–5, F.
61 *Mirador*] Mirador Q1–5, F, D.
74 *s.d.* Abdel.] Q2–3, Q5, F, D; *Abdel.* Q1, Q4.
83 Beware, brave] D; beware, brave Q1–5, F.

Then drew; and from his Saddle bending low, ⎫
90 Just where the neck did to the shoulders grow, ⎬
With his full force discharg'd a deadly blow. ⎭
Not heads of Poppies, (when they reap the grain)
Fall with more ease before the lab'ring Swayn,
Then fell this head:———
It fell so quick, it did even death prevent:
And made imperfect bellowings as it went.
Then all the Trumpets Victory did sound:
And yet their clangors in our shouts were drown'd.
                                [A confus'd noise within.
    Boab. Th' Alarm-bell rings from our *Alhambra* walls,
100 And, from the Streets, sound Drums, and *Ataballes.*
                      [Within, a Bell, Drumms & Trumpets.
How now! from whence proceed these new alarms?

              To them a Messenger.

    Mess. The two fierce factions are again in arms:
And, changing into blood the dayes delight,
The *Zegrys* with th' *Abencerrages* fight,
On each side their Allies and Friends appear;
The *Maças* here, the *Alabezes* there:
The *Gazuls* with th' *Abencerrages* joyn,
And, with the *Zegrys,* all great *Gomels* line.
    Boab. Draw up behind the *Vivarambla* place;
110 Double my guards, these factions I will face;
And try if all the fury they can bring
Be proof against the presence of their King.
                                    [Exit Boabdelin.

    The Factions appear; At the head of the Abencerrages,
Ozmyn; *at the head of the* Zegrys, Zulema, Hamet, Gomel,

---

100   *Ataballes*] Ataballes Q1–5, F, D.
101+   *s.d. To*] [∼ Q1–5, F, D (*right justified*).
104   th' *Abencerrages*] Q2–3, D; the *Abencerrages* Q1, Q4–5, F.
107   th' *Abencerrages*] the *Bencerrages* Q1–5, D; the *Abencerrages* F.
112   King.] Q3, D; ∼: Q1–2, Q4–5, F.
112+   *s.d.* [*Exit*] Q4–5, F, D; ∧∼ Q1–3.
112+   *s.d.* Boabdelin] Q2–3, Q5, F, D; *Boabdelin* Q1, Q4.

and Selin: Abenamar *and* Abdelmelech *joyned with the* Abencerrages.

Zulema. The faint *Abencerrages* quit their ground:
Press 'em; put home your thrusts to every wound.
     Abdelmelech. Zegry, on manly force our Line relyes;
Thine, poorly takes th' advantage of surprize.
Unarm'd, and much outnumber'd we retreat;
You gain no fame, when basely you defeat:
If thou art brave, seek nobler Victory;   ⎫
120 Save *Moorish* blood; and, while our bands stand by,   ⎬
Let two to two an equal combat try.   ⎭
     Hamet. 'Tis not for fear the Combat we refuse;
But we our gain'd advantage will not loose.
     Zul. In combating, but two of you will fall;
And we resolve we will dispatch you all.
     Ozmyn. Wee'l double yet th' exchange before we dye;
And each of ours two lives of yours shall buy.

          Almanzor *enter's betwixt them, as they stand ready*
                         to engage.

     Almanz. I cannot stay to ask which cause is best;
But this is so to me because opprest.   [*Goes to the* Abencerrages.

     To them Boabdelin *and his Guards going betwixt them.*

130   *Boab.* On your Allegiance, I command you stay;
Who passes here, through me must make his way.
My life's the *Isthmos;* through this narrow line
You first must cut, before those Sea's can joyn.
What fury, *Zegrys,* has possest your minds,
What rage the brave *Abencerrages* blinds?
If, of your Courage you new proofs wou'd show,
Without much travel you may find a foe.
Those foes are neither so remote nor few,

112+   *s.d.* Abenamar] Q2–3, D; Abenamat Q1, Q4–5, F.
117   retreat;] F, D; ~ᴧ Q1; ~, Q2–5.   120   *Moorish*] D; Moorish Q1–5, F.
129   *s.d.* Abencerrages] Q5, F, D; *Abencerrages* Q1–4.

That you shou'd need each other to pursue.
140 Lean times, and foreign Warrs should minds unite,
When poor, men mutter, but they seldome fight.
O holy *Alha*, that I live to see
Thy *Granadins* assist their Enemy.
You fight the Christians battels; every life
You lavish thus, in this intestine strife,
Does from our weak foundations, take one prop
Which helpt to hold our sinking Country up.
      Ozmyn. 'Tis fit our private Enmity should cease;
Though injur'd first, yet I will first seek peace.
150   *Selin.* No, Murd'rer, no; I never will be won
To peace with him whose hand has slain my Son.
      Ozmyn. Our Prophets curse————
On me, and all th' *Abencerrages* light
If unprovok'd I with your Son did fight.
      Abdelmel. A band of *Zegry's* ran within the Place,
Match'd with a Troop of thirty of our race.
Your Son and *Ozmyn* the first squadrons led,
Which, ten by ten, like *Parthyans*, charg'd and fled.
The Ground was strow'd with Canes, where we did meet,
160 Which crackled underneath our Coursers feet.
When *Tarifa*, (I saw him ride apart)
Chang'd his blunt Cane for a steel-pointed Dart,
And meeting *Ozmyn* next,
Who wanted time for Treason to provide,
He, basely, threw it at him, undefy'd.
      Ozmyn. Witness this blood————which, when by Treason
            sought,
That follow'd, Sir, which to my self I ought.
      Zulema. His hate to thee was grounded on a grudge
Which all our generous *Zegrys* just did judge;
170 Thy villain blood thou openly didst place
Above the purple of our Kingly race.

150   *Selin.*] *Zulem.* Q1–5, F, D.
162   steel-pointed] Q2–3, D; steel pointed Q1, Q4–5, F.
165   undefy'd.] Q2–3, F, D; ~: Q1, Q4–5.
166   *Ozmyn.* Witness] Q2–3; [*Ozmyn showing his arm.* / Witness Q1, Q4–5; [*Ozmyn showing his Arm.* / *Osmyn.* Witness F; *Ozm.* [*showing his Arm.*] Witness D.

Boabd. From equal Stems their blood both houses draw,
They from *Morocco*, you from *Cordova.*

Hamet. Their mungril race is mixt with Christian breed,
Hence 'tis that they those Dogs in prisons feed.

Abdel. Our holy Prophet wills, that Charity
Shoud, ev'n to birds and beasts extended be:
None knows what fate is for himself design'd;
The thought of humane Chance should make us kind.

180   *Gomel.* We waste that time we to revenge shou'd give:
Fall on; let no *Abencerrago* live.   [*Advancing before the
rest of his Party.*

Almanz. Upon thy life pass not this middle space;

     [*Advancing on the other side; and
describing a line with his sword.*

Sure Death stands guarding the forbidden place.

Gomel. To dare that death, I will approach yet nigher,
Thus, wer't thou compass'd in with circling fire.

     [*They fight.*

Boab. Disarm 'em both; if they resist you, kill.

     [Almanzor, *in the midst of the Guards
kills* Gomel, *and then is disarmed.*

Almanz. Now, you have but the Leavings of my will.

Boab. Kill him; this insolent Unknown shall fall,
And be the Victime to attone you all.

190   *Ozmyn.* If he must die, not one of us will live,
That life he gave for us, for him we give.

Boab. It was a Traytors voice that spoke those words;
So are you all, who do not sheath your swords.

Zulema. Outrage unpunish'd when a Prince is by,
Forfeits to scorn the rights of Majesty:
No Subject his Protection can expect
Who, what he ows himself, does first neglect.

Abenamar. This stranger, Sir is he,
Who lately in the *Vivarambla* place

---

173 *Morocco*] Q2–5, F, D; *Marocco* Q1.   182 *Almanz.* Upon] F, D; Upon Q1–5.
182+ s.d. [*Advancing . . . sword.*] Almanzor, *advancing . . . sword.* Q1–5, F, D
(*preceding l. 182 in Q1–5, F; run in with s.d. for l. 181 in D;* [Almanzor, . . . F).
184 nigher,] ~. Q1–5, F; ~; D.   186+ s.d. [Almanzor] F, D; ∧~ Q1–5.

200 Did, with so loud applause, your Triumphs grace.
　　Boab. The word which I have giv'n, Ile not revoke;
If he be brave he's ready for the stroke.
　　Almanz. No man has more contempt than I, of breath;
But whence hast thou the right to give me death?
Obey'd as Soveraign by thy Subjects be,
But know, that I alone am King of me.
I am as free as Nature first made man ⎞
'Ere the base Laws of Servitude began ⎬
When wild in woods the noble Savage ran. ⎠
210 　　*Boab.* Since, then, no pow'r above your own you know,
Mankind shou'd use you like a common foe,
You shou'd be hunted like a Beast of Prey;
By your own law, I take your life away.
　　Almanz. My laws are made but only for my sake,
No King against himself a Law can make.
If thou pretendst to be a Prince like me,
Blame not an Act which should thy Pattern be.
I saw th' opprest, and thought it did belong
To a King's office to redress the wrong:
220 I brought that Succour which thou oughtst to bring,
And so, in Nature, am thy Subjects King.
　　Boab. I do not want your Councel to direct,
Or aid to help me punish or protect.
　　Almanz. Thou wantst 'em both, or better thou wouldst know
Then to let Factions in thy Kingdom grow.
Divided int'rests while thou thinkst to sway,
Draw like two brooks thy middle stream away:
For though they band, and jar, yet both combine
To make their greatness by the fall of thine.
230 Thus, like a buckler, thou art held in sight,
While they, behind thee, with each other fight.
　　Boab. Away; and execute him instantly.　　[*To his Guards.*
　　Almanz. Stand off; I have not leisure yet to dye.

To them Abdalla *hastily.*

202　stroke.] Q2–5, F, D; ~∧ Q1.
233+　*s.d. right justified* Q1–5, F, D (*with right bracket prefixed in Q2–4, F, D*).
233+　*s.d.* Abdalla] Q2–5, F, D; *Abdalla* Q1.

Abdalla. Hold, Sir, for Heav'n sake hold.
Defer this noble Strangers punishment,
Or your rash orders you will soon repent.
    Boab. Brother, you know not yet his insolence.
    Abdal. Upon your self you punish his offence:
If we treat gallant Strangers in this sort,
240 Mankind will shun th' inhospitable Court.
And who, henceforth, to our defence will come,
If death must be the brave *Almanzors* doom?
From *Africa* I drew him to your ayd;
And for his succour have his life betray'd.
    Boab. Is this th' *Almanzor* whom at *Fez* you knew,
When first their swords the *Xeriff* Brothers drew?
    Abdalla. This, Sir, is he who for the Elder fought,
And to the juster cause the Conquest brought:
Till the proud *Santo*, seated in the Throne,
250 Disdain'd the service he had done, to own:
Then, to the vanquish'd part, his fate he led;
The vanquish'd triumph'd, and the Victor fled;
Vast is his Courage; boundless is his mind,
Rough as a storm, and humorous as wind;
Honour's the onely Idol of his Eyes:
The charms of Beauty like a pest he flies:
And, rais'd by Valour, from a birth unknown,
Acknowledges no pow'r above his own.
    Boabdelin. Impute your danger to our ignorance;
                                        [*Coming to* Almanzor.
260 The bravest men are subject most to chance:
Granada much does to your kindness owe: ⎞
But Towns, expecting Sieges, cannot show ⎬
More honour, then t' invite you to a foe. ⎠
    Almanzor. I do not doubt but I have been to blame:
But, to pursue the end for which I came,

---

234 *Abdalla*] Q2–5, F, D; *Abdella* Q1.
257 unknown] Q2–5, F, D; unknwn Q1.
259 *Boabdelin.* Impute . . . ignorance; [*Coming to* Almanzor.] *Boabdelin coming*
to Almanzor. / Impute . . . ignorance; Q1–5, F, D ([Boabdelin Q4–5, F, D; Almanzor. / *Boab.* Impute D).
264 to] Q4–5, F, D; too Q1–3.

Unite your Subjects first; then let us goe,
And poure their common rage upon the foe.
    Boab. Lay down your Arms; and let me beg you cease
Your Enmities.   *[To the Factions.*
    Zulema. ———We will not hear of peace,
270 Till we by force have first reveng'd our slain.
    Abdel. The Action we have done we will maintain.
    Selin. Then let the King depart, and we will try
Our cause by armes.
    Zul. ———————For us and Victory.
    Boab. A King intreats you.
    Almanz. What Subjects will precarious Kings regard?
A Begger speaks too softly to be heard.
Lay down your Armes; 'tis I command you now.
Do it———or by our Prophets soul I vow,
My hands shall right your King on him I seize.
280 Now, let me see whose look but disobeys.
    Omnes. Long live King *Mahomet Boabdelin!*
    Alman. No more; but hush'd as midnight silence go:
He will not have your Acclamations now,
Hence you unthinking Crowd———
                    [The common people go off
                            on both parties.

Empire, thou poor and despicable thing,
When such as these unmake, or make a King!
    Abdalla. How much of vertue lies in one great Soul
Whose single force can multitudes controll!   *[Embracing him.*
                            [A trumpet within.

        Enter a Messenger.

268–269 *Boab.* Lay . . . cease / . . . [*To the Factions.*] *Boab. to the Factions.* / Lay
. . . cease Q1–5, F; *Boab.* [*To the Factions.*] Lay . . . cease D.
270 slain.] Q3, F, D; ~: Q1–2, Q4–5.   273 armes.] F, D; ~: Q1–5.
275 regard?] Q3, F, D; ~: Q1–2, Q4–5.   276 heard.] F; ~: Q1–5, D.
281 *Boabdelin!*] ~: Q1, Q4–5; ~. Q2–3, F, D.
282 but hush'd Q2–5, F, D; bu husht'd Q1.
284+ s.d. [*The*] Q2–5, F, D; ᴧ~ Q1.
288 s.d. *Embracing*] Q2–5, F, D; *embracing* Q1.
288+ s.d. [*A*] Q2–5, F, D; ᴧ~ Q1.
288+ s.d. *Enter a Messenger.*] Q2–5, F, D; Enter a Messenger. Q1.

Messen. The Duke of *Arcos*, Sir,———

290 Does with a trumpet from the Foe appear.

    Boab. Attend him, he shall have his Audience here.

Enter the Duke of Arcos.

    Arcos. The Monarchs of *Castile* and *Arragon* ⎞
Have sent me to you, to demand this Town: ⎬
To which their just, and rightful claim is known. ⎠

    Boab. Tell *Ferdinand* my right to it appears
By long possession of eight hundred years.
When first my Ancestors from *Affrique* sail'd,
In *Rodriques* death your *Gothique* title fail'd.

    Arcos. The Successours of *Rodrique* still remain;

300 And ever since have held some part of *Spain.*
Ev'n in the midst of your victorious pow'rs
Th' *Asturia's*, and all *Portugal* were ours.
You have no right, except you force allow;
And if yours then was just, so ours is now.

    Boab. 'Tis true; from force the noblest title springs;
I therefore hold from that, which first made Kings.

    Arcos. Since then by force you prove your title true,
Ours must be just; because we claim from you.
When with your Father you did joyntly reign,

310 Invading with your *Moores* the South of *Spain,*
I, who that day the Christians did command,
Then took; and brought you bound to *Ferdinand.*

    Boab. Ile hear no more; defer what you would say:
In private wee'l discourse some other day.

    Arcos. Sir, you shall hear, however you are loath,
That, like a perjur'd Prince, you broke your oath.
To gain your freedom you a Contract sign'd,
By which your Crown you to my King resign'd;
From thenceforth as his Vassail holding it,

320 And paying tribute, such as he thought fit:

291+   *s.d. Enter the Duke of* Arcos.] Q2–5, F, D; Enter the Duke of *Arcos.* Q1.
310   *Moores*] Q2–3, F, D; Moores Q1, Q4–5.
318   resign'd;] ~. Q1–5, F, D.

Contracting, when your Father came to dye,
To lay aside all marks of Royalty:
And at *Purchena* privately to live;
Which, in exchange, King *Ferdinand* did give.
   Boab. The force us'd on me, made that Contract voyd.
   Arcos. Why have you then its benefits enjoy'd?
By it you had not only freedome then,
But since had ayd of mony and of men.
And, when *Granada* for your Uncle held,
330 You were by us restor'd, and he expel'd.
Since that, in peace we let you reap your grain,
Recall'd our Troops that us'd to beat your Plain,
And more————
   Almanz. ————Yes, yes, you did with wondrous care
Against his Rebels prosecute the war,
While he secure in your protection, slept,
For him you took, but for your selves you kept.
Thus, as some fawning usurer does feed
With present summs th' unwary Unthrifts need;
You sold your kindness at a boundless rate,
340 And then orepaid the debt from his Estate:
Which, mouldring piecemeal, in your hands did fall;
Till now at last you came to swoop it all.
   Arcos. The wrong you do my King I cannot bear;
Whose kindness you would odiously compare.
Th' Estate was his; which yet, since you deny,
He's now content in his own wrong to buy.
   Almanz. And he shall buy it dear what his he calls:
We will not give one stone from out these Walls.
   Boab. Take this for answer, then————
350 What 'ere your arms have conquer'd of my land
I will, for peace, resign to *Ferdinand*:
To harder terms my mind I cannot bring;
But as I still have liv'd, will dye a King.
   Arcos. Since thus you have resolv'd, henceforth prepare
For all the last extremities of war:

---

325   voyd.] F, D; ~: Q1–5.   326   Why] Q2–5, F, D; Whey Q1.
341   your] Q2–5, F, D; you Q1.

My King his hope from heavens assistance draws.

    Almanz. The *Moors* have Heav'n and me t' assist their cause.

                                           [Exit Arcos.

Enter Esperanza.

    Esper. Fair *Almahide*

(Who did with weeping eyes these discords see,

360 And fears the omen may unlucky be:)

Prepares a *Zambra* to be danc'd this Night,

In hope soft pleasures may your minds unite.

    Boab. My Mistris gently chides the fault I made: ⎫

But tedious business has my love delay'd;   ⎬

Business, which dares the joyes of Kings invade. ⎭

    Almanz. First let us sally out, and meet the foe.

    Abdalla. Led on by you we unto Triumph goe.

    Boab. Then, with the day let war and tumult cease:

The night be sacred to our love and peace:

370 'Tis just some joyes on weary Kings should waite;

'Tis all we gain by being slaves of State.

                                     [Exeunt omnes.

ACT II.

Abdalla, Abdelmelech, Ozmyn, Zulema, Hamet,
as returning from the Sally.

    Abdal. This happy day does to *Granada* bring

A lasting peace; and triumphs to the King:

356   draws.] F, D; ∼: Q1–5.

357   *Moors*] Q2–3, F, D; Moors Q1, Q4–5.

357+ *s.d.* [*Exit*] Q4–5, F, D; ∧∼ Q1–3.

357+ *s.d. Enter* Esperanza.] Q2–5, F, D; Enter *Esperanza.* Q1.

358   *Almahide*] Q3, F, D; ∼. Q1–2, Q4–5.

360   omen] D; *omen* Q1–5, F.

366   foe.] F, D; ∼: Q1–5.

367   unto] Q3; to Q1–2; on to Q4–5, F, D.

370   should] Q2–5, F, D; shoul Q1.

371+ *s.d.* [*Exeunt*] Q4–5, F, D; ∧∼ Q1–3.

ACT] Q2–3, Q5, F, D; ∼. Q1, Q4.

s.d. Abdalla . . . *Sally.*] Q4–5, F, D (*Enter* Abdalla D); *romans and italics reversed in Q1–3.*

The two fierce factions will no longer jarr,
Since they have now been brothers in the war:
Those, who apart in Emulation fought,
The common danger to one body brought;
And to his cost the proud *Castillian* finds
Our *Moorish* Courage in united minds.
    Abdelmel. Since to each others ayd our lives we owe,
10 Loose we the name of Faction and of foe,
Which I to *Zulema* can bear no more,
Since *Lyndaraxa's* beauty I adore.
    Zul. I am oblig'd to *Lyndaraxa's* charms
Which gain the conquest I should loose by Arms;
And wish my Sister may continue fair
That I may keep a good,
Of whose possession I should else despair.
    Ozmyn. While we indulge our common happiness
He is forgot by whom we all possess;
20 The brave *Almanzor* to whose arms we owe
All that we did, and all that we shall do;
Who, like a Tempest that out rides the wind,
Made a just battle 'ere the bodies joyn'd.
    Abdalla. His Victories we scarce could keep in view,
Or polish 'em so fast as he rough drew.
    Abdel. Fate after him, below with pain did move,
And Victory could scarce keep pace above.
Death did at length so many slain forget;
And lost the tale, and took 'em by the great.

To them Almanzor, *with the Duke of* Arcos *prisoner.*

30   *Hamet.* See here he comes,
And leads in Triumph him who did command
The vanquish'd Army of King *Ferdinand.*

---

8 *Moorish*] Q2–3, F, D; Moorish Q1, Q4; moorish Q5.
12, 13 *Lyndaraxa's*] Q2–3; *Lindaraxa's* Q1, Q4–5, F, D (*and similarly throughout the act, unless noted*).
29+ *s.d. right justified in Q1–5, F, D.* ([*To* Q4–5, F, D).
32 *Ferdinand.*] F, D; ∼: Q1–5 (Ferdinand Q1).

Almanzor. Thus far your Masters arms a fortune find
Below the sweld ambition of his mind: [*To the Duke of* Arcos.
And *Alha* shuts a mis-believers raign
From out the best and goodliest part of *Spain.*
Let *Ferdinand Calabrian* Conquests make,
And from the *French* contested *Millan* take,
Let him new worlds discover to the old,
40 And break up shining Mountains big with Gold,
Yet he shall finde this small Domestique foe
Still sharp, and pointed to his bosome grow.
  Duke of Arc. Of small advantages too much you boast,
You beat the outguards of my Masters hoast:
This little loss in our vast body, shews
So small, that half have never heard the news.
Fame's out of breath 'ere she can fly so farr
To tell 'em all, that you have 'ere made warr.
  Almanz. It pleases me your Army is so great:
50 For now I know there's more to conquer yet.
By Heav'n I'le see what Troops you have behinde;
I'le face this Storm that thickens in the winde:
And, with bent forehead, full against it goe,
Till I have found the last and utmost foe.
  Duke. Believe you shall not long attend in vain;
To morrow's dawn shall cover all your Plain.
Bright Arms shall flash upon you from afar;
A wood of Launces, and a moving warr.
But I, unhappy in my bands, must yet
60 Be onely pleas'd to hear of your defeat:
And, with a slaves inglorious ease remain,
Till conquering *Ferdinand* has broke my chain.
  Almanz. Vain man, thy hopes of *Ferdinand* are weak!
I hold thy chain too fast for him to break.

33–34 *Almanzor.* Thus . . . find / . . . [*To the Duke of* Arcos.] *Almanzor* to the
Duke of *Arcos.* / Thus . . . find Q1; Almanzor *to the Duke of* Arcos. / Thus . . . find
Q2–5, F ([Almanzor Q4–5, F; *Almanz.* Thus F); *Almanz.* [*To the Duke of* Arcos.]
Thus . . . find D.
38 *French*] Q2–5, F, D; French Q1.
43 *Duke of Arc.*] Duke of *Arc.* Q1–5; *Duke of* Arc. F; D. *Arcos.* D.
44 You] Q2–5, F, D; Yout Q1.   56 dawn] Q2–5, F, D; daun Q1.

But since thou threatn'st us, I'le set thee free,
That I again may fight and conquer thee.
    Duke. Old as I am I take thee at thy word,
And will tomorrow thank thee with my sword.
    Almanz. I'le go and instantly acquaint the King:
70 And suddain orders for thy freedom bring.
Thou canst not be so pleas'd at Liberty,
As I shall be to find thou darst be free.

>   [*Exeunt* Almanzor, Arcos; *and*
>   *the rest; excepting only* Ab-
>   dalla *and* Zulema.

    Abdalla. Of all those Christians who infest this town,
This Duke of *Arcos* is of most renown.
    Zulema. Oft have I heard, that in your Fathers reign,
His bold Advent'rers beat the Neighbring Plain;
Then, under *Ponce Leon's* name he fought,
And from our Triumphs many Prizes brought:
Till in disgrace, from *Spain* at length he went,
80 And since, continued long in banishment.
    Abdalla. But see, your beauteous Sister does appear.

To them Lyndaraxa.

    Zulema. By my desire she came to find me here.

>   [Zulema *and* Lyndaraxa *whisper;*
>   *then* Zulema *goes out; and* Lyn-
>   daraxa *is going after.*

    Abdalla. Why, fairest *Lyndaraxa,* do you fly   [*Staying her.*
A Prince, who at your feet is proud to dye?
    Lyndaraxa. Sir I should blush to own so rude a thing,
As 'tis to shun the Brother of my King.   [*Staying.*

72+   *s.d.* [*Exeunt*] Q4–5, F, D; ‸~ Q1–3.
78   brought:] ~. Q1–5, F, D.
81+   *s.d. To*] [~ Q1–5, F, D (*right justified*).
81+   *s.d.* Lyndaraxa] Q2–3; *Lindaraxa* Q1; Lindaraxa Q4–5, F, D.
82   here.] D; ~: Q1–5, F.
82+   *s.d.* [Zulema] Q4–5, F, D; ‸~ Q1–3.
82+   *s.d.* Lyndaraxa (*bis*)] Q2–3; Lindaraxa Q1, Q4–5, F, D.
83 *s.d.,* 86 *s.d. Staying*] Q2–3, F, D; *staying* Q1, Q4–5.

Abdal. In my hard fortune I some ease should find
Did your disdain extend to all Mankind.
But give me leave to grieve, and to complain,
90 That you give others what I beg in vain.
   Lyndar. Take my Esteem, if you on that can live,
For, franckly, Sir, 'tis all I have to give.
If, from my heart you ask or hope for more,
I grieve the place is taken up before.
   Abdal. My Rivall merits you.
To *Abdelmelech* I will Justice doe,
For he wants Worth who dares not praise a Foe.
   Lynd. That for his Vertue, Sir, you make defence,
Shows in your own a Noble confidence:
100 But him defending, and excusing me,
I know not what can your advantage be.
   Abdal. I fain would ask, ere I proceed in this,
If, as by choice, you are by promise, his?
   Lyndar. Th' Engagement only in my Love does lye;
But that's a knot which you can ne're untye.
   Abdal. When Cities are besieg'd and treat to yeild,
If there appear Relievers from the Field,
The Flagg of Parley may be taken down,
Till the success of those without be known.
110   *Lyndar.* Though *Abdelmelech* has not yet possest,
Yet I have seal'd the Treaty for my brest.
   Abdal. Your Treaty has not ty'd you to a day,
Some chance might break it, would you but delay:
If I can judge the Secrets of your heart,
Ambition in it has the greatest part;
And wisdome then will shew some difference
Betwixt a private Person and a Prince.
   Lyndar. Princes are Subjects still:———
Subject and Subject can small diff'rence bring:
120 The diff'rence 'twixt Subjects and a King.
And since, Sir, you are none, your hopes remove;
For less then Empire I'le not change my love.
   Abdal. Had I a Crown, all I should prize in it,
Should be the pow'r to lay it at your feet.

Lyn. Had you that Crown which you but wish not hope,
Then I, perhaps, might stoop, and take it up.
But till your wishes, and your hopes agree,
You shall be still a private Man with me.
    Abdall. If I am King, and if my Brother dye————
130   *Lyndar.* Two if's, scarce make one possibility.
    Abd. The rule of happiness by reason scan;
You may be happy with a Private man.
    Lyndar. That happiness I may enjoy, 'tis true;
But then that Private man must not be you.
Where e're I love, I'm happy in my choice;
If I make you so, you shall pay my price.
    Abdall. Why wou'd you be so great?
    Lyndar. ————————————————Because I've seen
This day, what 'tis to hope to be a Queen.
Heav'n, how y' all watch'd each motion of her Eye:
140 None could be seen while *Almahide* was by.
Why wou'd I be a Queen? because my Face
Wou'd wear the Title with a better grace.
If I became it not, yet it wou'd be
Part of your duty, then, to Flatter me.
These are not half the Charms of being great:
I wou'd be somewhat————that I know not yet:
Yes; I avowe th' ambition of my Soul,
To be that one, to live without controul:
And that's another happiness to me
150 To be so happy as but one can be.
    Abdall. Madam, (because I would all doubts remove,)
Wou'd you, were I a King, accept my Love?
    Lynd. I wou'd accept it; and to show 'tis true;
From any other man as soon as you.
    Abdall. Your sharp replies make me not love you less;
But make me seek new paths to Happiness.
What I design, by time will best be seen.

130, 133, 137 *Lyndar.*] Q3; *Lindar.* Q1–2, Q4–5, F, D.
140 could] Q2–5, F, D; conld Q1.
140 by.] ~; Q1–5, F; ~, D (*Q1, Q4–5, F, D have an additional line:* Because she is to be her Majesty.).
141 Queen?] D; ~! Q1–5, F.   153 *Lynd.*] Q3; *Lind.* Q1–2, Q4–5, F, D.

You may be mine; and yet may be a Queen:
When you are so, your Word your Love assures.
160　　*Lynd.* Perhaps not love you———but I will be yours.
　　　　　　　　[He offers to take her hand and kiss it.
Stay Sir; that grace I cannot yet allow;
Before you set the Crown upon my Brow.
That favour which you seek———
Or *Abdelmelech*, or a King must have,
When you are so, then you may be my slave.
　　　　　　　[Exit: but looks smiling back on him.
　　Abdal. How 'ere imperious in her words she were,
Her parting looks had nothing of severe.
A glancing smile allur'd me to command;
And her soft fingers gently prest my hand.
170　I felt the pleasure glide through every part;
Her hand went through me to my very heart.
For such another pleasure, did he live,
I could my Father of a Crown deprive.
What did I say!
Father! that impious thought has shock'd my mind:
How bold our Passions are, and yet how blind!
She's gone; and now
Methinks there is less glory in a Crown;
My boyling passions settle and goe down:
180　Like Amber chaf't, when she is near she acts,
When farther off, inclines, but not attracts.

　　　　　　　To him Zulema.

Assist me, *Zulema*, if thou wouldst be
That friend thou seem'st, assist me against me.
Betwixt my love and vertue I am tost;
This must be forfeited or that be lost:
I could do much to merit thy applause;
Help me to fortify the better cause.

160　*Lynd.*] Q3; *Lind.* Q1–2, Q4–5, F, D.
160+　*s.d.* [*He*] Q4–5, F, D; ∧~ Q1–3.
165+　*s.d.* [*Exit*] Q4–5, F, D; ∧~ Q1–3.　　　　172　pleasure,] F, D; ~∧ Q1–5.

My Honour is not wholly put to flight;
But would, if seconded, renue the fight.
190   *Zul.* I met my sister; but I do not see
What difficulty in your choice can be:
She told me all; and 'tis so plain a case
You need not ask, what council to embrace.
    Abdalla. I stand reprov'd, that I did doubt at all;
My waiting Vertue stay'd but for thy call:
'Tis plain that she who for a Kingdom, now
Would sacrifice her love, and break her vow,
Not out of Love but int'rest, acts alone,
And wou'd,
200 Ev'n in my arms, lie thinking of a throne.
    Zulema. Add to the rest this one reflection more,
When she is married, and you still adore,
Think then, and think what comfort it will bring,
She had been mine————
Had I but onely dar'd to be a King!
    Abdalla. I hope you only would my honour try;
I'm loath to think you vertue's enemy.
    Zulema. If, when a Crown and Mistress are in place,
Vertue intrudes with her lean holy face;
210 Vertues then mine, and not I vertues foe;
Why does she come where she has nought to do?
Let her with Anchorit's not with Lovers lye;
States-men and they keep better Company.
    Abdal. Reason was giv'n to curb our headstrong will.
    Zulema. Reason but shews a weak Physitians skill:
Gives nothing while the raging fit does last;
But stayes to cure it when the worst is past.
Reason's a staff for age, when Nature's gone;
But Youth is strong enough to walk alone.
220   *Abdall.* In curst ambition I no rest should find;
But must for ever loose my peace of mind.

---

188   flight;] Q2–5, F; ∼. Q1; ∼, D.
199–200   And wou'd, / Ev'n] *one line in* Q1–5, F, D (ev'n Q2–5, F, D).
214   will.] Q3, F, D; ∼: Q1–2, Q4–5.
216   last;] Q4–5, F, D; ∼. Q1–2; ∼: Q3.

Zul. Methinks that peace of mind were bravely lost;
A Crown, what e're we give, is worth the cost.
  Abdal. Justice distributes to each man his right,
But what she gives not should I take by might?
  Zulem. If Justice will take all and nothing give,
Justice, methinks, is not distributive.
  Abdal. Had fate so pleas'd, I had been eldest born;
And then, without a Crime, the Crown had worn.
230 *Zul.* Would you so please, Fate yet a way would find;
Man makes his fate according to his mind.
The weak low Spirit Fortune makes her slave;
But she's a drudge, when Hector'd by the brave.
If Fate weaves common Thrid, he'l change the doom:
And with new purple spread a Nobler loom.
  Abdal. No more;————I will usurp the Royal Seat;
Thou who hast made me wicked, make me great.
  Zulema. Your way is plain; the Death of *Tarifa*
Does, on the King, our *Zegry's* hatred draw;
240 Though with our Enemies in show we close,
'Tis but while we to purpose can be foes.
Selin, who heads us, would revenge his Son;
But favour hinders justice to be done.
Proud *Ozmyn* with the king his pow'r maintains:
And, in him, each *Abencerrago* reigns.
  Abdalla. What face of any title can I bring?
  Zul. The right an eldest Son has to be King.
Your Father was at first a private man;
And got your brother 'ere his reign began.
250 When, by his Valour, he the Crown had won,
Then you were born, a Monarch's eldest Son.
  Abdal. To sharp ey'd reason this would seem untrue;
But reason, I through Loves false Optiques view.
  Zul. Loves mighty pow'r has led me Captive too:
I am in it, unfortunate as you.
  Abdalla. Our Loves and fortunes shall together go,
Thou shalt be happy when I first am so.

---

223   what e're] Q2–3; what 're Q1, Q4; what e'r Q5; whate'er F; what e'er D.

Zul. The *Zegry's* at old *Selin*'s house are met;
Where in close Council, for revenge they sit,
260 There we our common int'rest will unite;
You their revenge shall own, and they your right.
One thing I had forgot which may import;
I met *Almanzor* coming back from Court;
But with a discompos'd and speedy pace,
A fiery colour kindling all his face:
The King his Pris'ners freedom has deny'd:
And that refusal has provok'd his pride.
   Abdal. Would he were ours!
I'le try to guild th' injustice of the cause;
270 And court his valour with a vast applause.
   Zulema. The bold are but the Instruments o' th' wise:
They undertake the dangers we advise.
And while our fabrick with their pains we raise,
We take the profit, and pay them with praise.

                                        [*Exeunt.*

ACT III.

Almanzor, Abdalla.

Alman. That he should dare to do me this disgrace!
Is fool or Coward writ upon my face?
Refuse my Pris'ner! I such means will use
He shall not have a Pris'ner to refuse.
   Abdal. He said you were not by your promise ty'd;
That he absolv'd your word when he deny'd.
   Almanz. He break my promise and absolve my vow!
'Tis more then *Mahomet* himself can do.
The word which I have giv'n shall stand like Fate;

261   right.] Q1 (*some copies*), Q4–5, F, D; ∼. —— Q1 (*some copies*), Q2–3.
263   Court;] Q2–3; ∼. Q1, Q4–5, F; ∼, D.
274+   *s.d.* [*Exeunt*] Q4–5, F, D; ∧∼ Q1–3.
ACT] Q2, Q5, F, D; ∼. Q1, Q3–4.
s.d. Almanzor, Abdalla.] Q4–5, D; *Almanzor, Abdalla.* Q1–3, F.
2   fool] Q1a; Fool Q1b.   8   then] Q1a; than Q1b.

10 Not like the King's, that weathercock of State.
   He stands so high, with so unfix't a mind,
   Two Factions turn him with each blast of wind.
   But now he shall not veer: my word is past:
   I'll take his heart by th' roots, and hold it fast.
       Abdal. You have your Vengeance in your hand this hour,
   Make me the humble Creature of your pow'r:
   The *Granadins* will gladly me obey;
   (Tir'd with so base and impotent a sway.)
   And when I shew my Title, you shall see
20 I have a better right to reign, than he.
       Almanz. It is sufficient that you make the claim:
   You wrong our friendship when your right you name.
   When for my self I fight, I weigh the cause;
   But friendship will admit of no such Laws:
   That weighs by th' lump, and, when the Cause is light,
   Puts kindness in to set the Ballance right.
   True, I would wish my friend the juster side:
   But in th' unjust my kindness more is try'd.
   And all the Opposition I can bring,
30 Is, that I fear to make you such a King.
       Abdal. The Majesty of Kings we should not blame,
   When Royal minds adorn the royal name:
   The vulgar, greatness too much idolize,
   But haughty Subjects it too much despise.
       Almanz. I onely speake of him,
   Whom Pomp and greatness sit so loose about
   That he wants Majesty to fill 'em out.
       Abdal. Haste, then, and loose no time————
   The business must be enterpriz'd this night:
40 We must surprise the Court in its delight.
       Almanzor. For you to will; for me 'tis to obey;

---

11 unfix't] Q1a; unfixt Q1b.	14 heart] Q1a; Heart Q1b.
15 Vengeance] Q1a; Veng'ance Q1b.	20 reign] Q1a; Reign Q1b.
22 friendship . . . right] Q1a; Friendship . . . Right Q1b.	
24 friendship] Q1a; Friendship Q1b.	25 Cause] Q1a; cause Q1b.
29 Opposition] Q1a; opposition Q1b.	32 royal name] Q1a; Royal name Q1b.
38 loose] Q1a; lose Q1b.	40 surprise] Q1a; surprize Q1b.
41 *Almanzor.* . . . will;] Q1a; *Almanz.* . . . Will, Q1b.	

But I would give a Crown in open day:
And, when the *Spaniards* their assault begin,
At once beat those without, and these within.

[*Exit* Almanzor.

Enter Abdelmelech.

Abdelm. Abdalla, hold; there's somewhat I intend
To speak, not as your Rival, but your Friend.
    Abdal. If as a Friend, I am oblig'd to hear;
And what a Rival says I cannot fear.
    Abdelm. Think, brave *Abdalla*, what it is you do: ⎫
50 Your Quiet, Honour, and our Friendship too,   ⎬
All for a fickle Beauty you foregoe.   ⎭
Think, and turn back before it be too late;
Behold, in me th' example of your Fate.
I am your Sea-mark, and though wrack'd and lost,
My Ruines stand to warn you from the Coast.
    Abdal. Your Councels, noble *Abdelmelech*, move
My reason to accept 'em; not my Love.
Ah, why did Heav'n leave Man so weak defence
To trust frail reason with the rule of Sence?
60 'Tis over-pois'd and kick'd up in the Air,
While sence weighs down the Scale; and keeps it there.
Or, like a Captive King, 'tis born away:
And forc'd to count'nance its own Rebels sway.
    Abdelm. No, no; our Reason was not vainly lent;
Nor is a slave but by its own consent.
If Reason on his Subjects Triumph wait,
An easie King deserves no better Fate.
    Abdal. You speak too late; my Empire's lost too far,
I cannot fight.

---

43   *Spaniards*] Q1a, Q3–5, F, D; Spaniards Q1b, Q2.
43   assault Q1a; Aslault Q1b.
44+s.d.–107+ s.d. [*Exit* . . . [*Exit* Abdalla.] Q1b, Q2–5, F, D (∧*Exit (bis)* Q1b, Q2–3);
As they go out, Abdelmelech *enters, leading* Lindaraxa: *she smiles on* Abdalla. Q1a.
59   Sence?] ∼! Q1b–5, F, D.
65   consent.] Q3, F; ∼, Q1b–2, Q4–5; ∼: D.

Abdelm. ——Then make a flying War,
70 Dislodge betimes before you are beset.
 Abdal. Her tears, her smiles, her every look's a Net.
Her voice is like a Syren's of the Land;
And bloody Hearts lie panting in her hand.
 Abdelm. This do you know, and tempt the danger still?
 Abdal. Love like a Lethargy has seiz'd my Will.
I'm not my self, since from her sight I went;
I lean my Trunck that way; and there stand bent.
As one, who in some frightful Dream, would shun
His pressing Foe, labours in vain to run;
80 And his own slowness in his sleep bemoans,
With thick short Sighs, weak Cries, and tender Groans,
So I———
 Abdelm. ———Some Friend in Charity, should shake
And rowse, and call you loudly till you wake.
Too well I know her blandishments to gain,
Usurper-like, till setled in her Reign;
Then proudly she insults, and gives you cares
And jealousies; short hopes, and long despairs.
To this hard yoke you must hereafter bow;
Howe're she shines all Golden to you now.
90 *Abdal.* Like him, who on the ice———
Slides swiftly on, and sees the water near,
Yet cannot stop himself in his Carrear:
So am I carry'd. This enchanted place,
Like *Circe*'s Isle, is peopled with a Race
Of dogs and swine, yet, though their fate I know,
I look with pleasure and am turning too.

   Lyndaraxa *passes over the Stage.*

 Abdelm. Fly, fly, before th' allurements of her face; ⎫
'Ere she return with some resistless grace, ⎬
And with new magique covers all the place. ⎭
100 *Abdalla.* I cannot, will not; nay I would not fly;
I'le love; be blind, be cousen'd till I dye.

———

76 I'm] Q2–3, Q5, F, D; ∼, Q1b, Q4. 94 *Circe*'s] Q4–5, F, D; *Cyrce*'s Q1b–3.

And you, who bid me wiser Counsel take,
I'le hate, and if I can, I'le kill you for her sake.
    Abdel. Ev'n I that counsell'd you, that choice approve,
I'le hate you blindly, and her blindly love:
Prudence, that stemm'd the stream, is out of breath;
And to go down it, is the easier death.

Lyndaraxa re-enters and smiles on Abdalla.

[Exit Abdalla.

    Abdelm. That Smile on Prince *Abdalla*, seem's to say
You are not in your killing mood to day.
110 Men brand, indeed, your sex with Cruelty,
But you'r too good, to see poor Lovers dye.
This Godlike pity in you I extoll;
And more, because, like heav'ns, 'tis general.
    Lyndarax. My smile implies not that I grant his suit:
'Twas but a bare return to his salute.
    Abdelm. It said, you were ingag'd and I in place:
But, to please both, you would divide the grace.
    Lyndar. You've cause to be contented with your part:
When he has but the look, and you the heart.
120   *Abdel.* In giving but that look, you give what's mine:
I'le not one corner of a glance resign:
All's mine; and I am cov'tous of my store:
I have not love enough; I'le tax you more.
    Lyndarax. I gave not love; 'twas but Civility,
He is a Prince; that's due to his Degree.
    Abdel. That Prince you smil'd on is my Rival still:
And shou'd, if me you lov'd, be treated ill.
    Lynd. I know not how to show so rude a spight.
    Abdel. That is, you know not how to love aright;
130 Or, if you did, you would more difference see

---

103   sake.] Q2–5, F, D; ~, Q1b.   108   Smile] Q1a; smile Q1b.
109   day.] Q1a, Q3; ~, Q1b, Q2, Q4–5; ~: F; ~; D.
114   *Lyndarax.*] *Lindarax.* Q1a; *Lynd.* Q1b.
115   to] Q1a; of Q1b.   117   But,] Q1a; ~ˌ Q1b.
117   grace.] Q3, Q5, F, D; ~: Q1–2, Q4.
118   *Lyndar.*] Q1a; *Lynd.* Q1b.
124   *Lyndarax.*] Q2–5, F, D; *Lindarax.* Q1.

Betwixt our Souls, then 'twixt our Quality.
Mark if his birth makes any difference,
If, to his words, it adds one grain of Sence:
That duty which his birth can make his due
I'le pay; but it shall not be paid by you.
For if a Prince Courts her whom I adore,
He is my Rival, and a Prince no more.
   Lynd. And when did I my pow'r so far resigne,
That you should regulate each Look of mine?
140   *Abdel.* Then, when you gave your Love, you gave that pow'r.
   Lynd. 'Twas during pleasure, 'tis revok'd this hour.
Now call me false, and rail on Woman-kind,
'Tis all the remedy you're like to find.
   Abdel. Yes, there's one more,
I'le hate you; and this visit is my last.
   Lynd. Do't, if you can; you know I hold you fast.
Yet, for your quiet, would you could resigne
Your love, as easily as I do mine.
   Abdel. Furies and Hell, how unconcern'd she speaks!
150 With what indifference all her Vows she breaks!
Curse on me but she smiles.
   Lynd. That smile's a part of Love; and all's your due:
I take it from the Prince, and give it you.
   Abdel. Just heav'n, must my poor heart your May-game prove
To bandy, and make Childrens play in Love?   [*Half crying.*
Ah! how have I this Cruelty deserv'd?
I who so truly and so long have serv'd!
And left so easily! oh cruel Maid.
So easily! 'twas too unkindly said.
160 That Heart which could so easily remove,
Was never fix'd, nor rooted deep in Love.
   Lynd. You Lodg'd it so uneasie in your Brest,
I thought you had been weary of the Guest.
First I was Treated like a stranger there;
But, when a Houshold Friend I did appear,
You thought, it seems, I could not live elsewhere.

155 Love?] Q3, Q5, F, D; ~. Q1-2, Q4.
156 Ah! ... deserv'd?] Q5, F, D; ~∧ ... ~, Q1-4.

Then, by degrees, your feign'd respect withdrew:
You mark'd my Actions; and my Guardian grew.
But, I am not concern'd your Acts to blame:
170   My heart to yours, but upon liking came.
And, like a Bird, whom prying Boys molest,
Stays not to Breed, where she had built her Nest.
　　Abdel. I have done ill————
And dare not ask you to be less displeas'd:
Be but more Angry, and my Pain is eas'd.
　　Lynd. If I should be so kind a Fool to take
This little Satisfaction which you make,
I know you would presume some other time
Upon my Goodness, and repeat your Crime.
180   *Abdel.* Oh never, never: upon no pretence:
My Life's too short to expiate this Offence.
　　Lynd. No; now I think on't, 'tis in vain to try;
'Tis in your Nature, and past remedy.
You'll still disquiet my too loving Heart:
Now we are friends 'tis best for both to part.
　　Abdel. By this————will you not give me leave to swear?
　　　　　　　　　　　　　　　　[*Taking her Hand.*
　　Lynd. You wou'd be perjur'd if you should I fear.
And when I talk with Prince *Abdalla* next
I with your fond Suspitions shall be vext.
190   *Abdel.* I cannot say I'le conquer Jealousie:
But if you'll freely pardon me, I'le try.
　　Lynd. And, till you that submissive Servant prove,
I never can conclude you truly love.

　　　　To them, the King, Almahide, Abenamar, Esperanza,
　　　　　　　　Guards, Attendants.

　　King. Approach, my *Almahide*, my charming fair;
Blessing of Peace, and recompence of War.
This Night is yours; and may your Life still be
The same in Joy, though not Solemnity.

─────────
186+   *s.d. above l. 186 in* Q*1*-*5*, F, D.　　187   *Lynd.*] Q2-5, F, D; *Lind.* Q1.
190   cannot] Q2-5, F, D; canot Q1.

S O N G.

1.

Beneath a Myrtle shade
Which Love for none but happy Lovers made,
I slept, and straight my Love before me brought
Phillis *the object of my waking thought;*
Undress'd she came my flames to meet,
While Love strow'd flow'rs beneath her feet;
Flow'rs, which so press'd by her, became more sweet.

2.

From the bright Visions head
A careless vail of Lawn was loosely spread:
From her white temples fell her shaded hair,
Like cloudy sunshine not too brown nor fair:
Her hands, her lips did love inspire;
Her every grace my heart did fire:
But most her eyes which languish'd with desire.

3.

Ah, Charming fair, said I,
How long can you my bliss and yours deny?
By Nature and by love this lonely shade
Was for revenge of suffring Lovers made:
Silence and shades with love agree:
Both shelter you and favour me;
You cannot blush because I cannot see.

4.

No, let me dye, she said,
Rather than loose the spotless name of Maid:

197+   SONG.] Q2–3, M1; SONG. *Misplac'd. Sung at the dance, or* Zambra *in the third* Act. Q1 *(after the epilogue);* The Zambra *Dance. SONG.* Q4–5, F, D; *A Song at the King's House.* Os1a, Os2a, Os3–4; *A Vision.* Os1b, Os2b; *Song* 6. Os5; *no title* Fs1–3, M2; *A SONG.* Ds5.
198–232   *romans and italics reversed from Q1.*

Faintly me thought she spoke, for all the while
She bid me not believe her, with a smile.
Then dye, said I. She still deny'd:
And, is it thus, thus, thus she cry'd
You use a harmless Maid? And so she dy'd!

5.
I wak'd, and straight I knew
I lov'd so well it made my dream prove true:
Fancy, the kinder Mistress of the two,
Fancy had done what Phillis *wou'd not do!*
230   *Ah, Cruel Nymph, cease your disdain,*
While I can dream you scorn in vain;
Asleep or waking you must ease my pain.

The Zambra *Dance.*

[*After the Dance, a tumultuous noise of Drums and Trumpets.*

To them Ozmyn; *his Sword drawn.*

Oz. Arm, quickly, arm, yet all, I fear too late:
The Enemy's already at the Gate.
    K. Boab. The Christians are dislodg'd; what Foe is near?
    Ozm. The *Zegry's* are in Arms, and almost here.
The Streets with Torches shine, with Shoutings ring,
And Prince *Abdalla* is proclaim'd the King.
What Man cou'd do I have already done,
240 But Bold *Almanzor* fiercely leads 'em on.
    Abenam. Th' *Alhambra* yet is safe in my Command,
Retreat you thither while their shock we stand.   [*To the King.*
    Boab. I cannot meanly for my life provide:
Ile either perish in't, or stemm this Tyde.

---

223 *I. She*] Q3, M1; ∼, she Q1–2, Q4–5, F, Os1–5, Fs1–3, Ds5, M2; ∼: *She* D.
225 *Maid? And*] Os1b, Os2b, Fs2–3, Ds5 (and); ∼, and Q1–5, F, D, Os1a, Os2a,
Os3–5, Fs1, M2; ∼; and M1.
232+ *The* Zambra *Dance.*] *included in brace with the following s.d. in Q1–3;*
centered preceding the song in Q4–5, F, D.
236 *Zegry's*] Q2–3, F, D; Zegry's Q1, Q4–5.

To guard the Palace, *Ozmyn*, be your care;
If they o'recome, no sword will hurt the fair.
   Ozm. I'le either dye, or I'le make good the place.
   Abdel. And I, with these, will bold *Almanzor* face.
               [*Exeunt all but the Ladies. An Alarm within.*
   Almah. What dismal Planet did my Triumphs light?
250 Discord the Day, and Death does rule the Night:
The noise, my Soul does through my Sences wound.
   Lynd. Me thinks it is a noble, sprightly Sound.
The Trumpets clangor, and the clash of Arms!
This noyse may chill your Blood, but mine it warms:
            [*Shouting and clashing of Swords within.*
We have already past the *Rubicon.*
The Dice are mine: now Fortune for a Throne.
       [*A shout within, and clashing of swords afar off.*
The sound goes farther off; and faintly dies,
Curse of this going back, these ebbing cryes!
Ye Winds waft hither sounds more strong, and quick:
260 Beat faster, Drums, and mingle Deaths more thick.
I'le to the Turrets of the Palace goe,
And add new fire to those that fight below.
Thence, *Hero*-like, with Torches by my side,
(Farr be the Omen, though,) my Love I'le guide.
No; like his better Fortune I'le appear: ⎫
With open Arms, loose Vayl, and flowing Hair, ⎬
Just flying forward from my rowling Sphere.   ⎭
My Smiles shall make *Abdalla* more then Man;
Let him look up and perish if he can.   [*Exit.*

    An Alarm, nearer: then Enter Almanzor; *and* Selin, *in
the head of the* Zegrys; Ozmyn *Pris'ner.*

270   *Almanz.* We have not fought enough; they fly too soon:
And I am griev'd the noble sport is done.

245 care;] F, D; ∼. Q1–4; ∼, Q5.
248+ *s.d.* [*Exeunt*] Q5, F, D; ∧Exeunt Q1; ∧*Exeunt* Q2–3; [Exeunt Q4.
249 light?] Q3, D; ∼: Q1–2, Q4–5, F.   255 *Rubicon*] D; Rubicon Q1–5, F.
256+ *s.d.* [*A*] Q2–5, F, D; ∧∼ Q1.   264 Omen] D; *Omen* Q1–5, F.
269+ *s.d.* Zegrys;] D; *Zegrys.* Q1, Q4–5; Zegrys. Q2–3, F.

This onely man of all whom chance did bring
                              [*Pointing to* Ozmyn.
To meet my Arms, was worth the Conquering.
His brave resistance did my Fortune grace;
So slow, so threatning forward he gave place.
His Chains be easie and his Usage fair.
   Selin. I beg you would commit him to my care.
   Alm. Next, the brave *Spaniard* free without delay:
And with a Convoy send him safe away.
                              [*Exit a Guard.*

       To them Hamet *and others.*

280   *Hamet.* The King by me salutes you: and, to show
That to your Valour he his Crown does owe,
Would, from your Mouth I should the Word receive;
And, that to these, you would your Orders give.
   Alm. He much o're-rates the little I have done.
                 [Almanzor *goes to the door, and there*
                      seems to give out Orders, by sending
                      People several ways.
   Selin. Now to revenge the Murder of my Son.
To morrow for thy certain death prepare: [*To* Ozmyn.
This night I onely leave thee to despair.
   Ozmyn. Thy idle Menaces I do not fear:
My business was to die, or conquer here.
290 Sister, for you I grieve I could no more:
My present State betrays my want of pow'r.
But, when true Courage is of force bereft,
Patience, the noblest Fortitude, is left.
                              [*Exit cum* Selin.

   Alma. Ah, *Esperanza*, what for me remains
But Death; or, worse than Death, inglorious Chains!

278 *Spaniard*] Q3, F, D; Spaniard Q1–2, Q4–5.
279+ *s.d. Exit*] Q4–5, F, D; Exit. Q1; *Exit.* Q2–3.
279+ *s.d. others.*] Q2–5, F, D; ~ₐ Q1.
284+ *s.d.* [Almanzor] Q4–5, F, D; ₐ~ Q1–3.
285–286 *Selin.* Now . . . prepare: [*To* Ozmyn.] *Selin to Ozmin.* / Now . . . prepare:
Q1–5 (*Ozmyn* Q2–5); *Selin to Ozmyn.* Now . . . prepare: F, D.

Esper. Madam, you must not to Despair give place;
Heav'n never meant misfortune to that Face.
Suppose there were no justice in your cause,
Beauty's a Bribe that gives her Judges Laws.
300 That you are brought to this deplor'd estate,
Is but th' ingenious Flatt'ry of your Fate;
Fate fears her Succor like an Alms to give:
And would, you, God-like from your self should live.
    Almah. Mark but how terrible his Eyes appear!
And yet there's something roughly noble there,
Which, in unfashion'd Nature, looks Divine;
And like a Gemm does in the Quarry shine.

                              [Almanzor *returns; she falls at*
                                    his feet being veyld.

    Almah. Turn, Mighty Conqu'ror, turn your Face this way,
Do not refuse to hear the wretched pray.
310   *Almanz.* What business can this Woman have with me?
    Almah. That of th' afflicted to the Deity.
So may your Arms success in battels find:
So may the Mistris of your vows be kind,
If you have any; or, if you have none,
So may your Liberty be still your own.
    Almanz. Yes, I will turn my face; but not my mind:
You bane, and soft destruction of mankind,
What would you have with me?
    Almahide. ————————I beg the grace   [*Unveyling.*
You would lay by those terrours of your face.
320 Till calmness to your eyes you first restore
I am afraid, and I can beg no more.
    Almanzor. Well; my fierce visage shall not murder you:
                           [*Looking fixedly on her.*
Speak quickly, woman; I have much to do.

———————
307+   *s.d.* [Almanzor] Q4, F, D; ∧~ Q1–3, Q5.
318   *s.d. Unveyling*] Q2–5, F, D; *unveyling* Q1.
322   *Almanzor.* Well; . . . you: [*Looking fixedly on her.*] *Almanzor looking fixedly
on her.* / Well; . . . you: Q1–5 ([Almanzor Q2–5); [Almanzor *looking fixedly on her.*
/ *Almanz.* Well, . . . you: F; *Almanz.* [*Looking fixedly on her.*] Well; . . . you: D.

Almah. Where should I finde the heart to speake one word?
Your voice, Sir, is as killing as your sword.
As you have left the lightning of your eye,
So would you please to lay your thunder by?
    Alman. I'me pleas'd and pain'd since first her eyes I saw,
As I were stung with some *Tarantula:*
330 Armes, and the dusty field I less admire;
And soften strangely in some new desire.
Honour burns in me, not so fiercely bright;
But pale, as fires when master'd by the light.
Ev'n while I speak and look, I change yet more;
And now am nothing that I was before.
I'm numm'd, and fix'd and scarce my eyeballs move;
I fear it is the Lethargy of Love!
'Tis he; I feel him now in every part:
Like a new Lord he vaunts about my Heart,
340 Surveys in state each corner of my Brest,
While poor fierce I, that was, am dispossest.
I'm bound; but I will rowze my rage again: ⎫
And, though no hope of Liberty remaine, ⎬
I'll fright my Keeper when I shake my chaine. ⎭
You are———   *[Angrily.*
    Almah. ———I know I am your Captive, Sir.
    Alman. You are———You shall———And I can scarce for-
      bear———
    Almah. Alas!
    Almanz. ———'Tis all in vain; it will not do: *[Aside.*
I cannot now a seeming anger show:
My Tongue against my heart no aid affords,
350 For Love still rises up, and choaks my words.
    Almah. In half this time a tempest would be still.
    Almanz. 'Tis you have rais'd that tempest in my will,
I wonnot love you, give me back my heart.
But give it as you had it, fierce and brave:

324   word?] F, D; ∼, Q1–2, Q4–5; ∼; Q3.
327   by?] ∼! Q1–5, F; ∼. D.
345   s.d. Angrily] Q2–3, D; angrily Q1; Angerly Q4–5, F.
345   Sir.] D; ∼: Q1–5, F.
347   s.d. Aside] Q4–5, F, D; aside Q1–3.

It was not made to be a womans slave:
But Lyon-like has been in desarts bred;
And, us'd to range, will ne're be tamely led.
Restore its freedom to my fetter'd will
And then I shall have pow'r, to use you ill.
360   *Almah.* My sad condition may your pity move;
But look not on me with the eyes of Love.————
I must be brief, though I have much to say.
    Almanz. No, speak: for I can hear you now, all day.   [*Softly.*
Her suing sooths me with a secret pride: [*Aside.*
A supplyant beauty cannot be deni'd:
Ev'n while I frown, her charms the furrows seize;
And I'm corrupted with the pow'r to please.
    Almah. Though in your worth no cause of fear I see;
I fear the insolence of Victory:
370 As you are Noble, Sir, protect me then,
From the rude outrage of insulting men.
    Almanz. Who dares touch her I love? I'm all o're love:
Nay, I am Love; Love shot, and shot so fast,
He shot himself into my brest at last.
    Almah. You see before you, her who should be Queen,
Since she is promis'd to *Boabdelin.*
    Almanz. Are you belov'd by him? O wretched fate,
First that I love at all; then, love too late!
Yet, I must love!
    Almah. ————Alas it is in vain;
380 Fate for each other did not us ordain.
The chances of this day too clearly show
That Heav'n took care that it should not be so.
    Almanz. Would Heav'n had quite forgot me this one day,
But fate's yet hot————
I'le make it take a bent another way.
              [*He walks swiftly and discomposedly studying.*
I bring a claim which does his right remove:
You're his by promise, but you're mine by Love.
'Tis all but Ceremony which is past:

363   s.d. *Softly*] Q2–3, F, D; *softly* Q1, Q4–5.
364   s.d. *Aside*] F, D; *aside* Q1–5.   377   him?] ~! Q1–5, F, D.

The knot's to tie which is to make you fast.
390 Fate gave not to *Boabdelin* that pow'r:
He woo'd you, but as my Ambassadour.
    Almah. Our Souls are ty'd by holy Vows above.
    Almanz. He sign'd but his: but I will seal my love.
I love you better; with more Zeale then he.
    Almah. This day———
I gave my faith to him, he his to me.
    Almanz. Good Heav'n thy book of fate before me lay,
But to tear out the journal of this day.
Or, if the order of the world below
400 Will not the gap of one whole day allow,
Give me that Minute when she made her vow.
"That Minute, ev'n the happy, from their bliss might give:
And those who live in griefe, a shorter time would live."
So small a link, if broke, th' eternal chain
Would, like divided waters, joyn again.
It wonnot be; the fugitive is gone;
Prest by the crowd of following Minutes on:
That precious Moment's out of Nature fled:
And in the heap of common rubbish layd,
410 Of things that once have been, and are decay'd.
    Almah. Your passion, like a fright suspends my pain:
It meets, 'ore-powr's, and bears mine back again.
But, as when tydes against the Current flow,
The Native stream runs its own course below:
So, though your griefs possess the upper part,
My own have deeper Channels in my heart.
    Almanz. Forgive that fury which my Soul does move,
'Tis the Essay of an untaught first love.
Yet rude, unfashion'd truth it does express:
420 'Tis love just peeping in a hasty dress.
Retire, fair Creature to your needful rest;
There's something noble, lab'ring in my brest:
This raging fire which through the Mass does move,

---

389 knot's] Q2–3, Q5, F, D; knots Q1, Q4.
407 crowd] Q4–5, F, D; crow'd Q1–3.

Shall purge my dross, and shall refine my Love.

                [*Exeunt* Almahide, *and* Esperanza.

She goes; And I, like my own Ghost appear:

It is not living, when she is not here.

    To him Abdalla *as King, attended by* Hamet *and others.*

    Abdal. My first acknowledgments to heav'n are due:

My next, *Almanzor*, let me pay to you.

    Alm. A poor surprize and on a naked foe:

430 What ever you confess, is all you owe.

And I no merit own, or understand

That fortune did you justice by my hand.

Yet, if you will that little service pay

With a great favour, I can shew the way.

    Abdal. I have a favour to demand of you;

That is to take the thing for which you sue.

    Alman. Then, briefly, thus; when I th' *Albayzin* won,

I found the Beauteous *Almahide* alone:

Whose sad condition did my pity move:

440 And that compassion did produce my love.

    Abdal. This needs no sute; in justice, I declare

She is your Captive by the right of war.

    Alm. She is no Captive, then; I set her free. ⎞

And rather then I will her Jaylour be,   ⎬

I'le Nobly loose her, in her liberty.   ⎠

    Abdal. Your generosity I much approve,

But your excess of that, shows want of Love.

    Alman. No, 'tis th' excess of love, which mounts so high

That, seen far off, it lessens to the eye.

450 Had I not lov'd her, and had set her free

That, Sir, had been my generosity:

But 'tis exalted passion when I show

424+   s.d. [*Exeunt*] Q4–5, F; ∧~ Q1–3, D.

426+   s.d. *attended by* Hamet *and others.*] attended. Q1–5, F, D.

429   foe:] ~. Q1–5, F; ~, D.

431   own,] Q3, F, D; ~∧ Q1–2, Q4–5.

437   *Albayzin*] Q3; *Albayzyn* Q1–2, Q4–5, F, D.

445   I'le] Q2–5, F, D; 'Ile Q1.

I dare be wretched not to make her so.
And, while another Passion fills her brest,
I'le be all wretched rather then half blest.
    Abdalla. May your heroique Act so prosperous be,
That *Almahide* may sigh you set her free.

Enter Zulema.

    Zulema. Of five tall tow'rs which fortifie this Town,
All but th' *Alhambra* your dominion own.
460 Now therefore boldly I confess a flame
Which is excus'd in *Almahida's* name.
If you the merit of this night regard,
In her possession I have my reward.
    Almanz. She your reward! why she's a gift so great————
That I my self have not deserv'd her yet.
And therefore, though I wonn her with my sword,
I have, with awe, my sacrilege restor'd.
    Zul. What you deserve————
Ile not dispute because I do not know,
470 This, onely I will say, she shall not goe.
    Almanz. Thou, single, art not worth my answering,
But take what friends, what armyes thou canst bring;
What worlds; and when you are united all,
Then, I will thunder in your ears, ————She shall.
    Zul. I'le not one tittle of my right resign;
Sir, your implicite promise made her mine.
When I in general terms my love did show,
You swore our fortunes should together goe.
    Abdalla. The merits of the cause I'le not decide,
480 But, like my love, I would my gift divide.
Your equal titles, then, no longer plead;
But one of you, for love of me recede.
    Alm. I have receded to the utmost line,
When, by my free consent, she is not mine.
Then let him equally recede with me,

---

454 fills] Q2–5, F, D; fils Q1.   458 *Zulema.*] Q2–5, F, D; ∼, Q1.
474 She] Q3–5, F, D; she Q1–2.

And both of us will join to set her free.

Zul. If you will free your part of her you may;
But, Sir, I love not your Romantique way.
Dream on; enjoy her Soul; and set that free;
490 I'me pleas'd her person should be left for me.

Alman. Thou shalt not wish her thine; thou shalt not dare
To be so impudent, as to despair.

Zul. The *Zegrys*, Sir, are all concern'd to see
How much their merit you neglect in me.

Hamet. Your slighting *Zulema*, this very hour
Will take ten thousand Subjects from you'r pow'r.

Almanz. What are ten thousand subjects such as they?
If I am scorn'd———I'le take my self away.

Abdalla. Since both cannot possess what both pursue;
500 I grieve, my friend, the chance should fall on you.
But when you hear what reasons I can urge———

Almanz. None, none that your ingratitude can purge.
Reason's a trick, when it no grant affords:
It stamps the face of Majesty on words.

Abdal. Your boldness to your services I give:
Now take it as your full reward to live.

Almanz. To live!
If from thy hands alone my death can be,
I am immortal; and a God, to thee.
510 If I would kill thee now, thy fate's so low
That I must stoop 'ere I can give the blow.
But mine is fix'd so far above thy Crown,
That all thy men
Pil'd on thy back can never pull it down.
But at my ease thy destiny I send,
By ceasing from this hour to be thy friend.
Like Heav'n I need but onely to stand still;
And, not concurring to thy life, I kill.
Thou canst no title to my duty bring:
520 I'm not thy Subject, and my Soul's thy King.
Farewell: when I am gone

---

497 they?] D; ~; Q1–5, F.   518 kill.] D; ~, Q1, Q4–5, F; ~: Q2–3.
521 Farewell:] D; ~, Q1–5, F.

There's not a starr of thine dare stay with thee:
I'le whistle thy tame fortune after me:
And whirl fate with me wheresoe're I fly,
As winds drive storms before 'em in the sky.

[Exit.

   Zulema. Let not this Insolent unpunish'd goe;
Give your Commands; your Justice is too slow.

[Zulema, Hamet and others, are going after him.

   Abdal. Stay: and what part he pleases let him take;
I know my Throne's too strong for him to shake.
530 But my fair Mistriss I too long forget:
The Crown I promis'd is not offer'd yet.
Without her presence, all my Joys are vain;
Empire a Curse; and life it self a pain.

[Exeunt.

ACT IV.

Boabdelin, Abenamar, *Guards.*

   Boab. Advise, or aid, but do not pity me;
No Monarch born can fall to that degree.
Pity descends from Kings to all below;
But can no more then fountains upward flow.
Witness just heav'n, my greatest grief has been
I could not make your *Almahide* a Queen.
   Aben. I have too long th' effects of Fortune known,
Either to trust her smiles, or fear her frown.
Since in their first attempt you were not slain,
10 Your safety bodes you yet a second reign.
The people, like a headlong torrent goe;
And, every dam, they break, or overflow:

---

523 me:] *some copies of Q1 have period.*
525+ *s.d.* [Exit] Q4–5, D; ⋏~ Q1–3, F.
527+ *s.d.* [Zulema, Hamet *and*] Q2–5, F, D; ⋏*Zulema, Hamet* and Q1.
533+ *s.d.* [Exeunt] Q4–5, F, D; ⋏~ Q1–3.
ACT] Q2–5, F, D; ~. Q1.
s.d. Boabdelin, Abenamar,] Q4–5, F, D; *Boabdelin, Abenamar,* Q1–3.

But, unoppos'd, they either loose their force,
Or wind in volumes to their former course.

    Boab. In walls we meanly must our hopes inclose,
To wait our friends, and weary out our foes,
While *Almahide*
To lawless Rebels is expos'd a prey,
And forc'd the lustful Victor to obey.

20   *Aben.* One of my blood, in rules of Vertue bred!
Think better of her; and believe she's dead.

To them Almanzor.

    Boab. We are betray'd; the Enemy is here;
We have no farther room to hope or fear.

    Almanz. It is indeed *Almanzor* whom you see,
But he no longer is your Enemy.
You were ungrateful, but your foes were more;
What your injustice lost you, theirs restore.
Make profit of my vengeance while you may,
My two-edg'd sword can cut the other way.

30 I am your fortune; but am swift like her,
And turn my hairy front if you defer:
That hour when you delib'rate is too late:
I point you the white moment of your fate.

    Aben. Believe him sent as Prince *Abdalla*'s spy;
He would betray us to the Enemy.

    Alman. Were I, like thee, in cheats of State grown old, ⎫
(Those publick Markets where for foreign gold   ⎬
The poorer Prince is to the Richer sold;)   ⎭
Then, thou might'st think me fit for that low part:

40 But I am yet to learn the Statesman's art.
My kindness and my hate unmask'd I wear;
For friends to trust, and Enemies to fear.
My hearts so plain,
That men on every passing thought may look,

---

13   But,] *some copies of* Q1 *lack comma.*
21   and] Q1 (*some copies*), Q4–5, F, D; and I Q1 (*some copies*), Q2; I Q3.
36   I,] Q1 (*some copies*), Q3–5, F, D; ~ₐ Q1 (*some copies*), Q2.
37   where] Q1 (*some copies*), Q3–4, F, D; were Q1 (*some copies*), Q2, Q5.

Like fishes gliding in a Chrystal brook:
When troubled most, it does the bottom show,
'Tis weedless all above; and rockless all below.
   Aben. 'Ere he be trusted let him first be try'd,
He may be false who once has chang'd his side.
50   *Almanz.* In that you more accuse your selves than me:
None who are injur'd can unconstant be.
You were unconstant; you who did the wrong;
To do me justice does to me belong.
Great Souls by kindness onely can be ti'd;
Injur'd again, again I'le leave your side.
Honour is what my self and friends I owe;
And none can loose it who forsake a foe.
Since, then, your Foes now happen to be mine,
Though not in friendship we'll in int'rest join.
60 So while my lov'd revenge is full and high,
Il'e give you back your Kingdom by the by.
   Boab. That I so long delai'd what you desire [*Embracing him.*
Was not to doubt your worth, but to admire.
   Alman. This Councellor an old mans caution shows, ⎫
Who fears that little he has left, to loose: ⎬
Age sets to fortune; while youth boldly throw's. ⎭
But let us first your drooping Souldiers cheere:
Then seek out danger, 'ere it dare appear.
This hour I fix your Crown upon your brow,
70 Next hour fate gives it; but I give it now.

                                         [*Exeunt.*

SCENE II.

Lyndaraxa *alone.*

   Lynd. O could I read the dark decrees of fate,
That I might once know whom to love or hate!

---

55 I'le] Q2–5, F, D; i'le Q1.
62 *Boab.* That . . . desire [*Embracing him.*] D; *Boabdelin embracing him.* |
That . . . desire Q1–5, F ([Boabdelin Q2–3, F).
70+ *s.d.* [*Exeunt*] Q5, F, D; ‸~ Q1–4.
s.d. Lyndaraxa] Q2–5, F, D; *Lindaraxa* Q1.   1 *Lynd.* O] F, D; O Q1–5.

For I my self scarce my own thoughts can ghess,
So much I find 'em varied by success.
As in some wether-glass my Love I hold;
Which falls or rises with the heat or cold.
I will be constant yet, if Fortune can;
I love the King: let her but name the Man.

To her Halyma.

Hal. Madam, a Gentleman to me unknown
10 Desires that he may speak with you alone.
     Lynd. Some Message from the King: let him appear.

To her Abdelmelech: *who, Entring, throws
off his Disguise. She starts.*

Abdelm. I see you are amaz'd that I am here.
But let at once your Fear and Wonder end;
In the Usurpers Guard I found a Friend,
Who led me to you safe in this Disguise.
     Lynd. Your Danger brings this Trouble in my Eyes.
But what affair this vent'rous visit drew?
     Abdel. The greatest in the world; the seeing you.
     Lynd. The Courage of your Love I so admire
20 That to preserve you, you shall straight retire.
                         [*She leads him to the door.*
Go, Dear, each Minute does new dangers bring;
You will be taken; I expect the King.
     Abdel. The King! the poor Usurper of an Hour,
His Empire's but a Dream of Kingly Pow'r.
I warn you, as a Lover and a Friend,
To leave him e're his short Dominion end.
The Soldier I suborn'd will wait at night;

7   Fortune] Q3, F, D; fortune Q1–2, Q4–5.
8+   s.d. Halyma] Q2–5, F; *Halyma* Q1, D.
11   *Lynd.*] Q2–5, F, D; *Lind.* Q1 (*and similarly below except as noted*).
11+   s.d. *To*] Q5, D; *in* Q1–4, F, *preceded by a brace.*
11+   s.d. starts.] Q2–5, F, D; ~: Q1.   23   *Abdel.*] Q3–5, F, D; *Abdal.* Q1–2.

And shall alone be conscious of your flight.
 Lynd. I thank you that you so much care bestow;
30 But, if his Reign be short, I need not goe.
For why should I expose my life and yours,
For what, you say, a little time assures?
 Abdel. My danger in th' attempt is very small:
And, if he loves you, yours is none at all.
But, though his Ruine be as sure as Fate,
Your proof of Love to me would come too late.
This Tryal, I in Kindness wou'd allow;
'Tis easie; if you love me, show it now.
 Lynd. It is because I love you, I refuse:
40 For all the World my Conduct would accuse
If I should go, with him I love, away:
And therefore, in strict Vertue, I will stay.
 Abdel. You would in vain dissemble Love to me:
Through that thinn Veyle your Artifice I see.
You would expect th' event, and then declare:
But do not, do not drive me to despair.
For if you now refuse with me to fly,
Rather then love you after this, I'le die.
And therefore weigh it well before you speak;
50 My King is safe; his force within not weak.
 Lynd. The Counsel you have giv'n me, may be wise:
But, since th' affair is great, I will advise.
 Abdel. Then that delay, I for denial take.——— [*Is going.*
 Lynd. Stay; you too swift an Exposition make.
If I should go, since *Zulema* will stay,
I should my Brother to the King betray.
 Abdel. There is no fear: but, if there were, I see
You value still your Brother more than me.
Farewel; some ease I in your falshood find;
60 It lets a Beam in, that will clear my mind.
My former weakness I with shame, confess:

29 bestow;] Q2–3, F, D; ∼. Q1; ∼, Q4–5.
38 easie;] Q3; ∼, Q1–2, Q4–5, F, D.
53 s.d. [*Is*] Q2–5, F, D; (*is* Q1.
54 *Lynd.*] *sic in* Q1.

And when I see you next shall love you less.   [*Is going again.*
  Lynd. Your faithless dealing you may blush to tell: [*Weeping.*
This is a Maids Reward who loves too well.   [*He looks back.*
Remember that I drew my latest breath
In charging your unkindness with my death.
  Abdel. Have I not answered all you can invent;
Ev'n the least shadow of an Argument?   [*Coming back.*
  Lynd. You want not cunning what you please to prove;
70 But my poor Heart knows onely how to Love.
And, finding this, you Tyrannize the more:————
'Tis plain, some other Mistriss you adore:
And now, with studied tricks of subtilty,
You come prepar'd to lay the fault on me.
                    [*Wringing her hands.*
But oh, that I should love so false a man!
  Abdel. Hear me; and then disprove it, if you can.
  Lynd. I'le hear no more; your breach of Faith is plain:
You would with Wit, your want of Love maintain.
But, by my own Experience, I can tell,
80 They who love truly cannot argue well.
Go Faithless Man!
Leave me alone to mourn my Misery:
I cannot cease to love you, but I'le die.
                [*Leans her Head on his Arm.*
  Abdel. What Man but I so long unmov'd could hear
Such tender passion, and refuse a Tear?   [*Weeping.*
But do not talk of dying any more,
Unless you mean that I should die before.
  Lynd. I fear your feign'd Repentance comes too late:

62 *s.d.* [*Is . . . again.*] Q2–5, F, D; (*is . . . again.*) Q1.
63 *Lynd.*] *sic in Q1.*
63 tell:] D; ~. Q1–4; ~ₐ Q5; ~; F.
67–68 *Abdel.* Have . . . invent; / . . . [*Coming back.*] [*Abdel. coming back.* / Have
. . . invent Q1–5 (invent, Q3); [*Abdel. coming back.* / *Abdel.* Have . . . invent F;
Abdelm. [*coming back.*] Have . . . invent, D.
77 plain:] *some copies of Q1 have period.*
83+ *s.d.* Leans . . . *Arm.*] Q4–5, F, D; (~ . . . ~.) Q1–3.
84–85 *Abdel.* What . . . hear / . . . [*Weeping.*] D; [*Abdelmelech weeping.* / What
. . . hear Q1–5, F (*some copies of Q1 have "Abdel." before "What"*).
85 Tear?] Q3; ~! Q1–2, Q4–5, F, D.

I dye to see you still thus obstinate.
90 But yet, in Death, my truth of Love to show,
Lead me; if I have strength enough, I'le goe.
　Abdel. By Heav'n you shall not goe: I will not be
O'recome in Love or Generosity.
All I desire, to end th' unlucky strife,
Is but a Vow that you will be my Wife.
　Lynd. To tie me to you by a Vow, is hard;
It show's my Love, you as no Tie regard.
Name any thing but that, and I'le agree.
　Abdel. Swear then, you never will my Rival's be.
100 　*Lynd.* Nay, prithee, this is harder then before;
Name any thing, good Dear, but that thing more.
　Abdel. Now I too late perceive I am undone:
Living and seeing, to my Death I run.
I know you false; yet in your Snares I fall;
You grant me nothing; and I grant you all.
　Lynd. I would grant all; but I must curb my will:
Because I love to keep you jealous still.
In your Suspicion I your Passion find:
But I will take a time to cure your mind.
110 　*Halyma.* Oh, Madam, the new King is drawing neer!
　Lynd. Hast quickly hence; least he should find you here.
　Abdel. How much more wretched then I came, I goe: ⎫
I more my Weakness, and your Falshood know; ⎬
And now must leave you with my greatest Foe! ⎭
　　　　　　　　　　　　　　[*Exit* Abdelmelech.
　Lynd. Go; how I love thee Heav'n can onely tell.
And yet I love thee, for a Subject, well.————
Yet, whatsoever Charms a Crown can bring,
A Subject's greater then a little King.
I will attend till Time this Throne secure;
120 And, when I climb, my footing shall be sure.
　　　　　　　　　　　　　[*Musique without.*
　Musique! and I believe, addrest to me.

97　show's] Q2–5, F, D; ～, Q1.　　　114+　s.d. [*Exit*] Q4–5, F, D; ∧～ Q1–3.
115　*Lynd.*] *sic in Q1, and similarly hereafter.*
121　I] Q2–3, F, D; ～, Q1, Q4–5.

SONG.

1.

Wherever I am, and whatever I doe;
My Phillis *is still in my mind:*
When angry I mean not to Phillis *to goe,*
My Feet of themselves the way find:
Unknown to my self I am just at her door,
And when I would raile, I can bring out no more,
Than Phillis *too fair and unkind!*

2.

When Phillis *I see, my Heart bounds in my Breast,*
130   *And the Love I would stifle is shown:*
But asleep, or awake, I am never at rest
   When from my Eyes Phillis *is gone!*
Sometimes a sad Dream does delude my sad mind,
But, alas, when I wake and no Phillis *I find*
   How I sigh to my self all alone.

3.

Should a King be my Rival in her I adore
   He should offer his Treasure in vain:
O let me alone to be happy and poor,
   And give me my Phillis *again:*
140 *Let* Phillis *be mine, and for ever be kind*
I could to a Desart with her be confin'd,
   And envy no Monarch his Raign.

4.

Alas, I discover too much of my Love,
   And she too well knows her own power!

---

135   *alone.*] Q2, Os5, M3; ∼: Q1; ∼! Q3, Q5, F, D, Ds2, Fs1–3, Ds5, M1; ∼? Q4;
∼, Ds1, Ds3–4, Os1–4, M4 (*line partly or fully repeated*).
140   *for ever*] Q2–3, F, M1, M4; *but ever* Q1, Q4–5, D, Ds1–4, M3; *ever* Os1–5,
Fs1–3, Ds5.

She makes me each day a new Martyrdom prove,
And makes me grow jealous each hour:
But let her each minute torment my poor mind
I had rather love Phillis *both False and Unkind,*
Then ever be freed from her Pow'r.

Abdalla *enters with* Selin, *Guards.*

150   *Abdal.* Now, Madam, at your Feet, a King you see:
Or, rather, if you please, a Scepter'd Slave;
'Tis just you should possess the pow'r you gave.
Had Love not made me yours, I yet had bin
But the first Subject to *Boabdelin.*
Thus Heav'n declares the Crown I bring, your due:
And had forgot my Title, but for you.
    Lynd. Heav'n to your Merits will, I hope be kind;
But, Sir, it has not yet declar'd its mind.
'Tis true, it holds the Crown above your Head;
160 But does not fix it till your Brother's dead.
    Abdal. All, but th' *Alhambra,* is within my pow'r;
And that, my forces goe to take this hour.
    Lynd. When, with its Keys, your Brothers Head you bring
I shall believe you are indeed a King.
    Abdal. But, since th' events of all things doubtful are,
And, of Events, most doubtful those of Warre,
I beg to know before, if Fortune frown,
Must I then loose your Favour with my Crown?
    Lynd. You'll soon return a Conquerour again;
170 And therefore, Sir, your question is in vain.
    Abdall. I think to certain Victory I move;
But you may more assure it by your Love.
That grant will make my arms invincible.
    Lynd. My pray'rs and wishes your success foretell.
Go then, and fight, and think you fight for me;

149+   *s.d. with* Selin,] *with* Q1–5, F, D.
161   pow'r;] Q3; ~. Q1–2, Q4–5, D; ~: F.
168   your] Q2–5, F, D; yonr Q1.

I wait but to reward your Victory.
    Abdal. But if I loose it, must I loose you too?
    Lynd. You are too curious if you more would know.
I know not what my future thoughts, will be:
180 Poor womens thoughts are all *Extempore.*
Wise men, indeed,
Before hand a long chain of thoughts produce;
But ours are onely for our present use.
    Abdal. Those thoughts you will not know, too well declare
You mean to waite the final doom of Warr.
    Lynd. I finde you come to quarrel with me now:
Would you know more of me then I allow?
Whence are you grown that great Divinity
Who with such ease into my thoughts can pry?
190 Indulgence does not with some tempers sute;
I see I must become more absolute.
    Abdalla. I must submit;
On what hard terms so e're my peace be bought.
    Lynd. Submit? you speak as you were not in fault!
'Tis evident the injury is mine;
For why should you my secret thoughts divine?
    Abdal. Yet if we might be judg'd by Reasons Laws!
    Lynd. Then you would have your reason judge my cause?
Either confess your fault or hold your tongue;
200 For I am sure I'm never in the wrong.
    Abdalla. Then I acknowledge it.
    Lynd. ————————————Then I forgive.
    Abdall. Under how hard a Law poor Lovers live!
Who, like the vanquish'd, must their right release:
And with the loss of reason, buy their peace.   *[Aside.*
Madam, to show that you my pow'r command,
I put my life and safety in your hand:
Dispose of the *Albayzin* as you please:
To your fair hands I here resign the keyes.

---

189 Who] Q2–3; That Q1, Q4–5, F, D.
194 Submit? . . . fault!] ∼! . . . ∼? Q1–2, Q4–5; ∼! . . . ∼. Q3, F, D.
204 *s.d. Aside*] Q4–5, F, D; *aside* Q1–3.

Lyn. I take your gift because your love it shows;
210 And faithful *Selin* for *Alcalde* choose.
  Abdall. Selin, from her alone your Orders take.
This one request, yet, Madam, let me make
That, from those turrets, you th' assault will see;
And Crown, once more, my arms with Victorie.
       [*Leads her out.* Selin *remains with*
        Gazul *and* Reduan *his Servants.*
  Selin. Gazul, go tell my daughter that I waite.
You, *Reduan,* bring the Pris'ner to his fate.
       [*Exeunt* Gazul *and* Reduan.
'Ere of my charge I will possession take,
A bloody sacrifice I mean to make:
The *Manes* of my son shall smile this day,
220 While I in blood my Vows of Vengeance pay.

    Enter, at one door Benzayda *with* Gazul,
    at the other Ozmyn *bound, with* Reduan.

  Selin. I sent, *Benzaida,* to glad your eies:
These rites we owe your brothers Obsequies.
You two th' accurst *Abencerrago* bind, [*To* Gazul *and* Reduan.
You need no more t' instruct you in my mind.
      [*They bind him to one corner of the Stage.*
  Benz. In what sad Object am I call'd to share,
Tell me, what is it, Sir, you here prepare?
  Selin. 'Tis, what your dying brother did bequeath,
A Scene of Vengeance, and a Pomp of death.
  Benz. The horrid Spectacle my Soul does fright;
230 I want the heart to see the dismal sight.
  Selin. You are my principal invited ghest:

---

211 take.] Q5, F; ~: Q1–4, D.   214+ *s.d.* [*Leads*] Q2–5, F, D; ˄~ Q1.
215 waite.] ~: Q1–5, F, D.   219 *Manes*] F; Manes Q1–5, D.
221 *Selin.*] Q2–5, F, D; *Selyn.* Q1.
223 *s.d.* [*To* Gazul *and* Reduan.] Q2–5, F, D (Gazul. Q4); ˄*To Gazul. and Reduan.*
Q1.
224+ *s.d.* [*They*] Q2–5, F, D; ˄~ Q1.   226 prepare?] Q3–5, F, D; ~. Q1–2.

Whose eies I would not onely feed but feast:
You are to smile at his last groaning breath,
And laugh to see his eye-balls rowle in death:
To judge the lingring Souls convulsive strife;
When thick short breath, catches at parting life.
    Benz. And of what Marble do you think me made?
    Selin. What, can you be of just revenge afraid?
    Benz. He kill'd my Brother in his own defence,
240 Pity his youth, and spare his innocence.
    Selin. Art thou so soon, to pardon murder, won?
Can he be innocent who kill'd my son?
Abenamar shall mourn as well as I;
His *Ozmyn* for my *Tarifa* shall die.
But, since thou plead'st so boldly; I will see
That Justice thou woud'st hinder, done by thee:
                                [*Gives her his sword.*
Here, take the sword; and do a Sisters part;
Pierce his, fond Girl; Or I will pierce thy heart.
    Ozmyn. To his commands I joyn my own request,
250 All wounds from you are welcome to my brest:
Think onely when your hand this act has done,
It has but finish'd what your eies begun.
I thought, with silence to have scorn'd my doom;
But now your noble pity has ore'come:
Which I acknowledge with my latest breath;
The first who 'ere began a love in death.
    Benz. Alas, what aid can my weak hand afford?   [*To* Selin.
You see I tremble when I touch a sword.
The brightness dazles me; and turnes my sight:
260 Or, if I look, 'tis but to aim less right.
    Ozmy. I'le guide the hand which must my death convay;
My leaping heart shall meet it half the way.

246+ *s.d.* [*Gives*] Q2–5, F, D; ˌ~ Q1.
248 his,] Q2–5, F, D; ~ˌ Q1.
257 *Benz.* Alas, . . . afford? [*To* Selin.] *Benz. to* Selin. / Alas, . . . afford; Q1–5;
Benz. Alas, . . . afford? [Benzayda *to* Selin. F; *Benz. to* Selin. Alas, . . . afford. D.
258 sword.] F; ~? Q1–5; ~: D.
261 convay;] Q3, F, D; ~ˌ Q1–2, Q4–5.

Selin. Waste not the precious time in idle breath.   [*To* Benz.
Benz. Let me resign this instrument of death.
                    [*Giving the sword to her father;*
                                and then pulling it back.

Ah, no: I was too hasty to resign;
'Tis in your hand more mortal then in mine.

                To them Hamet.

Ham. The King is from th' *Alhambra* beaten back;
And now preparing for a new attacque;
To favour which, he wills, that, instantly,
270 You reinforce him with a new supply.
    Selin. Think not, although my duty calls me hence, [*To* Benz.
That with the breach of yours I will dispence:
'Ere my return, see my commands you do;
Let me find *Ozmyn* dead; and kill'd by you.
Gazul and *Reduan* attend her still;
And if she dares to fail, perform my will.
                    [*Exeunt* Selin *and* Hamet.

        [Benzayda, *looks languishing on him with her sword down;*
        Gazul *and* Reduan, *standing with drawn swords by her.*

    Ozmyn. Defer not, fair *Benzaida*, my death;
Looking on you——
I should but live to sigh away my breath.

_____

263   *Selin.* Waste . . . breath. [*To* Benz.] *Selin to Benz.* / Waste . . . breath. Q1–5
(Wast Q5); [Selin *to* Benzayda. / *Selin.* Wast . . . Breath. F; *Selin to Benz.* Waste
. . . Breath. D.
264+   s.d. [*Giving*] Q2–5, F, D; ∧*giving* Q1.
266+   s.d. Hamet] Q2–5, F, D; *Hamet* Q1.
268   attacque;] Q2–3; ~. Q1, Q4–5; ~: F, D.
271   *Selin.* Think . . . hence, [*To* Benz.] *Selin to Benz.* / Think . . . hence, Q1–5;
[Selin *to* Benz. / *Selin.* Think . . . hence, F; *Selin to Benz.* Think . . . hence, D.
274   *Ozmyn*] Q3–5, F, D; *Ozmin* Q1–2.
276+   s.d. [*Exeunt*] Q4–5, F, D; ∧~ Q1–3.
276+   s.d. [Benzayda] F, D; ∧~ Q1–5.
276+   s.d. down;] F; ~. Q1–5, D.
277   *Ozmyn*] Q4–5; *Ozmin* Q1; *Ozm.* Q2–3, F, D.
277   *Benzaida*] Q2; *Benzaiida* Q1; *Benzayda* Q3–5, F, D.

BENZAYDA GUARDING OZMYN, ACT IV, SCENE II
FROM *The Dramatick Works of John Dryden, Esq.* (1735)

280 My eyes have done the work they had to do; ⎞
I take your Image with me, which they drew;   ⎬
And, when they close, I shall dye full of you. ⎠
    Benz. When Parents their Commands unjustly lay
Children are priviledg'd to disobey.
Yet from that breach of duty I am clear,
Since I submit the penalty to bear.
To dye or kill you is th' alternative;
Rather then take your life, I will not live.
    Ozm. This shows th' excess of generosity;
290 But, Madam, you have no pretence to die.
I should defame th' *Abencerrages* Race
To let a Lady suffer in my place.
But neither could that life you would bestow ⎞
Save mine: nor do you so much pity owe   ⎬
To me, a stranger, and your houses foe.   ⎠
    Benz. From whence-soe're their Hate our Houses drew,
I blush to tell you, I have none for you.
'Tis a Confession which I should not make,
Had I more time to give, or you to take.
300 But, since death's near, and run's with so much force,
We must meet first and intercept his course.
    Ozmyn. Oh, how unkind a comfort do you give!
Now, I fear death again, and wish to live.
Life were worth taking could I have it now, ⎞
But 'tis more good than Heav'n can e're allow, ⎬
To one man's portion, to have life and you. ⎠
    Benz. Sure, at our Births,
Death with our meeting Planets danc'd above;
Or we were wounded by a Mourning Love!
                                    [*Shouts within.*
310   *Redu.* The noise returns, and doubles from behind;
It seems as if two adverse Armies joyn'd:
Time presses us.
    Gaz. ———If longer you delay
We must, though loath, your Fathers Will obey.

---

291   *Abencerrages*] Q5, F, D; *Abencerrage's* Q1–4.
313   your] Q2–3, Q5, F, D; yours Q1, Q4.

Ozm. Haste, Madam, to fulfil his hard Commands:
And rescue me from their ignoble Hands.
Let me kiss yours, before my wound you make;
Then, easie Death I shall with pleasure take.
    Benz. Ah, gentle Soldiers, some short time allow,
                               [*To* Gaz. *and* Red.
My Father has repented him e're now;
320 Or will repent him when he finds me dead:
My clue of Life is twin'd with *Ozmyn's* Thred.
    Red. 'Tis fatal to refuse her, or obey:
But where is our excuse? what can we say?
    Benz. Say; any thing————
Say, that to kill the Guiltless you were loath.
Or, if you did, say, I would kill you both.
    Gaz. To disobey our Orders is to die:
I'le do't, who dare oppose it.
    Red. ————————————That dare I.
        [Reduan *stands before* Ozmyn, *and fights with* Gazul.
          Benzayda *unbinds* Ozmyn; *and gives him her Sword.*
    Benz. Stay not to see the issue of the Fight;   [Red. *kills* Gaz.
330 But haste to save your self by speedy flight.
    Ozmyn. Did all Mankind against my Life conspire
                   [*Kneeling to kiss her hand.*
Without this Blessing I would not retire.
But, Madam, can I goe and leave you here?
Your Fathers anger now for you I fear:
Consider you have done too much to stay.
    Benz. Think not of me, but fly your self away.
    Red. Haste quickly hence; the Enemies are nigh:
From every part I see our Soldiers fly;
The Foes not only our Assailants beat,

---

316   before . . . you make] Q2–3; when you . . . begin Q1, Q4–5, F, D.
317   I shall . . . take] Q2–3; will slide . . . in Q1, Q4–5, F, D.
328+   *s.d.* Gazul. Benzayda . . . *Sword.*] ~.] [~ . . . ~.] Q1, Q4; ~·ᴧ [~ . . . ~·ᴧ
Q2–3, Q5, F, D.
329   *s.d. kills*] Q3–5, F, D; *kils* Q1–2.
331   *Ozmyn.* Did . . . conspire [*Kneeling . . . hand.*] [Ozmyn *kneeling . . . hand.* /
Did . . . conspire Q1–5, F, D (*hand.*] Q1; *kneels* D; *Ozm.* Did F, D).

340 But fiercely sally out on their Retreat;
And, like a Sea broke loose, come on amain.

> *To them* Abenamar; *and a party with their swords*
> *drawn: driving in some of the Enemies.*

Aben. Traytors, you hope to save your selves in vain,
Your forfeit Lives shall for your Treason pay;
And *Ozmyn*'s Blood shall be reveng'd this day.
    Ozmyn. No Sir, your *Ozmyn* lives, and lives to own
A Fathers piety to free his Son.   [*Kneeling to his Father.*
    Aben. My *Ozmyn!* O thou blessing of my age!
And art thou safe from their deluded rage?   [*Embracing him.*
Whom must I praise for thy Deliverance,
350 Was it thy Valour or the work of Chance?
    Ozmyn. Nor Chance nor Valour could deliver me;
But 'twas a noble Pity set me free.
My Life, and what your Happiness you call,
We to this charming Beauty owe it all.
    Abenam. Instruct me, visible Divinity,   [*To her.*
Instruct me by what Name to worship thee.
For to thy Vertue I would Altars raise:
Since thou art much above all humane praise.
But see————

> *Enter* Almanzor, *his sword bloody, leading*
> *in* Almahide, *attended by* Esperanza.

360 My other blessing, *Almahide* is here:
Ile to the King, and tell him she is neer.

345–346 *Ozmyn.* . . . own / . . . [*Kneeling to his Father.*] D; *Ozmyn, kneeling to his*
Father. / Ozmyn. . . . own Q1–5, F (to his Father. Q1).
347–348 *Aben.* . . . age! / . . . [*Embracing him.*] D; [*Abenamar embracing him.* /
Aben. . . . age! Q1–5, F.
348 rage?] ∼! Q1–5, F, D.
353 My Life, and . . . you] Q2–3; My Liberty and Life, / And . . . you're pleas'd to
Q1, Q4–5, F, D.
355 *Abenam.* Instruct . . . Divinity, [*To her.*] D; [*Abenam. to her. /* Instruct . . .
Divinity, Q1–5, F (*Abenam:* Q1; *Aben* Instruct F).

You *Ozmyn*, on your fair deliverer wait:
And with your Joys the publick Celebrate.

[*Exeunt.*

Almanzor, Almahide, Esperanza.

Alman. The work is done; now, Madam, you are free:
At least if I can give you Liberty.
But you have Chains which you your self have chose;
And, oh, that I could free you too from those.
But, you are free from force, and have full pow'r
To goe, and kill my hopes and me, this hour.
370 I see, then, you will go; but yet my toyl
May be rewarded with a looking while.
    Almah. Almanzor can from every Subject raise
New matter for our Wonder and his Praise.
You bound and freed me, but the difference is,
That show'd your Valour; but your Vertue this.
    Almanz. Madam, you praise a Fun'ral Victory;
At whose sad pomp the Conquerour must die.
    Almah. Conquest attends *Almanzor* every where,
I am too small a Foe for him to fear:
380 But Heroes still must be oppos'd by some,
Or they would want occasion to ore'come.
    Almanz. Madam, I cannot on bare praises live:
Those who abound in praises seldom give.
    Almah. While I to all the world your worth make known,
May Heav'n reward the pity you have shown.
    Almanz. My Love is languishing and sterv'd to death,
And would you give me charity, in breath?
Pray'rs are the Alms of Church-men to the Poor:
They send to Heaven's; but drive us from their door.
390   *Almah.* Cease; cease a Sute
So vain to you and troublesome to me,
If you will have me think that I am free.

363   Joys] Q2–3; private Joys Q1, Q4–5, F, D.
363+   s.d. [*Exeunt.*] Q4–5, F, D; ∧~ Q1–3.
363+   s.d. Almanzor, Almahide, Esperanza.] *italics in Q1.*

If I am yet a Slave my bonds I'le bear,
But what I cannot grant, I will not hear.
   Almanz. You wonnot hear! you must both Hear and grant;
For, Madam, there's an impudence in want.
   Almah. Your way is somewhat strange to ask Relief;
You ask with threatning, like a begging Thief.
Once more *Almanzor,* tell me, am I free?
₄₀₀   *Almanz.* Madam, you are from all the World————but me.
But as a Pyrate, when he frees the Prize
He took from Friends, sees the rich Merchandize,
And after he has freed it, justly buys,
So when I have restor'd your Liberty,————
But, then, alas, I am too poor to buy!
   Almah. Nay now you use me just as Pyrats do:
You free me; but expect a ransome too.
   Almanz. You've all the freedom that a Prince can have:
But Greatness cannot be without a Slave.
₄₁₀ A Monarch never can in private move;
But still is haunted with officious Love.
So small an inconvenience you may bear,
'Tis all the Fine Fate sets upon the Fair.
   Almah. Yet Princes may retire when e're they please;
And breath free Air from out their Palaces:
They goe sometimes unknown to shun their State;
And then, 'tis manners not to know or wait.
   Almanz. If not a Subject then a Ghost I'le be;
And from a Ghost, you know, no place is free.
₄₂₀ Asleep, Awake, I'le haunt you every where;
From my white shrowd, groan Love into your Ear.
When in your Lovers Arms you sleep at night,
I'le glide in cold betwixt, and seize my Right.
And is't not better in your Nuptial Bed
To have a living lover than a dead?
   Almah. I can no longer bear to be accus'd,
As if what I could grant you I refus'd.
My Fathers choice I never will dispute;
And he has chosen e're you mov'd your Sute.
₄₃₀ You know my Case, if equal you can be,

Plead for your self, and answer it for me.
   Almanz. Then, Madam, in that hope you bid me live:
I ask no more then you may justly give:
But, in strict justice there may favour be:
And may I hope you can have that for me?
   Almah. Why do you thus my secret thoughts pursue,
Which known, hurt me, and cannot profit you?
Your knowledge but new troubles does prepare,
Like theirs who curious in their Fortunes are.
440 To say I could with more content be yours,
Tempts you to hope; but not that hope assures.
For since the King has right,
And favour'd by my Father in his Sute,
'Tis but a blossom which can bear no Fruit.
Yet, if you dare attempt so hard a task,
May you succeed; you have my leave to ask.
   Almanz. I can with courage now my hopes pursue,
Since I no longer have to combate you.
That did the greatest difficulty bring:
450 The rest are small, a Father, and a King!
   Almah. Great Souls discern not when the leap's too wide,
Nor view the passage, but the farther side.
What ever you desire you think is neer:
But, with more reason, the success I fear.
   Almanz. No; there is a necessity in Fate,
Why still the brave bold man is Fortunate:
He keeps his object ever full in sight,
And that assurance holds him firm, and right.
True, 'tis a narrow path that leads to bliss,   ⎫
460 But right before there is no precipice: ⎬
Fear makes men look aside, and then their footing miss. ⎭
   Almah. I do your merit all the right I can;
Admiring Vertue in a private man:
I onely wish the King may grateful be,

435   hope you can] Q2–3; hope that you Q1, Q4–5, F, D.
444   'Tis but] Q2–3; It is Q1, Q4–5, F, D.
452   Nor view the passage, but] Q2–3; Because they onely view Q1, Q4–5, F, D.
454   success] Q2–3; event Q1, Q4–5, F, D.

And that my Father with my Eyes may see.
Might I not make it as my last request
(Since humble carriage sutes a Suppliant best)
That you would somewhat of your fierceness hide:
That inborn fire; I do not call it pride.
470   *Almanz.* Born, as I am still to command, not sue,
Yet you shall see that I can beg for you.
And if your Father will require a Crown,
Let him but name the Kingdom, 'tis his own.
I am, but while I please, a private man;
I have that Soul which Empires first began:
From the dull crowd which every King does lead,
I will pick out whom I will choose to head:
The best and bravest Souls I can select,
And on their Conquer'd Necks my Throne erect.

                                        [*Exeunt.*

ACT V.

Abdalla *alone, under the walls of the* Albayzin.

Abd. While she is mine, I have not yet lost all:
But, in her Arms, shall have a gentle fall:
Blest in my Love, although in war o'recome,
I fly, like *Anthony* from *Actium*,
To meet a better *Cleopatra* here.
You of the Watch: you of the Watch: appear.

Souldier *above.*

Sould. Who calls below? What's your demand?
Abdal. ————————————————'Tis I:
Open the Gate with speed; the Foe is nigh.

---

478   select,] Q2–5, F, D; ~. Q1.
479+   s.d. [*Exeunt*] Q4–5, F, D; ∧~ Q1–3.
ACT] Q2, Q5, F, D; ~. Q1, Q3–4.
6+   s.d. *Souldier*] Q4–5; [~ Q1–3, F; *for D see next.*
7   *Sould.* Who] Who Q1–5, F; *Sold. above.* Who D.

Sol. What Orders for admittance do you bring?

10   *Abdal.* Slave, my own Orders; look and know the King.

    Sold. I know you, but my charge is so severe

That none, without exception, enter here.

    Abdal. Traytor, and Rebel, thou shalt shortly see

Thy Orders are not to extend to me.

Lyndaraxa above.

    Lynd. What saucy slave so rudely does exclaim,

And brands my Subject with a Rebels name?

    Abdal. Dear *Lyndaraxa* haste; the Foes pursue.

    Lynd. My Lord the Prince *Abdalla,* is it you?

I scarcely can believe the words I hear:

20 Could you so coursly Treat my Officer?

    Abdal. He forc'd me, but the danger nearer draws,

When I am enterd you shall know the cause.

    Lynd. Enterd! Why, have you any business here?

    Abdal. I am pursu'd; the Enemy is neer.

    Lynd. Are you pursu'd, and do you thus delay

To save your self? make haste, my Lord, away.

    Abdal. Give me not cause to think you mock my grief:

What place have I, but this, for my relief?

    Lynd. This favour does your handmaid much oblige:

30 But we are not provided for a siege.

My Subjects few; and their provision thin;

The foe is strong without, we weak within.

This to my noble Lord may seem unkind,

But he will weigh it in his Princely mind:

And pardon her, who does assurance want

So much, she blushes, when she cannot grant.

    Abdal. Yes, you may blush; and you have cause to weep:

Is this the faith you promis'd me to keep?

Ah yet, if to a Lover you will bring

14+   *s.d.* Lyndaraxa] Q4–5; [~ Q1–3, F; *for* D *see next.*

15   *Lynd.* What] What Q1–5, F; *Lyndar. above.* What D.

23   Why,] Q2–3, F; ~∧ Q1, Q4–5, D.

37   weep:] F; ~, Q1–2, Q4–5; ~. Q3, D.

40 No succour; give your succour to a King.

    Lynd. A King is he whom nothing can withstand;
Who men and money can with ease command:
A King is he whom fortune still does bless:
He is a King, who does a Crown possess.
If you would have me think that you are he,
Produce to view your marks of Soveraignty.
But, if your self alone for proof you bring,
You're but a single person; not a King.

    Abdal. Ingrateful Maid, did I for this rebel?
50 I say no more; but I have lov'd too well.

    Lynd. Who but your self did that Rebellion move?
Did I 'ere promise to receive your Love?
Is it my fault you are not fortunate?
I love a King, but a poor Rebel hate.

    Abdal. Who follow Fortune still are in the right.——
But let me be protected here this night.

    Lynd. The place to morrow will be circled round;
And then no way will for your flight be found.

    Abdalla. I hear my Enemies just coming on;

                                       [Trampling within.
60 Protect me but one hour, till they are gone.

    Lynd. They'l know you have been here; it cannot be,
That very hour you stay will ruine me.
For if the foe behold our Enterview,
I shall be thought a Rebel too like you:
Haste hence; and that your flight, may prosperous prove;
I'le recommend you to the pow'rs above.

                  [Exit Lyndaraxa *from above.*

    Abdal. She's gone; ah faithless and ingrateful maid!
I hear some tread; and fear I am betrai'd:
I'll to the *Spanish* King; and try if he
70 To count'nance his own right, will succour me.
There is more faith in Christian Dogs, than thee.

                                      [Exit.

59+ *s.d.* [*Trampling*] Q2–5, F, D (*trampling* Q2–4); ∧*trampling* Q1.
61 *Lynd.*] Q2–5, F, D; *Lind.* Q1.   66+ *s.d.* [*Exit*] Q4–5, F, D; ∧~ Q1–3.
68 I hear] Q3, F, D; I fear Q1–2, Q4–5.   69 *Spanish*] Q4–5, F, D; Spanish Q1–3.
71+ *s.d.* [*Exit*] Q4–5, F, D; ∧~ Q1–3.

Ozmyn. Benzayda. Abenamar.

Benz. I wish (to merit this) I could have said ⎞
My pity onely did his vertue aid: ⎬
'Twas pity; but 'twas of a Lovesick Maid.   ⎠
His manly suffering my esteem did move;
That bred Compassion; and Compassion, Love.
   Ozmyn. O blessing sold me at too cheap a rate!
My danger was the benefit of fate.
But that you may my fair deliverer know,   [*To his father.*
80 She was not only born our house's foe,
But to my death by pow'rful reasons, led,
At least, in justice she might wish me dead.
   Aben. But why thus long do you her name conceale?
   Ozmyn. To gain belief for what I now reveal:
Ev'n thus prepar'd, you scarce can think it true ⎞
The Saver of my life, from *Selin* drew   ⎬
Her birth; and was his Sister whom I slew.   ⎠
   Aben. No more; it cannot, was not, must not be:
Upon my blessing, say not it was she.
90 The daughter of the onely man I hate!
Two Contradictions twisted in a fate!
   Ozmyn. The mutual hate which you and *Selin* bore,
Does but exalt her generous pity more.
Could she a brothers death forgive to me,
And cannot you forget her family?
Can you so ill requite the life I owe
To reckon her, who gave it, still your foe?
It lends too great a luster to her line
To let her vertue, ours so much out-shine.
100   *Aben.* Thou giv'st her line th' advantage which they have
By meanly taking of the life they gave.
Grant that it did in her a pity show,

71+ *s.d.* Ozmyn. Benzayda. Abenamar.] *italics in* Q1.
72 I wish (to merit this)] Q2–3; ———I wish / (To merit all these thanks) Q1,
Q4–5, F, D.
79 *s.d.* [*To*] Q2–5, F, D (*between 78 and 79* Q2–3); ∧∼ Q1 (*between 78 and 79*).
80 foe,] Q2–3, F, D; ∼. Q1, Q4–5.   85 Ev'n] Q2–5, F, D; E'ven Q1.

But would my Son be pity'd by a foe?
She has the glory of thy act defac'd:
Thou kild'st her brother; but she triumphs last:
Poorly for us our Enmity would cease;
When we are beaten we receive a peace.
    Benz. If that be all in which you disagree,
I must confess 'twas *Ozmyn* conquer'd me.
110 Had I beheld him basely beg his life,
I should not now submit to be his wife.
But when I saw his courage death control,
I paid a secret homage to his Soul;
And thought my cruel father much to blame;
Since *Ozmyn*'s vertue his revenge did shame.
    Aben. What constancy canst thou 'ere hope to finde
In that unstable, and soon conquer'd mind;
What piety canst thou expect from her
Who could forgive a Brothers Murderer?
120 Or, what obedience hop'st thou to be pay'd
From one who first her father disobey'd?
    Ozmyn. Nature that bids us Parents to obey,
Bids parents their commands by Reason weigh.
And you her vertue by your praise did own,
Before you knew by whom the act was done.
    Aben. Your reasons speak too much of insolence,
Her birth's a crime past pardon or defence.
Know, that as *Selin* was not won by thee,
Neither will I by *Selins* daughter be.
130 Leave her, or cease henceforth to be my Son:
This is my will: and this I will have done.

                                          [*Exit* Abenamar.

    Ozmyn. It is a murdring will!
That whirls along with an impetuous sway;
And like chain-shot, sweeps all things in its way.
He does my honour want of duty call;
To that, and love he has no right at all.
    Benz. No, *Ozmyn*, no, 'tis not so great an ill

114   to] Q4–5, F, D; too Q1–3.   131+   *s.d.* [*Exit*] Q4–5, F, D; ∧~ Q1–3.
137   'tis not so great an] Q2–3; it is much less Q1, Q4–5, F, D (a much F, D).

To leave me as dispute a Fathers will:
If I had any title to your love,
140 A parent's greater right does mine remove.
Your vows and faith I give you back agen;
Since neither can be kept without a sin.
    Ozmyn. Nothing but death my vows can give me back:
They are not yours to give, nor mine to take.
    Benz. Nay, think not, though I could your vows resign,
My love or vertue could dispence with mine.
I would extinguish your unlucky fire,
To make you happy in some new desire:
I can preserve enough for me and you:
150 And love, and be unfortunate for two.
    Ozmyn. In all that's good and great,
You vanquish me so fast, that in the end
I shall have nothing left me to defend.
From every Post you force me to remove;
But let me keep my last retrenchment, Love.
    Benz. Love then, my *Ozmyn;* I will be content
                                   [*Giving her hand.*
To make you wretched by your own consent:
Live poor, despis'd, and banish'd for my sake:
And all the burden of my sorrows take.
160 For, as for me, in what soe're estate,
While I have you, I must be fortunate.
    Ozmyn. Thus then, secur'd of what we hold most dear,
(Each others love,) we'll go————I know not where.
For where, alas, should we our flight begin?
The foes without; our parents are within.
    Benz. I'le fly to you; and you shall fly to me:
Our flight but to each others armes shall be.
To providence and chance permit the rest;
Let us but love enough and we are blest.
                                       [*Exeunt.*

138   as] Q2–3; than Q1, Q4–5, F, D.
140   A parent's] Q2–3; Your fathers Q1, Q4–5, F, D.
156+   s.d. *Giving*] Q4–5, F, D; *giving* Q1–3.
169+   s.d. [*Exeunt*] Q4–5, F, D; ∧~ Q1–3.

Enter Boabdelin, Abenamar, Abdelmelech, *Guard,*
Zulema, *and* Hamet *prisoners.*

170   *Abdel.* They're *Lyndaraxa's* brothers; for her sake
Their lives, and pardon my request I make.
    Boab. Then *Zulema* and *Hamet* live; but know
Your lives to *Abdelmelechs* sute you owe.
    Zul. The grace receiv'd so much my hope exceeds
That words come weak and short to answer deeds.
You've made a venture, Sir, and time must show,
If this great mercy you did well bestow.
    Boabd. You, *Abdelmelech,* haste before 'tis night;
And close pursue my Brother in his flight.
               [*Exeunt* Abdelmelech, Zulema, Hamet.

Enter Almanzor, Almahide, *and* Esperanza.

180 But see with *Almahide,*
The brave *Almanzor* comes, whose conquering sword
That Crown it once took from me, has restor'd.
How can I recompence so great desert?
    Almanz. I bring you, Sir, perform'd in every part
My Promise made; Your foes are fled or slain;
Without a Rival, absolute you reign.
Yet, though in justice, this enough may be,
It is too little to be done by me:
I beg to goe
190 Where my own Courage and your fortune calls,
To chase these Misbelievers from our Walls.
I cannot breath within this narrow space;
My heart's too big; and swells beyond the place.
    Boab. You can perform, brave warrior, what you please,
Fate listens to your voice, and then decrees.

169+   *s.d.* Abdelmelech,] Q2–3, Q5, F, D; ∼. Q1, Q4.
170   *Lyndaraxa's*] Q2–3, Q5, F, D; *Lindraxa's* Q1; *Lyndraxa's* Q4.
179+   *s.d.* [*Exeunt*] Q4–5, F, D; ∧∼ Q1–3.
183   desert?] F; ∼! Q1–5, D.

Now I no longer fear the *Spanish* pow'rs;
Already we are free and Conquerours.
    Almanz. Accept great King, tomorrow from my hand,
The captive head of conquer'd *Ferdinand.*
200 You shall not only what you lost regain,   }
But, 'ore the *Byscayn* Mountains to the Mayn, }
Extend your sway, where *Moor* did never reign. }
    Aben. What in another Vanity would seem,
Appears but noble Confidence in him.
No haughty boasting; but a manly pride:
A Soul too fiery, and too great to guide:
He moves excentrique, like a wandring star;
Whose Motion's just; though 'tis not regular.
    Boab. It is for you, brave Man, and only you
210 Greatly to speake, and yet more greatly do.
But, if your Benefits too far extend,
I must be left ungrateful in the end:
Yet somewhat I would pay
Before my debts above all reck'ning grow;
To keep me from the shame of what I owe.
But you————
Are conscious to your self of such desert,
That of your gift I fear to offer part.
    Almanz. When I shall have declar'd my high request,
220 So much presumption there will be confest,
That you will find your gifts I do not shun;
But rather much o're-rate the service done.
    Boab. Give wing to your desires, and let 'em fly;
Secure, they cannot mount a pitch too high.
So bless me *Alha* both in peace and war,
As I accord what 'ere your wishes are.
    Almanz. Emboldn'd by the promise of a Prince
                    [*Putting one knee on the ground.*
I ask this Lady now with Confidence.

196 *Spanish*] Q3, D; Spanish Q1–2, Q4–5, F.
202 *Moor* did never] Q2–3; never Moor did Q1, Q4–5, F, D (*Moor* D).
227 *Almanz.* Emboldn'd . . . Prince [*Putting one knee on the ground.*] D; *Almanz.*
putting one knee on the ground. / Emboldn'd . . . Prince Q1–5; [*Almanz. putting
one Knee to the Ground.* / *Almanz.* Embolden'd . . . Prince, F.

Boab. You ask the onely thing I cannot grant.

      [*The King and* Aben. *look amazedly on each other.*

230 But, as a stranger, you are ignorant

Of what by publick fame my Subjects know;

She is my Mistress.

    Aben. ————And my daughter too.

    Almanz. Believe, old Man, that I her father knew:

What else should make *Almanzor* kneel to you?

Nor doubt, Sir, but your right to her was known: ⎫

For had you had no claim but love alone,   ⎬

I could produce a better of my own.   ⎭

    Almah. Almanzor, you forget my last request: [*Softly to him.*

Your words have too much haughtiness exprest.

240 Is this the humble way you were to move?

    Almanz. I was too far transported by my love.   [*To her.*

Forgive me; for I had not learn'd to sue

To any thing before, but Heav'n and you.

Sir, at your feet, I make it my request————   [*To the King:*

           first line kneeling: second rising: and boldly.

Though, without boasting I deserve her best.

For you, her love with gaudy titles sought,

But I her heart with blood and dangers bought.

    Boab. The blood which you have shed in her defence

Shall have in time a fitting recompence:

250 Or, if you think your services delai'd,

Name but your price, and you shall soon be pai'd.

    Alman. My price! why, King, you do not think you deal

With one, who sets his services to sale?

Reserve your gifts for those who gifts regard;

And know I think my self above reward.

229+ *s.d.* [*The*] Q2–5, F, D; ᴧ~ Q1.

230 ignorant] Q3–5, F, D; ~. Q1; ~, Q2.

232 Mistress.] F; ~: Q1–5, D.

234 make *Almanzor*] Q2–3, F, D; ~ᴧ ~, Q1; ~, ~, Q4; ~, ~ᴧ Q5.

238 *Almah. Almanzor, . . .* request: [*Softly to him.*] *Almahide softly to him.* |
Almanzor, . . . request: Q1–5, F; *Almah. softly to him.* Almanzor, . . . Request: D.

241 *Almanz.* I . . . love. [*To her.*] *Almanzor to her.* / I . . . love. Q1–5; [Almanzor
to her. / *Almanz.* I . . . Love. F; *Almanz. to her.* I . . . Love. D.

244 *s.d.* [*To*] Q2–5, F, D; ᴧ~ Q1.

244 *s.d. King:*] ~. Q1–2, Q4–5, D; ~, Q3; ~ᴧ F.

Boab. Then sure you are some Godhead; and our care
Must be to come with Incence, and with Pray'r.
    Almanz. As little as you think your self oblig'd,
You would be glad to do't, when next besieg'd.
260 But I am pleas'd there should be nothing due;
For what I did was for my self not you.
    Boab. You, with contempt, on meaner gifts look down;
And, aiming at my Queen, disdain my Crown.
That Crown restor'd, deserves no recompence,
Since you would rob the fairest Jewel thence.
Dare not henceforth ungrateful me to call;
What 'ere I ow'd you, this has cancell'd all.
    Alman. I'll call thee thankless, King; and perjur'd both:
Thou swor'st by *Alha;* and hast broke thy oath.
270 But thou dost well: thou tak'st the cheapest way;
Not to own services thou canst not pay.
    Boab. My patience more then payes thy service past;
But know this insolence shall be thy last.
Hence from my sight, and take it as a grace
Thou liv'st, and art but banish'd from the place.
    Almanz. Where 'ere I goe there can no exile be;
But from *Almanzor*'s sight I banish thee:
I will not now, if thou wouldst beg me, stay;
But I will take my *Almahide* away.
280 Stay thou with all thy Subjects here: but know
We leave thy City empty when we go.
                          [Takes Almahide's *hand.*
    Boabdelin. Fall on; take; kill the Traytour.
                    [The Guards fall on him: he makes
                    at the King through the midst of
                    them; and falls upon him; they
                    disarm him; and rescue the King.
    Almanz. ————————————————Base, and poor,
Blush that thou art *Almanzor*'s Conquerour.
                    [Almahide wrings her hands: then
                    turns and veyles her face.

281+   *s.d.* [*Takes*] Q2–5, F, D; ˄~ Q1.
282+   *s.d.* [*The Guards*] Q4, F, D; ˄~~ Q1–3, Q5.
283+   *s.d.* [Almahide] Q4–5, F, D; ˄~ Q1–3.

Farewell my *Almahide!*
Life of it self will goe, now thou art gone,
Like flies in Winter when they loose the Sun.
      [Abenamar *whispers the King a little; then speaks alowd.*
   Aben. Revenge, and taken so secure a way,
Are blessings which Heav'n sends not every day.
   Boab. I will at pleasure now revenge my wrong;
290 And, Traytour, thou shalt feel my vengeance long:
Thou shalt not dye just at thy own desire,
But see my Nuptials, and with rage expire.
   Alman. Thou darst not marry her while I'm in sight;
With a bent brow thy Priest and thee I'le fright,
And in that Scene
Which all thy hopes and wishes should content,
The thought of me shall make thee impotent.
                 [*He is led off by Guards.*
   Boab. As some fair tulip, by a storm opprest,   [*To* Almahide.
Shrinks up; and folds its silken arms to rest;
300 Bends to the blast, all pale and almost dead,
While the loud wind sings round its drooping head:
So, shrowded up your beauty disappears;
Unvail my Love; and lay aside your fears.
The storm that caus'd your fright, is past and done.
     [Almahide *unveyling and looking round for* Almanzor.
   Almah. So flow'rs peep out too soon, and miss the Sun.
                 [*Turning from him.*
   Boab. What myst'ry in this strange behaviour lies?
   Almah. Let me for ever hide these guilty eyes
Which lighted my *Almanzor* to his tomb;

286+   *s.d.* [Abenamar] Q4–5, F, D; ∧~ Q1–3.
289   pleasure] Q2–3; leisure Q1, Q4–5, F, D.
295   *centered in Q1.*
297+   *s.d.* [*He*] Q2–5, F, D; ∧~ Q1.
298   *Boab.* As . . . opprest, [*To* Almahide.] D; *Boabdel.* to *Almahide.* | As . . . op-
prest, Q1–5, F.
300   Bends . . . almost dead] Q2–3; And, bending . . . dead Q1, Q4–5, F, D.
301   While the loud . . . sings . . . drooping head] Q2–3; Hears from within, the
. . . sing . . . head Q1, Q4–5, F, D.
304+   *s.d.* [Almahide] Q4–5, F, D; ∧~ Q1–3.
305   *Almah.* So] F, D; So Q1–5.
305   flow'rs] Q2–3, D; flowr's Q1; flower's Q4–5, F.
305+   *s.d. Turning*] Q4–5, F, D; *turning* Q1–3.

Or, let 'em blaze to shew me there a room.

310   *Boab.* Heav'n lent their lustre for a Nobler end:
A thousand torches must their light attend
To lead you to a Temple and a Crown.————
Why does my fairest *Almahida* frown?
Am I less pleasing then I was before,
Or is the insolent *Almanzor*, more?

   Almah. I justly own that I some pity have,
Not for the Insolent, but for the Brave.

   Aben. Though to your King your duty you neglect,
Know, *Almahide*, I look for more respect.

320 And, if a Parents charge your mind can move,
Receive the blessing of a Monarch's love.

   Almah. Did he my freedome to his life prefer,
And shall I wed *Almanzor*'s Murderer?
No, Sir; I cannot to your will submit:
Your way's too rugged for my tender feet.

   Aben. You must be driv'n where you refuse to go:
And taught, by force, your happiness to know.

   Almah. To force me, Sir, is much unworthy you;
And, when you would, impossible to do.   *[Smiling scornfully.*

330 If force could bend me, you might think with shame,
That I debas'd the blood from whence I came.
My soul is soft; which you may gently lay   ⎫
In your loose palm; but when tis prest to stay,   ⎬
Like water it deludes your grasp, and slips away. ⎭

   Boab. I finde I must revoke what I decreed;
Almanzors death my Nuptials must precede.
Love is a Magick which the Lover tyes;
But charms still end, when the Magician dyes.
Go; let me hear my hated Rival's dead;   *[To his guards.*

340 And to convince my eyes, bring back his head.

   Almah. Go on; I wish no other way to prove
That I am worthy of *Almanzor*'s love.
We will in death, at least, united be;

---

311   thousand] Q2–5, F, D; thousaud Q1.
328–329 *Almah.* To . . . you; / . . . [*Smiling scornfully.*] D; *Almahide smiling
scornfully.* / To . . . you; Q1–5, F (*Almah.* To F).

I'le shew you I can dye as well as he.
    Boab. What should I do? when equally I dread
Almanzor living, and *Almanzor* dead!————
Yet, by your promise you are mine alone.
    Almah. How dare you claim my faith, and break your own?
    Aben. This for your vertue is a weak defence:
350 No second vows can with your first dispence.
Yet, since the King did to *Almanzor* swear,
And, in his death ingrateful may appear,
He ought, in justice, first to spare his life,
And then to claim your promise, as his wife.
    Almah. What 'ere my secret inclinations be,
To this, since honor ties me, I agree.
Yet I declare and to the world will own,
That, far from seeking, I would shun the Throne,
And, with *Almanzor*, lead an humble life;
360 There is a private greatness in his wife.
    Boab. That little love I have, I hardly buy;
You give my Rival all, while you deny.
Yet, *Almahide*, to let you see your pow'r,
Your lov'd *Almanzor* shall be free this hour.
You are obey'd; but tis so great a grace,
That I could almost wish my Rivals place.
               [*Exeunt King &* Abenamar.
    Almah. How blest was I before this fatal day!
When all I knew of love, was to obey!
'Twas life becalm'd; without a gentle breath;
370 Though not so cold, yet motionless as death:
A heavy quiet state: but love all strife,
All rapid, is the Hurrican of life.
Had love not shown me, I had never seen
An Excellence beyond *Boabdelin.*
I had not, ayming higher, lost my rest;
But with a vulgar good been dully blest.

---

345 do?] ~! Q1–5, F, D.
366 almost wish] Q2–3; wish me in Q1, Q4–5, F, D.
366+ s.d. [*Exeunt*] Q4–5, F, D; ∧~ Q1–3.
370 death:] ~. Q1–5, F, D.   372 rapid,] Q3, F, D; ~; Q1–2; ~∧ Q4–5.

But, in *Almanzor*, having seen what's rare,
Now I have learnt too sharply to compare,
And, like a Fav'rite, quickly in disgrace,
380 Just know the value 'ere I loose the place.

To her Almanzor *bound and guarded.*

Almanz. I see the end for which I'me hither sent;
To double, by your sight, my punishment.   [*Looking down.*
There is a shame in bonds, I cannot bear;
Far more than death, to meet your eyes I fear.
Almah. That shame of long continuance shall not be:
The King, at my intreaty, sets you free.   [*Unbinding him.*
Alman. The King! my wonder's greater than before:
How did he dare my freedom to restore?
He like some Captive Lyon uses me;
390 He runs away before he sets me free:
And takes a sanctuary in his Court:
I'll rather loose my life than thank him for't.
Alm. If any subject for your thanks there be,
The King expects 'em not; you ow 'em me.
Our freedoms through each others hands have past;
You give me my revenge in winning last.
Almanz. Then fate commodiously for me has done;
To loose mine there where I would wish it won.
Almah. Almanzor, you too soon will understand
400 That what I win is on anothers hand.
The King (who doom'd you to a cruel fate)
Gave to my pray'rs both his revenge and hate,
But at no other price would rate your life
Then my consent, and oath to be his wife.
Almanz. Would you to save my life, my love betray? ⎫
Here; take me; bind me; carry me away;   ⎬ [*To the*
Kill me: I'll kill you if you disobey.   ⎭ *Guards.*

---

382   *s.d.* [*Looking*] Q2–5, F, D; ∧*looking* Q1.
385–386   *Almah.* That . . . be: / . . . [*Unbinding him.*] D; *Almahide unbinding him.*
/ That . . . be: Q1–5; Almahide *unbinding him.* / *Almah.* That . . . be: F.
398   wish] Q2–3; have Q1, Q4–5, F, D.   405   *Almanz.*] *on a line by itself in* Q1.
406   *s.d.* [*To*] Q4–5, F, D; ∧*to* Q1; ∧*To* Q2–3.

Almah. That absolute command your love does give
I take; and charge you, by that pow'r, to live.
410   *Alman.* When death, the last of comforts you refuse,
Your pow'r, like Heav'n upon the damn'd, you use,
You force me in my being to remain,
To make me last, and keep me fresh for pain.
What cause can I for living longer, give,
But a dull lazy habitude to live?
    Almah. Rash men, like you, and impotent of will,
Give chance no time to turn; but urge her still.
She wou'd repent; you push the quarrel on,
And once because she went, she must be gone.
420   *Alman.* She shall not turn: what is it she can do
To recompence me for the loss of you?
    Almah. Heav'n will reward your worth some better way;
At least, for me, you have but lost one day.
Nor is't a real loss which you deplore;
You sought a heart that was ingag'd before.
'Twas a swift love which took you in his way;
Flew only through your heart but made no stay.
'Twas but a dream; where truth had not a place:
A scene of fancy, mov'd so swift a pace
430 And shifted, that you can but think it was:
Let, then, the short vexatious Vision pass.
    Alman. My joyes indeed are dreams; but not my pain;
'Twas a swift ruin; but the marks remain.
When some fierce fire lays goodly buildings wast,
Would you conclude
There had been none, because the burning's past?
    Almah. Your Heart's, at worst, but so consum'd by fire
As Cities are, that by their falls rise high'r.
Build Love a Nobler Temple in my place;

---

414   What] Q2–3; When all my joys are gone / What Q1, Q4–5, F, D.
419   once] D; ∼, Q1–5, F.
421   you?] D; ∼! Q1–5, F.
422   way;] Q2–3; ∼. Q1, Q4–5, F, D.
432   pain;] Q2–3; ∼∧ Q1; ∼: Q4–5, F, D.
437   *Almah.* Your Heart's,] Q2–3; *Almah.* It was your fault that fire seiz'd all your brest, / You should have blown up some, to save the rest. / But tis, Q1, Q4–5, F, D.

440 You'l find the fire has but inlarg'd your space.
      Alman. Love has undone me; I am grown so poor ⎞
      I sadly view the ground I had before: ⎟
      But want a stock; and ne'r can build it more.   ⎠
      Almah. Then say what Charity I can allow;
      I would contribute; if I knew but how.
      Take friendship: or if that too small appear,
      Take love which Sisters may to Brothers bear.
      Alman. A Sisters love! that is so pall'd a thing!
      What pleasure can it to a Lover bring?
450 'Tis like thin food to men in feavours spent;
      Just keeps alive; but gives no nourishment.
      What hopes, what fears, what raptures can it move?
      'Tis but the Ghost of a departed Love.
      Almah. You like some greedy Cormorant, devour
      All my whole life can give you, in an hour.
      What more I can do for you, is to dy,
      And that must follow, if you this deny.
      Since I gave up my love that you might live
      You, in refusing life, my sentence give.
460   *Alman.* Far from my brest be such an impious thought:
      Your death would loose the quiet mine had sought.
      I'll live for you, in spight of misery:
      But you shall grant that I had rather dye.
      I'll be so wretched; fild with such despair,
      That you shall see, to live, was more to dare.
      Almah. Adieu, then, O my Souls far better part;
      Your Image sticks so close
      That the blood follows from my rending heart.
      A last farewel!
470 For since a last must come, the rest are vain!
      Like gasps in death, which but prolong our pain.
      But, since the King is now a part of me:
      Cease from henceforth to be his Enemy.

---

445   contribute] Q2–3, Q5, F, D; *Contribute* Q1, Q4.
452   raptures] Q2–3; transports Q1, Q4–5, F, D.
465   dare.] Q3–5, F, D; ~, Q1–2.
466   part;] Q2–3; ~∧ Q1; ~, Q4–5, F, D.

Go now, for pity go, for if you stay
I fear I shall have something still to say.
Thus———I for ever shut you from my sight.   [*Veyles.*
    Alman. Like one thrust out in a cold Winters night,
Yet shivering, underneath your gate I stay;
One look———I cannot go before 'tis day———
                [*She beckens him to be gone.*
480 Not one———Farewell: what 'ere my sufferings be ⎫
Within; I'le speak Farewell, as loud as she: ⎬
I will not be out-done in Constancy.———   ⎭
               [*She turns her back.*

Then like a dying Conquerour I goe;
At least I have look't last upon my foe.
I go———but if too heavily I move,
I walk encumbred with a weight of Love.
Fain I would leave the thought of you behind   ⎫
But still, the more I cast you from my mind,   ⎬
You dash, like water, back, when thrown against the wind. ⎭
                  [*Exit.*

      As he goes off the King meets him with Abenamar,
        they stare at each other without saluting.

490   *Boabd.* With him go all my fears: a guard there wait;
And see him safe without the City gate.

          To them Abdelmelech.

Now *Abdelmelech*, is my brother dead?
    Abdel. Th' Usurper to the Christian Camp is fled;
Whom as *Granada*'s lawful King they own;
And vow, by force to seat him in the throne.

---

476   s.d. *Veyles*] Q4–5, F, D; *veyles* Q1–3.   479+   s.d. *She*] Q2–5, F, D; *she* Q1.
480   Farewell] Q2–5, F, D; farwell Q1.   482+   s.d. *She*] Q2–5, F, D; *she* Q1.
489   wind.] Q2–5, F, D; ~∧ Q1.   489+   s.d. [*Exit*] Q4–5, F, D; ∧~ Q1–3.
489+   s.d. *As . . . saluting.*] *at right in* Q1–5, F, D.
491+   s.d. *at right in* Q1–5, F.
491+   s.d. Abdelmelech] Q2–5, F, D; Abdemelech Q1.
492   *Abdelmelech*] Q2–5, F, D; *Abdemelech* Q1.

Mean time the Rebels in th' *Albayzin* rest;
Which is, in *Lyndaraxa's* name, possest.
   Boab. Hast; and reduce it instantly by force.
   Abdel. First give me leave to prove a milder course.
500 She will, perhaps, on summons yield the place.
   Boab. We cannot, to your sute, refuse her grace.

       One enters hastily and whispers Abenamar.

   Aben. How fortune persecutes this hoary head!
My *Ozmyn* is with *Selin's* daughter fled.
But he's no more my Son———
My hate shall like a *Zegry* him pursue;
Till I take back what blood from me he drew.
   Boab. Let war and vengeance be to morrow's care:
But let us to the Temple now repair.
A thousand torches make the Mosque more bright:
510 This must be mine and *Almahida's* night.
Hence ye importunate affairs of State;
You should not Tyrannize on Love, but waite.
Had life no love, none would for business live;
Yet still from love the largest part we give:
And must be forc'd, in Empires weary toile,
To live long wretched to be pleas'd a while.

                               [Exeunt.

---

497   *Lyndaraxa's*] Q2–5, F, D; *Lindaraxa's* Q1.
498   force.] Q3, F, D; ∼: Q1–2, Q4–5.
501+   *s.d. One*] Q2–3; [∼ Q1, Q4–5, F, D *(right justified)*.
503   *Ozmyn*] Q2–5, F, D; *Ozmin* Q1.
516+   *s.d. [Exeunt]* Q4–5, F, D; ∧∼ Q1–3.

Epilogue.

SUCCESS, *which can no more than beauty last,*
   Makes our sad Poet mourn your favours past:
   For, since without desert he got a name,
He fears to loose it now with greater shame.
Fame, like a little Mistriss of the town,
Is gaind with ease; but then she's lost as soon.
For, as those taudry Misses soon or late
Jilt such as keep 'em at the highest rate:
(And oft the Lacquey, or the Brawny Clown,
Gets what is hid in the loose body'd gown;)
So, Fame is false to all that keep her long;
And turns up to the Fop that's brisk and young.
Some wiser Poet now would leave Fame first:
But elder wits are like old Lovers curst;
Who, when the vigor of their youth is spent,
Still grow more fond as they grow impotent.
This, some years hence, our Poets case may prove;
But, yet, he hopes, he's young enough to love.
When forty comes, if 'ere he live to see
That wretched, fumbling age of poetry;
T'will be high time to bid his Muse adieu:
Well he may please him self, but never you.
Till then he'l do as well as he began;
And hopes you will not finde him less a man.
Think him not duller for this years delay; ⎫
He was prepar'd, the women were away; ⎬
And men, without their parts, can hardly play. ⎭
If they, through sickness, seldome did appear, ⎫
Pity the virgins of each Theatre! ⎪
For, at both houses, 'twas a sickly year! ⎬
And pity us, your servants, to whose cost, ⎭
In one such sickness, nine whole Mon'ths are lost.

7 *Misses*] M5; ~, Q1–5, F, D.

Their stay, he fears, has ruin'd what he writ:
Long waiting both disables love and wit.
They thought they gave him leisure to do well:
But when they forc'd him to attend, he fell!
Yet though he much has faild, he begs to day
You will excuse his unperforming Play:
Weakness sometimes great passion does express;
40   *He had pleas'd better, had he lov'd you less.*

THE CONQUEST OF GRANADA

THE SECOND PART

Almanzor and *Almahide*,

Or, The

CONQUEST

OF

Granada

The Second Part.

As it is Acted at the

THEATER-ROYAL.

Written by *JOHN DRYDEN* Servant
to His Majesty.

————————*Stimulos dedit æmula virtus.*

Lucan.

In the *SAVOY*,

Printed by *T. N.* for *Henry Herringman*, and are to
be sold at the *Anchor* in the Lower Walk
of the *New Exchange.* 1672.

PROLOGUE
To the Second Part, OF THE
CONQUEST OF Granada.

T HEY *who write Ill, and they who ne'r durst write,*
 Turn Critiques, out of meer Revenge and Spight:
 A Play-house gives 'em Fame; and up there starts,
From a mean Fifth-rate Wit, a Man of Parts.
(So Common Faces on the Stage appear:
We take 'em in; and they turn Beauties here.)
Our Authour fears those Critiques as his Fate:
And those he Fears, by consequence, must Hate.
For they the Trafficque of all Wit, invade;
10 *As Scriv'ners draw away the Bankers Trade.*
Howe're, the Poet's safe enough to day:
They cannot censure an unfinish'd Play.
But, as when Vizard Masque appears in Pit,
Straight, every man who thinks himself a Wit,
Perks up; and, managing his Comb, with grace,
With his white Wigg sets off his Nut-brown Face:
That done, bears up to th' prize, and views each Limb,
To know her by her Rigging and her Trimm:
Then, the whole noise of Fopps to wagers go,
20 *Pox on her, 't must be she; and Damm'ee no:*
Just so I Prophecy, these Wits to day,
Will blindly guess at our imperfect Play:
With what new Plots our Second Part is fill'd;
Who must be kept alive, and who be kill'd.
And as those Vizard Masques maintain that Fashion,
To sooth and tickle sweet Imagination:

3 *A Play-house*] *A* Play-house Q1–5, F, D; *A* play house M5.
10–11 *between these lines* M5 *has:*
  Some of them seeme indeed yᵉ poetts freinds;
  But 'tis, as France courts England, for her ends.
  They build up this Lampoone, & th' other Songe,
  And Court him, to lye still, while they grow stronge.

So, our dull Poet keeps you on with Masquing;
To make you think there's something worth your asking:
But when 'tis shown, that which does now delight you,
30   *Will prove a Dowdy, with a Face to fright you.*

ALMANZOR AND ALMAHIDE,

OR, THE

CONQUEST OF GRANADA

BY THE SPANIARDS.

The Second Part.

ACT I.

SCENE *A Camp.*

King Ferdinand; *Queen* Isabel; Alonzo d'Aguilar;
Attendants: men and women.

K. Ferd. At length the time is come, when *Spain* shall be
From the long Yoke of *Moorish* Tyrants free.
All causes seem to second our design;
And Heav'n and Earth in their destruction join.
When Empire in its Childhood first appears,
A watchful Fate o'resees its tender years;
Till, grown more strong, it thrusts, and stretches out,
And Elbows all the Kingdoms round about:
The place thus made for its first breathing free,
10 It moves again for ease and Luxury:
Till, swelling by degrees, it has possest
The greater space; and now crowds up the rest.

ACT] Q3–5, F, D; ∼. Q1–2.
s.d. Isabel;] Q2–3; ∼. Q1, Q4–5 (Ysabel Q1); ∼, F, D.
s.d. Aguilar;] D; ∼. Q1–2, Q4–5; ∼, Q3, F.
2   *Moorish*] Q2–3, D; Moorish Q1, Q4–5, F.
6   o'resees] Q2–5, F, D; 'oresees Q1.

When from behind, there starts some petty State;
And pushes on its now unwieldy fate:
Then, down the precipice of time it goes,
And sinks in Minutes, which in Ages rose.
    Qu. Isabel. Should bold *Columbus* in his search succeed,
And find those Beds in which bright Metals breed;
Tracing the Sun, who seems to steal away,   ⎫
20 That Miser-like, he might alone, survey   ⎬
The wealth, which he in Western Mines did lay; ⎭
Not all that shining Ore could give my heart
The joy, this Conquer'd Kingdom will impart:
Which, rescu'd from these Misbelievers hands;
Shall now, at once shake off its double bands:
At once to freedom and true faith restor'd:
Its old Religion, and its antient Lord.
    K. Ferd. By that assault which last we made, I find,
Their Courage is with their Success declin'd:
30 *Almanzor*'s absence now they dearly buy,
Whose Conduct crown'd their Armes with Victory.
    Alonzo. Their King himself did their last Sally guide, ⎫
I saw him glist'ring in bright armour, ride   ⎬
To break a Lance in honour of his Bride.   ⎭
But other thoughts now fill his anxious brest;
Care of his Crown his Love has dispossest.

To them Abdalla.

    Qu. Isabel. But see the brother of the *Moorish* King;
He seems some news of great import to bring.
    Ferd. He brings a specious title to our side;
40 Those who would conquer, must their Foes divide.
    Abdal. Since to my Exile you have pity shown;
And giv'n me Courage, yet to hope a throne;
While you without, our Common Foes subdue,

---

17   *Qu. Isabel.*] D; Qu. *Ysabel.* Q1; Qu. *Isabel.* Q2–5, F.
28   *K.*] D; K. Q1–5, F.
37   *Qu. Isabel.*] D; Qu. *Ysabel.* Q1; Qu. *Isabel.* Q2–5, F.
37   *Moorish*] Q3, D; Moorish Q1–2, Q4–5, F.
42   throne;] Q3, F, D; ∼. Q1–2, Q4–5.

I am not wanting to my self, or you:
But have, within, a faction still alive;
Strong to assist, and secret to contrive:
And watching each occasion, to foment
The peoples fears into a discontent:
Which, from *Almanzor*'s loss, before were great
50 And now are doubled by their late defeat.
These Letters from their Chiefs, the news assures.
                          [*Gives Letters to the King.*
      K. Ferd. Be mine the honour; but the profit yours.

           To them the Duke of Arcos,
        with Ozmyn, *and* Benzayda *prisoners.*

      K. Ferd. That *tertia* of *Italians* did you guide
To take their post upon the River side?
      Arcos. All are according to your Orders plac'd:
My chearful Soldiers their intrenchments hast,
The *Murcian* foot have ta'ne the upper ground,
And now the City is beleaguer'd round.
      Ferd. Why is not then, their Leader here again?
60   *Arcos.* The Master of *Alcantara* is slain:
But he who slew him here before you stands;
It is that *Moor* whom you behold in bands.
      K. Ferd. A braver man I had not in my host:
His Murd'rer shall not long his Conquest boast.
But, Duke of *Arcos*, say, how was he slain?
      Arcos. Our Souldiers march'd together on the Plain,
We two rode on, and left them far behind,
Till, coming where we found the valley winde,
Wee saw these *Moors*, who, swiftly as they cou'd,
70 Ran on, to gain the Covert of the wood.
This we observ'd; and, having cross'd their way,

---

44   you:] F; ~. Q1–5, D.
51+   *s.d. Gives*] Q2–5, F, D; *gives* Q1.
53   *K.*] D; K. Q1–5, F.
53   *Italians*] Q2–3, D; Italians Q1, Q4–5, F.
62   *Moor*] Q2–3, D; Moor Q1, Q4–5, F.
69   *Moors*] Q2–3, D; Moors Q1, Q4–5, F.

51   assures.] Q3–5, F, D; ~; Q1; ~: Q2.
52   *K.*] D; K. Q1–5, F.
53   *tertia*] Q2–3; tertia Q1, Q4–5, F, D.
63   *K.*] D; K. Q1–5, F.

The Lady, out of breath, was forc'd to stay:
The Man then stood and straight his fauchion drew,
Then told us, we in vain did those pursue
Whom their ill fortune to despair did drive,
And yet, whom we shou'd never take alive.
Neglecting this, the Master straight spurr'd on;
But th' active *Moor* his horses shock did shun,
And 'ere his Rider from his reach could goe,
80 Finish'd the Combat with one deadly blow.
I, to revenge my Friend, prepar'd to fight,
But now our foremost Men were come in sight,
Who soon would have dispatch'd him on the Place,
Had I not sav'd him from a death so base;
And brought him to attend your Royal doom.
     K. Ferd. A Manly face; and in his ages bloom.
But to content the Souldiers, he must dye;
Go, see him executed instantly.
     Q. Isabel. Stay; I would learn his name before he goe;
90 You, Prince *Abdalla*, may the Pris'ner know.
     Abdalla. *Ozmyn*'s his name; and he deserves his fate;
His father heads that faction which I hate:
But, much I wonder, that I with him see
The daughter of his Mortal Enemy.
     Benz. 'Tis true; by *Ozmyns* sword my Brother fell;
But 'twas a death he merited too well.
I know a sister should excuse his fault;
But you know too, that *Ozmyn*'s death he sought.
     Abdall. Our Prophet has declar'd, by the Event,
100 That *Ozmyn* is reserv'd for punishment.
For, when he thought his guilt from danger clear;
He, by new Crimes, is brought to suffer here.
     Benz. In Love, or Pity, if a Crime you find;
We two have sin'd above all humane kind.
     Ozm. Heav'n in my punishment, has done a grace;
I could not suffer in a better place:

72   breath,] Q2–3, F, D; ~ₐ Q1, Q4–5.   78   *Moor*] Q2–3, D; Moor Q1, Q4–5, F.
89   *Isabel*] Q2–5, F, D; *Ysabel* Q1.   106   better] Q2–5, F, D; betters Q1.

That I should dye by Christians, it thought good;
To save your fathers guilt, who sought my blood.   [*To her.*
   Benz. Fate aims so many blows to make us fall,
110 That 'tis in vain, to think to ward 'em all:
And where misfortunes great and many are,
Life grows a burden; and not worth our care.
   Ozm. I cast it from me, like a Garment torn,
Ragged, and too undecent to be worn.
Besides, there is Contagion in my Fate;   [*To Benz.*
It makes your Life too much unfortunate.
But, since her faults are not ally'd to mine,
In her protection let your favour shine:
To you, Great Queen, I make this last request;
120 (Since pity dwells in every Royal Brest)
Safe, in your care, her Life and Honour be:
It is a dying Lovers Legacy.
   Benz. Cease, *Ozmyn*, cease so vain a sute to move;
I did not give you on those terms my Love.
Leave me to my own care; for, when you go,
My Love will soon instruct me what to do.
   Qu. Isa. Permit me, Sir, these Lovers doom to give:
My Sentence is, they shall together live.
The Courts of Kings,
130 To all Distress'd shou'd Sanctuaries be:
But most, to Lovers in Adversity.
Castille and *Arragon*
Which, long against each other, War did move,
My plighted Lord and I have joyn'd by love:
And, if to add this Conquest Heav'n thinks good,
I would not have it stain'd with Lovers blood.
   Ferd. Whatever *Isabella* shall Command
Shall always be a Law to *Ferdinand.*
   Benz. The frowns of Fate we will no longer fear:

---

108   *s.d. To her*] Q2–5, F, D; *to her* Q1.
115   *s.d. To* Benz.] Q2–5, F, D; *to Benz.* Q1.
125   me to my own care;] Q2–3; Me, the care of Me; Q1, Q4–5, F, D.
130   be:] Q2–3; ~. Q1, Q4–5; ~; F; ~, D.
138   *Ferdinand.*] Q3, D; ~: Q1–2, Q4–5, F.

140 Ill Fate, Great Queen, can never find us here.
    Isab. Your thanks some other time I will receive:
Henceforward, safe in my Protection live.
Granada, is, for Noble Loves renown'd;
Her best defence is in her Lovers found.
Love's a Heroique Passion which can find
No room in any base degenerate mind:
It kindles all the Soul with Honours Fire,
To make the Lover worthy his desire.
Against such Heroes I success should fear,
150 Had we not too an Hoast of Lovers here.
An Army of bright Beauties come with me;
Each Lady shall her Servants actions see:
The Fair and Brave on each side shall contest;
And they shall overcome who love the best.

                         [*Exeunt omnes.*

SCENE II.

The Alhambra.

Zulema *solus.*

    Zul. True; they have pardon'd me; but do they know
What folly 'tis to trust a pardon'd Foe?
A Blush remains in a forgiven Face;
It wears the silent Tokens of Disgrace:
Forgiveness to the Injur'd does belong;
But they ne'r pardon who have done the wrong.
My hopeful Fortune's lost! and what's above
All I can name or think, my ruin'd Love!
Feign'd Honesty shall work me into Trust;
10 And seeming Penitence conceal my Lust.
Let Heav'ns great Eye of Providence now take
One day of rest, and ever after wake.

---

1 *Zul.* True] F; True Q1–5, D.   2 Foe?] ~! Q1–5, F, D.

Enter King Boabdelin, Abenamar *and Guards.*

Boab. Losses on Losses! as if Heav'n decreed
Almanzors valour should alone succeed.
  Aben. Each Sally we have made since he is gone,
Serves but to pull our speedy ruine on.
  Boab. Of all Mankind, the heaviest Fate he bears
Who the last Crown of sinking Empire wears.
No kindly Planet of his Birth took care:
20 Heav'ns Out-cast; and the Dross of every Starr!
                    [*A tumultuous noise within.*

Enter Abdelmelech.

What new misfortune do these Cries presage?
  Abdel. They are th' effects of the mad Peoples rage.
All in despair tumultuously they swarm;
The farthest Streets already take th' Alarm;
The needy creep from Cellars, under-ground,
To them new Cries from tops of Garrets sound.
The aged from the Chimneys seek the cold;
And Wives from Windows helpless Infants hold.
  Boab. See what the many-headed Beast demands.
                    [*Exit* Abdelmelech.
30 Curst is that King whose Honour's in their hands.
In Senates, either they too slowly grant,
Or saucily refuse to aid my want:
And when their Thrift has ruin'd me in Warr,
They call their Insolence my want of Care.
  Aben. Curst be their Leaders who that Rage foment;
And vail with publick good their discontent:
They keep the Peoples Purses in their hands,
And Hector Kings to grant their wild demands.
But to each Lure a Court throws out, descend;

12+   s.d. and] Q2–5, F, D; and Q1.   20+   s.d. within.] Q2–5, F, D; ~∧ Q1.
23   they] Q2–5, F, D; thy Q1.

40 And prey on those, they promis'd to defend.
   Zul. Those Kings who to their wild demands consent,
Teach others the same way to discontent.
Freedom in Subjects is not, nor can be;
But still to please 'em we must call 'em free.
Propriety which they their Idoll make,
Or Law, or Law's Interpreters can shake.
   Aben. The name of Common-wealth is popular;
But there the People their own Tyrants are.
   Boab. But Kings who rule with limited Command
50 Have Players Scepters put into their Hand.
Pow'r has no ballance, one side still weighs down;
And either hoysts the Common-wealth or Crown.
And those who think to set the Skale more right,
By various turnings but disturb the weight.
   Aben. While People tugg for Freedom, Kings for Pow'r,
Both sink beneath some foreign Conquerour.
Then Subjects find too late they were unjust
And want that pow'r of Kings they durst not trust.

To them Abdelmelech.

   Abdel. The Tumult now is high and dangerous grown:
60 The People talk of rendring up the Town;
And swear that they will force the Kings consent.
   K. Boab. What Councel can this rising storm prevent?
   Abdel. Their fright to no Perswasions will give ear:
There's a deaf madness in a Peoples fear.

Enter a Messenger.

   Mess. Their fury now a middle course does take:
To yield the Town, or call *Almanzor* back.
   Boab. Ile rather call my death.————

43   not, ... be;] Q3, Q5, F, D; ∼; ... ∼, Q1–2, Q4.
48   are.] Q3–5, F, D; ∼: Q1–2.
56   Conquerour.] Q3; ∼.: Q1; ∼: Q2, Q4–5, F, D.
58+   *s.d. To*] Q4–5, D; [∼ Q1–3, F.

Go, and bring up my Guards to my defence:
Ile punish this outragious Insolence.

70   *Aben.* Since blind opinion does their reason sway,
You must submit to cure 'em their own way.
You to their Fancies Physick must apply:
Give them that Chief on whom they most relye;
Under *Almanzor* prosperously they fought:
Almanzor therefore must with Pray'rs be brought.

Enter a Second Messenger.

Sec. Mess. Haste all you can their fury to asswage:
You are not safe from their rebellious rage.

Enter a Third Messenger.

Third Mes. This Minute if you grant not their desire
They'll seize your Person and your Palace Fire.

80   *Abdel.* Your danger, Sir, admits of no delay.
Boab. In tumults, People Reign, and Kings obey.
Go, and appease 'em with the vow I make
That they shall have their lov'd *Almanzor* back.
                                    [*Exit* Abdelmelech.
Almanzor has th' Ascendant o're my Fate:
I'me forc'd to stoop to one I fear and hate.
Disgrac'd, distrest, in exile, and alone,
He's greater then a Monarch on his Throne.
Without a Realm a Royalty he gains;
Kings are the Subjects over whom he Raigns.
                             [*A shout of Acclamation within.*

90   *Aben.* These shouts proclaim the people satisfy'd.
Boab. We for another Tempest must provide.
To promise his return as I was loath,
So I want pow'r now to perform my oath.

---

70 does] Q2–3, Q5, F, D; ~, Q1, Q4.   77 rage.] Q3–5, F, D; ~: Q1–2.
83+ *s.d.* [*Exit*] Q4–5, F, D; ∧~ Q1–3. 83+ *s.d.* Abdelmelech.] Q2–5, F, D; ~, Q1.
84 has] Q2–5, F, D; *has* Q1.
89+ *s.d. Acclamation*] Q2–3; *Acclamation's* Q1; *Acclamations* Q4–5, F, D.

E're this, for *Affricque* he is sail'd from *Spain.*
    Aben. The adverse winds his passage yet detain;
I heard, last night his equipage did stay,
At a small Village short of *Malaga.*
    K. Boab. Abenamar, this ev'ning thither, haste;
Desire him to forget his usage past:
100 Use all your Rhet'rique; Promise; Flatter; Pray.

To them Qu. Almahide *attended.*

    Aben. Good Fortune shows you yet a surer way:
Nor Pray'rs nor Promises his mind will move;
'Tis inaccessible to all, but Love.
    K. Boab. Oh, thou hast rows'd a thought within my brest,
That will for ever rob me of my rest.
Ah, Jealousie, how cruel is thy sting!
I, in *Almanzor,* a lov'd Rival bring!
And now, I think, it is an equal strife
If I my Crown should hazard, or my Wife.
110 Where, Marriage is thy cure, which Husbands boast,
That, in possession, their desire is lost?
Or why have I alone that wretched taste
Which, gorg'd and glutted, does with hunger last?
Custome and Duty, cannot set me free,
Ev'n Sin it self has not a Charm for me.
Of marry'd Lovers I am sure the first:
And nothing but a King could so be curst.
    Q. Almah. What sadness sits upon your Royal Heart?
Have you a Grief, and must not I have part?
120 All Creatures else a time of Love possess:
Man onely clogs with cares his happiness:
And, while he shou'd enjoy his part of Bliss,
With thoughts of what may be, destroys what is.
    K. Boab. You guess'd aright; I am opprest with grief:
And 'tis from you that I must seek relief.

---

100 Pray.] Q3, F, D; ~: Q1–2, Q4–5.   108 think,] Q2–3; ~ˌ Q1, Q4–5, F, D.
111 lost?] ~! Q1–3; ~: Q4–5, F, D.   112 why] Q3–5, F, D; ~, Q1–2.
113 last?] Q4–5, F, D; ~! Q1–3.   116 first:] Q3; ~. Q1–2, Q4–5, F; ~, D.

Leave us, to sorrow there's a rev'rence due: [*To the Company.*
Sad Kings, like Suns Ecclips'd, withdraw from view.
                              [*The Attendants goe off: and Chairs*
                                       are set for the King and Queen.
      Almah. So, two kind Turtles, when a storm is nigh,
      Look up; and see it gath'ring in the Skie:
130   *Each calls his Mate to shelter in the Groves,
      Leaving, in murmures, their unfinish'd Loves.
      Perch'd on some dropping Branch they sit alone,
      And Cooe, and hearken to each others moan.
            Boab. Since, *Almahide,* you seem so kind a Wife,
                              [*Taking her by the hand.*
      What would you do to save a Husbands life?
            Almah. When Fate calls on that hard Necessity,
      I'll suffer death rather than you shall dye.
            Boab. Suppose your Countrey should in danger be;
      What would you undertake to set it free?
140   *Almah.* It were too little to resign my Breath:
      My own free Hand should give me nobler Death.
            Boab. That Hand, which would so much for Glory do,
      Must yet do more; for it must kill me too.
      You must kill Me, for that dear Countreys sake:
      Or what's all one, must call *Almanzor* back.
            Almah. I see to what your Speech you now direct;
      Either my Love or Vertue you suspect.
      But know, that when my person I resign'd,
      I was too noble not to give my mind:
150   No more the shadow of *Almanzor* fear;
      I have no room but for your Image, here.
            Boab. This, *Almahide* would make me cease to mourn,
      Were that *Almanzor* never to return:
      But now my fearful People mutiny;
      Their clamours call *Almanzor* back, not I.

Soliq; sedent in margine ripæ.
  Soli cantare periti, Arcades. Virg. [Dryden's note.]

130   *footnote added in* Q2–3.
134   *Boab.* Since, . . . Wife, / [*Taking . . . hand.*] D; [*Boab. taking . . . hand.* /
Since, . . . Wife, Q1–5, F.

Their safety, through my ruine, I pursue;
He must return; and must be brought by you.
   Almah. That hour when I my Faith to you did plight,
I banish'd him for ever from my sight.
160 His banishment was to my Vertue due;
Not that I fear'd him for my self, but you.
My Honour had preserv'd me innocent:
But I would your suspicion too prevent:
Which, since I see augmented in your mind,
I, yet more reason for his Exile find.
   K. Boab. To your intreaties he will yield alone:
And, on your doom, depend my Life and Throne.
No longer therefore my desires withstand;
Or, if desires prevail not, my Command.
170 *Q. Almah.* In his return too sadly I foresee
Th' effects of your returning jealousie;
But, your Command I prize above my life:
'Tis sacred to a Subject and a Wife:
If I have pow'r *Almanzor* shall return.
   Boab. Curst be that fatal hour when I was born!
                       [Letting go her hand and starting up.
You love; you love him; and that love reveal
By your too quick consent to his repeal.
My jealousie had but too just a ground;
And now you stab into my former wound.
180 *Q. Almah.* This suddain change I do not understand;
Have you so soon forgot your own Command?
   Boab. Grant that I did th' unjust injunction lay,
You should have lov'd me more then to obey.
I know you did this mutiny design;
But your Love-plot I'le quickly countermine.
Let my Crown go; he never shall return;
I, like a Phœnix in my Nest will burn.
   Almah. You please me well that in one common Fate
You wrap your Self and Me, and all your State:

---

163 prevent:] ∼. Q1–5, F, D.
175 *Boab.* Curst . . . born! / [*Letting . . . up.*] D; [*Boab. letting . . . up.* / **Curst
. . . born!** Q1–5, F.

190 Let us no more of proud *Almanzor* hear:
'Tis better once to die, than still to fear.
And better many times to dye, than be
Oblig'd past payment to an Enemy.
    Boab. 'Tis better; but you wives still have one way:
When e're your Husbands are oblig'd, you pay.
    Almah. Thou, Heav'n, who know'st it, judge my innocence:
You, Sir, deserve not I should make defence.
Yet, judge my Vertue by that proof I gave,
When I submitted to be made your Slave.
200   *Boab.* If I have been suspicious or unkind,
Forgive me; many cares distract my mind.
Love, and a Crown!
Two such excuses no one Man e're had;
And each of 'em enough to make me mad:
But now, my Reason re-assumes its Throne:
And finds no safety when *Almanzor*'s gone.
Send for him, then; I'le be oblig'd; and sue;
'Tis a less evil than to part with you.
I leave you to your thoughts; but love me still!
210 Forgive my Passion, and obey my Will.

                              [*Exit* Boabdelin.

                    Almahide *Sola.*

    Almah. My jealous Lord will soon to Rage return;
That Fire his Fear rakes up, does inward burn.
But Heav'n which made me great, has chose for me:
I must th' oblation for my People be.
I'le cherish Honour, then, and Life despise;
What is not Pure, is not for Sacrifice.
Yet, for *Almanzor* I in secret mourn!
Can Vertue, then, admit of his return?
Yes; for my Love I will, by Vertue, square;
220 My Heart's not mine; but all my Actions are.

---

196   innocence:] Q2–3, F; ~. Q1, Q4–5, D.
210+   s.d. [*Exit*] Q4–5, F, D; ˌ~ Q1–3.
211   *Almah.* My] F; My Q1–5, D.

I'le imitate *Almanzor,* and will be
As haughty, and as wretched too as he.
What will he think is in my Message meant?
I scarcely understand my own intent:
But Silk-worm-like, so long within have wrought,
That I am lost in my own Webb of thought.

> [*Exit* Almahide.

ACT II.

SCENE   *A Wood.*

Ozmyn *and* Benzayda.

Ozm. 'Tis true that our protection here has been
Th' effect of Honour in a *Spanish* Queen.
But, while I as a friend continue here,
I, to my Country, must a Foe appear.
  Benz. Think not my *Ozmyn,* that we here remain
As friends, but Pris'ners to the Pow'r of *Spain.*
Fortune dispences with your Countryes right;
But you desert your honour in your flight.
  Ozm. I cannot leave you here, and go away;
10 My Honour's glad of a pretence to stay.

> [*A noise within,* Follow, follow, follow————

Enter Selin; *his sword drawn; as pursued.*

Selin. I am pursu'd, and now am spent and done;
My limbs suffice me not with strength to run.

---

221 I'le imitate *Almanzor,* and will be] Q2–3 (be, Q2); I'le, like *Almanzor,* act;
and dare to be Q1, Q4–5, F, D.
223 meant?] Q4–5, F, D; ~! Q1–3.   226+ *s.d.* [*Exit*] Q4–5, F, D; ∧~ Q1–3.
ACT] Q2–5, F, D; ~. Q1.
s.d. Ozmyn *and* Benzayda.] Q2–5, F, D; *Ozmyn and* Benzayda. Q1.
2 in a] Q2–3; in the Q1, Q4–5, F, D.   2 *Spanish*] D; Spanish Q1–5, F.
8 flight.] Q3, F, D; ~: Q1–2, Q4–5.
10+ *s.d.* [*A . . . within,* Follow, follow, follow————] *A . . . within follow, follow,
follow*———— Q1–5, F, D ([*A* Q4–5, F, D; *within,* Q2–3, Q5, F, D; *Follow* D).

And, if I could, alas, what can I save?
A year, the dregs of life too, from the grave.
                                        [*Sits down on the ground.*
Here will I sit, and here attend my fate;   ⎫
With the same hoary Majesty and State   ⎬
As *Rome*'s old Senate for the *Galls* did wait. ⎭
   Ben. It is my father; and he seems distrest.
   Ozmyn. My honour bids me succour the opprest:
20 That life he sought, for his I'le freely give;
We'll dye together; or together live.
   Benz. I'le call more succour, since the Camp is near;
And fly on all the wings of Love and fear.
                                        [*Exit* Benz.

Enter Abenamar *and four or five* Moors.
He looks; and finds Selin.

   Aben. Ye've liv'd, and now behold your latest hour.
   Selin. I scorn your malice, and defy your pow'r.
A speedy death is all I ask you now;
And that's a favour you may well allow.
   Ozmyn. Who gives you death shall give it first to me;
Fate cannot separate our destiny.   [*Shewing himself.*
30 My father here! then Heav'n it self has laid   [*Knows his father.*
The snare, in which my vertue is betray'd.
   Aben. Fortune, I thank thee, thou hast kindly done,
To bring me back that fugitive my Son.
In armes too; fighting for my Enemy!
I'le do a *Roman* justice; thou shalt dy.
   Ozm. I beg not, you my forfeit life would save:
Yet add one Minute to that breath you gave.
I disobey'd you; and deserve my fate,

---

13 save?] Q3; ∼; Q1–2, Q4–5, F; ∼! D.   14 dregs] Q2–3, D; *dregs* Q1, Q4–5, F.
14+ *s.d. Sits*] Q2–5, F, D; *sits* Q1.   18 distrest.] Q3, F, D; ∼: Q1–2, Q4–5.
23+ *s.d. [Exit]* Q4–5, F, D; ∧∼ Q1–3.
28–29 *Ozmyn.* Who . . . me; / . . . [*Shewing himself.*] Ozmyn; shewing himself. /
Who . . . me; Q1–5, D (*one line in* D); Ozmyn, showing himself. / *Ozm.* Who . . .
me; F.
30 *s.d. [Knows]* Q2–5, F, D; ∧*knows* Q1.
35 *Roman*] Q2–3, D; Roman Q1, Q4–5, F.

But bury in my grave two houses hate.
40 Let *Selin* live; and see your Justice done
On me, while you revenge him for his Son:
Your mutual malice in my death may cease;
And equal loss perswade you both to peace.
   Aben. Yes; justice shall be done, on him and thee.
Haste; and dispatch 'em both immediately.   [*To a Sold.*
   Ozmyn. If you have honour, (since you Nature want)
For your own sake my last Petition grant:
And kill not a disarm'd, defenceless foe:
Whose death your cruelty, or fear will show.
50 My Father cannot do an Act so base:
My Father! I mistake: I meant, who was!
   Aben. Go, then, dispatch him first who was my Son.
   Ozmyn. Swear but to save his life, I'le yield my own.
   Aben. Nor tears, nor pray'rs thy life, or his shall buy.
   Ozmyn. Then Sir, *Benzayda*'s father shall not dye.
                [*Putting himself before* Selin.
And, since he'le want defence when I am gone,
I will, to save his life, defend my own.
   Aben. This justice Parricides like thee should have.
                [Aben. *and his party attacque them*
                both. Ozmyn *parryes his fathers*
                thrusts; and thrusts at the others.

Enter Benzayda, *with* Abdalla, *the Duke of* Arcos,
                and Spaniards.

   Benz. O help my father, and my *Ozmyn* save.
60   *Abdal.* Villains, that death you have deserv'd, is near.
   Ozmyn. Stay Prince; and know I have a father here.

44–45 *Aben.* Yes; . . . thee. / . . . [*To a Sold.*] D; *Aben. to a Sold.* / Yes; . . . thee:
Q1–5; Aben. to a Soldier. / *Aben.* Yes, . . . thee: F.
53   own.] Q3, Q5, F, D; ~; Q1–2, Q4.
55   *Ozmyn.* Then . . . dye. / [*Putting* . . . Selin.] D; *Ozmyn putting himself before*
Selin. / Then . . . dye. Q1–5; Ozmyn *putting himself before* Selin. / *Ozm.* Then,
. . . die. F.
58   have.] Q3, F, D; ~: Q1–2, Q4–5.   58+ *s.d.* [Aben.] Q4–5, F, D; ∧~ Q1–3.
61–62 *Ozmyn.* Stay . . . here. / . . . [*Stops his hand.*] D; *Ozmyn stops his hand.* /
Stay . . . here. Q1–5; Ozmyn *stops his Hand.* / *Ozm.* Stay . . . here. F.

I were that Parricide of whom he spoke   [*Stops his hand.*
Did not my piety prevent your stroke.
   Arcos. Depart, then, and thank Heav'n you had a Son.
                               [*To* Aben.
   Aben. I am not with these shows of duty won.
   Ozm. Heav'n know's I would that life you seek, resign,
But, while *Benzayda* lives it is not mine.   [*To his father.*
Will you yet pardon my unwilling crime?
   Aben. By no intreaties; by no length of time
70 Will I be won: but, with my latest breath,
I'le curse thee here: and haunt thee after death.
                     [*Exit* Abenamar *with his party.*
   Ozmyn. Can you be merciful to that degree
As to forgive my Fathers faults in me?   [*Kneeling to* Selin.
Can you forgive
The death of him I slew in my defence;
And, from the malice, separate th' offence?
I can no longer be your Enemy:
In short, now kill me, Sir, or pardon me.   [*Offers him his sword.*
In this your silence my hard fate appears!
80   *Selin.* I'le answer you, when I can speak for tears.
But, till I can———
Imagine what must needs be brought to pass: [*Embraces him.*
My heart's not made of Marble, nor of Brass.
Did I for you a cruel death prepare,
And have you———have you, made my life your care?
There is a shame contracted by my faults,
Which hinders me to speak my secret thoughts.
And I will tell you (when that shame's remov'd,)
You are not better by my Daughter lov'd.

---

64 *Arcos.* Depart, . . . Son. [*To* Aben.] *Arcos to Aben.* | Depart, . . . Son: Q1–5,
F, D (*same line* F, D; Son. Q3–5, F, D).
66–67 *Ozm.* Heav'n . . . resign, / . . . [*To his father.*] *Ozm. to his father.* | Heav'n
. . . resign, Q1–5, F, D (*same line* F, D).
68 crime?] Q4–5, F, D; ∼! Q1–3.   71+ *s.d.* [*Exit*] Q4–5, F, D; ∧∼ Q1–3.
72–73 *Ozmyn.* Can . . . degree / . . . [*Kneeling to* Selin.] F, D ([Ozmyn *kneeling* F);
Ozmyn kneeling to Selin. / Can . . . degree Q1–5.
76 offence?] D; ∼! Q1–5, F.   78 *s.d.* [*Offers*] Q2–5, F, D; ∧∼ Q1.
85 care?] Q3; ∼! Q1–2, Q4–5, F, D.   89 Daughter] Q2–5, F, D; Daugher Q1.

90 *Benzaida* be your's———I can no more.
    Ozmyn. Blest be that breath which does my life restore.
                                [Embracing his knees.
    Benz. I hear my father now; these words confess
That name; and that indulgent tenderness.
    Selin. Benzayda, I have been too much to blame;
But, let your goodness expiate for my shame;
You, *Ozmyn*'s vertue did in chains adore;
And part of me was just to him before.
My Son!   *[To him.*
    Ozmyn. My father!
    Selin. ———————Since by you I live,
I, for your sake, your family forgive.
100 Let your hard father still my life pursue;
I hate not him, but for his hate to you:
Ev'n that hard father yet may one day be
By kindness vanquish'd as you vanquish'd me.
Or, if my death can quench to you his rage,
Heav'n makes good use of my remaining age.
    Abdal. I grieve your joyes are mingled with my cares.
But all take interest in their own affairs:
And therefore I must ask how mine proceed.
    Selin. They now are ripe; and but your presence need:
110 For, *Lyndaraxa,* faithless as the wind,
Yet to your better Fortunes will be kind:
For, hearing that the Christians own your cause,
From thence th' assurance of a Throne she draws.
And since *Almanzor,* whom she most did fear,
Is gone; she to no Treaty will give ear;
But sent me her unkindness to excuse.
    Abdal. You much surprize me with your pleasing news.
    Selin. But, Sir, she hourly does th' assault expect:
And must be lost, if you her Aid neglect.

---

91 *Ozmyn.* Blest . . . restore. / [*Embracing his knees.*] D; *Ozmyn embracing his knees.* / [Blest . . . restore. Q1–5 (restore‸ Q5); [*Ozmyn embracing his knees. (on l. 90) / Oxm.* Blest . . . restore. F.
94 *Benzayda*] Q3–5, F, D; *Benzaida* Q1–2.
98 s.d. *To*] Q2–5, F, D; *to* Q1.
114 And . . . fear,] Q3; ∼,. . . ∼‸ Q1–2, Q4–5; ∼, . . . ∼, F, D.

120 For *Abdelmelech* loudly does declare
    He'll use the last extremities of War;
    Since she refus'd the Fortress to resigne.
        Abdal. The charge of hast'ning this Relief be mine.
        Selin. This, while I undertook, whether beset
    Or else by chance, *Abenamar* I met:
    Who seem'd in haste returning to the Town.
        Abdal. My Love must in my diligence be shown.
    And as my pledge of Faith to *Spain*, this hour
    I'le put the Fortress in your Masters pow'r.   [*To* Arcos.
130   *Selin.* An open way from hence to it there lies,
    And we with ease may send in large supplies,
    Free from the shot and Sallies of the Town.
        Arcos. Permit me, Sir, to share in your renown;
    First to my King I will impart the news,
    And then draw out what Succors we shall use.
                        [*Exit Duke of* Arcos.
        Abdal. Grant that she loves me not, at least I see   [*Aside.*
    She loves not others, if she loves not me.
    'Tis Pleasure when we reap the fruit of Pain;
    'Tis onely Pride to be belov'd again.
140 How many are not lov'd who think they are;
    Yet all are willing to believe the Fair:
    And, though 'tis Beauties known and obvious Cheat,
    Yet Man's self-love still favours the deceit.
                        [*Exit* Abdalla.
        Selin. Farewell, my Children; equally so dear
    That I my self am to my self less neer.
    While I repeat the dangers of the War,
    Your mutual safety be each others care.
    Your Father, *Ozmyn*, till the War be done,
    As much as Honour will permit, I'le shun.
150 If by his sword I perish; let him know
    It was because I would not be his Foe.
        Ozmyn. Goodness and Vertue all your Actions guide;

130   lies,] Q4–5, F, D; ~. Q1–3.   132   Town.] Q3, F; ~; Q1–2, Q4–5, D.
135+   *s.d.* [*Exit*] Q4–5, F, D; ~ Q1–3.   136   *s.d. Aside*] Q4–5, F, D; *aside* Q1–3.
143+   *s.d.* [*Exit*] Q4–5, F, D; ~ Q1–3.

You onely erre in choosing of your side.
That party I with Honour cannot take;
But can much less the care of you forsake.
I must not draw my sword against my Prince,
But yet may hold a Shield in your defence.
Benzayda, free from danger here shall stay:
And for a Father, and a Lover, pray.
160   *Benz.* No, no; I gave not on those terms my Heart,
That from my *Ozmyn* I should ever part.
That Love I vow'd when you did death attend
'Tis just that nothing but my death should end.
What Merchant is it who would stay behind,
His whole stock ventur'd to the Waves and Wind?
I'le pray for both; but both shall be in sight;
And Heav'n shall hear me pray, and see you fight.
    Selin. No longer, *Ozmyn*, combat a design,
Where so much Love and so much vertue joyn.
170   *Ozmyn.* Then Conquer, and your Conquest happy be [*To her.*
Both to your self, your Father, and to me.
With bended knees our freedom we'll demand
Of *Isabel*, and mighty *Ferdinand*.
Then, while the paths of Honour we pursue,
We'll int'rest Heav'n for us, in right of you.

                                                    [*Exeunt.*

SCENE II.

The Albayzin.

An Alarm within; then Soldiers running over the Stage.
Enter Abdelmelech *victorious with Soldiers.*

    Abdel. 'Tis won, 'tis won; and *Lyndaraxa*, now,

───────────
165   Wind?] Q3, F, D; ~. Q1–2, Q4–5.
170   *Ozmyn.* Then ... be [*To her.*] D; Ozmyn *to her.* / Then ... be Q1–5; [Ozmyn
to her. (*on l. 169*) / *Ozm.* Then ... be, F.
175+   s.d. [*Exeunt.*] Q5, F, D; ∧~∧ Q1; ∧~. Q2–4.
SCENE II.] Sᴄᴇɴᴇ. Q1–5, F, D.
s.d. *An*] [~ Q1–5, F, D.

Who scorn'd to Treat, shall to a Conquest bow.
To every sword I free Commission give;
Fall on, my Friends, and let no Rebel live.
Spare onely *Lyndaraxa;* let her be
In Triumph led to grace my Victory.
Since, by her falshood she betray'd my Love,
Great as that falshood my Revenge shall prove.

Enter Lyndaraxa, *as affrighted; attended
by women.*

Go take th' Enchantress, bring her to me bound.
10   *Lynd.* Force needs not, where resistance is not found:
I come, my self, to offer you my hands;
And, of my own accord, invite your bands.
I wish'd to be my *Abdelmelechs* Slave;
I did but wish, and easie Fortune gave.
    Abdel. O, more then Woman false! but 'tis in vain.
Can you e're hope to be believ'd again?
I'le sooner trust th' Hyæna than your smile;
Or, than your Tears, the weeping Crocodile.
In War and Love none should be twice deceiv'd;
20 The fault is mine if you are now believ'd.
    Lynd. Be overwise, then, and too late repent;
Your Crime will carry its own punishment.
I am well pleas'd not to be justify'd:
I owe no satisfaction to your pride.
It will be more advantage to my Fame,
To have it said, I never own'd a Flame.
    Abdel. 'Tis true; my pride has satisfy'd it self:
I have at length escap'd the deadly shelf.
Th' excuses you prepare will be in vain,
30 Till I am fool enough to love again.
    Lynd. Am I not lov'd?
    Abdel. ——————I must, with shame, avow

---

11 self,] Q2–3, D; ∼ˌ Q1, Q4–5, F.   15 Woman] D; *Woman* Q1–5, F (∼, Q1).
17 Hyæna] *Hyæna* Q1–5, F, D.   25 Fame,] Q2–5, F, D; ∼. Q1.
31 lov'd?] Q4–5, F, D; ∼! Q1–3.

I lov'd you once; but do not love you now.
    Lynd. Have I for this betray'd *Abdalla*'s Trust?
You are to me as I to him unjust.   [*Angrily.*
    Abdel. 'Tis like you have done much for love of me,
Who kept the Fortress for my Enemy.
    Lynd. 'Tis true, I took the Fortress from his hand;
But, since, have kept it in my own Command.
    Abdel. That act your foul Ingratitude did show.
40   *Lynd.* You are th' ungrateful, since 'twas kept for you.
    Abdel. 'Twas kept indeed, but not by your intent;
For all your kindness I may thank th' event.
Blush, *Lyndaraxa* for so grosse a cheat;
'Twas kept for me when you refus'd to Treat!   [*Ironically.*
    Lynd. Blind Man! I knew the weakness of the place:
It was my plot to do your Arms this Grace:
Had not my care of your renown been great,
I lov'd enough to offer you to Treat.
She who is lov'd must little Letts create;
50   But you bold Lovers are to force your Fate.
This force you us'd my Maiden blush will save;
You seem'd to take what secretly I gave.
I knew you must be Conquer'd; but I knew
What Confidence I might repose in you.
I knew you were too grateful to expose
My Friends and Soldiers to be us'd like Foes.
    Abdel. Well; though I love you not, their lives shall be
Spar'd out of Pity and Humanity.
Alferez, Goe, and let the slaughter cease.   [*To a Soldier.*
                                                    [*Exit the* Alferez.
60   *Lynd.* Then must I to your pity owe my peace?
Is that the tender'st term you can afford?
Time was, you wou'd have us'd another word.

───────────

33 Trust?] Q4–5, F, D; ~! Q1–3.   37 Fortress] Q2–5, F, D; Fottress Q1.
41 indeed, . . . intent;] Q3, F; ~; . . . ~, Q1–2, Q4–5, D.
43 *Lyndaraxa*] Q2–5, F, D; *Lindaraxa* Q1.
49 create;] Q3–5, F, D; ~. Q1–2.   53 you] Q2–3; we Q1, Q4–5, F, D.
59 s.d. on l. 58 in Q1–2, Q4–5.
59+ s.d. [*Exit*] Q4–5, F, D (s.d. after l. 60); ∧~ Q1–3 (s.d. after l. 60).
60 peace?] Q3; ~! Q1–2, Q4–5, F, D.   61 afford?] Q3, F, D; ~! Q1–2, Q4–5.

Abdel. Then, for your Beauty I your Soldiers spare;
For though I do not love you, you are fair.
    Lynd. That little Beauty, why did Heav'n impart
To please your Eyes, but not to move your Heart?
I'le shrowd this Gorgon from all humane view;
And own no Beauty, since it charms not you!
Reverse your Orders, and our Sentence give;
70 My Soldiers shall not from my Beauty live.
    Abdel. Then, from our Friendship they their lives shall gain;
Though love be dead, yet friendship does remain.
    Lynd. That friendship which from wither'd Love does shoot,
Like the faint Herbage of a Rock, wants root.
Love is a tender Amity, refin'd:
Grafted on friendship it exalts the kind.
But when the Graff no longer does remain
The dull Stock lives; but never bears again.
    Abdel. Then, that my Friendship may not doubtful prove,
80 (Fool that I am to tell you so,) I love.
You would extort this knowledge from my Brest;
And tortur'd me so long that I confest.
Now I expect to suffer for my Sin;
My Monarchy must end; and yours begin.
    Lynd. Confess not Love, but spare your self that shame:
And call your Passion by some other name.
Call this assault, your Malice, or your Hate;
Love owns no acts so disproportionate.
Love never taught this insolence you show,
90 To Treat your Mistriss like a conquer'd Foe.
Is this th' obedience which my Heart should move?
This usage looks more like a Rape than Love.
    Abdel. What proof of Duty would you I should give?
    Lynd. 'Tis Grace enough to let my Subjects live:
Let your rude Souldiers keep possession still;
Spoil, rifle, pillage, any thing but kill.

---

64 you are] Q2–5, F, D; your are Q1.   66 Heart?] ~! Q1–5, F, D.
89 show,] D; show, [*Alferez.* Q1–5, F (*s.d. on l. 90 in Q4–5, F*).
90 Foe.] Q3, F, D; ~, Q1–2, Q4–5.   91 move?] ~! Q1–5, F, D.
96 rifle] Q2–5, F, D; riflle Q1.

In short, Sir, use your fortune as you please;
Secure my Castle, and my person seize.
Let your true men my Rebels hence remove;
100 I shall dream on; and think 'tis all your love.
 Abdel. You know too well my weakness and your pow'r.
Why did Heav'n make a fool a Conquerour?
She was my slave; till she by me was shown
How weak my force is, and how strong her own.
Now she has beat my pow'r from every part;
Made her way open to my naked heart.
Go, strictly charge my Souldiers to retreat: *[To a Sold.*
Those countermand who are not enter'd yet.
On peril of your lives leave all things free.

            [Exit Souldier.

110 Now, Madam, love *Abdalla* more than me.
I only ask, in duty, you would bring
The keys of our *Albayzin* to the King:
I'le make your terms as gentle as you please.

      [Trumpets sound a charge within:
        and Souldiers shout.

What shouts; and what new sounds of war are these?
 Lynd. Fortune, I hope, has favour'd my intent   *[Aside.*
Of gaining time; and welcome succours sent.

     Enter Alferez.

 Alf. All's lost; and you are fatally deceiv'd:
The foe is enter'd: and the place reliev'd.
Scarce from the walls had I drawn off my men
120 When, from their Camp, the Enemy rush'd in:
And Prince *Abdalla* enter'd first the gate.

---

98 seize.] Q2–5, F, D; ~- Q1.   102 Conquerour?] ~! Q1–5, F, D.
104 is] Q2–3; was Q1, Q4–5, F, D. 106 heart.] Q3, F; ~: Q1–2, Q4–5, D
107 s.d. [*To a Sold.*] Q3, F; *on line above in* Q1–2, Q4–5, D.
109+ s.d. [*Exit*] Q4–5, F, D; ‸~ Q1–3.
112 *Albayzin*] Q2–3; *Albazin* Q1; *Albayzn* Q4–5, F; *Albayzyn* D.
113+ s.d. [*Trumpets*] Q2–5, F, D; ‸~ Q1. 115 *Lynd.*] Q2–5, F, D; *Lind.* Q1.
115 s.d. *Aside*] Q4–5, F, D; *aside* Q1–3.

Abdel. I am betray'd; and find it now too late.   [*To her.*
When your proud Soul to flatt'ries did descend,
I might have known it did some ill portend.
The wary Seaman stormy weather fears,
When winds shift often, and no cause appears.
You, by my bounty live————
Your Brothers, too, were pardon'd for my sake,
And this return your gratitude does make.————
130 *Lynd.* My Brothers best their own obligements know;
Without your charging me with what they owe.
But, since you think th' obligement is so great,
Il'e bring a friend to satisfie my debt.   [*Looking behind.*
Abdel. Thou shalt not triumph in thy base design,
Though not thy fort, thy person shall be mine.
          [*He goes to take her; she runs and cries* Help.

          Enter Abdalla, Arcos, Spaniards. Abdelmelech
          *retreats fighting: and is pursued by the adverse
          party off the Stage. An Alarm within.*

          Enter again Abdalla *and the Duke of* Arcos,
                    with Lyndaraxa.

Arcos. Bold *Abdelmelech* twice our *Spaniards* fac'd;
Though much outnumbred; and retreated last.
     Abdalla. Your Beauty, as it moves no common fire,
So it no common courage can inspire.   [*To* Lyndar.
140 As he fought well, so had he prosper'd too,

---

122 *s.d. To*] Q2–5, F, D; *to* Q1.
130 *Lynd.*] Q2–5, F, D; *Lind.* Q1.
133 *s.d.* [*Looking*] Q2–5, D (*looking* Q2–3); ₍looking Q1.
135+ *s.d.* [*He*] Q4–5, F, D; ₍~ Q1–3.
135+ *s.d.* Help.] *help*: Q1–2; *help.* Q3–5, F; *Help.* D.
135+ *s.d.* Spaniards] Q2–3, D; *Spaniards* Q1, Q4–5, F.
135+ *s.d.* Arcos,] Q3–4; ~. Q1–2; ~₍ Q5, F, D.
136 *Spaniards*] Q3, D; Spaniards Q1–2, Q4–5, F.
138–139 *Abdalla.* Your . . . fire, / . . . [*To* Lyndar.] D; Abdalla *to* Lyndar. / Your
     . . . fire, Q1–5, F (*Abdalla to Lyndar.* Q1).

If, Madam, he like me, had fought for you.
  Lynd. Fortune, at last has chosen with my eies;
And, where I would have giv'n it, plac'd the prize.
You see, Sir, with what danger I am just,
To keep this pledge committed to my trust:
But 'twas the love of you which made me fight,
And gave me Courage to maintain your right.
Now, by Experience you my faith may find;
And are to thank me that I seem'd unkind.
150 When your malicious fortune doom'd your fall
My care restrain'd you, then, from loosing all.
Against your destiny I shut the Gate:
And Gather'd up the Shipwracks of your fate.
I, like a friend, did ev'n your self withstand,
From throwing all upon a loosing hand.
  Abdal. My love makes all your Acts unquestion'd go:
And sets a Soveraign stamp on all you doe.
Your Love, I will believe with hoodwink'd eyes;
In faith, much merit in much blindness lies.
160 But now, to make you great as you are fair,
The *Spaniards* an Imperial Crown prepare.
  Lyn. That gift's more welcome, which with you I share:
Let us no time in fruitless courtship loose,
But sally out upon our frighted Foes.
No Ornaments of pow'r so please my eies
As purple, which the blood of Princes, dies.
                              [*Exeunt: He leading her.*

---

142 *Lynd.*] Q2–5, F, D; *Lind.* Q1.
144–145 *as in* Q2–3; *Q1, Q4–5, F, D have*: You see, Sir, with what hardship I have
kept / This precious gage which in my hands you left.
146 fight,] Q2–5, F, D; ~. Q1.
147 right.] Q2–5, F, D; ~ᴧ Q1.
161 *Spaniards*] Q2–3, F, D; Spaniards Q1, Q4–5.
162 *Lyn.*] Q2–5, F, D; *Lin.* Q1.
166+ *s.d.* [*Exeunt:*] F; ᴧExeunt. Q1–5, D([~ Q4–5, D).

SCENE III.

The Alhambra.

Boabdelin, Abenamar, Almahide; *Guards, &c.*
The Queen wearing a Scarfe.

Abenamar. My little journey has successfull been;
The fierce *Almanzor* will obey the Queen.
I found him, like *Achilles* on the shore,
Pensive, complaining much, but threatning more.
And, like that injur'd *Greek,* he heard our woes:
Which, while I told, a gloomy smile arose
From his bent brows; and still, the more he heard,
A more severe and sullen joy appear'd.
But, when he knew we to despair were driv'n,
10 Betwixt his teeth he mutter'd thanks to Heav'n.
    Boab. How I disdain this aid; which I must take
Not for my own, but *Almahida*'s sake.
    Aben. But, when he heard it was the Queen who sent;
That her command repeal'd his banishment,
He took the summons with a greedy joy,
And ask'd me how she would his sword employ?
Then bid me say, her humblest slave would come
From her fair mouth with joy to take his doom.
    Boab. Oh that I had not sent you! though it cost
20 My Crown; though I and it, and all were lost!
    Aben. While I to bring this news, came on before,
I met with *Selin*————
    Boab. ————————I can hear no more.

Enter Hamet.

SCENE III.] Scene, Q1–5, F, D (~∧ Q2–3, F, D; ~. Q5).
s.d. Boabdelin, Abenamar, Almahide;] *italics in Q1.*
5 *Greek*] F, D; Greek Q1–5.
12 Not] Q2–5, F, D; No Q1.

Hamet. Almanzor is already at the gate
And throngs of people on his entrance wait.
   Boab. Thy news does all my faculties surprize,
He bears two Basilisks in those fierce eyes.
And that tame Demon, which should guard my throne,
Shrinks at a Genius greater than his own.

[*Exit* Boabdelin, *with*
Aben. *and* Guards.

Enter Almanzor; *seeing* Almahide *approach him,
he speaks.*

   Alman. So *Venus* moves when to the thunderer
30 In smiles and tears she would some sute prefer.
When with her Cestos girt————
And drawn by Doves, she cuts the yielding skies,
And kindles gentle fires where 'ere she flies:
To every eye a Goddess is confest: ⎞
By all the Heav'nly Nation she is blest,   ⎬
And each with secret joy admits her to his brest. ⎠
Madam, your new Commands I come to know: [*To her bowing.*
If yet you can have any where I goe:
If to the Regions of the dead they be,
40 You take the speediest course, to send by me.
   Almah. Heav'n has not destin'd you so soon to rest:
Heroes must live to succour the distrest.
   Almanz. To serve such beauty all mankind should live:
And, in our service, our reward you give:
But, stay me not in torture, to behold
And ne're enjoy: as from anothers gold
The Miser hastens in his own defence,
And shuns the sight of tempting excellence;
So, having seen you once so killing fair,

28+ *s.d.* [*Exit*] Q4–5, F, D; ᴧ~ Q1–3.   28+ *s.d. seeing*] Q2–5, F, D; *seing* Q1.
30 and] Q2–3; or Q1, Q4–5, F, D.   32 yielding] Q2–3; liquid Q1, Q4–5, F, D.
37 *s.d.* [*To*] F, D; ᴧ~ Q1–5 (*after l. 36 in Q1–5, D*).
46 gold] Q4–5, F, D; ~; Q1–2; ~, Q3.

50 A second sight were but to move despair.
I take my eies from what too much would please,
As men in feavors famish their disease.
 Almah. No; you may find your Cure an easier way,
If you are pleas'd to seek it; in your stay.
All objects loose by too familiar view,
When that great charm is gone of being new.
By often seeing me, you soon will find
Defects so many in my face and mind,
That to be free'd from Love you need not doubt;
60 And, as you look'd it in, you'll look it out.
 Almanz. I, rather, like weak armies should retreat;
And so prevent my more entire defeat.
For your own sake in quiet let me goe:
Press not too far on a despairing foe:
I may turn back; and arm'd against you move
With all the furious trayn of hopeless love.
 Almah. Your honour cannot to ill thoughts give way;
And mine can run no hazard by your stay.
 Almanz. Do you, then, think I can with patience, see
70 That sov'raign good possest, and not by me?
No; I all day shall languish at the sight;
And rave on what I do not see, all night.
My quick imagination will present
The Scenes and Images of your Content:
When to my envy'd Rival you dispence
Joyes too unruly, and too fierce for sence.
 Almahide. These are the day-dreams which wild fancy yields,
Empty as shaddows are, that fly o're fields.
O, whether would this boundless fancy move?
80 'Tis but the raging Calenture of Love.
Like the distracted Passenger you stand,
And see, in Seas, imaginary Land,
Cool Groves, and Flow'ry Meads, and while you think

---

51 please,] F; ∼. Q1–2, Q4–5; ∼: Q3, D. 77 *Almahide.*] Q2–5, F, D; ∼, Q1.
77 yields,] Q3–5, F, D; ∼ʌ Q1–2. 79 move?] ∼! Q1–5, F, D.
82 Land,] Q3, F, D; ∼. Q1–2, Q4–5. 83 Flow'ry] Q3–5, F, D; Flow'rs Q1–2.

To walk, plunge in, and wonder that you sink.

   Alman. Love's Calenture too well I understand;
But sure your Beauty is no Fairy Land!
Of your own Form a Judge you cannot be;
For, Glow-worm-like, you shine, and do not see.

   Almah. Can you think this, and would you go away?

90   *Alman.* What recompence attends me if I stay?

   Almah. You know I am from recompence debarr'd;
But I will grant you merit a reward.
Your Flame's too noble to deserve a Cheat;
And I too plain to practise a Deceit.
I no return of Love can ever make;
But what I ask is for my Husband's sake.
He, I confess, has been ungrateful too;
But he and I are ruin'd if you goe.
Your Vertue to the hardest proof I bring:

100 Unbrib'd, preserve a Mistress and a King.

   Alman. I'le stop at nothing that appears so brave;
I'le do't: and know I no Reward will have.
You've given my Honour such an ample Field
That I may dye, but that shall never yield.
Spight of my self I'le Stay, Fight, Love, Despair;
And I can do all this, because I dare.*
Yet I may own one suit.————
That Scarfe, which since by you it has been born
Is Blest, like Relicks, which by Saints were worn.

110   *Almah.* Presents like this my Vertue durst not make
But that 'tis giv'n you for my Husbands sake.   [*Gives the Scarfe.*

   Alman. This Scarfe, to Honourable Raggs I'le wear:
As conqu'ring Soldiers tatter'd Ensigns bear.
But oh how much my Fortune I despise,
Which gives me Conquest, while she Love denies.

                                [*Exeunt.*

Possunt quia posse videntur. Virg. [Dryden's note.]

88   see.] Q3–5, F, D; ∼: Q1–2.   96   sake.] Q3; ∼, Q1–2; ∼: Q4–5, F, D.
102   know] now Q1–5, F, D.   106   *footnote added in* Q2–3.
109   worn.] Q3–5, F, D; ∼: Q1–2.   115+   *s.d.* [*Exeunt*] Q4–5, F, D; ∧∼ Q1–3.

ACT III.

SCENE, *The Alhambra.*

Almahide *and* Esperanza.

Espe. Affected Modesty has much of Pride;
That scarfe he begg'd, you could not have deny'd:
Nor does it shock the Vertue of a Wife,
When giv'n that man, to whom you owe your life.
    Almah. Heav'n knows from all intent of ill 'twas free:
Yet it may feed my Husbands jealousie,
And, for that cause, I wish it were not done.

To them Boabdelin; *and walks apart.*

See where he comes all pensive and alone;
A gloomy Fury has o're-spread his Face:
10 'Tis so! and all my Fears are come to pass.
    Boab. Marriage, thou curse of Love; and snare of Life, [*Aside.*
That first debas'd a Mistress to a Wife!
Love, like a Scene, at distance should appear;
But Marriage views the gross-daub'd Landschape neer.
Loves nauseous cure! thou cloyst whom thou shoudst please;
And, when thou cur'st, then thou art the disease.
When Hearts are loose, thy Chain our bodies tyes;
Love couples Friends; but Marriage Enemies.
If Love, like mine, continues after thee,
20 'Tis soon made sowr, and turn'd by Jealousie.

ACT] Q2–5, F, D; ∼. Q1.
s.d. Almahide *and* Esperanza.] D; *Almahide, Esperanza.* Q1–5, F (*Almahide and* Q2–3).
7+ *s.d. To*] Q4–5, D; [∼ Q1–3, F.   7+ *s.d. apart.*] Q2–5, F, D; ∼: Q1.
11 *Boab.* Marriage, . . . Life, [*Aside.*] D; [*Boabdelin aside.* / Marriage, . . . Life, Q1–3; Marriage, . . . Life. [*Boab. aside.* Q4–5, F.
15 please] Q2–5, F, D; pleas Q1.

No sign of Love in jealous Men remains
But that which sick men have of life; their pains.
    Almahide. Has my dear Lord some new affliction had?
Have I done any thing that makes him sad?   [*Walking to him.*
    Boab. You, nothing, You! but let me walk alone!
    Almah. I will not leave you till the cause be known:
My knowledge of the ill may bring relief.
    Boab. Thank ye: You never faile to cure my grief!
Trouble me not; my grief concerns not you.
30   *Almah.* While I have life I will your steps pursue.
    Boab. I'me out of humour now; you must not stay.
    Almah. I fear it is that Scarfe I gave away.
    Boab. No; 'tis not that:——but speak of it no more:
Go hence; I am not what I was before.
    Almah. Then I will make you so: give me your hand!
Can you this pressing, and these Tears withstand?
    Boab. O Heav'n, were she but mine, or mine alone!
                    [*Sighing and going off from her.*
Ah, why are not the Hearts of Women known?
False Women to new joys, unseen can move:
40 There are no prints left in the paths of Love.
All Goods besides by publick marks are known;
But what we most desire to keep, has none.
    Almah. Why will you in your Brest your passion croud
Like unborn Thunder rowling in a Cloud? [*Approaching him.*
Torment not your poor Heart; but set it free;
And rather let its fury break on me.
I am not married to a God; I know,
Men must have Passions, and can bear from you.
I fear th' unlucky Present I have made!

23–24 *Almahide.* Has . . . had? / . . . [*Walking to him.*] D; [Almahide *walking to him.* / Has . . . had? Q1–5 (ᴧAlmahide Q4–5); [Almahide *walking to him. (on l. 22*) / *Almah.* Has . . . had? F.
27 relief.] Q3–5, F, D; ∼; Q1–2.
37 *Boab.* O . . . alone! / [*Sighing . . . her.*] D; [Boab. *sighing . . . her. / O . . . alone!* Q1–5 (Boabᴧ Q1; ᴧ*Boab.* Q2–3); [*Boab. sighing . . . her. / Boab.* O . . . alone! F.
38 known?] ∼! Q1–5, F, D.
43–44 *Almah.* Why . . . croud / . . . [*Approaching him.*] D; [Almah. *approaching him.* / Why . . . croud Q1–5 (ᴧAlma. Q2–3); [Almah *approaching him. (on l. 42*) / *Almah.* Why . . . croud, F.

50   *Boab.* O pow'r of Guilt; how Conscience can upbraid!
It forces her not onely to reveal
But to repeat what she would most conceal!
    Almah. Can such a toy, and giv'n in publick too———
    Boab. False Woman, you contriv'd it should be so.
That publick Gift in private was design'd,
The Embleme of the Love you meant to bind.
Hence from my sight, ungrateful as thou art;
And, when I can, I'le banish thee my heart.   [*She weeps.*

To them Almanzor *wearing the scarfe:*
he sees her weep.

    Almanz. What precious drops are those
60 Which, silently, each others track pursue,
Bright as young Diamonds in their infant dew?
Your lustre you should free from tears maintain;
Like *Egypt,* rich without the help of rain.
Now curst be he who gave this cause of grief;
And double curst who does not give relief.
    Almah. Our common fears, and publick miseries
Have drawn these tears from my afflicted eies.
    Alman. Madam, I cannot easily believe
It is for any publick cause you grieve.
70 On your fair face the marks of sorrow lie;
But I read fury in your Husbands eye.
And, in that passion, I too plainly find
That you'r unhappy; and that he's unkind.
    Almah. Not new-made Mothers greater love express
Than he; when with first looks their babes they bless.
Not Heav'n is more to dying Martyrs Kind;
Nor guardian Angels to their charge assign'd.
    Boab. O goodness counterfeited to the life!
O the well acted vertue of a wife.
80 Would you with this my just suspitions blind?
You've given me great occasion to be kind!

---

58 *s.d. She*] Q2–5, F, D; *she* Q1.   63 *Egypt*] D; Egypt Q1–5, F.
77 assign'd] Q2–5, F, D; asign'd Q1.

The marks, too, of your spotless love appear;
Witness the badge of my dishonor there.
[Pointing to Almanzor's scarfe.

  Almanz. Unworthy owner of a gemme so rare!
Heav'ns, why must he possess, and I despair?
Why is this Miser doom'd to all this store:
He who has all, and yet believes he's poor?

  Almah. You'r much too bold, to blame a jealousy, [*To* Almanz.
So kind in him, and so desir'd by me.

90 The faith of wives would unrewarded prove,
Without those just observers of our love.
The greater care the higher passion shows;
We hold that dearest we most fear to loose.
Distrust in Lovers is too warm a Sun,
But yet 'tis Night in Love when that is gone.
And, in those Clymes which most his scorching know,
He makes the noblest fruits and Metals grow.

  Alman. Yes, there are mines of Treasure in your brest,
Seen by that jealous Sun; but not possest.

100 He, like a dev'l among the blest above,
Can take no pleasure in your Heaven of love.
Go, take her; and thy causeless fears remove;   [*To the K.*
Love her so well that I with rage may dy:
Dull husbands have no right to jealousie:
If that's allow'd, it must in Lovers be.

  Boab. The succor which thou bring'st me makes thee bold:
But know, without thy ayd, my Crown I'le hold.
Or, if I cannot, I will fire the place:
Of a full City make a naked space.

110 Hence, then, and from a Rival set me free:
I'le do; I'le suffer any thing, but thee.

  Almanz. I wonnot goe; I'le not be forc'd away:

83+   *s.d.* [*Pointing*] Q4–5, F, D; ~ Q1–3.
83+   *s.d.* Almanzor's] Q2–5, F, D; Almonzor's Q1.
85   despair?] F; ~! Q1–5, D.
88   *Almah.* You'r . . . jealousy, [*To* Almanz.] *Almah. to* Almanz. / You'r . . .
jealousy, Q1–5, D (*on same line in* D); Almahide *to* Almanzor. / *Almah.* You'r
. . . Jealousie, F.
102   *s.d.* [*To*] Q4–5, F, D; ~ Q1–3.

I came not for thy sake; nor do I stay.
It was the Queen who for my ayd did send;
And 'tis I only can the Queen defend:
I, for her sake thy Scepter will maintain;
And thou, by me, in spight of thee, shalt raign.
     Boab. Had I but hope I could defend this place
Three daies, thou shoud'st not live to my disgrace.
120 So small a time———
Might I possess my *Almahide*, alone,
I would live ages out 'ere they were gone.
I should not be of love or life bereft;
All should be spent before; and nothing left.
     Almah. As for your sake I for *Almanzor* sent,   [*To* Boab.
So, when you please, he goes to banishment.
You shall, at last, my Loyalty approve:
I will refuse no tryal of my love.
     Boab. How can I think you love me, while I see
130 That trophee of a Rivals Victory?
I'le tear it from his side.———
     Almanz. ———————I'le hold it fast
As life: and, when life's gone, I'le hold this last.
And, if thou tak'st it after I am slain,
I'le send my Ghost to fetch it back again.
     Almah. When I bestow'd that scarf, I had not thought
Or not consider'd, it might be a fau't.
But, since my Lord's displeas'd that I should make
So small a present, I command it back.
Without delay th' unlucky gift restore;
140 Or, from this minute, never see me more.
     Almanz. The shock of such a curse I dare not stand,
         [*Pulling it off hastily, and presenting it to her.*
Thus I obey your absolute command.   [*She gives it the King.*
Must he the spoils of scorn'd *Almanzor* wear?

---

117   raign.] Q3–5, F, D; ~, Q1–2.   118   place] Q5, F, D; ~; Q1–4.
125   *Almah.* As . . . sent, [*To* Boab.] *Almahide to Boabdelin.* / As . . . sent, Q1–5,
F, D (*on same line in F, D*).
141   *Almanz.* The . . . stand, / [*Pulling . . . her.*] D; *Almanz. pulling . . . her.* / The
. . . stand, Q1–5; [Almanzor *pulling . . . her.* / *Almanz.* The . . . stand, F.

May *Turnus* fate be thine; who dar'd to bear
The belt of murder'd *Pallas;* from afar
Mayst thou be known; and be the mark of War.
Live just to see it from thy shoulders torn
By common hands, and by some Coward worn.

                                              [*An Alarm within.*

            Enter Abdelmelech, Zulema, Hamet, Abenamar: *their*
                              swords drawn.

    Abdelm. Is this a time for discord or for grief?
150 We perish, Sir, without your quick relief.
I have been fool'd, and am unfortunate:
The foes pursue their fortune; and our fate.
    Zul. The Rebels with the *Spaniards* are agreed.
    Boab. Take breath; my guards shall to the fight succeed.
    Abenam. Why stay you, Sir? the conqu'ring foe is near:
Give us their courage; and give them our fear.   [*To* Alman.
    Hamet. Take Arms, or we must perish in your sight.
    Alman. I care not; perish; for I will not fight.
I wonnot lift an arm in his defence:
160 Yet will I not remove one foot from hence:
I to your Kings defence his town resign;
This onely spot whereon I stand, is mine.
Madam, be safe; and lay aside your fear,   [*To the Queen.*
You are, as in a Magique Circle, here.
    Boab. To our own Valour our success we'l owe:
Hast, *Hamet,* with *Abenamar* to go;

---

144   *Turnus*] Q4–5, F, D; *Turnu's* Q1–3.
148+ *s.d.* [*An*] Q2–5, F, D; ∧~ Q1.
151   unfortunate:] F; ~. Q1–4; ~, Q5, D.
153   *Spaniards*] Q2–3, D; Spaniards Q1, Q4–5, F.
155–156 *Abenam.* Why . . . Sir? . . . near: / . . . [*To* Alman.] *Abenam. to Alman.* /
Why . . . Sir, . . . near: Q1–5, F, D (Sir? Q3, D; near? Q5, F; *on same line in* F, D).
160   Yet will I not remove . . . hence:] Q2–3; And yet I wonnot stir . . . ~. Q1,
Q4–5, F, D.
163   *s.d. on l. 162 in* Q1–5, F.
163   *s.d. To*] Q2–5, F, D; *to* Q1.
165   owe:] Q2–3; ~. Q1, Q4–5, F, D.

You two draw up, with all the speed you may,
Our last reserves, and, yet redeem the day.

> [*Exeunt* Hamet *and* Abenamar,
> *one way, the King the other,*
> *with* Abdelmelech, &c.
> [*Alarm within.*

Enter Abdelmelech, *his sword drawn.*

　　Abdel. *Granada* is no more! th' unhappy King
170 Vent'ring too far, 'ere we could succour bring,
Was, by the Duke of *Arcos*, Pris'ner made;
And, past relief, is to the Fort convey'd.
　　Almanz. Heav'n, thou art just! go, now despise my aid.
　　Almah. Unkind *Almanzor*, how am I betray'd!
Betray'd by him in whom I trusted most!
But I will ne'er outlive what I have lost.
Is this your succour, this your boasted love?
I will accuse you to the Saints above!
Almanzor vow'd he would for honour fight;
180 And lets my husband perish in my sight.

> [*Exeunt* Almahide *and* Esperanza.

　　Almanz. O, I have err'd; but fury made me blind:
And, in her just reproach, my fault I find!
I promis'd ev'n for him to fight, whom I————
————But since he's lov'd by her he must not dye.
Thus, happy fortune comes to me in vain,
When I my self must ruine it again.

To him Abenamar, Hamet, Abdelmelech, Zulema;
　　　　Soldiers.

　　Aben. The foe has enter'd the Vermillion tow'rs;
And nothing but th' *Alhambra* now is ours.
　　Alman. Ev'n that's too much, except we may have more;

168+　s.d. [*Exeunt*] Q4–5, F, D; ∧~ Q1–3.　　177　love?] ~! Q1–5, F, D.
180+　s.d. [*Exeunt*] Q4–5, F, D; ∧~ Q1–3.
187　tow'rs] Q2–3, Q5, F, D; towr's Q1, Q4.

190 You lost it all to that last stake before:
Fate, now come back; thou canst not farther get;
The bounds of thy libration here are set.
Thou knowst this place,———
And, like a Clock wound up, strik'st here for me; ⎫
Now, Chance, assert thy own inconstancy: ⎬
And, Fortune, fight, that thou maist Fortune be. ⎭
They come; here, favour'd by the narrow place,   [*A noise*
I can, with few, their gross Battalion face.   *within.*
By the dead wall, you, *Abdelmelech*, wind;
200 Then, charge; and their retreat cut off behind.
                    [*Exeunt. An Alarm within.*

        Enter Almanzor *and his party, with* Abdalla *Prisoner.*

    Alman. You were my friend; and to that name, I owe
The just respect, which you refus'd to show.   [*To* Abdal.
Your liberty I frankly would restore;
But honour now forbids me to do more.
Yet, Sir, your freedom in your choice shall be;
When you command to set your Brother free.
    Abdalla. Th' exchange which you propose, with joy I take;
An offer, easier then my hopes could make.
Your benefits revenge my crimes to you:
210 For, I my shame in that bright Mirrour, view.
    Alman. No more; you give me thanks you do not ow,
I have been faulty; and repent me now.
But, though our Penitence a vertue be,
Mean Souls alone repent in misery.
The brave own faults when good success is giv'n:
For then they come on equal terms to Heav'n.
                    [*Exeunt.*

194–196 *brace omitted from Q1, Q4–5.*
200+ *s.d.* [*Exeunt. An Alarm within.*] Q4–5, F, D ([*An*); *An Alarm within. Exeunt.*
Q1–3.
201–202 *Alman.* You . . . owe / . . . [*To* Abdal.] D; *Alman. to Abdal.* / You . . . owe
Q1–5, F (*on same line in F*).
202 respect] Q2–3; regard Q1, Q4–5, F, D.
216+ *s.d.* [*Exeunt*] Q4–5, F, D; ∧∼ Q1–3.

SCENE II.

The Albayzin.

Ozmyn *and* Benzayda.

Benz. I see there's somewhat which you fear to tell;
Speak quickly, *Ozmyn*, is my father well?————
————Why cross you thus your arms; and shake your head?
Kill me at once, and tell me he is dead.
  Ozmyn. I know not more than you; but fear not less;
Twice sinking, I withdrew him from the press.
But the victorious Foe pursu'd so fast,
That flying throngs divided us at last.
As Seamen, parting in a gen'ral wreck,
10 When first the loosening planks begin to crack,
Each catches one, and straight are far disjoind,
Some born by tydes and others by the wind;
So, in this ruine, from each other rent,
With heav'd up hands we mutual farewells sent;
Methought his Eyes, when just I lost his view,
Were looking blessings to be sent to you.
  Benz. Blind Queen of Chance, to Lovers too severe,
Thou rul'st Mankind, but art a Tyrant here!
Thy widest Empyre's in a lovers brest:
20 Like open Seas we seldom are at rest.
Upon thy Coasts our wealth is daily cast;
And thou, like Pyrates, mak'st no peace to last.

  To them Duke of Arcos, Lyndaraxa, *and Guards.*

D. Arcos. We were surpriz'd when least we did suspect;
And justly suffer'd by our own neglect.

  Lynd. No; none but I have reason to complain!
So near a Kingdom, yet 'tis lost again!
O, how unequally in me were joynd
A creeping fortune, with a soaring mind!
O Lottery of fate! where still the wise
30 Draw blanks of Fortune; and the fools the prize!
These Cross ill-shuffled lots from Heav'n are sent,
Yet dull Religion teaches us content.
But, when we ask it where that blessing dwells,
It points to Pedant Colleges, and Cells:
There, shows it rude, and in a homely dress;
And that proud want mistakes for happiness.

           [*A Trumpet within.*

      Enter Zulema.

Brother! what strange adventure brought you here?
  Zul. The News I bring will yet more strange appear.
The little care you of my life did show,
40 Has of a Brother justly made a foe.
And *Abdelmelech*, who that life did save
As justly has deserv'd that love he gave.

  Lynd. Your business cools, while tediously it stays
On the low Theme of *Abdelmelechs* praise.

  Zul. This, I present from Prince *Abdalla*'s hands.
      [*Delivers a letter which she reads.*

  Lynd. He has propos'd, (to free him from his bands,)
That, with his Brother, an Exchange be made.

  Arcos. It proves the same design which we had laid.

---

25 complain!] D; ~, Q1, Q4–5; ~. Q2–3; ~; F.
34 Cells:] ~. Q1–5, F, D.   36+ *s.d.* [*A*] Q4–5, F, D; ∧~ Q1–3.
42 gave.] Q3–5, F, D; ~: Q1–2. 43 *Lynd.*] Q2–5, F, D; *Lind.* Q1.
44 *Abdelmelechs*] Q2–5, F, D; *Adelmelechs* Q1.
45 hands.] Q4–5, F, D; ~: Q1–3. 46 *Lynd.*] Q2–5, F, D; *Lind.* Q1.

Before the Castle let a bar be set;
50 And, when the Captives on each side are met,
With equal Numbers chosen for their Guard,
Just at the time the passage is unbarr'd,
Let both at once advance, at once be free.
    Lynd. Th' Exchange I will my self in person see.
    Benz. I fear to ask, yet would from doubt be freed,
Is *Selin* Captive, Sir, or is he dead?
    Zul. I grieve to tell you what you needs must know;
He's made a Pris'ner to his greatest Foe:
Kept, with strong guards, in the *Alhambra* Tour;
60 Without the reach ev'n of *Almanzor*'s pow'r.
    Ozmyn. With grief and shame I am at once opprest.
    Zul. You will be more, when I relate the rest.   [*To* Ozmyn.
To you I from *Abenamar* am sent;
And you alone can *Selin*'s death prevent.
Give up your self a Pris'ner in his stead;
Or, e're to morrow's dawn, believe him dead.
    Benz. E're that appear I shall expire with grief.
    Zul. Your action swift, your Council must be brief.
    Lynd. While for *Abdalla*'s freedom we prepare,
70 You, in each others Brest unload your care.
                [*Exeunt all but* Ozmyn *and* Benzayda.
    Benz. My wishes contradictions must imply;
You must not goe; and yet he must not dye.
Your Reason may, perhaps, th' extremes unite;
But there's a mist of Fate before my sight.
    Ozm. The two Extremes too distant are to close;
And Human Wit can no mid-way propose.
My duty therefore shows the neerest way,
To free your Father; and my own obey.
    Benz. Your Father, whom since yours, I grieve to blame,

---

54   *Lynd.*] Q2–5, F, D; *Lind.* Q1.
58   He's made] Q2–3; He is Q1, Q4–5, F, D.
58   Foe:] ∼. Q1–5, F, D.
59   *Alhambra*] Q2–3, Q5, F, D; *Almambra* Q1, Q4.
70+   s.d. [*Exeunt*] Q4–5, F, D; ∧∼ Q1–3.
78   obey.] Q2–5, F, D; ∼, Q1.

80 Has lost, or quite forgot a Parents name:
And, when at once possest of him and you,
Instead of freeing one, will murder two.
    Ozm. Fear not my Life; but suffer me to goe:
What cannot onely Sons with Parents do?
'Tis not my death my Father does pursue;
He onely would withdraw my Love from you.
    Benz. Now, *Ozmyn,* now your want of Love I see:
For, would you goe, and hazard loosing me?
    Ozm. I rather would ten thousand Lives forsake:
90 Nor can you e're believe the doubt you make.————
————This night I with a chosen Band will goe;
And, by surprize, will free him from the Foe.
    Benz. What Foe? ah whether would your Vertue fall?
He is your Father whom the Foe you call.
Darkness and Rage will no distinction make;
And yours may perish for my Fathers sake.
    Ozm. Thus, when my weaker Vertue goes astray,
Yours pulls it back; and guides me in the way:
I'le send him word, my being shall depend
100 On *Selin*'s Life and with his Death shall end.
    Benz. 'Tis that indeed would glut your Fathers rage:
Revenge on *Ozmyn*'s Youth, and *Selin*'s age.
    Ozm. What e're I plot, like *Sisyphus,* in vain
I heave a stone that tumbles down again!
    Benz. This Glorious work is then reserv'd for me;
He is my Father; and Ile set him free.
These Chains my Father for my sake does wear:
I made the fault; and I the pains will bear.
    Ozm. Yes; you no doubt have merited those pains:
110 Those hands; those tender Limbs were made for chains.
Did I not love you, yet it were too base
To let a Lady suffer in my place.
Those proofs of Vertue you before did show
I did admire: but I must envy now.

————

80 name:] ～. Q1-5, F, D.   84 do?] Q5, F, D; ～! Q1-4.
87 *Ozmyn,*] Q2-5, F, D; ～. Q1.   89 forsake:] Q4-5, F, D; ～. Q1-3.
93 Foe?...fall?] ～!...～! Q1-5, F, D.   94 He] Q2-3; It Q1, Q4-5, F, D.

Your vast ambition leaves no Fame for me
But grasps at universal Monarchy.
   Benz. Yes, *Ozmyn*, I shall still this Palm pursue;
I will not yield my Glory, ev'n to you.
I'le break those bonds in which my Father's ty'd:
120 Or, if I cannot break 'em, I'le divide.
What though my Limbs a Womans weakness show?
I have a Soul as Masculine as you.
And, when these Limbs want strength, my Chains to wear;
My Mind shall teach my body how to bear.
                                   [*Exit* Benzayda.

   Ozm. What I resolve I must not let her know;
But Honour has decreed she must not goe.
What she resolves I must prevent with care;
She shall not in my Fame or Danger share.
I'le give strict Order to the Guards which wait;
130 That, when she comes, she shall not pass the Gate.
Fortune, at last, has run me out of breath;
I have no refuge, but the arms of death:
To that dark Sanctuary I will goe:
She cannot reach me when I lie so low.

SCENE III.

The Albayzin.

Enter on the one side Almanzor, Abdalla, Abdelmelech,
Zulema, Hamet: *On the other side the Duke of* Arcos,
Boabdelin, Lyndaraxa, *and their party. At the same time*
Boabdelin *and* Abdalla *pass by each other, each to his party:
when* Abdalla *is past on the other side; the Duke of* Arcos
approaches, and calls to Almanzor.

---

121 show?] ~; Q1–5, F, D.   122 Masculine] D; *Masculine* Q1–5, F.
124+ *s.d. [Exit]* Q4–5, F, D; ∧~ Q1–3.   SCENE III.] Sᴄᴇɴᴇ Q1–5, F, D.
s.d. Hamet:] ~. Q1–5, F, D.
s.d. and their party] Q2–5, F, D; and their party Q1.
s.d. At the same] *After which the Barrs are opened; and at the same* Q1, Q4–5, F,
D; *The same* Q2–3.
s.d. approaches,] Q2–3; *approaches the Barrs,* Q1, Q4–5, F, D.

Arc. The hatred of the brave, with battails, ends;
And Foes, who fought for Honour, then, are Friends.
I love thee, brave *Almanzor*, and am proud
To have one hour when Love may be allowd.
This hand, in sign of that esteem, I plight:
We shall have angry hours enough to fight.

                                           [*Giving his hand.*

    Almanz. The Man who dares, like you, in fields appear,
And meet my Sword, shall be my Mistriss here.
If I am proud, 'tis onely to my Foes;
10 Rough but to such who Vertue would oppose.
If I some fierceness from a Father drew,
A Mothers Milk gives me some softness too.

    Arcos. Since, first you took, and after set me free,
(Whether a sence of Gratitude it be,
Or some more secret motion of my mind,
For which I want a name that's more then kind)
I shall be glad, by what e're means I can,
To get the friendship of so brave a man:
And would your unavailing valour call
20 From aiding those whom Heav'n has doom'd to fall.
We owe you that respect————
Which to the Gods of Foes besieg'd was shown;
To call you out before we take your Town.

    Almanz. Those whom we love, Sir, we should value too;
And not debauch that Vertue which we wooe.
Yet, though you give my Honour just offence,
I'le take your kindness in the better sence.
And, since you for my safety seem to fear,
I, to return your Bribe, should wish you here.
30 But, since I love you more then you do me,   ⎞
In all events preserve your Honour free: ⎬
For that's your own, though not your destiny. ⎠

    Arcos. Were you oblig'd in Honour by a Trust,

---

17   can,] Q3, F, D; ∼; Q1–2, Q4–5.
19   would ... valour] Q3–5, F, D; ∼, ... ∼, Q1–2.
24   Sir, we should value] Q2–3; we should esteem 'em Q1, Q4–5, F, D.
30–32   *brace omitted in* Q1, Q4–5, F.

I should not think my own proposals just.
But, since you fight for an unthankful King,
What loss of Fame can change of parties bring?
    Almanz. It will, and may with justice too, be thought,
That some advantage, in that change I sought.
And, though I twice have chang'd, for wrongs receiv'd,
40 That it was done for profit, none believ'd.
The Kings Ingratitude I knew before;
So that can be no cause of changing more.
If now I stand, when no reward can be;
'Twill show the fault before was not in me.
    Arcos. Yet, there is one reward to valour due;
And such it is, as may be sought by you:
That beauteous Queen: whom you can never gain,
While you secure her Husbands Life and Raign.
    Almanz. Then be it so: let me have no return

                    [*Here* Lyndaraxa *comes*
                         neer and hears them.

50 From him but Hatred, and from her, but Scorn.
There is this comfort in a noble Fate,
That I deserve to be more fortunate.
———You have my last resolve; and now farewell;
My boding Heart some Mischief does foretell:
But, what it is, Heav'n will not let me know;
I'me sad to death, that I must be your Foe.
    Arcos. Heav'n, when we meet, if fatal it must be,
To one; spare him; and cast the Lot on me.   [*They retire.*
    Lynd. Ah, what a noble Conquest were this Heart!
60 I am resolv'd I'le try my utmost Art:
In gaining him, I gain that Fortune too
Which he has Wedded, and which I but Wooe.
I'le try each secret passage to his mind;
And Loves soft Bands about his Heart-strings wind.

---

46 you:] ～. Q1–5, F, D.
47 beauteous] Q2–3, D; beaut'ous Q1, Q4–5, F.
47 Queen] Q2–5, F, D; Qneen Q1.
53 ———You] Q2–3; ∧～ Q1, Q4–5, F, D.
58 *s.d. retire*] Q2–5, F, D; *retiree* Q1.

Not his vow'd Constancy shall scape my snare;
While he, without, resistance does prepare,
I'le melt into him e're his Love's aware.

> [*She makes a gesture of invitation to* Almanzor
> *who returns again.*

You see, Sir, to how strange a remedy
A persecuted Maid is forc'd to fly:
70 Who, much distrest, yet scarce has confidence,
To make your noble pity her defence.

Almanz. Beauty, like yours, can no protection need;
Or, if it sues, is certain to succeed.
To whate're Service you ordain my hand,
Name your Request, and call it your Command.

Lynd. You cannot, Sir, but know, that my ill Fate
Has made me lov'd with all th' effects of Hate:
One Lover would, by force, my person gain;
Which one as guilty would by force detain.
80 Rash *Abdelmelechs* Love I cannot prize;
And fond *Abdalla's* passion I despise.
As you are brave, so you are prudent too,
Advise a wretched Woman what to do.

Almanz. Have courage, Fair one; put your trust in me;
You shall at least from those you hate, be free.
Resign your Castle to the King's Command;
And leave your Love-concernments in my hand.

Lynd. The King, like them, is fierce, and faithless too:
How can I trust him, who has injur'd you?
90 Keep for your self (and you can grant no less)
What you alone are worthy to possess:
Enter, brave Sir; for, when you speak the word,
These Gates will open of their own accord.
The Genius of the place its Lord will meet:
And bend its tow'ry forehead to your feet.
That little Cittadel, which now you see,
Shall then, the head of Conquer'd Nations be:

---

68 You] F; *Lynd.* You Q1–5, D.   69 fly:] F; ~. Q1–5, D.
90 self] Q4–5, F, D; ~; Q1–3.
91 possess:] Q2; ~, Q1; ~! Q3; ~. Q4–5, F, D.

And every Turret, from your coming, rise
The Mother of some great Metropolis.
100   *Almanz.* 'Tis pity words which none but Gods should hear,
Should loose their sweetness in a Soldiers Ear:
I am not that *Almanzor* whom you praise:
But your fair Mouth can fair Idea's raise:
I am a wretch, to whom it is deny'd
T' accept, with Honour, what I wish with Pride:
And since I fight not for my self, must bring
The fruits of all my Conquests to the King.
    Lynd. Say rather to the Queen; to whose fair Name
I know you vow the Trophies of your Fame.
110 I hope she is as kind as she is fair:
Kinder then unexperienc'd Virgins, are
To their first Loves; (though she has lov'd before,
And that first innocence is now no more:)
But, in revenge, she gives you all her Heart;
(For you are much too brave to take a part.)
Though blinded by a Crown she did not see
Almanzor greater than a King could be,
I hope her Love repairs her ill made choice:
Almanzor cannot be deluded, twice.
120   *Almanz.* No; not deluded; for none count their gains,
Who, like *Almanzor*, franckly give their pains.
    Lynd. Almanzor, do not cheat your self, and me;
Your Love is not refin'd to that degree.
For, since you have desires, and those not blest,
Your Love's uneasie, and at little rest.
    Almanz. 'Tis true; my own unhappiness I see:
But who, alas, can my Physician be?
Love, like a lazy Ague I endure,
Which fears the Water; and abhors the Cure.
130   *Lynd.* 'Tis a Consumption, which your life does waste:
Still flatt'ring you with hope till help be past.
But, since of cure from her you now despair;
You, like consumptive Men, should change your Air.

---

105 Pride:] ∼. Q1–5, F, D.   112 before,] Q3–5, F, D; ∼) Q1–2.
122 and] Q2–3; nor Q1, Q4–5, F, D.   124 desires,] F, D; ∼; Q1–5.

Love some-where else, 'tis a hard remedy;
But yet you owe your self so much, to try.
 Almanz. My Love's now grown so much a part of me,
That Life would, in the Cure, endanger'd be.
At least it like a Limb cut off, would show;
And better dye than like a Cripple goe.
140 *Lynd.* You must be brought like mad Men to their cure;
And darkness first and next new Bonds endure:
Do you dark absence to your self ordain:
And I, in Charity, will find the Chain.
 Almanz. Love is that madness which all Lovers have;
But yet 'tis sweet and pleasing so to Rave.
'Tis an Enchantment where the reason's bound:
But Paradice is in th' enchanted ground:
A Palace void of Envy, Cares and Strife:
Where gentle hours delude so much of Life.
150 To take those Charms away; and set me free
Is but to send me into misery.
And Prudence of whose Cure so much you boast,
Restores those Pains, which that sweet Folly lost.
 Lynd. I would not, like Philosophers, remove,
But show you a more pleasing shape of Love.
You a sad, sullen, froward, Love did see;
I'le show him kind, and full of gayety.
In short, *Almanzor*, it shall be my care
To show you Love; for you but saw Despair.
160 *Almanz.* I in the shape of Love Despair did see:
You, in his shape, would show Inconstancy.
 Lynd. There's no such thing as Constancy you call:
Faith ties not Hearts; 'tis Inclination all.
Some Wit deform'd or Beauty much decay'd,
First, constancy in Love, a Vertue made.
From Friendship they that Landmark did remove;
And, falsly, plac'd it on the bounds of Love.
Let the effects of change be onely try'd:
Court me, in jest; and call me *Almahide.*

---

147 ground:] ~. Q1–5, F, D.
168 the] F, D; th' Q1–5.

170 But this is onely Council I impart;
For I, perhaps, should not receive your heart.
    Almanz. Fair though you are———
As Summer mornings, and your Eyes more bright
Than Starrs that twinckle in a winters night;
Though you have Eloquence to warm, and move
Cold age, and praying Hermites into Love;
Though *Almahide*, with scorn rewards my care;
Yet; than to change, 'tis nobler to despair.
My Love's my Soul; and that from Fate is free:
180 'Tis that unchang'd; and deathless part of me.
    Lynd. The Fate of Constancy your Love pursue!
Still to be faithful to what's false to you.
                    [*Turns from him, and goes off angrily.*
    Almanz. Ye Gods, why are not Hearts first pair'd above;
But some still interfere in others Love?
E're each, for each, by certain marks are known,
You mould 'em off in haste, and drop 'em down.
And while we seek what carelesly you sort,
You sit in State; and make our pains your sport.
                    [*Exeunt on both sides.*

ACT IV.

SCENE I.

Abenamar, *and servants.*

Aben. Hast; and conduct the Pris'ner to my sight.
                    [*Exit servant, and immediately
                        enters with* Selin *bound.*
    Aben. Did you, according to my orders, write?   [*To* Selin.

---

172 *Almanz.*] Q2–5, F, D; ~, Q1.   176 age,] Q3, D; ~; Q1–2, Q4–5; ~ₐ F.
184 Love?] ~! Q1–5, D; ~. F.   ACT] Q2–5, F, D; ~. Q1.
SCENE I.] Q4–5, F, D; SCENE Q1–3.
s.d. Abenamar, *and servants.*] Q2–5, F, D; *Abenamar,* and servants. Q1.
1+ s.d. [*Exit*] D; ₐExit Q1–4; [Exit Q5, F.
2   according] Q3, Q5, F, D; ~, Q1–2, Q4.
2   s.d. *To* Selin] Q2–5, F, D; *to Selin* Q1.

And have you summon'd *Ozmyn* to appear?
 Selin. I am not yet so much a slave to fear:
Nor has your Son deserv'd so ill of me
That, by his death or bonds, I would be free.
 Aben. Against thy life thou dost the sentence give:
Behold how short a time thou hast to live————

        [*Drawing a Sword.*

 Selin. Make haste; and draw the Curtain while you may:
10 You but shut out the twilight of my day:
Beneath the burden of my age I bend;
You, kindly ease me 'ere my Journey's end.

    To them a servant, with Ozmyn;
      Ozmyn *kneels.*

 Aben. It is enough: my promise makes you free: [*To* Selin.
Resign your bonds; and take your liberty.
 Ozmyn. Sir, you are just; and welcome are these bands:
'Tis all th' inheritance a son demands.
 Selin. Your goodness, O my *Ozmyn,* is too great:
I am not weary of my fetters yet:
Already when you move me to resign:
20 I feel 'em heavier on your feet than mine.

     Enter a Souldier.

 Sold. A youth attends you in the outer room;
Who seems in hast; and does from *Ozmyn* come.
 Aben. Conduct him in:————
 Ozm. Sent from *Benzaida* I fear to me.

---

8 live———— [*Drawing a Sword.*] Q2–3; live. Q1, Q4–5, F, D.
13 *Aben.* It . . . free: [*To* Selin.] *Aben. to Selin.* / It . . . free: Q1–5; *Aben. to*
Selin] It . . . free: F, D (*Selin.* D).
15 welcome] Q2–5, F, D; welome Q1.
20+ s.d. *Enter a*] *Another* Q1–5, F; *Enter another* D.
20+ s.d. *Souldier*] *Souldier or Servant* Q1, Q4–5, F, D.
21 outer] Q2–3, D; outter Q1, Q4–5, F.
24 *Benzaida*] *Benzayda* Q1–5, F, D.

To them Benzayda *in the habit of a man.*

Benz. My *Ozmyn* here!
Ozmyn. —————————*Benzaida!* 'tis she!
Go, youth; I have no business for thee here: [*To her.*
Go to th' *Albayzin*; and attend me there.
I'le not be long away; I prithee goe;
By all our Love and friendship———
    Ben. —————————————*Ozmyn,* no.
30 I did not take on me this bold disguise,
For ends so low to cheat your watchmens eies.
When I attempted this; it was to doe
An Action, to be envy'd ev'n by you:
But you, alas, have been too diligent,
And, what I purpos'd, fatally prevent!
Those chains, which for my father I would bear,
I take with less content, to find you here:
Except your father will that mercy show,
That I may wear 'em both for him and you.
40   *Aben.* I thank thee, Fortune; thou hast, in one hour,
Put all I could have ask'd thee in my pow'r.
My own lost wealth thou giv'st not only back,
But driv'st upon my Coast my Pyrats wrack.
    Selin. With *Ozmyns* kindness I was griev'd before;
But yours, *Benzayda,* has undone me more.
    Aben. Go fetch new fetters, and the daughter binde. [*To Sold.*
    Ozm. Be just, at least, Sir, though you are not kind.
Benzayda, is not, as a Pris'ner, brought;
But comes to suffer for anothers fau't.
50   *Aben.* Then *Ozmyn,* mark; that justice which I doe,
I, as severely will exact from you.

———————

24+ *s.d. To*] D; [∼ Q1–5, F.
26   *s.d. To*] Q2–5, F; *to* Q1; *s.d. omitted from* D.
29   friendship] Q2–5, F, D; frindship Q1.   37   here:] ∼. Q1–5, F, D.
40   Fortune] Q2–3, F, D; fortune Q1, Q4–5.
45   *Benzayda*] Q3–5, F, D; *Benzaida* Q1–2.
46   *Aben.* Go . . . binde. [*To Sold.*] *Aben. to Sold.* / Go . . . binde. Q1–5, F, D
(binde∧ Q1; bind: F; *on same line in F, D; to a* D).

The father is not wholly dead in me:
Or you may yet revive it, if it be.
Like tapers new blown out, the fumes remain
To catch the light; and bring it back again.
————*Benzayda* gave you life, and set you free;
For that I will restore her liberty.
    Ozmyn. Sir, on my knees I thank you.
    Aben. ————————————*Ozmyn,* hold:
One part of what I purpose is untold:
60 Consider, then, it on your part remains,
When I have broke, not to resume your chains.
Like an Indulgent father, I have pai'd
All debts, which you, my Prodigal, have made.
Now you are clear, break off your fond design;
Renounce *Benzayda;* and be wholly mine.
    Ozmyn. Are these the termes? is this the liberty?
Ah, Sir, how can you so inhumane be?
My duty to my life I will prefer;
But life and duty must give place to her.
70   *Aben.* Consider what you say; for, with one breath,
You disobey my will; and give her death.
    Ozmyn. Ah, cruel father, what do you propose?
Must I, then, kill *Benzayda,* or must loose?
I can do neither; in this wretched state
The least that I can suffer is your hate:
And yet, that's worse than death: Ev'n while I sue,
And choose your hatred, I could dye for you.
Break quickly, heart; or let my blood be spilt
By my own hand, to save a fathers guilt.
80   *Benz.* Hear me, my Lord, and take this wretched life,
To free you from the fear of *Ozmyns* wife.
I beg but what with ease may granted be;
To spare your son; and kill your Enemy.
Or, if my death's a grace too great to give;

56 *Benzayda*] Q2–5, F, D; *Benzaida* Q1.
58 *Ozmyn,* hold:] D; ~ᴧ ~ᴧ Q1–2, Q4–5; ~ᴧ ~, Q3; ~ᴧ ~; F.
65 *Benzayda*] Q2–5, F, D; *Benzaida* Q1.   72 propose?] ~! Q1–5, F, D.
73 *Benzayda*] Q2–5, F, D; *Benzaida* Q1.

Let me, my Lord, without my *Ozmyn* live.
Far from your sight, and *Ozmyn*'s let me goe,
And take from him a Care; from you a foe.
    Ozmyn. How, my *Benzayda!* can you thus resign
That love, which you have vow'd so firmly mine?
90 Can you leave me for life and liberty?
    Ben. What I have done will show that I dare dy.
But I'le twice suffer death; and go away;
Rather than make you wretched by my stay;
By this my father's freedom will be won;
And to your father I restore a Son.
    Selin. Cease, cease, my children, your unhappy strife:
Selin will not be ransom'd by your life.
Barbarian, thy old foe defyes thy rage: [*To* **Aben.**
Turn from their Youth thy malice to my Age.
100 *Ben.* Forbear, dear father, for your *Ozmyn*'s sake:
Do not, such words to *Ozmyn*'s father speak.
    Ozm. Alas, 'tis counterfeited rage; he strives
But to divert the danger from our lives.
For, I can witness, Sir, and you might see
How in your person he consider'd me.
He still declin'd the Combate where you were;
And you well know it was not out of fear.
    Ben. Alas, my Lord, where can your vengeance fall?
Your justice will not let it reach us all:
110 *Selin* and *Ozmyn* both would suff'rers be;
And punishment's a favour done to me.
If we are foes: since you have pow'r to kill
'Tis gen'rous in you not to have the will.
But are we foes? look round, my Lord; and see;
Point out that face which is your Enemy.
Would you your hand in *Selins* blood embrue?
Kill him unarm'd, who, arm'd, shun'd killing you!
Am I your foe? since you detest my line,

86 *Ozmyn's*] Q2–5, F, D; *Ozmin's* Q1.   88 *Benzayda*] Q2–5, F, D; *Benzaida* Q1.
96 strife:] F; ~. Q1–3; ~; Q4–5, D.
98 *s.d. To* Aben.] Q2–5, F, D; *to Aben.* Q1.
108 fall?] Q3, F, D; ~: Q1–2, Q4–5.   110 *Ozmyn*] Q2–5, F, D; *Ozmin* Q1.

That hated name of *Zegry* I resign:
120 For you, *Benzayda* will her self disclaim:
Call me your daughter, and forget my name.
    Selin. This vertue wou'd even Savages subdue;
And shall it want the pow'r to vanquish you?
    Ozmyn. It has, it has: I read it in his eyes;
'Tis now not anger; 'tis but shame denyes:
A shame of errour; which great spirits find,
Which keeps down vertue strugling in the mind.
    Aben. Yes; I am vanquish'd! the fierce conflict's past:
And shame it self is now ore'come at last.
130 'Twas long before my stubborn Mind was won;
But, melting once, I on the suddain run.
Nor can I hold my headlong kindness, more
Than I could curb my cruel Rage before.
                    [*Runs to* Benz. *and embraces her.*
Benzayda, 'twas your Vertue vanquish'd me:
That, could alone surmount my Cruelty.
                    [*Runs to* Selin; *and unbinds him.*
Forgive me, *Selin*, my neglect of you!
But men, just waking, scarce know what they do.
    Ozm. O Father!
    Benz. ————Father!
    Aben. ——————Dare I own that name?
Speak; speak it often, to remove my shame!
                    [*They all embrace him.*
140 O *Selin*; O my Children, let me goe!
I have more kindness then I yet can show.
For my recov'ry, I must shun your sight:
Eyes, us'd to darkness, cannot bear the light.
                    [*He runs in, they following him.*

---

125 denyes:] ∼. Q1–5, F, D.   126 which] Q2–3; that Q1, Q4–5, F, D.
135+ *s.d.* [*Runs*] Q2–5, F, D; ∧∼ Q1.   138 name?] ∼! Q1–5, F, D.

SCENE II.

The Albayzin.

Almanzor, Abdelmelech, *Soldiers.*

Almanz. 'Tis War again; and I am glad 'tis so;
Success, shall now by force and courage goe.
Treaties are but the combats of the Brain,
Where still the stronger loose, and weaker gain.
    Abdelm. On this Assault, brave Sir, which we prepare,
Depends the Sum and Fortune of the War.
Encamp'd without the Fort the *Spaniard* lies;
And may, in spight of us, send in supplies.
Consider yet, e're we attacque the place,
10 What 'tis to storm it in an Armies face.
    Almanz. The minds of Heroes their own measures are,
They stand exempted from the rules of War.
One Loose, one Sallye of the Heroes Soul,
Does all the Military Art controul.
While tim'rous Wit goes round, or foords the shore;
He shoots the Gulph; and is already o're:
And, when th' Enthusiastique fit is spent,
Looks back amaz'd at what he underwent.
                    [Exeunt. An Alarm within.

Enter Almanzor *and* Abdelmelech *with their Soldiers.*

    Abdelm. They fly, they fly; take breath and charge agen.
20   *Almanz.* Make good your entrance, and bring up more men.

SCENE II.] Scene Q1–5, F, D.
s.d. Almanzor, Abdelmelech,] Q4–5, F, D; *Almanzor, Abdelmelech,* Q1–3.
7   *Spaniard*] Q2–3, D; Spaniard Q1, Q4–5, F.
16   o're:] ∼. Q1–5, F, D.
18+   s.d. Exeunt. An Alarm within.] Q4–5, F, D ([An]); An Alarm within. Exeunt.
Q1–3.
20   men.] Q3; ∼ˏ Q1; ∼: Q2, Q4–5, F; ∼; D.

I fear'd, brave Friend, my Aid had been too late.
    Abdelm. You drew us from the jaws of certain Fate.
At my approach————
The Gate was open, and the Draw-bridge down;
But, when they saw I stood, and came not on,
They charg'd with fury on my little Band;
Who, much o're-powr'd, could scarce the shock withstand.
    Almanz. E're night we will the whole *Albayzin* gain,
But see the *Spaniards* march along the Plain,
30 To its relief: you *Abdelmelech*, goe
And force the rest, while I repulse the Foe.
                                        [*Exit* Almanzor.

Enter Abdalla, *and some few Soldiers who seem fearful.*

    Abdal. Turn, Cowards, turn; there is no hope in flight;
You yet may live, if you but dare to fight.
Come, you brave few, who onely fear to fly:
We're not enow to Conquer but to Dye.
    Abdelm. No, Prince; that mean advantage I refuse:
'Tis in your pow'r a nobler Fate to choose.
Since we are Rivals, Honour does command,
We should not dye but by each others hand.
40 Retire; and if it prove my destiny   [*To his men.*
To fall; I charge you let the Prince goe free.
                        [*The Soldiers depart on both sides.*
    Abdal. O, *Abdelmelech*, that I knew some way
This debt of Honour which I owe, to pay.
But Fate has left this onely means for me,
To dye; and leave you *Lyndaraxa* free.
    Abdelm. He who is vanquish'd and is slain, is blest:
The wretched Conquerour can ne're have rest:
But is reserv'd a harder fate to prove;
(Bound in the Fetters of dissembled Love.)
50   *Abdal.* Now thou art base; and I deserve her more:

21   late.] Q3, D; ~, Q1–2, Q4–5, F.   28   will] Q2–3; shall Q1, Q4–5, F, D.
29   *Spaniards*] Q2–3, D; Spaniards Q1, Q4–5, F.
31+   *s.d.* [*Exit*] Q4–5, F, D; ˄~ Q1–3.   35   enow] Q2–3; enough Q1, Q4–5, F, D.
40   *s.d. after l. 39 in Q1–3.*

Without complaint I will to death adore.
Dar'st thou see faults: and yet dost Love pretend?
I will, ev'n *Lyndaraxa's* Crimes defend.
   Abdelm. Maintain her cause, then, better than thy own,
Than thy ill got, and worse defended Throne.
                 [They fight, Abdalla *falls.*
   Abdelm. Now ask your life.
   Abdal. ————————'Tis gone; that busy thing ⎞
The Soul, is packing up; and just on wing,   ⎟
Like parting Swallows, when they seek the Spring. ⎠
Like them, at its appointed time, it goes;
60 And flies to Countreys more unknown than those.

      Enter Lyndaraxa *hastily, sees them, and is going
              out again.*

   Abdelm. No; you shall stay; and see a Sacrifice; *[Stopping her.*
Not offer'd by my Sword but by your Eyes.
From those he first Ambitions poyson drew;
And swell'd to Empire for the love of you.
Accursed fair!
Thy Comet-blaze portends a Princes fate;
And suff'ring Subjects groan beneath thy weight.
   Abdal. Cease Rival, cease!
I would have forc'd you; but it wonnot be:
70 I beg you now, upbraid her not for me.
You, fairest, to my memory be kind: *[To* Lynd.
Lovers like me your sex will seldom find.
When I usurp'd a Crown for love of you,
I, then, did more than dying now I do.
I'me still the same as when my love begun: ⎞
And could I now this fate foresee or shun; ⎬
Would yet do all I have already done.   ⎠   *[Dyes.*
         *[She puts her handkerchief
            to her eies.*

---

57 wing,] D; ∼. Q1–5, F.
61 *Abdelm.* No; . . . Sacrifice; *[Stopping her.] Abdelmelech stopping her.* / No;
. . . Sacrifice; Q1–5, F, D *(on same line in F).*
71 *s.d. on l. 70 in Q1–3 (to Lynd.* Q1*).*
77 *s.d. on l. 76 in Q1–5, F (*∧*dyes* Q1–3*).*   77+ *s.d. She]* Q2–5, F, D; *she* Q1.

Abdelm. Weep on; weep on; for it becomes you now:
These tears you to that love may well allow.
80 His unrepenting Soul, if it could move   ⎫
Upward, in Crimes, flew spotted with your love; ⎬
And brought Contagion to the blest above.   ⎭

    Lynd. He's gone; and peace go with a constant mind:
His love deserv'd I should have been more kind.
But then your love and greater worth I knew:
I was unjust to him, but just to you.

    Abdelm. I was his Enemy and Rival too;
Yet I some tears to his misfortunes owe:
You ow him more; weep then; and join with me:
90 So much is due ev'n to Humanity.

    Lynd. Weep for this wretch, whose memory I hate!
Whose folly made us both unfortunate!
Weep for this fool, who did my laughter move;
This, whining, tedious, heavy lump of Love?

    Abdelm. Had Fortune favour'd him, and frown'd on me, ⎫
I then had been that heavy fool, not he: ⎬
Just this had been my fun'ral Elegy.   ⎭
Thy arts and falshood I before did know;
But this last baseness was conceal'd till now.
100 And 'twas no more than needful to be known;
I could be cur'd by such an act alone.
My love, halfblasted, yet in time would shoot;
But this last tempest rends it to the root.

    Lyn. These little picques, which now your Anger move,
Will vanish; and are onely signes of love.
You've been too fierce; and, at some other time,
I should not with such ease forgive your Crime.
But, in a day of publick joy, like this,
I pardon; and forget what ere's amiss.

110   *Abdelm.* These Arts have oft prevail'd; but must no more:
The spell is ended; and th' Enchantment 'ore.

---

83 *Lynd.*] Q2–5, F, D; *Lind.* Q1.   94 Love?] Q2; ∼! Q1, Q4–5, F, D; ∼. Q3.
106 You've] *some copies of Q1 have* You've have.

You have at last destroy'd, with much adoe,
That love, which none could have destroy'd, but you.
My love was blind to your deluding Art;
But blind men feel, when stabb'd so neer the heart.
    Lynd. I must confess there was some pity due:
But I conceal'd it out of Love to you.
    Abdelm. No, *Lyndaraxa;* 'tis at last too late:
Our loves have mingled with too much of fate.
120 I would; but cannot now my self deceive:
O that you still could cheat, and I believe!
    Lynd. Do not so light a quarrel long pursue:
You grieve your Rival was less lov'd than you.
'Tis hard, when men, of kindness, must complain!
    Abdelm. I'm now awake, and cannot dream again!
    Lynd. Yet hear———
    Abdelm. ————No more: nothing my heart can bend:
That Queen you scorn'd, you shall this night, attend:
Your life the King has pardon'd for my sake;
But, on your Pride, I some revenge must take.
130 See now th' effects of what your Arts design'd:
Thank your inconstant, and ambitious Mind.
'Tis just that she who to no Love is true,
Should be forsaken, and contemn'd, like you.
    Lynd. All Arts of injur'd Women I will try:
First I will be reveng'd; and then I'le die.
But like some falling Tow'r———
Whose seeming firmness does the sight beguile,
So hold I up my nodding head awhile,
Till they come under; and reserve my fall,
140 That with my ruines I may reach 'em all.
    Abdelm. Conduct her hence.———
                              [*Exit* Lyndaraxa *guarded.*

                    Enter a Soldier.

---

112 adoe,] Q2–3, F, D; ~; Q1, Q4–5.   138 awhile,] Q3, F, D; ~; Q1–2, Q4–5.
139 under; ... fall,] Q3, F, D; ~,...~; Q1–2, Q4–5.
141+ *s.d.* [*Exit*] Q4–5, F, D; ∧~ Q1–3.

Sold. Almanzor is victorious without fight;
The Foes retreated when he came in sight.
Under the Walls, this night, his men are drawn;
And mean to seek the *Spaniard* with the dawn.
      Abdel. The Sun's declin'd:
Command the Watch be set without delay;
And in the Fort let bold *Benducar* stay.
I'le haste to Court, where Solitude I'le fly;   [*Aside.*
150 And heard, like wounded Deer, in company.
But oh, how hard is passion to remove,
When I must shun my self to 'scape from Love!

                                             [*Exit.*

SCENE III.

The Alhambra, or a Gallery.

Zulema, Hamet.

Hamet. I thought your passion for the Queen was dead:
Or that your love had, with your hopes, been fled.
      Zulema. 'Twas like a fire within a furnace pent:
I smother'd it, and kept it long from vent.
But (fed with looks; and blown with sighs, so fast)
It broke a passage through my lips, at last.
      Ham. Where found you confidence your suit to move?
Our broken fortunes are not fit to love.
Well; you declar'd your love: what follow'd then?
10   *Zulema.* She look'd as Judges do on guilty men:
When big with fate they triumph in their doomes,

145   *Spaniard*] Q2–3, F, D; Spaniard Q1, Q4–5.
148   stay.] Q3; ∼: Q1–2, Q4–5, F, D.
149   *s.d. Aside*] Q3–5, F, D; *aside* Q1–2.
152+   *s.d.* [*Exit*] Q4–5, D; ∧∼ Q1–3; *omitted from F.*
SCENE III.] Scene. Q1–5, F, D.
s.d. Zulema, Hamet.] Q4–5, F, D; *Zulema, Hamet.* Q1–3.
9   love:] Q2–3; ∼:: Q1; ∼:———— Q4–5, F, D.

And smile before the deadly sentence comes.
Silent I stood as I were thunder-strooke;
Condemn'd and executed with a look.
　　Hamet. You shou'd, with haste, some remedy prepare:
Now you are in, you must break through the snare.
　　Zulema. She said she would my folly yet conceal,
But vow'd my next attempt she would reveal.
　　Hamet. 'Tis dark; and, in this lonely Gallery,
20　(Remote from noyse, and shunning every eye)
One hour each Evening she in private mourns,
And prayes, and to the Circle then returnes.
Now, if you dare, attempt her passing by.————
　　Zulema. These lighted tapers show the time is nigh.
Perhaps my Courtship will not be in vain:
At least few women will of force complain.

　　　At the other end of the Gallery, Enter Almanzor
　　　　　　　　and Esperanza.

　　Hamet. Almanzor and with him————
The favourite slave of the Sultana Queen.
　　Zul. E're they approach, let us retire unseen
30 And watch our time when they return agen.
Then force shall give, if favour does deny;
　　And, that once done, we'll to the *Spaniards* fly.

　　　　　　　　　　　　　　　　　　　[*Exeunt.*
　　Almanz. Now stand; th' Apartment of the Queen is neer,
And, from this place your voice will reach her ear.

　　　　　　　　　　　　　　[Esperanza *goes out.*

——————
15　shou'd] Q2–3; must Q1, Q4–5, F, D.　　22　Circle] Q2–5, F, D; Cercle Q1.
25　vain:] D; ~. Q1–3; ~; Q4–5, F.　　28　Queen.] Q3, F; ~: Q1–2, Q4–5, D.
29　unseen] Q2; ~. Q1, Q4–5; ~, Q3; ~; F, D.
30　agen.] Q3, F; ~ᴧ Q1, Q4; ~, Q2; ~: Q5, D.
32　*Spaniards*] Q2–3, F, D; Spaniards Q1, Q4–5.
32+　*s.d.* [*Exeunt*] Q5, F, D; ᴧ~ Q1–4.

Song, In two Parts.

He. *How unhappy a Lover am I*
  While I sigh for my Phillis *in vain;*
 All my hopes of Delight
 Are another man's Right,
  Who is happy while I am in pain!

2.

40 She. *Since her Honour allows no Relief,*
  But to pity the pains which you bear,
 'Tis the best of your Fate,
 (In a hopeless Estate,)
  To give o're, and betimes to despair.

3.

He. *I have try'd the false Med'cine in vain;*
  For I wish what I hope not to win:
 From without, my desire
 Has no Food to its Fire,
  But it burns and consumes me within.

4.

50 She. *Yet at least 'tis a pleasure to know*
  That you are not unhappy alone:
 For the Nymph you adore
 Is as wretched and more,
  And accounts all your suff'rings her own.

5.

He. *O ye Gods, let me suffer for both;*
  At the feet of my Phillis *I'le lye:*
 I'le resign up my Breath,
 And take pleasure in Death,
  To be pity'd by her when I dye.

53 *wretched*] Q2–3, F, D, Ds1, Ds3–5, Os1–5, Fs1–3, M1–2; *wretch'd* Q1, Q4–5.

6.

60 She. *What her Honour deny'd you in Life*
      In her Death she will give to your Love.
      Such a Flame as is true
      After Fate will renew,
      For the Souls to meet closer above.

      Enter Esperanza *again after the Song.*

  Almanz. Accept this Diamond, till I can present
Something more worthy my acknowledgement.
And now, farewell; I will attend, alone,
Her coming forth; and make my suff'rings known.
                              [*Exit* Esperanza.
A hollow wind comes whistling through that door;
70 And a cold shivering seizes me all o're.
My Teeth, too, chatter, with a suddain fright:
These are the raptures of too fierce delight!
The combate of the Tyrants, Hope and Fear;
Which Hearts, for want of Field-room, cannot bear.
I grow impatient, this, or that's the room:
I'le meet her; now, methinks, I hear her come.
                    [*He goes to the door; the Ghost of his*
                      Mother meets him, he starts back:
                      the Ghost stands in the door.
  Almanz. Well mayst thou make thy boast, whate're thou art;
Thou art the first e're made *Almanzor* start.
My Legs————
80 Shall bear me to thee in their own despight: ⎞
I'le rush into the Covert of thy Night,   ⎟
And pull thee backward by thy shrowd, to light. ⎠
Or else I'le squeeze thee, like a Bladder, there:
And make thee groan thy self away to Air.
                              [*The Ghost retires.*
So; art thou gone? thou canst no Conquest boast:

68+ *s.d.* [*Exit*] Q5, F, D; ∧~ Q1–4.   68+ *s.d.* Esperanza.] Q2–5, F, D; ~: Q1.
69 A] D; *Solus.* / A Q1–5, F.   76+ *s.d.* [*He*] Q4–5, F, D; ∧~ Q1–3.
85 gone?] ~! Q1–5, F, D.

I thought what was the courage of a Ghost.———
———The grudging of my Ague yet remains:
My blood, like Ysicles, hangs in my veins,
And does not drop: be master of that door,
90 We two, will not disturb each other more.
I err'd a little, but extremes may joyn;
That door was Hell's; but this is Heav'ns and mine.

> [*Goes to the other door and is
> met again by the Ghost.*

Again! by Heav'n I do conjure thee, speak!
What art thou, Spirit; and what dost thou seek?

The Ghost comes on, softly, after the Conjuration: and
Almanzor *retires to the middle of the Stage.*

Ghost. I am the Ghost of her who gave thee birth,
The Airy shadow of her mouldring Earth.
Love of thy Father me through Seas did guide;
On Sea's I bore thee, and on Sea's I dy'd.
I dy'd; and for my Winding-sheet, a Wave
100 I had; and all the Ocean for my Grave.
But, when my soul to bliss did upward move,
I wander'd round the Chrystal walls above;
But found th' eternal fence so steepy high, ⎞
That, when I mounted to the middle Sky, ⎬
I flagg'd, and flutter'd down; and could not fly. ⎠
Then, from the Battlements of th' Heav'nly Tow'r,
An Angel gave me charge to waite this hour;
And told me I had yet a task assign'd,
To warn that little pledge I left behind;
110 And to divert him, e're it were too late,
From Crimes unknown; and errors of his Fate.

---

93 speak!] ~. Q1–5, F, D.   95 *Ghost.*] Q4–5, F, D; ~! Q1–3.
95 birth,] ~: Q1–5, F, D.
107 An Angel gave me charge to] Q2–3; A Watchman Angel bid me Q1, Q4–5,
F, D.

Almanz. Speak, Holy Shade; thou Parent form, speak on: ⎱ [*Bow-*
Instruct thy mortal Elemented Son;   ⎰ *ing.*
(For here I wander to my self unknown.)
But oh, thou better part of Heav'nly Air,
Teach me, kind spirit, (since I am still thy care,)
My Parents names!
If I have yet a Father, let me know
To whose old age my humble youth must bow;
120 And pay its duty, if he mortal be,
Or Adoration, if a Mind like thee.
    Ghost. Then, what I may, I'le tell.————
From antient Blood thy Fathers Linage springs,
Thy Mothers thou deriv'st from stemms of Kings.
A Christian born, and born again, that day,
When sacred Water wash'd thy sins away.
Yet bred in errors thou dost mis-imploy
That strength Heav'n gave thee, and its stock destroy.
    Almanz. By Reason, Man a Godhead may discern:
130 But, how he would be worshipt, cannot learn.
    Ghost. Heav'n does not now thy Ignorance reprove;
But warns thee from known Crimes of lawless Love.
That Crime thou know'st, and knowing, dost not shun,
Shall an unknown, and greater Crime pull on:
But, if thus warn'd, thou leav'st this cursed place,
Then shalt thou know the Author of thy Race.
Once more I'le see thee, when my charge is done:
Far hence, upon the Mountains of the Moon
Is my abode, where Heav'n and Nature smile;
140 And strew with Flowers the secret bed of *Nyle.*
Blest Souls are there refin'd, and made more bright,
And, in the shades of Heav'n, prepar'd for light.

                                   [*Exit Ghost.*

---

112   *Almanz.* Speak, . . . on: [*Bowing.*] D (*bowing*); [Almanzor *bowing.* / Speak,
. . . on: Q1–5 (ᴧAlmanzor Q2–5); [Almanzor *bowing.* / *Almanz.* Speak, . . . on: F.
128   stock] Q2–3; flock Q1, Q3–5, F, D.   137   thee,] Q2–3; ~: Q1, Q4–5, D; ~; F.
137   done:] ~, Q1–4; ~; Q5; ~. F, D.   142+   *s.d.* [*Exit*] Q4–5, F, D; ᴧ~ Q1–3.

Almanz. Oh Heav'n, how dark a Riddle's thy Decree,
Which bounds our Wills, yet seems to leave 'em free!
Since thy fore-knowledge cannot be in vain,
Our choice must be what thou didst first ordain:
Thus, like a Captive in an Isle confin'd,
Man walks at large, a Pris'ner of the Mind:
Wills all his Crimes, (while Heav'n th' Indictment draws;)
150 And, pleading guilty, justifies the Laws.————
Let Fate be Fate; the Lover and the Brave
Are rank'd, at least, above the vulgar Slave:
Love makes me willing to my death to run;
And courage scorns the death it cannot shun.

Enter Almahide *with a Taper.*

Almah. My Light will sure discover those who talk.————
Who dares to interrupt my private Walk?
Almanz. He who dares love; and for that love must dy,
And, knowing this, dares yet love on, am I.
Almah. That love which you can hope, and I can pay
160 May be receiv'd and giv'n in open day;
My praise and my esteem you had before:
And you have bound your self to ask no more.
Almanz. Yes, I have bound my self, but will you take
The forfeit of that bond which force did make?
Almah. You know you are from recompence debarr'd,
But purest love can live without reward.
Almanz. Pure love had need be to it self a feast;
For, like pure Elements, 'twill nourish least.
Almah. It therefore yields the only pure content;
170 For it, like Angels, needs no Nourishment.
To eat and drink can no perfection be;
All Appetite implies Necessity.
Almanz. 'Twere well, if I could like a spirit live:
But do not Angels food to Mortals give?————

————————
149   (while ... draws;)] Q2–3; ∧~ ... ~; ∧ Q1, Q4–5, F, D.
155   talk.————] D; ~;———— Q1–5, F.   172   Necessity.] Q3–5, F, D; ~: Q1–2.
174   give?————] D; ~.———— Q1–4; ~∧———— Q5, F.

What if some Dæmon should my death foreshow,
Or bid me change, and to the Christians goe,
Will you not think I merit some reward,
When I my love above my life regard?
    Almah. In such a case your change must be allow'd;
180 I would, my self, dispence with what you vow'd.
    Almanz. Were I to dye that hour when I possess;
This minute should begin my happiness.
    Almah. The thoughts of death your passion would remove:
Death is a cold encouragement to love!
    Alman. No; from my joyes I to my death would run;
And think the business of my life well done.
But I should walk a discontented Ghost,
If flesh and blood were to no purpose lost.
    Almah. You love me not, *Almanzor;* if you did, ⎫
190 You would not ask what honour must forbid.   ⎬
    Alman. And what is Honour, but a Love well hid? ⎭
    Almah. Yes; 'tis the Conscience of an Act well done:
Which gives us pow'r our own desires to shun.
The strong, and secret curb of headlong Will;
The self reward of good; and shame of ill.
    Almanz. These, Madam, are the Maximes of the Day;
When Honour's present, and when Love's away.
The duty of poor Honour were too hard,
In Arms all day, at night to mount the Guard.
200 Let him in pity, now, to rest retire;
Let these soft hours be watch'd by warm desire.
    Almah. Guards, who all day on painful duty keep,
In dangers are not priviledg'd to sleep.
    Alman. And with what dangers are you threaten'd here?
Am I, alas, a foe for you to fear?
See, Madam, at your feet this Enemy: *[Kneels.*
Without your pity and your Love I die.
    Almah. Rise, rise: and do not empty hopes pursue:
Yet think, that I deny my self, not you.

183   remove:] Q4, F; ~. Q1–3; ~, Q5; ~; D.
197   Love's] Q2–5, F, D; Lov's Q1.   206   *s.d. Kneels*] Q4–5, F, D; *kneels* Q1–3.
209   self,] Q2–3, F, D; ~ʌ Q1, Q4–5.

210   *Alman.* A happiness so nigh, I cannot bear:
My loves too fierce; and you too killing fair.
I grow enrag'd to see such Excellence: ⎞
If words so much disorder'd, give offence, ⎬
My love's too full of zeal to think of sence. ⎠
Be you like me; dull Reason hence remove;
And tedious formes; and give a loose to love.
Love eagerly; let us be gods to night;
And do not, with half-yielding, dash delight.
    Almah. Thou strong Seducer, Opportunity!
220 Of womankind, half are undone by thee!
Though I resolve I will not be misled,
I wish I had not heard what you have sed!
I cannot be so wicked to comply;
And, yet, am most unhappy to deny!
Away!
    Alman. ————I will not move me from this place:
I can take no denial from that face!
    Almah. If I could yield; (but think not that I will:)
You and my self, I in revenge, should kill.
For I should hate us both, when it were done:
230 And would not to the shame of life be wonn.
    Alman. Live but to night; and trust to morrows mind:
'Ere that can come, there's a whole life behind.
Methinks already crown'd with joyes, I lie;
Speechless and breathless in an Extasie.
Not absent in one thought: I am all there:
Still closs; yet wishing still to be more near.
    Almah. Deny your own desires: for it will be
Too little now to be deni'd by me.
Will he who does all great, all noble seem,
240 Be lost and forfeit to his own Esteem?
Will he, who may with Heroes claim a place,
Belie that fame, and to himself be base?
Think how August and god-like you did look

218   half-yielding] Q2–3; half yielding Q1, Q4–5, F, D.
222   have] Q2–3, D; had Q1, Q4–5, F.   225   Away!] ∼: Q1–3; ∼. Q4–5, F, D.

ALMANZOR PREVENTING ALMAHIDE'S SUICIDE,
ACT IV, SCENE III
FROM *The Dramatick Works of John Dryden, Esq.* (1735)

When my defence, unbrib'd you undertook.
But, when an Act so brave you disavow,
How little, and how mercenary now!
    Almanz. Are, then, my Services no higher priz'd?
And can I fall so low to be despis'd?
    Almah. Yes; for whatever may be bought, is low,
250 And you your self, who sell your self, are so.
Remember the great Act you did this day:
How did your Love to Vertue then give way?
When you gave freedom to my Captive Lord;
That Rival, who possest what you ador'd.
Of such a deed what price can there be made?
Think well: is that an Action to be paid?
It was a Myracle of Vertue shown:
And wonders are with wonder paid alone.
And would you all that secret joy of mind
260 Which great Souls onely in great actions find,
All that, for one tumultuous Minute loose?
    Alman. I wou'd that minute before ages choose.
Praise is the pay of Heav'n for doing good;
But Loves the best return for flesh and blood.
    Almah. You've mov'd my heart, so much, I can deny
No more; but know, *Almanzor,* I can dye.
Thus far, my vertue yields; if I have shown
More Love, than what I ought, let this attone.
                              [Going to stab herself.
    Almanz. Hold, hold!
270 Such fatal proofs of love you shall not give:
Deny me; hate me; (both are just) but live!
Your Vertue I will ne'r disturb again:
Nor dare to ask, for fear I should obtain.
    Almah. 'Tis gen'rous to have conquer'd your desire;
You mount above your wish; and loose it higher.
There's pride in vertue; and a kindly heat:
Not feverish, like your love; but full as great.
Farewell; and may our loves hereafter, be,
But Image-like, to heighten piety.

280   *Almanz.* 'Tis time I should be gone!
Alas I am but half converted yet:
All I resolve, I with one look, forget:
And, like a Lyon whom no Arts can tame;
Shall tear, ev'n those, who would my rage reclaime.

> [*Exeunt severally.* Zulema *and* Hamet *watch*
> Almanzor: *and when he is gone, go in*
> *after the Queen.*

Enter Abdelmelech *and* Lyndaraxa.

Lynd. It is enough; you've brought me to this place:
Here stop: and urge no further, my disgrace.
Kill me: in death your mercy will be seen,
But make me not a Captive to the Queen.
Abdelm. 'Tis therefore I this punishment provide:
290   This only can revenge me on your pride.
Prepare to suffer what you shun in vain:
And know, you now are to obey, not raign.

Enter Almahide; *schrieking: her hair loose; she runs*
over the stage.

Almah. Help; help: oh heav'n, some help!

Enter Zulema *and* Hamet.

Zul. ——————————————————Make haste before,
And intercept her passage to the door.
Abdelm. Villains, what Act are you attempting here?
Almah. I thank thee, heav'n; some succour does appear.

---

282   forget:] F; ~. Q1-5, D.
284+   s.d. [*Exeunt*] Q4-5, F, D; ∧~ Q1-3.
288   Queen.] Q3, Q5, F, D; ~: Q1-2, Q4.
291   vain:] Q3; ~. Q1-2, Q4; ~; Q5, F, D.
293   some help!] Q5, F, D; ~~. Q1, Q3-4; ~~: Q2.
294   door.] Q3, Q5, F, D; ~: Q1-2, Q4.
295   here?] ~! Q1-5, F, D.

[*As* Abdelmelech *is going to help the Queen:*
Lyndaraxa *pulls out his Sword: and holds it.*
Abdelm. With what ill fate, my good design is curst!
Zul. We have no time to think: dispatch him first.
Abdelm. Oh for a sword!

[*They make at* Abdelmelech: *he goes off at one
door, while the Queen escapes at the other.*
Zul. Ruin'd!
Hamet. ——Undone!
Lynd. ——————And which is worst of all
He is escap'd.
Zul. ——I hear 'em loudly call.
Lynd. Your fear will loose you: call as loud as they,
I have not time to teach you what to say:
The Court, will in a moment, all be here,
But second what I say, and do not fear.
Call Help; run that way; leave the rest to me.

[Zulema *and* Hamet *retire, and
within cry,* Help.

Enter at several doors, the King, Abenamar, Selin,
Ozmyn, Almanzor, *with guards attending* Boabdelin.

Boab. What can the cause of all this tumult be?
And what the meaning of that naked sword?
Lynd. I'le tell, when fear will so much breath afford.
The Queen and *Abdelmelech.*——T'will not out——
Ev'n I, who saw it, of the truth yet doubt,
It seems so strange.
Almanz. ——Did she not name the Queen?
Haste; speak.
Lynd. ——How dare I speak what I have seen?

296+   s.d. [*As*] Q4–5, F, D; ∧~ Q1–3.
299+   s.d. [*They*] Q4–5, F, D; ∧~ Q1–3.
299+   s.d. Abdelmelech] Q2–5, F, D; Abdemelech Q1.
301   He is] Q3; He Q1–2, Q4–5, F, D.   301   escap'd.] Q5, F, D; ~: Q1–4.
302   they,] Q5; ~. Q1–4, F; ~: D.   304   here,] Q5; ~. Q1–4; ~; F, D.
306   Help] D; help Q1–5, F.   306+   s.d. [Zulema] Q4–5, F, D; ∧~ Q1–3.
306+   s.d. cry, Help] D (*Help*); cry help Q1–5, F.   312   Queen?] ~! Q1–5, F, D.
313   speak.] Q5, F; ~: Q1–4; ~, D.   313   seen?] ~! Q1–5, F, D.

With *Hamet,* and with *Zulema,* I went
To pay both theirs, and my acknowledgement
To *Almahide;* and by her Pow'r implore
Your Clemency, our Fortunes to restore.
We chose this hour, which we believ'd most free,
When she retir'd from noise and company.

320 The Antichamber past, we gently knockt,
(Unheard it seems) but found the Lodgings lockt.
In dutious silence while we waited there,
We, first a noise, and then long whispers hear:
Yet thought it was the Queen at Pray'rs alone,
Till she distinctly said,————If this were known
My Love, what shame, what danger would ensue!
Yet I (and sigh'd) could venture more for you!

   Boab. O Heav'n, what do I hear?
   Almanz. ————————————Let her go on. ⎫
   Lynd. And how, (then murmur'd in a bigger tone, ⎬
330 Another voice) and how should it be known?   ⎭
This hour is from your Court Attendants, free:
The King suspects *Almanzor;* but not me.

   Zulema. I find her drift: *Hamet* be Confident;   [*At the door.*
Second her words; and fear not the event.

      Zulema *and* Hamet *Enter. The King embraces them.*

   Boab. Welcome, my onely Friends; Behold in me
O Kings, behold th' effects of Clemency!
See here the gratitude of pardon'd foes!
That life I gave 'em, they for me expose!

   Hamet. Though *Abdelmelech* was our Friend before,
340 When Duty call'd us he was so no more.

   Almanz. Damn your delay, you Torturers proceed,
I will not hear one word, but *Almahide.*

---

316   Pow'r] Q2–3; Mouth Q1, Q4–5, F, D.   328   hear?] ~, Q1–5; ~! F, D.
328   *Almanz.* ————] F (*without the rule*); (*Almanz.*) Q1–5, D (*on same line as preceding speech; no parens in D*).
333   *Zulema.* I . . . Confident; [*At the door.*] D; [Zulema, *at the door.* / I . . . Confident; Q1–5, F (*on same line in F*).

Boab. When you, within, the Traitors voice did hear,
What did you, then?
  Zul. —————I durst not trust my Ear:
But, peeping through the Key-hole, I espy'd
The Queen; and *Abdelmelech* by her side:
She on the Couch, he on her bosom lay, ⎞
Her Hand, about his Neck, his Head did stay, ⎬
And, from his Forehead wip'd the drops away. ⎠
  Boab. Go on, go on my friends, to clear my doubt: 350
I hope I shall have life to hear you out.
  Zul. What had been, Sir, you may suspect too well:
What follow'd, Modesty forbids to tell:
Seeing, what we had thought beyond belief,
Our hearts so swell'd with anger and with grief,
That, by plain force, we strove the door to break:
He, fearful, and with guilt, or Love, grown weak,
Just as we enter'd, scap'd the other way:
Nor did th' amazed Queen behind him stay.
  Lynd. His sword, in so much haste he could not mind: ⎞ 360
But left this witness of his Crime behind.   ⎬
  Boab. O proud, ingrateful, faithless, womankind! ⎠
How chang'd, and what a Monster am I made!
My Love, my Honour, ruin'd and betray'd!
  Almanz. Your Love and Honour! mine are ruin'd worse:
Furies and Hell what right have you to curse?
Dull Husband as you are,———
What can your Love, or what your Honour be?
I am her Lover, and she's false to me.
  Boab. Goe, when the Authors of my shame are found, 370
Let 'em be taken instantly, and bound:
They shall be punish'd as our Laws require:
'Tis just, that Flames should be condemn'd to fire.
This, with the dawn of morning shall be done.
  Aben. You haste too much her Execution.
Her Condemnation ought to be deferr'd:

———————
350 doubt:] *some copies of Q1 lack the colon.*
359 stay.] Q3–5, F, D; ~: Q1–2.   366 curse?] Q3, D; ~! Q1–2, Q4–5, F.
367 Dull] Q3–5, F, D; ~, Q1–2.   368 be?] ~! Q1–5, F, D.

With justice, none can be condemn'd unheard.
   Boab. A formal Process, tedious is, and long:
Besides, the evidence is full and strong.
380   *Lynd.* The Law demands two witnesses; and she
Is cast; (for which Heav'n knows I grieve) by three.
   Ozm. Hold, Sir; since you so far insist on Law;
We can, from thence, one just advantage draw:
That Law, which dooms Adultresses to die,
Gives Champions, too, to slander'd Chastity.
   Almanz. And how dare you, who from my Bounty live,
Intrench upon my Loves Prerogative?
Your courage in your own concernments try;
Brothers are things remote while I am by.
390   *Ozm.* I knew not you thus far her cause would own;
And must not suffer you to fight alone:
Let two to two in equal combat joyn;
You vindicate her Person, I her Line.
   Lynd. Of all Mankind *Almanzor* has least right
In her defence, who wrong'd his Love, to fight.
   Almanz. 'Tis false; she is not ill, nor can she be;
She must be Chaste, because she's lov'd by me.
   Zul. Dare you, what Sence and Reason prove, deny?
   Almanz. When she's in question, Sence and Reason lye.
400   *Zul.* For Truth, and for my injur'd Soveraign,
What I have said, I will to death maintain.
   Ozm. So foul a falshood, who e'r justifies
Is basely born; and, like a Villain, lies.
In witness of that Truth, be this my Gage.
                [*Takes a Ring from his finger.*
   Hamet. I take it; and despise a Traytors Rage.
   Boab. The Combat's yours; a Guard the Lists surround;
Then raise a Scaffold in th' incompast ground:
And, by it, piles of Wood; in whose just fire,
Her Champions slain, th' Adultress shall expire.

---

387   Prerogative?] Q3; ~. Q1–2, Q4–5, F, D.
409   Champions] Q5, F, D; Champion's Q1–2, Q4; Champion Q3.

410   *Aben.* We ask no favour, but what Arms will yield.
     Boab. Choose then two equal Judges of the Field:
Next morning shall decide the doubtful strife;
Condemn th' unchaste, or quit the vertuous Wife.
     Almanz. But I am both wayes, curst.————
For *Almahide* must dye, if I am slain;
Or, for my Rival, I the Conquest gain.

                            [*Exeunt.*

ACT V.

Almanzor *Solus.*

I have out-fac'd myself: and justify'd
What I knew false to all the World, beside.
She was as faithless as her Sex could be:
And now I am alone, she's so to me.
She's faln! and now where shall we vertue find?
She was the last that stood of Woman-kind:
Could she so holily my flames remove;
And fall that hour to *Abdelmelechs* Love?
Yet her protection I must undertake;
10 Not now for Love; but for my Honours sake.
That mov'd me first, and must oblige me still,
My cause is good, however hers be ill;
I'le leave her, when she's freed; and let it be
Her punishment, she could be false to me.

To *him,* Abdelmelech, *guarded.*

     Abdelm. Heav'n is not Heav'n; nor are there Deities:
There is some new Rebellion in the Skies.

---

410   yield.] Q3, F, D; ~: Q1-2, Q4-5 (*some copies of Q1 have* yidld).
411   Field:] Q3, D; ~, Q1-2, Q4-5; ~. F.
416+   *s.d.* [*Exeunt.*] Q4-5, F, D; ₍~ Q1-3.
2   beside.] Q3, F, D; ~, Q1-2, Q4-5.   5   find?] Q3, D; ~; Q1-2, Q4; ~, Q5; ~! F.
14+   *s.d. To*] Q2-5, F, D; [~ Q1.   15   Deities:] F; ~. Q1-5, D.

All that was Good and Holy, is dethron'd,
And Lust, and Rapine are for justice own'd.
   Almanz. 'Tis true; what justice in that Heav'n can be
20 Which thus affronts me with the sight of thee?
Why must I be from just Revenge debarr'd?
Chains are thy Arms, and Prisons are thy Guard:
The death thou dy'st may to a Husband be
A satisfaction; but 'tis none to me.
My Love would justice to it self afford;
But now thou creep'st to Death, below my Sword.
   Abdelm. This threat'ning would show better, were I free.
   Almanz. No; wer't thou freed, I would not threaten thee.
This arme should then.————But now it is too late!————
30 I could redeem thee to a nobler Fate.
As some huge Rock
Rent from its Quarry, does the Waves divide,
So I,————
Wou'd fall upon thy guards, and dash 'em wide:
Then, to my rage left naked and alone,
Thy too much freedome thou shouldst soon bemoan:
Dar'd, like a Lark, that on the open plain
Pursu'd and cuffd, seeks shelter now in vain:
So on the ground wou'dst thou expecting lye,
40 Not daring to afford me victory.
But, yet thy fate's not ripe: it is decreed
Before thou dy'st that *Almahide* be freed.
My honour first her danger shall remove,
And then, revenge on thee my injur'd love.

                                 [Exeunt severally.

---

20   thee?] D; ∼! Q1–5, F.
21   debarr'd?] D; ∼! Q1–5, F.
27   free.] Q2–3, D; ∼, Q1, Q4–5; ∼ₐ F.
34   Wou'd fall] Q2–3; Would sowze Q1, Q4–5, F, D (W'ould Q1).
44+   *s.d.* [*Exeunt*] Q4–5, F, D; ₐ∼ Q1–3.

SCENE II.

The Scene changes to the Vivarambla; *and appears fill'd
with Spectators: A scaffold hung with black, &c.*

Enter the Queen, guarded, with Esperanza.

Almah. See how the gazing people crowd the place:
All gaping to be fill'd with my disgrace.

[A shout within.

That shout, like the hoarse peal of Vultures rings,
When, over fighting fields, they beat their wings.
Let never woman trust in Innocence;
Or think her Chastity its own defence;
Mine has betray'd me to this publick shame:
And vertue, which I serv'd, is but a name.
      Esper. Leave then that shaddow, and for succor fly
10 To him, we serve, the Christians Deity.
Vertue's no god, nor has she power divine:
But he protects it who did first enjoyn.
Trust, then, in him, and from his grace, implore
Faith to believe what rightly we adore.
      Almah. Thou Pow'r unknown, if I have err'd forgive:
My infancy was taught what I believe.
But if thy Christians truely worship thee,
Let me thy godhead in thy succour see:
So shall thy Justice in my safety shine,
20 And all my dayes, which thou shalt add, be thine.

Enter the King, Abenamar, Lyndaraxa, Benzayda:
then Abdelmelech *guarded: And after him,* Selin,
and Alabez, *as Judges of the field.*

SCENE II. | *The*] The Q1–5, F, D.   *s.d. fill'd*] Q2–5, F, D; *fil'd* Q1.
3   peal] Q2–3; peals Q1, Q4–5, F, D.   5   Innocence;] Q2–3; ~. Q1, Q4–5; ~, F, D.
20+   *s.d. guarded:*] ~. Q1–5, F, D.

Boab. You Judges of the field, first take your place:
Th' accusers and accus'd bring face to face.
Set guards, and let the Lists be open'd wide,
And may just Heav'n assist the juster side.
    Almah. What not one tender look, one passing word?
Farewel, my much unkind, but still lov'd Lord!
Your Throne was for my humble fate too high;
And therefore Heav'n thinks fit that I should dye.
My story be forgot when I am dead;
30 Least it should fright some other from your bed:
And, to forget me, may you soon adore
Some happier maid (yet none could love you more.)
But may you never think me innocent;
Least it should cause you trouble to repent.
    Boabd. 'Tis pity so much beauty should not live;   [*Aside.*
Yet, I too much am injur'd to forgive.   [*Goes to his seat.*

> *Trumpets: Then enter two* Moors *bearing two naked
> swords before the Accusers* Zulema *and* Hamet, *who
> follow them. The Judges seat themselves: the Queen,
> and* Abdelmelech *are led to the Scaffold.*

Alabez. Say for what end you thus in arms appear:
What are your names, and what demand you here?
    Zulema. The *Zegrys* antient Race our Linage claims;
40 And *Zulema* and *Hamet* are our names.
Like Loyal Subjects in these lists we stand,
And Justice in our Kings behalf demand.
    Hamet. For whom, in witness of what both have seen,
Bound by our duty, we appeach the Queen
And *Abdelmelech,* of adultery.
    Zul. Which, like true Knights we will maintain, or dy.

---

22 Th'] Q3, D; The Q1–2, Q4–5, F.   25 word?] Q3, D; ~; Q1–2, Q4–5; ~! F.
35 s.d. *Aside.*] Q4–5, F, D; *aside*ₐ Q1; *aside.* Q2–3.
36 s.d. *Goes*] Q4–5, F, D; *goes* Q1–3.
36+ s.d. Moors] D; *Moors* Q1–5, F (*Mores* Q1).
37 appear:] Q3, Q5, F, D; ~? Q1–2, Q4.   39 *Zegrys*] D; *Zegry's* Q1–5, F.

Alabez. Swear on the *Alcoran* your cause is right;
And *Mahomet* so prosper you in fight.
                    [*They touch their foreheads with*
                         the Alcoran, *and bow.*

Trumpets on the other side of the Stage: two Moors
as before, with bare swords before Almanzor *and* Ozmyn.

Selin. Say for what end you thus in armes appear:
50 What are your names, and what demand you here?
   Alman. Ozmyn is his, *Almanzor* is my name;
   We come as Champions of the Queens fair fame.
   Ozmyn. To prove these *Zegrys,* like false Traitors, lye;
   Which, like true Knights, we will maintain, or dye.
   Selin. Madam, do you for Champions take these two;
   By their success to live or dye?   [*To* Almahide.
   Almah. ─────────────I do.
   Selin. Swear on the *Alcoran* your Cause is right;
   And *Mahomet* so prosper you in fight.
                    [*They kiss the* Alcoran. Ozmyn *and* Benzayda
                         embrace, and take leave in dumb show:
                         while Lyndaraxa *speaks to her Brothers.*
   Lynd. If you 'orecome, let neither of 'em live:
60 But use with care th' advantages I give.
   One of their swords in fight shall useless be;
   The Bearer of it is suborn'd by me.

                    [*She and* Benzayda *retire.*

────────

48+   *s.d.* Alcoran] Q2–3, Q5, F, D; *Alcoran* Q1, Q4.
48+   *s.d.* Moors] D; *Moors* Q1–5, F.
52   fame.] Q3, Q5, F, D; ~: Q1–2, Q4.
53   Traitors] Q2, F, D; Trators Q1, Q4; Traytors Q3, Q5.
55–56   *Selin.* Madam, . . . two; / . . . [*To* Almahide.] *Selin.* to *Almahide.* / Madam,
. . . two; Q1–5, F, D (Selin‸ Q2–3, Q5; *on same line in F, D;* [*Selin to Almahide.*] F;
Selin to Almahide. D).
56   dye?] Q3–5, F, D; ~; Q1–2.
58+   *s.d.* Alcoran.] Q2–3, F, D; *Alcoran.* Q1, Q4–5.
59   *Lynd.*] Q2–3, Q5, F, D; *Lind.* Q1, Q4.
60   th'] Q3, D; the Q1–2, Q4–5, F.   60   give.] Q1–3, F; ~; Q4; ~: Q5, D.
61   fight] Q2–5, F, D; sight Q1.   62+   *s.d. She*] Q2–5, F, D; *she* Q1.
62+   *s.d.* Benzayda] Q3–5, F, D; *Benzaida* Q1; Benzaida Q2.

Alabez. Now, Principals and Seconds, all advance
And each of you assist his fellows chance.
Selin. The wind and Sun we equally divide;
So, let th' events of Arms the truth decide.
The chances of the fight, and every wound,
The trumpets, on the Victors part, resound.

[*The Trumpets sound;* Almanzor *and* Zulema *meet and fight:* Ozmyn *and* Hamet: *after some passes, the sword of* Ozmyn *breaks; he retires defending himself, and is wounded: the* Zegrys *trumpets sound their advantage:* Almanzor, *in the mean time, drives* Zulema *to the further end of the stage; till, hearing the trumpets of the adverse party, he looks back and sees* Ozmyns *misfortune: he makes at* Zulema *just as* Ozmyn *falls in retiring, and* Hamet *is thrusting at him.*

Ham. to Ozmyn. Our difference now shall soon determin'd be.
                                                            [*Thrusting.*

70   *Alman.* Hold, Traytor, and defend thy self from me.

[Hamet *leaves* Ozmyn *(who cannot rise,) and both he and* Zulema *fall on* Almanzor, *and press him: he retires and* Hamet, *advancing first, is run through the body and falls. The Queens trumpets sound.* Almanzor *pursues* Zulema.

Lynd. I must make haste some remedy to find:———
Treason, *Almanzor,* treason; look behind.

[Almanzor *looks behind him to see who calls, and* Zulema *takes the advantage and wounds him; the* Zegrys *trumpets sound:* Almanzor *turns upon* Zulema *and wounds him: he falls. The Queens trumpets sound.*

68+   *s.d.* [*The Trumpets*] D; ∧∼∼ Q1–5, F.
68+   *s.d.* Zegrys] D; Zegry's Q1–5, F.
69   *Ham. to Ozmyn.* Our . . . be. [*Thrusting.*] *Ham. to Ozmyn thrusting.* / Our
. . . be. Q1–5, F, D (be: Q1–3; *on same line in F;* [Hamet . . . thrusting.] F; *thrusting,* D).
70+   *s.d.* [Hamet *leaves*] D; ∧∼∼ Q1–5, F.
71   *Lynd.*] Q2–5, F, D; *Lind.* Q1.
72+   *s.d.* [Almanzor *looks*] D; ∧∼∼ Q1–5, F.

Alman. Now triumph in thy sisters treachery.   [*Stabbing him.*
Zul. Hold, hold; I have enough to make me dye,
But, that I may in peace resign my breath,
I must confess my crime before my death.
Mine is the guilt; the Queen is innocent;   ⎫
I lov'd her; and, to compass my intent,   ⎬
Us'd force, which *Abdelmelech* did prevent. ⎭
80 The lye my Sister forg'd: But, oh my fate
Comes on too soon, and I repent too late.
Fair Queen, forgive; and let my penitence
Expiate some part of———   [*Dies.*
Almah. ————Ev'n thy whole offence!
Almanzor. If ought remains in the Sultana's cause,
I here am ready to fulfil the Laws.   [*To the Judges.*
Selin. The Law is fully satisfy'd; and we
Pronounce the Queen and *Abdelmelech* free.
Abdelm. Heav'n thou art just!
              [*The Judges rise from their seats, and goe before*
              Almanzor, *to the Queens Scaffold: he unbinds*
              the Queen and Abdelmelech; *and they all goe*
              off, the people showting, and the Trumpets
              sounding the while.
Boab. Before we pay our thanks, or show our joy;
90 Let us our needful Charity employ.
Some skilful Surgeon speedily be found,
T' apply fit Remedies to *Ozmyn*'s wound.
Benzayda. That be my charge; my Linnen I will tear:
                        [*Running to* Ozmyn.
Wash it with Tears, and bind it with my Hair.

73   *s.d. Stabbing*] Q4–5, F, D; *stabbing* Q1–3.
83   of———] Q3–5, F, D; ∼.——— Q1–2.
83   *s.d. Dies.*] Q4–5, F, D; *dies*ᴧ Q1; *dies.* Q2–3.
84–85   *Almanzor.* If . . . cause, / . . . [*To the Judges.*] [Almanzor *to the Judges.* /
If . . . cause, Q1–5, F, D (*on same line in F, D*; ᴧAlmanzor Q4–5, D; *Judges.*] F).
88+   *s.d.* [*The Judges*] D; ᴧ∼∼ Q1–5, F.
88+   *s.d.* Abdelmelech] Q2, Q5, F, D; *Abdelmelech* Q1, Q3–4.
93   *Benzayda.* That . . . tear: / [*Running to* Ozmyn.] F (Benzayda *running*);
[Benzayda *running to* Ozmyn. / That . . . tear: Q1–5, D (ᴧBenzayda Q4–5, D; *on
same line in D*).

Ozm. With how much pleasure I my pains endure!
And bless the wound which causes such a cure.

> [*Exit* Ozmyn, *led by* Benzayda
> *and* Abenamar.

Boab. Some, from the place of Combat bear the slain:
Next *Lyndaraxa's* death I should ordain:
But let her who this mischief did contrive,
100 For ever banish'd from *Granada* live.

Lynd. Thou shou'dst have punish'd more, or not at all:
By her thou hast not ruin'd, thou shalt fall.   [*Aside.*
The *Zegry's* shall revenge their branded Line:
Betray their Gate, and with the Christians joyn.

> [*Exit* Lynd. *with* Alabez. *The Bodies of
> her Brothers are born after her.*

Almanzor, Almahide, Esperanza *re-enter
to the King.*

Almah. The thanks thus paid, which first to Heav'n were due,
My next, *Almanzor,* let me pay you:
Somewhat there is, of more concernment, too,
Which 'tis not fit you should, in publick, know.
First let your wounds be dress'd with speedy care;
110 And then you shall th' important Secret share.

Almanz. When e're you speak,
Were my wounds mortal, they should still bleed on;
And I would listen till my life were gone:
My Soul, should, ev'n for your last accent, stay; ⎫
And then shoot out, and with such speed obey; ⎬
It shou'd not bait at Heav'n to stop its way. ⎭

> [*Exit* Almanzor.

Boab. 'Tis true, *Almanzor* did her Honour save;   [*Aside.*
But yet what private business can they have?

96+   *s.d.* [*Exit*] Q4–5, F, D; ∧~ Q1–3.   102   *s.d. Aside*] Q4–5, F, D; *aside* Q1–3.
104+   *s.d.* [*Exit*] Q4–5, F, D; ∧~ Q1–3.   104+   *s.d. The*] *the* Q1–5, F, D.
116+   *s.d.* [*Exit*] Q4–5, F, D; ∧~ Q1–3.
117   *s.d. Aside.*] Q4–5, F, D; *aside*∧ Q1; *aside.* Q2–3.
118   have?] ~! Q1–5, F, D.

Such freedom, vertue will not sure, allow;
120 I cannot clear my heart; but must my brow.
                    [*He approaches* Almahide.
Welcome again my Vertuous, Loyal, Wife;
Welcome, to Love, to Honour, and to Life.————
             [*Goes to salute her, she starts back.*
You seem————
As if you from a loath'd embrace did goe!
   Almah. Then briefly I will speak, (since you must know
What to the World my future Acts will show:)
But, hear me first, and then my reasons weigh:
'Tis known how Duty led me to obey
My Fathers choice; and how I since did live,
130 You, Sir, can best your testimony give.
How to your aid I have *Almanzor* brought,
When by rebellious Crowds your life was sought,
Then, how I bore your causeless Jealousie,
(For I must speak;) and after set you free,
When you were Pris'ner by the chance of war;
These sure are proofs of Love.————
   Boab. ————————————I grant they are.
   Almah. And cou'd you, then, O cruelly unkind,
So ill reward such tenderness of mind?
Could you, denying what our Laws afford
140 The meanest subject, on a Traytors word,
Unheard, condemn, and suffer me to goe
To death, and yet no common pity show?
   Boab. Love fill'd my heart ev'n to the brim before:
And then, with too much jealousie, boil'd o're.
   Almah. Be 't Love or Jealousie, tis such a Crime,
That I'm forewarn'd to trust a second time.
Know then, my Pray'rs to Heav'n, shall never cease
To crown your Arms in War; your Wars with Peace:
But, from this day, I will not know your Bed:
150 Though *Almahide* still lives, your wife is dead:

---

120   brow.] Q3; ～: Q1–2, Q4–5, F, D.   120+   *s.d.* [*He*] Q3, F; ∧～ Q1–2, Q4–5, D.
138   mind?] ～! Q1–5, F, D.   142   show?] ～! Q1–5, F, D.
149   Bed:] ～. Q1–5, F, D.

And, with her, dies a Love so pure and true,
It could be kill'd by nothing but by you.

                                 [*Exit* Almahide.

   Boab. Yes, you will spend your life, in Pray'rs for me;
And yet this hour my hated Rival see.
She might a Husbands Jealousie forgive;
But she will onely for *Almanzor* live.
It is resolv'd, I will, my self, provide
That vengeance, which my useless Laws deny'd:
And, by *Almanzor*'s death, at once, remove
160 The Rival of my Empire, and my Love.

                                 [*Exit* Boabdelin.

SCENE III.

Enter Almahide, *led by* Almanzor; *and follow'd
by* Esperanza; *she speaks entring.*

   Almah. How much, *Almanzor*, to your aid I owe,
Unable to repay, I blush to know.
Yet, forc'd by need, e're I can clear that score,
I, like ill debtors, come to borrow more.

   Almanz. Your new Commands I on my knees attend:
I was created for no other end.
Born to be yours, I do by Nature, serve,
And, like the lab'ring Beast, no thanks deserve.

   Almah. Yet first your Vertue to your succor call,
10 For, in this hard Command, you'll need it all.

   Almanz. I stand prepar'd; and whatsoe're it be,
Nothing is hard to him who loves like me.

   Almah. Then know, I from your Love must yet implore
One proof:————that you would never see me more.

   Almanzor. I must confess,   [*Starting back.*
For this last stroke I did no Guard provide;

152+   *s.d.* [*Exit*] Q3–5, F, D; ∧~ Q1–2.   160+   *s.d.* [*Exit*] Q4–5, F, D; ∧~ Q1–3.
SCENE III. / Enter] Enter Q1–5, F, D.
15   *Almanzor.* I must confess, [*Starting back.*] D; [Almanzor *starting back.* / I
must confess, Q1–5, F (∧Almanzor Q2–5, F; *on same line in F*).

I could suspect no Foe was neer that side:
From Winds and thickning Clouds we Thunder fear:
None dread it from that quarter which is cleer.
20 And I would fain believe, 'tis but your Art
To shew you knew where you could wound my Heart.
    Almah. So much respect is to your passion due,
That sure I could not practise Arts on you.
But, that you may not doubt what I have sed,
This hour I have renounc'd my Husbands Bed:
Judge then how much my Fame would injur'd be,
If, leaving him, I should a Lover see!
    Almanz. If his unkindness have deserv'd that Curse,
Must I for loving well be punish'd worse?
30   *Almah.* Neither your Love nor Merits I compare;
But my unspotted Name must be my care.
    Almanz. I have this day establish'd its renown.
    Almah. Would you so soon, what you have rais'd, throw **down?**
    Almanz. But, Madam, Is not yours a greater Guilt
To ruine him who has that Fabrique built?
    Almah. No Lover should his Mistriss Pray'rs withstand:
Yet you contemn my absolute Command.
    Almanz. 'Tis not contempt,
When your Command is issu'd out too late:
40 'Tis past my pow'r; and all beyond is fate.
I scarce could leave you when to Exile sent,
Much less when now recall'd from banishment:
For if that heat your glances cast, were strong;
Your Eyes like Glasses, Fire, when held so long.
    Almah. Then, since you needs will all my weakness know,
I love you; and so well, that you must goe:
I am so much oblig'd; and have withal,
A Heart so boundless and so prodigal,
I dare not trust my self or you, to stay,
50 But, like frank gamesters, must forswear the play.
    Almanz. Fate thou art kind to strike so hard a blow;
I am quite stun'd; and past all feeling now.

Yet———can you tell me you have pow'r and will
To save my life, and, at that instant, kill?
 Alm. This, had you stay'd, you never must have known:
But now you goe, I may with honour own.
 Almanz. But, Madam, I am forc'd to disobey:
In your defence, my honour bids me stay.
I promis'd to secure your life and throne;
60 And, heav'n be thank'd, that work is yet undone.
 Alma. I here make void that promise which you made:
For now I have no farther need of ayd:
That vow which to my plighted Lord was giv'n,
I must not break; but may transfer to Heav'n:
I will with Vestals live:
There needs no guard at a Religious door;
Few will disturb the praying and the poor.
 Almanz. Let me but near that happy Temple stay,
And, through the grates, peep on you once a day.
70 To famish'd hope I would no banquet give:
I cannot sterve, and wish but just to live.
Thus, as a drowning man
Sinks often, and does still more faintly rise;
With his last hold catching what 'ere he spies;
So, faln from those proud hopes I had before,
Your Aid I for a dying wretch implore.

Boabdelin *and guards above.*

 Almah. I cannot your hard destiny withstand;
But slip, like bending rushes, from your hand:
Sink all at once, since you must sink at last.
80 *Almanz.* Can you that last relief of sight remove,
And thrust me out the utmost line of love?
Then, since my hopes of happiness are gone,
Deny'd all favours, I will seyze this one.
      [*Catches her hand and kisses it.*

---

54 kill?] D; ∼! Q1–5, F.
76+ *s.d. follows l. 77 in* Q1–5, D; *on l. 77* ([Boabdelin.) *in* F.
76+ *s.d.* Boabdelin] Q2–5, F, D; *Boabdelin* Q1.
81 love?] Q3; ∼! Q1–2, Q4–5, F, D.

Boab. My just revenge no longer I'le forbear;
I've seen too much; I need not stay to hear.   [*Descends.*
   Almanz. As a small Show'r
To the parch'd earth does some refreshment give,
So, in the strength of this, one day I'le live:
A day:————a year————an age————for ever now;
                    [*Betwixt each word he kisses her*
                    hand by force; she struggling.
90 I feel from every touch a new Soul flow.
                    [*She snatches her hand away.*
My hop'd Eternity of joy is past!
'Twas insupportable, and could not last.
Were heav'n not made of less, or duller joy,
'Twould break each Minute, and it self destroy.

           Enter King and guards below.

King Boab. This, this is he for whom thou didst deny
To share my bed:————Let 'em together dye.
   Almah. Hear me, my Lord.————
   Boab. ————————————Your flatt'ring Arts are vain.
Make haste; and execute what I ordain.   [*To Guards.*
   Almanz. Cut piece-meal in this cause,
100 From every wound I shou'd new Vigour take:
And every limb should new *Almanzors* make.
           [*He puts himself before the Queen; the guards*
           attaque him; with the King.

           Enter Abdelmelech.

Abdelm. What angry God, to exercise his spight,
Has arm'd your left hand to cut off your right?   [*To the King.*
                    [*The King turns, and the fight ceases.*

85   s.d. Descends.] Q4–5, F, D (∼∧ Q5); descends. Q1–3 (∼∧ Q1).
89+   s.d. Betwixt] Q2–5, F, D; betwixt Q1.
90+   s.d. She] Q2–5, F, D; she Q1.   97   vain.] ∼: Q1–5, F, D.
98   s.d. To] Q2–5, F, D; to Q1.   101+   s.d. [He] Q2–4, F, D; ∧∼ Q1, Q5.
102–103   Abdelm. What . . . spight, / . . . [To the King.] D; Abdelm. to the King. /
What . . . spight, Q1–5, F (on same line in F).
103   right?] D; ∼! Q1–5, F.

Hast, not to give but to prevent a Fate:
The foes are enter'd at th' *Elvira* gate:
False *Lyndaraxa* has the Town betray'd,
And all the *Zegrys* give the *Spanyards* ayd.
        Boab. O mischief, not suspected nor foreseen!
        Abdelm. Already they have gain'd the *Zacatin*,
110 And, thence, the *Vivarambla* place possest:
While our faint Souldiers scarce defend the rest.
The Duke of *Arcos* does one squadron head;
The next by *Ferdinand* himself is led.
        Almah. Now brave *Almanzor,* be a god again;
Above our Crimes, and your own passions reign:
My Lord has been, by Jealousy, misled
To think I was not faithful to his bed.
I can forgive him though my death he sought;
For too much love can never be a fault.
120 Protect him, then; and what to his defence
You give not, give to clear my innocence.
        Alman. Listen sweet Heav'n; and all ye blest above
Take rules of Vertue from a Mortal love.
You've rais'd my Soul; and if it mount more high,
'Tis as the Wren did on the Eagle fly.
Yes, I once more will my revenge neglect:
And whom you can forgive, I can protect.
        Boab. How hard a fate is mine, still doom'd to shame:
I make Occasions for my Rivals fame!
                        [*Exeunt. An Alarm within.*

        Enter Ferdinand, Isabel, Don Alonzo d'Aguilar;
                Spaniards, *and Ladies.*

---

105   at th'] Q2–3, D; at the Q1, Q4–5, F.
105   *Elvira*] Q2–3, F, D; Elvira Q1, Q4–5.
106   has] Q2–3, Q5, F, D; 'has Q1, Q4.
107   *Zegrys*] Q3, D; *Zegry's* Q1–2, Q4–5, F *(in Q1 apostrophe worked up into line above before* has).
107   *Spanyards*] Q2–3, D; Spanyards Q1, Q4–5, F.
116   been,] Q1 *(some copies)*, Q4–5, F, D; ~∧ Q1 *(some copies)*, Q2–3.
123   Take] *some copies of Q1 add a comma.*
129+   s.d. [Exeunt] Q4–5, F, D; ∧~ Q1–3.
129+   s.d. Spaniards] D; *Spaniards* Q1–5, F.

130   *Ferd.* Already more than half the Town is gain'd:
But there is yet a doubtful fight maintain'd.
    Alonz. The fierce young King the enter'd does attacque,
And the more fierce *Almanzor* drives 'em back.
    Ferd. The valiant *Moores* like raging Lyons, fight;
Each youth encourag'd by his Ladies sight.
    Qu. Isab. I will advance with such a shining train,
That *Moorish* beauties shall oppose in vain:
Into the press of clashing swords we'll goe;
And where the darts fly thickest, seek the foe.
140   *K. Ferd.* May Heav'n, which has inspir'd this gen'rous
          thought,
Avert those dangers you have boldly sought:
Call up more troops; the women, to our shame,
Will ravish from the men their part of fame.
                              [*Exeunt* Isabel *and Ladies.*

Enter Alabez: *and kisses the Kings hand.*

    Alabez. Fair *Lyndaraxa,* and the *Zegry* line
Have led their forces with your troops to join:
The adverse part, which obstinately fought,
Are broke; and *Abdelmelech* pris'ner brought.
    K. Ferd. Fair *Lyndaraxa* and her friends shall find
Th' effects of an oblig'd and grateful mind.
150   *Alabez.* But, marching by the *Vivarambla* place,
The combat carry'd a more doubtful face;
In that vast square the *Moors* and *Spaniards* met;
Where the fierce conflict is continued yet:
But with advantage on the adverse side,
Whom fierce *Almanzor* does to conquest guide.

---

130 *Ferd.*] Q2–5, F, D; ~∧ Q1.   131 maintain'd.] F, D; ~; Q1–5.
134 *Ferd.*] Q2–5, F, D; ~∧ Q1.   134 *Moores*] Q2–3, D; Moores Q1, Q4–5, F.
134 fight;] Q2–3, F, D; ~. Q1, Q4–5.   137 *Moorish*] D; Moorish Q1–5, F.
137 vain:] *some copies of Q1 have a semicolon.*
140 *K.*] D; K. Q1–5, F.   143+ *s.d.* [*Exeunt*] Q4–5, F, D; ∧~ Q1–3.
143+ *s.d.* Isabel] Isabella Q1–5, F, D.   144 *Zegry*] Q2–3, D; Zegry Q1, Q4–5, F.
152 *Moors* and *Spaniards*] Q2–3, D; Moors and Spaniards Q1, Q4–5, F.
153 yet:] ~. Q1–5, F, D.

K. Ferd. With my *Castilian* foot I'le meet his rage;
      [*Is going out: shouts within are*
       heard, Victoria, Victoria.
But these loud clamours better news presage.

 Enter the Duke of Arcos, *and Souldiers; their swords*
    drawn and bloody.

  D. of Arcos. *Granada* now is yours; and there remain
No *Moors,* but such as own the pow'r of *Spain.*
160 That squadron which their King in person led,
We charg'd; but found *Almanzor* in their head.
Three several times we did the *Moors* attacque,
And thrice, with slaughter, did he drive us back.
Our troops then shrunk; and still we lost more ground:
Till, from our Queen, we needful succour found.
Her Guards to our assistance bravely flew,
And, with fresh vigour, did the fight renew.
At the same time————
Did *Lyndaraxa* with her troops appear,
170 And, while we charg'd the front, ingag'd the rear.
Then fell the King (slain by a *Zegry*'s hand.)
  K. Ferd. How could he, such united force withstand?
  D. of Arcos. Discourag'd with his death, the *Moorish* pow'rs
Fell back; and, falling back, were press'd by ours.
But, as when winds and rain together crowd,
They swell till they have burst the bladder'd clowd:
And first the Lightning, flashing deadly clear,
Flyes, falls, consumes, 'ere scarce it does appear:
So, from his shrinking troops, *Almanzor* flew;
180 Each blow gave wounds, and with each wound he slew.
His force at once I envy'd and admir'd;

---

156 *Castilian*] Q2–3, D; Castilian Q1, Q4–5, F.
156+ *s.d. heard,* Victoria, Victoria.] D; *heard. Victoria, Victoria.* Q1–5, F (*heard,*
F).
157 presage.] Q3, F, D; ∼: Q1–2, Q4–5. 158 *Granada*] Q2–5, F, D; Granada Q1.
159, 162 *Moors*] Q2–3, D; Moors Q1, Q4–5, F.
171 hand.)] F, D; ∼:) Q1–5.   172 withstand?] Q4–5, F, D; ∼! Q1–3.
173 *Moorish*] Q2–3, D; Moorish Q1, Q4–5, F.
175 crowd] crow'd Q1; croud Q2–5, F, D.

And, rushing forward, where my men retir'd,
Advanc'd alone.
    K. Ferd. ———You hazarded too far
Your person, and the fortune of the Warr.
    D. of Arcos. Already, both our armes for fight did bare,
Already held 'em threatning in the air:
When Heav'n (it must be Heav'n) my sight, did guid, ⎫
To view his arm, upon whose wrist, I spy'd   ⎬
A ruby Cross in Diamond bracelets ty'd.   ⎭
190 And just above it, in the brawnier part,
By nature was engrav'd a bloody Heart.
Struck with these tokens, which so well I knew,
And stagg'ring back, some paces I withdrew;
He follow'd; and suppos'd it was my fear:
When, from above, a shrill voice reach'd his ear;
Strike not thy father, it was heard to cry;
Amaz'd; and casting round his wond'ring eye,
He stop'd: then, thinking that his fears were vain,
He lifted up his thundring arm again:
200 Again the voice withheld him from my death;
Spare, spare his life, it cry'd, who gave thee breath.
Once more he stop'd: then threw his sword away;
Blest shade, he said, I hear thee, I obey
Thy sacred voice: then, in the sight of all,
He at my feet, I on his neck did fall.
    Ferd. O blest Event!———
    Arcos. ——————The *Moors* no longer fought;
But all their safety, by submission, sought:
Mean time, my Son grew faint with loss of blood:
And, on his bending sword supported, stood.
210 Yet, with a voice beyond his strength, he cry'd,
Lead me to live, or dye, by *Almahide.*
    K. Ferd. I am not for his wounds less griev'd than you.
For if, what now my Soul divines, prove true,
This is that son, whom in his Infancy
You lost, when by my father forc'd to fly.

---

198   vain,] Q3, D; ~. Q1, Q4–5; ~; Q2, F.
206   *Moors*] Q2–3, D; Moors Q1, Q4–5, F.

D. Arcos. His Sisters beauty did my passion move,
(The crime for which I suffer'd was my love.)
Our marriage known, to Sea we took our flight,
There, in a storm, *Almanzor* first saw light.
220 On his right Arm, a bloody heart was grav'd,
(The mark by which this day, my life was sav'd.)
The Bracelets and the Cross, his mother ty'd
About his wrist, 'ere she in childbed dy'd.
How we were Captives made, when she was dead;
And how *Almanzor* was in *Africque* bred,
Some other hour you may at leisure hear,
For see, the Queen, in triumph, does appear.

Enter Qu. Isabel: Lyndaraxa: *Ladies:* Moors *and* Spaniards
mix'd as Guards: Abdelmelech, Abenamar, Selin, *Pris'ners.*

K. Ferdinand. All stories, which *Granada*'s Conquest tell,
Shall celebrate the name of *Isabel.* [*Embracing Qu. Isabel.*
230 Your Ladies too, who in their Countries cause,
Led on the men, shall share in your applause:
And for your sakes, henceforward, I ordain,
No Ladies dow'r shall question'd be in *Spain.*
Fair *Lyndaraxa,* for the help she lent,
Shall, under Tribute, have this Government.
Abdelm. O Heav'n, that I should live to see this day!
Lynd. You murmur now, but you shall soon obey.
I knew this Empyre to my fate was ow'd:
Heav'n held it back as long as 'ere it cou'd.
240 For thee, base wretch, I want a torture yet——— [*To* Abdelm.

227+ s.d. *Ladies:*] ~, Q1–5, F, D.
227+ s.d. Moors *and* Spaniards] D; *Moors and Spaniards* Q1–5, F.
227+ s.d. *Guards:*] ~. Q1–5, F, D.
228–229 *K. Ferdinand.* All ... tell, / ... [Embracing *Qu.* Isabel.] *K. Ferdinand* embracing *Qu.* Isabel. / All ... tell, Q1–5, D (*Qu*∧ Q1; *on same line in* D); *K. Ferd.*
All ... tell, [*King* Ferdinand *embracing Queen* Isabel. F.
232 And] *some copies of Q1 add a comma.*
238 ow'd:] *some copies of Q1 omit colon.*
240 s.d. *To*] Q2–5, F, D; *to* Q1.
240 s.d. Abdelm.] Q3–5, F, D; *Abdelm.* Q1–2.

————I'le cage thee, thou shalt be my *Bajazet*.
I on no pavement but on thee will tread;
And, when I mount, my foot shall know thy head.
   Abdelm. This first shall know thy heart.
                        [*Stabbing her with a Ponyard.*
   Lynd. ————————————————Oh! I am slain!
   Abdelm. Now boast, thy Country is betray'd to *Spain*.
   K. Ferd. Look to the Lady.————Seize the Murderer.
   Abdel. I'le do my self that Justice I did her. [*Stabbing himself.*
Thy blood I to thy ruin'd Country give,   [*To* Lynd.
But love too well thy murther to out live.
250 Forgive a love, excus'd by its excess,
Which, had it not been cruel, had been less.
Condemn my passion, then, but pardon me;
And think I murder'd him, who murder'd thee.   [*Dyes.*
   Lynd. Dye for us both; I have not leysure now;
A Crown is come; and will not fate allow:
And yet, I feel something like death, is near:
My guards, my guards;————
Let not that ugly skeleton appear.
Sure destiny mistakes; this death's not mine;
260 She dotes; and meant to cut another line.
Tell her I am a Queen;————but 'tis too late;
Dying, I charge Rebellion on my fate:
Bow down ye slaves————   [*To the* Moors.
Bow quickly down, and your Submission show.   [*They bow.*
I'me pleas'd to taste an Empyre 'ere I goe.   [*Dyes*
    Selin. She's dead and here her proud ambition ends.
    Aben. Such fortune still, such black designs attends.

---

244 *Abdelm.* This . . . heart. / [*Stabbing . . . Ponyard.*] F; *Abdelm. stabbing* . . .
Ponyard. / This . . . heart. Q1–5, D (*Abdelm*∧ Q1; [Abdelm. Q4–5; *on same line
in D*).
244 *Lynd.*] Q2–5, F, D; *Lind.* Q1.
246 Murderer] Q2–5, F, D; Murdere Q1.
247 *Abdel.* I'le . . . her. [*Stabbing himself.*] F; *Abdelmelech, stabbing himself.
/* I'le . . . her. Q1–5, D (*on same line in D*).
248 s.d. [*To* Lynd.] Q2–5, F, D; ∧*To Lynd.* Q1.
253 s.d. *Dyes*] Q4–5, F, D; *dyes* Q1–3.
263 s.d. [*To*] Q2–5, F, D; ∧∼ Q1.   263 s.d. Moors] Q2–3, D; *Moors* Q1, Q4–5, F.
264 s.d. *They*] Q2–5, F, D; *they* Q1   265 s.d. *Dyes*] Q4–5, F, D; *dyes* Q1–3.

Ferd. Remove those mournful Objects from our eyes;
And see perform'd their funeral Obsequies.

> [*The Bodies carried off.*

Enter Almanzor *and* Almahide, Ozmyn *and* Benzayda:
Almahide *brought in a chair:* Almanzor *led betwixt*
Souldiers: Isabel *salutes* Almahide *in dumb show.*

270   *Duke of Arcos.* See here that Son, whom I with pride call mine;

> [*Presenting* Almanzor *to the King.*

And who dishonours not your royal line.
    K. Ferd. I'me now secure this Scepter, which I gain,
Shall be continu'd in the pow'r of *Spain;*
Since he, who could alone my foes defend,
By birth and honour is become my friend.
Yet I can own no joy; nor Conquest boast,   [*To Almanz.*
While in this blood I see how dear it cost.
    Almanz. This honor to my veins new blood will bring:
Streams cannot fail, fed by so high a Spring:
280 But all Court-Customs I so little know
That I may fail in those respects I owe.
I bring a heart which homage never knew;
Yet it finds something of it self in you:
Something so kingly, that my haughty mind
Is drawn to yours; because 'tis of a kind.
    Qu. Isabel. And yet, that Soul, which bears it self so high,
If fame be true, admits a Soveraignty.
This Queen, in her fair eyes, such fetters brings,
As chain that heart, which scorns the pow'r of Kings.
290   *Almah.* Little of charm in these sad eyes appears;
If they had any, now 'tis lost in tears.
A Crown, and Husband ravish'd in one day!————

269+ *s.d.* [*The*] Q2–5, F, D; ∧~ Q1.   269+ *s.d.* Benzayda:] ~. Q1–5, D; ~; F.
270 *Duke of Arcos.* See . . . mine; / [*Presenting . . . King.*] F; *Duke of* Arcos *pre-*
senting . . . King. / See . . . mine; Q1–5, D (D. Arcos D; *on same line in D*).
272 *K.*] Q2, D; K. Q1, Q3–5, F.   275 friend.] Q3, F, D; ~, Q1–2, Q4–5.
276 *s.d. To Almanz.*] Q2–5, F, D; *to Almanz.* Q1.
279 Streams] Q2–5, F, D; Sreams Q1.
292 day!————] Q2–3; ~;∧ Q1, Q4–5, F; ~,∧ D.

Excuse a grief, I cannot choose but pay.

    Q. Isab. Have Courage, Madam, heav'n has joyes in store
To recompence those losses you deplore.

    Almah. I know your God can all my woes redress;
To him I made my vows in my distress.
And what a Misbeliever vow'd this day,
Though not a Queen, a Christian yet shall pay.

300   *Qu. Isabel.* That Christian name you shall receive from me;
And *Isabella* of *Granada* be.   [*Embracing her.*

    Benz. This blessed change, we all with joy receive:
And beg to learn that faith which you believe.

    Qu. Isabel. With reverence for those holy rites prepare;
And all commit your fortunes to my care.

    K. Ferd. You, Madam, by that Crown, you loose, may gain,
If you accept a Coronet of *Spain;*   [*To* Almahide.
Of which *Almanzor's* father stands possest.

    Qu. Isabel. May you in him; and he in you be blest.
                                  [*To* Almahide.

310   *Almahide.* I owe my life and honour to his sword;
But owe my love to my departed Lord.

    Almanzor. Thus, when I have no living force to dread,
Fate find's me Enemies amongst the dead.
I'me now to conquer Ghosts; and to destroy,
The strong impressions of a Bridale joy.

    Almah. You've yet a greater Foe, than these can be;
Vertue opposes you and Modesty.

    Almanz. From a false fear that Modesty does grow;
And thinks true love, because 'tis fierce, its foe.
320 'Tis but the wax whose seals on Virgins stay:
Let it approach Loves fire, 'twill melt away.

---

294 *Q.*] Q2, D; *Q.* Q1, Q3–5, F.
296 *Almah.*] Q3, D; *Qu. Almah.* Q1–2, Q4–5, F.
300–301 *Qu. Isabel.* That . . . me; / . . . [*Embracing her.*] *Qu. Isabel embracing her.* / That . . . me; Q1–5, F, D (/ *Q. Isab.* That F; *on same line in D*).
306–307 *K. Ferd.* You, . . . gain, / . . . [*To* Almahide.] *K. Ferd. to Almahide.* / You, . . . gain, Q1–5, F, D (*on same line in F, D*).
309 *Qu. Isabel.* May . . . blest. / [*To* Almahide.] *Qu. Isabel to Almahide.* / May . . . blest. Q1–5, F, D (*on same line in F, D*).
310 *Almahide.*] Q3, D; *Qu. Almahide.* Q1–2, Q4–5, F.
314 I'me] Q2–3, Q5, F, D; 'Ime Q1, Q4.

But I have liv'd too long; I never knew
When fate was conquer'd, I must combate you.
I thought to climb the steep ascent of Love;
But did not think to find a foe above.
'Tis time to dye, when you my bar must be,
Whose aid alone could give me Victory.
Without————
I'le pull up all the sluces of the flood:
330 And Love, within, shall boyl out all my blood.
     Q. Isab. Fear not your Love should find so sad success;
While I have pow'r to be your Patroness.
I am her Parent, now, and may command
So much of duty, as to give her hand.

                       [*Gives him* Almahides *hand.*

     Almah. Madam, I never can dispute your pow'r,
Or, as a Parent, or a Conquerour:
But, when my year of Widowhood expires,
Shall yield to your Commands and his desires.
     Almanz. Move swiftly, Sun; and fly a lovers pace;
340 Leave weeks and moneths behind thee in thy race!
     K. Ferd. Mean time, you shall my Victories pursue;
The *Moors* in woods and mountains to subdue.
     Almanz. The toyles of war shall help to wear each day;
And dreams of love shall drive my nights away.
Our Banners to th' *Alhambra*'s turrets bear;
Then, wave our Conqu'ring Crosses in the Aire;
And Cry, with showts of Triumph; Live and raign,
Great *Ferdinand* and *Isabel* of *Spain.*

                       [*Exeunt omnes.*

334+ *s.d. Gives*] Q2–5, F, D; *gives* Q1.   336 Conquerour:] ∼. Q1–5, F, D.
342 *Moors*] Q2–3, D; Moors Q1, Q4–5, F.   347 Live] Q3–5, F, D; live Q1–2.
348 *Spain*] Q2–5, F, D; Spain Q1.   348+ *s.d. omitted from Q1–5, F.*

EPILOGUE to the Second Part of *GRANADA*.

T HEY, *who have best succeeded on the Stage,*
 Have still conform'd their Genius to their Age.
 Thus Jonson *did Mechanique humour show,*
When men were dull, and conversation low.
Then, Comedy was faultless, but 'twas course:
Cobbs *Tankard was a jest, and* Otter's *horse.*
And as their Comedy, their love was mean:
Except, by chance, in some one labour'd Scene,
Which must attone for an ill-written Play:
10 *They rose; but at their height could seldome stay.*
Fame then was cheap, and the first commer sped;
And they have kept it since, by being dead.
But were they now to write when Critiques weigh
Each Line, and ev'ry word, throughout a Play,
None of 'em, no not Jonson, *in his height*
Could pass, without allowing grains for weight.
Think it not envy that these truths are told,
Our Poet's not malicious, though he's bold.
'Tis not to brand 'em that their faults are shown,
20 *But, by their errours, to excuse his own.*
If Love and Honour now are higher rais'd,
'Tis not the Poet, but the Age is prais'd.
Wit's now ariv'd to a more high degree;
Our native Language more refin'd and free.
Our Ladies and our men now speak more wit
In conversation, than those Poets writ.
Then, one of these is, consequently, true;
That what this Poet writes comes short of you,
And imitates you ill, (which most he fears)
30 *Or else his writing is not worse than theirs.*
Yet, though you judge, (as sure the Critiques will)

---

9 *Play:*] ~. Q1–5, F; ~, D.   11 *Fame*] Q2–3; Fame Q1, Q4–5, F, D.

That some before him writ with greater skill,
In this one praise he hath their fame surpast,
To please an Age more Gallant than the last.

---

33   *hath*] Q2–3; *has* Q1, Q4–5, F, D.

Defence of the Epilogue.
Or,
An Essay on the Dramatique Poetry
of the last Age.

HE promises of Authors, that they will write again, are in
effect, a threatning of their Readers with some new impertinence, and they who perform not what they promise,
will have their pardon on easy terms. 'Tis from this consideration that I could be glad to spare you the trouble which I am now
giving you, of a Postscript, if I were not oblig'd by many reasons
to write somewhat concerning our present Playes, and those of
our predecessors on the *English* stage. The truth is, I have so farr
ingag'd my self in a bold Epilogue to this Play, wherein I have
10 somewhat tax'd the former writing, that it was necessary for me
either not to print it, or to show that I could defend it. Yet, I
would so maintain my opinion of the present Age, as not to be
wanting in my veneration for the past: I would ascribe to dead
Authors their just praises, in those things wherein they have excell'd us: and in those wherein we contend with them for the
preheminence, I would acknowledge our advantages to the Age,
and claim no victory from our wit. This being what I have propos'd to my self, I hope I shall not be thought arrogant when I
inquire into their Errors. For, we live in an Age, so Sceptical,
20 that as it determines little, so it takes nothing from Antiquity
on trust: and I profess to have no other ambition in this Essay,
than that Poetry may not go backward, when all other Arts and
Sciences are advancing. Whoever censures me for this inquiry,
let him hear his Character from *Horace:*

Ingeniis non ille favet plauditque sepultis,
Nostra sed impugnat; nos nostraque Lividus odit.

---

1   will] Q2–3, D; wil! Q1.
8   *English*] Q3, D; English Q1–2.
21   trust:] Q2–3; ∼. Q1; ∼, D.

6   Postscript] Q2–3, D; Preface Q1.
9   Epilogue] *Epilogue* Q1–3, D.

He favours not dead wits, but hates the living.

It was upbraided to that excellent Poet that he was an enemy
to the writings of his Predecessor *Lucilius,* because he had said,
Lucilium lutulentum fluere, that he ran muddy: and that he
ought to have retrench'd from his Satyrs many unnecessary verses.
But *Horace* makes *Lucilius* himself to justifie him from the im-
putation of Envy, by telling you that he would have done the
same had he liv'd in an age which was more refin'd.

> *Si foret hoc nostrum, fato, delapsus in ævum,*
> *Detraheret sibi multa, recideret omne quod ultra*
> *Perfectum traheretur:* &c.

And, both in the whole course of that Satyr, and in his most
admirable Epistle to *Augustus,* he makes it his business to prove
that Antiquity alone is no plea for the excellency of a Poem: but,
that one Age learning from another, the last (if we can suppose
an equallity of wit in the writers,) has the advantage of knowing
more, and better than the former. And this I think is the state of
the question in dispute. It is therefore my part to make it clear,
that the Language, Wit, and Conversation of our Age are improv'd and refin'd above the last: and then it will not be difficult,
to inferr, that our Playes have receiv'd some part of those advantages.

In the first place, therefore, it will be necessary to state, in
general, what this refinement is of which we treat: and that I
think will not be defin'd amiss: *An improvement of our Wit,
Language, and Conversation: or, an alteration in them for the
better.*

To begin with Language. That an Alteration is lately made
in ours or since the Writers of the last Age (in which I compre-
hend *Shakespear, Fletcher* and *Jonson*) is manifest. Any man who

---

4　*lutulentum*] Q2–3; *luculentum* Q1, D.
10　*recideret*] Q2–3; *recederet* Q1, D.　　　17　And] Q2–3, D; and Q1.
26　*Conversation:*] D; ～. Q1–3.　　　28　Language] *Language* Q1–3, D.

reads those excellent Poets, and compares their language with
what is now written, will see it almost in every line. But, that this
is an *Improvement* of the Language, or an alteration for the better, will not so easily be granted. For many are of a contrary
opinion, that the *English* tongue was then in the height of its
perfection; that, from *Jonsons* time to ours, it has been in a con-
tinual declination; like that of the *Romans* from the Age of
Virgil to *Statius*, and so downward to *Claudian:* of which, not
onely *Petronius*, but *Quintilian* himself so much complains, under the person of *Secundus*, in his famous Dialogue *de causis cor-
ruptæ eloquentiæ.*

But, to shew that our Language is improv'd; and that those
people have not a just value for the Age in which they live, let us
consider in what the refinement of a language principally consists: that is, *either in rejecting such old words or phrases which
are ill sounding, or improper, or in admitting new, which are
more proper, more sounding and more significant.*

The Reader will easily take notice, that when I speak of rejecting improper words and phrases I mention not such as are
Antiquated by custome onely: and, as I may say, without any
fault of theirs: for in this case the refinement can be but accidental: that is when the words and phrases which are rejected
happen to be improper. Neither would I be understood (when
I speak of impropriety in Language) either wholly to accuse the
last Age, or to excuse the present; and least of all my self. For all
writers have their imperfections and failings: but I may safely
conclude in the general, that our improprieties are less frequent,
and less gross than theirs. One Testimony of this is undeniable,
that we are the first who have observ'd them: and, certainly, to
observe errours is a great step to the correcting of them. But,
malice and partiality set apart, let any man who understands
English, read diligently the works of *Shakespear* and *Fletcher;*
and I dare undertake that he will find, in every page either some
Solecism of Speech, or some notorious flaw in Sence: and yet
these men are reverenc'd when we are not forgiven. That their

5   *English*] D; English Q1–3.
29   them:] D; ∼. Q1–3.
34   Solecism] *Solecism* Q1–3, D.

26   failings:] Q2, D; ∼. Q1, Q3.
32   *English*] D; English Q1–3.

wit is great and many times their expressions noble, envy it self cannot deny.

> ————*Neque ego illis detrahere ausim*
> *Hærentem capiti, multa cum laude, coronam:*

but the times were ignorant in which they liv'd. Poetry was then, if not in its infancy among us, at least not arriv'd to its vigor and maturity: witness the lameness of their Plots: many of which, especially those which they writ first, (for even that Age refin'd it self in some measure,) were made up of some ridiculous, in-
10 coherent story, which, in one Play many times took up the business of an Age. I suppose I need not name *Pericles Prince of Tyre,* nor the Historical Plays of *Shakespear:* Besides many of the rest as the *Winters Tale, Love's labour lost, Measure for Measure,* which were either grounded on impossibilities, or at least, so meanly written, that the Comedy neither caus'd your mirth, nor the serious part your concernment. If I would expatiate on this Subject, I could easily demonstrate that our admir'd *Fletcher,* who writ after him, neither understood correct Plotting, nor that which they call *the Decorum of the Stage.* I
20 would not search in his worst Plays for examples: he who will consider his *Philaster,* his *Humorous Lieutenant,* his *Faithful Shepheardess;* and many others which I could name, will find them much below the applause which is now given them: he will see *Philaster* wounding his Mistriss, and afterwards his Boy, to save himself: Not to mention the Clown who enters immediately, and not only has the advantage of the Combat against the Heroe, but diverts you from your serious concernment, with his ridiculous and absurd Raillery. In his *Humorous Lieutenant* you find his *Demetrius* and *Leoncius* staying in the midst of a routed
30 observe errours is a great step to the correcting of them. But, afterwards appearing with a Pistol in his hand, in the next Age to *Alexander* the Great. And for his Shepheard, he falls twice

11 *of*] of Q1–3, D.   12 *Shakespear:*] ~. Q1–3, D.
21 his *Humorous Lieutenant,* his] Q2–3, D; *his Humorous Lieutenant, his* Q1.
22 *Shepheardess*] Q2–3, D; Shepheardess Q1.
23 given them:] Q2–3, D; ~~. Q1.   30 Lieutenant] *Lieutenant* Q1–3, D.
32 Shepheard] *Shepheard* Q1–3, D.

into the former indecency of wounding Women: but these absurdities, which those Poets committed, may more properly be call'd the Ages fault than theirs: for, besides the want of Education and Learning, (which was their particular unhappiness) they wanted the benefit of converse: but of that, I shall speak hereafter, in a place more proper for it. Their Audiences knew no better: and therefore were satisfy'd with what they brought. Those who call theirs the *Golden Age of Poetry,* have only this reason for it, that they were then content with Acorns, before

10 they knew the use of Bread: or that Ἅλις δρυός was become a Proverb. They had many who admir'd them, and few who blam'd them: and, certainly, a severe Critique is the greatest help to a good Wit: he does the Office of a Friend, while he designs that of an Enemy: and his malice keeps a Poet within those bounds, which the Luxuriancy of his Fancy would tempt him to overleap.

But it is not their Plots which I meant, principally to tax: I was speaking of their Sence and Language; and I dare almost challenge any man to show me a page together, which is correct in both. As for *Ben. Jonson,* I am loath to name him, because he

20 is a most Judicious Writer; yet he very often falls into these errors. And I once more beg the Readers pardon, for accusing him or them. Onely let him consider that I live in an age where my least faults are severely censur'd: and that I have no way left to extenuate my failings but my showing as great in those whom we admire.

Cædimus, inque vicem præbemus crura sagittis.

[I cast my eyes but by chance on *Catiline;* and in the three or four first pages, found enough to conclude that *Jonson* writ not correctly.

1 Women:] Q2–3, D; ∼. Q1.   3 theirs:] Q2–3; ∼. Q1, D.
5 converse:] Q2–3, D; ∼. Q1.   12 them:] Q2–3, D; ∼. Q1.
13 Wit:] Q2–3, D; ∼. Q1.   17 Language;] D; ∼. Q1–3.
19 *Jonson*] *Johnson* Q1–3, D.
20 Judicious] *some copies of Q1 have* Judicsous.
23 faults] *some copies of Q1 have* faulrs.
26 *Cædimus*] Q3; *Cœdimus* Q1–2, D.   26 *crura*] Q2–3; *cura* Q1, D.
27 *the bracketed passage (ends 210:21) was deleted by Dryden from Q2–3.*
28 *Jonson*] *Johnson* Q1, D.

> ————*Let the long hid seeds*
> *Of treason, in thee, now shoot forth in deeds*
> *Ranker than horrour.*

In reading some bombast speeches of *Macbeth,* which are not to
be understood, he us'd to say that it was horrour; and I am much
afraid that this is so.

> *Thy parricide, late on thy onely Son,*
> *After his mother, to make empty way*
> *For thy last wicked Nuptials, worse than they*
10 > *That blaze that act of thy incestuous life,*
> *Which gain'd thee at once a daughter and a wife.*

The Sence is here extreamly perplex'd: and I doubt the word
They is false Grammar.

> ————*And be free*
> *Not Heaven it self from thy impiety.*

A *Synchœsis,* or ill placing of words, of which *Tully* so much
complains in Oratory.

> *The Waves, and Dens of beasts cou'd not receive*
> *The bodies that those Souls were frighted from.*

20 The Preposition in the end of the sentence; a common fault with
him, and which I have but lately observ'd in my own writings.

> *What all the several ills that visit earth,*
> *Plague, famine, fire, could not reach unto,*
> *The Sword nor surfeits, let thy fury do.*

Here are both the former faults: for, besides that the Preposition
unto, is plac'd last in the verse, and at the half period, and is redundant, there is the former *Synchœsis,* in the words (*The Sword*

---

5   horrour;] D; ∼. Q1.

nor Surfeits) which in construction ought to have been plac'd before the other.

Catiline sayes of *Cethegus,* that for his sake he would

> *Go on upon the Gods; kiss Lightning, wrest*
> *The Engine from the Cyclops, and give fire*
> *At face of a full clowd, and stand his ire.*

To *go on upon,* is onely to go on twice. To *give fire at face of a full cloud,* was not understood in his own time: *(and stand his ire)* besides the antiquated word *ire* there is the Article *his,* which makes false construction: and Giving fire at the face of a cloud, is a perfect image of shooting, however it came to be known in those daies to *Catiline.*

> ———*others there are*
> *Whom Envy to the State draws and pulls on,*
> *For Contumelies receiv'd; and such are sure ones.*

Ones in the plural Number: but that is frequent with him; for he sayes, not long after,

> Cæsar *and* Crassus; *if they be ill men,*
> *Are Mighty ones.*
> *Such Men they do not succour more the cause,* &c.

They redundant.

> *Though Heav'n should speak with all his wrath at once;*
> *We should stand upright and unfear'd.*

His is ill Syntax with Heaven: and by *unfear'd* he means *un-affraid:* words of a quite contrary signification.

---

7   twice. To] D; ∼. to Q1.
7–8   *give fire at face of a full cloud*] give fire at face of a full cloud Q1, D.
8   *and stand his*] and stand his Q1, D.
9   *his*] His Q1, D.
17   after,] D; ∼. Q1.
24–25   *unfear'd . . . unaffraid:*] Unfear'd . . . Unaffraid. Q1, D (Unaffraid: D).

The Ports are open,

He perpetually uses *ports* for *gates:* which is an affected error in him, to introduce *Latine* by the loss of the *English* Idiom: as in the Translation of *Tully*'s Speeches he usually does.

Well placing of Words for the sweetness of pronunciation was not known till Mr. *Waller* introduc'd it: and therefore 'tis not to be wonder'd if *Ben. Jonson* has many such lines as these,

> *But being bred up in his father's needy fortunes,*
> *Brought up in 's sister's Prostitution,* &c.

10 But meanness of expression one would think not to be his error in a Tragedy, which ought to be more high and sounding than any other kind of Poetry, and yet amongst many others in *Catiline* I find these four lines together:

> *So Asia, thou art cruelly even*
> *With us, for all the blows thee given:*
> *When we, whose Vertues conquer'd thee,*
> *Thus, by thy Vices, ruin'd be.*

Be there is false *English,* for *are:* though the Rhyme hides it.

But I am willing to close the Book, partly out of veneration to 20 the Author, partly out of weariness to pursue an argument which is so fruitful in so small a compass.] And what correctness, after this, can be expected from *Shakespear* or from *Fletcher,* who wanted that Learning and Care which *Jonson* had? I will therefore spare my own trouble of inquiring into their faults: who had they liv'd now, had doubtless written more correctly. I suppose it will be enough for me to affirm (as I think I safely may) that these and the like errors which I tax'd in the most correct of the last Age, are such, into which we doe not ordinarily fall.

---

2 *ports ... gates*] Ports ... Gates Q1, D.   7 *Jonson*] Johnson Q1, D.
7 these,] D; ~_∧ Q1.   10 meanness] *some copies of Q1 read* meaness.
8–9 *as prose in Q1, D (&c. Q1).*
12 Poetry,] D; ~. Q1.   18 there] D; *there* Q1.
23 *Jonson*] Johnson Q1–3, D.

[I think few of our present Writers would have left behind them such a line as this,

> *Contain your Spirit in more stricter bounds.*

But that gross way of two Comparatives was then, ordinary: and therefore more pardonable in *Jonson*.]

As for the other part of refining, which consists in receiving new Words and Phrases, I shall not insist much on it. 'Tis obvious that we have admitted many: some of which we wanted, and, therefore our Language is the richer for them: as it would 10 be by importation of Bullion: others are rather Ornamental than Necessary; yet by their admission, the Language is become more courtly: and our thoughts are better drest. These are to be found scatter'd in the Writers of our Age: and it is not my business to collect them. They who have lately written with most care, have, I believe, taken the Rule of *Horace* for their guide; that is, not to be too hasty in receiving of Words: but rather to stay till Custome has made them familiar to us,

> *Quem penes, arbitrium est, & jus & norma loquendi.*

For I cannot approve of their way of refining, who corrupt our 20 *English* Idiom by mixing it too much with *French:* that is a Sophistication of Language, not an improvement of it: a turning *English* into *French,* rather than a refining of *English* by *French.* We meet daily with those Fopps, who value themselves on their Travelling, and pretend they cannot express their meaning in *English,* because they would put off to us some *French* Phrase of the last Edition: without considering that, for ought they know, we have a better of our own; but these are not the men who are to refine us: their Tallent is to prescribe Fashions, not Words: at best they are onely serviceable to a Writer, so as *Ennius* 30 was to *Virgil.* He may *Aurum ex stercore colligere;* for 'tis hard if, amongst many insignificant Phrases, there happen not something worth preserving: though they themselves, like *Indians,* know not the value of their own Commodity.

1–5   *the bracketed passage was deleted by Dryden from Q2–3.*
5   *Jonson*] Johnson Q1, D.
30   may . . . *colligere;*] Q2–3; ~. . . . ~. Q1; ~, . . . ~. D.
31   amongst] Q2–3, D; a- / amongst Q1.

There is yet another way of improving Language, which Poets especially have practic'd in all Ages: that is by applying receiv'd words to a new Signification, and this I believe, is meant by *Horace,* in that Precept which is so variously constru'd by Expositors:

> *Dixeris Egregié, notum si callida verbum,*
> *Reddiderit junctura novum.*

And, in this way, he himself had a particular happiness: using all the Tropes, and particularly Metaphors, with that grace
10 which is observable in his Odes: where the Beauty of Expression is often greater than that of thought, as in that one example, amongst an infinite number of others; *Et vultus nimium ulbricus aspici.*

And therefore though he innovated little, he may justly be call'd a great Refiner of the *Roman* Tongue. This choice of words, and height'ning of their natural signification, was observ'd in him by the Writers of the following Ages: for *Petronius* says of him, *& Horatii curiosa fælicitas.* By this graffing, as I may call it, on old words, has our Tongue been Beautified by the
20 three fore-mention'd Poets, *Shakespear, Fletcher* and *Jonson:* whose Excellencies I can never enough admire: and in this, they have been follow'd especially by Sir *John Suckling* and Mr. *Waller,* who refin'd upon them; neither have they, who now succeed them, been wanting in their endeavours to adorn our Mother Tongue: but it is not so lawful for me to praise my living Contemporaries, as to admire my dead Predecessors.

I should now speak of the Refinement of Wit: but I have been so large on the former Subject that I am forc'd to contract my self in this. I will therefore onely observe to you, that the wit of
30 the last Age, was yet more incorrect than their language. *Shakespear,* who many times has written better than any Poet, in any Language, is yet so far from writing Wit always, or expressing that Wit according to the Dignity of the Subject, that he writes

in many places, below the dullest Writer of ours, or of any precedent Age. Never did any Author precipitate himself from such
heights of thought to so low expressions, as he often does. He is
the very *Janus* of Poets; he wears, almost every where two faces:
and you have scarce begun to admire the one, e're you despise
the other. Neither is the Luxuriance of *Fletcher,* (which his
friends have tax'd in him,) a less fault than the carelessness of
Shakespear. He does not well always, and, when he does, he is a
true *Englishman;* he knows not when to give over. If he wakes
in one Scene he commonly slumbers in another: And if he pleases
you in the first three Acts, he is frequently so tir'd with his labor,
that he goes heavily in the fourth, and sinks under his burden
in the fifth.

For *Ben. Jonson,* the most judicious of Poets, he always writ
properly; and as the Character requir'd: and I will not contest
farther with my Friends who call that Wit: It being very certain,
that even folly it self, well represented, is Wit in a larger signification: and that there is Fancy, as well as Judgement in it; though
not so much or noble: because all Poetry being imitation, that of
Folly is a lower exercise of Fancy, though perhaps as difficult as
the other: for 'tis a kind of looking downward in the Poet; and
representing that part of Mankind which is below him.

In these low Characters of Vice and Folly, lay the excellency
of that inimitable Writer: who, when at any time, he aim'd at
Wit, in the stricter sence, that is Sharpness of Conceit, was forc'd
either to borrow from the Ancients, as, to my knowledge he did
very much from *Plautus:* or, when he trusted himself alone, often
fell into meanness of expression. Nay, he was not free from the
lowest and most groveling kind of Wit, which we call clenches;
of which, *Every Man in his Humour,* is infinitely full: and, which
is worse, the wittiest persons in the Drama speak them. His
other Comedies are not exempted from them: will you give me
leave to name some few? *Asper,* in which Character he person-
ates himself, (and he neither was, nor thought himself a fool)
exclaiming against the ignorant Judges of the Age, speaks thus,

---

  1 below the] D; below—the Q1–3.   12 fourth, and] Q2–3, D; $\sim_{\wedge}\sim$, Q1.
 14 *Jonson*] *Johnson* Q1–3, D.   16 Wit:] $\sim$. Q1–3, D.
 30 full:] Q2–3; $\sim$. Q1; $\sim$, D.   31 Drama] *Drama* Q1–3, D.
 34 fool)] Q3, D; $\sim$.) Q1–2.   35 thus,] Q2–3; $\sim$. Q1; $\sim$: D.

How monstrous and detested is 't, to see
A fellow, that has neither Art nor Brain,
Sit like an Aristarchus, *or* Stark-Ass,
Taking Mens Lines, with a Tobacco-Face,
In Snuffe, &c.

And presently after,

I mar'le whose wit 'twas to put a Prologue in yond Sackbut's
mouth? they might well think he would be out of Tune, and yet
you'd play upon him too.

10   Will you have another of the same stamp?

O, I cannot abide these limbs of Sattin, *or rather* Satan.

But, it may be you will object that this was *Asper, Macilente,*
or, *Carlo Buffone:* you shall, therefore, hear him speak in his
own person: and, that, in the two last lines, or sting of an Epigram; 'tis Inscrib'd to *Fine Grand:* who, he says, was indebted
to him for many things, which he reckons there: and concludes
thus;

Forty things more, dear Grand, *which you know true,*
For which, or pay me quickly, or I'le pay you.

20   This was then the mode of wit, the vice of the Age and not
Ben. Jonson's: for you see, a little before him, that admirable
wit, Sir *Philip Sidney,* perpetually playing with his words. In his
time, I believe, it ascended first into the Pulpit: where (if you
will give me leave to clench too) it yet finds the benefit of its
Clergy; for they are commonly the first corrupters of Eloquence,
and the last reform'd from vicious Oratory: as a famous *Italian*
has observ'd before me, in his Treatise of the Corruption of the

---

6   after,] Q3; ∼ₐ Q1–2, D.
21   *Jonson's:] Johnson's:* Q1–3, D (∼. Q1; ∼; D).
25   Clergy;] Q2–3, D; ∼. Q1.

Italian Tongue; which he principally ascribes to Priests and preaching Friars.

But, to conclude with what brevity I can; I will only add this in the defence of our present Writers, that if they reach not some excellencies of *Ben. Jonson;* (which no Age, I am confident, ever shall) yet, at least, they are above that meanness of thought which I have tax'd, and which is frequent in him.

That the wit of this Age is much more Courtly, may easily be prov'd by viewing the Characters of Gentlemen which were writ-
10 ten in the last. First, for *Jonson, True-Wit* in the *Silent Woman,* was his Master-piece, and *True-wit* was a Scholar-like kind of man, a Gentleman with an allay of Pedantry: a man who seems mortifi'd to the world, by much reading. The best of his discourse, is drawn, not from the knowledge of the Town, but Books, and, in short, he would be a fine Gentleman, in an University. *Shake-spear* show'd the best of his skill in his *Mercutio,* and he said himself, that he was forc'd to kill him in the third Act, to prevent being kill'd by him. But, for my part, I cannot find he was so dangerous a person: I see nothing in him but what was so ex-
20 ceeding harmless, that he might have liv'd to the end of the Play, and dy'd in his bed, without offence to any man.

Fletcher's Don John is our onely Bug-bear: and yet, I may affirm, without suspition of flattery, that he now speaks better, and that his Character is maintain'd with much more vigour in the fourth and fifth Acts than it was by *Fletcher* in the three former. I have always acknowledg'd the wit of our Predecessors, with all the veneration which becomes me, but, I am sure, their wit was not that of Gentlemen, there was ever somewhat that was ill-bred and Clownish in it: and which confest the conver-
30 sation of the Authors.

And this leads me to the last and greatest advantage of our writing, which proceeds from conversation. In the Age, wherein those Poets liv'd, there was less of gallantry than in ours; neither did they keep the best company of theirs. Their fortune has been much like that of *Epicurus,* in the retirement of his Gardens: to live almost unknown, and to be celebrated after their decease. I

1   Tongue] Q2–3; *Tongue* Q1, D.   11   Master-piece,] Q2–3, D; ∼. Q1.
14   Books,] Q2; ∼. Q1; ∼; Q3; ∼: D.

cannot find that any of them were conversant in Courts, except
Ben. Jonson: and his genius lay not so much that way, as to make
an improvement by it: greatness was not, then, so easy of access,
nor conversation so free as now it is. I cannot, therefore, conceive it any insolence to affirm, that, by the knowledge, and pattern of their wit, who writ before us, and by the advantage of our
own conversation, the discourse and Raillery of our Comedies
excell what has been written by them: and this will be deny'd by
none, but some few old fellows who value themselves on their
acquaintance with the *Black-Friars:* who, because they saw their
Playes, would pretend a right to judge ours. The memory of
these grave Gentlemen is their only Plea for being Wits: they can
tell a story of *Ben. Jonson,* and perhaps have had fancy enough
to give a supper in *Apollo* that they might be call'd his Sons: and
because they were drawn in to be laught at in those times, they
think themselves now sufficiently intitled to laugh at ours. Learning I never saw in any of them, and wit no more than they could
remember. In short, they were unlucky to have been bred in an
unpolish'd Age, and more unlucky to live to a refin'd one. They
have lasted beyond their own, and are cast behind ours: and not
contented to have known little at the age of twenty, they boast of
their ignorance at threescore.

Now, if any ask me, whence it is that our conversation is so
much refin'd? I must freely, and without flattery, ascribe it to the
Court: and, in it, particularly to the King; whose example gives
a law to it. His own mis-fortunes and the Nations, afforded him
an opportunity, which is rarely allow'd to Sovereign Princes, I
mean of travelling, and being conversant in the most polish'd
Courts of *Europe;* and, thereby, of cultivating a Spirit, which
was form'd by Nature, to receive the impression of a gallant and
generous education. At his return, he found a Nation lost as
much in Barbarism as in Rebellion: and as the excellency of his
Nature forgave the one, so the excellency of his manners reform'd the other. The desire of imitating so great a pattern, first

2   genius] *genius* Q1–3, D.   3   it:] Q2–3; ~. Q1, D.
7   Comedies] *Comedies* Q1–3, D.   8   them:] Q2–3; ~. Q1, D.
12 Wits:] Q2–3; ~. Q1, D.   30 impression] Q2–3; impressions Q1, D.
32 Rebellion:] Q2–3; ~. Q1, D.   34 The desire] Q2–3, D; the desire Q1.

waken'd the dull and heavy spirits of the *English,* from their natural reserv'dness: loosen'd them, from their stiff forms of conversation; and made them easy and plyant to each other in discourse. Thus, insensibly, our way of living became more free: and the fire of the *English* wit, which was before stifled under a constrain'd melancholy way of breeding, began first to display its force: by mixing the solidity of our Nation, with the air and gayety of our neighbours. This being granted to be true, it would be a wonder, if the Poets, whose work is imitation, should be the onely persons in three Kingdoms, who should not receive advantage by it: or, if they should not more easily imitate the wit and conversation of the present age, than of the past.

Let us therefore admire the beauties and the heights of *Shakespear,* without falling after him into a carelesness and (as I may call it) a Lethargy of thought, for whole Scenes together. Let us imitate, as we are able, the quickness and easiness of *Fletcher,* without proposing him as a pattern to us, either in the redundancy of his matter, or the incorrectness of his language. Let us admire his wit and sharpness of conceit; but, let us at the same time acknowledge that it was seldome so fix'd, and made proper to his characters, as that the same things might not be spoken by any person in the Play. Let us applaud his Scenes of Love; but, let us confess that he understood not either greatness or perfect honour in the parts of any of his women. In fine, let us allow, that he had so much fancy, as when he pleas'd he could write wit: but that he wanted so much Judgment as seldome to have written humour; or describ'd a pleasant folly. Let us ascribe to *Jonson* the height and accuracy of Judgment, in the ordering of his Plots, his choice of characters, and maintaining what he had chosen, to the end: but let us not think him a perfect pattern of imitation; except it be in humour: for Love, which is the foundation of all Comedies in other Languages, is scarcely mention'd in any of his Playes: and for humour it self, the Poets of this Age will be more wary than to imitate the meanness of his persons. Gentlemen will now be entertain'd with the follies of each other:

5 *English*] Q2–3, D; English Q1.   22 Let] Q2–3, D; let Q1.
25 so much] Q2–3, D; so- / much Q1.   30 end:] Q2–3; ∼. Q1, D.
32 Comedies] Q2–3; *Comedies* Q1, D.   33 Playes:] Q2–3, D; ∼. Q1.

and though they allow *Cob* and *Tib* to speak properly, yet they are not much pleas'd with their Tankard or with their Raggs: And, surely, their conversation can be no jest to them on the Theatre, when they would avoid it in the street.

To conclude all, let us render to our Predecessors what is their due, without confineing our selves to a servile imitation of all they writ: and, without assuming to our selves the Title of better Poets, let us ascribe to the gallantry and civility of our age the advantage which we have above them; and to our knowledge of the customs and manners of it, the happiness we have to please beyond them.

4 Theatre] Q2–3; *Theatre* Q1, D.

MARRIAGE A-LA-MODE

MARRIAGE
A-la-Mode.

A
COMEDY.

As it is Acted at the

THEATRE-ROYAL.

Written by *JOHN DRYDEN*, Servant
to His Majesty.

*———————— Quicquid sum ego, quamvis
Infra Lucilli censum ingeniumque, tamen me
Cum magnis vixisse, invita fatebitur usque
Invidia, & fragili quærens illidere dentem
Offendet solido.*

Horat. Serm.

LONDON,

Printed by *T. N.* for *Henry Herringman*, and are to be
sold at the *Anchor* in the Lower Walk of
the *New Exchange.* 1673.

TITLE PAGE OF THE FIRST EDITION (MACDONALD 77A)

To the Right Honourable,
The Earl of ROCHESTER.

My Lord,

I humbly Dedicate to Your Lordship that Poem, of which you were pleas'd to appear an early Patron, before it was Acted on the Stage. I may yet go farther, with your permission, and say, That it receiv'd amendment from your noble hands, e're it was fit to be presented. You may please likewise to remember, with how much favour to the Authour, and indulgence to the Play, you commended it to the view of His Majesty, then at *Windsor,* and by His Approbation of it in Writing, made way for its
10 kind reception on the Theatre. In this Dedication therefore, I may seem to imitate a Custom of the Ancients, who offer'd to their Gods the Firstlings of the Flock, which I think they call'd *Ver Sacrum,* because they help'd 'em to increase. I am sure, if there be any thing in this Play, wherein I have rais'd my self beyond the ordinary lowness of my Comedies, I ought wholly to acknowledge it to the favour, of being admitted into your Lordship's Conversation. And not onely I, who pretend not to this way, but the best Comick Writers of our Age, will joyn with me to acknowledge, that they have copy'd the Gallantries of Courts, the
20 Delicacy of Expression, and the Decencies of Behaviour, from your Lordship, with more success, then if they had taken their Models from the Court of *France.* But this, my Lord, will be no wonder to the world, which knows the excellencie of your Natural parts, and those you have acquir'd in a Noble Education. That which with more reason I admire, is, that being so absolute a Courtier, you have not forgot, either the ties of Friendship, or the practise of Generosity. In my little Experience of a Court (which I confess I desire not to improve) I have found in it much of Interest, and more of Detraction: Few men there have that

10 Theatre] *Theatre* Q1–4, F, D.

assurance of a Friend, as not to be made ridiculous by him, when they are absent. There are a midling sort of Courtiers, who become happy by their want of wit; but they supply that want, by an excess of malice to those who have it. And there is no such persecution as that of fools: they can never be considerable enough to be talk'd of themselves; so that they are safe onely in their obscurity, and grow mischievous to witty men, by the great diligence of their envy, and by being always present to represent and aggravate their faults. In the mean time they are forc'd,

10 when they endeavour to be pleasant, to live on the Offalls of their Wit, whom they decry; and either to quote it, (which they do unwillingly) or to pass it upon others for their own. These are the men who make it their business to chase Wit from the Knowledge of Princes, lest it should disgrace their ignorance. And this kind of malice your Lordship has not so much avoided, as surmounted. But if by the excellent temper of a Royal Master, always more ready to hear good than ill, if by his inclination to love you, if by your own merit and address, if by the charmes of your Conversation, the Grace of your Behaviour, your knowl-

20 edge of Greatness and Habitude in Courts, you have been able to preserve your self with Honour in the midst of so dangerous a Course; yet at least the remembrance of those Hazards has inspir'd you with pity for other men, who being of an inferiour Wit and Quality to you, are yet Persecuted, for being that in Little, which your Lordship is in Great. For the quarrel of those people extends it self to any thing of sense; and if I may be so vain to own it amongst the rest of the Poets, has sometimes reach'd to the very borders of it, even to me. So that, if our general good fortune had not rais'd up your Lordship to defend us,

30 I know not whether any thing had been more ridiculous in Court, than Writers. 'Tis to your Lordship's favour we generally owe our Protection and Patronage: And to the Nobleness of your Nature, which will not suffer the least shadow of your Wit to be contemn'd in other men. You have been often pleas'd not onely to excuse my imperfections, but to vindicate what was tolerable in my Writings from their censures. And what I never

---

20   have] F, D; having Q1–4.   36   censures.] Q2–4, F, D; ~∧ Q1.

can forget, you have not onely been careful of my Reputation,
but of my Fortune. You have been Sollicitous to supply my
neglect of my self; and to overcome the fatal Modesty of Poets,
which submits them to perpetual wants, rather then to become
importunate with those people, who have the liberality of Kings
in their disposing; and who dishonouring the Bounty of their
Master, suffer such to be in necessity, who endeavour at least to
please him: and for whose entertainment He has generously provided, if the Fruits of His Royal favour were not often stopp'd
in other hands. But your Lordship has given me occasion, not to
complain of Courts, whil'st you are there. I have found the effects
of your Mediation in all my Concernments; and they were so
much the more noble in you, because they were wholly volun-
tary. I became your Lordship's (if I may venture on the Simili-
tude) as the world was made, without knowing him who made it;
and brought onely a passive obedience to be your Creature. This
Nobleness of yours I think my self the rather oblig'd to own,
because otherwise it must have been lost to all remembrance: for
you are endued with that excellent quality of a frank Nature, to
forget the good which you have done.

But, my Lord, I ought to have consider'd, that you are as great
a Judge, as you are a Patron; and that in praising you ill, I shall
incurre a higher note of ingratitude, then that I thought to have
avoided. I stand in need of all your accustom'd goodness for the
Dedication of this Play: which though, perhaps, it be the best of
my Comedies, is yet so faulty, that I should have fear'd you, for
my Critick, if I had not with some policy given you the trouble
of being my Protector. Wit seems to have lodg'd it self more
Nobly in this Age, than in any of the former: and people of my
mean condition, are onely Writers, because some of the Nobility,
and your Lordship in the first place, are above the narrow praises
which Poesie could give you. But let those who love to see themselves exceeded, encourage your Lordship in so dangerous a
quality: for my own part, I must confess, that I have so much of
self-interest, as to be content with reading some Papers of your
Verses, without desiring you should proceed to a Scene or Play:
with the common prudence of those, who are worsted in a Duel,
and declare they are satisfied when they are first wounded. Your

Lordship has but another step to make, and from the Patron of
Wit, you may become its Tyrant: and Oppress our little Reputations with more ease then you now protect them. But these,
my Lord, are designs, which I am sure you harbour not; any
more then the *French* King is contriving the Conquest of the
Swissers. 'Tis a barren Triumph, which is not worth your pains,
and wou'd onely rank him amongst your Slaves, who is already,

My Lord,

Your Lordships

Most obedient and most
faithful Servant,

JOHN DRYDEN.

---

5   King] Q2–4, F, D; *King* Q1.

Prologue.

Lord, *how reform'd and quiet we are grown,*
 Since all our Braves and all our Wits are gone:
 Fop-corner now is free from Civil War:
White-Wig and Vizard make no longer jar.
France, and the Fleet, have swept the Town so clear,
That we can Act in peace, and you can hear.
'Twas a sad sight, before they march'd from home,
To see our Warriours, in Red Wastecoats, come,
With hair tuck'd up, into our Tireing-room.
But 'twas more sad to hear their last Adieu,
The Women sob'd, and swore they would be true;
And so they were, as long as e're they cou'd:
But powerful Guinnee *cannot be withstood,*
And they were made of Play house flesh and bloud.
Fate did their Friends for double use ordain,
In Wars abroad, they grinning Honour gain,
And Mistresses, for all that stay, maintain.
Now they are gone, 'tis dead Vacation here,
For neither Friends nor Enemies appear.
Poor pensive Punk now peeps ere Plays begin,
Sees the bare Bench, and dares not venture in:
But manages her last Half-crown with care,
And trudges to the Mall, *on foot, for Air.*
Our City Friends so far will hardly come,
They can take up with Pleasures nearer home;
And see gay Shows, and gawdy Scenes elsewhere:
For we presume they seldom come to hear.

10

20

---

6   *after this line Os2 has:*
      Those that durst fight are gone to get renown,
      And those that durst not, blush to stand in Town.
In Os3 the foregoing lines replace ll. 3–6.
19   *after this line M1 has:*
      All noise is husht within our Empty Walls
      The Old Cat-fac't Critick now noe longer Brawles
      But vents his treadbare jests in Hospitalls

But they have now ta'n up a glorious Trade,
And cutting Moorcraft *struts in Masquerade.*
30   *There's all our hope, for we shall show to day,*
A Masquing Ball, to recommend our Play:
Nay, to endear'em more, and let'em see,
We scorn to come behind in Courtesie,
We'll follow the new Mode which they begin,
And treat'em with a Room, and Couch within:
For that's one way, how e're the Play fall short,
T' oblige the Town, the City, and the Court.

---

29   Moorcraft] *Moorcraft,* Q1–4, F, D, M1.

Persons Represented.

MEN.

	By
Polydamas, Usurper of *Sicily*—————	Mr. *Wintershall.*
Leonidas, the Rightful Prince, unknown———	Mr. *Kynaston.*
Argaleon, Favourite to *Polydamas*———	Mr. *Lydall.*
Hermogenes, Foster-father to *Leonidas*———	Mr. *Cartwright.*
Eubulus, his Friend and Companion———	Mr. *Watson.*
Rhodophil, Captain of the Guards———	Mr. *Mohun.*
Palamede, a Courtier———————	Mr. *Hart.*

WOMEN.

	By
Palmyra, Daughter to the Usurper———	Mrs. *Coxe.*
Amalthea, Sister to *Argaleon*———	Mrs. *James.*
Doralice, Wife to *Rhodophil*———	Mrs. *Marshall.*
Melantha, an Affected Lady———	Mrs. *Bowtell.*
Philotis, Woman to *Melantha*———	Mrs. *Reeve.*
Beliza, Woman to *Doralice*———	Mrs. *Slade.*
Artemis, a Court-Lady———	Mrs. *Uphill.*

Scene, *SICILIE.*

———

Beliza] D; *Belisa* Q1–4, F.

MARRIAGE A-LA-MODE.

ACT I. SCENE I.

Walks near the Court.

Enter Doralice *and* Beliza.

Dor. Beliza, bring the Lute into this Arbor, the Walks are empty: I would try the Song the Princess *Amalthea* bad me learn.
[*They go in, and sing.*

1.

Why should a foolish Marriage Vow
*   Which long ago was made,*
Oblige us to each other now
*   When Passion is decay'd?*
We lov'd, and we lov'd, as long as we cou'd,
*   Till our love was lov'd out in us both:*
But our Marriage is dead, when the Pleasure is fled:
*   'Twas Pleasure first made it an Oath.*

2.

If I have Pleasures for a Friend,
*   And farther love in store,*
What wrong has he whose joys did end,
*   And who cou'd give no more?*

10

2+ *s.d.* [*They*] F, D; ∧∼ Q1–4.

> *'Tis a madness that he should be jealous of me,*
> *Or that I shou'd bar him of another:*
> *For all we can gain, is to give our selves pain,*
> *When neither can hinder the other.*

Enter Palamede, *in Riding Habit, and hears the Song.*
Re-enter Doralice *and* Beliza.

Bel. Madam, a Stranger.

20   *Dor.* I did not think to have had witnesses of my bad singing.

Pala. If I have err'd, Madam, I hope you'l pardon the curiosity of a Stranger; for I may well call my self so, after five years absence from the Court: But you have freed me from one error.

Dor. What's that, I beseech you?

Pala. I thought good voices, and ill faces, had been inseparable; and that to be fair and sing well, had been onely the priviledge of Angels.

Dor. And how many more of these fine things can you say to me?

30   *Pala.* Very few, Madam, for if I should continue to see you some hours longer: You look so killingly, that I should be mute with wonder.

Dor. This will not give you the reputation of a Wit with me: you travelling Monsieurs live upon the stock you have got abroad, for the first day or two: to repeat with a good memory, and apply with a good grace, is all your wit. And, commonly, your Gullets are sew'd up, like Cormorants: When you have regorg'd what you have taken in, you are the leanest things in Nature.

40   *Pala.* Then, Madam, I think you had best make that use of me; let me wait on you for two or three days together, and you shall hear all I have learnt of extraordinary, in other Countreys: And one thing which I never saw till I came home, that is, a Lady of a better voice, better face, and better wit, than any I have seen abroad. And, after this, if I should not declare my self most pas-

---

15–18   *In Q1–4, F, D all lines are equally indented; except in F, they are preceded by a line space and divided and capitalized as follows:* 'Tis . . . | Should . . . | Or . . . | For . . . | Is . . . | When. . . .

sionately in love with you, I should have less wit than yet you
think I have.

Dor. A very plain, and pithy Declaration. I see, Sir, you have
been travelling in *Spain* or *Italy,* or some of the hot Countreys,
50 where men come to the point immediately. But are you sure
these are not words of course? For I would not give my poor heart
an occasion of complaint against me, that I engag'd it too rashly,
and then could not bring it off.

Pala. Your heart may trust it self with me safely; I shall use
it very civilly while it stays, and never turn it away, without fair
warning to provide for it self.

Dor. First, then, I do receive your passion with as little consideration, on my part, as ever you gave it me, on yours. And now
see what a miserable wretch you have made your self.

60 *Pala.* Who, I miserable? Thank you for that. Give me love
enough, and life enough, and I defie Fortune.

Dor. Know then, thou man of vain imagination, know, to thy
utter confusion, that I am vertuous.

Pala. Such another word, and I give up the ghost.

Dor. Then, to strike you quite dead, know, that I am marry'd
too.

Pala. Art thou marry'd; O thou damnable vertuous Woman?

Dor. Yes, marry'd to a Gentleman; young, handsome, rich,
valiant, and with all the good qualities that will make you de-
70 spair, and hang yourself.

Pala. Well, in spight of all that, I'll love you: Fortune has cut
us out for one another; for I am to be marry'd within these three
days: Marry'd past redemption, to a young, fair, rich, and vertuous Lady: And, it shall go hard, but I will love my Wife as
little, as I perceive you do your Husband.

Dor. Remember I invade no propriety: My servant you are
onely till you are marry'd.

Pala. In the mean time, you are to forget you have a Husband.

Dor. And you, that you are to have a Wife.

80 *Bel.* (*Aside to her Lady*) O Madam, my Lord's just at the end
of the Walks; and, if you make not haste, will discover you.

61, 71 Fortune] *Fortune* Q1–4, F, D.   73   days:] F; ~. Q1–4, D.
80 *s.d.* (*Aside ... Lady*)] ∧~ ... ~. Q1–4, F, D.

Dor. Some other time, new Servant, we'll talk further of the premisses; in the mean while, break not my first commandment, that is, not to follow me.

Pala. But where, then, shall I find you again?

Dor. At Court. Yours for two days, Sir.

Pala. And nights, I beseech you, Madam.

                           [*Exit* Doralice *and* Beliza.

Pala. Well, I'll say that for thee, thou art a very dextrous Executioner; thou hast done my business at one stroke: Yet I must

90 marry another————and yet I must love this; and if it lead me into some little inconveniencies, as jealousies, and duels, and death, and so forth; yet while sweet love is in the case, *Fortune* do thy worst, and avant Mortality.

        Enter Rodophil, *who seems speaking to one within.*

Rho. Leave 'em with my Lieutenant, while I fetch new Orders from the King. How? *Palamede!*   [*Sees* Palamede.

Pala. Rhodophil!

Rho. Who thought to have seen you in *Sicily?*

Pala. Who thought to have found the Court so far from *Syracuse?*

100 *Rho.* The King best knows the reason of the progress. But answer me, I beseech you, what brought you home from travel?

Pala. The commands of an old rich Father.

Rho. And the hopes of burying him?

Pala. Both together, as you see, have prevail'd on my good nature. In few words, My old man has already marry'd me; for he has agreed with another old man, as rich and as covetous as himself; the Articles are drawn, and I have given my consent, for fear of being dis-inherited; and yet know not what kind of woman I am to marry.

110 *Rho.* Sure your Father intends you some very ugly wife; and has a mind to keep you in ignorance, till you have shot the gulf.

Pala. I know not that; but obey I will, and must.

Rho. Then, I cannot chuse but grieve for all the good Girls

87+   s.d. [*Exit*] Q2–4, F, D; ₍ₐ₎~ Q1.
95   s.d. [*Sees* Palamede] Q2–4, D (₍ₐ₎~ Q2–4); [*Sees Palamede* Q1, F (₍ₐ₎~ Q1).

and Curtizans of *France* and *Italy:* They have lost the most kind-hearted, doting, prodigal, humble servant, in *Europe.*

Pala. All I could do in these three years I stay'd behind you, was to comfort the poor Creatures, for the loss of you. But what's the reason that in all this time, a friend could never hear from you?

120   *Rho.* Alass, dear *Palamede,* I have had no joy to write, nor indeed to do any thing in the World to please me: The greatest misfortune imaginable is faln upon me.

Pala. Prithee, what's the matter?

Rho. In one word, I am marry'd; wretchedly marry'd; and have been above these two years. Yes, faith, the Devil has had power over me, in spight of my Vows and Resolutions to the contrary.

Pala. I find you have sold your self for filthy lucre; she's old, or ill-condition'd.

130   *Rho.* No, none of these: I'm sure she's young; and, for her humor, she laughs, sings, and dances eternally; and, which is more, we never quarrel about it, for I do the same.

Pala. You're very unfortunate indeed: Then the case is plain, she is not handsome.

Rho. A great beauty too, as people say.

Pala. As people say? Why, you should know that best your self.

Rho. Ask those, who have smelt to a strong perfume two years together, what's the scent.

Pala. But here are good qualities enough for one woman.

140   *Rho.* Ay, too many, *Palamede,* if I could put 'em into three or four women, I should be content.

Pala. O, now I have found it, you dislike her for no other reason, but because she's your wife.

Rho. And is not that enough? All that I know of her perfections now, is only by memory; I remember, indeed, that about two years ago I lov'd her passionately; but those golden days are gone, *Palamede:* Yet I lov'd her a whole half year, double the natural term of any Mistress, and think in my conscience I could have held out another quarter; but then the World began to

---

116   years] Q2–4; ∼, Q1, F, D.

150 laugh at me, and a certain shame of being out of fashion seiz'd
me: At last, we arriv'd at that point, that there was nothing left
in us to make us new to one another: yet still I set a good face
upon the matter, and am infinite fond of her before company;
but, when we are alone, we walk like Lions in a room, she one
way, and I another: and we lie with our backs to each other so
far distant, as if the fashion of great Beds was onely invented to
keep Husband and Wife sufficiently asunder.

Pala. The truth is, your disease is very desperate; but, though
you cannot be cur'd, you may be patch'd up a little; you must get
160 you a Mistress, *Rhodophil:* that, indeed, is living upon Cordials;
but, as fast as one fails, you must supply it with another. You're
like a Gamester, who has lost his estate; yet, in doing that, you
have learn'd the advantages of Play, and can arrive to live upon't.

Rho. Truth is, I have been thinking on't, and have just resolv'd to take your counsel; and, faith, considering the damn'd
disadvantages of a marry'd man, I have provided well enough,
for a poor humble sinner, that is not ambitious of great matters.

Pala. What is she, for a Woman?

Rho. One of the Stars of *Syracuse,* I assure you: Young enough,
170 fair enough, and, but for one quality, Just such a woman as I
would wish.

Pala. O Friend, this is not an age to be critical in Beauty:
when we had good store of handsome women, and but few Chapmen, you might have been more curious in your choice; but now
the price is enhanc'd upon us, and all Mankind set up for Mistresses, so that poor little creatures, without beauty, birth, or
breeding, but onely impudence, go off at unreasonable rates: and
a man, in these hard times, snaps at 'em, as he does at Broad-gold,
never examines the weight, but takes light, or heavy, as he can
180 get it.

Rho. But my Mistris has one fault that's almost unpardonable;
for, being a Town-Lady, without any relation to the Court, yet
she thinks her self undone, if she be not seen there three or four
times a day, with the Princess *Amalthea.* And for the King, she
haunts, and watches him so narrowly in a morning, that she pre-

---

150 fashion] Q2–4; ~, Q1, F, D.   170 but] Q2–4, F, D; ~, Q1.
172 *Pala.*] Q2–4, F, D; ~, Q1.

vents even the Chymists who beset his Chamber, to turn their Mercury into his Gold.

Pala. Yet, hitherto, me-thinks, you are no very unhappy man.

Rho. With all this, she's the greatest Gossip in Nature; for, besides the Court, she's the most eternal Visiter of the Town: and yet manages her time so well, that she seems ubiquitary. For my part, I can compare her to nothing but the Sun; for, like him, she takes no rest, nor ever sets in one place, but to rise in another.

Pala. I confess she had need be handsome with these qualities.

Rho. No Lady can be so curious of a new Fashion, as she is of a new *French* Word; she's the very Mint of the Nation; and as fast as any Bullion comes out of *France,* coins it immediately into our Language.

Pala. And her name is————

Rho. No naming; that's not like a Cavalier: Find her, if you can, by my description; and I am not so ill a painter, that I need write the name beneath the Picture.

Pala. Well, then, how far have you proceeded in your love?

Rho. 'Tis yet in the bud, and what fruit it may bear I cannot tell; for this insufferable humour, of haunting the Court, is so predominant, that she has hitherto broken all her assignations with me, for fear of missing her visits there.

Pala. That's the hardest part of your adventure: but, for ought I see, Fortune has us'd us both alike; I have a strange kind of Mistris too in Court, besides her I am to marry.

Rho. You have made haste to be in love then; for, if I am not mistaken, you are but this day arriv'd.

Pala. That's all one, I have seen the Lady already, who has charm'd me, seen her in these Walks, courted her, and receiv'd, for the first time, an answer that does not put me into despair.

To them, Argaleon, Amalthea, Artemis.

I'll tell you at more leisure my adventures. The Walks fill apace, I see. Stay, is not that the young Lord *Argaleon,* the Kings Favourite?

---

197 *French* Word] Q2–4, D (French Q2–4); French-word Q1; *French*-Word F.

220   *Rho.* Yes, and as proud as ever, as ambitious, and as revengeful.

     Pala. How keeps he the Kings favour with these qualities?

     Rho. Argaleon's father help'd him to the Crown: besides, he gilds over all his vices to the King, and, standing in the dark to him, sees all his inclinations, interests and humours, which he so times and sooths, that, in effect, he reigns.

     Pala. His sister *Amalthea,* who, I ghess, stands by him, seems not to be of his temper.

     Rho. O, she's all goodness and generosity.

     Arga. Rhodophil, the King expects you earnestly.

230   *Rho.* 'Tis done, my Lord, what he commanded: I onely wait-ed his return from Hunting. Shall I attend your Lordship to him?

     Arga. No; I go first another way.   [*Exit hastily.*

     Pala. He seems in haste, and discompos'd.

     Amal. (*To* Rhod. *after a short whisper.*) Your friend? then he must needs be of much merit.

     Rho. When he has kiss'd the King's hand, I know he'll beg the honour to kiss yours. Come, *Palamede.*

         [*Exeunt* Rhodo. *and* Pala. *bowing to* Amal.

     Arte. Madam, you tell me most surprising news.

     Amal. The fear of it, you see,

240 Has discompos'd my brother; but to me

All that can bring my Country good, is welcome.

     Arte. It seems incredible, that this old King,

Whom all the world thought childless,

Should come to search the farthest parts of *Sicily,*

In hope to find an Heir.

     Amal. To lessen your astonishment, I will

Unfold some private passages of State,

Of which you yet are ignorant: Know, first,

That this *Polydamas,* who Reigns, unjustly

250 Gain'd the Crown.

     Arte. Somewhat of this I have confus'dly heard.

     Amal. I'll tell you all in brief: *Theagenes,*

Our last great King,

Had, by his Queen, one onely Son, an Infant

---

234   s.d. (*To . . . whisper.*)] D; ∧~ . . . ~·∧ Q1–4, F.

236   kiss'd] Q2–4, F, D; kis'd Q1.   237+   s.d. [*Exeunt*] F, D; ∧~ Q1–4.

Of three years old, call'd, after him, *Theagenes;*
The General, this *Polydamas,* then marri'd:
The publick Feasts for which were scarcely past,
When a Rebellion in the heart of *Sicily*
Call'd out the King to Arms.
    Arte. ————————*Polydamas*
260 Had then a just excuse to stay behind.
    Amal. His temper was too warlike to accept it:
He left his Bride, and the new joys of marriage,
And follow'd to the Feild. In short, they fought,
The Rebels were o'rcome; but in the Fight
The too bold King receiv'd a mortal wound.
When he perceiv'd his end approaching near,
He call'd the General, to whose care he left
His Widow Queen, and Orphan Son; then dy'd.
    Arte. Then false *Polydamas* betray'd his trust?
270   *Amal.* He did; and with my father's help, for which
Heav'n pardon him, so gain'd the Soldiers hearts,
That in few days he was saluted King:
And when his crimes had impudence enough
To bear the eye of day,
He march'd his Army back to *Syracuse.*
But see how heav'n can punish wicked men
In granting their desires: the news was brought him
That day he was to enter it, that *Eubulus,*
Whom his dead Master had left Governour,
280 Was fled, and with him bore away the Queen,
And Royal Orphan; but, what more amaz'd him,
His wife, now big with child, and much detesting
Her husband's practises, had willingly
Accompani'd their flight.
    Arte. How I admire her vertue!
    Amal. ————————————What became
Of her, and them, since that, was never known;
Onely, some few days since, a famous Robber
Was taken with some Jewels of vast price,
Which, when they were delivered to the King,
290 He knew had been his Wife's; with these, a Letter,

Much torn, and sulli'd, but which yet he knew
To be her writing.
    Arte. —————Sure from hence he learn'd
He had a Son.
    Amal. ——It was not left so plain:
The Paper onely said, she dy'd in childbed:
But when it should have mention'd Son, or Daughter,
Just there it was torn off.
    Arte. —————————Madam, the King.

    To them, Polydamas, Argaleon, *Guards, and Attendants.*

    Arga. The Robber, though thrice Rack'd, confess'd no more
But that he took those Jewels near this place.
    Poly. But yet the circumstances strongly argue,
300 That those, for whom I search, are not far off.
    Arga. I cannot easily believe it.
    Arte. ————————————No,
You would not have it so.   [*Aside.*
    Poly. Those I employ'd, have, in the neighbouring Hamlet,
Amongst the Fishers Cabins, made discovery
Of some young persons, whose uncommon beauty,
And graceful carriage, make it seem suspicious
They are not what they seem: I therefore sent
The Captain of my Guards, this morning early,
With orders to secure and bring 'em to me.

    Enter Rhodophil *and* Palamede.

310 O here he is. Have you perform'd my will?
    Rho. Sir, those whom you commanded me to bring,
Are waiting in the Walks.
    Poly. —————————Conduct 'em hither.
    Rho. First, give me leave
To beg your notice of this Gentleman.
    Poly. He seems to merit it. His name and quality?

---

293 He] Q2–4, D; he Q1, F.   296+ *s.d. Guards*] *Guard* Q1–4, F, D.
302 *s.d. Aside.*] D; *aside.* Q1–4, F (~, Q2).

Rho. Palamede, son to Lord *Cleodemus* of *Palermo,*
And new return'd from travel.
    [Palamede *approaches, and kneels to kiss the Kings hand.*
    Poly. ―――――――――――You're welcome.
I knew your father well, he was both brave
And honest; we two once were fellow-soldiers
320 In the last Civil Wars.
    Pala. I bring the same unquestion'd honesty
And zeal to serve your Majesty; the courage
You were pleased to praise in him,
Your Royal prudence, and your Peoples love,
Will never give me leave to try like him
In Civil Wars, I hope it may in Foreign.
    Poly. Attend the Court, and it shall be my care
To find out some employment, worthy you.
Go, *Rhodophil,* and bring in those without.
                      [*Exeunt* Rho. *&* Pala.

Rhodophil *returns again immediately, and with him*
    Enter Hermogenes, Leonidas, *and* Palmyra.

330 Behold two miracles! [*Looking earnestly on* Leon. *and* Palmyra.
Of different sexes, but of equal form:
So matchless both, that my divided soul
Can scarcely ask the Gods a Son, or Daughter,
For fear of losing one. If from your hands,
You Powers, I shall this day receive a Daughter,
Argaleon, she is yours; but, if a Son,
Then *Amalthea*'s love shall make him happy.
    Arga. Grant, heav'n, this admirable Nymph may prove
That issue which he seeks.
340   *Amal. Venus Urania,* if thou art a Goddess,
Grant that sweet Youth may prove the Prince of *Sicily.*
    Poly. Tell me, old man, and tell me true, from whence
Had you that Youth and Maid?   [*To* Her.

―――――――
317+ *s.d.* [Palamede] F, D; ₍ₐ₎~ Q1–4.   329+ *s.d. Exeunt*] Q2–4, F, D; ~. Q1.
343 *s.d. To*] Q3–4, F, D; *to* Q1–2.

Her. —————————————From whence you had
Your Scepter, Sir: I had 'em from the Gòds.
    Poly. The Gods then have not such another gift.
Say who their Parents were.
    Her. —————————————My Wife, and I.
    Arga. It is not likely,
A Virgin of so excellent a beauty
Should come from such a Stock.
350   *Amal.* Much less, that such a Youth, so sweet, so graceful,
Should be produc'd from Peasants.
    Her. Why, Nature is the same in Villages,
And much more fit to form a noble issue
Where it is least corrupted.
    Poly. He talks, too like a man that knew the world
To have been long a Peasant. But the Rack
Will teach him other language. Hence with him.
    [*As the Guards are carrying him away, his Perruke falls off.*
Sure I have seen that face before. *Hermogenes!*
'Tis he, 'tis he who fled away with *Eubulus*,
360 And with my dear *Eudocia.*
    Her. Yes, Sir, I am *Hermogenes.*
And if to have been loyal be a crime,
I stand prepar'd to suffer.
    Poly. If thou would'st live, speak quickly,
What is become of my *Eudocia?*
Where is the Queen and young *Theagenes?*
Where *Eubulus?* and which of these is mine?
                    [*Pointing to* Leon. *and* Palm.
    Her. Eudocia is dead, so is the Queen,
The infant King her son, and *Eubulus.*
370   *Poly.* Traitor, 'tis false: produce 'em, or———
    Her. —————————————————Once more
I tell you, they are dead; but leave to threaten,
For you shall know no further.

———————

347–348   *one line in Q1–4, F, D* (a Virgin).
357+   *s.d. Guards*] Q2–4; *Guard* Q1, F, D.
360, 365, 368   *Eudocia*] *Eudoxia* Q1–4, F, D.
368   Queen,] Q3–4; ~. Q1–2, D; ~; F.

Poly. Then prove indulgent to my hopes, and be
My friend for ever. Tell me, good *Hermogenes,*
Whose Son is that brave Youth?
Her. —————————————Sir, he is yours.
Poly. Fool that I am, thou see'st that so I wish it,
And so thou flatter'st me.
Her. —————————By all that's holy.
Poly. Again. Thou canst not swear too deeply.
Yet hold, I will beleive thee:————yet I doubt.
380   *Her.* You need not, Sir.
Arga. Beleive him not; he sees you credulous,
And would impose his own base issue on you,
And fix it to your Crown.
Amal. Behold his goodly shape and feature, Sir,
Methinks he much resembles you.
Arga. I say, if you have any issue here,
It must be that fair creature;
By all my hopes I think so.
Amal. Yes, Brother, I believe you by your hopes,
390   For they are all for her.
Poly. ————————————Call the Youth nearer.
Her. Leonidas, the King would speak with you.
Poly. Come near, and be not dazled with the splendor,
And greatness of a Court.
Leon. I need not this incouragement.
I can fear nothing but the Gods.
And for this glory, after I have seen
The Canopy of State spread wide above
In the Abyss of Heaven, the Court of Stars,
The blushing Morning, and the rising Sun,
400   What greater can I see?
Poly. This speaks thee born a Prince, thou art thy self
That rising Sun, and shalt not see on earth,   [*Embracing him.*
A brighter then thy self.————All of you witness,
That for my son I here receive this Youth,
This brave, this————but I must not praise him further,
Because he now is mine.

Leon. I wonnot, Sir, believe   [*Kneeling.*
That I am made your sport;
For I find nothing in my self, but what
410 Is much above a scorn; I dare give credit
To whatsoe'r a King, like you, can tell me.
Either I am, or will deserve to be your Son.
    Arga. I yet maintain it is impossible
This young man should be yours; for, if he were,
Why should *Hermogenes* so long conceal him
When he might gain so much by his discovery?
    Her. I stay'd a while to make him worthy, Sir, of you.
But in that time I found   [*To the King.*
Somewhat within him, which so mov'd my love,
420 I never could resolve to part with him.
    Leon. You ask too many questions, and are   [*To* Argaleon.
Too sawcy for a subject.
    Arga. You rather over-act your part, and are
Too soon a Prince.
    Leon. —————Too soon you'l find me one.
    Poly. Enough, *Argaleon;*
I have declar'd him mine: and you, *Leonidas,*
Live well with him I love.
    Arga. Sir, if he be your Son, I may have leave
To think your Queen had Twins; look on this Virgin;
430 *Hermogenes* would enviously deprive you
Of half your treasure.
    Her. —————Sir, she is my daughter.
I could, perhaps, thus aided by this Lord,
Prefer her to be yours; but truth forbid
I should procure her greatness by a Lie.
    Poly. Come hither, beauteous Maid: are you not sorry
Your father will not let you pass for mine?
    Palm. I am content to be what heav'n has made me.
    Poly. Could you not wish your self a Princess then?
    Palm. Not to be Sister to *Leonidas.*
440   *Poly.* Why, my sweet Maid?

---

407   *s.d. Kneeling*] F, D; *kneeling* Q1–4.

Palm. ————————————Indeed I cannot tell;
But I could be content to be his Handmaid.
   Arga. I wish I had not seen her.   [*Aside.*
   Palm. I must weep for your good fortune;   [*To* Leonidas.
Pray pardon me, indeed I cannot help it.
Leonidas, (alas, I had forgot,
Now I must call you Prince) but must I leave you?
   Leon. I dare not speak to her; for if I should,   [*Aside.*
I must weep too.
   Poly. No, you shall live at Court, sweet Innocence,
450 And see him there. *Hermogenes,*
Though you intended not to make me happy,
Yet you shall be rewarded for th' event.
Come, my *Leonidas,* let's thank the Gods;
Thou for a Father, I for such a Son.
         [*Exeunt all but* Leonidas *and* Palmyra.
   Leon. My dear *Palmyra,* many eyes observe me,
And I have thoughts so tender, that I cannot
In publick speak 'em to you: some hours hence
I shall shake off these crowds of fawning Courtiers,
And then————   [*Exit* Leonidas.
460   *Palm.* Fly swift, you hours, you measure time for me in vain,
Till you bring back *Leonidas* again.
Be shorter now; and to redeem that wrong,
When he and I are met, be twice as long.   [*Exit.*

ACT II. SCENE I.

Melantha *and* Philotis.

   Phil. Count *Rhodophil's* a fine Gentleman indeed, Madam;
and I think deserves your affection.
   Mel. Let me die but he's a fine man; he sings, and dances *en
Francois,* and writes the *Billets doux* to a miracle.
   Phil. And those are no small tallents, to a Lady that under-
stands, and values the *French* ayr, as your Ladiship does.

————————
445 *indented in Q1 as if a new speech.*

Mel. How charming is the *French* ayr! and what an *étourdy
bete* is one of our untravel'd Islanders! when he would make his
Court to me, let me die, but he is just *Æsop*'s Ass, that would
imitate the courtly *French* in his addresses; but, in stead of those,
comes pawing upon me, and doing all things so *mal a droitly.*

Phil. 'Tis great pity *Rhodophil*'s a married man, that you may
not have an honourable Intrigue with him.

Mel. Intrigue, *Philotis!* that's an old phrase; I have laid that
word by: *Amour* sounds better. But thou art heir to all my cast
words, as thou art to my old Wardrobe. Oh Count *Rhodophil!*
Ah *mon cher!* I could live and die with him.

Enter Palamede *and a Servant.*

Ser. Sir, this is my Lady.

Pala. Then this is she that is to be Divine, and Nymph, and
Goddess, and with whom I am to be desperately in love.

[*Bows to her, delivering a Letter.*
This Letter, Madam, which I present you from your father,
has given me both the happy opportunity, and the boldness, to
kiss the fairest hands in *Sicily.*

Mel. Came you lately from *Palermo,* Sir?

Pala. But yesterday, Madam.

Mel. [Reading the Letter] *Daughter, receive the bearer of this
Letter, as a Gentleman whom I have chosen to make you happy;*
(O *Venus,* a new Servant sent me! and let me die but he has the
ayre of a gallant *homme*) *his father is the rich Lord* Cleodemus,
*our neighbour: I suppose you'l find nothing disagreeable in his
person or his converse; both which he has improv'd by travel.
The Treaty is already concluded, and I shall be in Town within
these three days; so that you have nothing to do, but to obey your
careful Father.*

(*To* Pala.) Sir, my Father, for whom I have a blind obedience,
has commanded me to receive your passionate addresses; but you
must also give me leave to avow, that I cannot merit 'em, from
so accomplish'd a Cavalier.

Pala. I want many things, Madam, to render me accomplish'd;

7   *étourdy*] *etourdy* Q1–4, F, D.

40 and the first and greatest of 'em, is your favour.

Mel. Let me die, *Philotis,* but this is extremely *French;* but yet Count *Rhodophil*————A Gentleman, Sir, that understands the *Grand mond* so well, who has hanted the best conversations, and who (in short) has voyag'd, may pretend to the good graces of any Lady.

Pala. (Aside) Hay day! *Grand mond! conversation! voyag'd!* and *good graces!* I find my Mistris is one of those that run mad in new *French* words.

Mel. I suppose, Sir, you have made the *Tour* of *France;* and
50 having seen all that's fine there, will make a considerable reformation in the rudeness of our Court: for, let me die, but an unfashion'd, untravel'd, meer *Sicilian,* is a *Bete;* and has nothing in the world of an *honete homme.*

Pala. I must confess, Madam, that————

Mel. And what new *Minouets* have you brought over with you? their *Minouets* are to a miracle! and our *Sicilian* Jigs are so dull and *fade* to 'em!

Pala. For *Minouets,* Madam————

Mel. And what new Plays are there in vogue? and who danc'd
60 best in the last Grand Ballet? Come, sweet Servant, you shall tell me all.

Pala. (Aside) Tell her all? why, she asks all, and will hear nothing————To answer in order, Madam, to your demands————

Mel. I am thinking what a happy couple we shall be! for you shall keep up your correspondence abroad, and every thing that's new writ, in *France,* and fine, I mean all that's delicate, and *bien tourné,* we will have first.

Pala. But, Madam, our fortune————

Mel. I understand you, Sir; you'l leave that to me: for the
70 mennage of a family, I know it better then any Lady in *Sicily.*

Pala. Alas, Madam, we————

Mel. Then, we will never make visits together, nor see a Play, but always apart; you shall be every day at the King's *Levé,* and I at the Queen's; and we will never meet, but in the Drawing-room.

56 you?] F; ~! Q1–4, D.   56 Jigs] F, D; *Jigs* Q1–4.
57 *fade*] fad Q1; sad Q2–4, F, D.

Phil. Madam, the new Prince is just pass'd by the end of the Walk.

Mel. The new Prince, say'st thou? Adieu, dear Servant; I have not made my court to him these two long hours. O, 'tis the sweet-
80 est Prince! so *obligeant, charmant, ravissant,* that———Well, I'll make haste to kiss his hands; and then make half a score visits more, and be with you again in a twinkling.

              [*Exit, running with* Philotis.

Pala. (*Solus*) Now heaven, of thy mercy, bless me from this tongue; it may keep the field against a whole Army of Lawyers, and that in their own language, *French Gibberish.* 'Tis true, in the day-time, 'tis tolerable, when a man has field-room to run from it; but, to be shut up in a bed with her, like two Cocks in a pit; humanity cannot support it: I must kiss all night, in my own defence, and hold her down, like a Boy at cuffs, nay, and
90 give her the rising blow every time she begins to speak.

Enter Rhodophil.

But here comes *Rhodophil.* 'Tis pretty odd that my Mistris should so much resemble his: the same News-monger, the same passionate lover of a Court, the same———But *Basta,* since I must marry her, I'll say nothing, because he shall not laugh at my misfortune.

Rho. Well, *Palamede,* how go the affairs of love? You've seen your Mistris?

Pala. I have so.

Rho. And how, and how? has the old *Cupid,* your Father,
100 chosen well for you? is he a good Woodman?

Pala. She's much handsomer then I could have imagin'd: In short, I love her, and will marry her.

Rho. Then you are quite off from your other Mistris?

Pala. You are mistaken, I intend to love 'em both, as a reasonable man ought to do. For, since all women have their faults, and imperfections, 'tis fit that one of 'em should help out t' other.

Rho. This were a blessed Doctrine, indeed, if our Wives would

---

80   *obligeant, charmant, ravissant,*] obligeant, charmant, ravissant, Q1–4, F, D.

hear it; but, they're their own enemies: if they would suffer us
110 but now and then to make excursions, the benefit of our variety
would be theirs; instead of one continu'd, lazy, tyr'd love, they
would, in their turns, have twenty vigorous, fresh, and active
loves.

Pala. And I would ask any of 'em, whether a poor narrow
Brook, half dry the best part of the year, and running ever one
way, be to be compar'd to a lusty Stream, that has Ebbs and
Flows?

Rho. Ay; or is half so profitable for Navigation?

Enter Doralice, *walking by, and reading.*

Pala. Ods my life, *Rhodophil,* will you keep my counsel?
120 *Rho.* Yes: where's the secret?

Pala. There 'tis.   [*Showing* Doralice.
I may tell you, as my friend, *sub sigillo,* &c. this is that very numerical Lady, with whom I am in love.

Rho. By all that's vertuous, my Wife!   [*Aside.*

Pala. You look strangely: how do you like her? is she not very
handsome?

Rho. Sure he abuses me.   [*Aside.*
Why the devil do you ask my judgment?   [*To him.*

Pala. You are so dogged now, you think no man's Mistris
130 handsome, but your own. Come, you shall hear her talk too; she
has wit, I assure you.

Rho. This is too much, *Palamede.*   [*Going back.*

Pala. Prethee do not hang back so: of an old try'd Lover, thou
art the most bashful fellow!   [*Pulling him forward.*

Dor. Were you so near, and would not speak, dear Husband?
                                                 [*Looking up.*

Pala. Husband, quoth a! I have cut out a fine piece of work
for my self.   [*Aside.*

Rho. Pray, Spouse, how long have you been acquainted with
this Gentleman?

135+   *s.d. Looking*] F, D; *looking* Q1–4.

140   *Dor.* Who, I acquainted with this Stranger? To my best knowledge, I never saw him before.

Enter Melantha, *at the other end.*

Pala. Thanks, Fortune, thou hast help'd me.   [*Aside.*
Rho. Palamede, this must not pass so: I must know your Mis-
tris a little better.
Pala. It shall be your own fault else. Come, I'll introduce you.
Rho. Introduce me! where?
Pala. There. To my Mistris.
          [*Pointing to* Melantha, *who swiftly passes over the Stage.*
Rho. Who? *Melantha!* O heavens, I did not see her.
Pala. But I did: I am an Eagle where I love; I have seen her
150 this half hour.
Dor. (*Aside*) I find he has wit, he has got off so readily; but it
would anger me, if he should love *Melantha.*
Rho. (*Aside*) Now I could e'en wish it were my Wife he lov'd:
I find he's to be marri'd to my Mistris.
Pala. Shall I run after, and fetch her back again, to present
you to her?
Rho. No, you need not; I have the honour to have some small
acquaintance with her.
Pala. (*Aside*) O *Jupiter!* what a blockhead was I not to find it
160 out! My Wife that must be, is his Mistris. I did a little suspect
it before; well, I must marry her, because she's handsome, and
because I hate to be dis-inherited for a younger Brother, which
I am sure I shall be if I disobey; and yet I must keep in with
Rhodophil, because I love his Wife.
(*To* Rhodo.) I must desire you to make my excuse to your
Lady, if I have been so unfortunate to cause any mistake; and,
withall, to beg the honour of being known to her.
    Rho. O, that's but reason. Hark you, Spouse, pray look upon

140–141   *printed as verse* (. . . | To . . .) *in* Q*1–4,* F.
147+   s.d. *after* l. *146 in* Q*1–4,* D.
148   *printed as verse* (. . . | O . . .) *in* Q*1–4,* F.
149–150   *printed as verse* (. . . | I have . . .) *in* Q*1–4,* F.
151   s.d. *Aside*] Q3–4, D; ∼. Q1–2, F.   159   s.d. *Aside*] Q4; ∼. Q1–3, F, D.

this Gentleman as my friend; whom, to my knowledge, you have
170 never seen before this hour.

Dor. I'm so obedient a Wife, Sir, that my Husbands commands
shall ever be a Law to me.

Enter Melantha *again, hastily, and runs to embrace* Doralice.

Mela. O, my dear, I was just going to pay my devoirs to you; I
had not time this morning, for making my Court to the King,
and our new Prince. Well, never Nation was so happy, and all
that, in a young Prince; and he's the kindest person in the World
to me, let me die, if he is not.

Dor. He has been bred up far from Court, and therefore————

Mel. That imports not: Though he has not seen the *Grand*
180 *mond,* and all that, let me die but he has the air of the Court,
most absolutely.

Pala. But yet, Madam, he————

Mel. O, Servant, you can testifie that I am in his good Graces.
Well, I cannot stay long with you, because I have promis'd him
this Afternoon to————But hark you, my dear, I'll tell you a
Secret.   [*Whispers to* Doralice.

Rho. The Devil's in me, that I must love this Woman. [*Aside.*

Pala. The Devil's in me, that I must marry this Woman.
                                                      [*Aside.*

Mel. (Raising her Voice) So the Prince and I————But you
190 must make a Secret of this, my dear, for I would not for the
World your Husband should hear it, or my Tyrant, there, that
must be.

Pala. Well, fair impertinent, your whisper is not lost, we hear
you.   [*Aside.*

Dor. I understand then, that————

Mel. I'll tell you, my dear, the Prince took me by the hand, and
press'd it *a la derobbée,* because the King was near, made the

186   *s.d.* [*Whispers*] Q3–4, F, D; ∧∼ Q1–2.
187   *Rho.*] Q2–4, F, D; *Rho*∧ Q1.
187, 188+   *s.d.* [*Aside*] Q3–4, F, D; ∧∼ Q1–2.
189   *s.d. (Raising her Voice)*] ∧∼∼∼. Q1–4, D; [∼∼∼.] F.
194   *s.d.* [*Aside*] Q3–4, F, D; ∧∼ Q1–2.
197   *a la*] D; *al a* Q1–4, F.

doux yeux to me, and *en suitte,* said a thousand *Gallanteries,* or let me die, my dear.

    200   *Dor.* Then I am sure you————

    Mel. You are mistaken, my dear.

    Dor. What, before I speak?

    Mel. But I know your meaning; you think, my dear, that I as-sum'd something of *fierté* into my Countenance, to *rebute* him; but, quite contrary, I regarded him, I know not how to express it in our dull *Sicilian* Language, *d'un ayr enjoué;* and said nothing but *a d'autre, a d'autre,* and that it was all *grimace,* and would not pass upon me.

Enter Artemis: Melantha sees her, and runs away
from Doralice.

    (*To* Artemis) My dear, I must beg your pardon, I was just making a loose from *Doralice,* to pay my respects to you: Let me die, if I ever pass time so agreeably as in your company, and if I would leave it for any Lady's in *Sicily.*

    Arte. The Princess *Amalthea* is coming this way.

Enter Amalthea: Melantha runs to her.

    Mel. O dear Madam! I have been at your Lodgings, in my new *Galeche,* so often, to tell you of a new *Amour,* betwixt two per-sons whom you would little suspect for it; that, let me die, if one of my Coach-horses be not dead, and another quite tyr'd, and sunk under the *fatigue.*

    Amal. O, *Melantha,* I can tell you news, the Prince is coming this way.

    Mel. The Prince, O sweet Prince! He and I are to————and I forgot it.————Your pardon, sweet Madam, for my abruptness.

198   *en*] *in* Q1–4, F, D.

198   *Gallanteries*] Gallanteries Q1–2; Gallantries Q3–4, F, D.

206   *enjoué*] enjouué Q1–4, F, D.

207   *a d'autre, a d'autre*] ad autre, ad autre Q1–4, F, D.

209   *s.d.* (*To* Artemis)] *To* Artemis. Q1–4 (*Aretemis* Q1); [*To* Artemis.] F; [*To* Ar-temis.] D.

Adieu, my dears. Servant, *Rhodophil;* Servant, Servant, Servant
All.   *[Exit running.*

    Amal. Rhodophil, a word with you.   *[Whispers.*

    Dor. (*To* Pala.) Why do you not follow your Mistress, Sir?

    Pala. Follow her? Why, at this rate she'll be at the *Indies* with-
in this half hour.

    Dor. However, if you can't follow her all day, you'll meet her
230 at night, I hope?

    Pala. But can you, in charity, suffer me to be so mortify'd,
without affording me some relief? If it be but to punish that sign
of a Husband there; that lazy matrimony, that dull insipid taste,
who leaves such delicious fare at home, to dine abroad, on worse
meat, and to pay dear for't into the bargain.

    Dor. All this is in vain: Assure your self, I will never admit of
any visit from you in private.

    Pala. That is to tell me, in other words, my condition is des-
perate.

240   *Dor.* I think you in so ill a condition, that I am resolved to pray
for you, this very evening, in the close Walk, behind the Terras;
for that's a private place, and there I am sure no body will disturb
my devotions. And so, good-night, Sir.   *[Exit.*

    Pala. This is the newest way of making an appointment, I ever
heard of: let women alone to contrive the means; I find we are
but dunces to 'em. Well, I will not be so prophane a wretch as to
interrupt her devotions; but to make 'em more effectual, I'll down
upon my knees, and endeavour to joyn my own with 'em. *[Exit.*

    Amal. (*To* Rhodophil) I know already they do not love each
250 other; and that my Brother acts but a forc'd obedience to the
Kings commands; so that, if a quarrel should arise betwixt the
Prince and him, I were most miserable on both sides.

    Rho. There shall be nothing wanting in me, Madam, to pre-
vent so sad a consequence.

    Enter the King, Leonidas; *the King whispers* Amalthea.

---

223 *Rhodophil*] Q2–4, D; *Rodophil* Q1, F.   224 *s.d.* [*Exit*] Q3–4, F, D; ₍ₐ₎~ Q1–2.
225 *Rhodophil*] Q2–4, D; *Rodophil* Q1, F.
225 *s.d.* [*Whispers*] Q3–4, F, D; ₍ₐ₎~ Q1–2.
226 *Dor.* (*To* Pala.)] *Dor. to Pala.* Q1–4, D (*To* Q2–4); [*Dor. to Pala.*] F.

(To himself) I begin to hate this *Palamede*, because he is to
marry my Mistris: yet break with him I dare not, for fear of being
quite excluded from her company. 'Tis a hard case when a man
must go by his Rival to his Mistris: but 'tis at worst but using him
like a pair of heavy Boots in a dirty journey; after I have foul'd
260 him all day, I'll throw him off at night.   *[Exit.*
    Amal. (*To the King*) This honour is too great for me to hope.
    Poly. You shall this hour have the assurance of it.
Leonidas, come hither; you have heard,
I doubt not, that the Father of this Princess
Was my most faithful friend, while I was yet
A private man; and when I did assume
This Crown, he serv'd me in that high attempt.
You see, then, to what gratitude obliges me;
Make your address to her.
270   *Leon.* Sir, I am yet too young to be a Courtier;
I should too much betray my ignorance,
And want of breeding, to so fair a Lady.
    Amal. Your language speaks you not bred up in Desarts,
But in the softness of some *Asian* Court,
Where luxury and ease invent kind words,
To cozen tender Virgins of their hearts.
    Poly. You need not doubt
But in what words soe're a Prince can offer
His Crown and Person, they will be receiv'd.
280 You know my pleasure, and you know your duty.
    Leon. Yes, Sir, I shall obey, in what I can.
    Poly. In what you can, *Leonidas?* Consider,
He's both your King, and Father, who commands you.
Besides, what is there hard in my injunction?
    Leon. 'Tis hard to have my inclination forc'd.
I would not marry, Sir; and, when I do,
I hope you'll give me freedom in my choice.
    Poly. View well this Lady,
Whose mind as much transcends her beauteous face,
290 As that excels all others.
    Amal. My beauty, as it ne'r could merit love,

261 *s.d. To*] Q2–4; *to* Q1, F, D.

So neither can it beg: and, Sir, you may
Believe that, what the King has offer'd you,
I should refuse, did I not value more
Your person then your Crown.
 Leon. ————————————Think it not pride,
Or my new fortunes swell me to contemn you;
Think less, that I want eyes to see your beauty;
And least of all think duty wanting in me
T' obey a father's will: but————
 Poly. ——————————————But what, *Leonidas?*
300 For I must know your reason; and be sure
It be convincing too.
 Leon. ————————Sir, ask the Stars,
Which have impos'd love on us, like a fate,
Why minds are bent to one, and fly another?
Ask why all beauties cannot move all hearts?
For though there may
Be made a rule for colour, or for feature;
There can be none for liking.
 Poly. Leonidas, you owe me more
Then to oppose your liking to my pleasure.
310 *Leon.* I owe you all things, Sir; but something too
I owe my self.
 Poly. You shall dispute no more; I am a King,
And I will be obey'd.
 Leon. You are a King, Sir; but you are no God;
Or if you were, you could not force my will.
 Poly. But you are just, you Gods; O you are just,   [*Aside.*
In punishing the crimes of my rebellion
With a rebellious Son!
Yet I can punish him, as you do me.
320 *Leonidas,* there is no jesting with   [*To him.*
My will: I ne'r had done so much to gain
A Crown, but to be absolute in all things.
 Amal. O, Sir, be not so much a King, as to
Forget you are a Father: Soft indulgence

———

316 *s.d. Aside.*] Q2–4, F, D; ~ ∧ Q1.   320 with [*To him.*] with Q1–4, F, D.

Becomes that name. Though Nature gives you pow'r
To bind his duty, 'tis with silken Bonds:
Command him, then, as you command your self:
He is as much a part of you, as are
Your Appetite, and Will, and those you force not,
330 But gently bend, and make 'em pliant to your Reason.
    Poly. It may be I have us'd too rough a way:
Forgive me, my *Leonidas;* I know
I lie as open to the gusts of passion,
As the bare Shore to every beating Surge:
I will not force thee, now; but I intreat thee,
Absolve a Father's vow to this fair Virgin:
A vow, which hopes of having such a Son
First caus'd.
    Leon. Show not my disobedience by your pray'rs,
340 For I must still deny you, though I now
Appear more guilty to my self, than you:
I have some reasons, which I cannot utter,
That force my disobedience; yet I mourn
To death, that the first thing you e'r injoyn'd me,
Should be that onely one command in Nature
Which I could not obey.
    Poly. I did descend too much below my self
When I intreated him. Hence, to thy Desart,
Thou'rt not my son, or art not fit to be.
350   *Amal.* Great Sir, I humbly beg you, make not me   [*Kneeling.*
The cause of your displeasure. I absolve
Your vow: far, far from me, be such designs;
So wretched a desire of being great,
By making him unhappy. You may see
Something so noble in the Prince his nature,
As grieves him more not to obey, then you
That you are not obey'd.
    Poly. ————————Then, for your sake,
I'll give him one day longer, to consider
Not to deny; for my resolves are firm

---

360 As Fate, that cannot change.   [*Exeunt King and* Amal.
     Leon. ————————————And so are mine.
This beauteous Princess, charming as she is,
Could never make me happy: I must first
Be false to my *Palmyra,* and then wretched.
But, then, a Father's anger!
Suppose he should recede from his own vow,
He never would permit me to keep mine.

          Enter Palmyra; Argaleon *following her, a little after.*

See, she appears!
I'll think no more of any thing, but her.
Yet I have one hour good ere I am wretched.
370 But, Oh! *Argaleon* follows her! so night
Treads on the foot-steps of a Winter's Sun,
And stalks all black behind him.
     Palm. ————————————————O *Leonidas,*
(For I must call you still by that dear name)
Free me from this bad man.
     Leon. I hope he dares not be injurious to you.
     Arga. I rather was injurious to my self,
Then her.
     Leon. That must be judg'd when I hear what you said.
     Arga. I think you need not give your self that trouble:
380 It concern'd us alone.
     Leon. You answer sawcily, and indirectly:
What interest can you pretend in her?
     Arga. It may be, Sir, I made her some expressions
Which I would not repeat, because they were
Below my rank, to one of hers.
     Leon. What did he say, *Palmyra?*
     Palm. I'll tell you all: First, he began to look,
And then he sigh'd, and then he look'd again;
At last, he said my eyes wounded his heart:
390 And, after that, he talk'd of flames, and fires;
And such strange words, that I believ'd he conjur'd.
     Leon. O my heart! Leave me, *Argaleon.*

Arga. Come, sweet *Palmyra,*
I will instruct you better in my meaning:
You see he would be private.
     Leon. ————————Go your self,
And leave her here.
     Arga. ————Alas, she's ignorant,
And is not fit to entertain a Prince.
     Leon. First learn what's fit for you; that's to obey.
     Arga. I know my duty is to wait on you.
400 A great King's Son, like you, ought to forget
Such mean converse.
     Leon. ————————What? a disputing Subject?
Hence; or my sword shall do me justice, on thee.
     Arga. Yet I may find a time————   [*Going.*
     Leon. ————————What's that you mutter,
To find a time?   [*Going after him.*
     Arga. ————To wait on you again————
(*Softly*) In the mean while I'll watch you.
               [*Exit, and watches during the Scene.*
     Leon. How precious are the hours of Love in Courts!
In Cottages, where Love has all the day,
Full, and at ease, he throws it half away.
Time gives himself, and is not valu'd, there;
410 But sells, at mighty rates, each minute, here.
There, he is lazy, unemploy'd, and slow;
Here, he's more swift; and yet has more to do.
So many of his hours in publick move,
That few are left for privacy, and Love.
     Palm. The Sun, methinks, shines faint and dimly, here;
Light is not half so long, nor half so clear.
But, Oh! when every day was yours and mine,
How early up! what haste he made to shine!
     Leon. Such golden days no Prince must hope to see;
420 Whose ev'ry Subject is more bless'd then he.
     Palm. Do you remember, when their tasks were done,
How all the Youth did to our Cottage run?

---

403 *s.d.* [*Going.*] Q2–3, F, D (~. Q1; [~ₐ Q4.
404 *s.d. Going*] Q3–4, F, D; *going* Q1–2.   421 *Palm.*] Q2–4, F, D; ~ₐ Q1.

While winter-winds were whistling loud without,
Our chearful hearth was circled round about:
With strokes in ashes Maids their Lovers drew;
And still you fell to me, and I to you.
    Leon. When Love did of my heart possession take,
I was so young, my soul was scarce awake:
I cannot tell when first I thought you fair;
430 But suck'd in Love, insensibly as Ayre.
    Palm. I know too well when first my love began,
When, at our Wake, you for the Chaplet ran:
Then I was made the Lady of the May,
And, with the Garland, at the Goal did stay:
Still, as you ran, I kept you full in view;
I hop'd, and wish'd, and ran, methought, for you.
As you came near, I hastily did rise,
And stretch'd my arm out-right, that held the prize.
The custom was to kiss whom I should crown:
440 You kneel'd; and, in my lap, your head laid down.
I blush'd, and blush'd, and did the kiss delay:
At last, my Subjects forc'd me to obey;
But, when I gave the Crown, and then the kiss,
I scarce had breath to say, Take that————and this.
    Leon. I felt, the while, a pleasing kind of smart;
The kiss went, tingling, to my very heart.
When it was gone, the sense of it did stay; ⎫
The sweetness cling'd upon my lips all day, ⎬
Like drops of Honey, loath to fall away. ⎭
450   *Palm.* Life, like a prodigal, gave all his store
To my first youth, and now can give no more.
You are a Prince; and, in that high degree,
No longer must converse with humble me.
    Leon. 'Twas to my loss the Gods that title gave;
A Tyrant's Son is doubly born a Slave:
He gives a Crown; but, to prevent my life
From being happy, loads it with a Wife.
    Palm. Speak quickly; what have you resolv'd to do?
    Leon. To keep my faith inviolate to you.
460 He threatens me with exile, and with shame,

To lose my birth-right, and a Prince his name;
But there's a blessing which he did not mean,
To send me back to Love and You again.
    Palm. Why was not I a Princess for your sake?
But Heav'n no more such miracles can make:
And, since That cannot, This must never be;
You shall not lose a Crown for love of me.
Live happy, and a nobler choice pursue;
I shall complain of Fate; but not of you.
470   *Leon.* Can you so easily without me live?
Or could you take the counsel which you give?
Were you a Princess would you not be true?
    Palm. I would; but cannot merit it from you.
    Leon. Did you not merit, as you do, my heart;
Love gives esteem; and then it gives desert.
But if I basely could forget my vow,
Poor helpless Innocence, what would you do?
    Palm. In Woods, and Plains, where first my love began,
There would I live, retir'd from faithless man:
480 I'd sit all day within some lonely shade,
Or that close Arbour which your hands have made:
I'd search the Groves, and ev'ry Tree, to find
Where you had carv'd our names upon the rind:
Your Hook, your Scrip, all that was yours, I'd keep,
And lay 'em by me when I went to sleep.
Thus would I live: and Maidens, when I die,
Upon my Hearse white True-love-knots should tie:
And thus my Tomb should be inscrib'd above,
Here the forsaken Virgin rests from love.
490   *Leon.* Think not that time or fate shall e'r divide
Those hearts, which Love and mutual Vows have ty'd:
But we must part; farewell, my Love.
    Palm. ————————————————Till when?
    Leon. Till the next age of hours we meet agen.
Mean time————we may
When near each other we in publick stand,
Contrive to catch a look, or steal a hand:

———————

465 Heav'n] Q2–4, F, D; Heav'en Q1.

Fancy will every touch, and glance improve;
And draw the most spirituous parts of Love.
Our souls sit close, and silently within;
500 And their own Web from their own Intrals spin.
And when eyes meet far off, our sense is such,
That, Spider-like, we feel the tender'st touch.   [*Exeunt.*

ACT III.   SCENE I.

Enter Rhodophil, *meeting* Doralice *and* Artemis.
Rhodophil *and* Doralice *embrace.*

Rho. My own dear heart!
Dor. My own true love!   [*She starts back.*
I had forgot my self to be so kind; indeed I am very angry with
you, dear; you are come home an hour after you appointed: If
you had staid a minute longer, I was just considering, whether
I should stab, hang, or drown my self.   [*Embracing him.*
Rho. Nothing but the King's business could have hinder'd
me; and I was so vext, that I was just laying down my Commission, rather then have fail'd my Dear.   [*Kissing her hand.*
10 *Arte.* Why, this is love as it should be, betwixt Man and Wife:
such another Couple would bring Marriage into fashion again.
But is it always thus betwixt you?
Rho. Always thus! this is nothing. I tell you there is not such
a pair of Turtles in all *Sicily;* there is such an eternal Cooing
and kissing betwixt us, that indeed it is scandalous before civil
company.
Dor. Well, if I had imagin'd I should have been this fond
fool, I would never have marri'd the man I lov'd: I marri'd to
be happy; and have made my self miserable, by over-loving.
20 Nay, and now, my case is desperate; for I have been marry'd
above these two years, and find my self every day worse and worse
in love: nothing but madness can be the end on't.
Arte. Doat on, to the extremity, and you are happy.
Dor. He deserves so infinitely much, that, the truth is, there

---

17   imagin'd] Q4; ∼, Q1–3, F, D.

can be no doating in the matter; but to love well, I confess, is a work that pays it self: 'tis telling gold, and after taking it for ones pains.

Rho. By that I should be a very covetous person; for I am ever pulling out my money, and putting it into my pocket again.

30 *Dor.* O dear *Rhodophil!*

Rho. O sweet *Doralice!*   *[Embracing each other.*

Arte. (Aside) Nay, I am resolv'd, I'll never interrupt Lovers: I'll leave 'em as happy as I found 'em.   *[Steals away.*

Rho. What, is she gone?   *[Looking up.*

Dor. Yes; and without taking leave.

Rho. Then there's enough for this time. *[Parting from her.*

Dor. Yes sure, the Scene's done, I take it.

> *They walk contrary ways on the Stage; he, with his hands in his pocket, whistling: she, singing a dull melancholly Tune.*

Rho. Pox o' your dull tune, a man can't think for you.

Dor. Pox o' your damn'd whistling; you can neither be com-
40 pany to me your self, nor leave me to the freedom of my own fancy.

Rho. Well, thou art the most provoking Wife!

Dor. Well, thou art the dullest Husband, thou art never to be provok'd.

Rho. I was never thought dull, till I marry'd thee; and now thou hast made an old knife of me, thou hast whetted me so long, till I have no edge left.

Dor. I see you are in the Husbands fashion; you reserve all your good humours for your Mistresses, and keep your ill for your
50 wives.

Rho. Prethee leave me to my own cogitations; I am thinking over all my sins, to find for which of them it was I marry'd thee.

Dor. Whatever your sin was, mine's the punishment.

Rho. My comfort is, thou art not immortal; and when that blessed, that divine day comes, of thy departure, I'm resolv'd I'll make one Holy-day more in the Almanack, for thy sake.

Dor. Ay, you had need make a Holy-day for me, for I am sure you have made me a Martyr.

---

36 time.] Q2–4, F, D; ~ˌ Q1.   44 provok'd.] Q2–4, F, D; ~, Q1.

Rho. Then, setting my victorious foot upon thy head, in the
60 first hour of thy silence, (that is, the first hour thou art dead, for
I despair of it before) I will swear by thy Ghost, an oath as terrible to me, as *Styx* is to the Gods, never more to be in danger of
the Banes of Matrimony.

Dor. And I am resolv'd to marry the very same day thou dy'st,
if it be but to show how little I'm concern'd for thee.

Rho. Prethee, *Doralice,* why do we quarrel thus a-days? ha? this
is but a kind of Heathenish life, and does not answer the ends of
marriage. If I have err'd, propound what reasonable atonement
may be made, before we sleep, and I shall not be refractory: but
70 withall consider, I have been marry'd these three years, and be
not too tyrannical.

Dor. What should you talk of a peace abed, when you can give
no security for performance of Articles?

Rho. Then, since we must live together, and both of us stand
upon our terms, as to matter of dying first, let us make our selves
as merry as we can with our misfortunes.

Why there's the devil on't! if thou couldst make my enjoying
thee but a little less easie, or a little more unlawful, thou shouldst
see, what a Termagant Lover I would prove. I have taken such
80 pains to enjoy thee, *Doralice,* that I have fanci'd thee all the fine
women in the Town, to help me out. But now there's none left
for me to think on, my imagination is quite jaded. Thou art a
Wife, and thou wilt be a Wife, and I can make thee another no
longer.   [*Exit* Rhodophil.

Dor. Well, since thou art a Husband, and wilt be a Husband,
I'll try if I can find out another! 'Tis a pretty time we Women
have on't, to be made Widows, while we are marry'd. Our Husbands think it reasonable to complain, that we are the same, and
the same to them, when we have more reason to complain, that
90 they are not the same to us. Because they cannot feed on one dish,
therefore we must be starv'd. 'Tis enough that they have a sufficient Ordinary provided, and a Table ready spread for 'em: if
they cannot fall to and eat heartily, the fault is theirs; and 'tis
pity, me-thinks, that the good creature should be lost, when many
a poor sinner would be glad on't.

_____

93   to] Q4; too Q1–3, F, D.

Enter Melantha, *and* Artemis *to her.*

Mel. Dear, my dear, pity me; I am so *chagrin* to day, and have had the most signal affront at Court! I went this afternoon to do my devoir to Princess *Amalthea,* found her, convers'd with her, and help'd to make her court some half an hour; after which,
100 she went to take the ayr, chose out two Ladies to go with her, that came in after me, and left me most barbarously behind her.

Arte. You are the less to be piti'd, *Melantha,* because you subject your self to these affronts, by coming perpetually to Court, where you have no business nor employment.

Mel. I declare, I had rather of the two, be *railly'd,* nay, *mal traittée* at Court, then be Deifi'd in the Town: for, assuredly, nothing can be so *ridicule,* as a meer Town-Lady.

Dor. Especially at Court. How I have seen 'em crowd and sweat in the Drawing-room, on a Holiday-night! for that's their time
110 to swarm, and invade the Presence. O, how they catch at a bow, or any little salute from a Courtier, to make show of their acquaintance! and rather then be thought to be quite unknown, they court'sie to one another; but they take true pains to come near the Circle, and press and peep upon the Princess, to write Letters into the Countrey how she was dress'd, while the Ladies that stand about make their court to her with abusing them.

Arte. These are sad truths, *Melantha;* and therefore I would e'en advise you to quit the Court, and live either wholly in the Town; or, if you like not that, in the Countrey.

120 *Dor.* In the Countrey! nay, that's to fall beneath the Town; for they live there upon our offals here: their entertainment of wit, is onely the remembrance of what they had when they were last in Town; they live this year upon the last years knowledge, as their Cattel do all night, by chewing the Cud of what they eat in the afternoon.

Mel. And they tell, for news, such unlikely stories; a letter from one of us is such a present to 'em, that the poor souls wait for the Carriers-day with such devotion, that they cannot sleep the night before.

---

96   *chagrin*] chagrin Q1–4, **F, D.**

130 *Arte.* No more then I can, the night before I am to go a journey.

Dor. Or I, before I am to try on a new Gown.

Mel. A Song that's stale here, will be new there a twelve-moneth hence; and if a man of the Town by chance come amongst 'em, he's reverenced for teaching 'em the Tune.

Dor. A friend of mine, who makes Songs sometimes, came lately out of the West, and vow'd he was so put out of coun-t'nance with a Song of his; for at the first Countrey-Gentleman's he visited, he saw three Tailors cross-leg'd upon the Table in the
140 Hall, who were tearing out as loud as ever they could sing,

————*After the pangs of a desperate Lover,* &c.

and all that day he heard nothing else, but the Daughters of the house and the Maids, humming it over in every corner, and the Father whistling it.

Arte. Indeed I have observ'd of my self, that when I am out of Town but a fortnight, I am so humble, that I would receive a Letter from my Tailor or Mercer for a favour.

Mel. When I have been at grass in the Summer and am new come up again, methinks I'm to be turn'd into *ridicule* by all that
150 see me; but when I have been once or twice at Court, I begin to value my self again, and to despise my Countrey-acquaintance.

Arte. There are places where all people may be ador'd, and we ought to know our selves so well as to chuse 'em.

Dor. That's very true; your little Courtiers wife, who speaks to the King but once a moneth, need but go to a Town-Lady, and there she may vapour, and cry, *The King and I,* at every word. Your Town-Lady, who is laugh'd at in the Circle, takes her Coach into the City, and there she's call'd your Honour, and has a Banquet from the Merchants Wife, whom she laughs at for her kind-
160 ness. And, as for my finical Cit, she removes but to her Countrey-house, and there insults over the Countrey Gentlewoman that never comes up; who treats her with Frumity and Custard, and

136 *Dor.*] Q2–4, F, D; *Dor*ͺQ1.
141 &c.] Q3–4, F, D; &c. Q1–2.
155 Town-Lady,] Q3–4; ∼; Q1, F, D; ∼ͺ Q2.

opens her dear bottle of *Mirabilis* beside, for a Jill-glass of it at parting.

Arte. At last, I see, we shall leave *Melantha* where we found her; for, by your description of the Town and Countrey, they are become more dreadful to her, then the Court, where she was affronted. But you forget we are to wait on the Princess *Amalthea.* Come, *Doralice.*

Dor. Farewell, *Melantha.*

Mel. Adieu, my dear.

Arte. You are out of charity with her, and therefore I shall not give your service.

Mel. Do not omit it, I beseech you; for I have such a *tendre* for the Court, that I love it ev'n from the Drawing-room to the Lobby, and can never be *rebutée* by any usage. But, hark you, my Dears, one thing I had forgot of great concernment.

Dor. Quickly then, we are in haste.

Mel. Do not call it my service, that's too vulgar; but do my *baise mains* to the Princess *Amalthea; that is *Spirituelle!*

Dor. To do you service then, we will *prendre* the *Carrosse* to Court, and do your *Baise mains* to the Princess *Amalthea,* in your phrase *Spirituellé.*   [*Exeunt* Artemis *and* Doralice.

Enter Philotis, *with a Paper in her hand.*

Mel. O, are you there, Minion? And, well, are not you a most precious damsel, to retard all my visits for want of language, when you know you are paid so well for furnishing me with new words for my daily conversation? Let me die, if I have not run the *risque* already, to speak like one of the vulgar; and if I have one phrase left in all my store that is not thrid-bare & *usé,* and fit for nothing but to be thrown to Peasants.

Phil. Indeed, Madam, I have been very diligent in my vocation; but you have so drain'd all the *French* Plays and Romances, that they are not able to supply you with words for your daily expences.

---

174   *tendre*] tender Q1–4, F, D.
188   *risque*] risque Q1–4, F, D.
189   & *usé*] & *use* Q1; & *usè* Q2–3, D; & *usé* Q4, F.

Mel. Drain'd? what a word's there! *Épuisée,* you sot you. Come, produce your morning's work.

    Phil. 'Tis here, Madam.   [*Shows the Paper.*

    Mel. O, my *Venus!* fourteen or fifteen words to serve me a whole day! Let me die, at this rate I cannot last till night. Come,
200 read your words: twenty to one half of 'em will not pass muster neither.

    Phil. Sottises.   [*Reads.*

    Mel. Sottises: bon. That's an excellent word to begin withall: as for example; He, or she said a thousand *Sottises* to me. Proceed.

    Phil. Figure: as what a *figure* of a man is there! *Naive,* and *Naiveté.*

    Mel. Naive! as how?

    Phil. Speaking of a thing that was naturally said; It was so
210 *naive:* or such an innocent piece of simplicity; 'twas such a *naiveté.*

    Mel. Truce with your interpretations: make haste.

    Phil. Foible, Chagrin, Grimace, Embarrasse, Double entendre, Équivoque, Éclaircissement, Suitte, Bévue, Façon, Panchant, Coup d'étourdy, and *Ridicule.*

    Mel. Hold, hold; how did they begin?

    Phil. They began at *Sottises,* and ended *en Ridicule.*

    Mel. Now give me your Paper in my hand, and hold you my Glass, while I practise my postures for the day.

                   [*Melantha laughs in the Glass.*
220 How does that laugh become my face?

    Phil. Sovereignly well, Madam.

    Mel. Sovereignly! Let me die, that's not amiss. That word shall

---

195 *Drain'd*] Drain'd Q1–4, F, D.   195 *Épuisée*] Epuisée Q1–4, F, D.
200 words] works Q1–4, F, D.   206 *a figure*] a figure Q1–4, F, D.
207 *Naiveté*] Q3–4, F, D; *Naivetè* Q1–2.
211 *naiveté*] Q2–3, F, D; *naivetè* Q1, Q4.
214 *Équivoque*] *Equivoque* Q1–4, F, D.
214 *Éclaircissement*] *Esclaircissement* Q1–4, F; *Eclaircissement* D.
214 *Suitte*] F; *Suittè* Q1–2, D; *Suitté* Q3–4.
214 *Bévue*] *Beveue* Q1–4, F, D.
214 *Façon*] *Facòn* Q1–4, D; *Facon* F.
215 *étourdy*] *etourdy* Q1–4, F, D.

not be yours; I'll invent it, and bring it up my self: my new
Point Gorget shall be yours upon't: not a word of the word, I
charge you.

Phil. I am dumb, Madam.

Mel. That glance, how sutes it with my face?

                          [*Looking in the Glass again.*

Phil. 'Tis so *languissant.*

Mel. Languissant! that word shall be mine too, and my last
230 *Indian*-Gown thine for't.

That sigh?   [*Looks again.*

Phil. 'Twill make many a man sigh, Madam. 'Tis a meer *In-
cendiary.*

Mel. Take my Guimp Petticoat for that truth. If thou hast
more of these phrases, let me die but I could give away all my
Wardrobe, and go naked for 'em.

Phil. Go naked? then you would be a *Venus,* Madam. O *Jupiter!* what had I forgot? this Paper was given me by *Rhodophil's*
Page.

240   *Mel. (Reading the Letter)*————Beg the favour from you
————Gratifie my passion————so far————assignation————
in the Grotto————behind the Terras————clock this evening
————Well, for the *Billets doux* there's no man in *Sicily* must
dispute with *Rhodophil;* they are so *French,* so *gallant,* and so
tendre, that I cannot resist the temptation of the assignation.
Now go you away, *Philotis;* it imports me to practise what I shall
say to my Servant when I meet him.   [*Exit* Philotis.
Rhodophil, you'll wonder at my assurance to meet you here; let
me die, I am so out of breath with coming, that I can render you
250 no reason of it. Then he will make this *repartee;* Madam, I have
no reason to accuse you for that which is so great a favour to me.
Then I reply, But why have you drawn me to this solitary place?
let me die but I am apprehensive of some violence from you.
Then, says he; Solitude, Madam, is most fit for Lovers; but by
this fair hand————Nay, now I vow you're rude. Sir. O fie, fie,

230 *Indian*-Gown] D; *Indian-Gown* Q1-4, F.
231 *s.d. again.*] Q3-4, F, D; ~: Q1-2.
240-241 you————] Q2-4, F; ~.———— Q1, D.

fie; I hope you'l be honourable?————You'd laugh at me if I
should, Madam————What do you mean to throw me down
thus? Ah me! ah, ah, ah.

Enter Polydamas, Leonidas, *and Guards.*

　　O *Venus!* the King and Court. Let me die but I fear they have
260　found my *foible,* and will turn me into *ridicule.* [*Exit running.*
　　Leon. Sir, I beseech you.
　　Poly. —————————Do not urge my patience.
　　Leon. I'll not deny
But what your Spies inform'd you of, is true:
I love the fair *Palmyra;* but I lov'd her
Before I knew your title to my bloud.

Enter Palmyra, *guarded.*

　　See, here she comes; and looks, amid'st her Guards,
Like a weak Dove under the Falcon's gripe.
O heav'n, I cannot bear it.
　　Poly. —————————Maid, come hither.
Have you presum'd so far, as to receive
270　My Son's affection?
　　Palm. Alas, what shall I answer? to confess it
Will raise a blush upon a Virgin's face;
Yet I was ever taught 'twas base to lie.
　　Poly. You've been too bold, and you must love no more.
　　Palm. Indeed I must; I cannot help my love;
I was so tender when I took the bent,
That now I grow that way.
　　Poly. He is a Prince; and you are meanly born.
　　Leon. Love either finds equality, or makes it:
280　Like death, he knows no difference in degrees,
But plains, and levels all.
　　Palm. Alas, I had not render'd up my heart,
Had he not lov'd me first; but he prefer'd me
Above the Maidens of my age and rank;
Still shun'd their company, and still sought mine;

I was not won by gifts, yet still he gave;
And all his gifts, though small, yet spoke his love.
He pick'd the earliest Strawberries in Woods,
The cluster'd Filberds, and the purple Grapes:
290 He taught a prating Stare to speak my name;
And when he found a Nest of Nightingales,
Or callow Linnets, he would show 'em me,
And let me take 'em out.
    Poly. This is a little Mistris, meanly born,
Fit onely for a Prince his vacant hours,
And then, to laugh at her simplicity,
Not fix a passion there. Now hear my sentence.
    Leon. Remember, ere you give it, 'tis pronounc'd
Against us both.
300   *Poly.* First, in her hand
There shall be plac'd a Player's painted Sceptre,
And, on her head, a gilded Pageant Crown;
Thus shall she go,
With all the Boys attending on her Triumph:
That done, be put alone into a Boat,
With bread and water onely for three days,
So on the Sea she shall be set adrift,
And who relieves her, dies.
    Palm. I onely beg that you would execute
310 The last part first: let me be put to Sea;
The bread and water, for my three days life,
I give you back, I would not live so long;
But let me scape the shame.
    Leon. ————————————Look to me, Piety;
And you, O Gods, look to my piety:
Keep me from saying that which misbecomes a son;
But let me die before I see this done.
    Poly. If you for ever will abjure her sight,
I can be yet a father; she shall live.
    Leon. Hear, O you Pow'rs, is this to be a father?
320 I see 'tis all my happiness and quiet

313 ————Look] ∧~ Q1–4, F, D.
313–314 Piety; / And] Piety; and Q1–4, F, D.

You aim at, Sir; and take 'em:
I will not save ev'n my *Palmyra's* life
At that ignoble price; but I'll die with her.
    Palm. So had I done by you,
Had Fate made me a Princess: Death, methinks,
Is not a terrour now;
He is not fierce, or grim, but fawns, and sooths me,
And slides along, like *Cleopatra's* Aspick,
Off'ring his service to my troubled breast.
330   *Leon.* Begin what you have purpos'd when you please,
Lead her to scorn, your triumph shall be doubled.
As holy Priests
In pity go with dying malefactours,
So will I share her shame.
    Poly. You shall not have your will so much; first part 'em,
Then execute your office.
    Leon. ————————No; I'll die   [*Draws his sword.*
In her defence.
    Palm. ———Ah, hold, and pull not on
A curse, to make me worthy of my death:
Do not by lawless force oppose your Father,
340 Whom you have too much disobey'd for me.
    Leon. Here, take it, Sir, and with it, pierce my heart:
        [*Presenting his sword to his father upon his knees.*
You have done more, in taking my *Palmyra.*
You are my Father, therefore I submit.
    Poly. Keep him from any thing he may design
Against his life, whil'st the first fury lasts;
And now perform what I commanded you.
    Leon. In vain; if sword and poison be deni'd me,
I'll hold my breath and die.
    Palm. Farewell, my last *Leonidas;* yet live,
350 I charge you live, till you believe me dead.
I cannot die in peace, if you die first.
If life's a blessing, you shall have it last.
    Poly. Go on with her, and lead him after me.

    Enter Argaleon *hastily, with* Hermogenes.

Arga. I bring you, Sir, such news as must amaze you,
And such as will prevent you from an action
Which would have rendred all your life unhappy.
                           [Hermogenes *kneels.*
  Poly. Hermogenes, you bend your knees in vain,
My doom's already past.
  Her. I kneel not for *Palmyra,* for I know
360 She will not need my pray'rs; but for my self:
With a feign'd tale I have abus'd your ears,
And therefore merit death; but since, unforc'd,
I first accuse my self, I hope your mercy.
  Poly. Haste to explain your meaning.
  Her. Then, in few words, *Palmyra* is your daughter.
  Poly. How can I give belief to this Impostor?
He who has once abus'd me, often may.
I'l hear no more.
  Arga. ————For your own sake, you must.
  Her. A parent's love (for I confess my crime)
370 Mov'd me to say, *Leonidas* was yours;
But when I heard *Palmyra* was to die,
The fear of guiltless bloud so stung my conscience,
That I resolv'd, ev'n with my shame, to save
Your daughter's life.
  Poly. But how can I be certain, but that interest,
Which mov'd you first to say your son was mine,
Does not now move you too, to save your daughter?
  Her. You had but then my word; I bring you now
Authentick testimonies. Sir, in short,
               [*Delivers on his knees a Jewel, and a Letter.*
380 If this will not convince you, let me suffer.
  Poly. I know this Jewel well; 'twas once my mothers,
                    [*Looking first on the Jewel.*
Which, marrying, I presented to my wife.
And this, O this, is my *Eudocia's* hand.
This was the pledge of love given to Eudocia,   [*Reads.*
Who, dying, to her young Palmyra *leaves it:*
And this when you, my dearest Lord, receive,

356+   *s.d. as in D; after l. 357 in Q1–4; on l. 357 in F.*

Own her, and think on me, dying Eudocia.
Take it; 'tis well there is no more to read,   [*To* Argaleon.
My eyes grow full, and swim in their own light.
                                        [*He embraces* Palmyra.

390   *Palm.* I fear, Sir, this is your intended Pageant.
You sport your self at poor *Palmyra's* cost;
But if you think to make me proud,
Indeed I cannot be so: I was born
With humble thoughts, and lowly, like my birth.
A real fortune could not make me haughty,
Much less a feign'd.
        Poly. _____This was her mother's temper.
I have too much deserv'd thou shouldst suspect
That I am not thy father; but my love
Shall henceforth show I am. Behold my eyes,

400 And see a father there begin to flow:
This is not feign'd, *Palmyra.*
        Palm. I doubt no longer, Sir; you are a King,
And cannot lie: falshood's a vice too base
To find a room in any Royal breast;
I know, in spight of my unworthiness,
I am your child; for when you would have kill'd me,
Methought I lov'd you then.
        Arga. Sir, we forget the Prince *Leonidas,*
His greatness should not stand neglected thus.

410   *Poly.* Guards, you may now retire: Give him his sword,
And leave him free.
        Leon. Then the first use I make of liberty
Shall be, with your permission, mighty Sir,
To pay that reverence to which Nature binds me.
                                    [*Kneels to* Hermogenes.
        Arga. Sure you forget your birth, thus to misplace
This act of your obedience; you should kneel
To nothing but to Heav'n, and to a King.
        Leon. I never shall forget what Nature owes,
Nor be asham'd to pay it; though my father

420 Be not a King, I know him brave and honest,

414+   *s.d. Kneels*] Q3–4, F, D; *kneels* Q1–2.

And well deserving of a worthier son.
    Poly. He bears it gallantly.
    Leon. Why would you not instruct me, Sir, before [*To* Herm.
Where I should place my duty?
From which, if ignorance have made me swerve,
I beg your pardon for an erring son.
    Palm. I almost grieve I am a Princess, since
It makes him lose a Crown.
    Leon. And next, to you, my King, thus low I kneel,
430 T' implore your mercy; if in that small time
I had the honour to be thought your son,
I pay'd not strict obedience to your will:
I thought, indeed, I should not be compell'd,
But thought it as your son; so what I took
In duty from you, I restor'd in courage;
Because your son should not be forc'd.
    Poly. You have my pardon for it.
    Leon. To you, fair Princess, I congratulate
Your birth; of which I ever thought you worthy:
440 And give me leave to add, that I am proud
The Gods have pick'd me out to be the man
By whose dejected fate yours is to rise;
Because no man could more desire your fortune,
Or franklier part with his to make you great.
    Palm. I know the King, though you are not his son,
Will still regard you as my Foster-brother,
And so conduct you downward from a Throne,
By slow degrees, so unperceiv'd and soft,
That it may seem no fall: or, if it be,
450 May Fortune lay a bed of down beneath you.
    Poly. He shall be rank'd with my Nobility,
And kept from scorn by a large pension giv'n him.
    Leon. You are all great and Royal in your gifts;   [*Bowing.*
But at the Donor's feet I lay 'em down:
Should I take riches from you, it would seem
As I did want a soul to bear that poverty
To which the Gods design'd my humble birth:
And should I take your Honours without merit,

It would appear, I wanted manly courage
460 To hope 'em, in your service, from my sword.
    Poly. Still brave, and like your self.
The Court shall shine this night in its full splendor,
And celebrate this new discovery.
Argaleon, lead my daughter: as we go
I shall have time to give her my commands,
In which you are concern'd.   [*Exeunt all but* Leonidas.
    Leon. Methinks I do not want
That huge long train of fawning followers,
That swept a furlong after me.
470 'Tis true, I am alone;
So was the Godhead ere he made the world,
And better serv'd Himself, then serv'd by Nature.
And yet I have a Soul
Above this humble fate. I could command,
Love to do good; give largely to true merit;
All that a King should do: But though these are not
My Province, I have Scene enough within
To exercise my vertue.
All that a heart, so fix'd as mine, can move,
480 Is, that my niggard fortune starves my love.   [*Exit.*

SCENE II.

Palamede *and* Doralice *meet: she with a Book in her hand,*
seems to start at sight of him.

Dor. 'Tis a strange thing that no warning will serve your turn;
and that no retirement will secure me from your impertinent
addresses! Did not I tell you, that I was to be private here at my
devotions?
    Pala. Yes; and you see I have observ'd my Cue exactly: I am
come to releive you from them. Come, shut up, shut up your
Book; the man's come who is to supply all your necessities.
    Dor. Then, it seems, you are so impudent to think it was an

assignation? this, I warrant, was your lewd interpretation of my
10 innocent meaning.

Pala. *Venus* forbid that I should harbour so unreasonable a
thought of a fair young Lady, that you should lead me hither
into temptation. I confess I might think indeed it was a kind of
honourable challenge, to meet privately without Seconds, and
decide the difference betwixt the two Sexes; but heaven forgive
me if I thought amiss.

Dor. You thought too, I'll lay my life on't, that you might as
well make love to me, as my Husband does to your Mistris.

Pala. I was so unreasonable to think so too.

20 *Dor.* And then you wickedly inferr'd, that there was some
justice in the revenge of it: or at least but little injury; for a
man to endeavour to enjoy that, which he accounts a blessing,
and which is not valu'd as it ought by the dull possessour. Confess your wickedness, did you not think so?

Pala. I confess I was thinking so, as fast as I could; but you
think so much before me, that you will let me think nothing.

Dor. 'Tis the very thing that I design'd: I have forestall'd all
your arguments, and left you without a word more, to plead for
mercy. If you have any thing farther to offer, ere Sentence pass
30 ———Poor Animal, I brought you hither onely for my diversion.

Pala. That you may have, if you'll make use of me the right
way; but I tell thee, woman, I am now past talking.

Dor. But it may be, I came hither to hear what fine things you
could say for your self.

Pala. You would be very angry, to my knowledge, if I should
lose so much time to say many of 'em———By this hand you
would———

Dor. Fie, *Palamede,* I am a woman of honour.

40 *Pala.* I see you are; you have kept touch with your assignation: and before we part, you shall find that I am a man of honour———yet I have one scruple of conscience———

Dor. I warrant you will not want some naughty argument or
other to satisfie your self———I hope you are afraid of betraying your friend?

Pala. Of betraying my friend! I am more afraid of being be-

tray'd by you to my friend. You women now are got into the way
of telling first your selves: a man who has any care of his reputation will be loath to trust it with you.

    50   *Dor.* O you charge your faults upon our Sex: you men are like
Cocks, you never make love, but you clap your wings, and crow
when you have done.

    Pala. Nay, rather you women are like Hens; you never lay, but
you cackle an hour after, to discover your Nest————But I'll
venture it for once.

    Dor. To convince you that you are in the wrong, I'll retire
into the dark Grotto, to my devotion, and make so little noise,
that it shall be impossible for you to find me.

    Pala. But if I find you————

    60   *Dor.* Ay, if you find me————But I'll put you to search in
more corners then you imagine.

                               [She runs in, and he after her.

              Enter Rhodophil *and* Melantha.

    Mel. Let me die, but this solitude, and that Grotto are scan-
dalous; I'll go no further; besides, you have a sweet Lady of your
own.

    Rho. But a sweet Mistris, now and then, makes my sweet Lady
so much more sweet.

    Mel. I hope you will not force me?

    Rho. But I will, if you desire it.

    Pala. (Within) Where the devil are you, Madam? S'death, I
    70 begin to be weary of this hide and seek: if you stay a little longer,
till the fit's over, I'll hide in my turn, and put you to the finding me.

        He enters, and sees Rhodophil *and* Melantha.

How! *Rhodophil* and my Mistris!

    Mel. My servant to apprehend me! this is *Surprenant au
dernier.*

————————

72+   s.d. *He*] Q4, F; [∼ Q1–3, D (*s.d. flush right in Q1–4, run into speech in D*).

Rho. I must on; there's nothing but impudence can help me out.

Pala. Rhodophil, How came you hither in so good company?

Rho. As you see, *Palamede;* an effect of pure friendship; I was
80 not able to live without you.

Pala. But what makes my Mistris with you?

Rho. Why, I heard you were here alone, and could not in civility but bring her to you.

Mel. You'll pardon the effects of a passion which I may now
avow for you, if it transported me beyond the rules of *bien
seance.*

Pala. But who told you I was here? they that told you that,
may tell you more, for ought I know.

Rho. O, for that matter, we had intelligence.

90 *Pala.* But let me tell you, we came hither so very privately,
that you could not trace us.

Rho. Us? what us? you are alone.

Pala. Us! the devil's in me for mistaking: me, I meant. Or us;
that is, you are me, or I you, as we are friends: that's us.

Dor. Palamede, Palamede.   [*Within.*

Rho. I should know that voice. Who's within there, that calls
you?

Pala. Faith I can't imagine; I believe the place is haunted.

Dor. Palamede, Palamede, All-cocks hidden.   [*Within.*

100 *Pala.* Lord, lord, what shall I do? Well, dear friend, to let you
see I scorn to be jealous, and that I dare trust my Mistris with
you, take her back, for I would not willingly have her frighted,
and I am resolv'd to see who's there; I'll not be danted with a
Bug-bear, that's certain: prethee dispute it not, it shall be so;
nay, do not put me to swear, but go quickly: there's an effect of
pure friendship for you now.

Enter Doralice, *and looks amaz'd, seeing them.*

Rho. Doralice! I am thunder-struck to see you here.

Pala. So am I! quite thunder-struck. Was it you that call'd me
within? (I must be impudent.)

96   voice. Who's] voice? who's Q1–4, F, D.

110 *Rho.* How came you hither, Spouse?

Pala. Ay, how came you hither? And, which is more, how could you be here without my knowledge?

Dor. (*To her husband*) O, Gentleman, have I caught you i'faith? have I broke forth in ambush upon you? I thought my suspicions would prove true.

Rho. Suspicions! this is very fine, Spouse! Prethee what suspicions?

Dor. O, you feign ignorance: why, of you and *Melantha;* here have I staid these two hours, waiting with all the rage of a pas-

120 sionate, loving wife, but infinitely jealous, to take you two in the manner; for hither I was certain you would come.

Rho. But you are mistaken, Spouse, in the occasion; for we came hither on purpose to find *Palamede,* on intelligence he was gone before.

Pala. I'll be hang'd then if the same party who gave you intelligence, I was here, did not tell your wife you would come hither: now I smell the malice on't on both sides.

Dor. Was it so, think you? nay, then, I'll confess my part of the malice too. As soon as ever I spi'd my husband and *Melantha*

130 come together, I had a strange temptation to make him jealous in revenge; and that made me call *Palamede, Palamede,* as though there had been an Intrigue between us.

Mel. Nay, I avow, there was an apparence of an Intrigue between us too.

Pala. To see how things will come about!

Rho. And was it onely thus, my dear *Doralice?*   [*Embraces.*

Dor. And did I wrong none, *Rhodophil,* with a false suspicion?   [*Embracing him.*

Pala. (*Aside*) Now am I confident we had all four the same de-

140 sign: 'tis a pretty odd kind of game this, where each of us plays for double stakes: this is just thrust and parry with the same motion; I am to get his Wife, and yet to guard my own Mistris. But I am vilely suspitious, that, while I conquer in the Right Wing, I shall be routed in the Left: for both our women will certainly betray their party, because they are each of them for

---

114   i'faith?] ~! Q1–4, F, D.   114   you?] ~! Q1–4, F, D.
116–117   *printed as verse in Q1–4, F* (Spouse! / Prethee).

gaining of two, as well as we; and I much fear,
  If their necessities and ours were known,
  They have more need of two, then we of one.

[Exeunt, embracing one another.

ACT IV.   SCENE I.

Enter Leonidas, *musing,* Amalthea *following him.*

Amal. Yonder he is, and I must speak, or die;
And yet 'tis death to speak; yet he must know
I have a passion for him, and may know it
With a less blush; because to offer it
To his low fortunes, shows I lov'd, before,
His person, not his greatness.
  Leon. First scorn'd, and now commanded from the Court!
The King is good; but he is wrought to this
By proud *Argaleon's* malice.
10 What more disgrace can Love and Fortune joyn
T' inflict upon one man? I cannot now
Behold my dear *Palmyra:* she, perhaps, too
Is grown asham'd of a mean ill-plac'd love.
  Amal. Assist me, *Venus,* for I tremble when   [*Aside.*
I am to speak, but I must force my self.
Sir, I would crave but one short minute with you,   [*To him.*
And some few words.
  Leon. ——————The proud *Argaleon's* sister!   [*Aside.*
  Amal. Alas, it will not out; shame stops my mouth.   [*Aside.*
Pardon my errour, Sir, I was mistaken,   [*To him.*
20 And took you for another.
  Leon. In spight of all his guards, I'll see *Palmyra;*   [*Aside.*
Though meanly born, I have a Kingly Soul yet.
  Amal. I stand upon a precipice, where fain   [*Aside.*
I would retire, but Love still thrusts me on:
Now I grow bolder, and will speak to him.

---

5   lov'd,] ∼∧ Q1–4, F, D.
19   mistaken, [*To him.*] mistaken, Q1–4, F, D.

Sir, 'tis indeed to you that I would speak,   [*To him.*
And if———

 Leon. O, you are sent to scorn my fortunes;
Your Sex and Beauty are your priviledge;
But should your Brother———

30 *Amal.* Now he looks angry, and I dare not speak.   [*Aside.*
I had some business with you, Sir,   [*To him.*
But 'tis not worth your knowledge.

 Leon. Then 'twill be charity to let me mourn
My griefs alone, for I am much disorder'd.

 Amal. 'Twill be more charity to mourn 'em with you:
Heav'n knows I pity you.

 Leon. ————Your pity, Madam,
Is generous, but 'tis unavailable.

 Amal. You know not till 'tis tri'd.
Your sorrows are no secret; you have lost
40 A Crown, and Mistris.

 Leon. ————Are not these enough?
Hang two such weights on any other soul,
And see if it can bear 'em.

 Amal. More; you are banish'd, by my Brother's means,
And ne'r must hope again to see your Princess;
Except as Pris'ners view fair Walks and Streets,
And careless Passengers going by their grates,
To make 'em feel the want of liberty.
But, worse then all,
The King this morning has injoyn'd his Daughter
50 T' accept my Brother's love.

 Leon. ————Is this your pity?
You aggravate my griefs, and print 'em deeper
In new and heavier stamps.

 Amal. 'Tis as Physicians show the desperate ill
T' indear their Art, by mittigating pains
They cannot wholly cure: when you despair
Of all you wish, some part of it, because

---

30 speak. [*Aside.*] speak. Q1–3, F, D; speak︿ Q4.
31 Sir, [*To him.*] Sir, Q1, F, D; Sir. Q2–4.

Unhop'd for, may be grateful; and some other————
   Leon. What other?
   Amal. Some other may————
60 My shame again has seiz'd me, and I can go   [*Aside.*
No farther————
   Leon. These often failings, sighs, and interruptions,
Make me imagine you have grief like mine:
Have you ne'r lov'd?
   Amal. ————I? never. 'Tis in vain;
I must despair in silence.   [*Aside.*
   Leon. You come as I suspected then, to mock,
At least observe my griefs: take it not ill
That I must leave you.   [*Is going.*
   Amal. You must not go with these unjust opinions.
70 Command my life, and fortunes; you are wise,
Think, and think well, what I can do to serve you.
   Leon. I have but one thing in my thoughts and wishes:
If by your means I can obtain the sight
Of my ador'd *Palmyra;* or, what's harder,
One minutes time, to tell her, I die hers.   [*She starts back.*
I see I am not to expect it from you;
Nor could, indeed, with reason.
   Amal. Name any other thing: is *Amalthea*
So despicable, she can serve your wishes
80 In this alone?
   Leon. ————If I should ask of heav'n,
I have no other suit.
   Amal. To show you, then, I can deny you nothing,
Though 'tis more hard to me then any other,
Yet I will do't for you.
   Leon. Name quickly, name the means, speak my good Angel.
   Amal. Be not so much o'rjoy'd; for, if you are,
I'll rather dye then do't. This night the Court
Will be in Masquerade;

---

62   failings,] Q3–4; failing, Q1–2; failing‸ F, D.
64   never. 'Tis] ~: 'tis Q1–4, F, D ('Tis Q3–4, D).
88   Masquerade] F, D; *Masquerade* Q1–4.

You shall attend on me; in that disguise
90 You may both see and speak to her,
If you dare venture it.
     Leon. Yes, were a God her Guardian,
And bore in each hand thunder, I would venture.
     Amal. Farewell then; two hours hence I will expect you:
My heart's so full, that I can stay no longer.   [*Exit.*
     Leon. Already it grows dusky; I'll prepare
With haste for my disguise. But who are these?

                Enter Hermogenes *and* Eubulus.

     Her. 'Tis he; we need not fear to speak to him.
     Eub. Leonidas.
     Leon. ————————Sure I have known that voice.
100   *Her.* You have some reason, Sir; 'tis *Eubulus,*
Who bred you with the Princess; and, departing,
Bequeath'd you to my care.
     Leon. My Foster-Father! let my knees express   [*Kneeling.*
My joys for your return!
     Eub. Rise, Sir, you must not kneel.
     Leon. ————————————————E'r since you left me,
I have been wandring in a maze of fate,
Led by false fires of a fantastick glory,
And the vain lustre of imagin'd Crowns,
But, ah! why would you leave me? or how could you
110 Absent your self so long?
     Eub. I'll give you a most just account of both:
And something more I have to tell you, which
I know must cause your wonder; but this place,
Though almost hid in darkness, is not safe.
Already I discern some coming towards us   [*Torches appear.*
With lights, who may discover me. *Hermogenes,*
Your lodgings are hard by, and much more private.
     Her. There you may freely speak.
     Leon. ————————————————Let us make haste;

99   *Leon.*] F, D; *Leonidas.* Q1–4.
103 Foster-Father] Q4, F; Foster, Father Q1–3; Foster Father D.

For some affairs, and of no small importance,
120 Call me another way.   [*Exeunt.*

Enter Palamede *and* Rhodophil, *with Vizor Masques in
their hands, and Torches before 'em.*

Pala. We shall have noble sport to night, *Rhodophil;* this Masquerading is a most glorious invention.

Rho. I believe it was invented first by some jealous Lover, to discover the haunts of his Jilting Mistris; or, perhaps, by some distressed servant, to gain an opportunity with a jealous man's wife.

Pala. No, it must be the invention of a woman, it has so much of subtilty and love in it.

Rho. I am sure 'tis extremely pleasant; for to go unknown, is
130 the next degree to going invisible.

Pala. What with our antique habits, and feign'd voices, do you know me? and I know you? Methinks we move and talk just like so many over-grown Puppets.

Rho. Masquerade is onely Vizor-masque improv'd, a heightning of the same fashion.

Pala. No; Masquerade is Vizor-masque in debauch; and I like it the better for't: for, with a Vizor-masque, we fool our selves into courtship, for the sake of an eye that glanc'd; or a hand that stole it self out of the glove sometimes, to give us a sample
140 of the skin: but in Masquerade there is nothing to be known, she's all *Terra incognita,* and the bold discoverer leaps ashoar, and takes his lot among the wild *Indians* and Salvages, without the vile consideration of safety to his person, or of beauty, or wholesomeness in his Mistris.

Enter Beliza.

Rho. Beliza, what make you here?

Bel. Sir, my Lady sent me after you, to let you know, she finds her self a little indispos'd, so that she cannot be at Court, but is retir'd to rest, in her own appartment, where she shall want the

142   Salvages] *Salvages* Q1–4, F, D.

happiness of your dear embraces to night.

150   *Rho.* A very fine phrase, *Beliza,* to let me know my wife desires to lie alone.

Pala. I doubt, *Rhodophil,* you take the pains sometimes to instruct your wife's Woman in these elegancies.

Rho. Tell my dear Lady, that since I must be so unhappy as
not to wait on her to night, I will lament bitterly for her absence. 'Tis true, I shall be at Court, but I will take no divertisement there; and when I return to my solitary bed, if I am
so forgetful of my passion as to sleep, I will dream of her; and
betwixt sleep and waking, put out my foot towards her side, for
160   mid-night consolation; and not finding her, I will sigh, and imagine my self a most desolate widower.

Bel. I shall do your commands, Sir.   [*Exit.*

Rho. (*Aside*) She's sick as aptly for my purpose, as if she had
contriv'd it so: well, if ever woman was a help-meet for man,
my Spouse is so; for within this hour I receiv'd a Note from
Melantha, that she would meet me this evening in Masquerade
in Boys habit, to rejoyce with me before she entred into fetters; for I find she loves me better then *Palamede,* onely because
he's to be her husband. There's something of antipathy in the
170   word Marriage to the nature of love; marriage is the meer
Ladle of affection, that cools it when 'tis never so fiercely boiling
over.

Pala. Dear *Rhodophil,* I must needs beg your pardon; there is
an occasion fall'n out which I had forgot: I cannot be at Court
to night.

Rho. Dear *Palamede,* I am sorry we shall not have one course
together at the herd; but I find your Game lies single: good
fortune to you with your Mistris.   [*Exit.*

Pala. He has wish'd me good fortune with his Wife: there's
180   no sin in this then, there's fair leave given. Well, I must go visit
the sick; I cannot resist the temptations of my charity. O what
a difference will she find betwixt a dull resty Husband, and a
quick vigorous Lover! he sets out like a Carrier's Horse, plod-
ding on, because he knows he must, with the Bells of Matrimony chiming so melancholly about his neck, in pain till he's at

his journeys end, and dispairing to get thither, he is fain to for-
tifie imagination with the thoughts of another woman: I take
heat after heat, like a well-breath'd Courser, and————But hark,
what noise is that? swords!   [*Clashing of Swords within.*
190   Nay, then have with you.   [*Exit* Palamede.

Re-enter Palamede, *with* Rhodophil: *and* Doralice *in man's*
habit.

Rho. Friend, your relief was very timely, otherwise I had been
oppress'd.
Pala. What was the quarrel?
Rho. What I did, was in rescue of this Youth.
Pala. What cause could he give 'em?
Dor. The cause was nothing but onely the common cause
of fighting in Masquerades: they were drunk, and I was sober.
Rho. Have they not hurt you?
Dor. No; but I am exceeding ill, with the fright on't.
200   *Pala.* Let's lead him to some place where he may refresh him-
self.
Rho. Do you conduct him then.
Pala. (*Aside*) How cross this happens to my design of going
to *Doralice!* for I am confident she was sick on purpose that I
should visit her. Hark you, *Rhodophil,* could not you take care
of the stripling? I am partly engag'd to night.
Rho. You know I have business: but come, Youth, if it must
be so.
Dor. (*To* Rhodophil) No, good Sir, do not give your self that
210   trouble; I shall be safer, and better pleas'd with your friend
here.
Rho. Farewell then; once more I wish you a good adventure.
Pala. Damn this kindness! now must I be troubled with this
young Rogue, and miss my opportunity with *Doralice.*
          [*Exit* Rhodophil *alone,* Palamede *with* Doralice.

---

187   I] Q2–4, F, D; ∼, Q1.
209   *s.d.* Rhodophil] Q2–4, F; *Rhodophil* Q1, D.

SCENE II.

Enter Polydamas.

Argaleon counsel'd well to banish him,
He has, I know not what,
Of greatness in his looks, and of high fate,
That almost awes me; but I fear my Daughter,
Who hourly moves me for him, and I mark'd
She sigh'd when I but nam'd *Argaleon* to her.
But see, the Maskers: hence my cares, this night,
At least take truce, and find me on my pillow.

Enter the Princess in Masquerade, with Ladies: at the other end,
Argaleon *and Gentlemen in Masquerade: then* Leonidas
leading Amalthea. *The King sits. A Dance. After the Dance,*

    Amal. (*To* Leonidas) That's the Princess;
10 I saw the habit ere she put it on.
    Leon. I know her by a thousand other signs,
She cannot hide so much Divinity.
Disguis'd, and silent, yet some graceful motion
Breaks from her, and shines round her like a Glory.
                          [*Goes to* Palmyra.
    Amal. Thus she reveals her self, and knows it not:
Like Love's Dark-lantern I direct his steps,
And yet he sees not that which gives him light.
    Palm. I know you; but, alas, *Leonidas,*   [*To* Leonidas.
Why should you tempt this danger on your self?
20   *Leon.* Madam, you know me not, if you believe
I would not hazard greater for your sake:
But you, I fear, are chang'd.
    Palm. No, I am still the same;
But there are many things became *Palmyra*

---

9 *s.d.* Leonidas] Q3–4; *Leonidas* Q1–2, F, D.

Which ill become the Princess.
 Leon. ————————————I ask nothing
Which Honour will not give you leave to grant:
One hours short audience, at my fathers house,
You cannot sure refuse me.
 Palm. Perhaps I should, did I consult strict vertue;
30 But something must be given to Love and you.
When would you I should come?
 Leon. This evening, with the speediest opportunity.
I have a secret to discover to you,
Which will surprise, and please you.
 Palm. ————————————'Tis enough.
Go now; for we may be observ'd and known.
I trust your honour; give me not occasion
To blame my self, or you.
 Leon. You never shall repent your good opinion.
[Kisses her hand, and Exit.
 Arga. I cannot be deceiv'd; that is the Princess:
40 One of her Maids betray'd the habit to me;
But who was he with whom she held discourse?
'Tis one she favours, for he kiss'd her hand.
Our shapes are like, our habits near the same:
She may mistake, and speak to me for him.
I am resolv'd, I'll satisfie my doubts,
Though to be more tormented.   [*Exit.*

SONG.

1.

Whil'st Alexis *lay prest*
In her Arms he lov'd best,
With his hands round her neck,
50 *And his head on her breast,*
He found the fierce pleasure too hasty to stay,
And his soul in the tempest just flying away.

2.
When Cœlia *saw this,*
With a sigh, and a kiss,
She cry'd, Oh my dear, I am robb'd of my bliss;
'Tis unkind to your Love, and unfaithfully done,
To leave me behind you, and die all alone.

3.
The Youth, though in haste,
And breathing his last,
60 *In pity dy'd slowly, while she dy'd more fast;*
Till at length she cry'd, Now, my dear, now let us go,
Now die, my Alexis, *and I will die too.*

4.
Thus intranc'd they did lie,
Till Alexis *did try*
To recover new breath, that again he might die:
Then often they di'd; but the more they did so,
The Nymph di'd more quick, and the Shepherd more slow.

Another Dance. After it, Argaleon *re-enters, and*
stands by the Princess.

Palm. Leonidas, what means this quick return? [*To* Arga.
Arga. O heav'n! 'tis what I fear'd. [*Aside.*
70 *Palm.* Is ought of moment happen'd since you went?
Arga. No, Madam, but I understood not fully
Your last commands.
Palm. ───────And yet you answer'd to 'em.
Retire; you are too indiscreet a Lover:
I'll meet you where I promis'd. [*Exit.*
Arga. O my curst fortune! what have I discover'd?
But I will be reveng'd. [*Whispers to the King.*
Poly. But are you certain you are not deceiv'd?
Arga. Upon my life.
Poly. ───────Her honour is concern'd.
Somewhat I'll do; but I am yet distracted,

80 And know not where to fix. I wish'd a child,
And Heav'n, in anger, granted my request.
So blind we are, our wishes are so vain,
That what we most desire, proves most our pain.

[Exeunt omnes.

SCENE III.

An Eating-house. Bottles of Wine on the Table. Palamede;
and Doralice *in Man's habit.*

Dor. (*Aside*) Now cannot I find in my heart to discover my
self, though I long he should know me.

Pala. I tell thee, Boy, now I have seen thee safe, I must be
gone: I have no leisure to throw away on thy raw conversation:
I am a person that understands better things, I.

Dor. Were I a woman, Oh how you'd admire me! cry up
every word I said, and scrue your face into a submissive smile; as
I have seen a dull Gallant act Wit, and counterfeit pleasantness,
when he whispers to a great Person in a Play-house; smile, and
10 look briskly, when the other answers, as if something of extraordinary had past betwixt 'em, when, heaven knows, there was
nothing else but, What a clock does your Lordship think it is?
and my Lord's *repertee* is, 'Tis almost Park-time: or, at most,
Shall we out of the Pit, and go behind the Scenes for an Act or
two? And yet such fine things as these, would be wit in a Mistris's
mouth.

Pala. Ay, Boy; there's Dame Nature in the case: he who cannot find wit in a Mistris, deserves to find nothing else, Boy. But
these are riddles to thee, child, and I have not leisure to instruct
20 thee; I have affairs to dispatch, great affairs; I am a man of business.

Dor. Come, you shall not go: you have no affairs but what you
may dispatch here, to my knowledge.

Pala. I find now, thou art a Boy of more understanding then
I thought thee; a very lewd wicked Boy: o' my conscience thou

---

5   understands] D; understand Q1–4, F.

wouldst debauch me, and hast some evil designs upon my person.

Dor. You are mistaken, Sir; I would onely have you show me a more lawful reason why you would leave me, then I can why you should not, and I'll not stay you; for I am not so young, but I understand the necessities of flesh and bloud, and the pressing occasions of mankind, as well as you.

Pala. A very forward and understanding Boy! Thou art in great danger of a Pages wit, to be brisk at 14, and dull at 20. But I'll give thee no further account; I must, and will go.

Dor. My life on't, your Mistris is not at home.

Pala. This Imp will make me very angry.   [*Aside.*
I tell thee, young Sir, she is at home; and at home for me; and, which is more, she is abed for me, and sick for me.

Dor. For you onely?

Pala. Ay, for me onely.

Dor. But how do you know she's sick abed?

Pala. She sent her Husband word so.

Dor. And are you such a novice in Love, to believe a Wife's message to her Husband?

Pala. Why, what the devil should be her meaning else?

Dor. It may be, to go in Masquerade as well as you; to observe your haunts, and keep you company without your knowledge.

Pala. Nay, I'll trust her for that: she loves me too well, to disguise her self from me.

Dor. If I were she, I would disguise on purpose to try your wit; and come to my servant like a Riddle, Read me, and take me.

Pala. I could know her in any shape: my good Genius would prompt me to find out a handsome woman: there's something in her, that would attract me to her without my knowledge.

Dor. Then you make a Load-stone of your Mistris?

Pala. Yes, and I carry Steel about me, which has been so often touch'd, that it never fails to point to the North Pole.

Dor. Yet still my mind gives me, that you have met her disguis'd to night, and have not known her.

---

37   angry. [*Aside.*] angry. Q1–4, F, D.

Pala. This is the most pragmatical conceited little fellow, he will needs understand my business better then my self.   [*Aside.* I tell thee, once more, thou dost not know my Mistris.

Dor. And I tell you, once more, that I know her better then you do.

Pala. The Boy's resolv'd to have the last word.   [*Aside.* I find I must go without reply.   [*Exit.*

Dor. Ah mischief, I have lost him with my fooling. *Palamede,*
70 *Palamede.*

> *He returns. She plucks off her Perruke, and puts it on again when he knows her.*

Pala. O Heavens! is it you, Madam?

Dor. Now, where was your good Genius, that would prompt you to find me out?

Pala. Why, you see I was not deceiv'd; you, your self, were my good Genius.

Dor. But where was the Steel, that knew the Load-stone? ha?

Pala. The truth is, Madam, the Steel has lost its vertue; and therefore, if you please, we'll new touch it.

> *Enter* Rhodophil; *and* Melantha *in Boy's habit.* Rhodophil *sees* Palamede *kissing* Doralice's *hand.*

Rho. Palamede again! am I fall'n into your quarters? What?
80 ingaging with a Boy? is all honourable?

Pala. O, very honourable on my side. I was just chastising this young Villain; he was running away, without paying his share of the reckoning.

Rho. Then I find I was deceiv'd in him.

Pala. Yes, you are deceiv'd in him: 'tis the archest rogue, if you did but know him.

Mel. Good *Rhodophil,* let us get off *a-la-derobbée,* for fear I should be discover'd.

Rho. There's no retiring now; I warrant you for discovery:

---

63   self. [*Aside.*] self. Q1–4, F, D.   67   word. [*Aside.*] word. Q1–4, F, D.
87   *a-la-derobbée*] Q3–4; *al-a derobbée* Q1–2, D; *a-la derobbée* F.

90 now have I the oddest thought, to entertain you before your
Servants face, and he never the wiser; 'twill be the prettiest jug-
ling trick to cheat him when he looks upon us.

Mel. This is the strangest *caprice* in you.

Pala. (*To* Doralice) This *Rhodophil's* the unluckiest fellow to
me! this is now the second time he has bar'd the Dice when we
were just ready to have nick'd him; but if ever I get the Box
again———

Dor. Do you think he will not know me? Am I like my self?

Pala. No more then a Picture in the Hangings.

100 *Dor.* Nay, then he can never discover me, now the wrong side
of the Arras is turn'd towards him.

Pala. At least, 'twill be some pleasure to me, to enjoy what
freedom I can while he looks on; I will storm the Out-works of
Matrimony even before his face.

Rho. What Wine have you there, *Palamede?*

Pala. Old *Chios,* or the rogue's damn'd that drew it.

Rho. Come, to the most constant of Mistresses; that I believe
is yours, *Palamede.*

Dor. Pray spare your Seconds; for my part I am but a weak
110 Brother.

Pala. Now, to the truest of Turtles; that is your Wife, *Rhodophil,* that lies sick at home in the bed of honour.

Rho. Now let's have one common health, and so have done.

Dor. Then, for once, I'll begin it. Here's to him that has the
fairest Lady of *Sicily* in Masquerade to night.

Pala. This is such an obliging health, I'll kiss thee, dear Rogue,
for thy invention.   [*Kisses her.*

Rho. He who has this Lady, is a happy man, without dispute.
———I'm most concern'd in this, I am sure.   [*Aside.*
120 *Pala.* Was it not well found out, *Rhodophil?*

Mel. Ay, this was *bien trouvée* indeed.

Dor. (*To* Melantha) I suppose I shall do you a kindness to enquire if you have not been in *France,* Sir?

Mel. To do you service, Sir.

---

98   *printed as verse* (. . . me? / Am . . .) *in* Q*1–4, F.*
107   Mistresses;] Q4; ∼, Q1–3, F, D.
122   *s.d.* Melantha] Q2–4, D (∼. Q3–4, D); *Melantha.* Q1, F.

Dor. O, *Monsieur, vot' valet bien humble.*   [*Saluting her.*

Mel. Votre esclaue, Monsieur, de tout Mon Cœur.

[*Returning the salute.*

Dor. I suppose, sweet Sir, you are the hope and joy of some
thriving Citizen, who has pinch'd himself at home, to breed you
abroad, where you have learnt your Exercises, as it appears most
130 aukwardly, and are returned with the addition of a new-lac'd
bosom and a Clap, to your good old father, who looks at you with
his mouth, while you spout *French* with your *Mon Monsieur.*

Pala. Let me kiss thee again for that, dear Rogue.

Mel. And you, I imagine, are my young Master, whom your
Mother durst not trust upon salt water, but left you to be your
own Tutour at fourteen, to be very brisk and *entreprenant,* to
endeavour to be debauch'd ere you have learnt the knack on't, to
value your self upon a Clap before you can get it, and to make it
the height of your ambition to get a Player for your Mistris.

140 *Rho.* (*Embracing* Mel.) O dear young Bully, thou hast tickled
him with a *repertee* i'faith.

Mel. You are one of those that applaud our Countrey Plays,
where drums, and trumpets, and bloud, and wounds, are wit.

Rho. Again, my Boy? let me kiss thee most abundantly.

Dor. You are an admirer of the dull *French* Poetry, which is
so thin, that it is the very Leaf-gold of Wit, the very Wafers and
whip'd Cream of sense, for which a man opens his mouth and
gapes, to swallow nothing: and to be an admirer of such profound
dulness, one must be endow'd with a great perfection of impu-
150 dence and ignorance.

Pala. Let me embrace thee most vehemently.

Mel. I'll sacrifice my life for *French* Poetry.   [*Advancing.*

Dor. I'll die upon the spot for our Countrey Wit.

Rho. (*To* Melantha) Hold, hold, young *Mars: Palamede,* draw
back your Hero.

Pala. 'Tis time; I shall be drawn in for a Second else at the
wrong weapon.

---

125 *O, Monsieur,*] O, Monsieur, Q1–4, F, D.   125 *vot'*] vot Q1–4, F; *votre* D.

126 *Votre*] Votrè Q1–3, F; *Votré* Q4, D.   132 *Mon*] Q4; *Man* Q1–3, F, D.

140 *s.d. Embracing*] Q3–4; *embracing* Q1–2, F, D.

154 *s.d. To* Melantha] Q4; *to* Melantha. Q1–3, D (*To* Q3); *to Melantha.* F.

155 Hero] F; *Hero* Q1–4, D.

Mel. O that I were a man for thy sake!
Dor. You'll be a man as soon as I shall.

Enter a Messenger to Rhodophil.

160   *Mess.* Sir, the King has instant business with you.
I saw the Guard drawn up by your Lieutenant
Before the Palace-gate, ready to march.
        Rhod. 'Tis somewhat sodain; say that I am coming.
                                        [*Exit Messenger.*
Now, *Palamede,* what think you of this sport?
This is some suddain tumult: will you along?
        Pala. Yes, yes, I will go; but the devil take me if ever I was less
in humour. Why, the pox, could they not have staid their tumult
till to morrow? then I had done my business, and been ready for
'em. Truth is, I had a little transitory crime to have committed
170 first; and I am the worst man in the world at repenting, till a sin
be throughly done: but what shall we do with the two Boys?
        Rho. Let them take a lodging in the house till the business be
over.
        Dor. What, lie with a Boy? for my part, I own it, I cannot en-
dure to lie with a Boy.
        Pala. The more's my sorrow, I cannot accommodate you with
a better bed-fellow.
        Mel. Let me die, if I enter into a pair of sheets with him that
hates the *French.*
180   *Dor.* Pish, take no care for us, but leave us in the streets; I
warrant you, as late as it is, I'll find my lodging as well as any
drunken Bully of 'em all.
        Rho. I'll fight in meer revenge, and wreak my passion   [*Aside.*
On all that spoil this hopeful assignation.
        Pala. I'm sure we fight in a good quarrel:
Rogues may pretend Religion, and the Laws;
But a kind Mistris is the *Good old Cause.*   [*Exeunt.*

SCENE IV.

Enter Palmyra, Eubulus, Hermogenes.

Palm. You tell me wonders; that *Leonidas*
Is Prince *Theagenes,* the late King's Son.
    Eub. It seem'd as strange to him, as now to you,
Before I had convinc'd him; But, besides
His great resemblance to the King his Father,
The Queen his Mother lives, secur'd by me
In a Religious House; to whom each year
I brought the news of his increasing virtues.
My last long absence from you both, was caus'd
10 By wounds which, in my journey, I receiv'd,
When set upon by thieves; I lost those Jewels
And Letters, which your dying Mother left.
    Her. The same he means, which, since, brought to the King,
Made him first know he had a Child alive:
'Twas then my care of Prince *Leonidas*
Caus'd me to say he was th' Usurpers Son;
Till, after forc'd by your apparent danger,
I made the true discovery of your birth,
And once more hid my Prince's.

Enter Leonidas.

20 *Leon. Hermogenes,* and *Eubulus,* retire;
Those of our party, whom I left without,
Expect your aid and counsel.   [*Exeunt ambo.*
    Palm. I should, *Leonidas,* congratulate
This happy change of your exalted fate;
But, as my joy, so you my wonder move;
Your looks have more of Business, then of Love:
And your last words some great design did show.
    Leon. I frame not any to be hid from you.
You, in my love, all my designs may see;

30 But what have love and you design'd for me?
Fortune, once more, has set the ballance right:
First, equall'd us, in lowness; then, in height.
Both of us have so long, like Gamesters, thrown,
Till Fate comes round, and gives to each his own.
As Fate is equal, so may Love appear:
Tell me, at least, what I must hope, or fear.
    Palm. After so many proofs, how can you call
My love in doubt? Fear nothing; and hope, all.
Think what a Prince, with honour, may receive,
40 Or I may give, without a Parents leave.
    Leon. You give, and then restrain the grace you show;
As ostentatious Priests, when Souls they wooe,
Promise their Heav'n to all, but grant to few:
But do for me, what I have dar'd for you.
I did no argument from duty bring:
Duty's a Name; and Love's a Real thing.
    Palm. Man's love may, like wild torrents, over-flow;
Woman's as deep, but in its banks must go.
My love is mine; and that I can impart;
50 But cannot give my person, with my heart.
    Leon. Your love is then no gift:
For when the person it does not convey,
'Tis to give Gold, and not to give the Key.
    Palm. Then ask my Father.
    Leon. ——————————He detains my Throne:
Who holds back mine, will hardly give his own.
    Palm. What then remains?
    Leon. ——————————That I must have recourse
To Arms; and take my Love and Crown, by force.
Hermogenes is forming the design;
And with him, all the brave and loyal joyn.
60   *Palm.* And is it thus you court *Palmyra's* bed?
Can she the murd'rer of her Parent wed?
Desist from force: so much you well may give
To Love, and Me, to let my Father live.
    Leon. Each act of mine my love to you has shown;

---

43 few:] ~. Q1–4, F, D.   54, 56 *Leon.*] Q2–4, F, D; ~ Q1.

But you, who tax my want of it, have none.
You bid me part with you, and let him live;
But they should nothing ask, who nothing give.
    Palm. I give what vertue and what duty can,
In vowing ne'r to wed another man.
70   *Leon.* You will be forc'd to be *Argaleon*'s wife.
    Palm. I'll keep my promise, though I lose my life.
    Leon. Then you lose Love, for which we both contend;
For Life is but the means, but Love's the end.
    Palm. Our Souls shall love hereafter.
    Leon. —————————————————I much fear, ⎞
That Soul which could deny the Body here,   ⎬
To taste of love, would be a niggard there.   ⎠
    Palm. Then 'tis past hope: our cruel fate, I see,
Will make a sad divorce 'twixt you and me.
For, if you force employ, by Heav'n I swear,
80 And all bless'd Beings,————
    Leon. —————————Your rash Oath forbear.
    Palm. I never————
    Leon. —————Hold once more. But, yet, as he
Who scapes a dang'rous leap, looks back to see;
So I desire, now I am past my fear,
To know what was that Oath you meant to swear.
    Palm. I meant that if you hazarded your life,
Or sought my Father's, ne'r to be your Wife.
    Leon. See now, *Palmyra,* how unkind you prove!
Could you, with so much ease, forswear my love?
    Palm. You force me with your ruinous design.
90   *Leon.* Your Father's life is more your care, then Mine.
    Palm. You wrong me: 'tis not; though it ought to be;
You are my Care, heav'n knows, as well as he.
    Leon. If now the execution I delay,
My Honour, and my Subjects, I betray.
All is prepar'd for the just enterprize;
And the whole City will to morrow rise.
The Leaders of the party are within,
And *Eubulus* has sworn that he will bring,
To head their Arms, the person of their King.

100   *Palm.* In telling this, you make me guilty too;
I therefore must discover what I know:
What Honour bids you do, Nature bids me prevent;
But kill me first, and then pursue your black intent.
   Leon. Palmyra, no; you shall not need to die;
Yet I'll not trust so strict a piety.
Within there.

Enter Eubulus.

———————*Eubulus,* a Guard prepare;
Here, I commit this pris'ner to your care.
         [Kisses Palmyra's *hand; then gives it to* Eubulus.
   Palm. Leonidas, I never thought these bands
Could e'r be giv'n me by a Lover's hands.
110   *Leon. Palmyra,* thus your Judge himself arraigns; *[Kneeling.*
He who impos'd these bonds, still wears your chains:
When you to Love or Duty false must be,
Or to your Father guilty, or to me,
These chains, alone, remain to set you free.
         [Noise of swords clashing.
   Poly. (Within) Secure these, first; then search the inner room.
   Leon. From whence do these tumultuous clamours come?

Enter Hermogenes, *hastily.*

   Her. We are betray'd; and there remains alone
This comfort, that your person is not known.

Enter the King, Argaleon, Rhodophil, Palamede, *Guards;*
some like Citizens as prisoners.

   Poly. What mean these midnight-consultations here,
120 Where I, like an unsummon'd guest, appear?
   Leon. Sir——
   Arga. ——————There needs no excuse; 'tis understood;
You were all watching, for your Prince's good.

———

110 *s.d. Kneeling]* Q3, F, D; *kneeling* Q1–2, Q4.
115 *s.d. Within]* Q2–4, F; *within* Q1, D.   119 these] F, D; this Q1–4.

Poly. My reverend City-friends, you are well met!
On what great work were your grave wisdoms set?
Which of my actions were you scanning here?
What *French* invasion have you found to fear?
    Leon. They are my friends; and come, Sir, with intent
To take their leaves before my banishment.
    Poly. Your exile, in both sexes, friends can find:
130 I see the Ladies, like the men, are kind.   [*Seeing* Palmyra.
    Palm. Alas, I came but———   [*Kneeling.*
    Poly. ————————————Adde not to your crime
A lie: I'll hear you speak some other time.
How? *Eubulus!* nor time, nor thy disguise,
Can keep thee, undiscover'd, from my eyes.
A Guard there; seize 'em all.
    Rho. Yield, Sir; what use of valour can be shown?
    Pal. One, and unarm'd, against a multitude!
    Leon. O for a sword!
    [*He reaches at one of the Guards Halberds, and is seiz'd behind.*
————————————I w' not lose my breath
In fruitless pray'rs; but beg a speedy death.
140   *Palm.* O spare *Leonidas,* and punish me.
    Poly. Mean Girl, thou want'st an Advocate for thee.
Now the mysterious knot will be unty'd;
Whether the young King lives, or where he dy'd:
To morrows dawn shall the dark riddle clear;
Crown all my joys; and dissipate my fear.   [*Exeunt omnes.*

ACT V. SCENE I.

Palamede, Straton. Palamede *with a Letter
in his hand.*

    Pal. This evening, say'st thou? will they both be here?
    Stra. Yes, Sir; both my old Master, and your Mistris's Father:
the old Gentlemen ride hard this journey; they say, it shall be

---

131   *s.d. Kneeling]* Q3–4, F, D; *kneeling* Q1–2.
138   *Leon.* O] F; O Q1–4, D.

the last time they will see the Town; and both of 'em are so pleas'd with this marriage, which they have concluded for you, that I am afraid they will live some years longer to trouble you, with the joy of it.

Pal. But this is such an unreasonable thing, to impose upon me to be marri'd to morrow; 'tis hurrying a man to execution, 10 without giving him time to say his pray'rs.

Stra. Yet, if I might advise you, Sir, you should not delay it: for your younger Brother comes up with 'em, and is got already into their favours. He has gain'd much upon my old Master, by finding fault with Inn-keepers Bills, and by starving us, and our Horses, to show his frugality; and he is very well with your Mistris's Father, by giving him Receipts for the Splene, Gout, and Scurvy, and other infirmities of old age.

Pal. I'll rout him, and his Countrey education: Pox on him, I remember him before I travell'd, he had nothing in him but 20 meer Jocky; us'd to talk loud, and make matches, and was all for the crack of the field: sense and wit were as much banish'd from his discourse, as they are when the Court goes out of Town to a Horse-race. Go now and provide your Master's Lodgings.

Stra. I go, Sir. [*Exit.*

Pal. It vexes me to the heart, to leave all my designs with *Doralice* unfinish'd; to have flown her so often to a mark, and still to be bob'd at retrieve: if I had but once enjoy'd her, though I could not have satisfi'd my stomach, with the feast, at least I should have relish'd my mouth a little; but now————

Enter Philotis.

30 *Phil.* Oh, Sir, you are happily met; I was coming to find you.

Pal. From your Lady, I hope.

Phil. Partly from her; but more especially from my self: she has just now receiv'd a Letter from her Father, with an absolute command to dispose her self to marry you to morrow.

Pal. And she takes it to the death?

Phil. Quite contrary: the Letter could never have come in a more lucky minute; for it found her in an ill humour with a

33 Father] Q2–4, F, D; Fathet Q1.

Rival of yours, that shall be nameless, about the pronunciation
of a *French* word.

40   *Pal.* Count *Rhodophil;* never disguise it, I know the *Amour:*
but I hope you took the occasion to strike in for me?

Phil. It was my good fortune to do you some small service in
it; for your sake I discommended him all over: cloaths, person,
humour, behaviour, every thing; and to sum up all, told her, It
was impossible to find a marri'd man that was otherwise; for they
were all so mortifi'd at home with their wives ill humours, that
they could never recover themselves to be company abroad.

Pal. Most divinely urg'd!

Phil. Then I took occasion to commend your good qualities:
50 as, the sweetness of your humour, the comeliness of your person,
your good Meene, your valour; but, above all, your liberality.

Pal. I vow to Gad I had like to have forgot that good quality
in my self, if thou had'st not remember'd me on't: here are five
Pieces for thee.

Phil. Lord, you have the softest hand, Sir! it would do a woman good to touch it: Count *Rhodophil's* is not half so soft; for I
remember I felt it once, when he gave me ten Pieces for my New-
years gift.

Pal. O, I understand you, Madam; you shall find my hand as
60 soft again as Count *Rhodophil's*: there are twenty Pieces for you.
The former was but a Retaining Fee; now I hope you'l plead
for me.

Phil. Your own merits speak enough. Be sure onely to ply her
with *French* words, and I'll warrant you'll do your business. Here
are a list of her phrases for this day: use 'em to her upon all occasions, and foil her at her own weapon; for she's like one of the
old *Amazons*, she'l never marry, except it be the man who has
first conquer'd her.

Pal. I'll be sure to follow your advice: but you'll forget to fur-
70 ther my design.

Phil. What, do you think I'll be ungrateful?————But, however, if you distrust my memory, put some token on my finger to
remember it by: that Diamond there would do admirably.

Pal. There 'tis; and I ask your pardon heartily for calling your

---

71   ungrateful?————But] D; ungrateful?———— / ————But Q1–4, F.

memory into question: I assure you I'll trust it another time,
without putting you to the trouble of another token.

Enter Palmyra *and* Artemis.

Art. Madam, this way the prisoners are to pass;
Here you may see *Leonidas.*
Palm. Then here I'll stay, and follow him to death.

Enter Melantha *hastily.*

80 *Mela.* O, here's her Highness! Now is my time to introduce my
self, and to make my court to her, in my new *French* phrases.
Stay, let me read my catalogue——*suitte, figure, chagrin,
naiveté,* and *let me die* for the Parenthesis of all.
   Pal. (Aside) Do, persecute her; and I'll persecute thee as fast
in thy own dialect.
   Mel. Madam the Princess! let me die, but this is a most horrid
spectacle, to see a person who makes so grand a *figure* in the
Court, without the *Suitte* of a Princess, and entertaining your
Chagrin all alone; (*Naiveté* should have been there, but the dis-
90 obedient word would not come in.)
   Palm. What is she, *Artemis?*
   Art. An impertinent Lady, Madam; very ambitious of being
known to your Highness.
   Pal. (To Melantha) Let me die, Madam, if I have not waited
you here these two long hours, without so much as the *Suitte* of
a single Servant to attend me; entertaining my self with my own
Chagrin, till I had the honour to see your Ladiship, who are a
person that makes so considerable a *figure* in the Court.
   Mel. Truce with your *douceurs,* good servant; you see I am
100 addressing to the Princess; pray do not *embarrass* me——*embarrass* me! what a delicious *French* word do you make me lose
upon you too!

79	follow] Q2–4, F, D; follôw Q1.	80	Now] *starts a new line in* Q1–4, F.
83	naiveté] naivete Q1–4, F, D.	83	let me die] Q4, F, D; let me die Q1–3.
84	s.d. Aside] Q2–4, D; aside Q1, F.	86	Madam] Q2–4, F; ~, Q1, D.
87	figure] figure Q1–4, F, D.	89	Naiveté] Naivete Q1–4, F, D.
94	s.d. To Melantha] to Melantha Q1–4, F, D (*To* Q4, D).		
98	figure] figure Q1–4, F, D.		

(*To the Princess*) Your Highness, Madam, will please to pardon the *Bévue* which I made, in not sooner finding you out to be a Princess: but let me die if this *Éclaircissement* which is made this day of your quality, does not ravish me; and give me leave to tell you————

Pal. But first give me leave to tell you, Madam, that I have so great a *tendre* for your person, and such a *panchant* to do you
110 service, that————

Mel. What, must I still be troubled with your *Sottises?* (There's another word lost, that I meant for the Princess, with a mischief to you.) But your Highness, Madam————

Pal. But your Ladiship, Madam————

Enter Leonidas *guarded, and led over the Stage.*

Mel. Out upon him, how he looks, Madam! now he's found no Prince, he is the strangest *figure* of a man; how could I make that *Coup d'étourdy* to think him one?

Palm. Away, impertinent————
My dear *Leonidas!*

Leon. ————My dear *Palmyra!*
120   *Palm.* Death shall never part us;
My Destiny is yours.   [*He is led off; she follows.*

Mel. Impertinent! Oh I am the most unfortunate person this day breathing: that the Princess should thus *rompre en visiere*, without occasion. Let me die but I'll follow her to death, till I make my peace.

Pal. (*Holding her*) And let me die, but I'll follow you to the Infernals till you pity me.

Mel. (*Turning towards him angrily*) Ay, 'tis long of you that this *Malheur* is fall'n upon me; your impertinence has put me
130 out of the good graces of the Princess, and all that, which has

---

104   *Bévue*] *Beveue* Q1–4, F, D.
105   *Éclaircissement*] *Eclaircissement* Q1–4, F, D.
109   *tendre*] tender Q1–4, F, D.   113   you.)] Q3–4; ~ₐ) Q1–2, F, D.
116   *figure*] figure Q1–4, F, D.   117   *étourdy*] etourdy Q1–4, F, D.
118–119   *Palm....Leonidas!*] one line in Q1–4, F, D.
119   *Leon.*————] ~.ₐ Q1–4, F, D.   126   s.d. *Holding*] Q2–4, D; holding Q1, F.
128   s.d. *Turning*] Q2–4, D; turning Q1, F.

ruin'd me and all that, and therefore let me die but I'll be reveng'd, and all that.

Pal. *Façon, façon,* you must and shall love me, and all that;
for my old man is coming up, and all that; and I am *désespéré*
au dernier, and will not be disinherited, and all that.

Mel. How durst you interrupt me so *mal a propos,* when you
knew I was addressing to the Princess?

Pal. But why would you address your self so much *a contre-
temps* then?

140   *Mel.* Ah *mal peste!*

Pal. Ah *J'enrage!*

Phil. *Radoucissez vous, de grace, Madame; vous êtes bien en
colere pour peu de chose. Vous n'entendez pas la raillerie gal-
lante.*

Mel. *A d'autres, a d'autres:* he mocks himself of me, he abuses
me: ah me unfortunate!   [*Cries.*

Phil. You mistake him, Madam, he does but accommodate his
phrase to your refin'd language. *Ah, qu'il est un Cavalier ac-
comply!* Pursue your point, Sir———   [*To him.*

150   *Pal.* *Ah qu'il fait beau dans ces boccages;*   [*Singing.*
      Ah que le ciel donne un beau jour!
There I was with you, with a *minouet.*

Mel. Let me die now, but this singing is fine, and extremely
French in him: [*Laughs.*
But then, that he should use my own words, as it were in con-
tempt of me, I cannot bear it.   [*Crying.*

Pal. *Ces beaux séjours, ces doux ramages*———   [*Singing.*

Mel. *Ces beaux séjours, ces doux ramages,* [*Singing after him.*
      Ces beaux séjours, nous invitent a l'amour!

160 Let me die but he sings *en Cavalier,* and so humours the Cadence.
                                        [*Laughing.*

Pal. *Voy, ma Clymene, voy soubs ce chesne,*   [*Singing again.*
      S' entrebaiser ces oiseaux amoreux!

---

134 *désespéré*] desesperé Q1–4, F, D.
141 *J'enrage*] l'enrage Q1, F, D; 'enrage Q2; l'enrage Q3–4.
142 *êtes*] étes Q1, F, D; ètes Q2–4.
145 *A d'autres, a d'autres*] Ad' autres, ad' autres Q1–4, F, D (ad . . . ad F).
146 s.d. *Cries.*] D; cries! Q1, F; Cries! Q2–4.
149 Pursue] F; pursue Q1–4, D.   152 *minouet*] minouét Q1–4, F, D.
157, 158, 159 *séjours*] sejours (Sejours l. 158, Q1–2) Q1–5, F, D.
160 Let] *does not begin a new line in* Q1–4, F, D.

Let me die now, but that was fine. Ah, now, for three or four
brisk *Frenchmen,* to be put into Masquing habits, and to sing it
on a Theatre, how witty it would be! and then to dance helter
skelter to a *Chanson a boire: toute la terre, toute la terre est a
moy!* what's matter though it were made, and sung, two or three
years ago in *Cabarets,* how it would attract the admiration, especially of every one that's an *éveillé!*

170   *Mel.* Well; I begin to have a *tendre* for you; but yet, upon condition, that————when we are marri'd, you————

                                      [*Pal. sings, while she speaks.*

     Phil. You must drown her voice: if she makes her *French* con-
ditions, you are a slave for ever.

     Mel. First, will you engage that————

     Pal. Fa, la, la, la, &c.   [*Louder.*

     Mel. Will you hear the conditions?

     Pal. No; I will hear no conditions! I am resolv'd to win you
en Francois: to be very aiery, with abundance of noise, and no
sense: Fa, la, la, la, &c.

180   *Mel.* Hold, hold: I am vanquish'd with your *gayeté d'esprit.*
I am yours, and will be yours, *sans nulle reserve, ny condition:*
and let me die, if I do not think my self the happiest Nymph in
Sicily————My dear *French* Dear, stay but a *minuite,* till I rac-
commode my self with the Princess; and then I am yours, *jusq'
a la mort.*
Allons donc————   [*Exeunt* Mel. Philot.

     Pal. (*Solus, fanning himself with his hat*) I never thought be-
fore that wooing was so laborious an exercise; if she were worth
a million, I have deserv'd her; and now, me-thinks too, with
190 taking all this pains for her, I begin to like her. 'Tis so; I have
known many, who never car'd for Hare nor Partridge, but those
they caught themselves would eat heartily: the pains, and the
story a man tells of the taking of 'em, makes the meat go down
more pleasantly. Besides, last night I had a sweet dream of her,
and, Gad, she I have once dream'd of, I am stark mad till I enjoy
her, let her be never so ugly.

---

163   Let] *does not begin a new line in Q1–4, F, D.*
169   *éveillé*] eveille Q1–4, **F, D.**
170   *tendre*] tender Q1–4, **F, D.**
174   that————] ———— that Q1–4, **F, D.**

Enter Doralice.

Dor. Who's that you are so mad to enjoy, *Palamede?*

Pal. You may easily imagine that, sweet *Doralice.*

Dor. More easily then you think I can: I met just now with a
200 certain man, who came to you with Letters, from a certain old
Gentleman, yclipped your father; whereby I am given to understand, that to morrow you are to take an Oath in the Church to
be grave henceforward, to go ill-dress'd and slovenly, to get heirs
for your estate, and to dandle 'em for your diversion; and, in
short, that Love and Courtship are to be no more.

Pal. Now have I so much shame to be thus apprehended in the
manner, that I can neither speak nor look upon you; I have
abundance of grace in me, that I find: But if you have any spark
of true friendship in you, retire a little with me to the next room
210 that has a couch or bed in't, and bestow your charity upon a poor
dying man: a little comfort from a Mistris, before a man is going
to give himself in Marriage, is as good as a lusty dose of Strong-
water to a dying Malefactour; it takes away the sense of hell, and
hanging from him.

Dor. No, good *Palamede,* I must not be so injurious to your
Bride: 'tis ill drawing from the Bank to day, when all your ready
money is payable to morrow.

Pal. A Wife is onely to have the ripe fruit, that falls of it self;
but a wise man will always preserve a shaking for a Mistris.

220 *Dor.* But a Wife for the first quarter is a Mistris.

Pal. But when the second comes——

Dor. When it does come, you are so given to variety, that you
would make a Wife of me in another quarter.

Pal. No, never, except I were married to you: marri'd people
can never oblige one another; for all they do is duty, and consequently there can be no thanks: but Love is more frank and
generous then he is honest; he's a liberal giver, but a cursed pay-
master.

---

209   room] ~, Q1–4, F, D.   221   comes——] ~. Q1–4, F, D.
226   Love] F, D; love Q1–4.

Dor. I declare I will have no Gallant; but, if I would, he
230 should never be a marri'd man; a marri'd man is but a Mistris's
half-servant, as a Clergy-man is but the King's half-subject: for
a man to come to me that smells o' th' Wife! 's life, I wou'd as
soon wear her old Gown after her, as her Husband.

Pal. Yet 'tis a kind of fashion to wear a Princess cast shoes, you
see the Countrey Ladies buy 'em to be fine in them.

Dor. Yes, a Princess shoes may be worn after her, because they
keep their fashion, by being so very little us'd; but generally a
marri'd man is the creature of the world the most out of fashion;
his behaviour is dumpish, his discourse his wife and family, his
240 habit so much neglected, it looks as if that were marri'd too; his
Hat is marri'd, his Perruke is marri'd, his Breeches are marri'd,
and if we could look within his Breeches, we should find him
marri'd there too.

Pal. Am I then to be discarded for ever? pray do but mark how
terrible that word sounds; For ever! it has a very damn'd sound,
Doralice.

Dor. Ay, for ever! it sounds as hellishly to me, as it can do to
you, but there's no help for't.

Pal. Yet if we had but once enjoy'd one another; but then
250 once onely, is worse then not at all: it leaves a man with such a
lingring after it.

Dor. For ought I know 'tis better that we have not; we might
upon trial have lik'd each other less, as many a man and woman,
that have lov'd as desperately as we, and yet when they came to
possession, have sigh'd, and cri'd to themselves, Is this all?

Pal. That is onely, if the Servant were not found a man of this
world; but if, upon trial, we had not lik'd each other, we had
certainly left loving; and faith, that's the greater happiness of the
two.

260 *Dor.* 'Tis better as 'tis; we have drawn off already as much of
our Love as would run clear; after possessing, the rest is but
jealousies, and disquiets, and quarrelling, and piecing.

Pal. Nay, after one great quarrel, there's never any sound piecing; the love is apt to break in the same place again.

Dor. I declare I would never renew a love; that's like him who

trims an old Coach for ten years together; he might buy a new
one better cheap.

Pal. Well, Madam, I am convinc'd, that 'tis best for us not to
have enjoy'd; but Gad, the strongest reason is, because I cann't
270 help it.

Dor. The onely way to keep us new to one another, is never to
enjoy, as they keep grapes by hanging 'em upon a line; they must
touch nothing if you would preserve 'em fresh.

Pal. But then they wither, and grow dry in the very keeping;
however I shall have a warmth for you, and an eagerness, every
time I see you; and if I chance to out-live *Melantha*————

Dor. And if I chance to out-live *Rhodophil*————

Pal. Well, I'll cherish my body as much as I can upon that
hope. 'Tis true, I would not directly murder the wife of my
280 bosome; but to kill her civilly, by the way of kindness, I'll put
as fair as another man: I'll begin to morrow night, and be very
wrathful with her, that's resolv'd on.

Dor. Well, *Palamede,* here's my hand, I'll venture to be your
second Wife, for all your threatnings.

Pal. In the mean time I'll watch you hourly, as I would the
ripeness of a Melon, and I hope you'll give me leave now and
then to look on you, and to see if you are not ready to be cut yet.

Dor. No, no, that must not be, *Palamede,* for fear the Gardener
should come and catch you taking up the glass.

Enter Rhodophil.

290   *Rho. (Aside)* Billing so sweetly! now I am confirm'd in my
suspicions; I must put an end to this, ere it go further.

(To Doralice) Cry you mercy, Spouse; I fear I have interrupted
your recreations.

Dor. What recreations?

Rho. Nay, no excuses, good Spouse; I saw fair hand convey'd
to lip, and prest, as though you had been squeezing soft wax to-

---

266   together;] ∼, Q1–4, F, D.
272   line;] F; ∼, Q1–4, D.
291   further.] D; further. [*Aside.* Q1–4, F.
292   *s.d.* Doralice] *Doralice* Q1–4, F, D.

Gravelot inv.   G V.de Gucht Sculp.

RHODOPHIL SURPRISING DORALICE AND PALAMEDE,
ACT V, SCENE I
FROM *The Dramatick Works of John Dryden, Esq.* (1735)

gether for an Indenture. *Palamede,* you and I must clear this reckoning; why would you have seduc'd my wife?

Pal. Why would you have debauch'd my Mistris?

Rho. What do you think of that civil couple, that play'd at a Game call'd, *Hide and Seek,* last evening, in the Grotto?

Pal. What do you think of that innocent pair, who made it their pretence to seek for others, but came, indeed, to hide themselves there?

Rho. All things consider'd, I begin vehemently to suspect, that the young Gentleman I found in your company last night, was a certain youth of my acquaintance.

Pal. And I have an odd imagination, that you could never have suspected my small Gallant, if your little villanous *Frenchman* had not been a false Brother.

Rho. Farther Arguments are needless; Draw off; I shall speak to you now by way of *Bilbo.*   [*Claps his hand to his sword.*

Pal. And I shall answer you by the way of *Danger-field.*

                          [*Claps his hand on his.*

Dor. Hold, hold; are not you two a couple of mad fighting fools, to cut one another's throats for nothing?

Pal. How for nothing? he courts the woman I must marry.

Rho. And he courts you whom I have marri'd.

Dor. But you can neither of you be jealous of what you love not.

Rho. Faith I am jealous, and that makes me partly suspect that I love you better then I thought.

Dor. Pish! a meer jealousie of honour.

Rho. Gad I am afraid there's something else in't; for *Palamede* has wit, and if he loves you, there's something more in ye then I have found: some rich Mine, for ought I know, that I have not yet discover'd.

Pal. 'S life, what's this? here's an argument for me to love *Melantha;* for he has lov'd her, and he has wit too, and, for ought I know, there may be a Mine: but, if there be, I am resolv'd I'll dig for't.

Dor. (*To* Rhod.) Then I have found my account in raising

---

313   *Danger-field*] F; Danger-field Q1–4, D.
331   s.d. *To* Rhod.] *to Rhod.* Q1–4, F, D (*To* Q2–4).

your jealousie: O! 'tis the most delicate sharp sawce to a cloy'd
stomach; it will give you a new edge, *Rhodophil.*

Rho. And a new point too, *Doralice,* if I could be sure thou art
honest.

Dor. If you are wise, believe me for your own sake: Love and
Religion have but one thing to trust to; that's a good sound faith.
Consider, if I have play'd false, you can never find it out by any
experiment you can make upon me.

340   *Rho.* No? Why, suppose I had a delicate screw'd Gun, if I left
her clean, and found her foul, I should discover, to my cost, she
had been shot in.

Dor. But if you left her clean, and found her onely rusty, you
would discover, to your shame, she was onely so for want of
shooting.

Pal. Rhodophil, you know me too well, to imagine I speak for
fear; and therefore in consideration of our past friendship, I will
tell you, and bind it by all things holy, that *Doralice* is innocent.

Rho. Friend, I will believe you, and vow the same for your
350   *Melantha;* but the devil on't is, how we shall keep 'em so?

Pal. What dost think of a blessed community betwixt us four,
for the solace of the women, and relief of the men? Methinks it
would be a pleasant kind of life: Wife and Husband for the
standing Dish, and Mistris and Gallant for the Desert.

Rho. But suppose the Wife and the Mistris should both long
for the standing Dish, how should they be satisfi'd together?

Pal. In such a case they must draw lots: and yet that would not
do neither; for they would both be wishing for the longest cut.

Rho. Then I think, *Palamede,* we had as good make a firm
360   League, not to invade each others propriety.

Pal. Content, say I. From henceforth let all acts of hostility
cease betwixt us; and that in the usual form of Treaties, as well
by Sea as by Land, and in all Fresh waters.

Dor. I will adde but one *Proviso,* That who ever breaks the
League, either by war abroad, or by neglect at home, both the
Women shall revenge themselves, by the help of the other party.

Rho. That's but reasonable. Come away, *Doralice;* I have a
great temptation to be sealing Articles in private.

350   so?] Q2–4; ∼. Q1, F, D.   358   cut.] F; out? Q1–4, D (∼. Q2–4, D).

Palam. Hast thou so?   [*Claps him on the shoulder.*
370 Fall on, *Macduff,*
And curst be he that first cries, Hold, enough.

Enter Polydamas, Palmyra, Artemis, Argaleon: *after them,*
          Eubulus, *and* Hermogenes, *guarded.*

Palm. Sir, on my knees I beg you.
Pol. Away, I'll hear no more.
Palm. For my dead Mother's sake; you say you lov'd her,
And tell me I resemble her. Thus she
Had begg'd.
Pol. _____And thus had I deny'd her.
Palm. You must be merciful.
Arga. _____You must be constant.
Pol. Go, bear 'em to the torture; you have boasted
You have a King to head you: I would know
380 To whom I must resign.
Eub. _____This is our recompence
For serving thy dead Queen.
Her. _____And education
Of thy daughter.
Arga. You are too modest, in not naming all
His obligations to you: why did you
Omit his Son, the Prince *Leonidas?*
Pol. That Imposture
I had forgot; their tortures shall be doubled.
Her. You please me, I shall die the sooner.
Eub. No; could I live an age, and still be rack'd,
390 I still would keep the secret.   [*As they are going off,*

Enter Leonidas, *guarded.*

Leon. Oh whither do you hurry innocence?
If you have any justice, spare their lives;
Or if I cannot make you just, at least
I'll teach you to more purpose to be cruel.

---

370 *Macduff*] D; *Machduff* Q1-4, F.   391 innocence?] ∼! Q1-4, F, D.

Palm. Alas, what does he seek?

Leon. Make me the object of your hate and vengeance!
Are these decrepid bodies worn to ruine,
Just ready, of themselves, to fall asunder,
And to let drop the soul,
400 Are these fit subjects for a Rack, and Tortures?
Where would you fasten any hold upon 'em?
Place pains on me; united fix 'em here;
I have both youth, and strength, and soul to bear 'em:
And if they merit death, then I much more;
Since 'tis for me they suffer.

Her. ————————————Heav'n forbid
We should redeem our pains, or worthless lives,
By our exposing yours.

Eub. Away with us: Farewell, Sir.
I onely suffer in my fears for you.

410 *Arga.* So much concern'd for him? then my   [*Aside.*
Suspicion's true.   [*Whispers the King.*

Palm. Hear yet my last request, for poor *Leonidas;*
Or take my life with his.

Arga. Rest satisfi'd; *Leonidas* is he.   [*To the King.*

Pol. I am amaz'd: what must be done?

Arga. Command his execution instantly;
Give him not leisure to discover it;
He may corrupt the Soldiers.

Pol. Hence with that Traitour; bear him to his death:
420 Haste there, and see my will perform'd.

Leon. Nay, then I'll die like him the Gods have made me.
Hold, Gentlemen; I am———   [*Argaleon stops his mouth.*

Arga. Thou art a Traitor; 'tis not fit to hear thee.

Leon. I say I am the———   [*Getting loose a little.*

Arga. So; gag him, and lead him off.

[*Again stopping his mouth.*
[*Leonidas, Hermogenes, Eubulus, led
off. Polydamas and* Argaleon *follow.*

_____

395 seek?] ~! Q1–4, F, D.   410 s.d. Aside.] Q2–4, F, D; ~∧ Q1.
411 s.d. as in Q4, F, D; centered on a separate line, with final bracket in Q1–2;
flush right but with final bracket in Q3.

Palm. Duty and Love, by turns possess my soul,
And struggle for a fatal victory:
I will discover he's the King; Ah, no:
That will perhaps save him;
430 But then I am guilty of a father's ruine.
What shall I do, or not do? either way
I must destroy a Parent, or a Lover.
Break heart; for that's the least of ills to me,
And Death the onely cure.   [*Swoons.*
  Arte. ————————Help, help the Princess.
  Rho. Bear her gently hence, where she may have
More succour.   [*She is born off,* Arte. *follows her.*
                            [*Shouts within, and clashing of swords.*
  Pal. What noise is that?

Enter Amalthea, *running.*

  Amal. Oh, Gentlemen, if you have loyalty,
Or courage, show it now: *Leonidas*
440 Broke on the sudden from his Guards, and snatching
A sword from one, his back against the Scaffold,
Bravely defends himself; and owns aloud
He is our long lost King, found for this moment;
But, if your valours help not, lost for ever.
Two of his Guards, mov'd by the sense of virtue,
Are turn'd for him, and there they stand at Bay
Against an host of foes.
  Rho. ————————Madam, no more;
We lose time: my command, or my example,
May move the Soldiers to the better cause.
450 You'll second me?   [*To* Pal.
  Pal. Or die with you: no Subject e'r can meet
A nobler fate, then at his Sovereign's feet.   [*Exeunt.*
                            [*Clashing of swords within, and shouts.*

434 *Arte.*————] ~·ᴧ Q1–4, F, D.
435–436 may have / More] may / Have more Q1–4, F, D.

Enter Leonidas, Rhodophil, Palamede, Eubulus,
Hermogenes, *and their party, victorious;*
Polydamas *and* Argaleon, *disarm'd.*

Leon. That I survive the dangers of this day,
Next to the Gods, brave friends, be yours the honour.
And let Heav'n witness for me, that my joy
Is not more great for this my right restor'd,
Than 'tis, that I have power to recompence
Your Loyalty and Valour. Let mean Princes
Of abject souls, fear to reward great actions;
460 I mean to show,
That whatsoe'r subjects, like you, dare merit,
A King, like me, dares give————
 Rho. You make us blush, we have deserv'd so little.
 Pal. And yet instruct us how to merit more.
 Leon. And as I would be just in my rewards,
So should I in my punishments; these two,
This the Usurper of my Crown, the other
Of my *Palmyra*'s love, deserve that death
Which both design'd for me.
 Pol. ————————————And we expect it.
470 *Arga.* I have too long been happy to live wretched.
 Pol. And I too long have govern'd, to desire
A life without an Empire.
 Leon. You are *Palmyra*'s father; and as such,
Though not a King, shall have obedience paid
From him who is one. Father, in that name,
All injury's forgot, and duty own'd. [*Embraces him.*
 Pol. O, had I known you could have been this King,
Thus God-like, great and good, I should have wish'd
T' have been dethron'd before. 'Tis now I live,
480 And more then Reign; now all my joys flow pure,
Unmix'd with cares, and undisturb'd by conscience.

———————
452+ *s.d. victorious;*] ∼. Q1–4, **F, D.**
476 injury's] injuries Q1–4, **F, D.**

Enter Palmyra, Amalthea, Artemis, Doralice,
and Melantha.

Leon. See, my *Palmyra* comes! the frighted bloud
Scarce yet recall'd to her pale cheeks,
Like the first streaks of light broke loose from darkness,
And dawning into blushes.————Sir, you said,   [*To* Polyda.
Your joys were full; Oh, would you make mine so!
I am but half-restor'd without this blessing.

Pol. The Gods, and my *Palmyra,* make you happy,
As you make me.   [*Gives her hand to* Leonidas.

Palmy. ————Now all my prayers are heard:
490 I may be dutiful, and yet may love.
Virtue, and patience, have at length unravell'd
The knots which *Fortune* ty'd.

Mel. Let me die, but I'll congratulate his Majesty: how admirably well his Royalty becomes him! Becomes! that is *luy sied,* but our damn'd Language expresses nothing.

Pal. How? does it become him already? 'twas but just now you said, he was such a *figure* of a man.

Mel. True, my dear, when he was a private man he was a *figure;* but since he is a King, methinks he has assum'd another
500 *figure:* he looks so grand, and so August.   [*Going to the King.*

Pal. Stay, stay; I'll present you when it is more convenient. I find I must get her a place at Court; and when she is once there, she can be no longer ridiculous; for she is young enough, and pretty enough, and fool enough, and *French* enough, to bring up a fashion there to be affected.   [*Aside.*

Leon. (*To* Rhodophil) Did she then lead you to this brave attempt?
(*To* Amalthea) To you, fair *Amalthea,* what I am,
And what all these, from me, we joyntly owe:

493–495   *printed partly as verse (. . . his / Majesty . . . Royalty / Becomes . . .) in* Q*1–4,* F.
497, 499, 500   *figure*] figure Q1–4, F, D.
505   affected. [*Aside.*] affected. Q1–4, F, D.   506   *s.d. To*] Q3–4; *to* Q1–2, F, D.

510 First, therefore, to your great desert, we give
　　Your Brother's life; but keep him under guard,
　　Till our new power be setled. What more grace
　　He may receive, shall from his future carriage
　　Be given, as he deserves.
　　　　Arga. I neither now desire, nor will deserve it;
　　My loss is such as cannot be repair'd,
　　And to the wretched, life can be no mercy.
　　　　Leon. Then be a prisoner always: thy ill fate,
　　And pride will have it so: but since, in this, I cannot,
520 Instruct me, generous *Amalthea,* how
　　A King may serve you.
　　　　Amal. ——————————I have all I hope,
　　And all I now must wish; I see you happy.
　　Those hours I have to live, which Heav'n in pity
　　Will make but few, I vow to spend with Vestals:
　　The greatest part, in pray'rs for you; the rest
　　In mourning my unworthiness.
　　Press me not farther to explain my self;
　　'Twill not become me, and may cause you trouble.
　　　　Leon. Too well I understand her secret grief,　　　　*[Aside.*
530 But dare not seem to know it.————Come my
　　　　　　fairest,　　　　　　　　　　　　　　　　*[To* Palmyra.
　　Beyond my Crown, I have one joy in store;
　　To give that Crown to her whom I adore.　　　*[Exeunt omnes.*

———————

528　you] your Q1–4, F, D.

Epilogue.

THUS *have my Spouse and I inform'd the Nation,*
And led you all the way to Reformation:
Not with dull Morals, gravely writ, like those,
Which men of easie Phlegme, with care compose;
Your Poets of stiff words, and limber sense,
Born on the confines of indifference:
But by examples drawn, I dare to say,
From most of you, who hear, and see the Play.
There are more Rhodophils *in this Theatre,*
10 *More* Palamedes, *and some few Wives, I fear.*
But yet too far our Poet would not run,
Though 'twas well offer'd, there was nothing done.
He would not quite the Women's frailty bare,
But stript 'em to the waste, and left 'em there.
And the men's faults are less severely shown,
For he considers that himself is one.
Some stabbing Wits, to bloudy Satyr bent,
Would treat both Sexes with less complement:
Would lay the Scene at home, of Husbands tell,
20 *For Wenches, taking up their Wives i' th'* Mell,
And a brisk bout which each of them did want,
Made by mistake of Mistris and Gallant.
Our modest Authour, thought it was enough
To cut you off a Sample of the stuff:
He spar'd my shame, which you, I'm sure, would not,
For you were all for driving on the Plot:
You sigh'd when I came in to break the sport,
And set your teeth when each design fell short.

---

2   *Reformation:*] Os2–3; ∼. Q1–4, F, D; ∼, M1.
4   *compose;*] ∼. Q1–4, Os2–3; ∼: F, D; ∼, M1.
5   *Poets*] F, D, Os2–3, M1; *Poet's* Q1–4.
6   *indifference:*] ∼. Q1–4, F, D; ∼; Os2–3; ∼, M1.
13   *Women's*] M1; *Woman's* Q1–4, F, D; Women Os2–3.
20   Mell] F; *Mell* Q1–4, D, Os2–3, M1.

To Wives, and Servants all good wishes lend,
30   *But the poor Cuckold seldom finds a friend.*
Since therefore Court and Town will take no pity,
I humbly cast my self upon the City.

THE ASSIGNATION

OR

LOVE IN A NUNNERY

THE
ASSIGNATION:
OR,
Love in a Nunnery.

As it is ACTED,

At the *THEATRE-ROYAL.*

Written by *JOHN DRYDEN* Servant
to His MAJESTY.

Succeſſum dea dira negat————
Virg.

LONDON:
Printed by *T. N.* for *Henry Herringman*, and are to be ſold
at the *Anchor* in the Lower Walk of the
New Exchange. 1673.

TITLE PAGE OF THE FIRST EDITION (MACDONALD 78A)

TO MY MOST HONOUR'D FRIEND
Sir CHARLES SEDLEY, Baronet.

Sir,

THE Design of Dedicating Playes, is as common and unjust, as that of desiring Seconds in a Duel. 'Tis engaging our Friends (it may be) in a senceless quarrel, where they have much to venture, without any concernment of their own. I have declar'd thus much before-hand, to prevent you from suspicion, that I intend to interest either your judgment or your kindness, in defending the Errours of this Comedy. It succeeded ill in the representation, against the opinion of many the best
10 Judges of our Age, to whom you know I read it e're it was presented publickly. Whether the fault was in the Play it self, or in the lameness of the Action, or in the number of its Enemies, who came resolv'd to damn it for the Title, I will not now dispute: that wou'd be too like the little satisfaction which an unlucky Gamester finds in the relation of every cast by which he came to lose his Money. I have had formerly so much success, that the miscarriage of this Play was onely my giving Fortune her revenge: I ow'd it her; and she was indulgent that she exacted not the paiment long before. I will therefore deal more reasonably with
20 you, than any Poet has ever done with any Patron: I do not so much as oblige you for my sake to pass two ill houres in reading of my Play. Think, if you please, that this Dedication is onely an occasion I have taken to do my self the greatest honour imaginable with Posterity; that is, to be recorded in the number of those Men whom you have favour'd with your Friendship and esteem. For, I am well assur'd, that besides the present satisfaction I have, it will gain me the greatest part of my reputation with after-Ages, when they shall find me valuing my self on your kindness

---

2 Dedicating Playes] *Dedicating Playes* Q1–3, F, D.
3 Duel] *Duel* Q1–3, F, D.   8 Comedy] *Comedy* Q1–3, F, D.
17 Fortune] F, D; fortune Q1–3.

to me: I may have reason to suspect my own credit with them,
but I have none to doubt of yours. And they who perhaps wou'd
forget me in my Poems, wou'd remember me in this Epistle.

This was the course which has formerly been practis'd by the
Poets of that Nation who were Masters of the Universe. *Horace*
and *Ovid,* who had little reason to distrust their Immortality;
yet took occasion to speak with honour of *Virgil, Varius, Tibullus,* and *Propertius* their Contemporaries: as if they sought in
the testimony of their Friendship a farther evidence of their
10 fame. For my own part, I, who am the least amongst the Poets,
have yet the fortune to be honour'd with the best Patron, and the
best Friend. For, (to omit some Great Persons of our Court, to
whom I am many wayes oblig'd, and who have taken care of me,
even amidst the Exigencies of a War,) I can make my boast to
have found a better *Mæcenas* in the person of my Lord Treasurer
Clifford, and a more Elegant *Tibullus* in that of Sir *Charles
Sedley.* I have chosen that Poet to whom I would resemble you,
not onely because I think him at least equal, if not superiour to
Ovid in his *Elegies:* nor because of his quality for he was (you
20 know) a *Roman* Knight as well as *Ovid:* but for his Candour, his
Wealth, his way of Living, and particularly because of this testimony which is given him by *Horace,* which I have a thousand
times in my mind apply'd to you.

> *Non tu Corpus eras sine pectore; Dii tibi formam,*
> *Dii tibi divitias dederant, artemq; fruendi.*
> *Quid voveat dulci Nutricula majus Alumno*
> *Quam sapere, & fari possit quæ sentiat, & cui*
> *Gratia, forma, valetudo contingat abunde;*
> *Et mundus victus, non deficiente crumena?*

30 Certainly the Poets of that Age enjoy'd much happiness in the
Conversation and Friendship of one another. They imitated the
best way of Living, which was to pursue an innocent and in-
offensive Pleasure; that which one of the Ancients called *Eruditam voluptatem.* We have, like them, our Genial Nights; where
our discourse is neither too serious, nor too light; but alwayes

3 Epistle] *Epistle* Q1-3, F, D.

pleasant, and for the most part instructive: the raillery neither too sharp upon the present, nor too censorious on the absent; and the Cups onely such as will raise the Conversation of the Night, without disturbing the business of the Morrow. And thus far not only the Philosophers, but the Fathers of the Church have gone, without lessening their Reputation of good Manners, or of Piety. For this reason I have often Laugh'd at the ignorant and ridiculous Descriptions which some Pedants have given of the Wits (as they are pleas'd to call them:) which are a Genera-
10 tion of Men as unknown to them, as the People of *Tartary* or the *terra Australis* are to us. And therefore as we draw Giants and *Anthropophagi* in those vacancies of our Maps, where we have not Travell'd to discover better; so those wretches Paint leudness, Atheism, Folly, ill-Reasoning, and all manner of Extravagances amongst us for want of understanding what we are. Oftentimes it so falls out, that they have a particular picque to some one amongst us; and then they immediately interest Heaven in their quarrel: As 'tis an usual trick in Courts; when one designs the ruine of his Enemy, to disguise his malice with some con-
20 cernment of the Kings: and to revenge his own cause, with pretence of vindicating the Honour of his Master. Such Wits as they describe, I have never been so unfortunate to meet in your Company: but have often heard much better Reasoning at your Table, than I have encounter'd in their Books. The Wits they describe, are the Fops we banish: for Blasphemy and Atheism, if they were neither Sin nor Ill Manners, are Subjects so very common, and worn so Thredbare, that people who have sence avoid them, for fear of being suspected to have none. It calls the good Name of their Wit in question, as it does the Credit of a
30 Citizen when his Shop is fill'd with Trumperies, and Painted Titles in stead of Wares: we conclude them Bankrupt to all manner of understanding: and, that to use Blasphemy, is a kind of applying Pigeons to the Soles of the Feet: it proclaims their Fancy as well as judgment, to be in a desperate condition. I am sure for your own particular, if any of these Judges had once the happiness to converse with you, to hear the Candour of your

---

11 Giants] Q3; *Giants* Q1–2, F, D.   12 vacancies] Q3, F, D; vacances Q1–2.
12 Maps] *Maps* Q1–3, F, D.   31 Bankrupt] Q3, F, D; Bancrupt Q1–2.

Opinions; how freely you commend that wit in others, of which
you have so large a Portion your self; how unapt you are to be
censorious; with how much easiness you speak so many things,
and those so Pointed, that no other Man is able to excell, or perhaps to reach by Study; they wou'd, in stead of your Accusers,
become your Proselites. They wou'd reverence so much good
Sence, and so much good Nature in the same person: and come,
like the Satyre, to warm themselves at that Fire, of which they
were ignorantly afraid, when they stood at distance. But, you
10 have too great a Reputation to be wholly free from Censure: 'tis
a fine which Fortune sets upon all extraordinary persons, and
from which you should not wish to be deliver'd till you are dead.
I have been us'd by my Critiques much more severely, and have
more reason to complain, because I am deeper tax'd for a less
Estate. I am ridiculously enough accus'd to be a contemner of
Universities, that is in other words, an Enemy of Learning: without the Foundation of which I am sure no Man can pretend to
be a Poet. And if this be not enough I am made a Detractor from
my Predecessors, whom I confess to have been my Masters in
20 the Art. But this latter was the accusation of the best Judge, and
almost the best Poet in the *Latine* Tongue. You find *Horace*
complaining, that for taxing some Verses in *Lucilius,* he himself
was blam'd by others, though his Design was no other than mine
now, to improve the Knowledge of Poetry: and it was no defence
to him, amongst his Enemies, any more than it is for me, that he
Prais'd *Lucilius* where he deserv'd it; *Paginâ laudatur eâdem.*
'Tis for this reason I will be no more mistaken for my good
meaning: I know I honour *Ben Johnson* more than my little
Critiques, because without vanity I may own, I understand him
30 better. As for the Errors they pretend to find in me, I could
easily show them that the greatest part of them are Beauties: and
for the rest, I could recriminate upon the best Poets of our Nation, if I could resolve to accuse another of little faults, whom
at the same time I admire for greater Excellencies. But I have
neither concernment enough upon me to write any thing in my
own Defence, neither will I gratifie the ambition of two wretched
Scriblers, who desire nothing more than to be Answer'd. I have

---

13   been] Q2–3, F, D; ∼, Q1.   21   *Latine*] Q3, D; Latine Q1–2, F.

not wanted Friends, even amongst Strangers, who have defended
me more strongly, than my contemptible Pedant cou'd attacque
me. For the other: he is onely like *Fungoso* in the Play, who follows the Fashion at a distance, and adores the *Fastidious Brisk*
of *Oxford*. You can bear me witness, that I have not consideration enough for either of them to be angry: Let *Mævius* and
Bavius admire each other, I wish to be hated by them and their
Fellows, by the same reason for which I desire to be lov'd by
you. And I leave it to the world, whether their judgment of my
Poetry ought to be preferr'd to yours; though they are as much
prejudic'd by their Malice, as I desire you should be led by your
Kindness, to be partial to, Sir,

> *Your most Humble*
> *and most Faithful Servant*

John Dryden.

---

4 *Fastidious*] *Fastidius* Q1–3, F, D.

Prologue.

PROLOGUES, *like Bells to Churches, toul you in*
With Chimeing Verse; till the dull Playes begin:
With this sad difference though, of Pit and Pue;
You damn the Poet, *but the* Priest *damns you.*
But Priests can treat you at your own expence:
And, gravely, call you Fooles, without offence.
Poets, poor Devils, have ne'r your Folly shown
But, to their cost, you prov'd it was their own.
For, when a Fop's presented on the Stage,
10 *Straight all the Coxcombs in the Town ingage:*
For his deliverance, and revenge they joyn:
And grunt, like Hogs, about their Captive Swine.
Your Poets daily split upon this shelfe:
You must have Fooles, yet none will have himself.
Or, if in kindness, you that leave would give,
No man could write you at that rate you live:
For some of you grow Fops with so much haste, ⎫
Riot in nonsence, and commit such waste,   ⎬
'Twould Ruine Poets should they spend so fast. ⎭
20 *He who made this, observ'd what Farces hit,*
And durst not disoblige you now with wit.
But, Gentlemen, you overdo the Mode:
You must have Fooles out of the common Rode.
Th' unnatural strain'd Buffoon is onely taking:
No Fop can please you now of Gods own making.
Pardon our Poet if he speaks his Mind,
You come to Plays with your own Follies lin'd:
Small Fooles fall on you, like small showers, in vain:
Your own oyl'd Coates keep out all common raine.
30 *You must have* Mamamouchi *such a Fop*
As would appear a Monster in a Shop:
Hee'l fill your Pit and Boxes to the brim,

---

30 Mamamouchi] D; *Mamamouchi,* Q1–3, F.

Where, Ram'd in Crowds, you see your selves in him.
Sure there's some spell our Poet never knew,
In Hullibabilah da, *and* Chu, chu, chu.
But Marabarah sahem *most did touch ye,*
That is: Oh how we love the Mamamouchi!
Grimace and habit sent you pleas'd away:
You damn'd the Poet, and cry'd up the Play.
40   *This thought had made our Author more uneasie,*
But that he hopes I'm Fool enough to please ye:
But here's my griefe; though Nature joyn'd with art,
Have cut me out to act a Fooling Part;
Yet, to your praise, the few wits here will say,
'Twas imitating you taught Haynes *to Play.*

---

35   Hullibabilah da] F, D; *hullibabilah da* Q1–3.
35   Chu, chu, chu] F, D; *Chu, chu, chu* Q1–3.
36   Marabarah sahem] F, D; *Marabarah sahem* Q1–3.
36   *ye*] *you* Q1–3, F, D.
37   Oh how we love the Mamamouchi!] *Oh how we love the Mamamouchi!* Q1–3,
F, D (Mamamouchi F, D).

Persons Represented.

		By
Duke of *Mantoua*—————————————	—Major *Mohun.*	
Prince *Frederick* his Son————————	—Mr. *Kynaston.*	
Aurelian a *Roman* Gentleman————	—Mr. *Hart.*	
Camillo his Friend—————————	—Mr. *Burt.*	
Mario Governor of *Rome*——————	—Mr. *Cartwright.*	
Ascanio, Page of Honour to the Prince———	—Mrs. *Reeve.*	
Benito, Servant to *Aurelian*————	—Mr. *Haynes.*	
Valerio, Confident to the Duke————		
Fabio, Servant to *Mario*————		

Sophronia, Abbess of the *Torr' di Specchi.*———	—Mrs. *James.*	
Lucretia, a Lady design'd to be a Nun———	—Mrs. *Marshall.*	
Hippolita, a Nun—————————	—Mrs. *Knep.*	

Laura
  and   } Sisters, Neeces to *Mario*———— { Mrs. *Bowtel.*
Violetta {Mrs. *Cox.*

Scene, *ROME.*

THE
ASSIGNATION:
OR,
LOVE IN A NUNNERY.

SCENE *a Room.*

A Great Glass Plac'd.

Enter Benito, *with a Guittar in his hand.*

Benito bowing to the Glass. Save you, sweet Signior *Benito;* by
my faith I am glad to see you look so bonily to day: Gad, Sir,
every thing becomes you to a miracle! your Perruke, your Cloaths,
your Hat, your Shoo-tyes; and, Gad, Sir, let me tell you, you become every thing; you walk with such a grace, and you bow so
pliantly———

Aurelian within. Benito, Where are you, Sirrah?

Ben. Sirrah! That my damn'd Master should call a man of my
extraordinary indowments, Sirrah! A man of my indowments?

10 Gad, I ask my own pardon, I mean, a person of my indowments;
for a man of my parts and tallents, though he be but a *Valet de
Chambre,* is a person; and, let me tell my Master———Gad, I
frown too, as like a person as any Jack-Gentleman of 'em all; but,
Gad, when I do not frown, I am an absolute beauty: whatever this
Glass sayes to the contrary: and, if this Glass deny it, 'tis a base,
lying Glass, so I'll tell it to its face, and kick it down into the
bargain.

Aurelian within. Why *Benito,* How long shall we stay for you?

---

s.d. *a Room.*] D; *ROME* Q1–3, F.   15   Glass sayes] Q2–3, F, D; Class sayes Q1.
18   *Aurelian*] F; *Aurelia* Q1–3; *Aur.* D.

Ben. I come, Sir. What the Devil would he have? But, by his
20 favour, I'll first survey my Dancing, and my Singing.
  [*He playes on the Guittar, and Dances and Sings to the Glass.*
I think that was not amiss: I think so.   [*Layes down the Guittar.*
Gad, I can Dance, and play no longer, I am in such a rapture
with my self. What a villanous base fate have I! with all these excellencies, and a profound wit, and yet to be a Serving-man!

Enter Aurelian *and* Camillo.

Aur. Why, you Slave, you Dog, you Son of twenty Fathers, am
I to be serv'd at this rate eternally? A pox o' your conceited coxcomb.
  Camillo. Nay, prythee, *Aurelian,* be not angry.
  Aur. You do not know this Rogue, as I do, *Camillo.* Now, by
30 this Guittar, and that great looking-glass, I am certain how he
has spent his time. He courts himself every morning in that Glass,
at least an hour: there admires his own person, and his parts, and
studies postures and grimaces, to make himself yet more ridiculous, than he was born to be.
  Cam. You wrong him sure.
  Aur. I do; for he is yet more fool than I can speak him: I never
send him on a message, but he runs first to that Glass, to practice
how he may become his errand. Speak, Is this a lye, Sirrah?
  Ben. I confess, I have some kindness for the mirrour.
40   *Aur.* The mirrour! there's a touch of his Poetry too, he could
not call it a Glass. Then the Rogue has the impudence to make
Sonnets, as he calls 'em; and, which is a greater impudence, he
sings 'em too: there's not a Street in all *Rome* which he does not
nightly disquiet with his villanous Serenades: with that Guittar
there, the younger brother of a Cittern, he frights away the
Watch; and for his Violin, it squeaks so lewdly, that Sir *Tibert* in
the gutter mistakes him for his Mistriss. 'Tis a meer Cat-call.
  Cam. Is this true *Benito?*
  Ben. to Cam. aside. My Master, Sir, may say his pleasure; I

19 I ... have?] *set as a line of verse in Q1–3, F.*   20+   *s.d.* [*He*] F, D; ₐ~ Q1–3.
23 I!] ~? Q1–3, F, D.   37 send] F; sent Q1–3, D.

50 divert my self sometimes with hearing him: Alass, good Gentleman, 'tis not given to all persons to penetrate into Mens parts and
qualities; but I look on you, Sir, as a man of judgment, and therefore you shall hear me play and sing.

    [He takes up the Guittar and begins.

    Aur. Why, you invincible Sot you, will nothing mend you?
Lay 't down, or———

    Ben. to Camillo. Do ye see, Sir, this Enemy to the Muses? he
will not let me hold forth to you.   *[Layes down the Guittar.*
O Envy, and Ignorance, Whither will you!———But, Gad, before I'll suffer my parts to be kept in obscurity———

60   *Aur.* What will you do, Rascal?

    Ben. I'll take up the Guittar, and suffer heroically.

    [He Playes, Aure. *Kicks.*

    Aur. What? Do you Mutiny?

    Ben. Ay, do, kick till your toes ake; I'll be baffled in my Musick
by ne'r a foot in Christendome.

    Aur. I'll put you out of your time, with a vengeance to you.

    [As Aurelian *kicks harder,* Benito *sings*
    faster, and sometimes cryes out.

    Cam. holding Aur. Nay, then 'tis time to stickle. Hold, *Au-*
relian, prythee spare *Benito,* you know we have occasion for
him.

    Aur. I think that was well kick'd.

70   *Ben.* And I think that was well Sung too.

    Cam. Enough, *Aurelian.*

    Ben. No, Sir; let him proceed to discourage vertue, and see
what will come on't.

    Cam. Now to our business: but we must first instruct *Benito.*

    Aur. Be rul'd by me, and do not trust him: I prophesie he'll
spoil the whole affair; he has a Worm in's head as long as a
Conger, a brain so barren of all sence, and yet so fruitful of foolish plots, that if he does not all things his own way, yet at least
he'll ever be mingling his designs with yours, and go halves with
80 you, so that what with his ignorance, what with his plotting,
he'll be sure to ruine you, with an intention to serve you. For my

53+ *s.d.* [*He*] F, D; ₍ₐ₎~ Q1–3.   61+ *s.d.* [*He*] Q3, F, D; ₍ₐ₎~ Q1–2.
65+ *s.d.* [*As*] F, D; ₍ₐ₎~ Q1–3.   81 he'll] *some copies of Q1 have* h'll.

part I had turn'd him off long since; but that my wise Father, commanded me the contrary.

Cam. Still you speak, as if what we did were choice, and not necessity: you know their Uncle is suspicious of me, and consequently jealous of all my Servants; but if we employ yours, who is not suspected, because you are a stranger; I doubt not to get an Assignation with the younger Sister.

Aur. Well, use your own way, *Camillo:* but if it ever succeed, 90 with his management————

Cam. You must understand then, *Benito,* that this old Signior *Mario,* has two Neeces, with one of which I am desperately in Love, and————

Ben. aside to him. I understand you already, Sir, and you desire Love reciprocal: Leave your business in my hands, and, if it succeed not, think me no wiser than my Master.

Cam. Pray take me with you. These Sisters are great Beauties and vast Fortunes; but, by a Clause in their Fathers Will, if they Marry without their Uncles Consent, are to forfeit all. Their 100 Uncle, who is covetous, and base to the last degree, takes advantage of this Clause, and under pretence of not finding fit Matches for them, denies his consent to all who love 'em.

Ben. Denies 'em marriage: very good, Sir.

Cam. More than this, he refuses access to any Suitor, and immures 'em in a mean appartment on the garden side, where he barbarously debars 'em from all humane Society.

Ben. Uses them most barbarously: Still better and better.

Cam. The younger of these Sisters, *Violetta,* I have seen often in the Garden, from the Balcony in this Chamber, which looks 110 into it, have divers times shot Tickets on the point of an Arrow, which She has taken, and by the signes she made me I find they were not ill receiv'd.

Ben. I'll tell you now, just such an Amour as this had I once with a young Lady, that————

Aur. Quote your self agen, you Rogue, and my feet shall renew their acquaintance with your Buttocks.

---

94   *him.*] Q3, D; ~, Q1–2; ~∧ F.   106   Society] Q2–3, F, D; Socitey Q1.
108   Sisters] Q3, F, D; *Sisters* Q1–2.

Cam. Dear *Benito,* take care to convey this Ticket to *Violetta:* I saw her just now go by to the next Chappel; be sure to stand ready to give her Holy-water, and slip the Ticket into the hand
120 of her Woman *Beatrix;* And take care the elder Sister *Laura* sees you not, for she knows nothing of our Amour.

Ben. A word to the wise.
Have you no Service to *Laura?*   [*To* Aurelian.

Aur. None that I shall trouble you withall: I'll see first what returns you make from this Voyage, before I put in my venture with you. Away; be gone, Mr. *Mercury.*

Ben. I fly, Mr. *Jupiter.*   [*Exit.*

Aur. This Lady *Laura* I have seen from your Balcone, and was seen by her: methought, too, she lookt with a languishing eye
130 upon me, as who should say, Are you a man, and have no pitty for a poor distressed Virgin? For my part, I never found so much disposition in my self to Love any woman at first sight: handsome she is, of that I am certain.

Cam. And has Wit, I dare assure you; but I have not heard she has admitted of any Gallantry.

Aur. Her hour is not come yet; she has not met with a man to Love: when that happens (as I am resolv'd to push my fortune) you shall see that, as her love warms, her vertue will melt down, and dissolve in it; for there's no such Baud to a woman, as her
140 own wit is.

Cam. I look upon the Assignation, as certain: Will you promise me to go? You and *Benito* shall walk in the Garden, while I search the Nymph within the shade; one thing I had forgot to tell you, that our General of the Church, the Duke of *Mantoua,* and the Prince his Son, are just approaching the Gates of *Rome:* Will you go see the Ceremony of their Entrance?

Aur. With all my heart. They say, he has behav'd himself gallantly against the *French,* at their return from *Naples:* besides, I have a particular knowledge of young Prince *Frederick,* ever
150 since he was last at our *Venetian* Carnival.

Cam. Away, then, quickly; least we miss the Solemnity.
        [*Exeunt.*

151+   *s.d.* [*Exeunt*] F, D; ∧~ Q1–3.

Enter Laura, *and* Violetta *striving about a Letter, which*
Laura *holds.*

Vio. Let it go, I say.

Lau. I say, let you go.

Vio. Nay, sweet Sister *Laura.*

Lau. Nay, dear *Violetta,* 'tis in vain to contend, I am resolv'd
I'll see it.   [*Plucks the Paper from* Violetta.

Vio. But I am resolv'd you shall not read it. I know not what
authority this is which you assume, or what priviledge a year or
two can give you, to use this Soveraignty over me.

160   *Lau.* Do you rebell young Gentlewoman? I'll make you know
I have a double right over you: one, as I have more years; and
the other as I have more wit.

Vio. Though I am not all Ayr and Fire, as you are, yet that
little wit I have, will serve to conduct my Affairs, without a
Governess.

Lau. No, Gentlewoman, but it shall not: are you fit at Fifteen
to be trusted with a Maidenhead? 'Tis as much as your betters
can manage at full twenty.

> *For 'tis of a nature so subtil,*
170 > *That, if 'tis not Luted with care*
> *The Spirit will work through the Bottel,*
> *And vanish away into Ayr.*
> *To keep it, there's nothing so hard is,*
> *'Twill go betwixt waking and sleeping,*
> *The Simple too weak for a guard is,*
> *And no Wit would be plagu'd with the keeping.*

Vio. For ought I see, you are as little to be trusted with your
Madness, as I with my Simplicity; and therefore pray restore my
Letter.

180   *Lau. reading it.* What's here? An humble Petition for a private
Meeting? Are you twittering at that sport already, Mistriss Novice?

Vio. How! I a Novice, at ripe Fifteen? I would have you to

---

152   say.] F, D; ~: Q1–3.   167   much as] Q3, F, D; much Q1–2.

know, that I have kill'd my Man before I was Fourteen, and now
am ready for another execution.

 Lau. A very forward Rose-bud: you open apace, Gentlewoman. I find indeed your desires are quick enough; but where will
you have cunning to carry on your business with decency and
secrecy? Secrecy, I say, which is a main part of chastity in our Sex.
190 Where wit, to be sensible of the delicacies of Love? the tenderness
of a farewell-sigh? for an absence? the joy of a return? the zeal of
a pressing-hand? the sweetness of little quarrels, caus'd, and cur'd,
by the excess of Love? and, in short, the pleasing disquiets of the
Soul, always restless, and wandring up and down in a paradise
of thought, of its own making?

 Vio. If I understood not thus much before, I find you are an excellent instructer, and that argues you have had a feeling of the
cause in your time too, Sister.

 Lau. What have I confess'd before I was aware? She'll find out
200 my inclination to that stranger, whom I have only seen, and to
whom I have never spoken⸺   [*Aside.*
No, good *Violetta,* I never was in Love; all my experience is from
Playes and Romances: But who is this man, to whom you have
promis'd an Assignation?

 Vio. You'll tell my Uncle.

 Lau. I hate my Uncle more than you do.

 Vio. You know the man, 'tis Signior *Camillo:* his Birth and
Fortunes are equal to what I can expect; and he tells me his in-
tentions are Honourable.

210 *Lau.* Have I not seen him lately in his Balcone, which looks
into our Garden, with another handsome Gentleman in his
Company, who seems a stranger?

 Vio. They are the same. Do you think it a reasonable thing,
dear *Laura,* that my Uncle should keep us up so strictly, that we
must be beholden to hearsay, to know a young Gallant is in the
next house to us?

 Lau. 'Tis hard, indeed, to be mew'd like Hawks, and never
Man'd: to be lock'd in like Nuns here.

---

199 aware?] ~! Q1–3, F, D.
201 s.d. [*Aside*] F, D; ͚~ Q1–3 (*no space preceding; followed by next sentence on
same line in Q1–3, F*).
215 hearsay] D; heresay Q1–3, F.

Vio. They that look for Nuns flesh in me shall be mistaken.

220 *Lau.* Well, What answer have you return'd to this Letter?

Vio. That I would meet him at eight this evening, in the close walk in the Garden, attended onely by *Beatrix* my Woman.

Lau. Who comes with him?

Vio. Only his friend's Man *Benito;* the same who brought me the Letter which you took from me.

Lau. Stay, let me think a little. Do *Camillo,* or this *Benito,* know your Maid *Beatrix?*

Vio. They have never talk'd with her; but only seen her.

Lau. 'Tis concluded then; you shall meet your Servant, but I'll
230 be your *Beatrix:* I'll go in stead of her, and counterfeit your wait-ing-woman: in the dark I may easily pass for her: By this means I shall be present to instruct you; for you are yet a Callow Maid: I must teach you to Peck a little, you may come to Prey for your self in time.

Vio. A little teaching will serve my turn: if the old one left me to my self, I could go near to get my Living.

Lau. I find you are eager, and Baiting to be gone already, and I'll not hinder you when your hour approaches. In the mean time go in, and sigh, and think fondly, and ignorantly of your ap-
240 proaching pleasures:

Love, in young hearts, is like the must of Wine;
'Tis sweetest then; but elder 'tis more fine.   [*Exeunt.*

ACT II.   SCENE I.

The Front of a Nunnery.

Prince Frederick, Aurelian, Camillo, *and* Ascanio
the Princes Page.

Fred. My Father's antient, and may repose himself, if he pleases, after the Ceremony of his Entrance; but we, who are younger, should think it a sin, to spend any part of day-light in

242 *s.d.* [*Exeunt*] F, D; ∧~ Q1–3.   ACT] Q3, F, D; ~. Q1–2.
s.d. Princes Page] *Princes Page* Q1–3, F, D.
1 Father's] Q3, F, D; Fathers' Q1; Fathers Q2.

a Chamber. What are your wayes of living here?

Cam. Why Sir, we pass our time, either in conversation alone, or in Love alone, or in Love and Conversation together.

Fred. Come, explain, explain, my Counsel learned in the Laws of Living.

Cam. For conversation alone; that's either in going to Court, with a Face of Business, and there discoursing of the affairs of *Europe,* of which, *Rome,* you know, is the publick Mart; or, at best, meeting the *Vertuosi,* and there, wearying one another with rehearsing our own works, in Prose and Poetry.

Fred. Away with that dry method, I will have none on't. To the next.

Cam. Love alone, is either plain wenching, where every Curtizan is your Mistriss, and every Man your Rival; or else, what's worse, plain whining after one Woman: that is, walking before her door by day, and haunting her street by night, with Guittars, dark Lanthorns, and Rondaches.

Aur. Which, I take it, is, or will be our case, *Camillo.*

Fred. Neither of these will fit my humour: if your third prove not more pleasant, I shall stick to the old *Almaine* recreation; the Divine bottel, and the bounteous glass, that tun'd up old *Horace* to his *Odes.*

Aur. You shall need to have no recourse to that; for Love, and Conversation will do your business: that is, Sir, a most delicious Curtizan, I do not mean down-right Punk, but Punk of more than ordinary sence in Conversation: Punk in Ragou, Punk who playes on the Lute, and Sings; and, to sum up all, Punk who Cooks and Dresses up her self, with Poynant Sawce, to become a new Dish every time she is serv'd up to you.

Fred. This I believe, *Aurelian,* is your method of living, you talk of it so savorily.

Aur. There is yet another more insipid sort of Love and Conversation: as for example, look you there, Sir; the Courtship of our Nuns.   [*Pointing to the Nunnery.*
They talk prettily; but, a Pox on 'em, they raise our appetites, and then starve us. They are as dangerous as cold Fruits without Wine, and are never to be us'd but where there are abundance

---

23 *Almaine*] Q3, D; Almaine Q1-2, F.   37 *s.d. Nunnery.*] Q3, F, D; ~∧ Q1-2.

of Wenches in readiness, to qualifie 'em.

Cam. But yet they are ever at hand, and easie to come by; and if you'l believe an experienc'd sinner, easiness in Love is more than half the pleasure of it.

Fre. This way of chatting pleases me; for debauchery, I hate it; and, to Love, is not in my nature, except it be my Friends. Pray, What do you call that Nunnery?

Cam. 'Tis a House of *Benedictines,* call'd the *Torr' di Specchi,* where only Ladies of the best Quality are Profess'd.

Lucretia *and* Hippolita *appear at the Grates.*

50 *Aur.* Look you, yonder, Sir, are two of the pretty Magpies, in white and black: if you will lull your self into a Platonick Dream you may: but, consider your sport will be but dull, when you play without Stakes.

Fred. No matter, I'll fool away an hour of Courtship; for I never yet was engag'd in a serious love, nor I believe can be. Farewell, Gentlemen; at this time I shall dispence with your attendance: nay, without Ceremony, because I would be incognito.

Cam. Come then, *Aurelian,* to our own affairs.

[*Exeunt* Aur. *and* Camillo. *The* Prince
and Ascanio *approach.*

Fred. to Lu. For what Crime, fair Creature, were you con-
60 demn'd to this perpetual Prison?

Luc. For Chastity and Devotion, and two or three such melancholly vertues: they first brought me hither, and now must keep me company.

Fred. I should rather have guess'd it had been Murder, and that you are veil'd, for fear of doing more mischief with those Eyes: for, indeed, they are too sharp to be trusted out of the Scabbard.

Luc. Cease, I beseech you, to accuse my Eyes, till they have done some execution on your heart.

---

47 Nunnery?] ~. Q1–3, F, D.   48 *Torr'*] *Torre* Q1–3, F, D.
49+ *s.d. right justified in Q1–3, F, D (with bracket preceeding in F, D).*
50 you,] Q3; ~ˬ Q1–2, F, D.   58+ *s.d.* [*Exeunt*] F, D; ˬ~ Q1–3.
58+ *s.d. The . . . approach.] centered on separate line in Q1–3, F, D.*
59 *to*] D; to Q1–3, F.

70 *Fred.* But I am out of reach, perhaps.

Luc. Trust not to that; they may shoot at a distance, though they cannot strike you near at hand.

Fred. But, if they should kill, you are ne'r the better: there's a Grate betwixt us, and you cannot fetch in the dead Quarry.

Luc. Provided we destroy the Enemy, we do not value their dead bodies: but you, perhaps, are in your first error, and think we are rather Captives than Warriours; that we come like Prisoners to the Grate, to beg the Charity of Passengers for their love.

Fre. to Ascanio. Inquire as dexterously as you can, what is the 80 Name and Quality of this Charming Creature.

Luc. to Hip. Be sure, if the Page approaches you, to get out of him his Masters Name.   [*The* Prince *and* Lucretia *seem to talk.*

Hip. to Asca. By that short whisper which I observ'd you took with your Master, I imagine, Mr. Page, you come to ask a certain question of me.

Asca. By this thy question, and by that whisper with thy Lady, (O thou Nymph of Devotion!) I find I am to impart a secret, and not to ask one: therefore, either confess thou art yet a meer Woman under that Veil, and by consequence most horribly inquisi-90 tive, or thou shalt lose thy longing, and know nothing of my Master.

Hip. By my Virginity, you shall tell first.

Asca. You'll break your Oath, on purpose to make the forfeit.

Hip. Your Master is call'd———

Asca. Your Lady is Yclip'd———

Hip. For decency, in all matters of Love, the Man should offer first, you know.

Asca. That needs not, when the Damsel is so willing.

Hip. But I have sworn not to discover first, that her Name is 100 Madam *Lucretia;* fair, as you see, to a Miracle, and of a most charming conversation; of Royal blood, and Neece to his Holiness; and, if she were not espous'd to Heaven, a Mistriss for a Soveraign Prince.

Asca. After these Encomiums, 'twere vain for me to praise my Master: he is only poor Prince *Frederick,* otherwise call'd the

Prince of *Mantoua;* liberal, and valiant, discreet and handsome, and, in my simple judgment, a fitter Servant for your Lady, than his old Father, who is a Soveraign.

Hip. Dare you make all this good you have said of your Master?

110 *Asca.* Yes, and as much more of my self to you.

Hip. I defy you upon't, as my Lady's Second.

Asca. As my Masters, I accept it. The time?

Hip. Six this evening.

Asca. The place?

Hip. At this Grate.

Asca. The Weapons?

Hip. Hands, and it may be Lips.

Asca. 'Tis enough: expect to hear from me.

[*They withdraw and whisper to their Principals.*
After the Whisper.

Fred. to Luc. Madam, I am glad I know my enemy; for since it

120 is impossible to see, and not admire you, the name of *Lucretia* is the best excuse for my defeat.

Luc. Persons, like Prince *Frederick,* ought not to assault Religious Houses; or to pursue Chastity and Virtue to their last retreat.

Fred. A Monastery is no retreat for Chastity; 'tis only a hiding place for bad faces, where they are thrust in Crowds together, like heaps of rubbish out of the way, that the world may not be peopled with deform'd persons, and that such who are out of Play themselves, may pray for a blessing on their endeavours, who are

130 getting handsome Children: and carrying on the work for publick benefit.

Luc. Then you would put off Heaven with your leavings, and use it like them who play at Cards alone, take the Courts for your selves, and give the refuse to the Gentleman.

Fred. You mistake me, Madam; I would so contrive it, that Heaven and we might be serv'd at once: we have occasion for Wit and Beauty; now Piety and Ugliness will do as well for Heaven; that playes at one Game, and we at another, and therefore heaven may make its hand with the same Cards that we put out.

140 *Luc.* I could easily convince you if the argument concern'd

---

118+   *s.d.* [*They*] F, D; ∧~ Q1–3.

me; but I am one of those, whom, for want of wit and beauty, you have condemn'd to Religion: and therefore am your humble Servant to Pray for your handsome Wife and Children.

Fred. Heaven forbid, Madam, that I should condemn you, or indeed any handsome woman, to be Religious. No, Madam; the occasions of the World are great and urgent for such as you: and, for my part, I am of opinion, that it is as great a Sin for a Beauty to enter into a Nunnery, as for an ugly woman to stay out of it.

Luc. The Cares of the World are not yet upon you; but as soon as ever you come to be afflicted with Sickness, or visited with a Wife, you'll be content I should pray for you.

Fre. Any where, rather than in a Cloyster; for, truly, I suppose, all your Prayers there will be how to get out of it; and, upon that supposition, Madam, I am come to offer you my service for your redemption. Come, faith, be perswaded, the Church shall lose nothing by it: I'll take you out, and put in two or three Crooked Apostles in your place.   [*Bell rings within.*

Luc. Hark, the Bell rings, I must leave you: 'tis a summons to our Devotion.

Fred. Will you leave me for your Prayers, Madam? You may have enough of them at any time, but remember you cannot have a Man so easily.

Luc. Well, I'll say my Beads for you, and that's but Charity, for I believe I leave you in a most deplorable condition.

[*Exeunt* Women.

Fred. Not deplorable neither, but a little altred: if I could be in Love, as I am sure I cannot, it should be with her, for I like her conversation strangely.

Asca. Then, as young as I am, Sir, I am before-hand with you; for I am in Love already. I would fain make the first proof of my Manhood upon a Nun: I find I have a mighty grudging to Holy Flesh.

Fred. I'll ply *Lucretia* again, as soon as ever her Devotion's over. Methinks these Nuns divide their time most admirably: from Love to Prayers; from Prayers to Love: that is, just so much Sin, just so much Godliness.

157   *s.d.* [*Bell*] Q3, F, D; ∧~ Q1–2.   160   Prayers] Q2–3, F, D; Prayets Q1.
164+   *s.d.* [*Exeunt* Women] ∧*Exeunt Women* Q1–3, F, D ([~ F, D).

Asca. Then I can claim that Sister's Love by merit:
Half Man, half Boy; for her half Flesh, half Spirit.　　　[*Exeunt.*

SCENE II.　*A Street.*

Aurelian *and* Camillo.

Aur. I'll proceed no farther, if *Benito* goes: I know his folly
will produce some mischief.

Cam. But *Violetta* desir'd me, in her Note, to bring him, on
purpose to pass the time with her Woman *Beatrix.*

Aur. That objection is easily remov'd: I'll supply *Benito's*
place; the darkness will prevent discovery, and, for my discourse,
I'll imitate the half Wit, and patch'd breeding of a *Valet de
Chambre.*

Cam. But how shall we get rid of him?

10　*Aur.* Let me alone for that.

Enter Benito.

Ben. Come, Are we ready, Gallants? the Clock's upon the
stroke of Eight.

Aur. But we have alter'd our resolution: we go another way to
night.

Ben. I hope you have not broke my Assignation.

Aur. Why do you hope so?

Ben. Because my reputation is engag'd in't: I 'ave stipulated
upon my honour that you shall come.

Aur. I shall beat you if you follow me. Go, Sirrah, and adjourn

20　to the great looking-glass, and let me hear no more from you till
to morrow morning.

Ben. Sir, my fidelity, and, if I may be so vain, my discretion
may stand you in some stead.

Aur. Well, come along then, they are brave Fellows who have
challeng'd us, you shall have fighting enough, Sir.

Ben. How, Sir, Fighting?

177　s.d. [*Exeunt*] F, D; ∧~ Q1–3.

Aur. You may scape with the loss of a Leg, or an arm, or some such transitory limb.

Ben. No, Sir; I have that absolute obedience to your com-
30 mands, that I will bridle my courage, and stay at home. [*Exit.*

Cam. You took the only way to be rid of him. There's the wall: behind yond pane of it we'll set up the Ladder. [*Exeunt.*

SCENE III. *A Night-piece of a Garden.*

Enter Laura *and* Violetta.

Vio. Remember your waiting-womans part, *Laura.*

Lau. I warrant you, I'll wait on you by night as well as I govern'd you by day.

Vio. Hark, I hear foot-steps; and now, methinks, I see something approaching us.

Lau. They are certainly the Men whom we expect.

Enter Aurelian *and* Camillo.

Cam. I hear Womens voices.

Aur. We are right, I warrant you.

Cam. Violetta, my Love!

10 *Vio.* My dear *Camillo!*

Cam. O speak those words again: my own name never sounded so sweetly to me, as when you spoke it, and made me happy by adding Dear to it.

Vio. Speak softly then. I have stoln these few minutes from my watchful Uncle and my Sister, and they are as full of danger as they are of love. Something within me checks me too, and sayes, I was too forward in ventring thus to meet you.

Cam. You are too fearful rather, and fear's the greatest enemy to Love.

20 *Vio.* But night will hide my blushes, when I tell you I love you much, or I had never trusted my virtue and my person in your hands.

---

30 *s.d.* [*Exit*] F, D; ∧∼ Q1–3.   32 *s.d.* [*Exeunt*] D; ∧∼ Q1–3; *omitted from* F.

Cam. The one is sacred, and the other safe; but this auspicious minute is our first of near converse. May I not hope that favour, which strangers, in civility, may claim even from the most reserv'd? [*Kisses her hand.*

Vio. I fear you'll censure me.

Cam. Yes, as the blest above tax heaven for making them so happy. [*They walk farther off.*

30 *Aur. stepping towards Lau.* Damsel of darkness, advance, and meet my flames.

Lau. stepping forward. Right trusty Valet, heard, but yet unseen, I have advanced one step on reputation.

Aur. Now, by laudable custome, I am to love thee vehemently.

Lau. We should do well to see each other first: You know 'tis ill taking Money without light.

Aur. O, but the coyn of Love is known by the weight only, and you may feel it in the dark: Besides, you know 'tis Prince-like to Love without seeing.

40 *Lau.* But then you may be serv'd as Princes are sometimes.

Aur. Let us make haste however, and dispatch a little Love out of the way: we may do it now with ease, and save our selves a great deal of trouble, if we take it in time, before it grows too fast upon our hands.

Lau. Fie, no; let us Love discreetly, we must manage our passion, and not love all our love out at one meeting, but leave some for another time.

Aur. I am for applying the Plaister whilst the wound is green, 'twill heal the better. [*Takes her by the hand.*

50 *Lau.* Let go my hand: What crime has the poor wretch committed that you press it thus? I remember no mischief it has done you.

Aur. O 'tis a hainous malefactour, and is press'd by Law, because it will confess nothing. Come, withdraw a little farther, we have urgent business with one another.

Lau. 'Twere a shame to quit my ground upon the first charge; yet if you please to take truce a little, I will consent to go behind the Lovers, and listen with you.

Aur. I wonder you defer'd the Proposition so long. I were nei-

---

57 yet] Q2–3, F, D; yer Q1.

60 ther true Valet, nor you true Woman, if we could not Eves-
drop.

> [*They retire behind the other two, who
> come forward upon the Stage.*

Cam. kissing Violetta's hand. Give me another yet, and
then———

Vio. ———And then
Will you be satisfy'd?

Cam.———————And then I'll ask
A thousand more, and ne'r be satisfy'd.
Kisses are but thin nourishment, they are
Too soon digested, and hungry Love craves more.

Vio. You feed a Wolf within you.

Cam. Then feast my Love with a more solid dyet.
He makes us now a Misers Feast, and we
70 Forbear to take our fill. The silent night,
And all these downy hours were made for Lovers:
Gently they tread, and softly measure time,
That no rude noise may fright the tender Maid,
From giving all her soul to melting joyes.

Vio. You do not love me; if you did, you would not
Thus urge your satisfaction in my shame;
At best, I see you would not love me long,
For they who plunder do not mean to stay.

Cam. I haste to take possession of my own.

80 *Vio.* E're Heaven and holy vows have made it so?

Cam. Then witness Heaven, and all these twinkling Stars———

Vio. Hold, hold; you are distemper'd with your love:
Time, place, and strong desires now swear, not you.

Cam. Is not Love love without a Priest and Altars?
The Temples are inanimate, and know not
What Vows are made in them; the Priest stands ready
For his hire, and cares not what hearts he couples,
Love alone is marriage.

Vio. I never will receive these Mid-night Vows;

61+ *s.d.* [*They*] F, D; ~ Q1–3.
62–74 *Vio. . . .* joyes.] *as prose in* Q1–3, F, D (will . . . a thousand . . . too . . . forbear . . . and all . . . that . . . from).

90 But when I come hereafter to your Arms,
I'll bring you a sincere, full, perfect bliss,
Then you will thank me that I kept it so,
And trust my faith hereafter.

   Lau. There's your destiny, Lover mine: I am to be honest by
infection; my Lady will none you see.

   Aur. Truth is, they are a lost couple, unless they learn grace by
our example. Come, shall we begin first, and shame them both?
                              [*Takes her by the hand again.*

   Lau. You'll never be warn'd of this hand, *Benito.*

   Aur. Oh, 'tis so soft, as it were made on purpose to take hearts,
100 and handle them without hurting. These Taper fingers too, and
even joynts, so supple, that methinks I mould 'em as they pass
through mine: nay, in my conscience, tho' it be nonsense to say
it, your hand feels white too.

   Lau. Methinks yours is not very hard, for a Serving-mans: but
where, in the name of wonder, have you learn'd to talk so courtly?
you are a strange *Valet de Chambre.*

   Aur. And you are as strange a Waiting-woman: you have so
stab'd me with your Repartees to night, that I should be glad to
change the weapon to be reveng'd on you.

110   *Lau.* These, I suppose, are fragments which you learn'd from
your wild Master *Aurelian:* many a poor woman has pass'd
through his hands, with these very words. You treat me just like
a Serving-man, with the cold Meat which comes from your Masters Table.

   Aur. You could never have suspected me for using my Masters
wit, if you had not been guilty of purloining from your Lady. I
am told, that *Laura,* your Mistresses Sister, has wit enough to
confound a hundred *Aurelians.*

   Lau. I shall do your commendations to *Laura* for your com-
120 plement.

   Aur. And I shall not fail to revenge my self by informing
Aurelian of yours.

                    Enter Benito *with a Guittar.*

---

97   both?] Q2, F, D; ~ˌ Q1; ~. Q2.   102   tho' it] Q3, F, D; th' it Q1; tho i' Q2.

Ben. The poor souls shall not lose by the bargain, though my foolish gadding Masters have disappointed them. That Ladder of ropes was doubtless left there by the young Lady in hope of them.

Vio. Hark, I hear a noise in the Garden.

Lau. I fear we are betray'd.

Cam. Fear nothing, Madam, but stand close.

130 *Ben.* Now, *Benito,* is the time to hold forth thy tallent, and to set up for thy self. Yes, Ladies, you shall be Serenaded, and when I have display'd my gifts, I'll retire in Triumph over the Wall, and hug my self for the adventure.   [*He fums on the Guittar.*

Vio. Let us make haste, Sister, and get into Covert, this Musick will raise the House upon us immediately.

Lau. Alass, we cannot, the damn'd Musician stands just in the door where we should pass.

Ben. Singing.   *Éveillez vous, Belles endormies;*
                   Éveillez vous: car il est jour:
140   *Mettez la tete a la fenestre*
                   Vous entendrez parler d'amour.

Aur. aside to Cam. Camillo, this is my incorrigible rogue; and I dare not call him *Benito,* for fear of discovering my self not to be *Benito.*

Cam. The alarm's already given through the house. Ladies, you must be quick: secure your selves, and leave us to shift.
                                        [*Exeunt* Women.

Within. This way, this way.

Aur. I hear 'em coming; and, as ill luck will have it, just by that quarter where our Ladder is plac'd.

150 *Cam.* Let us hide in the dark walk till they are past.

Aur. But then *Benito* will be caught, and being known to be my man, will betray us.

Ben. I hear some in the Garden: Sure they are the Ladies, that are taken with my melody. To't again *Benito;* this time I will absolutely inchant 'em.   [*Fums again.*

Aur. He's at it again. Why *Benito,* Are you mad?

138, 139 *Éveillez*] *Eveillez* Q1–3, F, D.   146+ *s.d.* Women] *Women* Q1–3, F, D.

Ben. Ah, Madam! Are you there? this is such a favour to your poor unworthy Servant. [*Sings.*

> *But still between kissing* Amintas *did say,*
160 > *Fair* Phillis *look up, and you'll turn night to day.*

Aur. Come away, you unsufferable rascal, the House is up, and will be upon us immediately.
Ben. O Gemini, Is it you, Sir?
Within. This way; follow, follow.
Aur. Leave your scraping and croaking, and step with us into this Arbor.
Ben. Scraping and Croaking! 'Sfoot, Sir, either grant I sing and play to a Miracle, or I'll justifie my Musick, though I am caught, and hang'd for't.

Enter Mario *and* Servants.

170 *Mar.* Where is this Serenading Rascall? If I find him, I'll make him an example to all midnight Caterwaulers, of which this Fidler is the lewdest.
Ben. O that I durst but Play my Tune out to convince him! Soul of harmony! Is this lewd? [*Playes and Sings softly.*
Cam. Peace, dear *Benito:* We must flatter him.
Ben. Singing softly. Mettez la tete: the Notes which follow are so sweet, Sir, I must sing 'em, though it be my ruin———*Parler d'amour.*

Laura *and* Violetta *in the Balcone.*

Lau. Yes, we are safe, Sister; but they are yet in danger.
180 *Vio.* They are just upon 'em.
Lau. We must do something: Help, help; Thieves, thieves; we shall be murder'd.
Mar. Where? Where are they?

174+   s.d. [*Playes*] Q3, D; ∧~ Q1–2, F (*s.d. centered on separate line*).
178+   s.d. *right justified in* Q1–3, F, D (*bracket preceding in F, D*).
180   'em.] F, D; ~: Q1–3.

Lau. Here, Sir, at our Chamber door, and we are run into the Balcone for shelter: Dear Uncle, come and help us.

Mar. Back again quickly: I durst have sworn they had been in the Garden. 'Tis an *Ignis fatuus* I think that leads us from one place to another.   [*Exeunt* Mar. *and* Servants.

Vio. They are gone. My dear *Camillo,* make haste, and pre-
190 serve your self.

Cam. May our next Meeting prove more propitious.

Aur. to Benito. Come, Sirrah, I shall make you sing another note when you are at home.

Ben. Such another word, and I'le sing again.

Aur. Set the Ladder, and mount first, you Rogue.

Ben. Mount first your self, and fear not my delaying:
If I am caught, they'll spare me for my playing.
                              [*Sings as he goes off.*

Vous entendrez parler d'amour.

                              [*Exeunt omnes.*

ACT III.   SCENE I.

The Front of the Nunnery.

Ascanio, *and* Hippolita *at the Grate.*

Hip. I see you have kept touch, Brother.

Asca. As a man of honour ought, Sister, when he is challeng'd: and now, according to the Laws of Duel, the next thing is to strip, and, in stead of seconds, to search one another.

Hip. We'll strip our hands, if you please, Brother; for they are the only weapons we must use.

Asca. That were to invite me to my loss, Sister; I could have made a full meal in the World, and you would have me take up

with hungry commons in the Cloyster. Pray mend my fare, or I
10 am gone.

Hip. O, Brother, a hand in a Cloyster, is fare like flesh in *Spain*,
'tis delicate, because 'tis scarce. You may be satisfy'd with a hand,
as well as I am pleas'd with the Courtship of a Boy.

Asca. You may begin with me Sister, as *Milo* did, by carrying a
Calfe first, you may learn to carry an Oxe hereafter: In the mean
time produce your hand, I understand Nuns flesh better than
you imagine: give it me, you shall see how I will worry it.

[She gives her hand.

Now could not we thrust out our lips, and contrive a Kiss too?

Hip. Yes, we may; but I have had the experience of it: it will
20 be but half flesh, half Iron.

Asca. Let's try however.

Hip. Hold, *Lucretia* is here.

Asca. Nay, if you come with odds upon me, 'tis time to call
Seconds.   [Ascanio *Hems.*

The Prince and Lucretia appear.

Luc. Sir, though your Song was pleasant, yet there was one
thing amiss in it, that was your Rallying of Religion.

Fred. Do you speak well of my Friend Love, and I'll try to
speak well of your friend Devotion.

Luc. I can never speak well of Love: 'twas to avoid it that I
30 entred here.

Fred. Then, Madam, you have met your Man: for, to confess
the truth to you, I have but counterfeited Love to try you; for I
never yet could love any Woman: and, since I have seen you, and
do not, I am certain now I shall scape for ever.

Luc. You are the best man in the World, if you continue this
resolution. Pray, then, let us vow solemnly these two things: the
first, to esteem each other better than we do all the world besides; the next, never to change our amity to love.

Fre. Agreed Madam: shall I kiss your hand on't?

40 *Luc.* That's too like a Lover: or, if it were not, the narrowness
of the Grate will excuse the ceremony.

---

18   could] Q2–3, F, D; Could Q1.   24   *s.d.* [Ascanio] F, D; ∧~ Q1–3.

Hip. No, but it will not, to my knowledge: I have try'd every bar many a fair time over, and, at last, have found out one where a hand may get through, and be gallanted.

Luc. giving her hand. There, Sir; 'tis a true one.

Fre. kissing it. This, then, is a Seal to our perpetual friendship; and a defiance to all Love.

Luc. That seducer of virtue.

Fre. That disturber of quiet.

50   *Luc.* That madness of youth.

Fre. That dotage of old age.

Luc. That enemy to good humour.

Fre. And, to conclude all, that reason of all unreasonable actions.

Asca. This Doctrine is abominable, do not believe it Sister.

Hip. No, if I do, Brother, may I never have comfort from sweet youth at my extremity.

Luc. But remember one article of our friendship, that though we banish Love, we do not Mirth, nor Gallantry; for I declare, I
60 am for all extravagancies, but just loving.

Fre. Just my own humour; for I hate gravity and melancholy next to love.

Asca. Now it comes into my head, the Duke of *Mantoua* makes an entertainment to night in Masquerade: if you love extravagancy so well, Madam, I'll put you into the head of one; lay by your Nun-ship for an hour or two, and come amongst us in disguise.

Fre. My Boy is in the right, Madam. Will you venture? I'll furnish you with Masking-habits.

70   *Hip.* O my dear Sister, never refuse it: I keep the Keyes you know, I'll warrant you we'll return before we are miss'd. I do so long to have one fling into the sweet World again before I die. Hang't, at worst, 'tis but one sin more, and then we'll repent for all together.

Asca. But if I catch you in the World, Sister, I'll make you have a better opinion of the Flesh and the Devil for ever after.

Luc. If it were known, I were lost for ever.

---

47   defiance] Q3, F, D; defyance Q1–2.
53–54   actions.] *period missing in some copies of Q1.*
68–69   *last sentence on a separate line in Q1–3, F.*

Fre. How should it be known? you have her on your side, there, that keeps the Keyes: and, put the worst, that you are taken in
80 the World; the World's a good World to stay in; and there are certain occasions of waking in a morning, that may be more pleasant to you than your *Matins*.

Luc. Fie, Friend, these extravagancies are a breach of Articles in our Friendship: but well, for once, I'll venture to go out; Dancing and Singing are but petty transgressions.

Asca. My Lord, here's company approaching: we shall be dis-cover'd.

Fred. Adieu then, *jusqu'au revoir; Ascanio* shall be with you immediately, to conduct you.

90 *Asca.* How will you disguise, Sister? Will you be a Man, or a Woman?

Hip. A Woman, Brother Page, for life: I should have the strangest thoughts if I once wore Breeches.

Asca. A Woman, say you? Here's my hand, if I meet you in place convenient, I'll do my best to make you one.   [*Exeunt.*

Enter Aurelian *and* Camillo.

Cam. But, Why thus melancholy, with Hat pull'd down, and the hand on the Region of the Heart, just the reverse of my Friend *Aurelian,* of happy memory?

Aur. Faith, *Camillo,* I am asham'd on't, but cannot help it.

100 *Cam.* But to be in Love with a Waiting-woman! with an eater of Fragments, a Simperer at lower end of a Table, with mighty Golls, rough-grain'd, and red with Starching, those discouragers and abaters of elevated love!

Aur. I could Love Deformity it self, with that good humour. She who is arm'd with Gayety and Wit, needs no other Weapon to conquer me.

Cam. We Lovers are the great Creators of wit in our Mistrisses. For *Beatrix,* she is a meer utterer of Yes and No, and has no more Sence than what will just dignifie her to be an arrant waiting-

---

88   *jusqu'au*] *jusqu'a* Q1–3, F, D.
90   How will] F, D; How, Will Q1–3.   92   Page] *Page* Q1–3, F, D.
103   abaters] F; abettors Q1–3, D.   108   she is] Q3; she Q1; she's Q2, F, D.

110 woman: that is, to lye for her Lady, and take your Money.

Aur. It may be then I found her in the exaltation of her wit;
for, certainly, women have their good and ill dayes of talking, as
they have of looking.

Cam. But, however, she has done you the courtesy to drive out
Laura: and so one Poyson has expell'd the other.

Aur. Troth, not absolutely neither; for I dote on *Laura*'s beauty, and on *Beatrix*'s wit: I am wounded with a forked Arrow,
which will not easily be got out.

Cam. Not to lose time in fruitless complaints, let us pursue our
120 new contrivance, that you may see your two Mistresses, and I my
one.

Aur. That will not now be difficult: this plot's so laid, that I
defy the Devil to make it miss. The Woman of the house, by
which they are to pass to Church, is brib'd; the Ladies are, by her,
acquainted with the design; and we need only to be there before
them, and expect the prey, which will undoubtedly fall into the
net.

Cam. Your Man is made safe, I hope, from doing us any mischief.

130 *Aur.* He has dispos'd of himself, I thank him, for an hour or
two: the Fop would make me believe that an unknown Lady is
in love with him, and has made him an Assignation.

Cam. If he should succeed now, I should have the worse opinion of the Sex for his sake.

Aur. Never doubt but he'll succeed: your brisk Fool that can
make a Leg, is ever a fine Gentleman among the Ladies, because
he's just of their tallent, and they understand him better than a
Wit.

Cam. Peace, the Ladies are coming this way to the Chappel,
140 and their Jaylor with 'em: let 'em go by without saluting, to avoid
suspicion; and let us go off to prepare our Engine.

Enter Mario, Laura, *and* Violetta.

Aur. I must have a look before we go. Ah, you little Divine
rogue! I'le be with you immediately.   [*Exeunt* Aur. *and* Cam.

114   courtesy] Q2–3, F, D; courtisy Q1.

Vio. Look you, Sister, there are our Friends, but take no notice.
Lau. I saw them. Was not that *Aurelian* with *Camillo?*
Vio. Yes.
Lau. I like him strangely. If his person were joyn'd with *Benito's* Wit, I know not what would become of my poor heart.

Enter Fabio, *and whispers with* Mario.

Mar. Stay, Neeces, I'll but speak a word with *Fabio,* and go
150 with you immediately.
Vio. I see, Sister, you are infinitely taken with *Benito's* wit;
but I have heard he is a very conceited Coxcomb.
Lau. They who told you so, were horribly mistaken: you shall
be judge your self, *Violetta;* for, to confess frankly to you, I have
made him a kind of an appointment.
Vio. How! Have you made an Assignation to *Benito?* A Serving-man! a Trencher-carrying Rascal!
Lau. Good words, *Violetta!* I only sent to him from an unknown Lady near this Chappel, that I might view him in passing
160 by, and see if his person were answerable to his conversation.
Vio. But how will you get rid of my Uncle?
Lau. You see my project; his man *Fabio* is brib'd by me, to hold
him in discourse.

Enter Benito, *looking about him.*

Vio. In my conscience this is he. Lord, what a Monster of a
Man is there! With such a Workiday rough-hewn face too! for,
faith, Heaven has not bestow'd the finishing upon't.
Lau. 'Tis impossible this should be *Benito;* yet he stalks this
way: from such a piece of animated Timber, sweet Heaven deliver me.
170   *Benito aside.* This must of necessity be the Lady who is in Love
with me. See, how she surveyes my Person! Certainly one Wit
knows another by instinct. By that old Gentleman, it should be
the Lady *Laura* too. Hum! *Benito,* thou art made for ever.

---

165 Workiday rough-hewn] Q2, F, D; Workiday-rough-hewn Q1; Workiday-
rough hewn Q3.

Lau. He has the most unpromising Face, for a Wit, I ever saw; and yet he had need have a very good one, to make amends for his face. I am half cur'd of him already.

Ben. What means all this Surveying, Madam? you bristle up to me, and wheel about me, like a Turkey-cock that is making Love: Faith, How do you like my Person, ha?

180 *Lau.* I dare not praise it, for fear of the old Complement, that you should tell me, 'Tis at my service. But, pray, Is your Name *Benito?*

Ben. Signior *Benito,* at your service, Madam.

Lau. And have you no Brother, or any other of your Name, one that is a Wit, attending on Signior *Aurelian?*

Ben. No, I can assure your Ladiship: I my self am the only wit who does him the honour, not to attend him, but to bear him company.

Lau. But sure it was another you, that waited on *Camillo* in the 190 Garden, last night.

Ben. It was no other Me, but me Signior *Benito.*

Lau. 'Tis impossible.

Ben. 'Tis most certain.

Lau. Then I would advise you to go thither again, and look for the wit which you have left there, for you have brought very little along with you: your voice, methinks, too, is much alter'd.

Ben. Only a little over-strain'd, or so, with Singing.

Lau. How slept you, after your adventure?

Ben. Faith, Lady, I could not sleep one wink, for Dreaming of 200 you.

Lau. Not sleep for Dreaming! When the place falls, you shall be Bull-master-General at Court.

Ben. *Et tu Brute!* Do you mistake me for a Fool too? then, I find there's one more of that opinion besides my Master.

Vio. Sister, look to your self, my Uncle's returning.

Lau. I am glad on't; he has done my business: he has absolutely cur'd me. Lord, that I could be so mistaken!

Vio. I told you what he was.

Lau. He was quite another thing last night: never was Man so 210 alter'd in four and twenty hours. A pure Clown, meer Elementary earth, without the least spark of Soul in him!

Ben. But, tell me truly, Are not you in Love with me? Confess the truth: I love plain-dealing: you shall not find me refractory.

Lau. Away, thou Animal; I have found thee out for a high and mighty fool, and so I leave thee.

Mar. Come, now I am ready for you; as little Devotion, and as much good Huswifery as you please: take example by me; I assure you no body debauches me to Church, except it be in your Company.   [*Exeunt.*

Manet Benito.

220   *Ben.* I am undone for ever: What shall I do with my self? I'll run into some Desart, and there I'll hide my opprobrious head. No, hang't, I won't neither; all Wits have their failings sometimes, and have the fortune to be thought fools once in their lives. Sure this is but a copy of her countenance; for my heart's true to me, and whispers to me, she loves me still: well, I'll trust in my own merits, and be confident.

[*A noise of throwing down water within.*

Enter Mario, Fabio, Laura, *and* Violetta.

Lau. shaking her Cloaths. Oh Sir, I am wet quite through my Cloaths, I am not able to endure it.

Vio. Was there ever such an insolence?

230   *Mar.* Send in to see who lives there: I'll make an example of 'em.

Enter Frontona.

Fab. Here's the Woman of the House her self, Sir.

Fron. Sir, I submit, most willingly, to any punishment you shall inflict upon me; for, though I intended nothing of an affront to these sweet Ladies, yet I can never forgive my self the misfortune of which I was the innocent occasion.

Vio. O I am ready to faint away.

Fron. Alass, poor sweet Lady, she's young and tender, Sir: I

219+   *s.d. Manet*] F, D; Manet Q1–3.   227   *Cloaths.*] Q2–3, F, D; ∼, Q1.

beseech you, give me leave to repair my offence, with offering my
240 self, and poor House, for her accommodation.

Ben. I know that Woman: there's some villanous Plot in this,
I'll lay my life on't. Now, *Benito,* cast about for thy credit, and
recover all again.

Mar. Go into the Coach, Neeces, and bid the Coach-man drive
apace. As for you, Mistriss, your smooth Tongue shall not excuse
you.

Lau. By your favour, Sir, I'll accept of the Gentlewoman's civility; I cannot stir a step farther.

Fro. Come in, sweet Buds of Beauty, you shall have a Fire in an
250 inner Chamber, and if you please to repose your self a while, Sir,
in another Room, they shall come out, and wait on you immediately.

Mar. Well, if it must be so.

Fron. whispering the Ladies. Your Friends are ready in the
Garden, and will be with you as soon as we have shaken off your
Uncle.

Ben. A Cheat, a cheat, a rank one; I smell it, old Sir, I smell it.

Mar. What's the matter with the Fellow? Is he distracted?

Ben. No, 'tis you are more likely to be distracted; but that
260 there goes some wit to the being mad, and you have not the least
grain of wit to be gull'd thus grosly.

Fron. What does the fellow mean?

Ben. The Fellow means to detect your villany, and to recover
his lost reputation of a Wit.

Fron. Why, Friend, What villany? I hope my house is a civil
house.

Ben. Yes, a very civil one; for my master lay in of his last Clap
there, and was treated very civilly to my knowledge.

Mar. How's this, How's this?

270 *Fron.* Come, you are a dirty Fellow, and I am known to be a
person that———

Ben. Yes, you are known to be a person that———

Fron. Speak your worst of me, What person am I known to be?

Ben. Why, if you will have it, you are a little better than a pro-
curess: you carry messages betwixt party and party, and, in one
word Sir, she's as arrant a Fruit-woman as any is about *Rome.*

Mar. Nay, if she be a Fruit-woman, my Neeces shall not enter into her doors.

Ben. You had best let them enter, you do not know how they
280 may fructify in her house, for I heard her with these Eares whisper to 'm, that their Friends were within call.

Mar. This is palpable, this is manifest; I shall remember you, Lady Fruiterer, I shall have your baskets search'd when you bring Oranges again. Come away, Neeces; and thanks honest Fellow for thy discovery.   [*Exeunt* Mario *and* Women.

Ben. Hah couragio: Il Diavolo e morto. Now I think I have tickled it; this discovery has re-instated me into the Empire of my wit again. Now, in the pomp of this atchievement, will I present my self before Madam *Laura,* with a Behold, Madam, the happy
290 restauration of *Benito.*

Enter Aurelian, Camillo, *and* Frontona, *overhearing him.*

Oh, now, that I had the Mirrour, to behold my self in the fulness of my glory! and, oh, that the domineering Fop my Master were in presence, that I might triumph over him! that I might even contemn the wretched wight, the mortal of a groveling Soul, and of a debased understanding.

          [*He looks about him and sees his Master.*

How the Devil came these three together? nothing vexes me but that I must stand bare to him, after such an enterprize as this is.

Aur. Nay, put on, put on again, sweet Sir; Why should you be
300 uncover'd before the Fop your Master? the wretched wight, the mortal of a groveling Soul.

Ben. Ay, Sir, you may make bold with your self at your own pleasure: But for all that, a little bidding would make me take your Counsel and be cover'd, as Affairs go now.

Aur. If it be lawful for a man of a debased understanding to confer with such an exalted wit, pray what was that glorious atchievement which rapt you into such an extasy?

Ben. 'Tis a sign you know well how matters go, by your asking

---

295+   s.d. [*He*] Q3, D; ∧~ Q1–2, F (*s.d. centered*).

me so impertinent a question.

310　　*Aur. putting off his Hat to him.* Sir, I beg of you, as your most humble Master, to be satisfy'd.

Ben. Your Servant, Sir; at present I am not at leisure for conference. But hark you, Sir, by the way of friendly advice, one word, henceforward tell me no more of the adventure of the Garden, nor of the great Looking-glass————

Aur. You mean the Mirror.

Ben. Yes, the Mirror; tell me no more of that, except you could behold in it a better, a more discreet, or a more able face for stratagem, than I can, when I look there.

320　　*Aur.* But, to the business; What is this famous enterprise?

Ben. Be satisfy'd, without troubling me farther, the business is done, the Rogues are defeated, and your Mistriss is secur'd: if you would know more, demand it of that Criminal, [*Pointing to* Frontona] and ask her how she dares appear before you, after such a signal treachery, or before me, after such an overthrow?

Fron. I know nothing, but only that, by your Masters Order, I was to receive the two Ladies into my house, and you prevented it.

Ben. By my Master's Order? I'll ne'r believe it. This is your stratagem, to free your self, and defraud me of my reward.

330　　*Cam.* I'll witness what she sayes is true.

Ben. I am deaf to all asseverations that make against my honour.

Aur. I'll swear it then. We two were the two Rogues, and you the discoverer of our Villany.

Ben. Then, woe, woe, to poor *Benito!* I find my abundance of wit has ruin'd me.

Aur. But come a little nearer: I would not receive a good office from a Servant, but I would reward him for his diligence.

Ben. Virtue, Sir, is its own reward: I expect none from you.

340　　*Aur.* Since it is so, Sir, you shall lose no further time in my service: henceforward pray know me for your humble Servant; for your Master I am resolv'd to be no longer.

Ben. Nay, rather than so, Sir, I beseech you let a good honest sufficient beating attone the difference.

Aur. 'Tis in vain.

324　Frontona]] ∼. Q1, Q3; ∼,] Q2, F; ∼.] D.

Ben. I am loath to leave you without a guide.

Aur. He's at it again, do you hear, *Camillo?*

Cam. Prethy, *Aurelian,* be molify'd, and beat him.

Fron. Pray, Sir, hear reason, and lay 't on, for my sake.

350   *Aur.* I am obdurate.

Cam. But, What will your Father say, if you part with him?

Aur. I care not.

Ben. Well, Sir, since you are so peremptory, remember I have offer'd you satisfaction, and so long my conscience is at ease: what a Devil, before I'll offer my self twice to be beaten, by any Master in Christendome, I'll starve, and that's my resolution, and so your Servant that was Sir.   [*Exit.*

Aur. I am glad I am rid of him; he was my Evil Genius, and was alwayes appearing to me, to blast my undertakings: Let me

360   send him never so farr off, the Devil would be sure to put him in my way, when I had any thing to execute. Come, *Camillo,* now we have chang'd the Dice, it may be we shall have better fortune.
                                                            [*Exeunt.*

SCENE II.

Enter the Duke of Mantoua *in Masquerade,* Frederick,
Valerio, *and others. On the other side Enter*
Lucretia, Hippolita, *and* Ascanio.

Luc. to Asca. The Prince I know already, by your description of his Masking-habit; but, Which is the Duke his Father?

Asca. He whom you see talking with the Prince, and looking this way. I believe he has observ'd us.

Luc. If he has not, I am resolv'd we'll make our selves as remarkable as we can: I'll exercise my tallent of Dancing.

Hip. And I mine of Singing.

Duke to Frederick. Do you know the Company which came in last?

———————
355   I'll] Q2–3, F, D; I'lll Q1.   357   *s.d.* [*Exit*] D; ∧~ Q1–3, F.
362+   *s.d.* [*Exeunt.*] F (*without bracket*); *omitted from* Q1–3, D.
SCENE] Q2–3, F, D; ~. Q1.

Fred. I cannot possibly imagine who they are.
At least I will not tell you———   [*Aside.*

Duke. There's something very uncommon in the Ayre of one
of them.

Fred. Please you, Sir, I'll discourse with her, and see if I can
satisfie your Highness.

Duke. Stay, there's a Dance beginning, and she seems as if she
wou'd make one.

SONG and DANCE.

Long betwixt Love and fear Phillis *tormented,*
Shun'd her own wish yet at last she consented:
But loath that day shou'd her blushes discover,
  Come gentle Night She said,
  Come quickly to my aid,
  And a poor Shamefac'd Maid
  Hide from her Lover.

Now cold as Ice I am, now hot as Fire,
I dare not tell my self my own desire;
But let Day fly away, and let Night hast her:
  Grant yee kind Powers above,
  Slow houres to parting Love,
  But when to Bliss we move,
  Bid 'em fly faster.

How sweet it is to Love when I discover,
That Fire which burns my Heart, warming my Lover;
'Tis pitty Love so true should be mistaken:
  But if this Night he be
  False or unkinde to me,
  Let me dye ere I see
  That I'me forsaken.

10–11 are. / At] are: at Q1–3, F, D.   11 *s.d.* [*Aside*] D; ∧∼ Q1–3, F.

After the Dance. My curiosity redoubles, I must needs hale
40 that unknown Vessel, and enquire whither she's bound, and what
fraight she carries.

Fred. She's not worth your trouble, Sir: she'll either prove
some common Courtizan in disguise, or at best, some homely person of Honour, that only dances well enough to invite a sight of
her self, and would look ill enough to fright you.

Duke. That's maliciously said; all I see of her is charming, and
I have reason to think her face is of the same piece, at least I'll try
my fortune.

Fred. What an unlucky accident is this! If my father should
50 discover her, she's ruin'd: if he does not, yet I have lost her conversation to night.

[Duke *approaches* Lucretia.

Asca. 'Tis the Duke himself who comes to court you.

Luc. Peace, I'll fit him; for I have been inform'd to the least
tittle of his actions since he came to Town.

Duke to Lucretia. Madam, the Duke of *Mantoua,* whom you
must needs imagine to be in this company, has sent me to you,
to know what kind of face there is belonging to that excellent
shape, and to those charming motions which he observ'd so lately
in your Dancing.

60 *Luc.* Tell his Highness, if you please, that there is a Face within
the Masque, so very deform'd, that if it were discover'd, it would
prove the worst Vizor of the two; and that, of all Men, he ought
not to desire it should be expos'd, because then something would
be found amiss in an entertainment which he has made so splendid and magnificent.

Duke. The Duke I am sure would be very proud of your complement, but it would leave him more unsatisfy'd than before, for
he will find in it so much of Gallantry, as, being added to your
other graces, will move him to a strange temptation of knowing
70 you.

Luc. I should still have the more reason to refuse him; for
'twere a madness, when I had charm'd him by my motion and
converse, to hazard the loss of that conquest by my eyes.

Duke aside. I am on fire till I discover her.

51+   *s.d.* [Duke] ∧~ Q1-3, F, D (*s.d. centered* Q1-3, D; *Duke* Q1-2, F, D).

At least, Madam, tell me of what Family you are.

Luc. Will you be satisfy'd if I tell you I am of the *Colonne?*
you have seen *Julia* of that House.

Duke. Then you are she.

Luc. Have I not her Stature most exactly?

80   *Duke.* As near as I remember.

Luc. But, by your favour, I have nothing of her shape; for, if I
may be so vain to praise my self, she's a little thicker in the
shoulders, and, besides, she moves ungracefully.

Duke. Then you are not she again.

Luc. No not she: but you have forgotten *Emilia* of the *Ursini,*
whom the Duke saluted yesterday at her Balcone, when he enter'd. Her Ayre and Motion———

Duke. Are the very same with yours. Now I am sure I know
you.

90   *Luc.* But there's too little of her to make a Beauty: my stature
is much more advantagious.

Duke. You have cozen'd me again.

Luc. Well, I find at last I must confess my self. What think you
of *Eugenia Beata?* the Duke seem'd to be infinitely pleas'd last
night, when my Brother presented me to him at the *Belvedere.*

Duke. Now I am certain you are she; for you have both her
stature, and her motion.

Luc. But, if you remember your self a little better, there's some
small difference in our wit: for she has indeed the Ayre and Beau-
100   ty of a *Roman* Lady, but all the dulness of a *Dutch*-woman.

Duke. I see, Madam, you are resolv'd to conceal your self, and
I am as fully resolv'd to know you.

Luc. See which of our resolutions will take place.

Duke. I come from the Duke, and can assure you he is of an
humour to be obey'd.

Luc. And I am of an humour not to obey him. But, Why should
he be so curious?

Duke. If you would have my opinion, I believe he is in love
with you.

110   *Luc.* Without seeing me?

---

76 *Colonne?*] Q2, F, D; ~; Q1, Q3.   100 *Roman*] Q3, D; Roman Q1–2, F.
100 *Dutch*-woman] D; Dutch-woman Q1–3, F.

Duke. Without seeing all of you: Love is love, let it wound us from what part it please; and if he have enough from your shape and conversation, his business is done, the more compendiously, without the face.

Luc. But the Duke cannot be taken with my conversation, for he never heard me speak.

Duke aside. 'Slife, I shall discover my self.

Yes, Madam, he stood by, incognito, and heard me speak with you: but———

120 *Luc.* I wish he had trusted to his own courtship, and spoke himself; for it gives us a bad impression of a Princes wit, when we see fools in favour about his person.

Duke. What ever I am, I have it in Commission from him to tell you, He's in Love with you.

Luc. The good old Gentleman may dote, if he so pleases; but love, and fifty years old, are stark non-sense.

Duke. But some men, you know, are green at fifty.

Luc. Yes, in their understandings.

Duke. You speak with great contempt of a Prince, who has 130 some reputation in the world.

Luc. No; 'tis you that speak with contempt of him, by saying he is in love at such an Age.

Duke. Then, Madam, 'tis necessary you should know him better for his reputation: and, that shall be, though he violate the Laws of Masquerade, and force you.

Fred. I suspected this, from his violent temper.   [*Aside.*
Sir, the Emperour's Ambassador is here, in Masquerade, and I believe this to be his Lady: it were well if you inquir'd of him, before you forc'd her to discover.

140 *Duke.* Which is the Ambassador?

Fred. That farthermost.   [Duke *retires farther.*

Fred. to Luc. Take your opportunity to escape, while his back is turn'd, or you are ruin'd. *Ascanio,* wait on her.

Luc. I am so frighted, I cannot stay to thank you.

[*Exeunt* Luc. Asca. *and* Hippolita.

Duke to Fred. 'Tis a mistake, the Ambassador knows nothing

117–119 *second sentence begins on same line as first in* Q1–3, F, D.

of her: I'm resolv'd I'll know it of her self, ere she shall depart.
Ha! Where is she? I left her here.

   Fred. aside. Out of your reach, Father mine, I hope.

   Duke. She has either shifted places, or else slipt out of the As-
150 sembly.

   Fred. I have look'd round: she must be gone, Sir.

   Duke. She must not be gone, Sir. Search for her every where:
I will have her.

   Fred. Has she offended your Highness?

   Duke. Peace, with your impertinent questions. Come hither,
Valerio.

   Valerio. Sir?

   Duke. O, *Valerio,* I am desperately in love: that Lady, with
whom you saw me talking, has————But I lose time; she's gone;
160 haste after her; find her; bring her back to me.

   Val. If it be possible.

   Duke. It must be possible; the quiet of my life depends upon
it.

   Val. Which way took she?

   Duke. Go any way, every way; ask no questions: I know no
more, but that she must be had.   [*Exit* Valerio.

   Fred. Sir, the assembly will observe, that————

   Duke. Damn the assembly, 'tis a dull insignificant crowd, now
she is not here: break it up, I'll stay no longer.

170   *Fred. aside.* I hope she's safe, and then this fantastick love of
my Fathers will make us sport to morrow.   [*Exeunt.*

SCENE III.

Lucretia, Ascanio, Hippolita.

   Luc. Now, that we are safe at the gate of our Covent, methinks
the adventure was not unpleasant.

---

163   it] *in some copies of Q1 the* i *is in the line above.*
166   must] Q3; must must Q1; must, must Q2, F, D.
166   s.d. [*Exit*] Q3, F, D; ∧~ Q1–2.   170   *Fred.*] Q2–3, F, D; ~∧ Q1.
171   to] Q2–3, F, D; too Q1.   171   s.d. [*Exeunt*] Q3, F, D; ∧~ Q1–2.

Hip. And now that I am out of danger, Brother, I may tell you what a Novice you are in love, to tempt a young Sister into the wide World, and not to show her the difference betwixt that and her Cloyster: I find I may venture safely with you another time.

Asca. O, Sister, you play the Brazen-head with me; you give me warning when Time's past: but that was no fit opportunity: I hate to snatch a morsel of Love, and so away; I am for a set-meal, where I may enjoy my full gust; but when I once fall on, you shall find me a brave man upon occasion.

Luc. 'Tis time we were in our Cells. Quick, *Hippolita,* where's the Key?

Hip. Here, in my pocket————No, 'tis in my other Pocket ————Ha————'tis not there, neither. I am sure I put it in one of them.

Luc. What should we do, if it should be lost now?

Hip. I have search'd my self all over, and cannot find it.

Asca. A woman can never search her self all over; let me search you, Sister.

Luc. Is this a time for Raillery? Oh, sweet heaven! speak comfort quickly; Have you found it?

[*Here* Ascanio *slips away. Exit.*

Hip. Speak you comfort, Madam, and tell me you have it, for I am too sure that I have none on't.

Luc. O unfortunate that we are! day's breaking; the handy-crafts shops begin to open. [*Clock strikes.*

Hip. The Clock strikes two: within this half hour we shall be call'd up to our Devotions. Now, good *Ascanio*————Alass he's gone too! we are left miserable, and forlorn.

Luc. We have not so much as one place in the Town for a Retreat.

Hip. O, for a Miracle in our time of need! that some kind good-natur'd Saint would take us up, and heave us over the Wall into our Cells.

Luc. Dear Sister, Pray; for I cannot: I have been so sinful, in

---

8 opportunity] Q2–3, F, D; opportun y Q1.
22+ *s.d.* [*Here . . . away. Exit.*] F; *Here . . . away.* [*Exit.* Q1–3 (*first sentence centered*); [*Here . . . away.* D.
26 *s.d.* [*Clock*] F, D; ∧∼ Q1–3.

leaving my Cloyster for the World, that I am asham'd to trouble
my Friends above to help me.

Hip. Alass, Sister, with what face can I Pray, then! Yours were
but little vanities; but I have sin'd swingingly, against my Vow;
40 yes, indeed, Sister, I have been very wicked; for I wish'd the Ball
might be kept perpetually in our Cloyster, and that half the
handsome Nuns in it might be turn'd to Men, for the sake of the
other.

Luc. Well, if I were free from this disgrace, I would never
more set foot beyond the Cloyster, for the sake of any Man.

Hip. And here I Vow, if I get safe within my Cell, I will not
think of Man again these seven years.

Ascanio *Re-enters.*

Asca. Hold, *Hippolita,* and make no more rash Vows: if you
do, as I live, you shall not have the Key.
50 *Hip.* The Key! why, Have it you, Brother?

Luc. He does but mock us: I know you have it not, *Ascanio.*

Asca. Ecce signum; Here it is for you.

Hip. O, sweet Brother, let me kiss you.

Asca. Hands off, sweet Sister; you must not be forsworn: you
vow'd you would not think of a man these seven years.

Hip. Ay, Brother, but I was not so hasty, but I had wit enough
to cozen the Saint to whom I vow'd; for you are but a Boy, Brother, and will not be a Man these seven years.

Luc. But, Where did you find the Key, *Ascanio?*
60 *Asca.* To confess the truth, Madam, I stole it out of *Hippolita's*
Pocket, to take the Print of it in Wax; for, I'll suppose, you'll
give my Master leave to wait on you in the Nunnery-garden, after
your Abbess has walk'd the Rounds.

Luc. Well, well, good morrow: when you have slept, come to
the Grate for a Letter to your Lord. Now will I have the headach,
or the Meagrim, or some excuse, for I am resolv'd I'll not rise to
Prayers.

Hip. Pray, Brother, take care of our Masking-habits, that they
may be forth-coming another time.

70   *Asca.* Sleep, sleep, and dream of me, Sister: I'll make it good,
if you dream not too unreasonably.
    Luc. Thus dangers in our Love make joyes more dear;
And Pleasure's sweetest, when 'tis mixt with fear.   [*Exeunt.*

ACT IV. SCENE I.

A Dressing-Chamber.
The Masking-habits of Lucretia *and* Hippolita
laid in a Chair.

Fred. *and* Ascanio.

Fred. I never thought I should have lov'd her. Is't come to
this, after all my boastings and declarations against it? Sure I
lov'd her before, and did not know it, till I fear'd to lose her:
there's the reason. I had never desir'd her, if my Father had not.
This is just the longing of a Woman: she never finds the appetite
in her self, till she sees the Meat on anothers Plate. I'm glad however, you took the impression of the Key; but 'twas not well to
fright them.
    Asca. Sir, I could not help it; but here's the effect on't: the
10 Workman sate up all night to make it.   [*Gives a Key.*
    Fred. This Key will admit me into the *Seraglio* of the Godly.
The Monastery has begun the War, in Sallying out upon the
World, and therefore 'tis but just that the World should make
Reprizals on the Monastery.
    Asca. Alass, Sir, you and *Lucretia* do but skirmish; 'tis I and
Hippolita that make the War: 'tis true, opportunity has been
wanting for a Battel, but the forces have been stoutly drawn up
on both sides. As for your concernment, I come just now from the
Monastery, and have Orders from your Platonick Mistriss to tell
20 you, she expects you this evening in the Garden of the Nunnery;
withall, she deliver'd me this Letter for you.

ACT] Q3, F, D; ~. Q1–2.   10 *s.d.* [*Gives*] F, D; ‸~ Q1–3.

Fred. Give it me.

Asca. O, Sir, the Duke your Father!

> [*The* Prince *takes the Letter, and thinking*
> *to put it up hastily, drops it.*

Enter Duke.

Duke. Now, *Frederick!* not abroad yet?

Fred. Your last nights entertainment left me so weary, Sir, that I over-slept my self this morning.

Duke. I rather envy you, than blame you: our sleep is certainly the most pleasant portion of our lives. For my own part, I spent the night waking, and restless.

30   *Fred.* Has any thing of moment happen'd to discompose your Highness?

Duke. I'll confess my follies to you: I am in love with a Lady I saw last night in Masquerade.

Fred. 'Tis strange she should conceal her self.

Duke. She has, from my best search; yet I took exact notice of her Masking habit, and describ'd it to those whom I employ'd to find her.

Fred. aside. 'Sdeath, it lies there unremov'd; and, if he turns himself, full in his eye. Now, now 'twill be discover'd.

40   *Duke.* For 'twas extreamly remarkable. I remember very well 'twas a loose long Robe, streak'd black and white, girt with a large Silver Ribband, and the Vizor was a *Moor's* Face.

> [Frederick *running to the Chair where*
> *the Habits are, sits down.*

Fred. Sir, I beg pardon of your Highness for this Rudeness, I am————O, Oh————

Duke. What's the Matter?

Fred. I am taken so extreamly ill o' the sudden, that I am forc'd to sit before you.

---

22   me.] Q3, F, D; ∼, Q1–2.   23+   *s.d.* [*The*] Q3, F, D; ∧∼ Q1–2.
23+   *s.d.* Prince] Q2–3, F, D; prince Q1.
42+   *s.d.* [Frederick *running . . . down.*] ∧*Fred. Running . . . down.* Q1–3, F (Frederick Q3; *centered in all*); ∧*Fred.* [*Running . . . down.*] D.
43   *Fred.* Sir] Sir Q1–3, F, D.

Duke. Alass, What's your distemper?

Fred. A most violent griping, which pulls me together on a
50 heap.

Duke. Some cold, I fear, you took last night. [*Runs to the Door.*
Who waites there? Call Physitians to the Prince.

Fred. Ascanio, remove these quickly.

> [*Ascanio takes away the habits, and Exit.*

Duke returning. How do you find your self?

Fred. arising. Much better, Sir: that which pain'd me is remov'd: as it came unexpectedly, so it went as suddenly.

Enter Valerio.

Duke. The Ayre, perhaps, will do you good. If you have health,
you may see those Troops drawn out, which I design for *Milan.*

Fred. Shall I wait your Highness?

60 *Duke.* No, leave me here with *Valerio;* I have a little business,
which dispatch'd, I'll follow you immediately. [*Exit* Frederick.
Well, What success, *Valerio?*

Val. Our indeavours are in vain, Sir: there has been inquiry
made about all the Pallaces in *Rome,* and neither of the Masking-
habits can be discover'd.

Duke. Yet, it must be a Woman of Quality. What Paper's that
at my foot?

Val. taking up the Letter. 'Tis Seal'd, Sir, and directed to the
Prince.

70 *Duke, taking the Letter.* 'Tis a Womans hand. Has he got a
Mistriss in Town so soon? I am resolv'd to open it, though I do
not approve my own curiosity.   [*Opens and Reads it.*

*Now my fear is over, I can laugh at my last nights adventure:
I find that at Fifty all Men grow incorrigible, and Lovers especially; for, certainly, never any Creature could be worse treated
than your Father,* (How's this, *Valerio?* I am amaz'd) *and yet the
good, old, out of fashion Gentleman heard himself Raillied, and
bore it with all the patience of a Christian Prince.* (Now 'tis plain,

---

53+ *s.d.* [Ascanio] F, D; ₳~ Q1–3.   55 *Fred.*] Q3, F, D; *Fre.* Q1–2.
55 better,] Q2–3, F, D; ~. Q1.   58 *Milan*] Q3; *Millan* Q1–2, F, D.
61 *s.d. on line below in* Q1–3, F, D.   72 *s.d.* [Opens] F, D; ₳~ Q1–3.

the Lady in Masquerade is a Mistriss of my Son's, and the un-
dutiful wretch was in the Plot to abuse me.) Ascanio *will tell*
you the latter part of our misfortune, how hardly we got into the
Cloyster, (A Nun too! Oh, the Devil!) *when we meet next, pray*
provide to laugh heartily, for there is subject sufficient for a plen-
tiful fit, and fop enough to spare for another time.

Lucretia.

Val. Lucretia! now the Mistery is unfolded.
Duke. Do you know her?
Val. When I was last at *Rome,* I saw her often; she is near Kins-
woman to the present Pope; and, before he placed her in this
Nunnery of *Benedictines,* was the most celebrated Beauty of the
Town.
Duke. I know I ought to hate this Woman, because she has
affronted me thus grossly; but yet I cannot help it, I must love
her.
Val. But, Sir, you come on too much disadvantage to be your
Son's Rival.
Duke. I am deaf to all considerations: pr'ythee do not think of
giving a Mad-man Counsel: pity me, and cure me, if thou canst;
but remember there's but one infallible Medicine, that's enjoy-
ment.
Val. I had forgot to tell you, Sir, that the Governour Don *Mario*
is without, to wait on you.
Duke. Desire him to come in.

Enter Don Mario.

Mar. I am come, Sir, to beg a favour from your Highness, and
'tis on the behalf of my Sister *Sophronia,* Abbess of the *Torr' di*
Specchi.
Val. Sir, she's Abbess of that very Monastery where your Mis-
triss is inclos'd.   [*Aside, to the* Duke.
Duke. I should be glad to serve any Relation of yours, Don
Mario.
Mar. Her request is, That you would be pleas'd to grace her

---

108   s.d. Duke] *Duke* Q1–3, F, D.

Chappel this afternoon. There will be Musick, and some little Ceremony, in the Reception of my two Neeces, who are to be plac'd in Pension there.

Duke. Your Neeces, I hear, are fair, and great Fortunes.

Mar. Great vexations I'm sure they are; being daily haunted by a company of wild Fellows, who buz about my house like Flies.

Duke. Your design seems reasonable; Women in hot Coun-
120 tryes are like Oranges in cold: to preserve them, they must be perpetually hous'd. I'll bear you company to the Monastery. Come, *Valerio;* this opportunity is happy beyond our expectation. [*Exeunt.*

SCENE II.

Camillo, Aurelian.

Cam. He has smarted sufficiently for this offence: pr'ythee, dear *Aurelian,* forgive him; he waits without, and appears peni-tent; I'll be responsible for his future carriage.

Aur. For your sake, then, I receive him into grace.

Cam. at the door. Benito, you may appear, your peace is made.

Enter Benito.

Aur. But, it must be upon conditions.

Ben. Any conditions that are reasonable; for, as I am a Wit, Sir, I have not eaten———

Aur. You are in the path of perdition already; that's the prin-
10 cipal of our Conditions, you are to be a Wit no more.

Ben. Pray, Sir, if it be possible, let me be a little Wit still.

Aur. No, Sir: you can make a Leg, and Dance; those are no Tallents of a Wit: you are cut out for a brisk fool, and can be no other.

Ben. Pray, Sir, let me think I am a Wit, or my heart will break.

123 *s.d. Exeunt.*] Q2, Q3 (*some copies*), D; ~ₐ Q1, Q3 (*some copies*); *omitted from F.*
s.d. Camillo, Aurelian] Q3; *Camillo, Aurelian* Q1-2, F, D.

Cam. That you will naturally do, as you are a Fool.

Aur. Then, no farther medling with adventures, or contrivances of your own: they are all belonging to the Territories of wit, from whence you are banish'd.

20 *Ben.* But what if my imagination should really furnish me with some———

Aur. Not a Plot, I hope?

Ben. No, Sir, no Plot; but some expedient then, to molify the word, when your invention has fail'd you?

Aur. Think it a temptation of the Devil, and believe it not.

Ben. Then farewel all the happiness of my life.

Cam. You know your doom, *Benito,* and now you may take your choice, whether you will renounce wit, or eating.

Ben. Well, Sir, I must continue my Body at what rate soever:
30 and the rather, because now there's no farther need of me in your adventures; for I was assur'd, by *Beatrix,* this morning, that her two Mistrisses are to be put in Pension in the Nunnery of *Benedictines,* this afternoon.

Cam. Then I am miserable.

Aur. And you have defer'd the telling it till it is past time to study for prevention.

Cam. Let us run thither immediately, and either perish in't, or free them. You'll assist me with your Sword?

Aur. Yes, if I cannot do't to more purpose, with my counsel.
40 Let us first play the fairest of our Game, 'tis time enough to snatch when we have lost it.   [*Exeunt.*

SCENE III.

A Chappel.

The Duke, Valerio, Attendants. *At the other door,* Laura,
Violetta, Beatrix, Mario. *Instrumental and vocal Musick,*
in the time of which, Enter Aurelian *and* Camillo. *After*
the Musick, Enter Sophronia, Lucretia,
Hippolita, *and other* Nuns.

---

s.d. *Musick, in*] ∼. *In* Q1–3, F, D.

Duke to Valerio, who had whisper'd to him. I needed not those markes to know her. She's one continu'd excellence; she's all over Miracle.

Soph. to the Duke. We know, Sir, we are not capable, by our Entertainments, of adding any thing to your pleasures, and therefore we must attribute this favour of your presence, to your piety and devotion.

Duke. You have treated me with Harmony so excellent, that I believ'd my self among a quire of angels; especially, when I be-
10 held so fair a Troop behind you.

Soph. Their Beauty, Sir, is wholly dedicated to Heaven, and is no way ambitious of a commendation, which from your mouth might raise a pride in any other of the Sex.

Cam. I am impatient, and can bear no longer. Let what will happen———

Aur. Do you not see your ruine inevitable? Draw in a holy place! and in the presence of the Duke!

Mar. I do not like *Camillo*'s being here: I must cut short the Ceremony.   [*Whispers* Sophronia.
20 *Soph. to Lau. and Violet.* Come, fair Cousins, we hope to make the Cloysteral life so pleasing, that it may be an inducement to you to quit the wicked world for ever.

Violetta passing by Camillo. Take that, and read it at your leasure.   [*Conveys a Note into his hand.*

Cam. A Ticket, as I live, *Aurelian.*

Aur. Steal off, and be thankful: If that be my *Beatrix* with *Laura*, she's most confoundedly ugly. If ever we had come to Love-work, and a Candle had been brought us, I had faln back from that face, like a Buck Rabbet in coupling.

[*Exeunt* Camillo *and* Aurelian.
30 *Soph.* Daughters, the time of our Devotion calls us. All happiness to your Highness.

Luc. to Hip. Little thinks my venerable old Love there, that his Mistriss in Masquerade is so near him. Now do I e'en long to abuse that Fop-gravity again.

Hip. Methinks he looks on us.

---

1   *Valerio*] F, D; *Valeria* Q1–3.   3   Miracle.] Q2–3, F, D; ~, Q1.
19   *s.d.* Sophronia.] Q2–3, F, D; ~, Q1.   25   *Cam.*] Q2–3, F, D; ~∧ Q1.

Luc. Farewell, poor love, I am she, I am, for all my demure
looks, that treated thee so inhumanely last night.
　　　　　　　　　　　　[*She is going off, after* Sophronia.
Duke following her. Stay Lady; I would speak with you.
Luc. Ah! (*Screaking.*)
40　　*Soph.* How now, Daughter? What's the meaning of that undecent noise you make?
　　Luc. aside. If I speak to him, he will discover my voice, and
then I am ruin'd.
　　Duke. If your name be *Lucretia*, I have some business of con-
cernment with you.
　　Luc. to Soph. Dear Madam, for Heavens sake make haste into
the Cloyster, the Duke pursues me on some ill design.
　　Soph. to the Duke. 'Tis not permitted, Sir, for Maids once
entred into Religion, to hold discourses here of worldly things.
50　　*Duke.* But my discourses are not worldly Madam;
I had a Vision in the dead of night,
Which show'd me this fair Virgin in my sleep,
And told me, that from her I should be taught
Where to bestow large Almes, and great Endowments,
On some near Monastery.
　　Soph. ————————Stay, *Lucretia*,
The Holy Vision's will must be obey'd. [*Exeunt* Soph. *cum suis.*
　　Luc. aside. He does not know me, sure; and yet I fear
Religion is the least of his business with me.
　　Duke. I see, Madam,
60　Beauty will be beauty in any habit:
Though I confess, the splendor of a Court
Were a much fitter Scene for yours, then is
A Cloyster'd privacy.
　　Luc. counterfeiting her voice. The World has no temptations
　　　　for a mind
So fix'd, and rais'd above it,
This humble Cell contains and bounds my wishes.
My Charity gives you my Prayers, and that's

37+　*s.d.* Sophronia] Q3, F, D; Sophonia Q1–2.
39　*s.d. Screaking*] screaking Q1–3, F; *Shreiking* D.
60　habit:] ~. Q1–3, F, D.
67–68　that's / All my Converse] D; that's all my / Converse Q1–3, F.

All my Converse with humane kind.

Duke. Since when, Madam, have the World and you been
70　upon these equal termes of hostility? time was you have been
better friends.

Luc. No doubt I have been vain, and sinful; but, the remembrance of those dayes cannot be pleasant to me now, and therefore, if you please, do not refresh their Memory.

Duke. Their memory! you speak as if they were Ages past.

Luc. You think me still what I was once, a vain, fond, giddy
creature; I see, Sir, whether your discourses tend, and therefore
take my leave.

Duke. Yes, Madam, I know you see whither my discourses
80　tend, and therefore 'twill not be convenient that you should take
your leave. Disguise your self no farther; you are known, as well
as you knew me in Masquerade.

Luc. I am not us'd enough to the World, to interpret Riddles;
therefore, once more, heaven keep you.

Duke. This will not do: your voice, your meen, your stature,
betray you for the same I saw last night: you know the time and
place.

Luc. You were not in this Chappel; and, I am bound by vow
to stir no farther.

90　*Duke.* But you had too much wit to keep that vow.

Luc. If you persist, Sir, in this raving madness,
I can bring witness of my innocence.　　　　　　[*Is going.*

Duke. To save that labour, see if you know that hand,
And let that justifie you.　　　　　　(*Shows her Letter.*)

Luc. What do I see! my ruine is inevitable.

Duke. You know you merit it:
You us'd me ill, and now are in my power.

Luc. But you, I hope,
Are much too noble to destroy the Fame
100　Of a poor silly Woman?

Duke. Then, in few words, for I am bred a Souldier,
And must speak plain, it is your Love I ask:
If you deny, this Letter is produc'd;

98–100　*two lines in Q1–3, F, D* (noble / To Q1–3; Noble / to F; to / Destroy D).

You know the consequence.
    Luc. —————————I hope I do not:
For, though there are appearances against me,
Enough to give you hope I durst not shun you;
Yet, could you see my heart, 'tis a white Virgin-Tablet,
On which no Characters of earthly love
Were ever writ: and, 'twixt the Prince and me;
If there were any Criminal affection,
May heaven this minute————
    Duke. —————————Swear not; I believe you:
For could I think my Son had e're enjoy'd you,
I should not be his Rival. Since he has not,
I may have so much kindness for my self
To wish that happiness.
    Luc. —————————You ask me what
I must not grant, nor if I lov'd you would:
You know my vow of Chastity.
    Duke. Yet again that senceless argument?
The Vows of Chastity can ne're be broken,
Where Vows of secrecy are kept: those I'll swear with you.
But 'tis enough, at present, you know my resolution.
I would perswade, not force you to my Love;
And to that end I give you this nights respite.
Consider all, that you may fear or hope;
And think that on your grant, or your denial,
Depends a double welfare, yours and mine.   [*Exit.*
    Luc. A double ruine rather, if I grant:
For what can I expect from such a Father,
When such a Son betrayes me? Could I think
Of all Mankind, that *Frederick* could be base,
And, with the vanity of vulgar Souls
Betray a Virgins fame? one who esteem'd him,
And I much fear did more than barely so————

---

104   *Luc.*————] ~·‚ Q1–3, F, D.
111   *Duke.*————] ~·‚ Q1–3, F, D.
115–117   *Luc.*. . . . Chastity.] *two lines in* Q1–3, F, D (‚You ask . . . / Nor . . . you know . . .).
127–133   *as prose in* Q1–3, F (when . . . of all . . . betray . . . and I).
129   me?] ~! Q1–3, F, D.
130   base,] ~. Q1, Q3; ~? Q2, F, D.   132   fame?] F; ~: Q1–3, D.

But I dare not examine my self farther; for fear of confessing to my own thoughts, a tenderness of which he is unworthy.

Enter Hippolita.

Hip. I watch'd till your old Gallant was gone, to bring you news of your young one. A mischief on these old dry Lovers, they are good for nothing but tedious talking; Well, yonder's the Prince at the Grate; I hope I need say no more to you.

140 *Luc.* I'll come when I have recover'd my self a little. I am a wretched creature, *Hippolita;* the Letter I writ the Prince————

Hip. I know it, is faln into his Fathers hands by accident. He's as wretched as you too. Well, well, it shall be my part to bring you together; and then, if two young people that have opportunity, can be wretched and melancholy————I'll go before and meet *Ascanio.*   [*Exit.*

Luc. I am half unwilling to go, because I must be accessary to her Assignation with *Ascanio;* but, for once, I'll meet the Prince in the Garden walk: I am glad however that he is less criminal

150 than I thought him.   [*Exit.*

SCENE IV.

The Nunnery-Garden.

Hippolita, Ascanio, *meeting* Laura *and* Violetta.

Hip. I hear some walking this way. Who goes there?

Lau. We are the two new Pensioners, *Laura* and *Violetta.*

Hip. Go in, to your devotion: these undue hours of walking savour too much of worldly thoughts.

Lau. Let us retire to the Arbor, where, by this time, I believe our Friends are. Goodnight, Sister.

Hip. Good Angels guard you.   [*Exit* Laura *and* Violetta.

Now, Brother, the coast is clear, and we have the Garden to our

---

140–141 *as verse in* Q*1–3*, F, D (little. / I . . . Letter / I).
150 *s.d. Exit*] *Exeunt* Q1–3, F, D.

selves. Do you remember how you threatened me? but that's all
10　one, how good soever the opportunity may be, so long as we two
resolve to be vertuous.

Asca. Speak for your self, Sister, for I am wickedly inclin'd. Yet,
I confess, I have some remorse, when I consider you are in Religion.

Hip. We should do very well to consider that, both of us; for,
indeed, What should young people do, but think of Goodness
and Religion; especially when they love one another, and are
alone too, Brother?

Asca. A curse on't, here comes my Lord, and *Lucretia.* We
20　might have accomplish'd all, and been repenting by this time;
yet who the Devil would have thought they should have come so
soon?————Ah————　　　　　　　　*[Sets his Teeth.*

Hip. Who the Devil would have put it to the venture? This is
always the fault of you raw Pages: you that are too young, never
use an opportunity; and we that are elder can seldome get one.
————Ah!　　　　　　　　　　　　　　*[Sets her Teeth.*

Enter Frederick *and* Lucretia.

Luc. I believe, indeed, it troubled you to lose that Letter.

Fred. So much, Madam, that I can never forgive my self that
negligence.

30　*Luc.* Call it not so, 'twas but a casualty, though, I confess, the
consequence is dangerous; and therefore have not both of us reason to defy Love, when we see a little Gallantry is able to produce
so much mischief?

Fred. aside. Now cannot I, for my heart, bring out one word
against this Love.

Luc. Come, you are mute, upon a Subject that is both easie
and pleasant. A man in Love is so ridiculous a creature————

Fred. Especially to those that are not.

Luc. True; for to those that are, he cannot be so: they are like
40　the Citizens of *Bethlehem,* who never find out one anothers
Madness, because they are all tainted. But for such antient Fops,

as (with reverence) your Father is, What reason can they have to be in Love?

Fred. Nay, your old Fop's unpardonable, that's certain———— But————

Luc. But What? Come, laugh at him.

Fred. But, I consider, he is my Father, I can't laugh at him.

Luc. But, if it were another, we should see how you would insult over him.

50 *Fred.* Ay, if it were another————And yet I don't know neither, 'tis no part of good nature to insult: a man may be overtaken with a passion, or so, I know it by my self.

Luc. How, by your self? you are not in love, I hope?
Oh that he would confess first now!   [*Aside.*

Fred. But, if I were, I should be loath to be laugh'd at.

Luc. Since you are not in Love, you may the better counsel me: What shall I do with this same troublesome Father of yours?

Fred. Any thing, but love him.

Luc. But you know he has me at a Bay; my Letter is in his pos-
60 session, and he may produce it to my ruine: therefore if I did allow him some little favour, to mollify him————

Fred. How, Madam? would you allow him Favours? I can never consent to it: not the least look or smile; they are all too precious, though they were to save his life.

Luc. What, Not your Father?
Oh that he wou'd confess he lov'd me first!   [*Aside.*

Fred. What have I done? I shall betray my self, and confess my love, to be laugh'd at, by this hard-hearted Woman.   [*Aside.*
'Tis true, Madam, I had forgot; he is, indeed, my Father, and
70 therefore you may use him as kindly as you please.

Luc. He's insensible: now he inrages me.   [*Aside.*
What if he proposes to Marry me? I am not yet profess'd, and 'twould be much to my advantage.

Fred. Marry you! I had rather dye a thousand deaths, than suffer it.

Luc. This begins to please me.   [*Aside.*
But, Why should you be so much my enemy?

Fred. Your enemy, Madam? Why, Do you desire it?

65–66 *sentences not on separate lines in Q1–3, F, D.*

Luc. Perhaps I do.

80 *Fred.* Do it, Madam, since it pleases you so well.

Luc. But you had rather dye, than suffer it.

Fred. No, I have chang'd my mind: I'll live, and not be concern'd at it.

Luc. Do you contradict your self so soon? Then know, Sir, I did intend to do it; and I am glad you have given me advice so agreeable to my inclinations.

Fred. Heaven! that you should not find it out! I deliver'd your Letter on purpose to my Father, and 'twas my business, now, to come and mediate for him.

90 *Luc.* Pray, then, carry him the news of his good success. Adieu, sweet Prince.

Fred. Adieu, dear Madam.

Asca. Hey day! What will this come to? they have cozen'd one another into a quarrel; just like friends in Fencing, a chance thrust comes, and then they fall to't in earnest.

Hip. You and I, Brother, shall never meet upon even termes, if this be not piec'd. Faces about, Madam, turn quickly to your Man, or by all that's virtuous, I'll call the Abbess.

Asca. I must not be so bold with you, Sir; but, if you please,
100 you may turn towards the Lady, and I suppose you would be glad I durst speak to you with more authority, to save the credit of your willingness.

Fred. Well, I'll shew her I dare stay, if it be but to confront her Malice.

Luc. I am sure I have done nothing to be asham'd of, that I should need to run away.

Asca. Pray give me leave, Sir, to ask you but one question; Why were you so unwilling that she should be Marry'd to your Father?

Fred. Because then, her Friendship must wholly cease.

110 *Asca.* But, you may have her Friendship, when she is Marry'd to him.

Fred. What, when another had enjoy'd her?

Asca. Victoria, Victoria, he loves you, Madam; let him deny it if he can.

Luc. Fie, fie, love me, *Ascanio!* I hope he would not forswear

---

79 do.] Q3, F, D; ~, Q1–2.   90–91 *sentences on separate lines in Q1–3, F.*

himself, when he has rail'd so much against it.

Fred. I hope I may love your mind, Madam; I may Love Spiritually.

Hip. That's enough, that's enough: let him love the mind
120 without the body if he can.

Asca. Ay, ay, when the love is once come so far, that Spiritual Mind will never leave pulling, and pulling, till it has drawn the beastly body after it.

Fred. Well, Madam, since I must confess it, (though I expect to be laugh'd at, after my railing against Love) I do love you all over, both Soul and Body.

Asca. Lord, Sir, What a Tygress have you provok'd! you may see she takes it to the death that you have made this declaration.

Hip. I thought where all her anger was: Why do you not raile,
130 Madam? Why do you not banish him? the Prince expects it; he has dealt honestly, he has told you his Mind, and you make your worst on't.

Luc. Because he does expect it, I am resolv'd I'll neither satisfie him nor you; I will neither raile nor laugh: let him make his worst of that, now.

Fred. If I understand you right, Madam, I am happy beyond either my deserts or expectation.

Luc. You may give my words what interpretation you please, Sir, I shall not envy you their meaning in the kindest sence. But
140 we are near the Jessamine-walk, there we may talk with greater freedom, because 'tis farther from the House.

Fred. I wait you, Madam.   [*Exeunt.*

SCENE V.

Aurelian *with a dark Lanthorn,* Camillo
and Benito.

Cam. So, we are safe got over into the Nunnery-Garden; for what's to come, trust Love and Fortune.

---

131   has dealt] *some copies of Q1 have* hast dealt.
SCENE] Q2–3, F, D; ~. Q1.

Aur. This must needs be the walk she mention'd; yet, to be sure, I'll hold the Lanthorn while you read the Ticket.

Cam. reads. I prepar'd this Ticket, hoping to see you in the Chappel: come this evening over the Garden-wall, on the right hand, next the Tiber.

Aur. (We are right, I see.)

Cam. Bring only your discreet Benito *with you, and I will meet*
10 *you, attended by my faithful* Beatrix.   Violetta.

Ben. Discreet *Benito!* Did you hear that, Sir?

Aur. Mortifie thy self for that vain thought; and, without enquiring into the mystery of these words, which I assure thee were not meant to thee, plant thy self by that Ladder without motion, to secure our retreat; and be sure to make no noise.

Ben. But, Sir, in case that————

Aur. Honest *Benito,* no more questions: *Basta* is the word. Remember, thou art only taken with us, because thou hast a certain evil *Dæmon* who conducts thy actions, and would have been sure,
20 by some damn'd accident or other, to have brought thee hither to disturb us.

Cam. I hear whispering not far from us, and I think 'tis *Violetta*'s voice.

Aur. to Benito. Retire to your Post; avoid, good Sathan.

[*Exit* Benito.

Enter Laura *with a dark Lanthorn hid, and* Violetta.

Cam. Ours is the honour of the Field, Madam; we are here before you.

Vio. Softly, dear friend, I think I hear some walking in the Garden.

Cam. Rather, let us take this opportunity for your escape from
30 hence; all things are here in readiness.

Vio. This is the second time we e're have met; let us discourse,

---

5–7   *I* . . . Tiber] F; *all romans* Q1–3; *romans and italics reversed* D.
9–10   *Bring* . . . Violetta] F; *romans and italics reversed in* Q1–3, D (Violetta D).
24+   *s.d.* [*Exit*] F, D; ∧~ Q1–3.

and know each other better first: that's the way to make sure of some love before-hand; for, as the world goes, we know not how little we may have when we are Marry'd.

Cam. Losses of opportunity are fatal, in war, you know, and Love's a kind of warfare.

Vio. I shall keep you yet a while from close fighting.

Cam. But, Do you know what an hour in Love is worth? 'Tis more precious than an Age of ordinary life; 'tis the very Quintes-
40 sence and Extract of it.

Vio. I do not like your Chymical preparation of love; yours is all Spirit, and will fly too soon: I must see it fix'd, before I trust you. But we are near the Arbor; now our out-guards are set, let us retire a little, if you please; there we may talk more freely.

[*Exeunt.*

Aur. to Laura. My Ladies Woman, methinks you are very re-serv'd to night: pray advance into the Lists; though I have seen your countenance by day, I can endure to hear you talk by night. Be cunning, and set your wit to show which is your best commodi-ty: it will help the better to put off that drug, your Face.

50 *Lau.* The coursest ware will serve such customers as you are: let it suffice, Mr. Servingman, that I have seen you too. Your face is the original of the ugliest Vizors about Town; and for wit, I would advise you to speak reverently of it, as a thing you are never like to understand.

Aur. Sure, *Beatrix,* you came lately from looking in your Glass, and that has given you a bad opinion of all faces. But since when am I become so notorious a fool?

Lau. Since yesterday; for t' other night you talk'd like a man of sence: I think your wit comes to you, as the sight of Owles
60 does, only in the dark.

Aur. Why, When did you discourse by day with me?

Lau. You have a short memory. This afternoon, in the great street. Do you not remember when you talk'd with *Laura?*

Aur. But what was that to *Beatrix?*

Lau. aside. 'Slife, I had forgot that I am *Beatrix.*
But, pray, When did you find me out to be so ugly?

Aur. This afternoon, in the Chappel.

39–40 Quintessence] Q2, F, D; Quintesence Q1, Q3.

Aurelian and Laura Discovering
Each Other's Identity, Act IV, Scene V
From *The Dramatick Works of John Dryden, Esq.* (1735)

Lau. That cannot be, for I well remember you were not there, *Benito:* I saw none but *Camillo,* and his friend the handsome
70 stranger.

Aur. aside. Curse on't, I have betray'd my self.

Lau. I find you are an Impostor; you are not the same *Benito:* your language has nothing of the Serving-man.

Aur. And yours, methinks, has not much of the Waiting-woman.

Lau. My Lady is abus'd, and betray'd by you: but I am resolv'd I'll discover who you are.   [*Holds out a Lanthorn to him.* How? the Stranger!

Aur. Nay, Madam, if you are good at that, I'll match you there
80 too.   [*Holds out his Lanthorn.* O prodigy! Is *Beatrix* turn'd to *Laura?*

Lau. Now the question is, which of us two is the greatest cheat?

Aur. That's hardly to be try'd, at so short warning: Let's Marry one another, and then, twenty to one, in a Twelve Moneth we shall know.

Lau. Marry! Are you at that so soon, Signior? *Benito* and *Beatrix,* I confess, had some acquaintance; but *Aurelian* and *Laura* are meer strangers.

Aur. That ground I have gotten as *Benito,* I am resolv'd I'll
90 keep as *Aurelian.* If you will take State upon you, I have treated you with Ceremony already; for I have woo'd you by Proxy.

Lau. But you would not be contented to bed me so; or give me leave to put the Sword betwixt us.

Aur. Yes, upon condition you'll remove it.

Lau. Pray let our Friends be judge of it; if you please, we'll find 'em in the Arbor.

Aur. Content; I am then sure of the Verdict, because the Jury is brib'd already.   [*Exeunt.*

SCENE VI.

Benito *meeting* Frederick, Ascanio, Lucretia
and Hippolita.

Ben. Knowing my own merits, as I do, 'tis not impossible but
some of these Harlotry Nuns may love me: Oh, here's my Master!
now if I could but put this into civil termes, so as to ask his leave,
and not displease him————

Asca. I hear one talking, Sir, just by us.

Ben. I am stoln from my post, Sir, but for one minute only, to
demand permission of you, since it is not in our Articles, that if
any of these Nuns should cast an eye or so————

Fred. 'Slife, we are betray'd; but I'll make this Rascal sure.

[Draws and runs at him.

10   *Ben.* Help, Murder, Murder.   [*Runs off.*

Enter Aurelian *and* Camillo; Laura *and* Violetta
after them.

Aur. That was *Benito*'s voice: we are ruin'd.

Cam. Oh, here they are; we must make our way.

[Aur. and the Prince make a Pass or two confusedly,
and fight off the Stage. The Women Schreek.

Asca. Never fear, Ladies. Come on, Sir; I am your Man.

Cam. stepping back. This is the Prince's Page, I know his
voice. *Ascanio?*

Asca. Signior *Camillo!*

Cam. If the Prince be here, 'tis *Aurelian* is engag'd with him.
Let us run in quickly, and prevent the mischief.

[All go off. A little Clashing within.

After which they all re-enter.

12+ *s.d.* [Aur.] F, D; ∧~ Q1–3.   12+ *s.d.* Women] *Women* Q1–3, F, D.
15 voice.] F, D; ~, Q1–3.   18+ *s.d.* [All] D; ∧~ Q1–3; [*Exeunt* F.

Fred. to Aur. I hope you are not wounded.

20   *Aur.* No, Sir; but infinitely griev'd that————

Fred. No more; 'twas a mistake: but which way can we escape?
the Abbess is coming, I see the Lights.

Luc. You cannot go by the Gate then. Ah me, unfortunate!

Cam. But over the Wall you may: we have a Ladder ready.
Adieu, Ladies. Curse on this ill luck, where we had just perswaded e'm to go with us!

Fred. Farewell, sweet *Lucretia.*

Lau. Goodnight, *Aurelian.*

Aur. I, it might have prov'd a good one: Faith, shall I stay, yet,
30 and make it one, in spite of the Abbess, and all her Works?

Lau. The Abbess is just here; you will be
Caught in the Spiritual Trap, if you should tarry.

Aur. That will be time enough when we two Marry.

                      [*Exeunt severally.*

ACT V.   SCENE I.

Enter Sophronia, Lucretia, Laura, Violetta.

Soph. By this, then, it appears you all are guilty;
Only your ignorance of each others crimes
Caus'd first that tumult, and this discovery.
Good Heavens, that I should live to see this day!
Methinks these Holy Walls, the Cells, the Cloysters,
Should all have strook a secret horror on you:
And when, with unchast thoughts,
You trod these lonely walks, you should have look'd
The venerable Ghost of our first Foundress
10 Should with spread arms have met you in her Shroud,
And frighted you from Sin.

Luc. Alass, you need not aggravate our crimes,
We know them to be great beyond excuse,

21   escape?] Q2, F, D; ~, Q1, Q3.
31–32   be / Caught in] D; be caught / In Q1–3, F.
33+   *s.d. [Exeunt]* F, D; ∧~ Q1–3.   ACT] Q3, F, D; ~. Q1–2.

And have no hope, but only from your mercy.

    Lau. Love is, indeed, no plea within these Walls;
But, since we brought it hither, and were forc'd,
Not led by our own choice, to this strict life————

    Vio. Too hard for our soft youth, and bands of love,
Which we before had knit————

    Lau. ————————Pity your blood,
20 Which runs within our veins, and since Heaven puts it
In your sole power to ruine or to save,
Protect us from the sordid avarice
Of our domestick Tyrant, who deserves not
That we should call him Uncle, or you Brother.

    Soph. If, as I might, with Justice I should punish,
No penance could be rigorous enough;
But I am willing to be more indulgent.
None of you are Profess'd: and since I see
You are not fit for higher happiness,
30 You may have what you think the world can give you.

    Luc. Let us adore you, Madam.

    Soph. ————————————You, *Lucretia,*
I shall advise within.

    Vio. ————————But for us, Madam?

    Soph. For you, dear Neeces, I have long consider'd
The injuries you suffer from my Brother,
And I rejoyce it is in me to help you:
I will endeavour, from this very hour,
To put you both into your Lovers hands,
Who, by your own confession, have deserv'd you;
But so as (though 'tis done by my connivance)
40 It shall not seem to be with my consent.

    Lau. You do an act of noble charity,
And may just heaven reward it.

            Enter Hippolita *and whispers* Lucretia.

    Soph. Oh, you're a faithful Portress of a Cloyster.
What is't you whisper to *Lucretia?*

———————

19 knit————] ~. Q1–3, F, D.

On your Obedience tell me.

Luc. ——————Since you must know, Madam,
I have receiv'd a Courtship from the Prince
Of *Mantoua.* The rest *Hippolita* may speak.

 Hip. His Page *Ascanio* is at the grate,
To know, from him, how you had scap'd this danger;
50 And brings with him those Habits——

 Soph. I find that here has been a long commerce.
What Habits?

 Luc. I blush to tell you, Madam. They were Masking Habits,
in which we went abroad.

 Soph. O strange Impiety! Well, I conclude
You are no longer for Religious cloathing:
You would infect our Order.

 Luc. kneeling. Madam, you promis'd us forgiveness.

 Soph. I have done; for 'tis indeed too late to chide.

60 *Hip.* With *Ascanio,* there are two Gentlemen: *Aurelian* and
Camillo I think they call themselves, who came to me, recom-
mended from the Prince, and desir'd to speak with *Laura* and
Violetta.

 Soph. I think they are your Lovers, Neeces.

 Vio. Madam, they are.

 Hip. But, for fear of discovery from your Unckle *Mario,* whose
House you know, joyns to the Monastery, are both in Masquerade.

 Soph. to Laura and Violetta. This opportunity must not be lost.
70 You two shall take the Masking-habits instantly,
And, in them, scape your jealous Unckle's eyes.
When you are happy,
Make me so, by hearing your success.

      [*Kisses them. Exeunt* Lau. *and* Vio.

 Luc. A sudden thought is sprung within my mind,
Which, by the same indulgence you have shown,
May make me happy too. I have not time
To tell you now, for fear I lose this opportunity.

---

61 *Camillo*] Q1 *(text);* ~, Q1 *(catchword),* Q2–3, F, D.
72–73 *one line in* Q1–3, F, D (make). 73+ *s.d.* [*Kisses*] D; ∧~ Q1–3, F.
73+ *s.d.* Lau. *and* Vio.] Q3, F, D; *Lau. and Vio.* Q1–2.

When I return from speaking with *Ascanio*,
I shall declare the secrets of my Love,
80 And crave your farther help.
      Soph. ————————————In all that virtue
Will permit you shall not fail to find it.   [*Exit* Lucretia.
      Hip. Madam, the foolish Fellow whom we took grows trouble-
some; What shall we do with him?
      Soph. Send for the Magistrate; he must be punish'd————
Yet hold; that would betray the other secret.
Let him be strait turn'd out, on this Condition,
That he presume not ever to disclose
He was within these walls. I'll speak with him:
Come, and attend me to him.   [*Exit* Sophronia.
90 *Hip.* You fit to be an Abbess? We that live out of the World,
should at least have the common sence of those that live farr from
Town; if a Pedler comes by 'em once a year, they will not let him
go without providing themselves with what they want.
                                        [*Exit after* Sophronia.

SCENE II.

The Street.

Aurelian, Camillo, Laura, Violetta: *all in Masking habits.*

      Cam. This generosity of the Abbess is never to be forgot; and it
is the more to be esteem'd because it was the less to be expected.
      Vio. At length, my *Camillo*, I see my self safe within your
Armes; and yet, methinks, I can never be enough secure of you:
for, now I have nothing else to fear, I am afraid of you; I fear your
constancy: they say possession is so dangerous to Lovers, that
more of them die of Surfeits than of Fasting.
      Lau. You'll be rambling too, *Aurelian*, I do not doubt it, if I
would let you; but I'll take care to be as little a Wife, and as much
10 a Mistriss to you, as is possible: I'll be sure to be alwayes pleasant,
and never suffer you to be cloy'd.

80–81 *prose in Q1–3, F, D* (ᴧIn ... will).   81 *s.d.* [*Exit*] **F, D;** ᴧ~ Q1–3.
89 *s.d.* [*Exit*] **F, D;** ᴧ~ Q1–3.   93+ *s.d.* [*Exit*] **F, D;** ᴧ~ Q1–3.

Aur. You are certainly in the right: pleasantness of humour makes a Wife last in the sweet meat, when it will no longer in the Fruit. But pray let's make haste to the next honest Priest, that can say Grace to us, and take our appetites while they are coming.

Cam. That way leads to the *Austin*-Fryers, there lives a Father of my acquaintance.

Lau. I have heard of him; he has a mighty stroke at Matrimonies, and mumbles 'em over as fast, as if he were teaching us
20 to forget 'em all the while.

Enter Benito, *and over-hears the last speech.*

Ben. Cappari; that's the voice of Madam *Laura.* Now, *Benito,* is the time to repair the lost honour of thy wit, and to blot out the last adventure of the Nunnery.

Vio. That way I hear company; let's go about by this other street, and shun 'em.

Ben. That voice I know too; 'tis the younger Sister, *Violetta's.* Now have these two most treacherously convey'd themselves out of the Nunnery, for my Master and *Camillo,* and given up their persons to those lewd Rascals in Masquerade; but I'll prevent
30 'em. Help there, Thieves and Ravishers, villanous Maskers, stop Robbers, stop Ravishers.

Cam. We are pursu'd that way, let's take this street.

Lau. Save your selves, and leave us.

Cam. We'll rather dye than leave you.

Enter at several doors Duke of Mantoua *and* Guards,
and Don Mario *and* Servants, *with Torches.*

Aur. So, now the way is shut up on both sides. We'll dye merrily however:————have at the fairest.

[Aurelian *and* Camillo *fall upon the* Dukes Guards, *and are seiz'd behind by* Mario's *Servants. At the drawing of Swords,* Benito *runs off.*

16   *Austin*-Fryers] *Austin-Fryers* Q1–3, F, D.
21   Now] *starts a new line in Q1–3, F.*
34+   *s.d.* Guards] *Guards* Q1–3, F, D.
36+   *s.d.* [Aurelian . . . Dukes Guards . . . Servants] ∧~ . . . *Dukes Guards . . . Servants* Q1–3, F, D.

Duke. Are these insolencies usually committed in *Rome* by night? it has the fame of a well-govern'd City; and methinks, Don *Mario,* it does somewhat reflect on you to suffer these Disorders.

40   *Mar.* They are not to be hinder'd in the Carnival: you see, Sir, they have assum'd the Priviledge of Maskers.

Lau. to Au. If my Unckle know us, we are ruin'd; therefore be sure you do not speak.

Duke. How then can we be satisfy'd this was not a device of Masking, rather than a design of Ravishing?

Mar. Their accuser is fled, I saw him run at the beginning of the scuffle; but I'll examine the Ladies.

Vio. Now we are lost.

        [Duke *coming near* Laura *takes notice of her Habit.*

Duke aside. 'Tis the same, 'tis the same; I know *Lucretia* by 50 her Habit: I'm sure I am not mistaken. Now, Sir, you may cease your examination, I know the Ladies.

Aur. to Cam. How the Devil does he know 'em?

Cam. 'Tis alike to us; they are lost both wayes.

Duke taking Laura aside. Madam, you may confess your self to me. Whatever your design was in leaving the Nunnery, your reputation shall be safe. I'll not discover you, provided you grant me the happiness I last requested.

Lau. I know not, Sir, how you could possibly come to know me, or of my design in quitting the Nunnery; but this I know, that 60 my Sister and my self are both unfortunate, except your Highness be pleas'd to protect us from our Unckle; at least, not to discover us.

Duke. His Holiness your Unckle, shall never be acquainted with your flight, on Condition you will wholly renounce my Son, and give your self to me.

Lau. Alass, Sir, For whom do you mistake me?

Duke. I mistake you not, Madam: I know you for *Lucretia.* You forget that your Disguise betrayes you.

Lau. Then, Sir, I perceive I must disabuse you: if you please 70 to withdraw a little, that I may not be seen by others, I will pull

---

40   Carnival] *Carnival* Q1–3, F, D.
48+   *s.d.* [Duke] F, D; ∧∼ Q1–3.
68   *set as a line of verse in Q1–3, F.*

off my Mask, and discover to you that *Lucretia* and I have no resemblance, but only in our misfortunes.

Duke. 'Tis in vain, Madam, this dissembling: I protest if you
pull off your Mask, I will hide my Face, and not look upon you,
to convince you that I know you.

Enter Benito.

Ben. So, now the fray is over, a man may appear again with
safety. Oh, the Rogues are caught I see, and the Damsels deliver'd. This was the effect of my valour at the second hand.

Aur. Look, look, *Camillo,* it was my perpetual Fool that caus'd
all this, and now he stands yonder, laughing at his mischief, as the
Devil is pictur'd, grinning behind the Witch upon the Gallows.

Ben. to Mario. I see, Sir, you have got your Women, and I am
glad on't: I took 'em just flying from the Nunnery.

Duke to Lau. You see that Fellow knows you too.

Mar. Were these Women flying from a Nunnery?

Ben. These Women? Hey day! then, it seems, you do not know
they are your Neeces.

Duke. His Neeces, say you? Take heed, Fellow, you shall be
punish'd severely if you mistake.

Cam. Speak to *Benito* in time, *Aurelian.*

Aur. The Devil's in him, he's running down-hill full speed,
and there is no stopping him.

Mar. My Neeces?

Ben. Your Neeces? Why, Do you doubt it? I praise Heaven I
never met but with two half-wits in my life, and my Master's one
of 'em; I will not name the other, at this time.

Duke. I say they are not they.

Ben. I am sure they are *Laura* and *Violetta,* and that those two
Rogues were running away with 'em, and that I believe with
their consent.

Vio. Sister, 'Tis in vain to deny our selves; you see our ill fortune pursues us unavoidably.   [*Turning up her Masque.*
Yes, Sir, we are *Laura* and *Violetta,* whom you have made unhappy by your Tyranny.

75+   *s.d.* Benito] Q2–3, F, D; *Benito* Q1.

Lau. turning up her Mask. And these two Gentlemen are no
Ravishers, but———

Ben. How, no Ravishers? yes, to my knowledge, they are———
            [*As he speaks,* Aurelian *pulls off his Mask.*
no Ravishers, as Madam *Laura* was saying; but two as honest
Gentlemen as e're broke bread: My own dear Master, and so forth!
            [*Runs to* Aurelian, *who thrusts him back.*

Enter Valerio, *and whispers the* Duke, *giving him a Paper,*
which he reads, and seemes pleas'd.

110   *Mar. Aurelian* and *Camillo!* I'll see you in safe custody, and,
for these Fugitives, go, carry 'em to my Sister, and desire her to
have a better care of her Kinswomen.

Vio. We shall live yet to make you refund our Portions. Farewell *Camillo;* comfort your self; remember there's but a Wall
betwixt us.

Lau. And I'll cut through that Wall with Vineger, but I'll
come to you, *Aurelian.*

Aur. I'll cut through the Grates with *Aqua-fortis,* but I'll meet
you. Think of these things, and despair and dye, old Gentleman.
            [Aurelian *and* Camillo *are carry'd off on one side,*
                    and Laura *and* Violetta *on the other.*

120   *Ben.* All things go cross to men of sence: would I had been
born with the brains of a Shop-keeper, that I might have thriven
without knowing why I did so. Now must I follow my Master to
the Prison, and, like an ignorant Customer that comes to buy,
must offer him my back-side, tell him I trust to his honesty, and
desire him to please himself, and so be satisfy'd.   [*Exit.*

Duke to Valerio. I am overjoy'd, I'll see her immediately: now
my business with Don *Mario* is at an end, I need not desire his
company to introduce me to the Abbess, this Assignation from
Lucretia shows me a nearer way. Noble Don *Mario,* it was my
130 business when this accident happen'd in the street to have made

107+   *s.d.* [*As*] Q3, D; ₍~ Q1–2, F (*line centered*).
109+   *s.d.* [*Runs*] Q3, F, D; ₍~ Q1–2.
109+   *s.d.* Duke] *Duke* Q1–3, F, D.
111   for] Q1 (*catchword*), Q2–3, F, D; ~, Q1 (*text*).
119+   *s.d.* [Aurelian] F, D; ₍~ Q1–3.

you a visit; but now I am prevented by an occasion which calls me another way.

Mar. I receive the intention of that honour as the greatest happiness that cou'd befall me: in the mean time, if my attendance————

Duke. By no means, Sir, I must of necessity go in private, and therefore, if you please, you shall omit the ceremony.

Mar. A happy even to your Highness. Now will I go to my Sister the Abbess, before I sleep, and desire her to take more care
140 of her Flock, or, for all our Relation, I shall make complaint, and indeavour to ease her of her charge.   [*Exit.*

Duke. So, now we are alone. What said *Lucretia?*

Val. When first I press'd her to this Assignation, she spoke like one in doubt what she should do; she demur'd much upon the decency of it, and somewhat too she seem'd to urge, of her Engagement to the Prince: in short, Sir, I perceiv'd her wavering; and clos'd with the opportunity.

Duke. O, when women are once irresolute, betwixt the former love and the new one, they are sure to come over to the latter: the
150 wind, their nearest likeness, seldome chops about to return into the old corner.

Val. In conclusion, she consented to the interview, and for the rest, I urg'd it not, for I suppose she will hear reason sooner from your mouth than mine.

Duke. Her Letter is of the same tenor with her Discourse; full of doubts and doubles, like a hunted Hare when she's near tyr'd. The Garden, you say, is the place appointed?

Val. It is, Sir; and the next half hour the time: but, Sir, I fear the Prince your Son will never bear the loss of her with patience.
160 *Duke.* 'Tis no matter; let the young Gallant storm to night, to morrow he departs from *Rome.*

Val. That, Sir, will be severe.

Duke. He has already receiv'd my commands to travel into *Germany:* I know it stung him to the quick; but he's too dangerous a Rival: the Souldiers love him too; when he's absent they

---

142 alone.] Q2, F, D; ~, Q1, Q3.
143–147 *as verse in* Q1–3, F, D (. . . / She spoke . . . / She demur'd . . . / And somewhat . . . / Engagement . . . / I).

will respect me more. But I defer my happiness too long; dismiss
my Guards there.   [*Exeunt* Guards.
    The pleasures of old age brook no delay:
Seldome they come, and soon they fly away.   [*Exeunt.*

SCENE III.

Prince *and* Ascanio.

Fred. 'Tis true, he is my Father; but when Nature
Is dead in him, Why should it live in me?
What have I done, that I am banish'd *Rome,*
The Worlds delight, and my Souls joy *Lucretia,*
And sent to reel with midnight Beasts in *Almain?*
I cannot, will not bear it.
    Asca. I'm sure you need not, Sir: the Army is all yours; they
wish a youthful Monarch, and will resent your injuries.
    Fred. Heaven forbid it.
10 And yet I cannot lose *Lucretia.*
There's something I would do, and yet would shun
The ill that must attend it.
    Asca. You must resolve, for the time presses. She told me, this
hour, she had sent for your Father: what she means I know not,
for she seem'd doubtful, and would not tell me her intention.
    Fred. If she be false;————yet, Why should I suspect her? yet,
Why should I not? she's a Woman; that includes ambition, and
inconstancy: then, she's tempted high: 'twere unreasonable to
expect she should be faithful: well, something I have resolv'd
20 and will about it instantly: and if my Friends prove faithful I
shall prevent the worst.

Enter Aurelian *and* Camillo *guarded.*

Aurelian and *Camillo?* How came you thus attended?
    Cam. You may guess at the occasion, Sir; pursuing the adven-

---

167   *s.d. at end of preceding sentence in Q1–3.*
167   *s.d.* Guards] Guards Q1–3, F, D.   9–10   *one line in Q1–3, F, D.*

ture which brought us to meet you in the Garden, we were taken
by Don *Mario*.

Aur. And, as the Devil would have it, when both we and our
Mistresses were in expectation of a more pleasant lodging.

Fred. Faith, that's very hard, when a man has charg'd and
prim'd, and taken aim, to be hinder'd of his shoot———Soul-
30 diers, release these Gentlemen; I'll answer it.

Cap. Sir, we dare not disobey our Orders.

Fred. I'll stand betwixt you and danger. In the mean time take
this, as an acknowledgment of the kindness you do me.

Cap. Ay, marry, there's Rhetorique in Gold: Who can deny
these arguments? Sir, you may dispose of our prisoners as you
please; we'll use your name if we are call'd in question.

Fred. Do so. Good-night good Souldiers.   [*Exeunt* Souldiers.
Now, Gentlemen, no thanks, you'll find occasion instantly to re-
imburse me of my kindness.

40   *Cam.* Nothing but want of liberty could have hinder'd us from
serving you.

Fred. Meet me, within this half hour, at our Monastery; and if,
in the mean time, you can pick up a dozen of good Fellows, who
dare venture their lives bravely, bring them with you.

Aur. I hope the Cause is bad too, otherwise we shall not deserve your thanks: may it be for demolishing that cursed Monastery.

Fred. Come, *Ascanio,* follow me.   [*Exeunt severally.*

SCENE IV.

The Nunnery-Garden.

Duke, Lucretia.

Luc. In making this appointment,
I go too far, for one of my profession;
But I have a divining Soul within me,
Which tells me, trust repos'd in noble natures
Obliges them the more.

---

37   s.d. Souldiers] *Souldiers* Q1–3, F, D.

Duke. I come to be commanded, not to govern,
Those few soft words you sent me, have quite alter'd
My rugged nature; if it still be violent,
'Tis only fierce and eager to obey you,
10 Like some impetuous flood, which Master'd once,
With double force bends backward.
The place of Treaty shows you strongest here;
For still the vanquish'd sues for peace abroad,
While the proud Victor makes his termes at home.
 Luc. That peace, I see, will not be hard to make
When either side shows confidence of noble
Dealing from the other.
 Duke. And this, sure, is our case, since both are met alone.
 Luc. 'Tis mine, Sir, more than yours.
20 To meet you single, shows I trust your virtue;
But you appear distrustful of my Love.
 Duke. You wrong me much, I am not.
 Luc. Excuse me, Sir, you keep a curb upon me:
You awe me with a Letter, which you hold
As Hostage of my Love; and Hostages
Are ne'r requir'd but from suspected Faith.
 Duke. We are not yet in termes of perfect peace;
When e're you please to seal the Articles,
Your pledge shall be restor'd.
30 *Luc.* That were the way to keep us still at distance;
For what we fear, we cannot truly love.
 Duke. But how can I be then secure, that when
Your fear is o're your love will still continue?
 Luc. Make tryal of my gratitude; you'll find
I can acknowledge kindness.
 Duke. But that were to forego the faster hold
To take a loose, and weaker.
Would you not judge him mad who held a Lion
In chains of Steel, and chang'd e'm for a twine?
40 *Luc.* But love is soft,
Not of the Lion's nature, but the Dove's;

16–17 noble / Dealing from] noble dealing / From Q1–3, F, D.
27 *Duke.*] Q2–3, F, D; ~ˌ Q1.

An Iron chain would hang too heavy on
A tender neck.
    Duke. Since on one side there must be confidence,
Why may not I expect, as well as you,
To have it plac'd in me? Repose your trust
Upon my Royal word.
    Luc. As 'tis the priviledge of womankind
That men should court our Love,
50 And make the first advances; so it follows
That you should first oblige; for 'tis our weakness
Gives us more cause of fear, and therefore you,
Who are the stronger Sex, should first secure it.
    Duke. But, Madam, as you talk of fear from me,
I may as well suspect design from you.
    Luc. Design! of giving you my Love more freely,
Of making you a Title to my heart,
Where you by force would reign.
    Duke. O that I could believe you! but your words
60 Are not enough disorder'd for true love;
They are not plain, and hearty, as are mine;
But full of art, and close insinuation:
You promise all, but give me not one proof
Of love before; not the least earnest of it.
    Luc. And, What is then this midnight conversation?
These silent hours divided from my sleep?
Nay, more; stoln from my Prayers with Sacriledge,
And here transfer'd to you? This guilty hand,
Which should be us'd in dropping holy Beads,
70 But now, bequeath'd to yours? This heaving heart,
Which only should be throbbing for my sins,
But which now beats uneven time for you?
These are my arts! and these are my designs!
    Duke. I love you more, *Lucretia,* than my Soul;
Nay, than yours too, for I would venture both
That I might now enjoy you; and if what
You ask me did not make me fear to lose you,

42–43 *one line in Q1–3, F, D* (a tender).   55 you.] Q2, F, D; ~, Q1, Q3.
70 throbbing] F, D; throbing Q1–3.

Though it were even my life, you should not be deny'd it.
 Luc. Then I will ask no more.
80 Keep my Letter, to upbraid me with it;
To Say, when I am sully'd with your Lust,
And fit to be forsaken, Go, *Lucretia*,
To your first love; for this, for this, I leave you.
 Duke. Oh, Madam, never think that day can come!
 Luc. It must, it will, I read it in your looks;
You will betray me when I'm once engag'd.
 Duke. If not my Faith, your Beauty will secure you.
 Luc. My Beauty is a Flower upon the stalk,
Goodly to see; but, gather'd for the scent,
90 And once with eagerness press'd to your nostrils,
The sweet's drawn out, 'tis thrown with scorn away.
But I am glad I find you out so soon:
I simply lov'd, and meant (with shame I own it)
To trust my Virgin-honour in your hands;
I ask'd not wealth, for hire; and, but by chance,
(I wonder that I thought on't) beg'd one tryal,
And, but for form, to have pretence to yield,
And that you have deny'd me. Farewell: I could
Have lov'd you, and yet, perhaps, I———
100 *Duke.* O speak, speak out, and do not drown that word,
It seem'd as if it would have been a kind one,
And yours are much too precious to be lost.
 Luc. Perhaps———I cannot yet leave loving you.
There 'twas. But I recall'd it in my mind,
And made it false before I gave it Ayr.
Once more, farewell———I wonnot;
Now I can say I wonnot, wonnot love you.   [*Going.*
 Duke. You shall; and this shall be the Seal of my affection.
            [*Gives the Letter.*
There, take it, my *Lucretia;* I give it with more joy,
110 Than I with grief receiv'd it.
 Luc. Good night; I'll thank you for't some other time.
 Duke. You'll not abuse my love?

---

96 tryal,] Q2–3, F, D; ∼. Q1.

Luc. No; but secure my Honour.
Duke. I'll force it from your hands.　　　　[Lucretia *runs.*
Luc. Help, help, or I am ravish'd; help, for heavens sake.

> Hippolita, Laura, *and* Violetta *within,*
> *in several places.*

Within. Help, help *Lucretia;*
They bear away *Lucretia* by force.
Duke. I think there is a Devil in every corner.

> *Enter* Valerio.

Val. Sir, the design was lay'd on purpose for you,
120 And all the women plac'd to cry. Make haste
Away; avoid the shame for heavens sake.
Duke going. O, I could fire this Monastery!

> *Enter* Frederick *and* Ascanio.

(Frederick *entring speaks as to some behind him*)
Fred. Pain of your lives, let none of you presume
To enter but my self.
Duke. My Son!
O, I could burst with spite, and dye with shame,
To be thus apprehended! this is the baseness
And cowardise of guilt: an Army now
Were not so dreadful to me as that Son,
130 O're whom the right of Nature gives me power.
Fred. Sir, I am come———
Duke. To laugh at first, and then to blaze abroad
The weakness, and the follies of your Father.
Val. Sir, he has Men in Armes attending him.
Duke. I know my doom then.

116–117　*as prose in Q1–3, F, D* (they).
119–121　*as prose in Q1–3, F, D* (and . . . away).
123–124　*as prose in Q1–3, F, D* (to).
125–130　*as prose in Q1–3, F, D* (to be . . . and cowardise . . . were . . . o're).
135–138　*as prose in Q1–3, F, D* (fit).

You have taken a popular occasion;
I am now a ravisher of chastity,
Fit to be made prisoner first, and then depos'd.
        Fred. You will not hear me, Sir.
140   *Duke.* No, I confess I have deserv'd my fate;
For, What had these gray haires to do with Love?
Or, if th' unseemly folly would possess me,
Why should I choose to make my Son my Rival?
        Fred. Sir, you may add you banish'd me from *Rome,*
And from the light of it, *Lucretia's* eyes.
        Duke. Nay, if thou aggravat'st my crimes, thou giv'st
Me right to justify 'em: thou doubly art my slave,
Both Son and Subject. I can do thee no wrong,
Nor hast thou right t' arraign or punish me:
150 But thou inquir'st into thy Fathers years;
Thy swift ambition could not stay my death,
But must ride post to Empire. Lead me now:
Thy crimes have made me guiltless to my self,
And given me face to bear the publick scorn.
You have a guard without?
        Fred. ————————I have some friends.
        Duke. Speak plainly your intent.
I love not a sophisticated truth,
With an allay of lye in't.
        Fred. kneeling. This is not, Sir, the posture of a Rebel,
160 But of a suppliant, if the Name of Son
Be too much honour to me.
What first I purpos'd, I scarce know my self.
Love, Anger, and Revenge then rowl'd within me,
And yet, ev'n then, I was not hurry'd farther
Than to preserve my own.
        Duke. ————————Your own! What mean you?
        Fred. My Love, and my *Lucretia;* which I thought
In my then boyling passion, you pursu'd
With some injustice, and much violence;
This led me to repell that force by force.

---

143   Rival?] F, D; ~: Q1-3.   155 ————I] ∧~ Q1-3, F, D.

170 'Twas easie to surprize you, when I knew
Of your intended visit.
  Duke. ——————Thank my folly.
  Fred. But reason now has reassum'd its place,
And makes me see how black a crime it is
To use a force upon my Prince and Father.
  Duke. You give me hope you will resign *Lucretia*
  Fred. Ah no: I never can resign her to you;
But, Sir, I can my life: which, on my knees,
I tender, as th' attoning Sacrifice.
Or if your hand (because you are a Father)
180 Be loath to take away that life you gave,
I will redeem your crime, by making it
My own: So you shall still be innocent, and I
Dye bless'd, and unindebted for my being.
  Duke embracing him. O *Frederick,* you are too much a Son,
And I too little am a Father: You,
And you alone, have merited *Lucretia.*
'Tis now my only grief,
I can do nothing to requite this virtue;
For to restore her to you
190 Is not an act of generosity,
But a scant, niggard Justice; yet I love her
So much, that even this little which I do
Is like the bounty of an Usurer;
High to be priz'd from me,
Because 'tis drawn from such a wretched mind.
  Fred. kissing his hands. You give me now a second, better life;
But, that the gift may be more easie to you,
Consider, Sir, *Lucretia* did not Love you:
I fear to say ne'r would.
  Duke. ——————You do well,
200 To help me to o'recome that difficulty:
I'll weigh that, too, hereafter. For a love,
So violent as mine, will ask long time,
And much of reason, to effect the cure.

———————

199–200 *Duke. . . .* difficulty:] *on one line in* Q*1–3,* F, D (ᴧYou . . . to help . . .).

My present care shall be to make you happy;
For that will make my wish impossible,
And then the remedies will be more easie.

Enter Sophronia, Lucretia, Violetta, Laura, Hippolita.

Soph. I have, with joy, o'reheard this happy change,
And come, with blessings, to applaud your conquest,
Over the greatest of Mankind, your self.
210   *Duke.* I hope 'twill be a full, and lasting one.
    Luc. kneeling. Thus, let me kneel, and pay my thanks and duty
Both to my Prince, and Father.
    Duke. Rise, rise, too charming Maid; for yet I cannot
Call you Daughter: that first name, *Lucretia,*
Hangs on my lips, and would be still pronounc'd.
Look not too kindly on me; one sweet glance,
Perhaps, would ruine both: therefore, I'll go
And try to get new strength to bear your eyes.
Till then, Farewell. Be sure you love my *Frederick,*
220 And do not hate his Father.   *[Exeunt* Duke *and* Valerio.
    Fred. at the door. Now, friends, you may appear.

Enter Aurelian, Camillo, Benito.

Your pardon, Madam, that we thus intrude
On holy ground: your self best know it could not
Be avoided, and it shall be my care it be excus'd.
    Soph. Though Soveraign Princes bear a priviledge,
Of entring when they please within our walls,
In others, 'tis a crime past dispensation:
And therefore, to avoid a publick scandal,
Be pleas'd, Sir, to retire, and quit this Garden.
230   *Aur.* We shall obey you, Madam: But, that we may do it with
less regret, we hope you will give these Ladies leave to accompany us.
    Soph. They shall.

---

211 duty] ~. Q1–3, F, D.   212 Father.] D; ~? Q1–3, F.
220 *s.d. [Exeunt]* F, D; ∧~ Q1–3.   222 pardon,] Q2–3, F, D; ~. Q1.

And Neeces, for my self, I only ask you
To justify my conduct to the world,
That none may think I have betray'd a trust,
But freed you from a Tyranny.

   Lau. Our duty binds us to acknowledge it.

   Cam. And our gratitude, to witness it.

240   *Vio.* With a holy, and lasting remembrance of your favour.

   Fred. And it shall be my care, either by reason to bend your Unckle's will, or, by my Father's interest, to force your Dowry from his hands.

   Ben. to Aur. Pray, Sir, let us make haste over these Walls again, these Gardens are unlucky to me: I have lost my reputation of Musick in the one of 'em, and of wit in the other.

   Aur. to Lau. Now, *Laura,* you may take your choice betwixt the two *Benito's,* and consider whether you had rather he should Serenade you in the Garden, or I in Bed to night.

250   *Lau.* You may be sure I shall give Sentence for *Benito;* for, the effect of your Serenading would be to make me pay the Musick nine Moneths hence.

   Hip. to Asca. You see, Brother, here's a General Jayle-delivery: there has been a great deal of bustle and disturbance in the Cloyster to night; enough to distract a Soul which is given up, like me, to contemplation: and therefore, if you think fit, I could e'en be content to retire, with you, into the World; and, by way of Penance, to Marry you; which, as Husbands and Wives go now, is a greater Mortification than a Nunnery.

260   *Asca.* No, Sister, if you love me, keep to your Monastery: I'll come now and then to the Grate and beg you a Recreation. But I know my self so well, that, if I had you one twelve Moneth in the world, I should run my self into a Cloyster, to be rid of you.

   Soph. Neeces, once more farewell. Adieu, *Lucretia.*
My wishes and my prayers attend you all.

   Luc. to Fred. I am so fearful,
That, though I gladly run to your embraces,
Yet, ventring in the World a second time,

238 it.] *some copies of Q1 have comma.*   246 Musick] Q3, F, D; *Musick* Q1–2.
251 Musick] Q3, F, D; *Musick* Q1–2.   256 e'en] Q2–3, F, D; een Q1.
259 Nunnery] F, D; *Nunnery* Q1–3.   264 *Lucretia.*] Q3, F; ∼: Q1–2, D.

Methinks I put to Sea in a rough storm,
270 With shipwracks round about me.
    Fred. My Dear, be kinder to your self, and me,
And let not fear fright back our coming joyes;
For we, at length, stand reconcil'd to fate:
And now to fear, when to such bliss we move,
Were not to doubt our Fortune, but our Love.

                                         [Exeunt.

275+   s.d. *[Exeunt.] omitted from Q1–3, F, D.*

Epilogue.

S OME *have expected from our Bills to day*
      To find a Satyre *in our* Poet's Play.
         The Zealous Rout *from* Coleman-street *did run,*
To see the Story of the Fryer *and* Nun.
Or Tales, yet more Ridiculous to hear,
Vouch'd by their Vicar of Ten pounds a year;
Of Nuns, who did against Temptation Pray,
And Discipline laid on the Pleasant way:
Or that to please the Malice of the Town,
Our Poet *should in some close Cell have shown*
Some Sister, Playing at Content alone:
This they did hope; the other side did fear,
And both you see alike are Couzen'd here.
Some thought the Title of our Play *to blame,*
They lik'd the thing, but yet abhor'd the Name:
Like Modest Puncks, *who all you ask afford,*
But, for the World, *they would not name that word.*
Yet, if you'll credit what I heard him say,
Our Poet *meant no Scandal in his* Play;
His Nuns are good which on the Stage are shown,
And, sure, behind our Scenes *you'll look for none.*

---

14   Play] *Play* Q1–3, F, D.

COMMENTARY

List of Abbreviated References

Allen: Ned Bliss Allen, *The Sources of John Dryden's Comedies,* Ann Arbor, 1935

Avery: *The London Stage, 1660–1800,* Part 2: 1700–1729, ed. Emmett L. Avery, Carbondale, Ill., 1960.

Beaurline and Bowers: *John Dryden: Four Comedies,* ed. L. A. Beaurline and Fredson Bowers, Chicago, 1967.

Bentley: Gerald Eades Bentley, *The Jacobean and Caroline Stage,* 1941–1956

BH: Samuel Johnson, *Lives of the English Poets,* ed. George Birkbeck Hill, Oxford, 1905

Bulstrode Papers: The Bulstrode Papers, ed. Alfred Morrison, 1897

Calderón: Pedro Calderón de la Barca, *Con Quien Vengo, Vengo,* in *Obras Completas,* ed. Angel Valbuena Briones, 2d ed., Madrid, 1960, II, 1129–1165

Cibber: *An Apology for the Life of Mr. Colley Cibber,* ed. Robert W. Lowe, 1889

CSPD: Calendar of State Papers Domestic

DNB: Dictionary of National Biography

Downes: John Downes, *Roscius Anglicanus,* 1708

ELH: A Journal of English Literary History

Evelyn, *Diary: The Diary of John Evelyn,* ed. E. S. de Beer, Oxford, 1955

Highfill: Philip H. Highfill, Jr., Kalman A. Burnim, and Edward A. Langhans, *A Biographical Dictionary of Actors, Actresses, Musicians, Dancers, Managers & Other Stage Personnel in London, 1660–1800,* 1973–1975

HLB: Harvard Library Bulletin

HLQ: Huntington Library Quarterly

Hobbes, *Leviathan:* Thomas Hobbes, *Leviathan,* ed. Michael Oakeshott, Oxford, 1960

Hume: Robert D. Hume, *The Development of English Drama in the Late Seventeenth Century,* Oxford, 1976

Jonson, *Works: Ben Jonson,* ed. C. H. Herford and Percy Simpson, Oxford, 1925–1952

JWCI: Journal of the Warburg and Courtauld Institutes

Ker: *Essays of John Dryden,* ed. W. P. Ker, Oxford, 1926

Kinsley: *The Poems of John Dryden,* ed. James Kinsley, Oxford, 1958

Langbaine: Gerard Langbaine, *An Account of the English Dramatick Poets,* 1691

Macdonald: Hugh Macdonald, *John Dryden: A Bibliography of Early Editions and of Drydeniana,* Oxford, 1939

Malone: *Critical and Miscellaneous Prose Works of John Dryden,* ed. Edmond Malone, 1800

MLN: Modern Language Notes

MLR: Modern Language Review

Moore: Frank Harper Moore, *The Nobler Pleasure: Dryden's Comedy in Theory and Practice,* Chapel Hill, 1963

MP: *Modern Philology*
NCD: *A New Canting Dictionary*, 1725
N&Q: *Notes and Queries*
Nicoll: Allardyce Nicoll, *A History of Restoration Drama, 1660–1700*, 4th ed., Cambridge, 1952
Noyes: *Poetical Works of Dryden*, ed. George R. Noyes, rev. ed., Cambridge, Mass., 1950
Noyes, *Selected Dramas: Selected Dramas of John Dryden*, ed. George R. Noyes, Chicago, 1910
OED: *Oxford English Dictionary*
Ogg: David Ogg, *England in the Reign of Charles II*, 2d ed., Oxford, 1955
Pepys, *Diary: The Diary of Samuel Pepys*, ed. Robert Latham and William Matthews, Berkeley and Los Angeles, 1970–1976
Pérez: Ginés Pérez de Hita, *Guerras Civiles de Granada*, ed. Paula Blanchard-Demouge, Madrid, 1913–1915
PMLA: *Publications of the Modern Language Association of America*
PQ: *Philological Quarterly*
RES: *Review of English Studies*
Rodd: Thomas Rodd, trans., *The Civil Wars of Granada; and the History of the Factions of the Zegries and Abencerrages, Two Noble Families of that City, To the Final Conquest by Ferdinand and Isabella. . . . By Ginés Pérez De Hita*, 1803
SEL: *Studies in English Literature*
SP: *Studies in Philology*
Spingarn: *Critical Essays of the Seventeenth Century*, ed. J. E. Spingarn, Bloomington, Ind., 1957
S-S: *The Works of John Dryden*, ed. Sir Walter Scott and George Saintsbury, 1882–1893
Summers: Dryden's *Dramatic Works*, ed. Montague Summers, 1931
Sutherland: *Marriage A-la-Mode*, ed. J. R. Sutherland, 1934
Tasso, *Discourses:* Torquato Tasso, *Discourses on the Heroic Poem*, trans. Mariella Cavalchini and Irene Samuel, Oxford, 1973
Tilley: M. P. Tilley, *A Dictionary of the Proverbs in England in the Sixteenth and Seventeenth Centuries*, Ann Arbor, 1950
Van Lennep: *The London Stage, 1660–1800*, Part 1: 1660–1700, ed. William Van Lennep, with Critical Introduction by Emmett L. Avery and Arthur H. Scouten, Carbondale, Ill., 1965
Ward, *Letters: The Letters of John Dryden*, ed. Charles E. Ward, Durham, N.C., 1942
Ward, *Life:* Charles E. Ward, *The Life of John Dryden*, Chapel Hill, 1961
Watson: *John Dryden: Of Dramatic Poesy and Other Critical Essays*, ed. George Watson, 1962
Wilson: John Harold Wilson, *All the King's Ladies*, Chicago, 1958
Works: Dryden's works in the present edition

The Conquest of Granada

Lady Mary Bertie wrote to Katherine Noel on 2 January 1671 telling her "there is letely come out a new play writ by Mr. Dreyden who made the *Indian Emperor*. It is caled the *Conquest of Grenada*. My brother Norreys tooke a box and carryed my Lady Rochester and his mistresse and all us to, and on Tuestay wee are to goe see the second part of it which is then the first tim acted."[1] This testimony—the earliest that is reasonably precise—dates the first performance of Part I to December 1670 and sets the first performance of Part II on Tuesday, 3 or 10 January 1671. One Jeffrey Boys of Gray's Inn saw Part I on 26 January, Part II on 31 January 1671.[2] Performances were by the King's Company in the old Theatre Royal. John Evelyn confided to his diary on 9 February 1671 that he "saw the greate Ball danced by the Queene & greate Ladies at White hall Theater: & next day was acted there the famous Play, cald the Siege of *Granada* two days acted successively: there were indeede very glorious scenes & perspectives, the worke of Mr. Streeter, who well understands it."[3] Mrs. Evelyn also saw the play[4] during its first season, perhaps in January 1671, and recorded her impressions in a letter to Dr. Bohun:

> I have seene "The Siege of Grenada," a play so full of ideas that the most refined romance I ever read is not to compare with it: love is made so pure, and valor so nice, that one would imagine it designed for an Utopia rather then our stage. I do not quarrell with the poet, but admire one borne in the decline of morality should be able to feigne such exact virtue: and as poetick fiction has been instructive in former ages, I wish this the same event in ours.[5]

We have no record of performance after the season of 1670–71 until 21 December 1675, when Part I was acted at Drury Lane,[6] and the next indication of public performance comes after an even longer interval. Dryden wrote to Tonson in the late summer or early fall of 1684 telling him of Betterton's preparations for a revival of the play in the forthcoming season.[7] The play may also have been revived—although there is no certain evidence

---

[1] *Rutland MSS, HMC, 12th Report, Appendix*, Pt. V (1889), p. 22.

[2] G. J. Gray, "The Diary of Jeffrey Boys of Gray's Inn, 1671," *N&Q*, CLIX (1930), 455–456.

[3] Evelyn, *Diary*, III, 569–570. The "greate Ball" may have been danced on Monday, 6 February 1671 (Van Lennep, p. 180). De Beer finds no other evidence that *The Conquest of Granada* received a court performance at this time and accordingly questions Evelyn's record.

[4] We call the complete ten-act drama "the play," and distinguish where necessary between first and second parts.

[5] *Diary and Correspondence of John Evelyn*, ed. William Bray and Henry B. Wheatley (1906), IV, 56–57.

[6] Van Lennep, p. 241.

[7] Ward, *Letters*, pp. 23–24.

—in the seasons of 1677–78, 1686–87, and 1694–95.[8] A version of the play was apparently staged sometime before February 1698, when Dryden published his complimentary poem to Granville and referred dismissively to the actors'

> Murd'ring Plays, which they miscal Reviving.
> Our Sense is Nonsense, through their Pipes convey'd;
> Scarce can a Poet know the Play He made.

The actors' retort to this general charge came a few months later in George Powell's preface to an anonymous play called *The Fatal Discovery:*

> 'Tis true, I think we have reviv'd some pieces of Dryden, as his *Sebastian, Maiden Queen, Marriage A-la-mode, King Arthur,* &c. But ... his more particular picque against us, as he has declared himself, is in Relation to our Reviving his *Almanzor.* There indeed he has reason to be angry for our waking that sleeping Dowdy, and exposing his nonsense, not ours.[9]

Nearly thirty years separate Powell's "sleeping Dowdy" from Mrs. Evelyn's play of "such exact virtue," and we would scarcely notice Powell's phrase were it not last in a long train of dismissive references to *The Conquest of Granada* on the Restoration stage. Even amateur theatricals provoked jests, as we know from two poems by Thomas Shipman indicating that the play, or one of its parts, was privately acted in 1677 at Belvoir Castle, the seat of the Earl of Rutland.[10] Both poems, one of them serving "in way of Prologue" and entitled "The Huffer," deal roughly with the play and especially its hero.

The habit of attacking and defending Almanzor and his play was established well before Shipman wrote his Belvoir poems. The habit, indeed, belongs as much to the play's publication as to its theatrical history. By the time Henry Herringman entered *The Conquest of Granada* in the *Stationers' Register* on 25 February 1671, Dryden had already promised to discuss heroic plays and perhaps *"to treat of the improvement of our Language since* Fletcher's *and* Johnson's *dayes"* when he came to *"publish the* Conquest of Granada."[11] Dryden fulfilled that promise a year later by publishing the play with a prefatory discourse *Of Heroique Playes,* much of it defending Almanzor, and a concluding *Defence of the Epilogue.* By February 1672 Almanzor had undergone mutation into Drawcansir of *The Rehearsal,* while the term catalogue listing Dryden's play also listed a piece entitled *Al-Man-Sir or, Rhodomontados of the most Horrible Terrible and Invincible Captain Sr Fredrick Fight-all. English and French.*[12] When Almanzor and his play first appeared in print, they were already launched

---

8 Van Lennep, pp. 262, 351, 440. For three performances in the first decade of the eighteenth century see Avery, pp. 64, 124, 187.

9 *The Fatal Discovery: Or, Love in Ruines* (1698), sig. A2v.

10 Van Lennep, p. 248. For the poems see Thomas Shipman, *Carolina: or, Loyal Poems* (1683), p. 190–191.

11 Preface to *An Evening's Love* (*Works,* X, 202). *An Evening's Love* was listed in the term catalogue licensed on 13 February 1671.

12 *Term Catalogues,* I, 97; cf. Macdonald, p. 194. This curious collection of boasts, tall tales, and extravagant oaths seems only to have capitalized upon Almanzor's name and to have no other connection with Dryden's play.

into a literary and theatrical notoriety which was merely confirmed in spring 1673 by four so-called Rota pamphlets, two attacking and two defending *The Conquest of Granada*. Moreover, Dryden's seeming presumption in defending an epilogue by criticizing Shakespeare, Jonson, and Fletcher moved at least one adversary to raise "the *Posse-comitatus* upon this Poetick Almanzor . . . [and] put a stop to his Spoils upon his own Country-men." [13]

Such responses to early performances and editions—and there were others —prompt questions about *The Conquest of Granada* we need to answer if we are to locate the work in its age and its author's career. The glorious scenes and perspectives remarked by Evelyn no doubt contributed to the popular success Dryden claimed for his play (and even Langbaine admitted he had seen it "acted with great Applause" [p. 157]). Mrs. Evelyn's comparison of the play with romances sends us to sources and to the analogues touched upon by Dryden in his prefatory *Of Heroique Playes*. Her description of it as utopian encourages us to ask how far removed from the manners of the age are the play's precepts and examples. To answer such a question we must consider the dedication of the published work to James, Duke of York, the epilogue to the second part, and its prose defense arguing a greater correspondence between the age's manners and the play's than Mrs. Evelyn acknowledged. Possible discrepancy between stage and age prompts the further question of Almanzor's rant and Dryden's prefatory defense of it. The age, we know, spun a coin with panegyric head and satiric tail. The play's bid for wonder, admiration, not only met with the derision of *The Rehearsal* and two of the Rota pamphlets; it was also framed by the ironic prologue to the second part and the epilogue's appeal to refinement and wit. But the epilogue's notion of refinement—*"Love and Honour now are higher rais'd"*—corresponds in part to Mrs. Evelyn's and sends us to sources.

⟨⟩

Sources are innocent things in the accounts of modern scholars, but show darkly in the stern forensic of Gerard Langbaine. Dryden, he assures us, borrowed, stole, copied, or took all the actions and characters of his play from French and Spanish romances.[14] Langbaine calls five victims to the stand, but principally examines one rifled romance, the *Almahide* of Georges de Scudéry (1660–1663),[15] documenting his charges by reference to the 1677 translation of John Phillips. Part III, Book III of *Almahide* figures prominently in the examination, and Langbaine demonstrates strikingly close correspondences between play and romance. But Scudéry left his romance incomplete. Part III, Book III was the work of Phillips, who ap-

---

[13] Langbaine, p. 133.

[14] *Ibid.*, pp. 158–160.

[15] The romance has frequently been attributed to Madeleine de Scudéry, but would seem to be principally her brother's work. See Jerome W. Schweitzer, *Georges de Scudéry's "Almahide": Authorship, Analysis, Sources and Structure,* in The Johns Hopkins Studies in Romance Literatures and Languages, XXXIV (1939).

parently drew upon the play published five years before his translation.[16]

Dryden certainly used Scudéry's *Almahide,* finding there his heroine's name, if little of her character. He could also have found his hero's name in Scudéry, who tells us early in the romance that after the king of Granada had temporarily halted the fighting between Zegrys and Abencerrages, he returned to the Alhambra attended, among others, by Almanzor.[17] But Almanzor plays no significant role in the romance. We are told later that a pageant representing the city of Morocco was "chiefly remarkable for the Magnificence of Almansor's Palace, that Wise and Just Prince, whose Renown is so far spread among the Moors, and whose Memory is so well belov'd by them."[18] Dryden, in fact, could have found his hero's name in other places than Scudéry's romance. Many Mohammedan princes called themselves Almanzor, the "victorious." One such Almanzor was the subject of a biography translated from the Spanish. This Almanzor won thirteen set battles, captured five gentile kings, suffered no losses, "and even with a few Souldiers, in regard of those that came against him, he performed great Exploits."[19] He was "worthily called the Conquerour," his epitaph proclaimed, "being never overcome."[20]

If Dryden could have found his hero's name in more than one place, his hero's character could also have been variously derived. Dryden himself acknowledged models in Homer's Achilles, Tasso's Rinaldo, and the Artaban of La Calprenède's *Cléopâtre.*[21] Rough, passionate, and proud, irresistible in battle, La Calprenède's Artaban also changes sides with facility. Like Almanzor after him, Artaban comes upon a fight between unequal forces, takes the weaker and overcomes the stronger side.[22] He leads the Armenian army to victory, then requests that two of his noble prisoners be released. When the Armenian king refuses, Artaban joins the Medes, whom he has just overcome.[23] Now conqueror for the Medes, Artaban storms a city housing the Parthian queen and princess. He generously stops the slaughter, secures the ladies from harm, and asks the Median king to release them. The king at first grants the request, but then sees the princess, who has already been overwhelmed by Artaban's bearing and generosity. The king is overwhelmed by the princess and refuses to free her. Artaban in a rage joins the Parthians and leads them from triumph to triumph until the Parthian king promises to grant anything he asks. Artaban asks for the Parthian princess; the king haughtily refuses. Infuriated though he is, Artaban cannot seek to revenge himself upon his mistress's father.[24] At

---

16 See Jerome W. Schweitzer, "Dryden's Use of Scudéry's *Almahide,*" *MLN,* LIV (1939), 190–192.

17 *Almahide, or the Captive Queen,* trans. John Phillips, Pt. I, Bk. I, p. 7.

18 *Ibid.,* Pt. I, Bk. II, p. 95.

19 Robert Ashley, *Almansor The Learned and Victorious King that conquered Spaine. His Life and Death* (1627), p. 48.

20 *Ibid.,* p. 73.

21 See above, 14:22–25.

22 *Hymen's Præludia or Loves Master-peice. Being That so much admired Romance, Intituled Cleopatra* (1674), Pt. XII, Bk. II, 2d pag., p. 505. The translation, first published in 1654–55, was by Robert Loveday and others.

23 *Ibid.,* Pt. V, Bk. I, 1st pag., pp. 383–386.

24 *Ibid.,* Pt. III, Bk. III, 1st pag., pp. 214 ff.

last Artaban becomes king of Parthia, and marries his lady.[25] Summarized in this way, the doings of Dryden's Almanzor would sound as odd, although leaving his subordinates anonymous might help elucidate the equally intricate lines of his career.

But Dryden obviously could not have filled ten busy acts with a hero and heroine alone. He needed subordinates, and Scudéry's *Almahide* supplied hints toward names, if not characters, that appear in *The Conquest of Granada*. Scudéry has a Boaudilin, Zilama, and Lindarache, an Abdalla, Esperance de Hitta, and Hamet. Scudéry also has a subplot of Abdalla and Fatima, who are as star-crossed as Dryden's Ozmyn and Benzayda, as Romeo and Juliet. Like Dryden's, Scudéry's young lovers have fathers at enmity who in turn refuse to accept an enemy child into the family. Like Dryden's, Scudéry's young lovers overcome paternal obstinacy by generously offering to sacrifice themselves one for the other.[26]

If Dryden found Lyndaraxa's name in Georges de Scudéry's Lindarache, he probably, as Langbaine charged (pp. 158–159), found some part of her character in the Elibesis of Madeleine de Scudéry's *Grand Cyrus*.[27] The younger brother of a reigning queen falls in love with Elibesis, who already has a lover but whose dominant passion, she admits, is ambition. Elibesis tells the prince she has promised never to reject her lover except to become queen. But she promises the prince not to marry her lover for a year and to accept the man who would make her queen. The prince listens to a villain who urges him to seize the throne because his right exceeds his sister's. Fired by love and false counsel, the prince decides to revolt. As he prepares to battle the lover of Elibesis, he asks her to promise that he will not lose her should he lose the battle. Elibesis equivocates, seeming to promise with her eyes what she will not speak. The prince is defeated; she rejects him. Finally, she loses prince, lover, and beauty, as, her fate more lingering than Lyndaraxa's, she withers in melancholy.

Langbaine neglected to subpoena Ginés Pérez de Hita's *Guerras Civiles de Granada*, but Dryden may nonetheless have drawn upon this romance or historical novel, which was published toward the end of the sixteenth century and was available in French as well as Spanish.[28] Since Georges de

---

25 The story of Artaban and the Parthian princess has been summarized by H. W. Hill, *La Calprenède's Romances and the Restoration Drama*, in University of Nevada Studies, II (1910), 14–15; in III (1911), 78–81, Hill discusses parallels between Almanzor and Artaban.

26 For the story of Abdalla and Fatima see *Almahide*, trans. Phillips, Pt. II, Bk. III, pp. 204 ff. For a merciful summary of their story see Schweitzer, *Georges de Scudéry's "Almahide,"* pp. 38–41. For the argument that Dryden used their story see Jerome W. Schweitzer, "Another Note on Dryden's Use of Georges de Scudéry's *Almahide,"* *MLN*, LXII (1947), 262–263. Summers (III, 12) argues that Dryden may have drawn upon "The Sequele of the History of Osman and Alibech" in Madeleine de Scudéry's *Ibrahim* (*Ibrahim. or the Illustrious Bassa*, trans. Henry Cogan [1652], Pt. IV, Bk. IV, pp. 194–210). Madeleine de Scudéry offers the same general situation of young lovers and hostile fathers, but Dryden's subplot seems closer in detail to her brother's version.

27 See "The History of The Prince Ariantes, of Elibesis, of Adonacris, and of Noromante," in *Artamenes, or The Grand Cyrus*, trans. F. G. (1653–1655), Vol. II, Pt. IX, Bk. 1, pp. 12–73.

28 The modern edition is by Paula Blanchard-Demouge (1913–1915). An Eng-

Scudéry based the main plot of *Almahide* on Pérez de Hita, Dryden could have found some details, including names of characters, in both works. But two matters in particular suggest that Dryden knew Pérez de Hita as well as Scudéry. The hostility between Dryden's Zegrys and Abencerrages resumes when Ozmyn kills Tarifa. Pérez de Hita also describes a mock battle with canes, for which the Zegrys treacherously substitute lances. A Zegry wounds an Abencerrago, as Tarifa wounds Ozmyn. The Abencerrago kills the Zegry, as Ozmyn kills Tarifa.[29] More important, Pérez de Hita describes fully, while Scudéry only implies, a charge of adultery against the queen and her subsequent trial by combat. A Zegry falsely tells King Boabdil that the Abencerrages are plotting his death and that one of their leaders is engaged in adultery with the queen. Boabdil declares the Abencerrages must die. He accuses the queen of adultery and confines her, but gives her leave to appoint four knights to combat four of her accusers, decreeing her death by burning if her champions are overcome.[30] Protesting innocence, the queen vows never to return to Boabdil's bed.[31] She contemplates suicide, but is won back for life when her slave, Esperanza de Hita, discourses persuasively of Christian consolation. Esperanza recommends a Spanish nobleman as Christian champion in the trial by combat. He agrees to serve and enlists three other Spanish knights.[32] Together they defeat the four accusers as the queen watches from the scaffold with Esperanza. The original Zegry accuser dies in the lists confessing his deceit,[33] and Boabdil seeks to win back the queen, but she, true to her vow, rejects him.[34] Granada surrenders to Ferdinand, and Boabdil goes off to Africa to be killed. The queen embraces Christianity, is named Isabella of Granada, marries a nobleman, and frees Esperanza.[35] Pérez de Hita certainly appears to have contributed to Dryden's concluding scenes.

Some distance behind Pérez de Hita's romance lies the historical fact of Moorish Granada's submission to King Ferdinand of Spain in the last decade of the fifteenth century. Langbaine supplies a summary list of pertinent historians (p. 161), but Dryden probably turned to Juan de Mariana's *Historia general de España*, published first in Latin, then in Spanish, at the turn of the sixteenth and seventeenth centuries and well known in England.[36] In Mariana's twenty-fifth book, entirely devoted to the Granadan wars, Dryden could have read of Moorish factions, rival kings, Boabdil's capture by the Spanish, and his humiliating submission to Ferdinand. Mariana also describes the city of Granada, Queen Isabella's visit to the Spanish camp outside its walls, and its surrender to Ferdinand.[37]

lish translation by Thomas Rodd appeared in 1803 with the title *The Civil Wars of Granada; and the History of the Factions of the Zegries and Abencerrages, Two Noble Families of that City, To the Final Conquest by Ferdinand and Isabella.*

[29] Rodd, pp. 75–78; Pérez, I, 58–61.
[30] Rodd, pp. 221–226; Pérez, I, 170–173.
[31] Rodd, pp. 250–251; Pérez, I, 189.
[32] Rodd, pp. 284–292; Pérez, I, 214–221.
[33] Rodd, pp. 305–322; Pérez, I, 228–245.
[34] Rodd, p. 328; Pérez, I, 249.
[35] Rodd, pp. 383–384; Pérez, I, 289–290.
[36] See John Loftis, *The Spanish Plays of Neoclassical England* (1973), p. 222.
[37] For further details see *ibid.*, pp. 222–226.

The Scudérys and La Calprenède, Mariana and Pérez de Hita, supplied Dryden with many details of character and action. But, as Dryden makes clear in the prefatory *Of Heroique Playes*, he drew also on material less precisely relevant than his "sources." Such material provides contexts for the Restoration heroic play, not just *The Conquest of Granada*. It includes—to list only the more widely debated topics—the epic, especially the Renaissance epic, prose romance, the plays of at least Fletcher and Corneille, Caroline court drama, the opera.[38] Since heroic plays are manifestly dramas of ideas, scholars have sought to identify the origins of those ideas, a quest that usually involves at some point gazing upon the hard face of Hobbes.[39] The common decorum of such inquiry insists that the scholar confront all topics, summarily dispatch those he deems of small moment, and grapple fiercely with the one or two he believes guardians of truth. The debate should and will continue because it concerns the point at which scholarly pursuit of sources and analogues gives way to critical discrimination between significances, relevancies, emphases. No one will ever settle the matter to the satisfaction of all other readers, and if, as seems unlikely, there is a proper place at which to try to close a critical debate, that place is certainly not an edition. The endeavor here must be to touch upon a few points of special concern for *The Conquest of Granada*. We

---

[38] A useful survey of many of these topics is provided by Eugene M. Waith, *Ideas of Greatness: Heroic Drama in England* (1971); Waith discusses contexts without arguing the priority of one or another. An earlier survey by B. J. Pendlebury, *Dryden's Heroic Plays: A Study of the Origins* (1923), esp. pp. 1–44, stresses contexts in Italian epic theory and French romance. A similar emphasis is supplied by A. E. Parsons, "The English Heroic Play," *MLR*, XXXIII (1938), 1–14, and by William S. Clark, "The Sources of the Restoration Heroic Play," *RES*, IV (1928), 49–63. The argument from native rather than continental antecedents is supplied by, among others, Kathleen M. Lynch, "Conventions of Platonic Drama in the Heroic Plays of Orrery and Dryden," *PMLA*, XLIV (1929), 456–471, and Alfred Harbage, *Cavalier Drama: An Historical and Critical Supplement to the Study of the Elizabethan and Restoration Stage* (1936), esp. pp. 48–71. Arthur C. Kirsch, *Dryden's Heroic Drama* (1965), esp. pp. 46–65, has stressed the Cornelian context. For further discussion of antecedents in *Works* see VIII, 284–289; IX, 297–298.

[39] See Thomas Fujimura, "The Appeal of Dryden's Heroic Plays," *PMLA*, LXXV (1960), 37–45, with the discussion by Kirsch, *Dryden's Heroic Drama*, pp. 41–42. See also Anne T. Barbeau, *The Intellectual Design of John Dryden's Heroic Plays* (1970), esp. pp. 25–40. Applying Hobbist ideas to Dryden's plays has produced at least two problems. Some have felt that modern scholars and critics turn too easily to the familiar and available *Leviathan* for documentation of ideas widely disseminated in the age, often in forms closer to Dryden's own royalism than Hobbes provides (the levies upon Filmer in recent years have prompted similar feelings). Of course, Restoration familiarity with Hobbes can be more easily documented than familiarity with many other writers (something similar is true of Filmer, at least after 1680). The other problem concerns the degree to which Hobbist positions, if present in the plays, are offered for criticism or approbation. Those arguing their presence find them variously used: more or less straightforwardly; selectively, for the identification of villainy and wrong opinion; satirically or ironically, in order to show the absurdity of conclusions drawn from Hobbist premises. The first two emphases are summarized in *Works*, IX, 301. The third is illustrated by Bruce King, *Dryden's Major Plays* (1966), esp. pp. 64–78.

may take our direction from Dryden and consider first the relation of heroic play to heroic poem.

Dryden's acknowledged debts, however general, to Homer, Ariosto, Tasso, and La Calprenède, like his borrowings from the Scudérys and Pérez de Hita, suffice to associate his play with epic and romance. The association brings chivalric ideals upon the Restoration stage. Homer, it is true, might seem an odd companion for such knightly quests. But *Of Heroique Playes* makes clear that Dryden is principally concerned with the first Iliad's quarrel between king and hero over a mistress,[40] a situation assimilable to the world of later romance by, for instance, thinking Briseis more important in herself than Homer allows, important as potential subject, not just object.[41] The voice of Homer's Achilles may sound different to us from the voice of Almanzor, but when Dryden came to translate the first Iliad at the end of his life, he made Achilles sound very like Almanzor of earlier days.

Dryden said later that he copied the moral of *The Conquest of Granada* from Homer: "*Union preserves a Common-wealth, and discord destroys it.*"[42] His debts to Renaissance epic were larger and more diffuse, as we can see by setting his play against Tasso's *Discourses on the Heroic Poem.*[43] Among other things, Tasso's *Discourses* contributed to an existing and lively debate over unity and multiplicity of action, over the respective contributions of concentration and variety to heroic effect.[44] The debate frequently instanced the unity of Tasso's own *Gerusalemme Liberata* to con-

---

[40] See above, 14:25–15:18 and nn.

[41] When Briseis is handed over to Agamemnon's heralds, we learn only that she went with them unwillingly, ἀέκουσ' ἅμα τοῖσι (*Iliad*, I, 348). But Dryden's Briseis "wept, and often cast her Eyes behind: / Forc'd from the Man she lov'd" (*Ilias*, I, 484–485). For Achilles as romance hero see also Tasso, *Discourses*, p. 47: "we are speaking of chivalric love, such as that of Achilles for Polyxena was or might have been."

[42] Preface to *Troilus and Cressida* (1679, sig. a3v; Watson, I, 248). Dryden acknowledges that he took from René Le Bossu the general rule that heroic poems should be based upon some "*precept of morality*," and he may also have taken from Le Bossu the particular precept he attributes to the *Iliad*. The *Iliad*, Le Bossu claimed, reveals that "il n'y avoit que la subordination, & la bonne intelligence qui pût faire réüssir des desseins formez, & conduits par plusieurs Chefs: & au-contraire, que la mes-intelligence, l'ambition de Commander, & le refus de se soumettre, ont toûjours été les pestes infaillibles & inévitables de ces confédérations" (*Traité du Poëme Epique* [Paris, 1675], I, viii, pp. 45–46). Dryden may, then, have retrospectively attributed to *The Conquest of Granada* a Homeric moral he came upon in a treatise published several years after his play. But Dryden's Homeric moral differs from Le Bossu's in directing its attention to commonwealths rather than to confederacies, and Dryden could easily have recalled, when writing *The Conquest of Granada*, such a maxim, by then commonplace, as that from Sallust, *Jugurtha*, X.vi: *nam concordia parvae res crescunt, discordia maxumae dilabuntur* (Loeb trans.: "for harmony makes small states great, while discord undermines the mightiest empires").

[43] Cf. John C. Sherwood, "Dryden and the Critical Theories of Tasso," *Comparative Literature*, XVIII (1966), 351–359.

[44] See Bernard Weinberg, *A History of Literary Criticism in the Italian Renaissance* (1961), II, 991–1073.

trast with the variety and multiplicity of Ariosto's *Orlando Furioso*. There were those who argued for generic differences between classical epic and Renaissance romance, the first favoring unity, the second multiplicity. Dismissing the distinction, Tasso urged unity upon romance as well as epic.[45] Without Aristotelian analysis of an action, we sometimes have difficulty separating unity from multiplicity in stories so incident crammed. But *The Conquest of Granada* may help us to an instance. Dryden's meditation upon the deficiencies of *The Siege of Rhodes* led him to note, unimpeachably, that it "wanted the fulness of a Plot, and the variety of Characters."[46] To make his own drama just, Dryden supplied several plots with associated causes. We may isolate the plots of Almanzor, Almahide, and Boabdelin, of Lyndaraxa and her entourage of swains, and of Ozmyn and Benzayda. However variously derived, all three plots proceed from, capitalize upon, or are fueled by the strife between Zegrys and Abencerrages. But only the first two tend, if intricately, to further the action, which is, after all, to conquer Granada for Spain. Ozmyn and Benzayda illustrate that discord destroys the little commonwealth of families while union preserves it, but Ozmyn and Benzayda contribute nothing to the conquest of Granada, despite their sojourn among the Spanish. Their plot, like their characters, adds variety at the expense of unified action.

As Tasso realized, one problem with the fullness yielded by variety is that it easily destroys a needed economy. "Anyone," he noted, "who chooses too ample a matter is forced to prolong the poem beyond a seemly limit."[47] The ten acts of Dryden's play seem to illustrate the truth of this maxim precisely. Part One, after all, does not constitute a just drama in itself, and Part Two is scarcely more self-contained. We should not think of Dryden's needing, say, eight acts to cultivate discord, two to harvest its consequences. We should see, rather, that all relationships between characters produce discords which seem to resolve only to renew themselves. In scene after scene waves of discord beat upon Granada, then dissipate, to be succeeded by other waves and still others. But the progress of each discord in itself, not its ultimate significance for Granada, holds the attention from moment to moment. Plots, we can say, obscure action, and the play may accordingly tax readers who struggle to remember Lyndaraxa's last duplicity, Almanzor's last change of sides, when presented with the next one.

Dryden no doubt sought to approximate in drama the social range of epic. His "Homeric" moral, the precept to be deduced from his action, addresses itself entirely to public causes and consequences, suppressing individual needs. The action promised by his title obviously corresponds to those Tasso thought properly noble and excellent: "the deliverance of Italy from the Goths, which gave Trissino his subject . . . [and] the enterprises happily . . . undertaken to establish the faith or exalt the Church and Empire."[48] The epic of Christendom numbers among its curious progeny such works from Protestant England as *The Siege of Rhodes* and *The Indian Emperour* as well as *The Conquest of Granada*, perhaps because "we can

---

[45] Tasso, *Discourses*, pp. 65–79.
[46] See above, 9:26.
[47] Tasso, *Discourses*, p. 55.
[48] *Ibid.*, p. 50.

easily invent many fictions about faraway peoples and unfamiliar lands
without costing the fable its credibility."[49]

If Dryden found material in a story apt for epic and gave form to matter
in part with an epic moral, the final cause of his play points also toward
epic effects. "Heroic poems," Tasso remarked, "should naturally interest
no one more than those who enjoy reading about deeds like their own and
their ancestors' because in such poems they may see an image, as it were,
of the very glory that gets them considered superior to others." Presented
with that image, "they try to raise their own minds to its example."[50] Dryden offers his version of this Renaissance commonplace in the opening
paragraphs of the dedication. We all acquire the protective habit of reading through commonplaces inattentively, assuming, justly for the most part,
that where the writer seems to rest his mind, relaxing among agreed propo-
sitions, we too may rest. But we should notice that Dryden speaks of heroic
play not as if it were in some respects like heroic poem, but as if it actually
were one, using the same materials for the same end and limiting its audience to the agreed, aristocratic audience for epic. Heroic play, then, joins
"Historique and Panegyrique" poems, which Dryden had earlier called
"branches" of "Epique Poesie,"[51] and seeks its obvious audience among
those men, leaders or potential leaders, who served as subjects for panegyric
in heroic couplet or dedicatory prose and found themselves and their ancestors cast, as Sidney would have it, in golden images, not brazen. "For all
men," Hobbes sourly observed, "love to behold, though not to practise,
Vertue," and proceeded with grim gallantry to enlarge the audience with
women: "the work of an Heroique Poem is to raise admiration, principally,
for three Vertues, Valour, Beauty, and Love; to the reading whereof Women
no less than Men have a just pretence, though their skill in Language be
not so universal."[52] Mrs. Evelyn is thus accommodated.[53]

But the habit of describing one literary kind in terms of another has
dangerous consequences. Dryden seems uncertain in dedication and preface whether to argue from heroic poem or heroic play, just as he defends
the epilogue undecided whether to address the gallantry of comedy or of
serious play.[54] At one point in the preface he seeks to distinguish between
heroic and "common Drama" by the authority of epic. The heroic dramatist
should draw "all things as far above the ordinary proportion of the Stage,
as that is beyond the common words and actions of humane life."[55] Now,
said Tasso, "the wonder that almost stuns us as we see one man alone dis-
maying an entire army with his threats and gestures would be inappropriate
to tragedy, yet makes the epic poem marvellous. . . . We gladly read in epic

---

49 *Ibid.*

50 *Ibid.*, p. 5.

51 Preface to *Annus Mirabilis* (*Works*, I, 56).

52 Preface to *Homer's Odysses* (Spingarn, II, 68).

53 For the contention that heroic plays especially appealed to women see Anne
Righter, "Heroic Tragedy," in *Restoration Theatre*, ed. John Russell Brown and
Bernard Harris (1965), pp. 138–139.

54 The "confusion" exists also in the epilogue's praise for the Restoration's
higher degree both of "wit" and of "Love and Honour." The difficult derivation
of social chivalry from knightly adventure has long proved troublesome.

55 See above, 10:27–29.

about many wonders that might be unsuitable on stage, both because they are proper to epic and because the reader allows many liberties which the spectator forbids."[56] Dryden, in contrast, called Horace to testify that drama has the advantage of representing "to view, what the Poem onely does relate,"[57] but early responses to his play show that its spectators forbade much, even if they allowed some.

Dryden sought, he assures us, "an absolute dominion over the minds of the Spectators," sought "to raise the imagination of the Audience, and to perswade them, for the time, that what they behold on the Theater is really perform'd."[58] This endeavor explained his "frequent use of Drums and Trumpets; and [his] representations of Battels."[59] The endeavor may also have been assisted by those scenes, the work of Robert Streater, which caught the attention of Evelyn. We have no indication in the printed text of Streater's designs. But the play evidently calls for nothing like the notorious scene that closed the second act of Lee's *Sophonisba* by picturing the ancient notion, still current in the Restoration, that great battles are frequently preceded by the clash of aerial armies.[60] More probably, the terse directions—scene: a camp, a wood, the Albayzin—summoned from Streater something comparable to "the scene before the first entry" of *The Siege of Rhodes:*

> The curtain being drawn up, a lightsome sky appear'd, discov'ring a maritime coast, full of craggy rocks, and high cliffs, with several verdures naturally growing upon such scituations; and afar off, the true prospect of the City of RHODES, when it was in prosperous estate; with so much view of the gardens and hills about it as the narrowness of the room could allow the scene. In that part of the horizon, terminated by the sea, was represented the Turkish fleet, making towards a promontory, some few miles distant from the town.[61]

The translation of such elaborate scenery into words constitutes *topographia*, the figure of geographical description recommended for literary or historical narrative. Made into picture, the scenery gives narrative perspective to the actions represented before it, and may help persuade audiences that what they see on the stage "is really perform'd," the actors having

---

[56] Tasso, *Discourses*, p. 16.

[57] See above, 13:24–25.

[58] See above, 14:2–5.

[59] See above, 13:28–29.

[60] *The Works of Nathaniel Lee*, ed. Thomas B. Stroup and Arthur L. Cooke (1954), I, 102: "The SCENE drawn, discovers a Heaven of blood, two Suns, Spirits in Battle, Arrows shot to and fro in the Air: Cryes of yielding Persons, &c. Cryes of Carthage is fal'n, Carthage, &c." Modern commentators have sometimes used this scene to exemplify the absurdity of Restoration spectacle. Cf. [Owen Lloyd], *The Panther-Prophesy. . . . To which is added, An Astrological Discourse Concerning That strange Apparition of an Army of Horse seen in Wales, near Mountgomery, December the 20th. 1661* (1662), p. 7: Jupiter "sends down an Incorporeal Army, consisting of 1000 Horse."

[61] Davenant, *Love and Honour and The Siege of Rhodes*, ed. James W. Tupper (1909), p. 192.

become not persons of the drama but people inhabiting something other than a stage. To be sure, the principal because most obvious purpose of such scenery must have been to provide visual excitement to complement the hoped-for emotional and intellectual excitement of the actors' words. Audiences still applaud fine sets along with well-delivered soliloquies and arias. In the Restoration, we may suppose, scene and spectacle associated heroic plays with masque, opera, royal or civic pageant rather than "the common Drama." The designer was challenged more excitingly by the Alhambra than by a chocolate house.

However useful the designer's contributions, it was the poet's task "to endeavour an absolute dominion over the minds of the Spectators." He might seek to do so by representing exciting actions on stage or by allowing the audience to "hear from behind the Scenes, the sounding of Trumpets, and the shouts of fighting Armies." [62] But, as we know from Dryden's earlier criticism if only glancingly from the essay *Of Heroique Playes,* the poet should rather "seek out truth in the Passions then . . . record the truth of Actions." [63] The phrase was Davenant's in the preface to *Gondibert* and provided one more variation upon the venerable distinction between history —sometimes oratory—and poetry. Truth of passions constituted an Aristotelian universal because it enabled men to "contemplate the general History of Nature," while truth of actions supplied only "a selected Diary of Fortune." [64] Dryden, of course, could not rest with so simple an antithesis. He needed four voices to speak his mind in the essay *Of Dramatick Poesie* and to test often conflicting dramatic principles against equally conflicting, or at least shifting, theatrical facts. Eugenius addresses himself at one point to a matter of considerable importance for *The Conquest of Granada:*

> Any sudden gust of passion (as an extasie of love in an
> unexpected meeting) cannot better be express'd than in
> a word and a sigh, breaking one another. Nature is dumb
> on such occasions, and to make her speak, would be to
> represent her unlike her self. But there are a thousand
> other concernments of Lovers, as jealousies, complaints,
> contrivances and the like, where not to open their minds
> at large to each other, were to be wanting to their own
> love, and to the expectation of the Audience; who watch
> the movements of their minds, as much as the changes
> of their fortunes. For the imaging of the first is properly
> the work of a Poet, the latter he borrows from the His-
> torian.[65]

The constantly renewed discords of *The Conquest of Granada* supply the changes in fortune which make necessary, justify, scenes displaying the movement of minds, as characters explicate their passions to one another. Their explications unfold causes or conditions; they may define—"Love's

---

62 See above, 13:31–33.

63 Spingarn, II, 3.

64 *Ibid.* For an interesting account of the distinction see Dean T. Mace, "Dryden's Dialogue on Drama," *JWCI,* XXV (1962), 87–112.

65 *Works,* XVII, 31–32.

a Heroique Passion"[66]—or they may recall some contemporary theory of passions.[67]

The movement of minds on stage should produce an emotional excitement sufficient to hold the attention of spectators and thus, so the program runs, help the poet to his wished-for dominion over their minds. But minds move among reasons as well as passions, especially when characters, like Dryden's, are required to debate the reasons for their passions. Their reasons are more often ethical and political than psychological. Love's motions and conditions, it is true, often receive psychological explanation or diagnosis. But love finds itself in frequent conflict if occasional harmony with rules and sanctions governing conduct in families, societies, states. Changes in fortune constantly juxtapose the obligations of prince, subject, father, child, friend, lover. Characters' minds move among these obligations, exploring allegiances, disputing topics, and seeking, at times successfully, always strenuously, to reconcile conflicting obligations and thus settle the conscience in order to act.

As Mrs. Evelyn recognized, the scrupulous accounting for obligation, the sifting of motive—making love pure and valor nice—came to the heroic play in part from the long literature of courtly romance. We also know that dramatists before Dryden had set characters to debating vows and promises, to arguing duty and reputation. But Dryden's contexts were not limited to stories whether narrated or represented. Concern with the ethical and political bases of conduct showed also in a large literature devoted to resolving doubts and settling consciences, the literature of casuistry.

Seventeenth-century English casuistry, whether Anglican or Puritan, addressed itself to the task of training individual Christians to elect truly pious conduct in situations where differing, often conflicting, duties might leave the untutored conscience confused. Casuistical discourse typically moved through hypothetical cases:

> If a son swear that he will perform some lawfull thing, and his father ignorant thereof lay some other command upon him which hinders the performance of his oath, the son is not obnoxious to the oath: because by divine and naturall Law, he is bound to obey his fathers commands.[68]

Such hypothetical cases might actualize themselves in the lives of individual Christians, who could therefore find in casuistry the conduct they should elect. But Protestant casuistry was also heuristic, elucidating the principles

---

66 2 *Conquest of Granada*, I, i, 145.

67 The psychological theories—Descartes', Hobbes's, Charleton's, e.g.—to which characters sometimes appear to speak have been variously surveyed. Although he does not treat English sources, there is much relevant material in Anthony Levi, *French Moralists: The Theory of the Passions, 1585 to 1649* (1964). Clarence De-Witt Thorpe, *The Aesthetic Theory of Thomas Hobbes*, in University of Michigan Publications: Language and Literature, XVIII (1940), discusses the influence of psychological upon critical theory in the work of Hobbes, Davenant, Charleton, and Dryden, among others. For annotation of characters' words from psychological theory, see *Works*, X, 418–419, 469, 479.

68 Robert Sanderson, *De Juramento. Seven Lectures concerning the Obligation of Promissory Oathes* (1655), p. 56.

upon which conduct should be based and training consciences to discrimi-
nate for themselves between possible responses. In this respect it differed
from the casuistry of the medieval church, which was regulatory, legislative
even, offering an encyclopedia of proper conduct and setting the penances
to be imposed by confessors upon improper conduct.[69]

By seeking to discipline while still respecting the liberty of individual
consciences, Protestant casuistry found much in common with the practical
ethics of Seneca's *De Beneficiis,* which argues through actual and hypothetical cases the morality of gratitude, of obligations incurred and imposed.[70]
In its concern with individual conduct, casuistry also overlapped with such
popular devotional manuals as Lewis Bayly's *The Practice of Piety.* By 1650
large public events and issues had come to dominate individual conduct,
and casuistry was ready to advise. During the civil war Robert Sanderson
delivered in Latin his Oxford lectures on the obligations of conscience and
promissory oaths.[71] Their subsequent popularity is attested by the editions
and translations they received in the Interregnum and Restoration. When
Sanderson addresses himself in these lectures, as he frequently does, to
rules of conduct and conscience in times of national crisis, his discourse
seems indistinguishable from that of political pamphlet or treatise. He can
sound like Hobbes by insisting that "an oath maketh not a former obligation void";[72] Hobbes would say "a former covenant, makes void a later."[73]
He can agree with Hobbes that ransoms promised to thieves should be
paid.[74] Like Filmer he can offer "directions for obedience to government
in dangerous or doubtful times,"[75] tackling the slippery question of passive
obedience during usurpations.[76]

Sanderson's casuistical blend of private conduct and public obligation
provides a discursive counterpart to the dramatized debates of *The Conquest of Granada.* To say so is by no means to claim Sanderson as source of
ideas in Dryden's play. Those ideas certainly could have and probably did
come to Dryden from texts as venerable as Aristotle's, as adolescent as
L'Estrange's. Most tracts recapitulated past and present arguments and
thus gave even recondite texts a secondhand currency. We know that many
cited Bracton; we may guess that few read him. Early in the second part of
The Conquest of Granada Boabdelin, Zulema, and Abenamar illustrate the
precept Dryden claimed for his play by discussing constitutional principles
that produce destructive discord.[77] Their discussion could figure as ap-

---

[69] For a useful summary of Protestant and medieval casuistry see William
Whewell, *Lectures on the History of Moral Philosophy* (Cambridge, 1862), pp.
18–39.

[70] The relevance of Seneca's *De Beneficiis* to Dryden's plays has been argued by
John M. Wallace, "John Dryden's Plays and Restoration Politics," a paper read
at the William Andrews Clark Memorial Library on 27 February 1976.

[71] *De Obligatione Conscientiae* and *De Juramenti Promissorii Obligatione.*

[72] *De Juramento,* p. 58.

[73] *Leviathan,* I, xiv, ed. Michael Oakeshott (1960), p. 91.

[74] *De Juramento,* p. 139; *Leviathan,* p. 91.

[75] *Patriarcha and other Political Works,* ed. Peter Laslett (1949), pp. 231–235.

[76] *De Juramento,* pp. 120–121.

[77] 2 *Conquest of Granada,* I, ii, 30–58.

pendix to the chapter Hobbes gloomily entitled "Of those things that weaken, or tend to the dissolution of a commonwealth."[78] It could also be glossed from numerous tracts more orthodox than *Leviathan* in their arguments for strong central monarchy. Sanderson on the obligations of prince and subject was similarly anticipated and recapitulated in countless works. Sanderson, then, is important not as influence, but as illustration. Sanderson illustrates the habit of converting political principles into situations where duties collide. His persistent concern with oath, vow, promise, and allegiance finds a parallel in *The Conquest of Granada,* where action constantly settles into confrontations permitting debate of conflicting obligations. Dryden's characters might make and break promises, discuss duties, in part because the characters of antecedent drama and romance had done so. But the promises and duties of Dryden's characters concern, though not exclusively, the preservation or destruction of a commonwealth and remind us that his play was written and performed during the great age of English casuistry, when casuistry had pressed deeply into the matter of constitutional obligations. Then, too, Almanzor might trace his lineage to Artaban or to some Cornelian hero centered upon *la gloire.* He might even, though it seems unlikely, represent "Men in a Hobbian State of War."[79] But this hero without established political allegiance manifestly generates constantly changing situations chiefly remarkable for the intricate cases of conscience and obligation they involve, for the casuistical opportunities they supply.

◈

Casuistry, it should be stressed, was no mere discipline for school divines in the seventeenth century. Sanderson's Oxford lectures on promissory oaths and the obligations of conscience were succeeded in 1648 by parliamentary forces come to deprive him and other royalists of their chairs. Charles I, Walton tells us, translated Sanderson's *De Juramento* while in prison.[80] The hypothetical cases of casuistical treatises jostled the actual cases of casuistical polemic as the age tried to come to terms with a series of constitutional crises, all of them concerning in some way the obligations of princes and people.[81] The restoration of Charles II had seemingly settled the crisis of civil war, execution, interregnum. But by the early months of 1672 court and country were settling toward exclusion crisis and Popish Plot.

---

[78] *Leviathan,* II, xxix.

[79] Richard Leigh, *The Censure of the Rota* (1673), p. 3.

[80] *The Life of Dr. Sanderson* (1678), sigs. f1v–f2r. But the 1655 title page of *De Juramento* claims only that it was "Translated into English by His late Majesties speciall Command, and afterwards Revised and approved under His Majesties own hand."

[81] One such crisis of political conscience produced the engagement controversy of the early Interregnum; see the summary and analysis by John M. Wallace, *Destiny His Choice: The Loyalism of Andrew Marvell* (1968), pp. 43–68. A similar crisis produced the nonjuring controversy of 1689–90; see the summary by Charles F. Mullett, "A Case of Allegiance: William Sherlock and the Revolution of 1688," *HLQ,* X (1946), 83–103.

Dryden no more than other men could foresee the five-year hysteria which would commence so improbably in the fall of 1678. But by the time his play was first acted, the Duke of York had avowed Roman Catholicism and the King's interest in a French alliance had produced the Treaty of Dover. Even the public version of that treaty—without the secret clause promising Charles II's declared conversion to Rome—could give pause to those stern members of the so-called cavalier parliament who had for some years resisted the King's requests for supplies and had pressed so hard upon the conduct of the second Dutch war. By the time Dryden's play was published with its dedication to James, the Duke's Protestant wife was nearly a year dead and negotiations for a second marriage to a Roman Catholic were already advanced, although they were not concluded until September 1673. For some months before the end of 1671 England was evidently moving—or being moved by royal policy—toward a third Dutch war in accordance with the Treaty of Dover.

Men may not have seen clearly, but, as Marvell was to argue later, the growth of popery and arbitrary government in England had already begun.[82] It was certainly as clear in 1670–1672 as it had been a generation before that "union preserves a commonwealth, and discord destroys it." It was time for loyal poets to celebrate greatness, to warn against weakness in kings, dissidence in subjects, vulnerability to foreign conquest. It was time to remind Englishmen of countries beyond their island, to remind them of their mercantile destiny by dwelling in a dedication upon the triumph at Lowestoft and touching upon the humiliation of Chatham only to arouse them to further triumphs.[83] Dryden's own *Annus Mirabilis* figures, and importantly, among the numerous literary antecedents of *The Conquest of Granada*.[84]

To a point, then, the exotic and spectacular stage life corresponds to the life of its audience. The correspondence may seem to be more with its potential than its actual life.[85] But Dryden insists in the dedication that the Duke of York's conduct as heroic young general and admiral complemented stage fiction with contemporary fact. Dryden similarly concludes the preface by turning from Almanzor's literary antecedents to the recorded heroism of such as Julius Caesar and the Duke of Guise. We misunderstand plays like *The Conquest of Granada* if we suppose that, because they glance away from so many contemporary acts and attitudes, they offered only escapist anodynes. Such misunderstandings are certainly licensed by Mrs. Evelyn's response to *The Conquest of Granada*. But we should remember that Dry-

---

[82] Marvell concentrates on events of the two years preceding publication of his famous tract in 1677, but fetches his beginning from the second Anglo-Dutch war of 1665–1667. See *An Account of the Growth of Popery, and Arbitrary Government in England* (1677), p. 17.

[83] See above, 5:3–11; 5:32–34.

[84] For some elaboration of this point see Barbeau, *Intellectual Design of Dryden's Heroic Plays*, pp. 192–193, 205.

[85] Unless we take that correspondence to consist, as *The Censure of the Rota* (1673), p. 18, puts it, in Dryden's "framing the character of a Huff of the Town, one that from breaking Glass-windows, and combating the watch, starts up an Heroe." For further discussion and illustration of this curious correspondence see Kirsch, *Dryden's Heroic Drama*, pp. 43–44.

den's heroic decade, the decade of heroic plays, roughly from mid-sixties to mid-seventies, was generated in part by the euphoria of restoration, with prince and people seemingly reunited, the country seemingly big with greatness through the advancement of science, letters, trade.

To speak in this way is to raise, if only to dismiss, the question of allegory, at least of historical allegory.[86] The association of James and Almanzor, it must be said, exists in the dedication, not in the play. Dryden's already performed play supplies his subsequently written dedication with one more analogue for the greatness of James, contributing to a host of possible analogues in history and fiction. Dryden's dedication reminds readers that "the World is govern'd by precept and Example."[87] The example of Almanzor's acts supplies general precepts, some of them also supplied by the example of the Duke's different acts. Such precepts vary the moral Dryden placed at the center of his play by insisting that troubled states need strong generals as well as wise kings, Achilles as well as Agamemnon, or—fictional example translated by precept into historical instance—that England needs both Stuart brothers to achieve greatness.[88] *The Conquest of Granada* is obviously not concerned to solve the problems faced by England at the beginning of the century's eighth decade. But it is concerned with the public issues raised by such problems, concerned to please and instruct by dramatizing those issues into fictional examples. The play seeks to work upon general manners, not particular opinions. It seeks to inculcate by positive and negative example a decency and moral discipline of potential use in national affairs, rather than to persuade men how to deal with particular affairs.

The decency and moral discipline taught by the play consist for the most part in proper discrimination between the often conflicting obligations of conscience, consist, that is, in recognizably casuistical practices. The casuistical treatises, we have seen, addressed hypothetical cases. They also classified those cases according to the moral, political, or religious issues they were thought to involve. Thus Sanderson:

> When a Prince swears unto his favorite, to give him in acknowledgement of his faithfull service whatsoever he shall desire; or a friend, or servant, swears unto his friend or master to obey what he shall command . . . this kind of oath, if it be simply understood according to the tenor of the words, is unlawful. He injureth God, whose servant every man is, who maketh himself a servant to man and slave to anothers rashnesse. . . . Something else must necessarily be understood to make it lawfull. For example, I swear to doe as you will have me, meaning whatsoever is just, honest, possible; and so far, and in this sense it obligeth.[89]

---

86 See the discussions by John M. Wallace, "Dryden and History: A Problem in Allegorical Reading," *ELH*, XXXVI (1969), 265–290, and " 'Examples are Best Precepts': Readers and Meanings in Seventeenth-Century Poetry," *Critical Inquiry*, I (1974), 273–290. See also *Works*, XVIII, 428–434.

87 See above, 3:11.

88 See above, 5:34–6:9.

89 *De Juramento,* pp. 95–96.

Although *The Conquest of Granada* names its princes, servants, friends, although it seems to individualize them, the play tends markedly to classify them and their situations into cases: the case of the arrogant individual without political allegiance, the weak king, the honorable wife. Action assists classification by contriving situations in which obligations are to be debated, the words principally addressed to a generalizing issue of morality, politics, or religion. Moreover, the couplet Dryden still favored for serious plays encourages, although it does not demand, the classification of experience because its typical syntax places the components of experience in nice parallel or pointed antithesis, closing up the comparison with a rhyme that emphasizes sententiousness. But full experience consists not merely of issues and significances; it consists also of events, particular occasions, gestures, impulses, feelings which escape full classification. Dryden's characters have no difficulty classifying their feelings, explaining them, comparing and contrasting them with related feelings. Thus Abdalla asks Almanzor to help him usurp his brother's throne, assuring Almanzor he has "a better right to reign" than his brother. Almanzor replies:

> It is sufficient that you make the claim:
> You wrong our friendship when your right you name.
> When for my self I fight, I weigh the cause;
> But friendship will admit of no such Laws:
> That weighs by th' lump, and, when the Cause is light,
> Puts kindness in to set the Ballance right.
> True, I would wish my friend the juster side:
> But in th' unjust my kindness more is try'd.[90]

The neat answering of wrong by right, just by unjust, the nicely contrasted methods of weighing, declare that Friendship has been classified into a set of rules for occasions both hypothetical and actual. Any sense of a particular relationship with its own nuances and contradictions has been obliterated. Words fly to the definition of Friendship, neglecting the fact of a particular friendship. When the words are also big words, loud words, as they are here and elsewhere in the play, we easily sense discrepancies between diction and occasion. The age designated such discrepancies rant, bombast, rodomontade.

⟳〰⟲

Rodomontade and spectacle may, as Dryden supposed in the dedication of *The Spanish Fryar*, impose upon theater audiences.[91] But certainly in the closet, where spectacle shrinks to stage direction, and probably in the theater for the skeptically alert, they court the ludicrous. A familiar episode illustrates the point. On 4 October 1664 Pepys went

> after dinner to a play, to see [Orrery's] *The Generall;*
> which is so dull and so ill acted, that I think it is the worst

---

[90] *1 Conquest of Granada*, III, i, 21–28. For an interesting discussion of this and other passages in the play, see Alan S. Fisher, "Daring to Be Absurd: The Paradoxes of *The Conquest of Granada*," *SP*, LXXIII (1976), 414–439.

[91] 1681, sig. A2v; Watson, I, 275–276.

I ever saw or heard in all my days. I happened to sit next
to Sir Ch. Sidly; who I find a very witty man, and did at
every line take notice of the dullness of the poet and bad-
ness of the action, and that most pertinently; which I was
mightily taken with—and among others, where by Alte-
mira's command Clarimont the Generall is commanded
to rescue his Rivall whom she loved, Lucidor, he after a
great deal of demurre breaks out—"Well—Ile save my
Rivall and make her confess. That I deserve, while he
doth but possesse." "Why, what! Pox!" says Sir Ch. Sydly,
"would he have him have more, or what is there more to
be had of a woman then the possessing her?"

Sedley anticipates Horner's outburst against the affected virtue of Lady
Fidget and Mrs. Squeamish. Cynics on stage and in audiences look only to
carnal facts.

The Restoration founded much of its best comedy upon skeptical ques-
tioning of words that defined situations in terms of ethical significances
and ignored particular impulses. Since Restoration comedy ridiculed those
of its characters who talked exclusively of honor, reputation, virtue, we
should expect the age to ridicule the characters in heroic plays, who either
talked exclusively in this way or supplied villainous foils to those who did.
The acceptable converse to the language of heroic virtue proved not to be
the language of heroic vice, which merely counters simple positive with simple negative, but language that was satiric, ironic, witty in self-deprecation,
countering what ought to be with what was thought to be. So we should
not be surprised that the age elected at some point to ridicule heroic plays.
But we need to ask why *The Conquest of Granada* figured so prominently
in the onslaught that it has come down to us as the defining example of
Restoration heroic play not just for its matter, not just because of the
theoretical discourse with which Dryden prefaced the published version,
but also for the responses it prompted. If you wish to understand *The Rehearsal*, handbooks assure us, read any heroic play, but preferably *The
Conquest of Granada*.

The Conquest of Granada's centrality issues from several causes, of which
the least important appears to be a rivalry between theatrical companies,
with King's men and Duke's competing for audiences and applause. Such
rivalry evidently accounts, say, for dismissive references in the prologues
to Ravenscroft's *The Citizen Turn'd Gentleman* and Arrowsmith's *The
Reformation*.[92] It also accounts in part for the debate over Settle's *The
Empress of Morocco*, and Settle's retorting to the hostile examen of his play
by Dryden, Shadwell, and Crowne with an equally hostile examen of *The
Conquest of Granada*.[93] Far more important than insults exchanged with
the rival Duke's Company was the performance on or about 7 December
1671 by Dryden's own company, the King's, of *The Rehearsal*, the work of
Buckingham and others.

---

[92] For these quarrels see Macdonald, pp. 196–197, 204–205, 207–208, and *The
Critical Heritage*, ed. James and Helen Kinsley (1971), pp. 109–110.

[93] See *The Empress of Morocco and Its Critics*, introd. Maximillian E. Novak
(1968).

The story of *The Rehearsal* has been told many times.[94] Conceived roughly eight years before first performance and apparently existing in some form by the end of 1664, this much delayed and altered burlesque of heroic plays was revised for the season of 1671–72 to include among the many plays parodied *The Conquest of Granada* from the preceding season. The most obvious addition of 1671 is the minor character of Drawcansir, who burlesques Almanzor by exploding into the fourth act to answer the stern question "What man is this, that dares disturb our Feast?" with "He that dares drink, and for that drink dares dye, / And, knowing this, dares yet drink on, am I."[95] Subsequent annotations call attention to *The Rehearsal*'s parody of particular moments in *The Conquest of Granada*. But the attack is by no means restricted to the odd farrago of dramatic conventions and particulars that makes up the formless, mindless play which is intermittently rehearsed. The attack is also conveyed through the figure of Mr. Bayes, author of the farrago, who is made to explain his dramatic principles and practice to Smith and Johnson. Smith and Johnson show themselves properly witty men-about-town by their relentlessly skeptical dismissal of rhymed heroics. They need not concern us further. But the object of their covert derision concerns us greatly. *The Rehearsal* satirizes Dryden not only through Drawcansir and the absurd two kings of Brentford, but also, and more decisively, through what has been aptly called "the voice of Mr. Bayes."[96]

Bayes seems to have been as much a farrago as his aborted play. Tradition has it that during *The Rehearsal*'s long gestation its embryonic butt changed from a Davenant into a Howard into a Dryden. Scholars have detected features from earlier versions in the final one, and certainly the Bayes who "design'd a Conquest, that Cannot possibly, I gad, be acted in less than a whole week"[97] could have served to satirize the author of *The Siege of Rhodes* almost as readily as the author of *The Conquest of Granada*. But in December 1671 whatever remained from earlier versions must have been assimilated to the laureate of the day. Satiric characters, after all, are not circumstantial biographies. They are deliberate fictions which interpret facts to the disadvantage of historical subjects, as Buckingham subsequently discovered when Dryden wrote him up and off as Zimri.[98] So, however the character began, when Bayes was first impersonated on stage, he must have constituted a fiction interpreting Dryden to Dryden's disadvantage. Dryden as laureate contributed a name and little else to Bayes. Dryden as heroic playwright obviously contributed much. Dryden as critic seems to have contributed most of all.

We can see now, what Dryden's contemporaries evidently and excusably could not see, that by December 1671 he was already the best critic of his

[94] See Macdonald, pp. 193–195; Noyes, *Selected Dramas*, pp. xxxi–xxxiii; and Dane Farnsworth Smith, *Plays about the Theatre in England* (1936), pp. 9–37.

[95] *The Rehearsal*, IV, i; 1675, p. 43 (1672, p. 37).

[96] Eugene M. Waith, "The Voice of Mr. Bayes," *SEL*, III (1963), 335–343.

[97] *The Rehearsal*, IV, i; 1675, p. 37 (1672, p. 32).

[98] See Buckingham's mortified verses on his characterization as Zimri (*Works*, II, 260).

age. He was so not only because, as Dr. Johnson put it, he sought "to determine upon principles the merit of composition,"[99] but because, seeking thus, he sought also to test closet principle against theatrical fact, fact against principle. Determining upon principles gave coherence as well as confidence not just to *Of Dramatick Poesie* but also to those prefaces and dedications in which Dryden had already shown his fondness for discoursing, like Bayes, of his own works. Such criticism is of an altogether different intellectual order from the scattered if modish aperçus of a Sedley on *The Generall* or, for that matter, of a Smith and a Johnson at a rehearsal. Testing principle against fact involved Dryden in qualification, concession, self-deprecation at times, and at times a stated modesty. The voice of Bayes wickedly and wittily distorts the voice of Dryden by shrinking modesty into obsequiousness, swelling confidence into arrogance, converting principle into idiotic commonplace, then testing it against theatrical facts drawn from the lowest farce, and adopting the accent of an ill-bred, ungentlemanly upstart thrusting himself among his social and intellectual superiors. The degree to which the voice of Bayes truly coincides with the voice of Dryden must be argued in essays concerned with tone. But in December 1671 it should have been clear that any attempt by Dryden to exercise his critical voice would attune the ears of adversaries to the mocking echo of Bayes. Prudence dictated silence for a while. But *The Conquest of Granada* was probably in or at least ready for press when *The Rehearsal* was first acted; the term catalogue listing it for sale was licensed two months later. With printed play came not only dedication and preface, but also, and crucially, a postscript defending the epilogue to the play's second part by offering *An Essay on the Dramatique Poetry of the last Age.*

The Defence of the Epilogue became the last of several reasons for *The Conquest of Granada*'s centrality in Restoration attacks upon heroic plays. Dryden's postscript begins with three excellent paragraphs declaring once more his lifelong sense of patriotic mission in criticism and his equally enduring impulse to turn to the ancients for analogy and precedent when identifying the needs and achievements of English literature.[100] But Dryden moves quickly to detailed defense of the epilogue's assertion that Restoration drama exceeds Jacobean in some ways because it is nourished and supplied with models by a society more civilized than that which existed earlier. Detailed defense rests upon a largely grammatical examination of errors in old dramatists, and, read without the modest exordium, such examination might sound to the ill-disposed like effrontery, like complacent self-congratulation, like Mr. Bayes, indeed. Speaking as Eugenius in *Of Dramatick Poesie*, Dryden had amused himself with the familiar legends upon which Athenians based their tragedies:

> The people so soon as ever they heard the Name of
> *Oedipus*, knew as well as the Poet, that he had kill'd his
> Father by a mistake, and committed Incest with his Moth-
> er, before the Play; that they were now to hear of a great
> Plague, an Oracle, and the Ghost of *Laius:* so that they

---

99 BH, I, 410.
100 See above, 203:1–204:22.

> sate with a yawning kind of expectation, till he was to
> come with his eyes pull'd out, and speak a hundred or
> more Verses in a Tragick tone, in complaint of his mis-
> fortunes.[101]

The implied principle is easily distorted into *The Rehearsal's* description of Bayes's "new way of writing," whose "grand design . . . is to keep the Auditors in suspence; for to guess presently at the plot, and the sence, tires 'em before the end of the first Act: now, here, every line surprises you, and brings in new matter."[102] Odd though it may now seem, Dryden evidently impressed some contemporaries (including the young Swift) as a mere up- start modern denigrating revered ancients in order to applaud himself and his times. Cursorily read, *The Defence of the Epilogue* supplies grounds for such an impression.

More than a year passed between publication of Dryden's play and post- script and publication of the first detailed responses.[103] Four anonymous pamphlets appeared in spring 1673, the first and best of them borrowing a title from an earlier controversy by calling itself *The Censure of the Rota. On Mr Driden's Conquest of Granada*.[104] A second attack was ironically dubbed *The Friendly Vindication of Mr. Dryden From the Censure of the Rota*, but its author unfortunately exhausted his wit upon the title. These attacks were succeeded by two labored defenses, *Mr. Dreyden Vindicated* and *A Description of the Academy of the Athenian Virtuosi*. The four pieces have been summarized elsewhere and recently reprinted.[105] We need con- cern ourselves only and briefly with the strategy of the first. After some preliminary jests about Dryden's play and preface, *The Censure of the Rota* proceeds to examine lapses of sense or grammar in Dryden's plays, espe- cially *The Conquest of Granada*, by recalling the methods of *The Defence of the Epilogue*. A "grave Gentleman" reminds the Athenian virtuosi gath- ered to censure Dryden that the object of their displeasure

> for the most part combated the dead; and the dead—send
> no Challenges; nor indeed need they, since through their
> sides he had wounded himselfe; for he ever play'd the
> Critick so unluckely, as to discover only his own faults

---

[101] *Works,* XVII, 24.

[102] *The Rehearsal,* I, i; 1675, p. 5 (1672, p. 5).

[103] But there was apparently an attempt to engage Dryden in dispute a few months after his play was printed. Martin Clifford (who had collaborated with Buckingham on *The Rehearsal*) seems to have written at this time some epistolary attacks on Dryden, especially on *The Conquest of Granada*. The attacks were subsequently published ten years after Clifford's death as *Notes upon Mr. Dry- den's Poems in Four Letters* (1687). The last letter is dated 1 July 1672 (p. 13); another claims "I was about six years since a little acquainted with a . . . [Dryden] who pilfer'd . . . an Essay of Dramatick Poetry" out of French critics (p. 8). The attacks have been reprinted in *Critical Heritage,* pp. 175–186.

[104] Cf. *The Censure of the Rota upon Mr. Milton's Book entituled, The Ready and Easie Way to Establish a Free Common-wealth* (1660).

[105] For summary see Macdonald, pp. 201–203; for the reprinted texts see *Critical Heritage,* pp. 54–108. For Dryden's dismissive reference to the exchange see the dedication of *The Assignation,* 322:28–323:12 above.

in other men, with the advantage of this aggravation, that
the Grammaticall Errors of older Poets, were but the
Errors of their Age, but being made his, were not the
Errors of this Age: since he granted this Age was refin'd
above those Solecismes of the last.[106]

The Censure of the Rota's strategy makes clear that the attack upon The
Conquest of Granada and other plays of "Rime and Non-sence"[107] was concerned not only with what some thought a foolish dramatic fashion; it was
concerned also, and perhaps as importantly, with the proper decorum of
literary criticism, its tone, method, and objects. When Dryden joined the
following year in a hostile examen of Settle's The Empress of Morocco,
Settle pointedly subtitled his reply "with Some few Errata's to be Printed
instead of the Postscript, with the next Edition of the Conquest of Granada."[108] Nearly twenty years later Langbaine could still justify his attack
on Dryden by recalling Dryden's old depredations "upon his own Country-
men."[109]

The confidence, at times self-congratulation of Dryden's prose—"I have
already swept the stakes"[110]—provoked adversaries to ironic or angry dismissal. The overbright images of greatness in his heroic plays prompted
satiric commentary upon their panegyric texts. But Dryden, too, was skeptically aware. He had already shown in defending Of Dramatick Poesie that
he could deal in irony and satire. By the time The Conquest of Granada was
published, The Rehearsal first acted, Dryden had written Marriage A-la-
Mode and probably had seen it performed.[111] Marriage A-la-Mode—Dryden's most brilliant play—courts a perhaps overbearing sophistication by
its counterpoise of two versions of pastoral, exquisite honor and elegant
innuendo, romance hero and man of mode. Even before 1671 Dryden had
shown in prologues and epilogues that he was aware of varied theatrical
responses to heroic plays by defending himself with irony and seeking to
anticipate depreciation with self-deprecation. Some adversaries, enjoying
the games that ironists play, cheerfully converted self-deprecation into depreciation. George Powell claimed in 1698 to have helped awaken a "sleeping Dowdy," but he was speaking, after all, of a play that Dryden himself,
prologizing to the second part, had long since predicted would "prove a

---

[106] Censure of the Rota (1673), p. 4; and see Clifford's similar contempt for
Dryden's "excess of Modesty . . . in your Postscript to Granada" (1687), p. 10. Dryden responded to attacks on his effrontery by removing from the second and
third editions the lengthy inquisition of Jonson's grammar in the first (207:27–
210:21; 211:1–5), retaining only his general remarks on Jonson's incorrectness. He
dropped the whole postscript from the last two editions published in his lifetime,
and it was not restored until Congreve's edition of 1717.

[107] Joseph Arrowsmith, prologue to The Reformation (1673).

[108] Settle was also retorting to the subtitle of Notes and Observations on the
Empress of Morocco. Or, Some few Erratas to be Printed instead of the Sculptures
with the Second Edition of that Play (1674).

[109] Langbaine, p. 133.

[110] See above, 18:6.

[111] See Robert D. Hume, "The Date of Dryden's Marriage A-la-Mode," HLB,
XXI (1973), 161–166.

Dowdy, with a Face to fright you." Similarly, Dryden's prefatory discussion of *furor poeticus* in heroic plays found a saucily ironic counterpart in the earlier prologue to *Tyrannick Love* (ll. 12–15):

> *Poets, like Lovers, should be bold and dare,*
> *They spoil their business with an over-care.*
> *And he who servilely creeps after sence,*
> *Is safe, but ne're will reach an Excellence.*

Five or six years later Johnson assured Smith in the third edition of *The Rehearsal* that Bayes "is too proud a man to creep servily after Sense."[112] What should the ironist do? Moreover, *The Rehearsal*'s description of Bayes's "new way of writing," where "every line surprises you, and brings in new matter," need not be mere ridicule of Eugenius on Oedipus. It could just as well echo Dryden's flippancy in the prologue to the second part of *The Conquest of Granada:*

> ... I Prophecy, these Wits to day,
> Will blindly guess at our imperfect Play:
> With what new Plots our Second Part is fill'd;
> Who must be kept alive, and who be kill'd.

Dryden was undoubtedly able to take heroics lightly as well as seriously. We know from Sedley's response to *The Generall* that at least some in the audience could greet love and honor with derision. Cibber later described how one actor played an heroic role for laughs. This sort of evidence—and there is more of it—is telling; unfortunately, we cannot be sure what it is trying to tell us. Some have thought the undoubted presence of irony in actors, audiences, prologues and epilogues argues the existence of ironies in serious dramatic texts, and they have thus embarked upon a critical adventure fraught with hazard. A familiar passage in Cibber's *Apology* illustrates the difficulty and danger:

> Here I cannot help observing upon a modest Mistake
> which I thought the late Mr. Booth committed in his act-
> ing the Part of Morat [in *Aureng-Zebe*]. There are in this
> fierce Character so many Sentiments of avow'd Barbarity,
> Insolence, and Vain-glory, that they blaze even to a ludi-
> crous Lustre, and doubtless the Poet intended those to
> make his Spectators laugh while they admir'd them; but
> Booth thought it depreciated the Dignity of Tragedy to
> raise a Smile in any part of it.[113]

Cibber goes on to praise Kynaston's different interpretation of Morat and softens his firm statement of authorial intention by placing it beyond the determination of an actor, "whose Business, sure, is to make the best of his Author's Intention, as in this Part Kynaston did, doubtless not without Dryden's Approbation."[114] When Kynaston came to speak one "heroical Rhodomontade" of Morat's, "*Risum Teneatis?*" It was impossible not to laugh and reasonably too, when this Line came out of the Mouth of Kynas-

---

[112] *The Rehearsal*, IV, ii; 1675, p. 47. Dryden's line was ridiculed before *The Rehearsal;* see the dedication of *Tyrannick Love* (*Works*, X, 112–113).

[113] Cibber, I, 121–122.

[114] *Ibid.*, p. 124.

ton, with the stern and haughty Look that attended it."[115] The critic's pudding here mixes author's intention, actor's interpretation, author's approval of an interpretation that changes intention, and audience response. Such puddings are or should be slow and heavy in the digestion, but critics still find them nourishing, and continue to argue that, because some spectators, some actors, evidently balanced heroic exaggeration with ironic flippancy, some authors' texts must reveal a similar balance.[116] Again, a critical debate should not be closed, but left open. We need note only a few points. Taking their lead from Cibber perhaps, critics in search of heroic irony tend to emphasize *Aureng-Zebe,* which followed the three-year onslaught upon "Rime and Non-sence" and may therefore have elicited from Dryden some concessions to skeptics in the audience. Critics have also responded more to possible irony in exaggerated villains than in exaggerated heroes, finding caricature in what seem the outrageous flippancies of a Morat or a Maximin. *The Conquest of Granada* has no character of that kind, unless it be, and at a considerable distance, Lyndaraxa. Finally, Dryden merely repented Almanzor's extravagance, or Maximin's for that matter; he did not seek to excuse it as hyperbole tempered with wit.

The Conquest of Granada came just after a decade that Dryden chiefly devoted to images and possibilities of greatness, finding them in restoration, coronation, fire and war, the advancement of learning and letters, the deeds of history and romance. Perhaps because the huge image of his ten-act play acquired a grotesque shadow in contemporary responses, Dryden's attitude toward heroism was persistently ambivalent for the rest of his career. He noted in the preface to *The State of Innocence* that heroic diction could be mockingly misapplied;[117] then showed how to do so in *Mac Flecknoe. Absalom and Achitophel* interleaves panegyric with satire. Heroes shrink at times into "a race of Men who can never enjoy quiet in themselves, 'till they have taken it from all the World,"[118] or play the buffoon to illustrate the power of Timotheus's music, or find that their "Wars brought nothing about."[119] At other times, Dryden's late heroes take on the old greatness, as he turned at the end of his life to translate the tale of Chaucer's knight and give English voice to "the *Achilles* of *Homer,*" who, years before, had supplied him with "the first Image" of Almanzor.[120] Like the hare he described to his cousin of Chesterton,[121] Dryden filled his circle, ending where he began, but with a difference.[122]

---

115 *Ibid.,* p. 125.

116 See King, *Dryden's Major Plays;* Eric Rothstein, *Restoration Tragedy: Form and the Process of Change* (1967), pp. 99–100; Novak, introd., *The Empress of Morocco and Its Critics,* pp. vi–vii; Robert S. Newman, "Irony and the Problem of Tone in Dryden's *Aureng-Zebe," SEL,* X (1970), 439–458.

117 1677, sig. clv; Watson, I, 205.

118 Dedication of *Examen Poeticum (Works,* IV, 374).

119 *The Secular Masque,* l. 88.

120 See above, 14:22–23.

121 *To My Honour'd Kinsman,* ll. 62–66.

122 For further discussion see H. T. Swedenberg, Jr., "Dryden's Obsessive Concern with the Heroic," *SP,* Extra Series 4 (1967), 12–26.

Conquest of Granada, The First Part

TITLE PAGE

Epigraph. *Aeneid*, VII, 44–45 (a greater series of events springs from me; I begin a greater task); Virgil promises to tell of the war in Latium. Cf. Dryden's *Aeneis*, VII, 66–67.

DEDICATION

P. 3 *His Royal Highness The Duke.* James, Duke of York, afterwards King James II.

3:2–3 *Virgil . . . Augustus Cæsar.* Augustus' interest in the *Aeneid* while Virgil was writing it and his commanding its preservation after Virgil's death were frequently remarked; Suetonius' life of Virgil is the principal source. But Virgil cannot properly be said to have "inscrib'd" his unperfected epic to Augustus, even if we understand by "inscribe" something less formal than, though akin to, "dedicate" (*OED*). Dryden perhaps had in mind the common assumption that the *Aeneid* celebrates Augustus through the figure of his putative ancestor, Aeneas. Some support for this assumption could be found in *Aeneid*, I, 286–290 (Dryden's *Aeneis*, I, 390–395). Dryden later availed himself of the common assumption in *The Character of St. Evremond* (1692, sig. A5r-v; Watson, II, 57–58) and in the dedication of *Aeneis* (1697, sigs. (b)2r-3v; Ker, II, 174–175). Earlier, he could have found it in John Ogilby's English translation of Virgil (2d ed., 1668, p. 127) or in the preface to Jean Regnauld de Segrais' *Traduction de l'Eneïde de Virgile* (Paris, 1668, p. 8).

3:3–4 *Tasso and Ariosto . . . house of Est.* Ludovico Ariosto dedicated *Orlando Furioso* (1516) to Cardinal Ippolito of Este: see the inscription at the head of Canto I in some editions and the dedication in I.iii. Torquato Tasso dedicated *Gerusalemme Liberata* (1581) to Alfonso II of Este, Duke of Ferrara: see I.iv.

3:25 *acknowledging.* Grateful.

3:28–31 *Even the first blossomes . . . . all other Captains.* James campaigned with the French army from 1652, when he was eighteen, to 1655, participating both in the civil war of the Fronde and the war with Spain in the Lowlands. All reports accounted him a brave cavalry officer and provided matter for later encomiasts. "He had no less a judge of his merits than the General of the French Army, Marshal Tureine [Turenne], under whom he performed such eminent services against the Spaniards, as had fixed upon him the deserved character of a most valiant and prudent Commander, insomuch that notwithstanding his youth he was made Lieutenant General of all the Army" (*A Short View of the Life and Actions of . . . James Duke of York* [1660], p. 15).

4:5–14 *You were then an honour . . . . whom they commanded.* A treaty between France and England signed late in 1655 provided that Charles, James, and their principal supporters be denied further refuge in France. In 1657 and 1658 James served with the Spanish army campaigning against France in the Lowlands. An Anglo-French treaty of March 1657 provided that the French army be reinforced with 6,000 English infantry, who landed in Flanders in May 1657. By the end of the summer's campaigning the English contingent was reduced to less than 4,000 by sickness and desertion. Some deserters returned to England; some joined the Spanish and found their way into the British regiments commanded by James. Desertions continued throughout the winter of 1657–58, as the English troops were unpaid and miserably garrisoned in Mardyke. The English captains were told to keep a stricter watch on their companies. (See Charles Harding Firth, *The Last Years of the Protectorate, 1656–1658* [1909], I, 279, 291–300.) Money, not Stuart loyalism, was evidently the motive for desertion, although James thought the English commander, Sir John Reynolds, was leaning toward the Stuarts. In an interview with James, Reynolds "used obscure expressions which showed that he hoped to be able one day to render service to the Duke" (*The Memoirs of James II*, trans. A. Lytton Sells [1962], p. 245). The interview is described in *A Short View of the Life and Actions of . . . James Duke of York*, p. 20.

4:15–21 *that Army . . . . to overcome*. Dryden describes the Battle of the Dunes, 4/14 June 1658, between the Anglo-French army and the Spanish army in which James served. Although briefer, Dryden's account is similar to that given in *A Short View of the Life and Actions of . . . James Duke of York*, p. 22. The Anglo-French victory forced the surrender of the Spanish-held Dunkirk on 15/25 June 1658.

4:24 *became a terror . . . they conquer'd*. Like Mardyke the year before, Dunkirk was handed over to the English in accordance with the treaty of March 1657. Many Frenchmen feared that England would use the garrisons to threaten France (see Firth, *Last Years of the Protectorate*, II, 202–204).

4:28–31 *When the Hollanders . . . were first protected*. Holland was aided by England during its war of independence from Spain in the last thirty years of the sixteenth century. For a similar reflection upon Dutch obligations to the English and subsequent ingratitude see Henry Stubbs, *A Justification of the Present War against the United Netherlands* (1672), pp. 13–26.

4:32 *a sordid parsimony*. Cf. Roger Palmer, Earl of Castlemaine, *A short and true Account of . . . the late War Between the English and Dutch* (1671), p. 91: "we can maintain a war far cheaper then they, which doubtless seems a Paradox, considering theirs as a frugal State, and ours as a Magnificent and Splendid Monarchy."

4:33 *dar'd . . . the Seas*. In the second Anglo-Dutch war, 1665–1667

5:3–9 *the most glorious victory . . . without an Admiral*. On 3 June 1665 the English fleet commanded by James defeated the Dutch off Lowestoft. Opdam, one of the Dutch admirals, was killed when his ship, the admiral ship, blew up; the Dutch returned without an admiral in both senses of the word. Dryden earlier described the Battle of Lowestoft in *Annus Mirabilis*, ll. 73–92, and in the opening paragraph of *Of Dramatick Poesie* (see *Works*, I, 62–63; XVII, 8, and nn). Pepys recorded the victory in his entry for 8 June 1665, and, as Crites prophesied in *Of Dramatick Poesie*, the victory was celebrated in "many ill verses" (*Works*, XVII, 9), among them Edward Howard's *A Panegyrick to his Highness the Duke of York, on his Sea-Fight with the Dutch June 3ᵈ 1665* (1666). The victory also prompted Edmund Waller's *Instructions to a Painter* (1665), which in turn stimulated a series of advice-to-a-painter poems, several of them dealing with the second Anglo-

Dutch war (see *Poems on Affairs of State,* I, ed. George deF. Lord [1963]). Dryden's insistence upon an *absolute* victory seems more than panegyric exultation. With the Battle of Lowestoft won, James ordered pursuit of the Dutch fleet and then retired to his cabin. While he slept, his secretary, Henry Brouncker, countermanded his orders, allowing the Dutch to escape and refit. Parliament's vigorous inquiry into the conduct of the war between 1666 and 1669 took note of Brouncker's interference (see Anchitell Grey, *Debates of the House of Commons* [1763], I, 139–141, 143–144). Brouncker's folly was still being explained away by a court apologist like Castlemaine some months after *The Conquest of Granada* was first performed. Castlemaine wrote of the Battle of Lowestoft (*A short and true Account of . . . the late War,* pp. 9–10):

> Triumph I may well say, since no victory was ever more
> clear, and yet it would have been greater, had his High-
> ness had less courage, or his people less passion for him;
> For least (after so much glory to the Kingdom) some ill
> chance might befall him (every one knowing he would
> be foremost in the new action) many were content, while
> he reposed, the flying enemy should not be so fiercely
> pursued that night, as we had opportunity to do, through
> their wretched state and condition.

5:10–11 *a dissembled day of publick Thanks-giving.* Although the Dutch at first claimed a victory at Lowestoft, they soon admitted defeat there (see Ogg, p. 288). Dryden's resentful allusion is apparently to the day of thanksgiving celebrated in the United Provinces on 6 July 1667 to mark the victorious attack on the English fleet at Chatham on 13 June 1667 (see *Description Exacte de tout ce qui s'est passé dans les Guerres entre le Roy d'Angleterre, le Roy de France, les Estats des Provinces Unies du Pays-bas, & l'Evesque de Munster* [Amsterdam, 1668], p. 229).

5:16–17 *when you were absent.* After Lowestoft Charles replaced James as admiral with the Earl of Sandwich, on the grounds that James was too valuable to risk in further engagements.

5:30–32 *a Nation eager to revenge . . . . a surprise.* The *Conquest of Granada* was published before Charles declared war on the Dutch on 17 March 1672. But the drift toward a third Dutch war was apparent months before the actual declaration (see headnote to *Marriage A-la-Mode,* pp. 460–461 below). Dryden's bellicose tone contrasts with the irenic note sounded by Castlemaine in *A short and true Account of . . . the late War,* which was included in the term catalogue licensed on 13 February 1671: "for the future I doubt not of a good understanding between these our late enemies and us, because they are with reason . . . reputed a wise and prudent Nation" (p. 103). Dryden's dedication was evidently written some months after such sentiments as Castlemaine's still corresponded with official policy. The Dutch surprise still to be revenged was the humiliating and destructive attack of 13 June 1667 upon the English fleet docked in Chatham.

5:32–34 *as the Samnites . . . are reveng'd.* In 321 B.C., during the second Samnite war, the Samnites camped near Caudium about fifteen miles from the Roman forces. Ten Samnite soldiers disguised as shepherds were sent to the vicinity of the Roman camp, where they told Roman pillagers the Samnites were besieging and about to capture Luceria in Apulia. Seeking to relieve Luceria, the Romans marched by the shortest route, through the narrow pass of the Caudine Forks (more usually *Furculae,* not *Furcae, Caudinae*). The Samnites trapped the Romans in the pass and forced humiliating terms of surrender upon them. The episode produced widespread mourning and anger at Rome and prompted a war of revenge in 320–319 B.C. which culminated in the defeat and humiliation of the Samnites at Luceria (see Livy, IX.ii–xv). For Dryden's later allusion to the episode see *The Duke of Guise,* Act IV (1683, p. 53; S-S, VII, 95).

6:5 *Achilles.* Two years earlier Dryden found an Achilles in Monmouth when dedicating *Tyrannick Love* to him (*Works,* X, 107). Now he finds an Achilles in James; in the next paragraph he finds one in Almanzor before consigning his hero to James's protection.

6:6–9 *I doubt not . . . the Poet.* As Summers notes, Dryden was both poet laureate and historiographer royal at this time, and evidently alludes here to his double office. He glances also at much debated distinctions between poetry and history. Dryden later defined *"Annals"* in *The Life of Plutarch* (1683) as "naked History; Or the plain relation of matter of fact. . . . The springs and motives of actions are not here sought, unless they offer themselves, and are open to every Mans discernment. . . . Counsels, guesses, politick observations, sentences, and Orations are avoyded: In few words a bare Narration is its business" (*Works,* XVII, 271–272). This definition should be set beside Davenant's observation in the preface to *Gondibert* (1650; Spingarn, II, 3):

> Lucan, who chose to write the greatest actions that ever were allowed to be true . . . did not observe that such an enterprize rather beseem'd an Historian then a Poet: For wise Poets think it more worthy to seek out truth in the Passions then to record the truth of Actions, and practise to describe Mankinde just as we are perswaded or guided by instinct, not particular persons as they are lifted or levell'd by the force of Fate.

6:15–18 *Homer and Tasso . . . . an Epick poem.* The precedents of Homer's Achilles and Tasso's Rinaldo are more fully considered in *Of Heroique Playes* (14:21–16:17).

6:24–26 *roughness of Character . . . an arrogance.* Summers cites Horace's account of Achilles in *Ars Poetica,* ll. 120–122, as the basis of this description. Dryden has already compared Achilles and Almanzor (6:13–18), and cites the lines of Horace when developing the comparison in *Of Heroique Playes* (15:16–18).

7:10–13 *By the suffrage . . . . of my friends.* These contrary votes were evidently cast in conversation. We do not know when Dryden wrote the dedication—sometime late in 1671 seems likely (see note to 5:30–32)—and *The Rehearsal* may already have been performed (7 December 1671), or Dryden may have known of its preparation (see Ward, *Life,* p. 84). But, *The Rehearsal* aside, written opinion of Almanzor and his play postdates publication of *The Conquest of Granada;* see headnote, pp. 412–413 above. Dryden's "Apology" for Almanzor in *Of Heroique Playes* (14:16–17:34) fails to reintroduce those "most and best," his "friends," who "acquitted" Almanzor in the dedication.

7:12 *stand to the award.* Accept the judgment.

OF HEROIQUE PLAYES

8:1–9:7 *Whether Heroique verse* . . . . *the Audience will receive it.* This paragraph offers to terminate more than seven years of dispute about the admission of rhyme into drama. Dryden first raised the matter in the dedication of *The Rival Ladies* (1664; *Works*, VIII, 98–101), pursued it in *Of Dramatick Poesie* (1668; *Works*, XVII, 64–80), and dealt in *A Defence of an Essay of Dramatique Poesie* (1668; *Works*, IX, 5–7) with objections to rhyme raised by Sir Robert Howard in his preface to *The Duke of Lerma* (1668). For discussion of the dispute see *Works*, VIII, 274–275; IX, 302–305, 306; XVII, 346–347. The prologue to *Aureng-Zebe* (1676), Dryden's last rhymed play, announced that he was "weary of his long-lov'd Mistris, Rhyme" (l. 8).

8:20–21 *because Shakespear . . . to be erected.* Alluding to the Pillars of Hercules supposedly set on either side of the Straits of Gibraltar and once the boundary of the known world. For Dryden's use of geographical discovery to exemplify intellectual advance see *To My Honored Friend, Dr. Charleton,* ll. 15–20 (*Works*, I, 43). Cf. Tasso, *Discourses,* p. 57:

> Many people think, my illustrious lord, that the same
> thing has happened with the noblest arts and sciences as
> with peoples, provinces, lands, and oceans, a number of
> which were not well known to the ancients, but have
> recently been discovered beyond the Pillars of Hercules
> to the west. . . . They compare the achievements of the
> poetic and rhetorical arts to the goals and other marks
> placed as boundaries to timid navigators.

9:8–25 *For Heroick Plays* . . . . *to make his design perfect.* The first version of *The Siege of Rhodes* was performed and published in 1656. Shortly after the Restoration, Davenant was granted a patent to operate the Duke's Company. He revised *The Siege of Rhodes* and added a second part for performance in 1661, publication in 1663. The dedication of the 1663 quarto to Clarendon contains perhaps the earliest extant use of the term "heroic plays" (see William S. Clark, "The Sources of the Restoration Heroic Play," *RES*, IV [1928], 54). Davenant died in 1668, leaving unperfected that "design" of establishing heroic plays on the London stage.

9:16–20 *The Original . . . some French Poets.* The early history of opera has been told many times (see, e.g., Ludovic Celler [Louis Leclercq], *Les Origines de l'Opéra et le Ballet de la Reine* [Paris, 1868]), and Dryden's remark seems unspecific. But Ker may be right in assuming (I, 308) a reference to the work of Giacomo Torelli, an Italian designer, stage engineer, and producer whom Mazarin brought to Paris in 1645. Late in 1645 Torelli staged with Italian singers Strozzi's *Finta Pazza*, "une comédie lyrique avec airs, duos, chœurs, dans laquelle les artistes chantaient, déclamaient et dansaient" (Celler, pp. 339–340). Torelli subsequently staged Pierre Corneille's *Andromède* (1650), a tragedy with elaborate scenery and singing gods in machines. Davenant obviously had available more Cornelian examples than *Andromède* for the heightening of characters.

9:25–28 *There wanted . . . the beauty of the stile.* Davenant conceded defects of plot and character (as well as scenery), at least in the 1656 version of *The Siege of Rhodes,* but failed to remark its deficiencies of style: "we are like to give no great satisfaction in the quantity of our argument, which is in story [Knolles's *Historie of the Turkes*] very copious; but shrinks to a small narration here, because we could not convey it by more than seven persons; being constrain'd to prevent the length of *recitative* musick, as well as to conserve, without incumbrance, the narrowness of the place" (*Love and Honour and The Siege of Rhodes,* ed. James W. Tupper [1909], p. 183). Davenant added more principal characters for the 1661 version.

10:1–2 *it is an easy thing to add to what already is invented.* Dryden makes English a proverbial Latin phrase, *facile est inventis addere,* he later used in the preface to *Fables* (1700, sig *D1; Watson, II, 289).

10:6–17 *I observ'd . . . . the Subject of it.* Ariosto's *Orlando Furioso* helps move Dryden's discourse from design and variety to love and valor not only because it sang of arms and love but also because it had been frequently celebrated or condemned for multiplicity and variety of both action and character (see headnote, pp. 418–419 above).

10:12–13 *Le Donne . . . io canto.* "Of Dames, of knights, of armes, of loves delight, / Of courtesies, of high attempts I speake" (Sir John Harington's translation, 1591).

10:16 *Love and Valour.* As Ker notes (I, 309), Dryden's "Heroick Poem" is the epic as interpreted by the Italian Renaissance to include chivalric love among its subjects; cf. Tasso, *Discourses,* pp. 45–47.

10:18–20 *as first Discoverers . . . saw not clearly.* Watson notes (I, 159) the occurrence of similar cartographical images in Davenant's preface to *Gondibert,* but we need not suppose a specific borrowing from Davenant, since the image was commonplace (cf. note to 8:20–21, above).

10:21 *The common Drama.* As opposed to heroic plays and, perhaps, operas.

10:22 *the Antients . . . great Action.* See Aristotle, *Poetics,* ch. 7.

10:23–24 *neither fill'd . . . with Characters.* Dryden distinguishes between roles—persons of the drama—as they may be simply enumerated and those roles as they are differentiated into *"characters"* by a particular *"composition of qualities"* (preface to *Troilus and Cressida,* 1679, sig. a4; Watson, I, 249–250). Dryden's notion of *"character"* apparently derives from the rhetorical figure known variously as *characterismus, personae descriptio, prosopographia,* and *notatio,* which served, among other things, as schoolboy exercise. Dryden's most important discussion of character, apart from that in the preface to *Troilus and Cressida,* occurs in *Of Dramatick Poesie* (*Works,* XVII, 59–61).

10:25–29 *The Laws . . . of humane life.* See headnote, pp. 420–421 above, for discussion of this remark.

10:30–31 *the scanting of . . . an Heroick Poem.* Dryden later modified this close analogy between heroic play and poem when he came to compare "Epick Poetry and Tragedy" in the dedication of *Aeneis:* "the work of Tragedy is on the Passions, and in Dialogue, both of them abhor strong Metaphors, in which the *Epopee* delights. A Poet cannot speak too plainly on the Stage: for *Volat irrevocabile verbum;* the sense is lost if it be not taken flying: but what we read alone we have leisure to digest" (1697, sig. (a)4; Watson, II, 233). The modification presumably resulted from Dryden's reflecting upon imagistic excesses in his own plays: see the preface to *The*

State of Innocence (1677, sig. c1v; Watson, I, 205), where Dryden defends a catachresis against his critics, and the dedication of *The Spanish Fryar* (1681, sig. A2v; Watson, I, 276), where he repents his "extravagance."

11:2–7 *That it ought to be . . . Antients or Moderns.* Dryden draws into one "judgment" scattered points and phrases in Davenant's preface to *Gondibert.* See especially: "give me leave (remembring with what difficulty the world can shew any Heroick Poem that in a perfect glass of Nature gives us a familiar and easie view of our selves) to take notice of those quarrels which the Living have with the Dead" (Spingarn, II, 1); "I chose a Story of such persons as profess'd Christian Religion . . . because the Principles of our Religion conduce more to explicable vertue . . . then any other Religion" (Spingarn, II, 9).

11:7–11 *thus he takes . . . our Acts.* See preface to *Gondibert* (Spingarn, II, 17).

11:22–26 *Non enim . . . fides.* See *Satyricon,* 118, and the translation by Sir Richard Fanshawe in the preface to his 1655 translation of Camoens' *The Lusiads,* ed. Geoffrey Bullough (1963), p. 37:

> For not *things done* should be comprehended in verse,
> (which is much better performed by Historians) but the
> free spirit must throw it self headlong in digressions
> [circumlocutions, perhaps], and in personatings [inter-
> ventions, perhaps] of Gods, and in fabulous ornaments
> [ornaments from legend, that is] upon the rack of inven-
> tion: that it may seem rather an ebullition of some pro-
> phetick truths, amidst a world of pleasant extravagancies,
> from a breast inflamed with fury; than a deposition, as
> of sworn witnesses to *tell the truth, all the truth, and
> nothing but the truth.*

Fanshawe's "and in fabulous ornaments upon the rack of invention" corresponds to *et fabulosum sententiarum tormentum,* a phrase omitted from all editions of Dryden's essay, although it occurs in seventeenth-century as well as modern editions of the *Satyricon.* The omission may have been an oversight by Dryden or his compositor, since Dryden proceeds to test Lucan against the Petronian formula and charges him not merely with neglecting "the ministry of the Gods"—*Deorumque ministeria*—but also "the help of his heathen Deities," which perhaps corresponds to *fabulosum sententiarum.* But Dryden's omission may have been deliberate, since he also charges Lucan with using too many "Sentences," *sententiae,* that is, while in the omitted phrase Petronius recommends the use of *sententiae* from myth or legend.

11:27–29 *In which sentence . . . the truth of history.* After prescribing the heroic poem, Petronius offers through the mouth of Eumolpus his own example of an *impetus*—a "rapture," as Fanshawe translates it—a three-hundred-line poem on the civil wars of Rome, the subject of Lucan's *Pharsalia.* Fanshawe translated the rapture and, noting in his postscript (ed. Bullough, p. 52) the common charge that Lucan was rather historian than poet, found the charge implied "in the Introduction [from which Dryden quotes] to this Essay [attempt at, example of an epic] (which glanceth particularly at LUCAN) and mended (as the Author thereof conceived) by the Essay itself, which is of a mixt nature between Fable and

History." See also the commentary in *Satyricon,* ed. Michael Hadrianides (Amsterdam, 1669), pp. 417–418. For additional discussion of Lucan as historian see *Works,* I, 270.

11:29–32 *crowded Sentences . . . of an Heroick Poem.* Cf. preface to *Annus Mirabilis* and note in *Works,* I, 53:17–20, and 272. Dryden's phrasing is partly synonymous, since the "sting" of an epigram was also its "point," a witty turn or application which closed up the whole; cf. *Discourse of Satire* (*Works,* IV, 13:22–24) and *The Art of Poetry,* ll. 329–364 (*Works,* II, 134–135). For discussion of the epigram as form see C. H. Herford and Percy Simpson, eds., *Ben Jonson,* II (1925), 342–360.

12:6–7 *The Oracle . . . of Erictho.* Lucan, *Pharsalia,* V, 65–224; VI, 507–830.

12:12–13 *Enthusiastick parts of Poetry.* Those resulting from inspiration or *furor poeticus.* Cf. preface to *The State of Innocence* (1677, sig. b4v; Watson, I, 203), *A Parallel betwixt Painting and Poetry* (1695, sig. lii; Watson, II, 205), and dedication of *Aeneis* (1697, sig. (f)1v; Watson, II, 249).

12:15–16 *the Ghost of Polydorus.* See *Aeneid,* III, 39–48; Dryden's *Aeneis,* III, 54–67.

12:16 *the Enchanted wood.* See *Gerusalemme Liberata,* XIII.ii–li, XVIII. iii–xl.

12:16–17 *the Bower of bliss.* See *The Faerie Queene,* II, xii, 42–87.

12:19–21 *if any man . . . by Magick.* Among those who so objected were Davenant in his preface to *Gondibert* and Hobbes in his answer to Davenant (Spingarn, II, 5, 61–62).

12:26–29 *'Tis enough . . . . for Poetry.* Cf. preface to *Tyrannick Love* (*Works,* X, 112).

12:30–34 *the whole Doctrine . . . conjectur'd.* Cf. Dryden's later discussion of guardian spirits in *Discourse of Satire* (*Works,* IV, 19:15–21:19 and nn). The doctrine and some of its literary applications have been surveyed by Robert Hunter West in *The Invisible World: A Study of Pneumatology in Elizabethan Drama* (1939), esp. pp. 24–27. For the objection of Hobbes, see *Leviathan,* III, xxxiv, pp. 255–265. Dryden prepares here for Almanzor's interview with the ghost of his mother in *2 Conquest,* IV, iii, 77–142.

13:2 *phlegmatick, heavy gown-man.* For response to this attack on the clergy, see note to dedication of *The Assignation,* pp. 522–524.

13:10–13 *Cowleys . . . fayery-land.* See "To Sir William Davenant, upon his two first Books of Gondibert":

Methinks heroick Poesie till now,
Like some fantastic fairy-land did show.

. . . .

Thou, like some worthy knight with sacred arms,
Dost drive the monsters thence, and end the charms.

13:11–12 *his authority is almost sacred to me.* For other expressions of Dryden's respect for Cowley see John M. Aden, *The Critical Opinions of John Dryden* (1963), pp. 37–38.

13:13–15 *his own Example. . . . in his Davideis.* See, e.g., *Davideis,* I, 71–311; II, 439–460.

13:15 *Tasso in his Godfrey.* See, e.g., *Gerusalemme Liberata,* I.vii–xvii; IV.i–xviii; VII.lxxix–lxxxii; IX.lv–lxvi; XVIII.xcii–xcvii.

13:25–26 *Segnius . . . fidelibus.* Horace, *Ars Poetica,* ll. 180–181 (Loeb trans.: "Less vividly is the mind stirred by what finds entrance through the ears than by what is brought before the trusty eyes"). Dryden substitutes *animum* and *aures* for *animos* and *aurem*.

13:28–30 *To those who object . . . frequently.* Cf. *Of Dramatick Poesie* (*Works*, XVII, 39, 50).

13:31–33 *Jonson shows no . . . Armies.* Neither stage directions nor exclamations in speeches call for the noise of offstage battles, which must therefore occur as the business of particular productions. *Catiline* was revived for the season of 1668–69; Pepys attended a performance on 19 December and saw "a fine Scene . . . of a fight."

14:7 *the Red Bull.* An open-air theater in Clerkenwell noted for ranting productions. Cf. *Of Dramatick Poesie* (*Works*, XVII, 35:15 and n).

14:24–25 *the Artaban of Monsieur Calprenede.* For Artaban in La Calprenède's *Cléopâtre* see headnote, pp. 414–415 above.

15:3–4 Οἰνοβαρὲς . . . *&c.* See *Iliad*, I, 225, 231 (Loeb trans.: "Thou heavy with wine, thou with the front of a dog but the heart of a deer"; "Folk-devouring king"). Cf. Dryden's *Ilias*, I, 335–336, 342–343.

15:7 Ἕλκετο . . . ξίφος. See *Iliad*, I, 194 (Loeb trans.: while he "was drawing from its sheath his great sword"). Cf. Dryden's *Ilias*, I, 295.

15:12–13 Ἀλλ' . . . ἀνάσσειν. See *Iliad*, I, 287–288 (Loeb trans.: "But this man is minded to be above all others; over all is he minded to hold sway and be king among all, and to all give orders"). Cf. Dryden's *Ilias*, I, 406–408.

15:16–18 *Honoratum . . . armis.* See *Ars Poetica*, ll. 120–122 (Loeb trans.: if "you bring back to the stage the honouring of Achilles, let him be impatient, passionate, ruthless, fierce; let him claim that laws are not for him, let him ever make appeal to the sword").

16:4–7 *Venga . . . genti.* See *Gerusalemme Liberata*, V.xliii, trans. Edward Fairfax (1600):

> Let Godfrey come or send, I will not hence,
> Until we know who shall this bargain rue;
> That of our tragedy, the late done fact
> May be the first, and this the second act.

16:8–10 *You see . . . by us.* Cf. preface to *All for Love* (1678, sig. b2r-v; Watson, I, 224–225).

16:16–17 *Cyrus and Oroondates.* The heroes, respectively, of Madeleine de Scudéry's *Artamène: ou le Grand Cyrus* (1649–1653; English trans. 1653–1655) and Gauthier de la Calprenède's *Cassandre* (1644–1650; English trans. 1652).

17:1–3 *Cethegus threatens . . . to look Cato dead.* Dryden partly misremembers Jonson's *Catiline*. "Rash CETHEGUS, / My executioner," as Catiline calls him (III, 723–724), indeed has some share in the play's rodomontades, although his share is smaller than Catiline's. Catiline it is who wishes to destroy nature; Cethegus retorts he would "force new nature out" of the chaos Catiline seeks (III, 175–181). Later, Cethegus and Curius vie with each other in wishing to ruin more Romes than one, more worlds, gods, natures (III, 594–595). It is Catiline again who threatens to look Cicero (not Cato) dead (IV, 501). But Cethegus indeed petitions to "kill all the Senate, for my share" of the rebellion (IV, 597; references to the edition of Herford and Simpson).

17:12–14 *Their King . . . tells us.* The hostility of Granadans for King Boabdelin is noted in Juan de Mariana, *Historia General de España* (Toledo, 1601), II, 660, 666–668. Mariana tells us (II, 667) that Boabdelin was called "el rey Chiquito" because he had authority over no one and commanded no respect.

17:15 *Juego de toros.* The bullfight in the first scene of *1 Conquest of Granada.*

17:16–18 *the character . . . just before.* See *1 Conquest,* I, i, 247–258.

17:20–21 *Cæsar . . . with a word.* Summers notes Suetonius, *Julius,* LXX. Caesar's word to the mutinous 10th Legion was *quirites,* "citizens," which prompted the mutineers to exclaim they were still Caesar's "soldiers." Cf. *The Duke of Guise,* Act IV (1683, p. 39; S-S, VII, 74).

17:22–24 *single before . . . their trenches.* For enemy forces deserting to Caesar on his approach with an army see, e.g., his *Civil War,* I, 13, 18, 23, 24, 74.

17:29–30 *If the History of . . . in Naples.* The *Memoires* of Henry of Lorraine, 5th Duke of Guise, were published at Paris in 1668, four years after his death, pirated in the Lowlands, and Englished in 1669. The *Memoires* describe Guise's "Passage to Naples, and heading there the Second Revolt of that People."

18:5 *Ast . . . Somnum.* Horace, *Ars Poetica,* l. 360: *verum operi longo fas est obrepere somnum* (Loeb trans.: "when a work is long, a drowsy mood may well creep over it").

PROLOGUE

1 *of t'other houses making.* That is, of course, the Duke's Company. The allusion to James Nokes (l. 7), comedian, seems to rest upon an episode when Nokes acted the part of Sir Arthur Addell in John Caryll's comedy *Sir Salomon; or, the Cautious Coxcomb* before the court at Dover in May 1670. Downes (p. 29) recalled the occasion:

> The French Court wearing then Excessive short Lac'd Coats; some Scarlet, some Blew, with Broad wast Belts; Mr. Nokes having at that time one shorter than the French Fashion, to Act Sir Arthur Addle in; the Duke of Monmouth gave Mr. Nokes his Sword and Belt from his Side, and Buckled it on himself, on purpose to Ape the French: That Mr. Nokes lookt more like a Drest up Ape, than a Sir Arthur: Which upon his first Entrance on the Stage, put the King and Court to an Excessive Laughter; at which the French look'd very Shaggrin.

16 *Meat, drink, and cloth, in Ale.* See Tilley, A103.

19 *the best Comedians.* Summers takes the reference to be to John Lacy and Joseph Haines. But the prologue is still talking about actors wearing broad-brimmed hats and has specified (ll. 7–8) James Nokes and Nell Gwyn.

20 *blocks.* That is, hat molds.

38 *French farce worn out at home.* Charles II encouraged French troupes to come to England and perform there. English playwrights naturally were not pleased with the competition. As early as 1663, Davenant, in *The Playhouse to be Let,* has the following exchange between the manager of a

French troupe and an English player (*Works* [1673], 2d pag., p. 68):

> *Mons.* Mi vil make Presentation of de Farce.
> *Tir. W.* Farces, what be those? New French
> Bobs for Ladies?
> *Play.* Pray peace; I understand the Gentleman.
> Your Farces are a kind of Mungril Plays.
> But, Sir, I believe all French Farces are
> Prohibited Commodities, and will
> Not pass current in England.
> *Mons.* Sir, pardon me; de Engelis be more
> Fantastick den de Fransh. De Farce
> Bi also very fantastick, and vil passe.
> *Play.* The Monsieur's in the right; for we have found
> Our Customers of late exceeding humorous.

Dryden had spoken contemptuously of farce in the preface to *An Evening's Love* (*Works*, X, 203), though he was not above writing farcical scenes.

I, i

10 *darted Cane.* A reference to the play of canes (*juego de cañas*), a "skirmish with throwing canes on horsebacke one at another . . ." (*OED*).

23 *Sierra Ronda.* Summers: "Serrania de Ronda, a mountain group difficult of access, which stretches out its sierras in all directions beyond the gorge of the Guadalhorce."

24 *Who, with high Nostrils* etc. Reuben A. Brower ("Dryden's Epic Manner and Virgil," in *Essential Articles for the Study of John Dryden*, ed. H. T. Swedenberg, Jr. [1966], p. 472) notes that the line echoes *Georgics*, I, 375–376:

> *bucula caelum*
> *suspiciens patulis captavit naribus auras.*

Dryden trans. (*Georgics*, I, 518–519):

> The Cow looks up, and from afar can find
> The change of Heav'n, and snuffs it in the Wind.

40 *launch'd.* Wounded. *OED* cites this line.

50–57 Brower ("Dryden's Epic Manner and Virgil," pp. 472–473) finds the passage reminiscent of Virgil, in particular *Georgics*, III, 51–55, 233–234.

61 *Mirador.* "A turret or belvedere on the top of a Spanish house" (*OED*, which cites this line).

70 *Escapade.* "A fit of plunging and rearing" (*OED*, which cites this line).

73 *What after pass'd.* An example of the hemistich or broken line. Noyes, *Selected Dramas*, observed that Dryden uses the device often in the heroic plays and that it also appears in *Absalom and Achitophel*. See note to l. 87 in *Works*, II, 242.

74 *Ventanna.* "A window" (*OED*, which cites this line).

92–98 Brower ("Dryden's Epic Manner and Virgil," p. 473) observes: "In this passage Dryden is not merely blending two parts of a Virgilian simile into one, or recalling, with no little success, the sonorous trumpets of the *Æneid*; he is writing in a style which in great part owes its variety of movement and mastery of sound to a thorough appreciation of Virgil's artistry." Brower notes in particular *Aeneid*, IX, 435–437:

> *purpureus veluti cum flos succisus aratro*

languescit moriens, lassove papavera collo
demisere caput, pluvia cum forte gravantur.

Dryden trans. (*Aeneis*, IX, 582–584):

Like a fair Flow'r by the keen Share oppress'd:
Like a white Poppy sinking on the Plain,
Whose heavy Head is overcharg'd with Rain.

95 *prevent.* Anticipate.

100 *Ataballes.* "A kind of kettle-drum or tabour used by the Moors" (*OED*).

109 *Vivarambla place.* "The Plaza de Bibarrambla . . . the scene of many jousts, bull-fights, gay fiestas and tournaments both under Moor and Christian" (Summers).

150 *Selin.* A. E. Morgan in *English Plays, 1660–1820* (1935) assigned this speech to Selin. Even though the early texts all give the speech to Zulema, the emendation seems sound, for subsequent passages (II, i, 242, and III, i, 285) show that it is Selin who seeks revenge for the death of his son Tarifa.

161–162 In Pérez de Hita (Pérez, I, 58–61; Rodd, pp. 75–78) an account is given of the game of canes between the Zegrys and Abencerrages, in which the Zegrys treacherously used lances instead of canes. Mahomet Zegry wounded Alabez, an Abencerrago, who in turn killed Mahomet.

167 *ought.* Owed.

175 *those Dogs.* That is, Christian prisoners.

245 *at Fez.* According to Pérez de Hita (Pérez, I, 20; Rodd, p. 29), the noble family of Almanzores came from Fez.

246 *Xeriff.* The ruling house of Morocco.

275 *precarious.* Supplicating. *OED* cites this line.

298 *Rodriques death.* Roderic, king of the Visigoths, was killed in battle in 711, leaving the Moors triumphant in Spain.

309–333 For seventeenth-century debate over the obligations of ransomed prisoners of war, see, e.g., Hobbes, *Leviathan*, I, xiv. Pérez de Hita recounts that some of the Moors chose Boabdil king and that he and his father, Muley-hascem, reigned jointly in Granada (Pérez, I, 16–17; Rodd, pp. 22–23). Relatives of the queen of Granada persuade Muley-hascem to appoint his brother, Abdallah, governor of Granada (Pérez, I, 199–200; Rodd, pp. 264–268). In battle with the Christians, Boabdil is taken prisoner and presented to Ferdinand. He is freed after swearing fealty to Ferdinand (Pérez, I, 259–260; Rodd, pp. 340–341). He agrees that once Ferdinand has conquered certain cities and towns, Boabdil will surrender the "city of Granada, the Alhambra, the Alcazaba, the Albaycin, the Red Towers, and the Castle of Bibatambin, and other forts of the city." In return he would be given Purchena and three other towns (Pérez, I, 275; Rodd, p. 363). In a war against his uncle Abdallah, Boabdil appeals to Ferdinand for help and receives it (Pérez, I, 267–268; Rodd, pp. 352–353). Ferdinand demands the surrender of Granada. Boabdil refuses (Pérez, I, 275–276; Rodd, pp. 363–364).

357+ *s.d. Esperanza.* In both Pérez de Hita and *Almahide,* the character appears as slave or servant to the queen. Anne Reeves, who acted the part in *The Conquest of Granada,* was reputed to be the mistress of Dryden. Cf. commentary on the actors, p. 547 below, and the frontispiece to this volume. According to the *Key to The Rehearsal* she acted the part of Amaryllis in

Buckingham's play. In the third edition Bayes is made to say that the actress
playing this part is his mistress and that he has already talked bawdy to her
(*The Rehearsal*, I, i; 1675, p. 6):

> *Johns.* Hast thou, faith? Pr'ythee how was that?
>
> *Bayes.* Why, Sir, there is, in the French Tongue, a cer-
> tain Criticism, which, by the variation of the Masculine
> Adjective instead of the Fœminine, makes a quite differ-
> ent signification of the word: as, for example, *Ma vie* is
> my life; but if, before *vie* you put *Mon* instead of *Ma*, you
> make it bawdy.
>
> *Johns.* Very true.
>
> *Bayes.* Now, Sir, I, having observed this, set a Trap for
> her, the other day in the Tyring-Room; for this said I,
> *Adieu bel Esperansa de mavie;* (which I gad is very pretty)
> to which she answer'd, I vow, almost as prettily, every jot;
> for said she, *Songes a mavie Mounsieur;* whereupon I
> presently snapt this upon her; *Non, non, Madam—Songes
> vous a mon,* by gad, and nam'd the thing directly to her.

361 *Zambra.* In *Almahide* (trans. John Phillips [1677], Pt. II, Bk. I, p. 46)
we read that at a sumptuous court entertainment "they began a grave and
serious Dance, which the Moors call Zambra, and which is something like
our first Branles, for they go round as in them, and with a soft and measured Cadence, which did not much busie the Body nor the Mind, but
left the last free enough to hold a certain kind of Conversation, whilst they
danc'd, with those they held by either hand."

II, i

29 *tale.* Count. *by the great.* "In the mass" (*OED*, which cites this line).

39–40 At the time of the action of the play, Columbus, of course, had not
set off on his first voyage, but he had been in Spain for some years trying
to get support from Ferdinand and Isabella.

77 *Ponce Leon's.* In *Almahide,* Ponce de Leon is a brave young warrior
in love with Almahide.

78 *our Triumphs.* That is, from victories over us.

180 *Amber chaf't.* A quality of amber, long known, is that it takes on an
electrical charge when rubbed.

227 *distributive.* "Distributive justice, one of the two divisions of Justice,
according to Aristotle (the other being COMMUTATIVE); that which consists
in the distribution of something in shares proportionate to the deserts of
each among the several parties" (*OED*).

231 *Man makes his fate.* As a Mohammedan, Zulema is being heterodox,
since his religion stressed determinism.

273 *fabrick.* That is, contrivance, edifice.

III, i

78–81 Brower ("Dryden's Epic Manner and Virgil," p. 473) compares the
dream simile to *Aeneid*, XII, 908–913. Dryden trans. (*Aeneis*, XII, 1312–
1318):

> And as, when heavy Sleep has clos'd the sight,
> The sickly Fancy labours in the Night:

> We seem to run; and destitute of Force
> Our sinking Limbs forsake us in the Course:
> In vain we heave for Breath; in vain we cry:
> The Nerves unbrac'd, their usual Strength deny;
> And, on the Tongue the falt'ring Accents dye.

89 Summers notes Horace, *Carmina*, I, v, 9: *qui nunc te fruitur credulus aurea* (Loeb trans.; "who now enjoys thee, fondly thinking thee all golden").

90–92 Cf. *Absalom and Achitophel*, ll. 198–199 (*Works*, II, 11):

> But wilde Ambition loves to slide, not stand;
> And Fortunes Ice prefers to Vertues Land.

197+ *Song.* Elkanah Settle (*Notes and Observations on the Empress of Morocco Revised* [1674], p. 4) comments ironically on the "Song":

> After such a plentiful treat of rank Bawdy, of Alma-hides preparing, I need not describe her Character. But perhaps Mr. Dryden will answer that a woman of her Quality might keep a Laureat, and the Bawdy entertain-ment was her Poets fault; or else he may tell us, that he wrote this to please the Age, who are best delighted with languishing Songs in this Style: And therefore the making a Woman of Honour, or a Jilt in a Comedy, talk Bawdy, or take pleasure in hearing it, is all alike to him.

232+ s.d. *The Zambra Dance.* See note to I, i, 361.

263–264 In Ovid, *Heroides*, XIX, 151–152, Hero writes that her lamp sputters, and she takes this as a favorable sign. But according to the myth, the lamp she was wont to light as a guide is blown out on the night that Leander drowns.

265–267 Cf. H. R. Patch, *The Goddess Fortuna in Mediaeval Literature* (1927), p. 59: "As Fortuna is very much at home at court, so she deals par-ticularly in royal favors, bestowing kingship, empire, and crown, and taking them back at will."

329 *Tarantula.* The bite of the tarantula was thought to produce strange effects in the victim. *OED* quotes, for example, Hoby's *Castiglione's Court-yer:* "Them that are bitten with a Tarrantula. . . . A kind of spiders, which being divers of nature cause divers effectes, some after their biting fal a singing, some laugh."

336–337 For the various symptoms of love, see *The Anatomy of Melan-choly*, III, ii, 3. Burton concludes "there is no end of love's symptoms, 'tis a bottomless pit."

402–403 The inverted commas before each line of this hexameter couplet in the first edition could signify one of three things: (1) a quotation; if so, its source has eluded the present editors; (2) lines omitted in the acting version; cf. the statement to the reader in the 1676 quarto of *Hamlet:*

> This Play being too long to be conveniently Acted, such places as might be least prejudicial to the Plot or Sense, are left out upon the Stage: but that we may no way wrong the incomparable Author, are here inserted according to the Original Copy with this Mark " [quoted by James G. McManaway, "The Two Earliest Prompt Books of *Hamlet*," *Papers of the Bibliographical Society of America*, XLIII (1949), 289].

(3) a *sententia;* see G. K. Hunter, "The Marking of *Sententiae* in Elizabethan Printed Plays, Poems, and Romances," *The Library,* 5th ser., VI (1951), 171–188. Hunter notes, however, that "the practice" of marking *sententiae* "seems to disappear" after 1660.

458 *five tall tow'rs.* Summers, citing Pérez de Hita, lists the Red Tower, the Alhambra, the Albaycin, the towers of the Elvira Gate, and the towers of Azeytuno.

IV, i

14 *in volumes.* That is, in convolutions.

31 *hairy front.* Fortune was sometimes depicted as having long hair that hung over her mouth (cf. Patch, *Goddess Fortuna,* p. 43). Geoffrey Whitney, *A Choice of Emblems* (1586), p. 181, has a cut of Occasion, i.e., Fortune, with a razor in one hand, with long hair streaming ahead of her, and with wings on her feet. The interpretive verses read:

> Why doest thou houlde a rasor in thy hande?
> *That men maie knowe I cut on everie side,*
> *And when I come, I armies can devide.*

> But wherefore hast thou winges uppon thy feete?
> *To showe, how lighte I flie with little winde.*
> What meanes longe lockes before? *that suche as meete,*
> *Maye houlde at firste, when they occasion finde.*
>   Thy head behinde all balde, what telles it more?
>   *That none shoulde houlde, that let me slippe before.*

33 *white.* Auspicious. Cf. *Astraea Redux,* l. 292 (*Works,* I, 30, 233).

66 *Age sets to fortune.* Noyes, *Selected Dramas,* noting that *sets to* means to gamble with, calls attention to ll. 53–54 of the second prologue to *Secret Love* (*Works,* IX, 121):

> Then, for his sake, ne're stint your own delight;
> Throw boldly, for he sets to all that write.

Noyes continues: "So the purport of this somewhat obscure passage seems to be: 'Age gambles (methodically) against fortune, while youth risks all on one bold throw.' "

IV, ii

52 *advise.* Consider.

54 *Exposition.* Interpretation.

418–425 Noyes, *Selected Dramas,* notes that a passage in *The Rehearsal* (IV, i; 1675, p. 41), which parodies a speech by Berenice in *Tyrannick Love,* also seems to glance at this speech of Almanzor. The passage begins:

> Since death my earthly part will thus remove
>   I'l come a Humble Bee to your chaste love.

430 *equal.* Impartial.

V, i

134 *chain-shot.* "A kind of shot formed of two balls, or half-balls, connected by a chain, chiefly used in naval warfare to destroy masts, rigging, and sails" (*OED*).

155 *retrenchment.* "An inner line of defence within a large work" (*OED*).

278–279 These lines seem to be parodied in *The Rehearsal*, IV, i (1675, p. 44):

> You shall not know how long I here will stay;
> But you shall know I'l take your Bowles away.

293–294 The lines are parodied in *The Rehearsal*, IV, i (1675, p. 44):

> Who e'er to gulp one drop of this dares think
> I'l stare away his very pow'r to drink.

298–304 This passage is also parodied in *The Rehearsal*, II, iii (1675, p. 18):

> As some tall Pine, which we, on Ætna, find
> T' have stood the rage of many a boist'rous wind,
> Feeling without, that flames within do play,
> Which would consume his Root and Sap away;
> He spreads his woorsted Arms unto the Skies,
> Silently grieves, all pale, repines and dies:
> So, shrowded up, your bright eye disappears.
> Break forth, bright scorching Sun, and dry my tears.

In *The Censure of the Rota* (1673), p. 7, Richard Leigh comments on Dryden's simile: "This Tulip that could hear the wind sing its Epicedium, after it was dead; you may be sure grew no where but in a Poets Garden."

437–440 Dryden seems to recall the Great Fire of London. In *Annus Mirabilis*, st. 295, a greater London rising from its ashes is envisioned (*Works*, I, 103):

> More great then humane, now, and more *August*,
>   New deifi'd she from her fires does rise:
> Her widening streets on new foundations trust,
>   And, opening, into larger parts she flies.

443 *stock.* Capital.

EPILOGUE

G. Thorn-Drury ("Some Notes on Dryden," *RES*, I [1925], 325) first called attention to a manuscript compiled by Sir William Haward containing a transcript of this epilogue. Haward states that it was spoken by Charles Hart, and he notes that ll. 23–24, 31–32, and 35–36 were "not spoke."

19 *When forty comes.* Dryden was thirty-nine when the play was first performed.

25 *for this years delay.* In late June 1669, *Tyrannick Love*, which preceded *The Conquest of Granada*, had been produced.

32 *nine whole Mon'ths are lost.* Nell Gwyn gave birth to her first child by Charles II in May 1670. Presumably other actresses were also incapacitated during the time to which the epilogue refers. In the Haward manuscript, *were* is substituted for *are* in this line.

Conquest of Granada, The Second Part

TITLE PAGE

Epigraph. *The Civil War*, I, 120 (Vying with excellence gave the spur). Perhaps as Noyes, *Selected Dramas*, notes, Dryden refers to his effort to surpass the first part of the play; or he may be referring to the several rivalries of his characters.

PROLOGUE

The Haward manuscript (see Textual Headnote, p. 564 below) says that the prologue was spoken by Michael Mohun and that it has four additional lines after l. 10. For the lines, see textual footnotes. Kinsley notes that this prologue may glance at the Buckingham circle and *The Rehearsal*.

10 *As Scriv'ners.* Scriveners were moneylenders and were often chided for sharp practices. Cf. Dryden's translation of the second epode of Horace, ll. 1–5 (*Works*, III, 85):

> How happy in his low degree
> How rich in humble Poverty, is he,
> Who leads a quiet country life!
> Discharg'd of business, void of strife,
> And from the gripeing Scrivener free.

13 *Vizard Masque.* Cf. prologue to *Marriage A-la-Mode*, l. 4n.

15–16 Combing the hair in public was the mark of a fop. Summers quotes an anonymous prologue of the time (*Covent Garden Drollery*, ed. Summers [1927], p. 26):

> He who comes hither with design to hiss,
> And with a bum revers'd, to whisper Miss,
> To comb a Perriwig, or to shew gay cloathes,
> Our Poet welcomes as the Muses friend,
> For hee'l by irony each Play commend.

Prologues and epilogues of the period constantly castigate the behavior of the gallants in the pit. See Van Lennep, p. clxviii.

I, i

5–16 Dryden has Ferdinand voice the Greco-Roman cyclic theory of history. See, for example, Polybius, *Histories*, VI, 9, 10. For the Christian view of the linear nature of history, see C. A. Patrides, *The Phoenix and the Ladder: The Rise and Decline of the Christian View of History*, University of California Publications: English Studies, no. 29 (1964).

17–21 Columbus was present at the surrender of Granada on 2 January 1492. For the theory of the growth of precious metals, see *Annus Mirabilis*, st. 139 and note (*Works*, I, 80, 296).

53 *tertia.* "A division of infantry" (*OED*, which cites this line).

78 *shock.* "The encounter of two mounted warriors or jousters charging one another" (*OED*).

132 Isabella was of Castile and Ferdinand of Aragon. Their marriage, of course, united the two kingdoms.

I, ii

21 This line and ll. 76–77 are parodied, rather feebly, in *The Rehearsal*, V, i (1675, pp. 51–52):

> *1 King.* What dreadful noise is this that comes and goes?
> *Enter a Souldier with his Sword drawn.*

Sould. Haste hence, great Sirs, your Royal persons save,
For the event of war no mortal knowes:
The Army, wrangling for the gold you gave,
First fell to words and then to handy-blows.

31–34 Boabdelin's complaint suggests that of Charles II in his attempts to get funds for the second Dutch war. See, for example, his speeches to Parliament on 18 January and 8 February 1667 (*The Letters, Speeches and Declarations of King Charles II*, ed. Arthur Bryant [1935], pp. 198–200).

45 *Propriety.* Property.

128–133 The speech is parodied in *The Rehearsal*, I, i (1675, p. 10):

So Boar and Sow, when any storm is nigh,
Snuff up, and smell it gath'ring in the Sky;
Boar beckons Sow to trot in Chestnut Groves,
And there consummate their unfinish'd Loves:
Pensive in mud they wallow all alone,
And snore and gruntle to each others moan.

In the second edition Dryden inserted the Latin quotation (And alone they sit on the edge of the banks. Arcadians alone sing skilfully), presumably as a justification of his simile. As Noyes pointed out, the second sentence is from *Eclogues*, X, 32–33. The first is not in Virgil.

132 *dropping.* Dripping.

212 *rakes up.* That is, covers up, as embers are covered by ashes.

II, i

16–17 For an account of the Roman elders sitting in their robes of state and calmly awaiting death by the conquering Gauls, see Livy, V, xli. Cf. *Annus Mirabilis*, ll. 251–252.

II, ii

17 *Hyæna.* The hyena was a synonym for a rapacious and deceitful person. Edward Topsell (*The History of Four-footed Beasts and Serpents* [1658], p. 341) reports one of its fabled techniques in luring man to destruction:

> They are great enemies to men, and for this cause Solinus reporteth of them, that by secret accustoming themselves to houses or yards, where Carpenters or such Mechanicks work, they learn to call their names, and so will come being an hungred and call one of them with a distinct and articulate voice, whereby he causeth the man many times to forsake his work and go to see the person calling him; but the subtile Hyæna goeth further off, and so by calling allureth him from help of company, and afterward when she seeth time devoureth him, and for this cause her proper Epithet is *Æmula vocis*, Voyce-counterfeiter.

28 *shelf.* "A sandbank in the sea or river rendering the water shallow and dangerous" (*OED*).

49 *Letts.* Hindrances.

59 *Alferez.* Ensign.

II, iii

3–4 Cf. *Iliad*, IX, 307–429.

27 *Demon.* Attendant spirit.

31 *Cestos.* The cestus, or girdle of Venus, which provoked love in all who looked upon it, both men and gods.

39 As Noyes, *Selected Dramas*, observed, Leigh (*Censure of the Rota*, p. 5) chides Dryden for using a form here which he finds false in Jonson: "Thus the using *be* for *are* the vice of those dull times, when Conversation was so low, that our Fathers were not taught to write and read good English, was frequent with Mr. Dryden in this politer Age." See *Defence of the Epilogue* (210:14–18 above).

80 *Calenture.* Feverish, burning passion. "A disease incident to sailors within the tropics, characterized by delirium in which the patient, it is said, fancies the sea to be green fields, and desires to leap into it" (*OED*).

105–106 These lines are parodied in *The Rehearsal*, IV, i (1675, p. 44):
> *Draw.* I drink I huff, I strut, look big and stare;
> And all this I can do, because I dare.

Possunt quia etc. *Aeneid*, V, 231. (Loeb trans.: "Strong are they, for strong they deem themselves.") Dryden added the quotation in the second edition, again apparently trying to justify the rant.

III, i

13–14 Editors have taken the figure to refer to stage scenery. It seems more likely that it is drawn from a commonplace of art criticism. See *Notes and Observations* (*Works*, XVII, 182, 410).

97 *Metals grow.* Cf. I, i, 17–21 and n.

144–145 In the *Aeneid*, X, 479–500, Turnus kills Pallas and takes his belt. At the end of the poem (XII, 919–952) Aeneas wounds Turnus and is tempted to spare him. But when he sees that Turnus is wearing the belt of Pallas, he dispatches him.

187 *Vermillion tow'rs.* See note to *1 Conquest of Granada*, I, i, 309–333.

198 *gross.* Main.

199 *dead.* Unbroken (*OED*, citing this line).

III, iii

127–129 The simile perhaps refers to taking the mineral waters. Dr. Lewis Rouse (*Tunbridge Wells: or a Directory for the Drinking of Those Waters* [1725], p. 6) writes that the waters "are of excellent Use for all Diseases which have their dependency upon Obstructions, as all long and tedious Agues." Warm baths were also sometimes prescribed for a quartan ague. See, for example, Nicholas Culpeper et al., *The Practice of Physick* (1655), p. 589.

IV, ii

58–60 The departure of the swallows before winter was often observed, but their abode in winter was conjectural. See *The Hind and the Panther*, III, 427–444, 450–452 and notes (*Works*, III, 173–174, 422–423).

66–67 For the concept of comets portending the fate of kings, see *Annus*

Mirabilis, ll. 69–72 and note (*Works,* I, 62, 281–282). Summers cites *Julius Caesar,* II, ii, 30–31.

> When beggars die, there are no comets seen;
> The heavens themselves blaze forth the death of princes.

102 *would shoot.* That is, would send forth shoots.

IV, iii

22 *Circle.* " 'An assembly surrounding the principal person' (J.), as at Court" (*OED*).

87 *grudging.* The *OED* defines *grudge* and marks it as rare in this sense: "To chatter with the teeth (? as in ague)."

95–284 Noyes, *Selected Dramas,* following Bishop Percy, notes that *The Rehearsal,* IV, i (1675, p. 43), seems to glance at parts of this passage.

138–142 *Mountains of the Moon . . . prepar'd for light.* For the moon as the abode of the blessed, cf. *Paradise Lost,* III, 460–462:

> Those argent Fields more likely habitants,
> Translated Saints, or middle Spirits hold
> Betwixt th' Angelical and Human kind.

140 *secret bed of Nyle.* Ptolemy (*Geographia,* 1.9.3–4) cited a traveler who had reported from East Africa that the inland Mountains of the Moon were the source of the Nile. Dryden apparently conflated the lunar mountains with the terrestrial.

157–158 This speech is parodied in *The Rehearsal,* IV, i (1675, p. 43):

> *Draw.* He that dares drink, and for that drink dares dye,
> And, knowing this, dares yet drink on, am I.

168 *pure Elements.* According to philosophers of the old science, the four elements are never found in a pure state. The pure element is simply a hypothesis, a product of man's mind. (See Lynn Thorndike, *A History of Magic and Experimental Science,* II [1929], 34, 53, 175.) So also, Almanzor implies, is pure love.

170 *Angels . . . Nourishment.* Dryden reflects the traditional opinion that angels were pure spirits without any matter or body, hence needed no nourishment and indeed could not truly eat because they were unable to convert food to their own substance (see Robert H. West, *Milton and the Angels* [1955], pp. 45–46, 56). In the well-known passage of *Paradise Lost* (V, 415 ff.), Milton expressly repudiates this doctrine.

279 *Image-like.* "The reference seems to be to the excuse for image-worship,—that the images are not intended to be directly adored, but merely to fix and stimulate the devotion of the worshipper" (Saintsbury).

363 *Monster.* Cuckold.

380 *two witnesses.* In English law two witnesses were required in a case of treason. Furthermore, "violating the Queen Consort is High Treason, and her yielding and consenting to it is Treason" (Giles Jacob, *A New Law-Dictionary,* 7th ed. [1756], under "Treason").

381 *Is cast.* Found guilty.

V, i

37 *Dar'd.* The *OED* gives, "*To dare larks,* to fascinate and daze them, in order to catch them."

38 *cuffd.* Buffeted with wings (*OED*).

V, ii

20+ *s.d. Enter . . . Alabez*. Although Alabez does not appear in the list of "Persons Represented," it is not uncommon to find a minor character omitted in this way.

44 *appeach*. Accuse.

V, iii

35 *Fabrique*. Edifice.

50 *frank*. Lavish.

79 *Sink . . . at last*. This line reads like the second line of a couplet, the first of which may have been lost in composition, thus accounting for the slight break in sense between lines 78 and 79.

125–126 For the fable of the wren riding on the eagle's back and thus winning the race in the sky, see *Babrius and Phaedrus*, ed. and trans. Ben Edwin Perry (1965), p. 508.

241–243 Bajazet, Turkish emperor, was conquered by Tamburlaine. In Marlowe's play, Tamburlaine sits on Bajazet, cages him, and taunts him. Bajazet dashes his brains out against his cage.

EPILOGUE

3 *Mechanique*. Vulgar, low.

6 Cob is a water-bearer in *Every Man in his Humour*. Otter is a "land, sea-Captaine" in *Epicoene*.

11–16 A metaphor from shopkeeping using some words in special senses —*pass* for "pass current, be acceptable coin," *grains* for either the "smallest units of weight" or "small particles of gold," *for weight* for "to make up weight"—and alluding in the final phrase to the practice of selling some commodities by weighing them in a balance against coin. The lines may be paraphrased as follows: "Fame could then be purchased for a small outlay of talent; so the first customers bought it up and took it with them to their graves. But if they tried to purchase fame nowadays from critics who weigh so precisely what authors offer in return, then not even Jonson's drama at its best could pass current without our granting it some small additional worth to make up the weight of his own coin." Even at its best, then, Jonson's drama fails, if narrowly, to meet Restoration standards.

DEFENCE OF THE EPILOGUE

203:1 *The promises of Authors*. In the preface to *An Evening's Love* (published in 1671, three years after the play was first performed), Dryden wrote that he had thought to have written something "*concerning the difference betwixt the Playes of our Age, and those of our Predecessors on the English Stage: to have shewn in what parts of Dramatick Poesie we were excell'd by* Ben. Johnson, *I mean, humour, and contrivance of Comedy; and in what we may justly claim precedence of* Shakespear *and* Fletcher, *namely in Heroick Playes: but this design I have wav'd on second considerations; at least deferr'd it till I publish the* Conquest of Granada, *where the discourse will be more proper*" (*Works*, X, 202).

203:19 *Age, so Sceptical.* For comment on Dryden and skepticism, see *Works,* II, 345–346; IX, 322.

203:25 *Ingeniis non ille favet* etc. Horace, *Epistles,* II, i, 88–89 (Loeb trans.: "that man does not favour and applaud the genius of the dead, but assails ours to-day, spitefully hating us and everything of ours").

204:4 *lutulentum fluere.* See Horace, *Satires,* I, x, 50.

204:9 *Si foret hoc nostrum* etc. *Satires,* I, x, 68–70 (Loeb trans.: "had he fallen by fate upon this our day, he would smooth away much of his work, would prune off all that trailed beyond the proper limit"). Dryden substitutes *detraheret* ("would remove") in the second line for *detereret* ("would rub away"), probably by memorial contamination from *traheretur* in the third line.

204:13 *Epistle to Augustus.* That is, *Epistles,* II, i.

204:19–20 *Language, Wit, and Conversation . . . are improv'd* etc. Dryden, of course, had made the same assertion in ll. 23–26 of the epilogue. See also the dedication of *Marriage A-la-Mode,* 233:28–29.

205:9 *Petronius.* The *Satyricon* opens with a speech on the decline of eloquence.

205:10 *famous Dialogue.* In the prooemium to Bk. VI of the *Institutio Oratoria,* Quintilian wrote: *Nam ita forte accidit, ut eum quoque librum, quem de causis corruptae eloquentiae emisi, iam scribere aggressus ictu simili ferirer* (Loeb trans.: "For it so chances that just at the moment when I began my book on the causes of the decline of eloquence, I was stricken by a like affliction"). Nothing remains of the book here referred to. Ker noted that the *Dialogus* of Tacitus was at times ascribed to Quintilian. Dryden assumes that the *Dialogus* is the work referred to by Quintilian in the sentence quoted above; the burden of it is indeed the decline of Roman oratory.

205:12 *our Language is improv'd.* In Dryden's time it was a commonplace to assert that the language had been refined over that of the preceding age. See James Sutherland, *English Literature of the Late Seventeenth Century* (1969), p. 407.

205:34 *Solecism of Speech.* On this passage Malone (I, ii, 232) sagely observed: "These *notorious flaws in sense,* I conceive, will be found only by those who are not well acquainted with the phraseology of Shakespeare's time, as undoubtedly our author was not when he wrote this piece."

206:3 *Neque ego* etc. Horace, *Satires,* I, x, 48–49 (Loeb trans.: "Nor would I dare to wrest from him the crown that clings to his brow with so much glory"). Editors have noted that Dryden has *illis* for *ille.*

206:19 *Decorum of the Stage.* The statements that follow imply a concept of decorum that was to be developed in detail a few years later by Rymer.

207:9 *content with Acorns* etc. Cf. Tilley, A21: "Acorns were good till bread was found."

207:10 Ἅλις δρυός. Enough of oak. Ker noted Cicero's use of the term in *Ad Atticum,* II, xix. The Loeb translator comments in a note: "A proverb alluding to a supposed acorn diet in the days before the use of corn was discovered."

207:26 *Cædimus* etc. Persius, IV, 42. Dryden trans. (ll. 99–100; see *Works,* IV, 319):

> Thus others we with Defamations wound,
> While they stab us; and so the Jest goes round.

207:27–28 *three or four first pages.* The first three quotations are from *Catiline*, I, 25–27, 32–36, 59–60. In l. 183, *gain'd* has been substituted for Jonson's *got*.

208:4–5 *Macbeth . . . that it was horrour.* Dryden is probably recalling oral tradition about Jonson's pronouncements. However, Herford and Simpson (*Ben Jonson*, II, 56), suggest that the stylistic extravagancies of *Lear* and *Macbeth* may have been in Jonson's mind when he wrote in the preface to *Volpone* about the contemporary stage as having "such plenty of solœcismes, such dearth of sense, so bold prolepse's, so rackt metaphors, with brothelry, able to violate the eare of a pagan, and blasphemy, to turn the bloud of a christian to water" (V, 19).

208:16–17 *Tully so much complains.* "Cicero discusses the placing of words in *Orator*, c. 44 *sqq.*; σύγχυσις is not found in this context, but is used in his letters, e.g., σύγχυσιν litterularum, *Att.* vi.9" (Ker). The reference to *Orator* is to Bk. III.

208:18–19 *The Waves* etc. *Catiline*, I, 250–251. For *Waves* read *mawes* in Jonson.

208:22–24 *Catiline*, I, 49, 51–52. Jonson's l. 50, "(Brought forth by night, with a sinister birth)," is omitted. For *Plague* read *Plagues* in Jonson.

209:4–6 *Catiline*, I, 143–145.

209:13–15 *Catiline*, I, 146–148. For *pulls* read *puts* in Jonson.

209:18–20 Lines 18–19 are in *Catiline*, IV, 530–531, not near the preceding passage, as Dryden says. Line 20 does not belong to the passage as quoted. It is in IV, 56.

209:22–23 *Catiline*, IV, 30, 32. Dryden omits l. 31 and part of l. 32.

210:1 *Catiline*, IV, 302.

210:8–9 *Catiline*, IV, 122–123. Jonson's first line reads *bred in's fathers.*

210:14–17 *Catiline*, I, 587–590. For *thou art cruelly* read *art thou cru'lly* in Jonson; for *Vertues* read *vertue.*

211:3 *Contain your Spirit* etc. Line 46 of the induction to *Every Man Out of his Humour.*

211:18 *Quem penes* etc. *Art of Poetry*, l. 72 (Loeb trans.: "in whose hands lies the judgement, the right and the rule of speech").

211:30 *Aurum ex* etc. "Gather gold from dung" (Noyes).

212:6–7 *Dixeris* etc. *Art of Poetry*, ll. 47–48 (Loeb trans.: "you will express yourself most happily, if a skilful setting makes a familiar word new").

212:12–13 *Et vultus* etc. *Odes*, I, xix, 8 (Loeb trans.: "and her face seductive to behold").

212:17–18 *Petronius says* etc. *Satyricon*, 118 (Loeb trans.: "and the studied felicity of Horace").

212:33 *Wit according to the Dignity of the Subject.* Several years later, in *The Authors Apology for Heroique Poetry; and Poetique Licence*, Dryden was to define wit as "*a propriety of Thoughts and Words; or in other terms, Thought and Words, elegantly adapted to the Subject*" (*The State of Innocence* [1677], sig. c2v; Watson, I, 207). It is the impropriety of some of Shakespeare to which he objects here. In the preface to *An Evening's Love* (*Works*, X, 206), he had written of the "*ornaments of wit*" and, though he makes no mention of them in the paragraph under consideration, he presumably wished that Shakespeare had made more use of them.

213:15–16 *I will not contest farther.* In the same preface (*Works,* X, 205), Dryden had argued that Jonson's representation of folly on the stage is the result of observation, which in turn is based on judgment. But these representations are not properly wit. Now he takes a more conciliatory stand in reply to Jonson's admirers.

214:1–5 Induction to *Every Man Out of his Humour,* ll. 177–181.

214:7–9 *Ibid.,* ll. 322–325. For *you'd* read *you'ld* in Jonson.

214:11 From *Every Man Out of his Humour,* IV, iv, 14–15. In the following two lines, Dryden implies that the second speech is spoken by the character Macilente. In fact, it as well as the third speech is spoken by Carlo Buffone.

214:15 *Fine Grand.* Epigram LXXIII.

214:24–25 *the benefit of its Clergy.* For the Restoration reaction against witty, outlandish preaching, see W. F. Mitchell, *English Pulpit Oratory from Andrewes to Tillotson* (1932), pp. 308 ff.

214:26 *a famous Italian.* Ker attempted to identify the author and work, but without success, and we have fared no better. For continental attacks on strained pulpit oratory in the seventeenth century, see Spingarn, I, xxxvi–xlv.

215:22 *Fletcher's Don John.* Don John is a witty character in *The Chances,* a play that the Duke of Buckingham altered, particularly, as Dryden says, in the last two acts. Pepys saw a performance (presumably the altered version) on 5 February 1667 and liked it very much.

216:14 *Apollo.* Upper room of the Old Devil tavern where Jonson and the Sons of Ben met.

216:23–24 *conversation . . . so much refin'd.* John Wilmot, Earl of Rochester, altered *Valentinian,* another play by Fletcher. In his preface to the printed version (1685), Robert Wolseley also commented on the refined language of gentlemen and of the court (Spingarn, III, 2–3): "it must be also confess'd that my Lord's [Rochester's] constant living at Court, and the Conversation of Persons of Quality, to which from his greenest Youth both his Birth and his Choice had accustom'd him, gave him some great Advantages above this so much and so justly applauded Author [Fletcher], ————I mean a nicer knowledge both of Men and Manners, an Air of good Breeding, and a Gentleman-like easiness in all he writ, to which Fletcher's obscure Education and the mean Company he kept had made him wholly a Stranger."

For further comment on the "Conversation of Gentlemen" in comedy, see Gunnar Sorelius, '*The Giant Race before the Flood': Pre-Restoration Drama on the Stage and in the Criticism of the Restoration* (1966), pp. 100–104.

217:27 *humour.* Sorelius (*'The Giant Race before the Flood,'* p. 105) observed: "Dryden sees the concept of humour not primarily as a manner of classifying human characters but as a way of achieving individuality with no sacrifice of dramatic effectiveness; it was one of the means by which English comedy was able to sustain diversity."

218:1 *Cob and Tib.* Characters in *Every Man in his Humour.*

Marriage A-la-Mode

In the graceful dedication of *Marriage A-la-Mode,* Dryden asks the Earl of Rochester, who read the play "before it was Acted," to remember "with how much favour to the Authour, and indulgence to the Play, you commended it to the view of His Majesty, then at *Windsor.*" The King, in turn, "by His Approbation of it in Writing, made way for its kind reception on the Theatre."[1] One might infer that the manuscript must therefore have been completed before Charles left Windsor on 13 July 1671 after a seven weeks' stay to return to Whitehall by way of Plymouth.[2] The play, preceded by such royal favor, would almost surely have received its first performance sometime, probably early, in the following theatrical season.[3] There is, however, no certain record of performance earlier than April 1674—some ten months after publication of the first edition[4]—and commentators, forced to speculate, have usually dated the first performance April or May 1672,[5] principally because the prologue alludes to preparations for the third Anglo-Dutch war, which was declared on 17 March 1672. But recently assembled evidence reinforces the argument for a first performance early rather than late in the theatrical season of 1671–72, most likely late in November or very early in December of 1671.[6] The play belonged to the King's Company, which performed in the Bridges Street Theatre, Drury Lane, until its destruction by fire on 25 January 1672, and then, after a hiatus of one month, completed the season in the Duke's old house in Lincoln's Inn Fields.[7]

The prologue's allusions to preparations for war—"*all our Braves and all*

---

[1] See 221:1–10 above.

[2] Charles went to Windsor on 26 May 1671, and his unusually lengthy sojourn there is thoroughly documented in *CSPD,* the *London Gazette,* and the *Bulstrode Papers* (see esp. I, 195–196). Buckingham's *The Rehearsal,* III, ii (1672, p. 28), likewise takes notice of the King's summer visit.

[3] See Charles Eugene Ward, "The Dates of Two Dryden Plays," *PMLA,* LI (1936), 786–788.

[4] See headnote to *The Assignation,* p. 519 below, for dates of the first edition's registration and advertisement.

[5] Malone (I, i, 106–107) assigns the date of the first performance to May 1672, as does G. Thorn-Drury in his edition of *Covent Garden Drollery* (1928), p. 116. Summers suggests a première about Easter 1672, and Nicoll (pp. 404–405), while believing an autumn date possible and speculating that the prologue may have been written for a later performance, concludes that *Marriage A-la-Mode* was acted "before the beginning of June 1672." Van Lennep (p. 194) places the play tentatively in April 1672.

[6] See Robert D. Hume, "The Date of Dryden's *Marriage A-la-Mode,*" *HLB,* XXI (1973), 161–166.

[7] See Van Lennep, p. 193. For information and conjecture on the plan and appearance of the Theatre Royal, Bridges Street, see Edward A. Langhans, "Pictorial Material on the Bridges Street and Drury Lane Theatres," *Theatre Survey,* VII (1966), 80–100; and Donald C. Mullin, "The Theatre Royal, Bridges Street: A Conjectural Restoration," *Educational Theatre Journal,* XIX (1967), 17–29.

our Wits are gone. . . . France, *and the Fleet, have swept the Town so clear"*
—find support in the official documentation of late 1671 as well as early
1672, and we know from state papers that English troops were already moving to France by mid-November 1671.[8] The *London Gazette*, we can add,
announced on 6 January 1672 that "His Majesty . . . . had already given
Orders, for the fitting and preparing a very considerable Fleet, to be ready
against the Spring."[9] And early in December Sir Richard Bulstrode, while
noting reports of continental activity between the two chief antagonists—
"In Holland they rayse men as fast as they doe in France"—also alludes to
diplomatic and military reverberations at home: "the Dutch Amb^r here
says he has orders to returne speedily home, and is therefore makeing prepa-
rac̃ons accordingly," and "it's said his Ma^{ty} will have a considerable fleet at
sea this next spring."[10] In addition to the notices in governmental papers,
the martial arrangements remarked upon in the prologue find close theatrical parallels in the prologues to John Crowne's *The History of Charles the
Eighth of France* and the Duke of Buckingham's *The Rehearsal* (as well as
in its text)[11] and in the epilogue to William Wycherley's *The Gentleman
Dancing Master*.[12] Crowne's play was probably performed by the end of
November 1671;[13] *The Rehearsal* was certainly on the stage by 14 December
and probably a week earlier;[14] and while the first definitely recorded performance of *The Gentleman Dancing Master* dates to early February 1672,
its prologue, "To the CITY, Newly after the Removal of the Dukes Company
from *Lincoln-Inn-fields* to their new Theatre," strongly indicates a premiere
some two months earlier. The Duke's "new Theatre" with its greater convenience to the City[15] to which Wycherley alludes is evidently referred to

---

[8] See esp. *CSPD* for 16 November and 2 and 6 December 1671; quoted in Hume,
"Date of Dryden's *Marriage A-la-Mode*," p. 166.

[9] *London Gazette*, 4–8 January 1671.

[10] *Bulstrode Papers*, I, 210–211 (for 2 and 9 December 1671); see I, 204–216
passim, for other notices of war preparations and troop movements.

[11] The reference to the soldiers' departure in the text of *The Rehearsal*, III, i
(1672, p. 22), comes in Prince Prettyman's boast to Tom Thimble: "Well, Tom,
I hope shortly I shall have another coyn for thee; for now the Wars come on, I
shall grow to be a man of mettal."

[12] Hume ("Date of Dryden's *Marriage A-la-Mode*," pp. 164–166) argues that a
rhetoric of reference both to "the City" and to the departing soldiers, as exempli-
fied by the prologue and epilogue to *The Gentleman Dancing Master*, was especially frequent in the fall of 1671.

[13] See Van Lennep, p. 190. According to Downes (p. 32), "the first new Play
Acted there [Dorset Garden], was King Charles the VIII. of France; it was all new
Cloath'd, yet lasted but 6 Days together."

[14] Macdonald (p. 193) gives the date of the first performance as 7 December 1671,
citing as evidence Anthony à Wood's *Athenae Oxonienses*, IV (1820), 209: "*The
Rehearsal, a Comedy.*—This . . . was first of all acted on the 7th of Dec. 1671."
(This information does not appear in Wood until the 1721 edition [II, 804].) John
Evelyn (III, 599) saw a performance of *The Rehearsal* on 14 December.

[15] Lincoln's Inn Fields, to which the King's Company moved after the Bridges
Street fire, was probably as convenient to the City as the new Dorset Garden
Theatre; the reference in lines 24–25 of the prologue to cits taking their pleasures
nearer home suggests, therefore, that *Marriage A-la-Mode* was first performed at

slightingly by Dryden as well in lines 24–26 of his own prologue. The splendid new playhouse of the Duke's Company in Dorset Garden opened on 9 November 1671,[16] handsomely equipped with machinery for the elaborate spectacles which threatened to outdraw the rival King's Company. The threat, well known in advance, exaggerated even further the ascendancy of the Duke's Company with its stable of younger performers and its responsiveness to popular taste for farce and spectacle.[17] The first play in their new house was Dryden's own much-performed, farcical *Sir Martin Mar-all*,[18] and the King's Company may well have replied with the new comedy that Dryden, their leading playwright and a shareholder, had ready at hand.

The evidence we have, then, certainly makes attractive a dating of the first performance of *Marriage A-la-Mode* toward the end of November 1671. The play was completed and therefore ready to be put into production by the beginning of the season of 1671–72. It was first acted sometime after the opening on 9 November of the Dorset Garden Theatre. And the prologue's reference to gallants going to the wars was at least as topical in November 1671 as it was after the official commencement of the war in March 1672. That is all we certainly know.

The final and most significant consideration in dating the initial performance of *Marriage A-la-Mode*—and the one that remains the most problematical—concerns the relationship between this play and Buckingham's *The Rehearsal*. *The Rehearsal* seems to include in its wide-ranging parody of heroic plays and conventions some details drawn from the heroic plot of *Marriage A-la-Mode* and to satirize in particular the character of Leonidas through the figure of Prince Prettyman. Indeed, two of the four notes that appear marginally in the "Seventh Edition" of *The Rehearsal*, in sections otherwise unchanged from the first edition, state directly the connection between Leonidas and Prettyman.[19] The similarity could, of course, originally have been accidental (each princeling deriving independently from romance and heroic literature and each moving on to his separate fate in opposed literary modes); the connection could have been made after the fact. Here there is no allusion so precise as that of Drawcansir to *The Conquest of Granada*'s Almanzor and the parody of *Marriage A-la-Mode* is in no manner so extensive as that of *The Conquest of Granada*. The difference in focus and intensity would, however, be understandable in terms of dating and mode. If *Marriage A-la-Mode* preceded *The Rehearsal* on the stage, it

---

Bridges Street and not at Lincoln's Inn Fields. See headnote to *The Assignation*, p. 506 below.

[16] The ground for the Duke's new playhouse had been leased since 11 August 1670, and construction must have occupied most of a year (see prologue, ll. 24–27n). John Evelyn, visiting the unfinished structure on 26 June 1671, reported with uncharacteristic enthusiasm (III, 583): "I went home, steping in at the Theater, to see the new Machines for the intended scenes, which were indeede very costly, & magnificent."

[17] The most careful and general commentaries on the rivalry of the two patent companies and their differing theatrical traditions and fortunes are to be found in Van Lennep, pp. xxi ff., and in Hume, pp. 19–31, 233–237, 280–299.

[18] See Van Lennep, p. 189; Downes, p. 31.

[19] II, iii (1701, pp. 12–13).

would have done so by no more than two or three weeks, and with a play so fresh in memory, even a glancing parody—as much a matter of gesture and accent as of text—could be perceived and enjoyed. *The Conquest of Granada*, performed some months before to applause and notice, would have been more familiar in broad outline, supporting—indeed, requiring—a parody at once more general and more specific. Moreover, Dryden's own treatment of Leonidas is itself briefer and less extravagant than that of Almanzor, and the noble plot of *Marriage A-la-Mode* is held in check by its own comic plot; it was therefore less open to full-scale remark and parody, less useful to Buckingham, than was *The Conquest of Granada*. In any event, the fact that all three plays were enacted by the same company, by many of the same players, probably in the same house with shared costumes and scenery, would have constituted an important dimension of *The Rehearsal*'s effectiveness.

The best argument for regarding *The Rehearsal* as a sporadic parody of *Marriage A-la-Mode* depends on three main incidents of plot and character as well as localized tricks of action and language.[20] Centrally, Buckingham seems to create Prince Prettyman as a pastiche of Leonidas in order to criticize the overinvolved plotting, anguish, and dizzying changes of fortune which surround Dryden's prince as arabesques of romantic grandeur. Buckingham's specific attention seems to be caught especially by Leonidas' halting exaltation from lowly fisherman's son to king, by Hermogenes' dangerous loss of his peruke (I, i, 367), which initiates the process of discovery, and by Polydamas' climactic threat (V, i, 375 ff.) to rack Hermogenes and Eubulus in order to discover once and for all Leonidas' true parentage. More generally, Princes Prettyman and Leonidas share a romantic softness that is overlooked in the power of Almanzor and the bluster of Drawcansir and Volscius. Second, Buckingham calls attention to the absurdly conventional device of letters and tokens of natal patent, seemingly catching Dryden's own confusion in *Marriage A-la-Mode* in defining pertinent information concerning the letter or paper that explains the royal children's true heritage. Third, and most problematical, Buckingham seems to attack the dramatic convenience and sentimental neatness of the bloodless coup that ends the heroic plot of *Marriage A-la-Mode*. Bayes points out proudly that "the chief hindge" of his play is in the competing claims of the two kings, Tweedles dee and dum, for the same throne. The 1701 edition of *The Rehearsal* does identify these two kings of Brentford, the "two Usurpers," specifically as "the two Kings in Granada,"[21] but *A Key to the Rehearsal* (1704), while maintaining that *Marriage A-la-Mode* was "writ since the first Publication of this Farce" and castigating "the Dulness of the State-part, [and] the obscurity of the Comic," sees *The Rehearsal* as moving satirically beyond *The Conquest of Granada* to other improbably dra-

---

[20] Although most of the potential references in *The Rehearsal* to *Marriage A-la-Mode* concern its noble rather than its comic plot, Noyes, *Selected Dramas* (p. 451), suggests that Bayes's proud boast of a "Scene of sheer Wit . . . a prize of Wit; for you shall see 'em come in upon one another snip snap, hit for hit" (*The Rehearsal*, III, i [1672, p. 21]) parodies generally the mode of repartee in the play's comic action. Subsequent annotation to lines of the text calls attention to more specific moments of parody.

[21] P. 19.

matic conclusions such as that represented by Leonidas' bloodless coup: "Such easy turns of State, are frequent in our Modern Plays; where we see Princes Dethron'd, and Governments Chang'd, by very feeble Means, and on slight Occasions: particularly, in *Marriage a la Mode*. . . . how easily the Fierce and Jealous Usurper is Depos'd, and the Right Heir plac'd on the Throne."[22] Seen through the fisheye of satire, "the State-part" of *Marriage A-la-Mode* is indeed, if one discounts its exceptionally fine language, conventional within a literary tradition, and this conventionality finally makes the dating of the play by reference to *The Rehearsal* an uneasy business. But while all three of these matters have general literary application and Buckingham's satire on *Marriage A-la-Mode* may be prescient and before the fact, one might also argue that their specific caustic would have been completely realized only if the King's audience knew *Marriage A-la-Mode* well and recently and that Dryden's play and Buckingham's parody would have offered a particularly effective and needed (if complex) counteroffensive to the popular offerings of the rival company. Nevertheless, the evidence for precise dating remains too general to find in *The Rehearsal* a terminus ad quem as convincing as the terminus a quo supplied by the opening of the Dorset Garden Theatre. Whether its first production preceded or followed that of *The Rehearsal*, Buckingham may well have known *Marriage A-la-Mode* in manuscript (like the King and Rochester), in rehearsal, or by detailed rumor; and if direct satire is intended he would certainly have needed that information to revise and rehearse his own glowing parody.

The theatrical history of *Marriage A-la-Mode* touches upon certainty only three times during Dryden's lifetime. The play was revived on 23 April 1674 and 19 June 1675,[23] and two decades later, on 18 June 1697, Lady Morley attended a performance at Drury Lane.[24] New editions of the play suggest revivals in the seasons of 1683–84, 1690–91, and 1697–98. George Powell's Dryden-baiting preface to *The Fatal Discovery*, published in 1698, includes *Marriage A-la-Mode* among plays by Dryden recently revived by the Drury Lane company,[25] and while Powell might be referring to the performance seen by Lady Morley, we cannot be certain.

The age of Dryden has left us disappointingly few records of performance, interpretation, or reception of Dryden's most elegant play, a play brilliant in its craft, wit, and sophistication, and a theater piece which offers to performers a luxurious variety of attractive roles. No sure memorandum survives of its opening performance, but *Gallantry A-la-mode* (1674), a lively poem about overfashionable London life which plays with Dryden's title and subject matter, pretends to recreate momentarily the initial performance:

> Already is the Play begun.
> 'Twas the first Time that e're was show'd
> That Play call'd *Marriage A-la-Mode;*

---

22 P. 8.
23 Van Lennep, pp. 215, 234.
24 *Ibid.*, p. 480.
25 See headnote to *The Conquest of Granada*, p. 412 above.

> The Name my Fancy did incline
> To think Concernment ith' Design.[26]

And in 1745, an old gentleman of eighty-seven claims to look back with remembered pleasure to the première: "This comedy, acted by his majesty's servants at the theatre royal, made its first appearance with extraordinary lustre. Divesting my self of the old man, I solemnly declare that you have seen no such acting, no not in any degree, since."[27] For its initial production the King's Company put forth the strongest cast at its disposal, and the two plots of honor and innuendo were headed by Edward Kynaston as Leonidas and Charles Hart as Palamede, with Elizabeth Boutell as Melantha. The roles were no doubt designed with these performers in mind, but we can only guess at their interpretations and abilities from records of their other roles and from later performances of the same roles by other artists.[28]

Fortunately, the next and subsequent ages have left fuller theatrical records, but *Marriage A-la-Mode* as Dryden designed it scarcely survived his own lifetime. The last performance of the full-length, double-plot play was evidently given on 29 November 1700.[29] Within three years of Dryden's death, the heroic and comic plots of the play were sundered, with the comic plot turned into a two-act piece sufficient to fill out a program.[30] A few years later, early in 1707,[31] Colley Cibber, that astute pragmatist of the stage, yoked the comic scenes of *Marriage A-la-Mode* to those of Dryden's *Secret Love*, mingling Florimel and Celadon with Melantha, Doralice, and their gallants for a feast of chatter and bustle.[32] Cibber called his ingenious "compilation" *The Comical Lovers; or, Marriage a la Mode*, and this version enjoyed frequent revivals throughout the first quarter of the century.[33] The popularity in the early 1740's of the series of Hogarth prints entitled "Marriage a la Mode,"[34] may have inspired Kitty Clive to revive *The Comical Lovers* as a benefit piece, for she used it as a showcase frequently in 1746 (and once in 1747 and in 1752).[35] In turn, Cibber's version was

---

[26] Pt. II, pp. 81–82.

[27] *The Gentleman's Magazine*, XV (February 1745), 99.

[28] See section on actors, pp. 547–557 below.

[29] Avery, p. 5.

[30] The 1703 adaptation of *Marriage A-la-Mode* was anonymous. Performances were on 1 and 11 February 1703 (Avery, pp. 31–32), the other piece on the program being a one-act version of Settle and Purcell's *The Fairy Queen*.

[31] The first performance took place on 4 February 1707 at the Queen's Theatre (Avery, p. 139).

[32] Cibber may also have drawn upon Act III of *An Evening's Love* for two scenes in Act IV of his "compilation"; see Marilyn Klawiter, "A Third Source for Cibber's 'The Comical Lovers,'" *N&Q*, n.s., XXII (1975), 488–489.

[33] See Avery, p. 139 and *passim*, which lists more than two dozen performances between 1707 and 1728. The two titles of Cibber's comedy were often reversed, and on the occasion of a third command performance in 1715 (on 3 June) the title was altered to *Court Gallantry; or, Marriage a la Mode*.

[34] Beyond their title these prints have no direct connection with Dryden's play.

[35] See Arthur H. Scouten, ed., *The London Stage, 1660–1800*, Pt. 3: 1729–1747 (1961), pp. 1223–1225, 1228, 1236, 1259, 1310; and George Winchester Stone, Jr., ed., Pt. 4: 1747–1776 (1962), pp. 290, 298, 308.

replaced in 1757 by Henry Dell's *The Frenchified Lady Never in Paris,* an adaptation that further narrowed the comic focus to the part of Melantha —"The gaudy effort of luxuriant art, / In all imagination's glitter drest"[36] —and which served with much success as a playlet for a series of famous actresses, chief among whom was Peg Woffington.[37] *The Frenchified Lady Never in Paris* functioned as part of an evening's entertainment which included such plays—all likewise much shortened and revised—as *Macbeth, Theodosius, Richard II, Hamlet,* and *The Fair Penitent.* The patterns that are noticeable, then, in the three eighteenth-century adaptations of *Marriage A-la-Mode* are their excision of the heroic on the one hand, and, on the other, their use of the emphasized role of Melantha as an effective vehicle for a leading comic actress (with their concomitant popularity as dependable benefit pieces). These patterns tell us something about the theatrical taste of the eighteenth century, which clearly appreciated Dryden's creation of joyful, actable comic characters and witty repartee. The tragic and pathetic modes certainly did not go unappreciated on the eighteenth-century stage—so much is clear from the use of a short *Hamlet* or a short *Fair Penitent* to make an evening's entertainment with *The Frenchified Lady*—but, in a decorum that seems less complex than that of the Restoration stage, they were not to be combined too intimately with comedy and farce, which were to be played as separate, refreshing addenda.

Such eighteenth-century simplifications are interesting not just as an index of temporal fashion, not just as items in the history of interpretation, but also because they confront the main critical issue, as much tonal as structural, of *Marriage A-la-Mode.* "The Comic Scenes of Dryden's *Marriage à la mode* and of his *Maiden Queen*" were combined, said Cibber of his Drydenian compilation, because "it was judg'd that, as these comic Episodes were utterly independent of the serious Scenes they were originally written to, they might . . . as well . . . make up five livelier Acts between them."[38] Cibber implies the question we need most to answer: are the wit and humorous character of the comic plot disjunctive from the elevation and distress of the heroic, or is there that ordered juxtaposition of

---

[36] This phrase describing the role of Melantha is taken from an encomium to an actress of the Drury Lane Company—"To Mrs. SYBILLA on her acting the Goddess of Dullness, and persuading her to attempt Melantha in Dryden's Marr. Alamode"—in *The Gentleman's Magazine,* XV (February 1745), 98. The praise continues, telling us something of the eighteenth-century appreciation of the gaiety, sense of motion, and variety to be found in the role of Melantha:

> O thou, or beauteous Woffington, display,
> What Dryden's self with pleasure might survey.
> Ev'n he, before whose visionary eyes,
> Melantha rob'd in ever-varying dies,
> Gay fancy's work, appears.

[37] The 1757 single edition of *The Frenchified Lady Never in Paris* was, as its title page announces, "Taken from Dryden and Colley Cibber, Poets Laureat, Acted at the Theatre-Royal in Covent-Garden, with Universal Applause."

[38] Cibber, II, 5. In the preface to *The Double Gallant* (1707), Cibber confesses (or boasts with possible exaggeration) that his popular "Alteration cost me but six days trouble."

Palmyra's world and Melantha's which would make for literary and theatrical meaning?

ᐧᐧᐧ

According to Gerard Langbaine, the most relentless accuser of Dryden as "plagiary," the text of *Marriage A-la-Mode* seems nothing more than an unassimilated assortment of borrowed and foreign literary parts. Langbaine, disregarding matters of theatrical effectiveness, as was his custom, begins his attack on the play's literary merit with a charge of false advertising: "This Play tho' stil'd in the Title-page a Comedy, is rather a Tragi-Comedy, and consists of two different Actions; the one Serious, the other Comick." Langbaine follows with the assumption that these "two Stories" are merely "tackt together," and then proceeds to his real mission, a listing of some four French narrative sources from which he believes *Marriage A-la-Mode* is reconstituted, a practice, Langbaine concludes, which "is usual with our Poet."[39]

Actually, only the first of Langbaine's imputed French sources figures extensively in *Marriage A-la-Mode*, in that "L'Histoire de Sesostris et Timarete" from Madeleine de Scudéry's *Artamène: ou le Grand Cyrus* does indeed provide the immediate and principal source for the heroic plot of Dryden's play.[40] "Sesostris and Timareta" tells in mazed detail the story of Apriez, king of Egypt, and his queen and of the king's usurping captain of the armies, Amasis, who has wed the queen's favorite, the Princess Ladice, although "his soule was filled fuller of secret ambition, then it was of love."[41] In transforming and dramatizing "Sesostris and Timareta," Dryden retains the essential personalities and functions of Scudéry's characters, but substitutes one set of romantic Mediterranean-sounding names for another in the following manner:[42] Sesostris/Leonidas; Timareta/

---

[39] Langbaine, p. 166 (all subsequent references to Langbaine in this headnote are to this page). For speculation on the cause of Langbaine's pedantic fury, see David Stuart Rodes's introduction to Gerard Langbaine, *Momus Triumphans* (1688 [1687]), Augustan Reprint (1971), pp. x–xii.

[40] (Paris, 1651), Tome VI, Livre 2, and continuing into Livre 3 (Vol. II, pp. 556–938), and briefly in Tome VII, Livres 1 and 2. The first English translation was published in London in five volumes bound in two (1653–1655) as *Artamenes, or The Grand Cyrus*. All the material that concerns *Marriage A-la-Mode* is to be found in the second bound volume; "Sesostris and Timareta" begins in Pt. VI, Bk. 2, pp. 75–125, continues briefly into Bk. 3 (pp. 126–128), and ends perfunctorily in Pt. VII, Bk. 1 (p. 13) and Pt. VII, Bk. 2 (p. 92). Quotations are taken from this English translation.

Summers recounts the plot of "Sesostris and Timareta" with gusto and intricacy, but without analysis; Allen (pp. 110–124 and 261–268) provides the most comprehensive survey of Langbaine's charges; and Leslie Howard Martin, Jr., "Conventions of the French Romances in the Drama of John Dryden" (Ph.D. dissertation, Stanford University, 1967), ch. 5, offers the best evaluation of Dryden's use of Scudéry.

[41] Vol. II, Pt. VI, Bk. 1, p. 77.

[42] The name of the young hero is emblematic of his noble strength and leonine power and may have been suggested by that of Leontes in *The Winter's Tale*.

Palmyra; Amasis/Polydamas; Heracleon/Argaleon; Liserina/Amalthea; Traseas/Hermogenes; Amenophis/Eubulus. In Scudéry's original tale, the queen, her young son Sesostris ("a miracle"), and the pregnant Ladice take secret refuge from the tyrant usurper on a romantically described island in the delta of the Nile where Ladice shortly gives birth to a daughter, Timareta ("a most perfect Miracle of Beauty").[43] Before she expires, Ladice writes a letter to her estranged husband, but because it arrives torn and because of the ill will and dispersal that derive from Amasis' usurpation, there succeeds a long series of intricate adventures, mistaken identities, and occasions for high sentiment. As is customary with works of art in the pastoral mode, Scudéry's long tale of growth, love, physical separation, and reestablishment poses the question of integrity of character in terms of the rival influences of nature and nurture and of country and court as that integrity is displayed and tested in the vortex of rapidly shifting fortune. At long last, when the true positions of Sesostris and Timareta are recognized, members of Cyrus's court wonder that the royal pair "ever were a Shepherd and Shepherdess" since they "carry themselves so admirably well, and spoke in such a noble manner."[44] But the disparity between their rural past and their courtly present is merely illusory. From the beginning the lovers have been stable in their affections and in their simple nobility, easily integrating in a distinguished rural shelter their royal birth (nature) and their princely tutelage (nurture) by the faithful courtier Amenophis. The only ironies are those presented externally by extravagantly changing circumstance and by the worldly ambition and misapprehension of others. To modern taste, loss of integrity in Scudéry's tale comes in the separation between action and character. Plot seems to have no fundamental effect on character, but simply demonstrates stability rather than testing or provoking growth or degeneration. Plot offers a series of discrete, variously decorated display boxes to show off virtue.[45]

Palmyra's name may also be emblematic in its association with the palm tree as a symbol of strength in adversity (see note to IV, i, 41–42) and as a symbol of triumph and joy. Allen (p. 123) speculates that Palamede's name may be taken from a character in Jean Des Marets de Saint Sorlin's romance *L'Ariane* (Paris, 1632). The name and something of the character of Doralice may originate in the talkative, "aimable" young lady-in-waiting Doralisa in Cyrus's court; see esp. Vol. II, Pt. VII, Bk. 1, pp. 10–11, for her opinions on the provocativeness and weaknesses of women. See also the description (Vol. I, Pt. V, Bk. 1, p. 9) of Doralisa's "pleasing and merry wit" which was "so full of reason, that she brought all the world unto her own sense of things" and of her "subtil and witty way of jesting, against which there was no defending ones self."

43 Vol. II, Pt. VI, Bk. 2, p. 83.
44 Vol. II, Pt. VII, Bk. 2, p. 92.
45 For further discussion of similar ideas in relation to heroic and tragic drama, see Eric Rothstein, *Restoration Tragedy: Form and the Process of Change* (1967). Some of this disconnection between plot and character in Scudéry's romance carries over into Dryden's heroic plot. On the other hand, the relationship of plot and character in Dryden's comic action may be perceived as virtually opposite: the characters of the four lovers adjust gracefully to accidents and vagaries of plot, and happy accidents of plot, not strength of character, may prevent the illicit action, which, according to the epilogue, was *"well offer'd"* but *"nothing done"*; see Allen, p. 119.

With professional dispatch and, we may imagine, some patience, Dryden dramatized, demystified, and condensed the action, time, and setting of Scudéry's leisurely, but busy, excursus. The wondrous travelogue of the Mediterranean world is gone and with it such tours de force of the romance as pronouncing oracles, lovingly detailed descriptions of combat with crocodiles, and a visit to the isle by the philosopher Pythagoras. Dryden has briskly eliminated the discursive narrative of the usurpation and exiled childhoods of Sesostris and Timareta, and he has gathered all his participants to one conveniently located island court. He has caused his Leonidas to seize the throne from Polydamas rather than have it handed over, as in Scudéry, to Sesostris by an Amasis psychosomatically blind with guilt. Dryden has also decreased in importance and malevolence the role of Leonidas' rival, Argaleon.[46] On the whole, then, "Sesostris and Timareta" is a convenience for Dryden, a specific and entertaining story that provides an organized or prearranged forum for the discussion of three pairs of ideas in tension: usurpation versus loyalty; shifting identities versus fidelity of being and affection; and reconciliation versus renunciation. All these Dryden might just as well have had by borrowing his plot from *Rosalynde or Euphues' Golden Legacy* or from *Pandosto*, but those romances were old, English, and already taken, and clearly between 1664 and 1675 Dryden was reading with attention and a soliciting eye the fashionable new French romances of Madeleine de Scudéry.

According to Langbaine, the characters of Rhodophil and Palamede are likewise derived from "The History of Timantes and Parthenia" in *The Grand Cyrus*.[47] In that story there are indeed two courtiers, the married Prince of Salamis and the bachelor "Gallant of high esteem" Timantes, both of whom find it unlikely that love and marriage often clap hands together. The prince asseverates that "there is no such extravagancy in the world, as for a Husband to be alwaies in love with his Wife; and if Parthenia would have kept me still in love with her, she should never have married me."[48] When Salamis dies, his widow and Timantes meet in a series of masked encounters; Timantes also becomes enamored of a Fair Unknown, whom he eventually discovers, with wonder at the consistency of his roving taste, to be Parthenia: "he was beyond all expectation joyed to find, that all he loved in two persons were conjoyned in one, and that his unknown Mistresse and Parthenia were one and the same."[49] A similar pattern of fashionable alienation and unexpected reconciliation occurs in "The His-

---

[46] Scudéry's story trails off (Vol. II, Pt. VII, Bk. 1, p. 13) in conventionally dispensed happiness and morality: "Timaretta was all hopes, and had nothing to fear; Sesostris was living, Sesostris was faithful, and Heracleon was dead; so that nothing wanted to compleat their contentment, but to return into Ægypt, where Amasis did earnestly desire them."

[47] Vol. II, Pt. VI, Bk. 1, pp. 17–68.

[48] Vol. II, Pt. VI, Bk. 1, p. 25. The prince continues (p. 26) to detail the staleness of his marriage: "that beauty which one enjoyes is like perfumes, which continuall custome brings one not to smell at all." Allen (p. 113) points to this passage as probably the only direct verbal borrowing Dryden makes from this story; compare I, i, 137–138 of *Marriage A-la-Mode*.

[49] Vol. II, Pt. VI, Bk. 1, p. 67.

tory of Nogaret and Mariana" from *The Annals of Love*,[50] where Nogaret rebukes a friend who praises his wife Mariana's beauty and wit: "you have kept such a stir with the names of Husband and Wife, that the very pronouncing them so often, hath given me the headach."[51] Langbaine suggests that "part of the Character of Doralice was possibly borrow'd" from this story, and it is true that in *The Annals of Love* Nogaret does make an assignation with his disguised wife only to discover—in bed—her true uxorial identity. After some vexation and some few embarrassments "this Couple took one another again, and loved one another as entirely, as when they were married at first."[52] Both of these stories of gallants and ladies are indeed apposite in parts to the wit plot of *Marriage A-la-Mode,* and Dryden no doubt knew at least Scudéry's tale,[53] but plots involving masquerading wives and fashionable opinion that, to quote an old French song, "les baisers permis sont fades" could be had for the asking on any street corner of the Strand or Saint Germain.

Langbaine assigns the source for Melantha's making court to herself in Rhodophil's name to a humorous vignette called "Naiveté d'une jeune Fille" in *Les Contes* of Antoine Le Métel, sieur D'Ouville, where a young girl practiced her airs, "repetant devant ce miroir les réponses qu'elle devoit faire quand elle se verroit carressée de quelque galand & disoit quelquefois, Ah! je pense que voire, Monsieur, qui vous croiroit, je sçai bien que je n'ai pas tant de merite, ni tant de beauté comme vous me le voulez persuader." Her beaux secretly overhear, and one of them surprises her "sur le fait, dont de honte & de confusion elle s'alla cacher."[54] Melantha shares with her possible prototype a comic and touching combination of energetic vanity and vulnerability, but perhaps a character from *The Grand Cyrus,* unnoticed by Langbaine, is closer to the point. Like Melantha, one Berisa in the "History of the King of Assyria, of Intaphernes, of Atergates, of Istrina, and of the Princesse of Bythinia"[55] is a "ubiquitary" who buzzes frantically from place to place in court and town, inserting her person and opinions where they are not wanted, always (p. 42) "whispering one after another with all she met, either upon matters of War or business of State, or Cabinet news, or business of Gallantry, or some tittle tattle or other." Berisa decries the country (whence she comes) and idolizes the court; and "though she had a hundred severall employments, yet she was hardly an

---

50 (1672), pp. 163–184. This collection of romantic tales, *Les Annales Galantes,* was written by Marie-Catherine Hortense Desjardins (Paris, 1670). The anonymous English translation, *The Annals of Love,* appears in the *Term Catalogues* as licensed on 20 November 1671, and it might therefore have been available to the English public just before *Marriage A-la-Mode* was first produced. For clear instances of Dryden's extensive use of *The Annals of Love,* see headnote and notes to *The Assignation,* below, and *Works,* XV, 387.

51 *The Annals of Love,* p. 169.

52 *Ibid.,* p. 184; Langbaine, p. 166.

53 Allen (p. 115n) believes that the story in *The Annals of Love* derives from the one in *The Grand Cyrus.*

54 Quoted in Summers.

55 Vol. II, Pt. VIII, Bk. 1, pp. 41–52. This prototype for Melantha was discovered and analyzed in careful detail by Leslie Howard Martin, Jr., in "The Source and Originality of Dryden's Melantha," *PQ,* LII (1973), 746–753.

hour from the Princess of Bythinia: Not that the Princess did love her; for on the contrary, she was very troublesom to her; But this woman did so intrude upon her, to the end that other Ladies of the Town might think her a Favourite, that she was one of the most burthensome creatures in the world" (p. 41). Melantha's behavior dramatizes these and other details of Berisa's assaults on decorum, but, unlike Berisa, Melantha is generously endowed with an eccentric charm, a capacity for friendship, an essential dignity, and an imaginative "voice": all these attributes remove her to a noticeable degree from the strict censure for ill breeding to which Scudéry subjects Berisa.

Melantha's dramatic vibrancy of language and her notions of courtship derived from French romance and Parisian high society connect her much more closely with Magdelon and Cathos, the title characters of Molière's *Les Précieuses Ridicules* (1660),[56] than with the French narrative sources themselves. Even then, we know Melantha better and like her more than Molière's two French country cousins, and the lessons of vanity, talkativeness, and busy modishness are taught more gently in the English play. Melantha is sycophant, fop, Francomaniac, busybody, and chatterer, a very compaction of types whose excesses have always provided matter for the comic view of life and art. She is also handsome, not unclever, and very rich, and her successors are as various and as memorable as Lady Fantast and Sir Fopling Flutter on the one hand and the exquisitely controlled and successful Millamant on the other.

Dryden borrows, then, when and where he needs—characters, situations, plots, topics, ideas. What he does not borrow for *Marriage A-la-Mode*, with the fewest exceptions, are language and turns of wit.[57] In this respect his practice differs, at least in degree, from his work in *Secret Love*, with its very similar sources for plot and character, but is in accord with his claim in the preface to *An Evening's Love* (1671) *"that I seldome use the wit and language of any Romance or Play which I undertake to alter."*[58] As Dryden himself seems to be aware (in his general criticism as in his dedication of *Marriage A-la-Mode*), the added power, subtlety, and freshness of his language constitute the binding and transforming art of his comedies: *"the price lyes wholly in the workmanship."*[59] And whether looking at his outside sources for *Marriage A-la-Mode* or at his borrowings from himself, we

---

56 Like Melantha, Magdelon rhapsodizes about Paris as "le grand bureau des merveilles, le centre du bon goût, du bel esprit et de la galanterie" (sc. ix). Her terminology and her expectations come from "la filofie dans *le Grand Cyre*" (as her hapless maid phrases it in sc. vi). Marriage, for the two would-be fashionables, "ne doit jamais arriver qu'après les autres aventures" (sc. iv). Despite these parallels, John Wilcox (*The Relation of Molière to Restoration Comedy* [1938], pp. 112–113) argues that Dryden's recall of Molière and of the subject of French *preciosité* was of only the most general sort; Beaurline and Bowers (p. 278), on the other hand, believe that Melantha derives from Mascarille, the valet and would-be gallant of Molière's comedy, but Allen (p. 121) had earlier dismissed similar comparisons with Mascarille (who, indeed, seems more a prototype for Benito in *The Assignation* than for Melantha).

57 Allen, p. 268.

58 *Works*, X, 211.

59 *Ibid.*, p. 212.

may agree that with *Marriage A-la-Mode* (and to a greater extent than with *An Evening's Love* to which he is specifically referring) Dryden has made a new and better vessel:

> *'Tis true, that where ever I have lik'd any story in a Romance, Novel, or forreign Play, I have made no difficulty, nor ever shall, to take the foundation of it, to build it up, and to make it proper for the* English *Stage. And I will be so vain to say it has lost nothing in my hands: But it alwayes cost me so much trouble to heighten it for our Theatre (which is incomparably more curious in all the ornaments of Dramatick Poesie, than the* French *or* Spanish) *that when I had finish'd my Play, it was like the Hulk of* Sir Francis Drake, *so strangely alter'd, that there scarce remain'd any Plank of the Timber which first built it.*[60]

The first planks of Dryden's timber are best uncovered in his own years of experience and reflection as playwright and critic,[61] and *Marriage A-la-Mode* incorporates the sensible ideas and tested components explored in his own earlier work: the flexible precepts concerning the management of time, place, and action;[62] the practicality of the double plot to support and order "the pleasure of variety" which the English dramatic tradition encourages;[63] and the psychological decorum of language which responds, on the one hand, to the measured aggrandizement of the heroic and, on the other, to the "chase of wit" of the comic.[64] *Secret Love*, with which *Marriage A-la-Mode* has the most affinity, was itself the outcome of a concentrated preoccupation with the formulas of comic success whose critical expression is found in *Of Dramatick Poesie* and in the preface to *Secret Love*. From *Secret Love*, *Marriage A-la-Mode* derives its basic structural identity of alternating comic and heroic plots. Each play is set in a Sicily that is both pastoral and courtly, distant and modern, and both plays glean their heroic plots from French romance. Each play commences with the return of a gallant and both include "gay couples"[65] who erupt in badinage and proviso as well as a noble woman who expresses in quiet plaint the pains of self-sacrifice.

But Dryden did not, of course, confine himself to formulas from *Secret Love*. The fashionable attitude toward marriage as a condition to be avoided until it must be endured is taken in *The Rival Ladies* (I, iii, 23–27; *Works*, VIII, 114) and in *The Wild Gallant* (I, ii, 52–54; *Works*, VIII, 13)

---

[60] *Ibid.*, pp. 210–211.

[61] Dryden was accused by Martin Clifford of plagiarism even from himself: "You are . . . a strange unconscionable Thief, that art not content to steal from others, but do'st rob thy poor wretched Self too" (*Notes upon Mr. Dryden's Poems in Four Letters* [1687], p. 7; also quoted in Allen, p. 123n). Clifford had the heroic plays, and principally *The Conquest of Granada*, in mind.

[62] See esp. *Of Dramatick Poesie* (*Works*, XVII, 52). Moore develops the relationships between Dryden's comedy and theory.

[63] The phrase is from *The Grounds of Criticism in Tragedy* but the critical principle is also discussed in *Of Dramatick Poesie* (*Works*, XVII, 46–47).

[64] *Of Dramatick Poesie* (*Works*, XVII, 48).

[65] See John Harrington Smith, *The Gay Couple in Restoration Comedy* (1948), pp. 69–71; *Works*, IX, 340–344; and Moore, pp. 107–108.

as well, and marriage discussed in terms of a legal treaty between nations concludes both *An Evening's Love* and *Marriage A-la-Mode*. The venerable Elizabethan device of female characters disguised as boys is transformed by Dryden into breeches roles in *The Rival Ladies* and then reworked to suit the fourth act of *Marriage A-la-Mode*.[66] Likewise, the quarrel between Doralice and Melantha reflects that between Hippolito and Angellina in *The Rival Ladies* (III, i). Furthermore, Dryden reworked two incidents from *An Evening's Love* to fit *Marriage A-la-Mode*. The earnest Melchor can inject only an occasional "but, Sir" into the tirade of the garrulous Alonzo (IV, i), much as an exhausted Palamede finally despairs of Melantha (II, i, 62–90) who "asks all, and will hear nothing. . . . bless me from this tongue." And Palamede must ply Philotis, Melantha's attendant, with gold coin, just as Melchor presses money into the palm of Aurelia's maid for aid in courtship.

Such a recital of indebtedness to self and others reveals merely that Dryden was able to draw upon and transform in a manner at once civilized, professional, and conservative the not inexhaustible store of literary situations and tropes. Thus, as noted above, both *Marriage A-la-Mode* and *An Evening's Love* include versions of the conventional scene that forces a gallant to advance a courtship by pressing money upon his mistress's maid or attendant.[67] In the earlier play Aurelia's maid, Camilla, assures Don Melchor she has been sent to him by "a fair Lady, who bears you no ill will," and adds that she has already sought him "in a thousand places." Among those places is "that shop where, out of your nobleness, you promis'd me a new Silk Gown." Melchor takes the hint, and gives Camilla money for a gown of her choice. Perhaps because only subordinate characters are involved, Dryden leaves the theatrical cliché as he found it, relying upon the agreed comedy of the situation to do his work for him and seeking to release that comedy with a single, simple joke. The situation recurs in *Marriage A-la-Mode*, but with far wittier, far more aware characters, as Palamede pays tax upon tax to Philotis, Melantha's walking word list and confidant, who receives five pieces for remarking upon Palamede's "liberality," a further twenty for recalling that Rhodophil once gave her ten pieces for a "New-years gift," and, when Palamede incautiously questions whether she will remember to forward his suit to Melantha, a diamond from his finger to stimulate her memory. The exchange between Philotis and Palamede renews the standard comic situation not only by offering three variations upon the single joke of *An Evening's Love,* but also by making the participants acutely conscious of their involvement in a sophisticated game with established rules and penalties.

Melantha's conversation—to take a similar case—is noticeably livelier than

---

[66] Rhodophil, with Palamede's help, rescues Doralice, who is unrecognized by the men while she is dressed in boy's attire, just as Gonsalvo rescues the disguised and adoring Hippolito in *The Rival Ladies* (I, ii). Not knowing the other's true gender and fearing to betray their own sexual identities, Hipolito and Angellina are horrified at the suggestion that they should sleep with each other, or another woman, or another man. Similarly Doralice and Melantha make strong protest at the suggestion that they "lie with a Boy" (IV, iii, 174–175).

[67] *An Evening's Love,* IV, i, 479–499 (*Works,* X, 284–285); *Marriage A-la-Mode,* V, i, 30–76.

Aurelia's in *An Evening's Love*. We have already seen that Melantha parallels Scudéry's Berisa in manner, and we can also see that her speech reflects Dryden's increased skill in the creation and deployment of repartee. In the earlier play Aurelia asks Camilla whether she is properly dressed for the evening's entertainment—"is nothing disorder'd in my head?"—and, distrusting Camilla's reassurances, calls for "the Counsellor of the Graces," a conceit that Camilla excusably fails to understand. Aurelia is forced to translate—"My Glass I mean"—and revenges herself upon Camilla by correcting the maid's *"Madam"* into *"Mam,"* her *"par-don"* into *"parn,"* her *"Ladyship"* into *"Laship."* The humor of the exchange is entirely lexical, seeking to amuse by setting affected speech against speech that is not merely unaffected, but simple, straightforward, and dull.[68] The comparable scene in *Marriage A-la-Mode* makes the unaffected speech of Philotis interesting, because witty and ironic, while Melantha's avid curiosity about words echoes with the slightly mad halloo of the dictionary huntress in full pursuit.[69] Melantha berates Philotis for delaying her "visits" by failing to supply "new words" for her "daily conversation." Philotis excuses herself by pointing out that Melantha has "so drain'd all the *French* Plays and Romances, that they are not able to supply you with words for your daily expences." Melantha singles out the unfortunate verb—*"Drain'd?* what a word's there! *Épuisée,* you sot you"—and orders Philotis to hold up a mirror while she consults the list of new words and practices her "postures for the day." The exchange between Melantha and Philotis complicates the wholly lexical humor of *An Evening's Love* with social activity both literal (visits and postures) and metaphorical (words to supply daily expenses). The sense of activity, of people doing things, provides a dramatic counterpart to the discursive vigor of Dryden's best critical essays.[70] Furthermore, while Melantha certainly has more personality and more and more striking things to say than has Aurelia, Philotis it is who makes the chief difference in the scenes between mistress and maid, just as she does in those between maid and gallant. Unlike Camilla, Philotis shares in the play's wit and sophistication and ministers in a way denied Camilla to our ironic enjoyment of Melantha's airs. *Marriage A-la-Mode* is quite simply richer in wit and ideas than the earlier *An Evening's Love*, and Dryden has used this richness to give comic dimension to a character whose counterpart in the earlier play he had left comparatively unrealized.

Similarly, Dryden's use of Sicily as his setting in *Marriage A-la-Mode* explores a landscape seen earlier in *Secret Love*; but whereas in *Secret Love* the setting is derived from the play's source, in *Marriage A-la-Mode* Dryden has chosen it for its aptness to a design at once less topical and more coordinated than that of his earlier play. The Sicily of *Marriage A-la-Mode*

---

[68] *An Evening's Love*, III, i, 86–100 (*Works*, X, 250–251).

[69] *Marriage A-la-Mode*, III, i, 184–236 above.

[70] T. S. Eliot believed, however, that Melantha was "still too 'humorous' in her French affectations" to compare with characters in "the finest Restoration comedy" and that, moreover, "in his comedies Dryden was not able to bring his prose to perfection; it is a transition prose; and I doubt anyway whether his heart was in it." In Eliot's view, Dryden, unlike Shakespeare or Congreve, "was not *naturally* a dramatist" (*John Dryden . . . Three Essays* [1932], p. 42).

combines in one intensified place of action the courtly Egyptian setting and extensive wanderings through romantic Mediterranean lands of Scudéry's "Sesostris and Timareta." Court busyness and a sense of pastoral retreat meld here efficiently in a single location. As the birthplace of Theocritus, "the Bucolick Poet,"[71] and the setting for innumerable dramas from *Amyntas, The Winter's Tale,* and *Philaster* to *The Siege of Rhodes* and *The Platonick Lovers,* Sicily is extraordinarily rich in poetic, pastoral reference,[72] and by its selection Dryden emphasizes the literary dimensions of *Marriage A-la-Mode.*[73] Moreover, although the play does not seem to be politically disposed, in a heroic plot where usurpation and rebellion are prominent Dryden is not unwise to choose a setting that invokes the other-world, fairy-tale quality of his play.[74] Sicily allows for a court that pertains

---

[71] The phrase is from Edmund Warcupp, *Italy, in its Original Glory, Ruine and Revival* (1660), p. 323, the most extensive and factual (but not likely firsthand) of the relatively few contemporary travel guides.

[72] In *An Index of Characters in English Printed Drama to the Restoration* (1975), Thomas L. Berger and William C. Bradford, Jr., list over forty plays with Sicilian settings.

[73] Warcupp, *Italy, in its Original Glory,* attests to the island's pastoral celebrity (p. 319): "modern authors as well as antient render a large testimony, though there are some who take it for a ridiculous opinion. It is esteemed for the salubrity of the Ayre, the abundance of terrene sustenance and plenty of all things necessarie for mans use very excellent." He then continues with an olio of attributions, strongly related to the island's literary reputation (p. 321): "Antient writers attribute the following things to the invention of the Sicilians, the art of Oratory, the Bucolick or pastoral verse, dyall making, the Catapulte a warlike engine, the illustrating of Pictures, the Art of Barbing, the use of skins of wilde beasts and Ryme."
    The reality of seventeenth-century Sicily was, of course, somewhat different from its picturesque description in pastoral idealization. In *A Voyage to Sicily and Malta* (1776), John Dryden, Jr., who visited the island in 1700, gives a personal account of Messina of another flavor (p. 12): "the city within does not at all answer the great idea which one has of it without, for the streets are nasty, and ill pav'd, and all broken, the houses bad, dark within." On visiting a seaside villa called *il Paradiso di Messina,* he saw nothing "worth remark, except an abundance of motto's all in Latine verse . . . all to expresse the happinesse of a retir'd life. As for it's garden, it was good for nothing, there not being so much as one level walk in it, but full of cabbage in the middle, (fit meat for a Messinese Prince,) all up hill, with a straggling tree here and there" (p. 20). Sicily was, then, probably nearer to Melantha's worst opinion than to the pastoral romance Dryden's heroic plot requires, though this account by his son did come after the aborted French seizure of the late 1670s and the particularly violent earthquake of the 1690s.

[74] On the other hand, the strongly literary bias of Sicily's repute and the virtual absence of a noteworthy modern political life rendered the island useful for satiric and political purposes as well, and its rich ancient and medieval history of tyrants (Dionysius, Agathocles) and revolt (the Sicilian Vespers) could be made to serve as analogy and precedent. For example, Sir William Sales's *Theophania: or Severall Modern Histories Represented by way of Romance: and Politickly Discours'd upon* (1655) laboriously recreates the rebel and loyalist intrigues of the English civil wars in the gentle setting of Sicily and Sardinia. Likewise, Richard Perrinchief in *The Sicilian Tyrant: or, the Life of Agathocles* (1676) offers thinly veiled parallels to Cromwell. The use of Sicily for literary heightening or as effective political mask was not always successful. In his adaptation of *Richard II,* acted briefly for

to European custom, yet its royal government can be efficiently overturned by brief offstage swordplay and its deposed tyrant neatly dissuaded from further treachery by the magnanimity of an unworldly, idealized youth. The heroic mode, as Dryden characteristically envisioned it, investigates other times and other places, but the ambiguity of reference—is this Restoration England or is it not?—is an inherent spatial and temporal part of its complexity. Since virtually nothing was known about its contemporary politics,[75] Sicily could serve as a noncontroversial (or nonintrusive) referent; but as an island just off the coast of continental Europe it might also obliquely suggest a sun-ripened England.[76] At once, Sicily as location partly justifies Melantha's implied complaint that it is not Paris, and yet it does not degrade (or actualize too realistically) the princelings who are to govern the isle. At the heroic level the purpose of setting is one of literary heightening and spatial and temporal distancing; on the other level the choice provides a festive setting beyond stiff drawing rooms and narrow streets, offering instead a comedy *en plein jardin*.

Verse form and vocabulary work with setting to give an impression of double time without insisting upon disjunction. The heroic speech glances back to the antique, the pastoral, and the emotively grand, while the comic banter projects the modern and pragmatical, the familiar and immediate. But the absence of specific and limiting allusion in the two plots, either in setting or in dialogue, makes for variety without schism.

The setting and the language, then, propose a certain ambiguity. This sense is further promoted geographically by the journey of mysterious purpose which the Sicilian court is about when the play opens. Palamede, returning from a five-year absence, is greeted by Rhodophil: "Who thought to have seen you in *Sicily?*" Palamede rejoins: "Who thought to have found the Court so far from *Syracuse?*" "The King," Rhodophil replies, "best knows the reason of the progress" (I, i, 97–99). The dislocation of the court carries with it suggestions of holiday: rules are temporarily weakened and decorums made more tenuous, and the peripatetic court turns in upon itself, leaving aside the politics of international diplomacy and battle as well as the day-to-day concerns of governmental bureaucracy. Instead, the traveling, self-diverting court is swayed by a politics of gossip. The suggested mingling of levels of society and weakening of normal responsibility are intensified in the fourth act by the masquerade ball, for "in Masquerade there is nothing to be known," in the masked diversion all is excitingly "*Terra incognita*" (IV, i, 140–141).

---

political reasons under the disguised title of *The Sicilian Usurper* (1681), Nahum Tate speaks (dedication, sigs. A2v–A3r) of the "great Disadvantage" caused by "the Change of the Scene, Names of Persons," and so forth: "I call'd my Persons Sicilians but might as well have made 'em Inhabitants of the Isle of Pines, or, World in the Moon, for whom an Audience are like to have small Concern."

[75] For instance, Sicily goes almost unnoticed in the political reporting of the *London Gazette* throughout 1671; it is mentioned less than a dozen times, usually in regard to pirates (nos. 570, 576, 577, 600) and (in December) to (unpastoral) corn shortages (nos. 633, 635, 636).

[76] This point is suggested in relation to the comic plot by both Allen (p. 262) and Moore (p. 107).

⟨✼⟩

The play Dryden designed for this Sicilian setting is crafted of a variety of parts, "manag'd so regularly that the beauty of the whole be kept intire."[77] But the beauty and unity were not always appreciated, as Langbaine's accusations suggest. Genest thought "the two distinct plots awkwardly united,"[78] and Scott speculated that "the state-intrigue bears evident marks of hurry and inattention; and it is at least possible, that Dryden originally intended it for the subject of a proper heroic play, but, startled at the effect of Buckingham's satire [*The Rehearsal*], hastily added to it some comic scenes . . . . Even the language has an abridged appearance."[79] This suggestion seems unlikely, even preposterous, for so composed and carefully crafted a play, but Dryden's own assertion that in *Marriage A-la-Mode* "there are manifestly two Actions, not depending on one another," must give pause. The context of his discussion in *The Grounds of Criticism in Tragedy* makes clear, however, that Dryden was speaking mainly of the genre of tragedy (and with some irony in this second response to Thomas Rymer's conservative *The Tragedies of the Last Age* [1678] and that he had in mind only strict narrative connection.[80] Nevertheless, critics have continued to be concerned with the construction, relationship, and effect of the two plots and their language.[81]

If we examine the play, we find not awkwardness and haste or unaccountable relationships between the two plots, but careful planning, much attention to coordinating detail, and an almost obsessive mutual interest in

---

[77] *Of Dramatick Poesie* (*Works*, XVII, 49).

[78] John Genest, *Some Account of the English Stage* (1832), I, 134.

[79] *The Life of John Dryden*, ed. Bernard Kreissman (1963), p. 123.

[80] See *The Grounds of Criticism in Tragedy*, prefixed to *Troilus and Cressida* (1679), sig. a2; Watson, 1, 243–244.

[81] Much of the nineteenth- and twentieth-century criticism of *Marriage A-la-Mode* may be classified, though very generally, by its defense or denial of a connection between the two plots of the play or by its focus on the comic plot to the relative neglect of the heroic. The position that the two plots are unrelated, or at least unsuccessfully related, was argued by Sutherland, p. xi; Clifford Leech, "Restoration Tragedy: A Reconsideration," *Durham University Journal*, XI (1950), reprinted in *Restoration Drama: Modern Essays in Criticism*, ed. John Loftis (1966), p. 149; and others. An effective connection between plots has been defended by Noyes, *Selected Dramas*, pp. xxxiv–xxxv; Summers, III, 186; Bonamy Dobrée, *John Dryden* (1956), p. 24 (although he had not mentioned the heroic plot in 1924 in *Restoration Comedy*); Beaurline and Bowers, p. 277; James Sutherland in a revised opinion, *English Literature of the Late Seventeenth Century* (1969), p. 101; as well as others. Far and away the major critical interest in *Marriage A-la-Mode*—praise or blame—has been devoted to the play's comic plot by such critics as S-S, IV, 251; Kathleen M. Lynch, *The Social Mode of Restoration Comedy* (1926), p. 160; P. F. Vernon, "Marriage of Convenience and the Moral Code of Restoration Comedy," *Essays in Criticism*, XII (1962), 370–387; John Harold Wilson, *A Preface to Restoration Drama* (1965), pp. 126–127; and Sutherland, *English Literature of the Late Seventeenth Century*, p. 101; and others. See also David J. Latt and Samuel Holt Monk, *John Dryden: A Survey and Bibliography of Critical Studies, 1895–1974* (1976).

themes and language. The two distinct narrative lines, which merge only tangentially to confirm Palamede and Rhodophil's brave standing and Melantha's effrontery, comment upon each other intellectually, if not emotionally, by their very separation and juxtaposition and confirm Dryden's aesthetic sense "that contraries when plac'd near, set off each other."[82] The two worlds of *Marriage A-la-Mode* alternate with precise regularity between the comic and the heroic, each comic scene followed by a heroic scene of about equal length, until the fifth act, where the comic overbalances the heroic, taking more than twice the number of lines to bring the play to its general comic conclusion and diffusing into itself the tragic tendencies of the heroic plot. Separately and combined the plots follow a four-part classical dramatic movement[83] and together they examine the fashionable and the idealized attitudes surrounding honor and "propriety," love and marriage, law and desire. Within the overall design of the play as a whole, each act has its individual keynote, expressed in the physical action and in the imagery and language of the act.

The prologue initiates the design, hinting to the audience of the comic version of themes and events to follow—love, low finance, inconstancy, masquerade—finally titillating the audience with coy reference to "a room and couch within" and employing the playfulness potential in the rhymed couplet to ease the spectator out of his daytime involvements—war preparations against the Dutch—into the gaiety and high tone of the play to follow.

The play proper opens with a song sung by Doralice—"*Why should a foolish Marriage Vow . . . Oblige us to each other now . . . ?*"—which sets the tone of soigné superiority among the comic characters toward constancy in marriage. The lyricism of the song undercuts somewhat its seriousness of intent and application, in keeping with the ritual ambiguity with which these witty couples often pursue their game of promiscuity. The scene proceeds quickly to a brisk bout of mutually recognized amatory overstatement between Palamede and Doralice, though Doralice is careful to set limits of decorum and time (ll. 76–77): "Remember I invade no propriety: My servant you are onely till you are marry'd." Their encounter is followed by a bracing dissection between the gallants of the boredom implicit in the cage of wedlock. We quickly learn that in modern life no strategy is too much trouble or too complex to gain a mistress (or, rather, to preserve fashionable notoriety) and no price too niggardly to begrudge in keeping the harmony of the married state. The first act, in the best Jonsonian manner,[84] defines the relationships of the couples, projects their subsequent entanglements, and prepares for the entrance of the humours character of Melantha. In the lower plot Palamede pursues Doralice, wife to Rhodophil; Rhodophil desires Melantha, intended for Palamede. In the heroic plot Leonidas adores Palmyra, whom Polydamas intends for Argaleon, and Palmyra remains faithful to Leonidas, who is immediately loved by the Princess

---

[82] The quotation from *Of Dramatick Poesie* (*Works*, XVII, 46) continues: "A continued gravity keeps the spirit too much bent; we must refresh it sometimes. . . . A Scene of mirth mix'd with Tragedy has the same effect upon us which our musick has betwixt the Acts."

[83] See *Of Dramatick Poesie* (*Works*, XVII, 23).

[84] *Ibid.*, p. 62.

Amalthea. At the conclusion of the first act each couple is divided, rightful partners separated from each other.

The second act introduces Melantha and briefly reunites each couple. After Melantha and Palamede anticipate in the first scene their future married life rich in Parisian connections and sophistication, Palmyra and Leonidas look backward in the second scene, recalling their early days of courtship in a simple fishing village. Language—and how language defines the individual—is specifically the theme of the second act. "Your language speaks you not bred up in Desarts," says Amalthea to Leonidas (II, i, 273), and Melantha betrays her affectations in her ridiculous barrage of French words and phrases.

The comic climax of the play comes in the third act where a game of hide-and-seek in the grotto becomes an obvious metaphor for the subterfuge employed in the world of fashionable manners. Under the pose of sophistication, these adults hide themselves from one another, concealed, appropriately enough, in an artifice of nature; and each hides as well from himself and from acknowledging to himself his appropriate relationships and rightful place in a connubial society. "There are places where all people may be ador'd, and we ought to know our selves so well as to chuse 'em," counsels Artemis (III, i, 152–153) to the unhearing Melantha. In contrast with the flitting affections of Melantha and the pretense of endearments by the comic characters to their respective partners, Palmyra and Leonidas personify the virtues of real loyalty and integrity on which an enduring relationship must be built. Palmyra maintains, "Yet I was ever taught 'twas base to lie" (III, i, 273). Constancy is embraced in the face of death by Palmyra and Leonidas, while the comic couples look to death as a handy means of release from each other.

Disguise and darkness dominate the fourth act and its masquerade ball. While questions of self-deception and propriety remain politely suppressed in the third act, in the fourth act the obfuscation extends to the most obvious situations. Leonidas does not recognize the love Amalthea bears him, Rhodophil and Palamede cannot discern the identities of their inamoratas in boys' clothing, and even Palmyra fails to differentiate between Argaleon and Leonidas dressed in "habits near the same" (IV, ii, 43). The dusk and darkness that engulf the palace are allied to the metaphysical state of confusion, and even the gold and yellow found in the imagery of coin and royalty of the first act are dulled into "Love's Dark-lantern" (IV, ii, 16). Echoing gently the near fatal loss of Hermogenes' disguise earlier (I, i, 357+ *s.d.*) in the heroic action, Doralice jauntily lifts her peruke (IV, iii, 70+ *s.d.*), revealing her true identity to Rhodophil. But here the terms are those of farce, comic aggression and embarrassment, and sexual misconstruction rather than potential death and state disorder. Against the comical confusion of the ball is sung the second song, "*Whil'st* Alexis *lay prest*," delineating the sexuality that animates the play. Clothed in euphonies of the pastoral, the sexual is only slightly muted. The final scene in the fourth act uses the word "design" repeatedly and prepares for the clearing of the "dark riddle" and the untying of the "mysterious knot" (IV, iv, 142–144).

In the fifth act there is a return to the more vigorous tone of the first act. A lively proviso scene never quite becomes a bargain in the offensive of Palamede's overwhelming torrent of French phrases, and the two gallants now "make a firm *League*, not to invade each others propriety" (ll. 359–360).[85] The celebratory ending properly unites and weds the couples, heroic as well as comic, reinstalls the rightful king, and suggests a reasonably revived romanticism as the proper settlement of the dalliance in the comic plot.

The epilogue concludes with mention of the playwright's manipulation of text and plot, returning the audience to the divided world of London where, though strategies in the world of free enterprise need be of each citizen's own making, the contract of marriage must be respected.

Dryden's elegant language embellishes and organizes his skillfully interwoven plots, both differentiating and connecting them. An obvious example is the imaginative play of identical language used in completely antithetical situations. For example, in the heroic plot Leonidas' "But let me die before I see this done" (III, i, 316) establishes physical death as a reality to be met, but a reality that must yield to spiritual requirements of honor and fidelity; in the lower plot Melantha's constant "Let me die" is to her a fashionable linguistic mannerism, devoid of the reality of denotation but hinting coyly at hidden levels of sexual intrigue and desire and potential embarrassment. Equally interesting is the transmutation in the first act of the yellow that glints in the comic scene in "coin" and "gold" and becomes in the heroic scene the "sun" and the "Splendor of royalty."

The play's supporting fabric of language is a witty vernacular of theological, legal, and commercial phrases and puns, cross-threaded with allusions to wit and words, French and France, and an innumerable brood of "clenches" on "dying" and "execution." Against this background appear clusters of references to animals, appetite and food, games and rules, water and navigation. "Poor Animal, I brought you hither onely for my diversion," says Doralice (III, ii, 30–31), melding into one sentence animal, sexual appetite, and game imagery. "Design" is a particularly important base word in the language of the play, inherent in the intensely wrought plotting of the play itself, appearing actively in both aesthetic and malicious senses as noun and verb, implicit in such images as "spiderweb" and "knot."

---

[85] Here the word "propriety" is virtually synonymous with "property," whereas in I, i, 76 it more nearly suggests "appropriateness of behavior." The two meanings, however, are not separate but each is a variant derivative of the word "own" (see notes to the appropriate lines below) and suggest, in somewhat circular fashion, both what one possesses and what is owing to one's sense of place. The happy circumstance of coming to love the heiress who has already been selected for one by one's father owes something to the literary assurance of the author toward his comic genre and something to the bracing proverbial notion that we see value in our possessions only when others want them. It is, then, the old comic solution: one's rival, in unconscious conspiracy with society, confers real (estate) value on the irrationality of love. Bruce King (*Dryden's Major Plays* [1966], ch. 5) argues for a direct Hobbesian reading of the comic plot as concerning man in his natural state permanently at war to conquer the property of others. For a subtler view of the way in which Palamede and Rhodophil's attitude comments on the "selfishness" of man, see Robert D. Hume, "Marital Discord in English Comedy from Dryden to Fielding," *MP*, LXXIV (1977), 269–270; and his "The Myth of the Rake in 'Restoration' Comedy," *Studies in the Literary Imagination*, X (1977), 25–55.

The predominance of religious terminology would seem at times to border on the sacrilegious. In context, however, such a phrase as "break not my first commandment, that is, not to follow me" (I, i, 83–84) appears not so much profane as satiric of the hypocrisy of reverse meaning which society finds practical, but the Almanzoresque presumption of Leonidas' "So was the Godhead ere he made the world" (III, i, 471) comes dangerously close to impiety.

The imagery may occasionally seem to verge on the bizarre. Not only does the heroic Leonidas compare himself to the Godhead, but he proclaims extravagantly, "I'll hold my breath and die" (III, i, 348).[86] Or in another direction, the love of Leonidas and Palmyra is such that (II, i, 499–502):

> Our souls sit close, and silently within;
> And their own Web from their own Intrals spin.
> And when eyes meet far off, our sense is such,
> That, Spider-like, we feel the tender'st touch.

"Spiders" and "Intrals" may not seem vocabulary strictly appropriate to the decorum of seventeenth-century princes, but as with the image of the tarantula in *1 Conquest of Granada* (III, i, 329), the unexpectedness and metaphysical conceit of the imagery constitute part of its intensity. Leonidas and Palmyra are spun-web heroic, and Dryden later points out that *"sublime Subjects ought to be adorn'd with the sublimist, and (consequently often) with the most figurative expressions."*[87] Behind such strained diction is Dryden's heartfelt search for an intensive language appropriate to heroic drama. The speeches of Palmyra and Leonidas must express their great carriage, just as the witty repartee of the gay couples signals their accommodating flexibility. Thus the heroic characters consistently speak in blank or rhymed verse, often sharing lines, while the comic characters speak and interrupt one another in prose. Occasionally, when the two plots touch there is an interesting change in the language as it transposes from one level to the other. In Act I (i, 217–237) the comic scene edges into an exposition and preparation for the heroic scene that follows. There is a subtle gathering of archaisms, a gently formalized quality to the speech, as the gallants await the entrance of the king. Such discreet movement unifies the play, ennobles the characters of Palamede and Rhodophil, making their philandering more witty and occasional, an interlude in their military service to the court. Dryden's style of language at any point in the play is intentional and decorous, as is his use of rhyme to underscore moments of tension. Rhyming couplets close each scene and act, emphasize emotional moments between Leonidas and Palmyra, and, in one instance, punctuate the royalist position which the play seems to defend. Palamede declares (V, i, 451–452): "no Subject e'r can meet / A nobler fate, then at his Sovereign's feet."[88]

---

[86] See note to III, i, 348, for other instances of this boast in Dryden.

[87] *The Authors Apology for Heroique Poetry; and Poetic Licence* prefixed to *The State of Innocence* (1677), sig. c2v; Watson, I, 207.

[88] This is one of three statements in the play which indicate directly its royalist inclinations; see also I, i, 321–326, and III, i, 416–417. The royalism partly derives, of course, from the source in French romance.

The language of the comic plot has its basis in the fashionable speech of the court, and the speech of Melantha, it has been argued, is not so much an innovation as an imitation of a dialect affected at court.[89] A fascination of the court and aristocratic circles with all things French had prevailed since Charles's return from France. And French affectations of clothes, manners, and talk offered the handiest of satiric butts for the insular English. Dryden himself did not approve of the French invasion of the English language, and in expressing this distaste he projects distinctly the foppish humor of Melantha:

> For I cannot approve of their way of refining, who cor-
> rupt our *English* Idiom by mixing it too much with the
> *French:* that is a Sophistication of Language, not an im-
> provement of it. . . . We meet daily with those Fopps, who
> value themselves on their Travelling, and pretend they
> cannot express their meaning in *English,* because they
> would put off to us some *French* Phrase of the last Edi-
> tion.[90]

Melantha's use of French is indeed unabsorbed and satirized, but it is vibrant and not vulgar. In use of language as well as foreign setting and European literary conventions, *Marriage A-la-Mode* functions as a glamorous attack on the parochial and mundane. However malapropian and superficial in practice, Melantha's desires for admiration and great elegance are not to be dismissed out of hand. In her love of words, Melantha is only the satiric outrunner of the play's interest in splendid language. She misuses words blithely while her fellows, her attendant, and her betters manipulate sentences with finesse and passion. The deployment of language in *Marriage A-la-Mode* is indeed so accomplished that it becomes not only an act of communication and lively characterization but of pleasure, fulfilling, perhaps for the first time in Restoration comedy, at least to so high a degree, Hobbes's definition of the fourth use of civilized speech: "to please and delight ourselves and others, by playing with our words, for pleasure or ornament, innocently."[91]

Though linguistic innocence is more often a characteristic of literature than of life, Dryden, in a dedicatory compliment which strives for a balance between the real and the hopeful, attributes the specific excellence of *Marriage A-la-Mode* to the witty and educated conversation of Lord Rochester: "if there be any thing in this Play, wherein I have rais'd my self beyond the ordinary lowness of my Comedies, I ought wholly to acknowledge it to the favour, of being admitted into your Lordship's Conversation." Dryden here treads a fine edge between a genuine gratitude to a clever and especially interesting nobleman and the creation of an idealized gentleman classically learned and acutely sensitive to "the Gallantries of Courts, the Delicacy of Expression, and the Decencies of Behaviour." The description of the nobleness of Rochester's character prepares the reader to accept the

---

[89] For a detailed listing of Melantha's hoard of French words and their currency, see E. A. Horsman, "Dryden's French Borrowings," *RES*, n.s., I (1950), 346–351.

[90] *Defence of the Epilogue,* 211:19–26; cf. Moore, pp. 106–108.

[91] Hobbes, *Leviathan,* I, iv, p. 19.

pattern of "exact virtue" established in the play by Leonidas, Palmyra, and Amalthea; like the pastoral couple in Scudéry, Rochester has completed "the excellencie of . . . [his] Natural parts" with "a Noble Education." The concentration on Rochester's conversation and wit—significantly, the dedication uses the word "wit" or "witty" eight times—makes us sensitive to the repartee and subjects of discussion in the play that follows. The primary topics of the dedication as of the play are language itself and the behavior of gallants at court (with references to food, friendship, games, the French, pastoralism, and design).

The dedication and the play, then, are both artistic strategies, each sharing interests, each reflecting favorably on the other, and together including the reader, dedicatee, poet, and characters in a flattering coterie of refinement. The play's two modes of heroism and wit are unified in the "character" of Rochester himself.

But the dedication also gives us a sharp and unpleasant glimpse of an unidealized court where there is "much of Interest, and more of Detraction." There one can find "a midling sort of Courtiers" who substitute malice for true wit and who can prove to be fools, sycophants, and mischiefmakers; there envious courtiers "live on the Offalls of their Wit, whom they decry," and "make it their business to chase Wit from the Knowledge of Princes, lest it should disgrace their ignorance" (221:28–222:14).[92] Perhaps there is a little of Melantha (and Argaleon) and the Sicilian court in this hard picture, and Doralice's description (III, i, 120–125) of the anxious "Town-Lady" seeking notice from the great at court is not a pleasant one. Artemis rebukes the deservedly snubbed Melantha (III, i, 117–119): "These are sad truths, *Melantha;* and therefore I would e'en advise you to quit the Court, and live either wholly in the Town; or, if you like not that, in the Countrey." But Melantha is an enthusiast, not scheming or malicious, and she does not have to undergo serious condescension nor is she banished to the country. The dedication seems to betray a sense of strain which the play itself does not. The play's satire is more carefully bounded by liveliness and sympathy.

The play has as final recommendation, beyond its well-designed plot and brilliant language, genuine good humor and generosity of spirit. Comedies do end in marriage, but that solution, especially in the Restoration, is often a forced or technical one. As one example, the title character in *Amorous Orontus: or The Love in Fashion* (1665) accepts wedlock more for the requirements of genre than for affection: "I must consent to Wed at last, for I / Have no way else to End this Comedy."[93] *Marriage A-la-Mode* concludes, however, just as much of its comic plot has proceeded, with sincere amicability. While the fate of the self-effacing Amalthea injects a sober note into the joyfulness, this single personal misfortune is held in

---

92 The reference to "Offalls" is repeated by Doralice (III, i, 121) in her description of a perverse ecology of wit in which the rurals feed on the detritus of the townspeople who in turn live off court debris.

93 This lame verse concludes (V, x) John Bulteel's translation (1665) of Thomas Corneille's *L'Amour à la Mode,* itself derived from a Spanish play, *El Amor al uso,* by Antonio de Solis. For further reference to Corneille's play, see *Works,* IX, 344; XVII, 379.

painless context by the Romance convention and the sense of timelessness of the heroic action, and it is offset by the return of Leonidas to his throne, his marriage to Palmyra, the regeneration of Polydamas, and the good-natured reconciliation of the two gay couples.

In his essays and prefaces Dryden spoke out against his moralistic detractors who seemed to argue for a simplistic or instantaneous distribution of terminal punishment and reward. If the comic poet *"works a cure on folly, and the small imperfections in mankind, by exposing them to publick view"*—and Dryden thinks he does—*"that cure is not perform'd by an immediate operation."* Dryden argues *"against the Law of Comedy, which is to reward virtue and punish vice. . . . [for] Comedy is not so much oblig'd to the punishment of the faults which it represents, as [is] Tragedy."* [94] The "faults" represented in *Marriage A-la-Mode* are human frailties, not so much set out with harsh realism or moral judgment as displayed in sporting fashion. The comic characters' praise of inconstancy is neither actualized nor is it intended to persuade, include, or criticize those who do not choose to play their game. (This is in contrast with the wits of, say, Etherege's *The Man of Mode* or Vanbrugh's *The Relapse* who insist on a rigorously high standard of misbehavior from all who count.) Rhodophil and Palamede practice a kind of laissez-faire immorality of language which does not call to ironic account the ideals of their betters or lead to the impregnation of their paramours, nor does it even disarrange the polite, controlled polish of their syntax. One does not (as one certainly does in Wycherley's sexualists) hear the insistence or the urgency of their commitment to infidelity in their prose rhythms. The sexuality is a game of conversation and convention, and one in which the poet himself engages the audience in the epilogue (ll. 27–28): *"You sigh'd when I came in to break the sport, / And set your teeth when each design fell short."*

If Dryden stooped to titillate—and he certainly did not neglect the bawdy, the innuendo, or the double entendre—ultimately he remained decorous, so much so that *Marriage A-la-Mode* was held up as a defense of the state of matrimony. In *Marriage Asserted: In Answer to a Book Entituled Conjugium Conjurgium* (1674) the essayist writes to defend the ends of marriage which are (sig. A5) "the continuation of the species of Mankind . . . and to avoid Fornication." Presumably Dryden's comic characters do not wish "to avoid Fornication" by too wide a mark and they are tantalized by the notion that one man's wife might be another's delight, but the writer has something of a point when he insists that "Mr. Dreydon," along with Mr. Cowley, has "celebrated Love and Marriage":

> What is either wicked or silly in modish colours he [Dryden] has so well painted, as would divert any person that is owner of the least ingenuity, from both: more particularly this of shunning Marriage, and being entred perfidiously to break a vow so easy to be kept, in his Play of *Marriage a-la-Mode:* a more gentile Satyre against this

---

[94] Preface to *An Evening's Love* (*Works*, X, 208–209).

sort of folly, no Pen can write, where he brings the very
assignations that are commonly used about Town upon
the stage; and to see both Boxes and Pitt so damnably
crouded, in order to see themselves abused, and yet neither to be angry or ashamed, argues such excess of stupidity,
that this great Pen it self . . . would be put to a nonplus
to express it.[95]

The abuse, however, if it can be called that, is very lightly spun, and Dryden's "Satyre" is gentle as well as genteel.

Dryden may well have found such defense acceptable, since he allowed
for instruction as the *"secondary end"* of comedy,[96] but the pedagogue
never so gracefully cedes the stage to the entertainer as in *Marriage A-la-
Mode.* The chief end of comedy remains for him *"divertisement and delight."*[97] Unlike *Secret Love, Marriage A-la-Mode* is specifically entitled
"A Comedy," and one must (pace Langbaine) probably accept Dryden at
his generic word. But whether we call it a tragicomedy or a comedy in two
different moods, one heroic, romantic, pastoral, absolutist, the other witty,
urbane, accommodating, and sexually provocative, what we have is a play
whose two plots both lead to forgiveness, marriage, and the refreshment of
society. The double-plot play seems a particularly appropriate vehicle for
one of Dryden's restless, diverse viewpoint, and it marks a culmination of
his abilities to incorporate any number of disparate ideas and ways of con-
fronting experience into a generously unified whole. While the "pattern
of highest human virtue" represented by Palmyra and Leonidas appears
unrelated to the libertinism of the comic characters, the two are in fact
distant (but not polar) marks on an ethical scale whose mean is a balance
of respect and sexual gaiety; the rational cynicism of the gay couple provides a needed corrective to the high sentiment of the heroic mode.[98] Of
course, the opposition is exaggerated for artistic effect, and both the comic
and the heroic are distortions of a practical mean or of any Restoration
reality. While much heightened, the exaggeration is not, however, nearly
so great as it could have been were the plot of wit farcical or really corrupt,
or if the heroic action ended tragically. One of the functions of the upper

---

[95] Pp. 75–76. The marriage controversy of which *Marriage Asserted* is an important part and to which Dryden's play bears only this one slight connection is
thoroughly discussed by Maximillian E. Novak, "Margery Pinchwife's 'London
Disease': Restoration Comedy and the Libertine Offensive of the 1670's," *Studies
in the Literary Imagination,* X (1977), 1–23; see also Moore, pp. 105–106, and
Hume, pp. 292–293.

[96] Preface to *An Evening's Love* (*Works,* X, 209). See preface to *Secret Love*
(*Works,* IX, 117), for a stronger statement of moral intent. Nevertheless, as Hume
(p. 292) points out, such a play as Joseph Arrowsmith's *The Reformation* (acted
by August 1673) attacks *Marriage A-la-Mode* on grounds of sexual license, suggesting that Dryden's play "was seen more as a contribution to sexual innuendo than
to morality"; see also note to epilogue, l. 2.

[97] Preface to *An Evening's Love* (*Works,* X, 209).

[98] For further discussion of the relationship of the satiric and the heroic, see
Earl Miner, ed., *Restoration Dramatists* (1966), pp. 1–18; John Traugott, "The
Rake's Progress from Court to Comedy: A Study in Comic Form," *SEL,* VI (1966),
381–407; and headnote to *The Conquest of Granada,* pp. 428–430, 433–435, above.

plot (and setting) is to elevate the proximate comic action while gently rebuking it for frivolity and lack of greatness. This technique of subtly managed and opposed relationships ministers to Dryden's continuing search for a "nobler" kind of comedy than the farces that so pleased the cits of London.[99] In turn, the comic plot does not degrade the heroism of the royal characters or neutralize their motives and values. Here is no Falstaff showing up the "honor" of Lancasters and Percys as codes of manipulation and self-deception. In *Marriage A-la-Mode* the two worlds of higher and lower courtiers relate almost unironically. Dryden himself did not regard conflicting attitudes as mutually exclusive, but insisted that the educated man would respond with sensitivity to a variety of criteria and perspectives. Dryden defends *Of Dramatick Poesie* as "a Dialogue sustain'd by persons of several opinions,"[100] and that same sense of range and option and civilized disinterest carries forward into this play. Dryden himself was not unmindful of the artistic success he had won in *Marriage A-la-Mode*. Writing in the dedication, he praised the play with modesty and justness as "perhaps . . . the best of my Comedies."

TITLE PAGE

Epigraph. *Quic quid sum ego . . . solido.* From Horace, *Satires,* II, i, 74–79. (Loeb trans.: "Such as I am, however far beneath Lucillius in rank and native gifts, yet Envy, in spite of herself, will ever admit that I have lived with the great, and, while trying to strike her tooth on something soft, will dash upon what is solid.") This is one of the closing lines in an imaginary conversation between Trebatius, a famous attorney, and Horace, who like Dryden is the object of many critical attacks and who is required to use his pen for protection since each man must use "the weapon in which he is strong." Dryden evidently alludes here to the attacks on him in the recently published Rota pamphlets which especially address themselves to *The Conquest of Granada* (see p. 432 above) and to which Dryden responds more directly in the dedication of *The Assignation* (see commentary, pp. 526–529 below). Dryden uses the epigraph both to mock his assailants and to prepare for his compliment upon Rochester's wit in the dedication.

DEDICATION

P. 221 *The Earl of Rochester.* John Wilmot, second Earl of Rochester (1647–1680), an excellent poet himself and an important literary figure in

---

[99] See especially the preface to *An Evening's Love,* (*Works,* X, 203): *"That I admire not any Comedy equally with Tragedy, is, perhaps, from the sullenness of my humor; but that I detest those Farces, which are now the most frequent entertainments of the Stage, I am sure I have reason on my side. . . . Farce . . . consists of forc'd humours, and unnatural events. Comedy presents us with the imperfections of humane nature: Farce entertains us with what is monstrous and chimerical."* Hume (p. 45) argues that in nominating his play a "Comedy" Dryden is making "a deliberate attempt to 'raise' comedy by emphasizing the 'admiration' he had once considered proper to tragedy."

[100] *Defence of an Essay of Dramatique Poesie* (*Works,* IX, 15).

the early Restoration. Much of his extraordinary celebrity derived, however, from his wit and his profligate behavior. On 10 October 1667 he was admitted to the House of Lords along with his contemporary, John Sheffield, third Earl of Mulgrave (1648–1721), who was later to become Dryden's chief patron. Rochester himself was briefly an important supporter of Dryden, as this dedication gracefully acknowledges, but a quarrel between Rochester and Mulgrave may have provoked Rochester to promote Shadwell over Dryden. Rochester's *An Allusion to Horace*, written in the winter of 1675–76, satirizes Dryden, who responded in kind in his preface to *All for Love* (1678). Eventually men of the theater, including Nathaniel Lee, Thomas Otway, and John Crowne, were divided into warring factions: Rochester-Shadwell against Mulgrave-Dryden (see David M. Vieth, ed., *The Complete Poems of John Wilmot, Earl of Rochester* [1968], pp. xxix ff.). Friendly relations between Rochester and Dryden were never resumed; in 1692 in his *Discourse concerning the Original and Progress of Satire* which serves as preface to the translations of Juvenal and Persius, Dryden alludes to Rochester as one "whose Ashes I will not disturb" (*Works*, IV, 6). Rochester's influence on seventeenth-century language and literature, as instanced in this dedication by Dryden personally (and genuinely, it seems), is increasingly recognized and documented by modern critics. See David M. Vieth, "Rochester and the Restoration: An Introductory Note and Bibliography," *Papers on Language and Literature*, XII (Summer 1976), 260–272.

221:8–9 *His Majesty, then at Windsor.* Charles II stayed at Windsor from 27 May to 13 July in 1671 (*CSPD*, vol. 11, pp. 279–382). See headnote, p. 460 above.

221:11–13 *Custom . . . call'd Ver Sacrum.* The custom was to sacrifice animals born in the spring to a god, usually Jupiter, to promote the welfare of the community. The sacrifice was often made either in propitiation during times of distress or in celebration when the yield was abundant (*Oxford Classical Dictionary*). Cf. Dryden's translation of Virgil's *First Pastoral*, ll. 9–10. By complimentary analogy, Dryden here offers the dedication to Rochester as a token for the abundance that Rochester's favor and assistance secured for him. He again expressed his gratitude to Rochester in a letter evidently written in reply to Rochester's "most handsom" acknowledgment of this dedication, there describing Rochester as "above any Incense I can give you" (Ward, *Letters*, pp. 7–11).

221:16–17 *the favour, of being admitted into your Lordship's Conversation.* I.e., into Rochester's circle of acquaintance. (Cf. Melantha's evocation [II, i, 42–46] of Palamede's fashionable *"conversation"* in the French *"Grand mond."*) Rochester was himself highly praised as a conversationalist by his contemporaries. In the epistle dedicatory to Rochester of Fane's *Love in the Dark, or The Man of Business* (1675) Sir Francis Fane says:

> I must confess, I never return from your Lordships most Charming and Instructive Conversation, but I am inspir'd with a new Genius, and improv'd in all those Sciences I ever coveted the knowledge of.

Robert Wolseley speaks of "the agreeable Mirth of his ordinary Conversation" in his preface to Rochester's *Valentinian* (1685). Three times in "Some Memoirs of the Life of John Earl of Rochester," attributed to St.

Evremond (*The Works of the Earls of Rochester, Roscommon, Dorset, the Duke of Devonshire, etc.* [1721], I), Rochester's conversation is described:

> He drew a Conversation so engaging, that none could enjoy without Admiration and Delight, and few without Love [p. ix]. . . . the uncommon Charms of my Lord's Conversation, drew every Man of Taste to engage him with a Bottle; his pleasing Extravagance increasing with his Liquor [p. x]. . . . The Pleasure he gave in his Conversation, was a Snare to him; for his Mirth increasing with his Liquor, many Persons of Quality of his Friends promoted the Glass to his Detriment, for their Satisfaction [p. xxi].

Similarly Congreve, in his dedication of *The Way of the World* (1700) to the Earl of Montague, ascribes the merit of his own comedy "to the Honour of your Lordship's admitting me into your Conversation."

221:17 *I, who pretend not to this way.* Dryden constantly professed that he had no ambitions to write comedy and did so only in deference to public demand. In *A Defence of an Essay of Dramatique Poesie* (*Works*, IX, 7–8) he writes:

> For I confess my chief endeavours are to delight the Age in which I live. If the humour of this, be for low Comedy, small Accidents, and Raillery, I will force my Genius to obey it, though with more reputation I could write in Verse. I know I am not so fitted by Nature to write Comedy: I want that gayety of humour which is required to it. My Conversation is slow and dull, my humour Saturnine and reserv'd: In short, I am none of those who endeavour to break Jests in Company, or make reparties, so that those who decry my Comedies do me no injury, except it be in point of profit: reputation in them is the last thing to which I shall pretend.

Furthermore, Dryden considered comedy "*inferiour to all sorts of Dramatick writing*" (preface to *An Evening's Love* [*Works*, X, 202]). Moore (pp. 64–68) argues convincingly for a reading of ll. 1–2 in the *Epilogue to the Wild Gallant reviv'd* which would indicate that Dryden held this opinion from the very early years of his career as a dramatist. See *Works*, VIII, 89, 262.

221:24 *Noble Education.* After the death in 1658 of Henry Wilmot, Rochester's father, Charles II himself supervised the education of the then eleven-year-old boy. After receiving his M.A. at Oxford on 9 September 1661, Rochester was sent on the grand tour with Sir Andrew Balfour, a tutor of Charles's appointing. Rochester returned to England three years later at the age of seventeen and was in court on Christmas Day 1664.

221:27 *In my little Experience of a Court.* Unlike Rochester, who was early accepted into the court circle, Dryden had sought court favor since 1660, with his praise of Charles in *Astraea Redux* and *To His Sacred Majesty, A Panegyrick on His Coronation* (1661), and further through his praise of Clarendon in *To My Lord Chancellor* (1662). The publication of *Annus Mirabilis* in January 1667, the return of *The Indian Emperour* to Bridges Street in the same month, and the outstanding success of *Secret Love* throughout the winter—so notable that Dryden states in the preface that

Charles "grac'd it with the Title of His Play" (*Works*, IX, 115)—apparently gained Dryden the entrance into court circles he desired. Confirmation of his new status came when he was made poet laureate in April 1668, but acquaintance with the intimates of the court seems possible from 1667 on. See James M. Osborn, *John Dryden: Some Biographical Facts and Problems*, rev. ed. (1965), pp. 215–216; Ward, *Life*, pp. 47 ff.

222:33–34 *the least shadow of your Wit . . . in other men.* That is, poets of less wit under Rochester's patronage. In fact, Rochester was notorious for his satirical lampoons and pranks against friends, admirers, and enemies alike. According to the "Memoirs" (*Works of the Earls of Rochester, Roscommon* [I, xi]):

> His Talent of Satire, was admirable, and in it he spar'd none, not even the King himself. . . . Yet, either by a too frequent Repetition, or a too close and poignant Violence, he banish'd him the Court, for a Satire made directly on him.

The anonymous memorialist may here refer to a well-known incident of early 1674 when "my Lord Rochester fled from Court some time since for delivering (by mistake) into the King's hands a terrible lampoon of his own making against the King, instead of another the King asked him for" (from an anonymous and secret correspondence quoted in K. H. D. Haley, *William of Orange and the English Opposition, 1672–4* [1953], pp. 60–61). Rochester's banishment, one of several, was brief; in 1674 he received from the King the post of keeper and ranger of Woodstock Park, a position he held until his death in 1680.

223:28–29 *Wit seems to have lodg'd it self more Nobly in this Age.* Charles's return to England with his French-style court and manners, and the contemporary self-consciousness toward language, gave rise to the belief among fashionable circles that the Restoration, while perhaps lacking in energy and originality, possessed greater refinement and wit than pre-Interregnum England. John Evelyn (*Diary*, III, 304), after seeing a performance of *Hamlet* on 26 November 1661, wrote: "now the old playe began [sic] to disgust this refined age; since his Majestie being so long abroad." Dryden expressed often and explicitly his conviction that greater wit and refinement of language and manners marked his own times. His *Defence of the Epilogue* was written (see 204:18–20 above) "to make it clear, that the Language, Wit, and Conversation of our Age are improv'd and refin'd above the last." In *Of Dramatick Poesie* (1668), Dryden had expressed this opinion (see *Works*, XVII, 17) as he did again later in the preface to *Troilus and Cressida* (1679, sig. A4v; Watson, I, 239): "*it must be allow'd to the present Age, that the tongue in general is so much refin'd since* Shakespear's *time, that many of his words, and more of his Phrases, are scarce intelligible.*" The poem *To my Dear Friend Mr. Congreve, On His Comedy, call'd, The Double-Dealer* (*Works*, IV, 432) opens with this same assertion:

> Well then; the promis'd hour is come at last;
> The present Age of Wit obscures the past.

223:36 *without desiring you should proceed to a Scene or Play.* Possibly only two or three years intervened between this writing and Rochester's alteration of Fletcher's *Valentinian*, a former Blackfriars play allowed to the King's Company in 1669 (Van Lennep, p. 152). Rochester may have planned his version for production during the 1675–76 season; a manuscript now in the British Library (MS Add. 28692, ff. 3a–69a) gives a cast that includes Mohun, Hart, Boutell, Marshall, and Cox, as well as other performers in the original cast of *Marriage A-la-Mode*. In 1684 *Valentinian* was finally and very successfully performed; the first edition appeared the following year (Van Lennep, pp. 152, 237, 325; Downes, p. 40).

224:4–6 *any more then the French King is contriving the Conquest of the Swissers.* "Swissers" refers to the politically unimportant Swiss cantons. The political ambitions of Louis XIV did not include conquest of the Swiss, who lacked political prestige and whose poverty made them proverbially available as mercenary soldiers. (See Tilley, M1089; cf. *The Hind and the Panther*, III, 177, in *Works*, III, 166). A report from Paris dated 24 September 1671 in the *London Gazette* gives exactly contemporary information on the relations between Louis and the Swiss cantons: they "not onely consent to the raising of 22000 Swisses, which the King intends to have on foot in his Service, but have likewise abated very considerably of the pensions they always received of this Crown." With this analogy, Dryden wittily and self-deprecatingly suggests that it was as unnecessary for Rochester to seek success as a playwright as for Louis XIV to be interested in conquering the paltry Swiss.

PROLOGUE

The prologue was first published in *Covent Garden Drollery* (1672), pp. 6–7, and is assigned to Charles Hart, who played Palamede. For an additional couplet printed there following l. 6 see the textual footnote.

1–2 *Lord, how reform'd and quiet etc.* Preparations for the third Dutch war, which was not declared until 17 March 1672, were well underway by November 1671, the month of the earliest possible first performance of *Marriage A-la-Mode*. Robert D. Hume ("The Date of Dryden's *Marriage A-la-Mode*," *HLB*, XXI [1973], 166) points out that the *CSPD* for 1671 (vols. 11, 12 *passim*) registers preparations for the war with the movements and departures of groups of men, many no doubt drawn from the gentry. This activity would explain the "quiet" in a theater without its most energetic male contingent, though it is a recurring artistic technique of Restoration prologues to divide contemporary audiences into economic, social, and sexual constituencies and send one group away, either to foreign parts, to the Wells, or back to the City.

3 *Fop-corner.* A front corner of the pit where the fops sat and chatted during a play. Summers quotes Alexander Radcliffe's *The Ramble* (1682) which describes satirically the would-be young man of fashion:

> Into Fop-corner you wou'd get,
> And use a strange obstreperous Wit,
> Not any quiet to the Pit Allowing.

3 *Civil War.* With rhythmic stress and ironic pun on "civil"; the fierce, primitive battle between the sexes as opposed to the impending international conflict between England and Holland.

4 *White-Wig and Vizard.* Synecdoches for men of fashion with powdered

wigs and prostitutes in face masks. For a similar connection, see prologue, 2 *Conquest of Granada,* ll. 13–16 above.

5–6 *France, and the Fleet, have swept the Town so clear.* The date for beginning the war in the spring had been publicly set in the bogus treaty with France signed by Charles II and the entire Cabal in December 1670, but the war had already been planned in a secret treaty made six months earlier (22 May 1670), in which Charles agreed to reconcile himself publicly to Catholicism at a time "left entirely to the discretion of the King of England" (Ogg, p. 345). For this public reconciliation, Louis had agreed to pay England the sum of 200,000 pounds sterling. According to the remaining terms of both treaties, England was to contribute to the Dutch war an army of foot of 6,000 and 60 men-of-war and ten fireships (Ogg, pp. 342–348). That this drain on the male population was already noticeable by the fall of 1671 in London is attested to by remarks in the prologues to John Crowne's *The History of Charles the Eighth of France* and Buckingham's *The Rehearsal* and in the epilogue to Wycherley's *The Gentleman Dancing Master* (Hume, "The Date of Dryden's *Marriage A-la-Mode,*" pp. 161–166).

6 *you can hear.* The noise and licentious behavior of the audience were perennial subjects of comment: "the Pit and Galleries are become downright Conventicles of Bawdery; one cannot hear a Play in 'em, for the Chattering of the fluttering Blades to a Company of Pockey-fac'd Creatures in Vizards" ([Thomas Rawlins], *Tom Essence: or, The Modish Wife* [1677], p. 67). See, too, Dryden's *Epilogue to the King and Queen* (*Works,* II, 198 and nn) for a full and lively description of this pandemonium.

9 *With hair tuck'd up.* The hair or wig is tied back in a queue for the forthcoming military campaign. In Thomas Shadwell's *Epsom-Wells* (performed by 2 December 1672), Carolina in a mask says about Bevil and Rains: "Ye don't look as if you would make Love, but War; ye have long Swords, and your hair tuck'd up" (II, i). Cf. also *Tunbridge Wells* (spring 1674), where Rochester describes "Some warlike men . . . With hair tied back, singing a bawdy song" (ll. 149 ff., in *Complete Poems of John Wilmot* ed. Vieth, p. 79).

13 *powerful Guinnee.* A guinea coin was the customarily inflated literary price for sexual favors. Macdonald (p. 110n) points to a borrowing by John Lacy in *Sir Hercules Buffoon:* "Prithee consider, Sister, Virtue cannot maintain thee; and when once 'tis known a handsom Woman is in want, then as the Poet worthily says, the powerful Guiney cannot be withstood." In a song (pp. 52–53) printed in *Bristol Drollery* (1674), a gallant boasts that "We'l tempt pretty Susan, and Marg'ret, and Jenny, / For mid night access, with the bribe of a Guiney." For general proverbial expressions of gold conquering all, see Horace, *Odes,* III, xvi, 1–8, and Tilley, L406 (Kinsley).

14 *made of Play house flesh and bloud.* This line evokes a complex of ideas concerning the deceptiveness of art, the parallelism of artfulness and sex, and the image of the theater as brothel, a place where one pays.

16 *grinning Honour gain.* I.e., death. See Falstaff's remark to Prince Hal over Sir Walter Blunt's corpse: "I like not such grinning honour as Sir Walter hath. Give me life . . ." (*1 Henry IV,* V, iii, 58–59).

18 *dead Vacation.* In a general sense, Dryden alludes to the lack of audi-

ence at the King's House; but "vacation" is more precisely one of the four periods of the year when the courts were not sitting, probably here the vacation between Michaelmas and Hilary terms (i.e., between 26 November and 10 January).

20 *Poor pensive Punk now peeps.* The soliciting whore looks into the theater and decides there are not enough potential customers to justify the half-crown price of admission to the pit. The same calculation, without Dryden's comic alliteration, is portrayed by Sir *C*[harles] *S*[edley] in his prologue to Shadwell's *Epsom-Wells* (1673):

> . . . if once the Pit grows thin,
> Your dear lov'd Masks, will hardly venture in.

22 *manages her last Half-crown with care.* A half crown was both the price of admission to the pit and a customary charge for a whore (Kinsley).

23 *the Mall.* The allée along the northern edge of St. James's Park fashionable for walking, sport, and procurement.

24-27 *Our City Friends . . . seldom come to hear.* For information on the opening, popularity, and accessibility to the City of the Duke's elaborate new theater in Dorset Garden, see headnote, pp. 461–462. Dryden's *Sir Martin Mar-all* and Etherege's *The Comical Revenge, or Love in a Tub*, apparently the first plays to be performed at Dorset Garden (Downes, pp. 31–32), may qualify as the *"gay Shows"* of Dryden's allusion, while John Crowne's *The History of Charles the Eighth of France*, "the first new Play Acted there" and "all new Cloath'd," (*ibid.*, p. 32) may well be the object of Dryden's jibe at *"gawdy Scenes."* Certainly several times in 1672 and 1674 Dryden refers with scorn to Dorset Garden's luxurious house, to its elaborate scenic effects, and to the citizens' vulgar preference generally for the spectacular. In the *Prologue Spoken at the Opening of the New House* (l. 6), e.g., Dryden describes Dorset Garden as *"Nero's* Palace, shining all with Gold" (see *Works*, I, 149, 353). Also, the actress speaking the *Prologue for the Women* when they acted at the theater in Lincoln's Inn Fields (*Works*, I, 144) expects an audience of "the *Lovers, Braves,* and *Wits,* / The Gaudy House with Scenes, will serve for *Citts"* (ll. 22–23). In turn, Dryden's condescensions of this kind are parodied in *The Rehearsal* (I, i [1672, p. 5]): "And, then, for Scenes, Cloaths and Dancing, we put 'em quite down, all that ever went before us."

29 *cutting Moorcraft.* Cutting means a "swaggering blade" (*OED*). Moorcraft is an important character in Beaumont and Fletcher's *The Scornful Lady*, a usurer who at the end of the play is declared a gallant (V, iv, 134) "now called, Cutting Moorecraft" (*The Dramatic Works*, ed. Fredson Bowers *et al.*, II [1970], 543). *The Scornful Lady* was well known to Restoration audiences. Pepys saw it at least seven times, and Langbaine (p. 214) refers to it as "a Comedy acted with good Applause even in these times, at the Theatre in Dorset-Garden." It was in fact assigned to the King's Company (not the Duke's, as Langbaine suggests) c. 12 January 1669 (Van Lennep, p. 152). Earlier it had been made the substance of at least one droll, *The false Heire and formal Curate*, published in *The Wits, or, Sport upon Sport. In Select Pieces of Drollery* (1662), but there Moorcraft does not undergo conversion. That the incidents so mangled in this droll could be considered recognizable and entertaining further attests to a tradition of long exposure of *The Scornful Lady* (see *The Wits or, Sport upon Sport,*

ed. John James Elson, in *Cornell Studies in English,* XVIII [1932], 68–77, 371–372).

Langbaine (p. 214) remembers that Dryden "condemn'd the Conclusion of this Play in reference to the conversation of Moor-craft the Usurer; but whether this Catastrophe be excusable, I must leave to the Criticks." In *An Essay of Dramatick Poesie (Works,* XVII, 42–43) Lisideius praises the French for not ending their plays with an abrupt or unprepared-for "conversion, or simple change of will." As an example of the English predilection for a fifth-act change of character, he cites "the conversion of the Usurer ["cutting Moorcraft"] in the *Scornful Lady,*" which seems to him

> a little forc'd; for being an Usurer, which implies a lover
> of Money to the highest degree of covetousness, (and such
> the Poet has represented him) the account he gives for
> the sudden change is, that he has been dup'd by the wilde
> young fellow, which in reason might render him more
> wary another time, and make him punish himself with
> harder fare and courser cloaths to get up again what he
> had lost: but that he should look on it as a judgment, and
> so repent, we may expect to hear in a Sermon, but I
> should never indure it in a Play.

In *A Parallel Betwixt Painting and Poetry* ([1695], p. xl; Watson, II, 198), Dryden again refers to "Cutting Moorcraft":

> So in the Persons of a *Play,* whatsoever is said or done by
> any of them, must be consistent with the manners which
> the *Poet* has given them distinctly: and even the Habits
> must be proper to the degrees, and humours of the Persons as well as in a *Picture.* He who enter'd in the first
> Act, a Young man like *Pericles* Prince of *Tyre,* must not
> be in danger in the fifth Act, of committing Incest with
> his Daughter: nor an Usurer, without great probability
> and causes of Repentance, be turn'd into a *Cutting Moorcraft.*"

In Dryden's version of Horace's second Epode (*Works,* III, 85), "*Morecraft*" stands for the corrupted urban man whose "prevailing love of pelf" (l. 100) prevents him from enjoying the bounties of pastoral life. In the present allusion, Moorcraft becomes the citizen-turned-rake, a formerly sober City man who, corrupted by his own delusions and by the "Glorious Trade" of sophisticated town and court manners, constantly attends masquerades.

31 *A Masquing Ball.* Masquerade balls and masked entertainments were fashionable from the beginning of the Restoration (see, for example, Pepys, 3 February 1665), particularly during the winter season, but judging by the many references, they seemed to have reached a new degree of popularity during the winters of 1671, 1672, and 1673. On 24 January 1671 the *Bulstrode Papers* (I, 168) report that "last night their Majesties were pleased to honour the French ambassador with their companyes at Yorke House at an entertainment prepaired, where was great danceing, and severall principall persons about the towne in mascarade"; and on the following Saturday "theire Majesties, accompanied by the Prince of Orange and most of the nobility and ladyes about y[e] Court in Mascarade were pleased to bee

present at yᵉ revells at Lincolne's Inn" (p. 169; see also p. 159). On 4 February 1671 the *CSPD* (vol. 11, p. 69) takes note of a "great revelling at Gray's Inn, where his Majesty was present, accompanied by most of the Court in masquerade." Lady Mary Bertie writes to her niece Katherine Noel of several masked balls at Whitehall during this season, and on 4 March 1671 inquires if "you have heard of the watchman that was killed. . . . They say the King hath put out a Proclamation to forbid maskerades" (*Rutland MSS, HMC, 12th Report, Appendix, Pt. V* [1889], p. 23). A newsletter on 7 March 1671, discussing the incident, describes the King as deploring "the many mischiefs that may arise and have lately by persons under pretence of masquerade" (*Le Fleming MSS, HMC, 12th Report, Appendix*, Pt. VII [1890], p. 76). See also *Bulstrode Papers*, I, 174–175. On 4 January 1672 Mrs. Evelyn writes of "the eclat of the wedding, mascarades which trebled their number the second night of the wedding [so] that there was great disorder and confusion caused by it" (*Diary and Correspondence of John Evelyn*, ed. William Bray and Henry B. Wheatley [1906], IV, 57). There are extended references to the masquerade and its manners in the epilogue to Thomas Shadwell's *The Miser*, which had its first performance at Bridges Street in January 1672:

> But as a fop that's dress'd in Masquerade,
> Will any place with impudence invade,
> And little rambling Punks dare be so rude,
> Among the best of Ladies to intrude:
> So Poets sure, though ill, may be allow'd
> Among the best in Masquerade to crowd.
> Our Poet who wrote this Incognito,
> Does boldly claim this priviledge as his due;
> He presses in, and will not be kept out,
> Though he deserves to stand amongst the rout,
> Those fifteen hundred Poets who have writ,
> And never could have one Play acted yet.
> But now hee's in, pray use him civilly,
> Let him, what e're he sayes, unquestion'd be,
> According to the Laws of Masquerade,
> Those sacred Laws by dancing Nations made,
> Which the young Gallants sure will ne're invade.

The Prologue to the Widdow, an anonymous piece in *London Drollery* ([1673], pp. 11–12], frankly deplores the popularity of the masquerade. This particular prologue, which internal evidence dates to the winter of 1672–73 and which incidentally is much in Dryden's style, suggests, as does the prologue to *Marriage A-la-Mode*, that the masquerade with its private advantages and direct sexual pleasures is preferred to the theater:

> Now that the Season of the War is past,
> We well had hop'd to see you here at last,
> But you this Winter find out other ways
> To kill your selves, and to destroy our Plays,
> You meet in Masquerade to pass your time
> Without the help of Reason or of Rime,
> You talk, and cheat each other in disguise,

And draw ten blanks of Beauty for one prize
Were Visor of[f], and all were bound to come,
And shew your homely Faces in the Room,
Each one would cry to see the rest appear,
Now what the Dev'l do these damn'd faces here.
Then he who seem'd a Lord in that dumb show,
Prove some young Spark of Pater-Noster-Row.
And she who in disguise appear'd so pretty,
Turns up her Masque and shews the Orange Betty.
Thus tir'd with want of pleasure home we creep,
And all next day, you lie a Bed and sleep,
Mean time our empty Seats, your absence mourn,
We sigh (but Poets think of you with scorn)
For Courting still your selves, you seem to say,
That you Heaven Love, you have more wit then they,
And that one Sceen o' th' Couch, is worth a Play.

Clearly, during at least two theater seasons, 1671–72 and 1672–73, masquerades were being attended, discussed, and satirized. Dapperwit, in Wycherley's *Love in a Wood*, ed. Gerald Weales (1966), boasts that "a man of wit may have the better of the dumb shew" (II, i, p. 30). Alternating between references to theater and real life as modes of disguise and as forums for illicit sexuality, Dryden and his fellow writers satirize the deceiving and stupid citizen who has become the mock hero in his own "dumb show."

That the masquerade finally and inevitably became notorious for the sexual dalliance and transmigration of class it licensed may be inferred from extensive contemporary evidence; and if the titillating value of "Room" and "Couch" is in question, the idea will be found specifically stated in the epilogue to Edward Ravenscroft's *The Citizen Turn'd Gentleman* (1st ed., [1672]), a play performed often in the summer of 1672:

They sup, they have the fiddles too and dance:
Tow'rds morning, when they think of going home,
Each Gallant on a Couch in the next room,
In's turn, takes gentle solace with his Punk;
Drops her a Guinney, and sends her home half drunk.

In the first four scenes of Act IV of *Marriage A-la-Mode* all the main characters are dressed in masquerade for the masked ball at court.

I, i

3–18 The music to the song that opens the play was written by Robert Smith (d. 1675), one of the group of musicians who reached maturity during the Commonwealth and was a part of that first generation of Restoration songwriters which included John Banister and Pelham Humphrey (see Ian Spink, *English Song: Dowland to Purcell* [1974], pp. 149–184). Smith was in steady demand by the theaters, particularly by the musically interested Dorset Garden. Ordinarily he wrote his songs in triple time, the dance-time measure popularly used with songs in the 1670's, but this setting is in common time, and at the date of the opening it would therefore have been a striking piece of music.

37 *your Gullets are sew'd up, like Cormorants.* Cormorants are large and

voracious seabirds (*OED*) used to catch fish. Cf. *1 Conquest of Granada*, V, i, 454. A leather thong tied around the lower part of its neck prevented a cormorant from swallowing its catch.

51 *words of course*. Said for form or fashion's sake; not meant. Cf. *The Medall*, ll. 84–85.

76 *propriety*. "Propriety" did not carry the modern meaning of "correctness of behavior or morals" until the late eighteenth century. It did, however, mean the "proper state or condition" of man's "own nature" as well as "appropriateness" and "property" (*OED*), all of which meanings are suggested here, as in V, i, 360. See headnote, p. 480n above.

111 *shot the gulf*. To have been successful in a daring enterprise (*OED*).

156 *great Beds*. Rhodophil seems to refer to the double beds that were becoming fashionable in Restoration houses (Beaurline and Bowers, p. 289).

160 *Cordials*. A cordial is a "medicine, food, or beverage which invigorates the heart and stimulates the circulation" (*OED*).

173–174 *Chapmen*. Persons engaged in buying and selling; a retail dealer or an agent in a commercial transaction (*OED*). The term has a lesser meaning of customer or purchaser, but the sense is that of one who will shortly turn over the goods he is buying.

178 *Broad-gold*. The twenty-shilling gold pieces were broader than the guineas introduced in 1663 and were known as broad gold or old gold. "He . . . was pulling out broad pieces (that have not seen the Sun these many years)" (Shadwell, *The Miser* [1672], III, iii). Despite severe penalties for mutilation of currency, these older coins were much clipped and devalued.

182 *Town-Lady*. Cf. epilogue, l. 32.

185–186 *prevents*. Arrives before (*OED*).

186 *Chymists*. Sutherland suspects a covert sexual allusion to Charles II and the treatment of venereal disease with mercury in return for payment of gold. The "Chymists" have found a medical treatment that brings surer profit than their alchemical investigations. The King was indeed interested in scientific experimentation (see, e.g., Pepys, 15 January 1669) as well as sexual pleasure, and a double meaning or sly reference to the English court seems likely here. Within the play the focus is upon Melantha's fervid desire to inflate her social position.

191 *ubiquitary*. Ubiquitous (*OED*). See headnote, p. 470 above.

200–203 Similarly, in Congreve's *Love for Love* (1695), I, i, Tattle coyly refuses to identify by name his portraits of "Women of Quality" and Scandal warns him to "take notice, if you are so ill a Painter, that I cannot know the Person by your picture of her, you must be condemn'd, like other bad Painters, to write the Name at the bottom."

290–296 *a Letter . . . torn off*. In *The Rehearsal*, III, ii ([1672], p. 24), Bayes and Smith likewise discuss letters of natal patent brought to Prince Volscius by his servants, as those of Polydamas are brought to him by his, and the unclear state of health of the fair Parthenope—dead or alive—is commented upon:

> *Cor.* At last,
> *Volscius* the great this dire resolve embrac'd:
> His servants he into the Country sent,
> And he himself to *Piccadillè* went.

Where he's inform'd, by Letters, that she's dead.
Ush. Dead! is that possible? Dead!
Phys. O ye Gods! [*Exeunt.*
Bayes. There's a smart expression of a passion; O ye Gods! That's one of my bold strokes, a gad.
Smi. Yes; but who is the fair person that's dead?
Bayes. That you shall know anon.
Smi. Nay, if we know it at all, 'tis well enough.
Bayes. Perhaps you may find too, by and by, for all this, that she's not dead neither.
Smi. Marry, that's good news: I am glad of that with all my heart.
In the colored light of romance, ghostly dictation has, from time to time, taken place, but Buckingham chooses to draw up his accounts with satiric brightness. See headnote, p. 463, and John Reichert, "A Note on Buckingham and Dryden," *N&Q,* CCVII (1962), 220–221.

340 *Venus Urania.* The daughter of Uranus who rules over beauty and generation.

II, i

9 *Æsop's Ass.* Who is vigorously repulsed when he awkwardly attempts to imitate the fawning of his master's pet dog.

18–82 *Sir . . . in a twinkling.* Cibber (I, 167–169) describes how Susanna Percival as Melantha played this first encounter with Palamede; see section on actors, p. 551 below.

44, 47 *good graces.* Sutherland suggests that because Palamede repeats this phrase along with the French words, Melantha may have pronounced "graces" with a French accent.

56 *Minouets . . . Jigs.* A minuet is a "slow, stately dance, in triple measure," for two dancers, imported from France in the later part of the seventeenth century (*OED*). A jig is a "lively, rapid, springy kind of dance" to music in triple rhythm (usually 6/8 or 12/8) (*OED*). Melantha, typically enough, has her adjectives reversed.

74 *at the Queen's.* Although Polydamas is a widower, Melantha is here concerned with her ideal world, not necessarily with the real one.

78–79 *I have not made my court to him these two long hours.* The Prince's presence has been known for only two hours, but Melantha has not yet met him.

85 *French Gibberish.* Until the beginning of the eighteenth century English lawbooks and statutes were written in legal French, an Anglo-Norman mixture of English, Latin, and French (S-S, IV, 281). Summers refers to Aphra Behn's *Sir Patient Fancy* (first performed 1678), where in Act IV books are described as uninteresting because "they are only English and some Law-French."

89 *at cuffs.* Fighting (*OED*).

90 *rising blow.* Sutherland suggests that this may be "a pugilistic term of the seventeenth century, with the meaning of upper-cut. . . . But Palamede's expression has probably an obscene significance as well."

93 *Basta.* Italian and Spanish for "enough."

100 *Woodman.* Hunter (*OED*).

122 *sub sigillo.* "Under seal," i.e., to swear under oath.

122–123 *numerical.* Identical (*OED* cites this passage).

210 *making a loose.* Getting away (Beaurline and Bowers).

215 *Galeche.* Also calash, calèche, gallesh. "A kind of light carriage with low wheels, having a removable folding hood or top" (*OED*). Summers cites Etherege's *The Man of Mode* (1676), III, ii, where Sir Fopling proudly asks, "Have you taken notice of the Gallesh I brought over [from France]?"

222–224 *Your pardon . . . Servant All.* Melantha's voluble leave-taking may find an echo in that of an overcorrect Bayes in *The Rehearsal*, I, i ([1672], p. 2): "Your most obsequious, and most observant, very servant, Sir."

336 *Absolve.* In the now obsolete sense of accomplish or perform completely (*OED*).

351 *absolve.* Used this time in the still current sense of set free from (*OED*).

425 *strokes in ashes* etc. "The maidens gathered about the hearth, and in the ashes which had fallen from the fire made marks or strokes, which, with a little imagination, could be easily interpreted as the initials of their lovers" (Sutherland).

432 *Wake.* The local annual festival an English parish observed originally on the feast of the church's patron saint (*OED*).

432 *Chaplet.* "A wreath for the head, usually a garland of flowers or leaves" (*OED*). Summers quotes from *Le Grand Cyrus*, VI, ii.

484 *Your Hook, your Scrip.* Shepherd's crook and bag.

487 *Upon my Hearse.* Sutherland suggests that this sort of melodious lament became a dramatic convention in the late seventeenth and early eighteenth centuries. See Aspatia's lament in Beaumont and Fletcher's *The Maid's Tragedy* (II, i).

491 *Love and mutual Vows have ty'd.* The vows between Leonidas and Palmyra are based on spiritual affinity, but they would have been, in England at any rate, legally binding as well, since mutual vows, even privately uttered, had the validity of a public marriage ceremony. See Gellert Spencer Alleman, *Matrimonial Law and the Materials of Restoration Comedy* (1942), p. 9.

III, i

14 *Turtles.* Turtledoves (*OED*).

63 *Banes of Matrimony.* Banes is an obsolete form of banns (*OED*), but there is a pun here on the deadliness of marriage (S-S, IV, 298).

128 *Carriers-day.* Mailman's delivery day; private individuals delivered letters until well into the eighteenth century.

141 *After the pangs of a desperate Lover.* The song is by Dryden himself, from *An Evening's Love*, II, i, 499–514 (*Works*, X, 245).

160 *finical Cit.* "Finical" is "over-nice or particular, affectedly fastidious" (*OED*). "Cit" is a derogatory appellation for a citizen of the City of London.

162 *Frumity.* "A dish made of hulled wheat boiled in milk, and seasoned with cinnamon, sugar, etc." (*OED*).

163 *Mirabilis.* Short for *Aqua Mirabilis*, "the wonderful water," prepared of wine and spices (*OED*). Summers quotes *The Queen's Closet Opened* (1655):

This water preserveth the Lungs without grievances, &
helpeth them; being wounded, it suffereth the Blood not
to putrifie, but multiplieth the same. This water suffereth
not the heart to burn, nor melancholy, nor the Spleen
to be lifted up above nature: it expelleth the Rheum,
preserveth the Stomach, conserveth Youth, & procureth
a good Colour: it preserveth Memory, it destroyeth the
Palsie: If this be given to one a dying, a spoonful of it
reviveth him; in the Summer use one spoonful a week
fasting; in the Winter two spoonfuls.

163 *Jill-glass.* "A measure for liquids, containing one fourth of a standard
pint" (*OED*).

184–247 For discussion of this exchange, see headnote, p. 474 above.

224 *Point Gorget.* A lace covering for the neck and breast (*OED*).

230 *Indian-Gown.* A dressing gown of Indian cloth. See Wycherley's *The
Gentleman Dancing Master* (1673), Act V, where a kept mistress expects a
"variety of new Gowns, and rich Petticoats, with her Dishabiliee or Flame-
colour Gown call'd Indian, and Slippers of the same."

232 *meer.* Absolute, perfect (*OED*).

234 *Guimp.* Lace in which a thicker thread called gimp makes a pattern
of figures, flowers, or other ornaments (*OED*).

257 *What do you mean.* What: Why (*OED*). Most modern editors have
treated "What" as an expletive, putting a comma after it. There is no authority for doing so, and the comma, as Sutherland notes, considerably
alters the meaning.

290 *Stare.* Starling (*OED*).

313–314 *Piety . . . piety.* Leonidas seems to use the word first in the sense
of "Virtue" to refer to Palmyra, and then in reference to his filial duty to
Polydamas.

348 *I'll hold my breath and die.* For similar threats of heroic self-control
see Indamora in *Aureng-Zebe,* V, i (1676, p. 70; S-S, V, 283); Don Sebastian
in *Don Sebastian,* V, i (*Works,* XV, 208); and Cleonidas in *Cleomenes,* IV, i
(1692, p. 48; S-S, VIII, 333).

349 *last Leonidas.* Saintsbury conjectures "lost" for "last," but incorrect-
ly, it seems. Other editors have inserted a comma after "last," but see *Don
Sebastian,* III, i, 312; V, i, 707–711; and notes in *Works,* XV, 136, 216–217,
440.

412–480 *Then the first use . . . starves my love.* In *The Rehearsal,* III, ii
([1672], pp. 25–27), while Smith and Johnson look on askance and Bayes
rhapsodizes (and while the old fisherman is dragged "hence / Till torture
of the Rack produce his sence"), Prince Prettyman displays his emotional
turmoil concerning his confused parentage:

> Bring in my Father, why d'ye keep him from me?
> Although a Fisherman, he is my Father,
> Was ever Son, yet, brought to this distress,
> To be, for being a Son, made fatherless?
> Oh, you just Gods, rob me not of a Father.
> The being of a Son take from me rather.
> . . . .

What Oracle this darkness can evince?
Sometimes a Fishers Son, sometimes a Prince.
It is a secret, great as is the world;
In which, I, like the soul, am toss'd and hurl'd.
In the blackest Ink of Fate, sure, was my Lot.
And, when she writ my name, she made a blot.

See headnote, p. 463 above.

III, ii

70 *hide and seek*. The *OED* cites this name of the children's game as the first recorded usage, but Professor Robert Dent (UCLA) has noticed that it is already listed as a "proverb" by John Clarke in *Paroemiologia Anglo-Latina* (1639), p. 2.

99 *All-cocks hidden*. Derived from the cry "all hid" in the children's game now usually called "hide-and-seek"; the variation used here probably carries an innuendo. See III, ii, 70; V, i, 301.

103–104 *danted with a Bug-bear*. "He thinks every bush a bugbear" (Tilley, B738). "Danted" is an obsolete form of "daunted" (*OED*).

137 *none*. An obsolete variant of "my own," according to Summers.

IV, i

37 *unavailable*. Unavailing.

41–42 *Hang . . . 'em*. The image that probably stands behind Leonidas's plaint is drawn from the familiar emblem of the growing palm tree weighed down on either side with two stones to make it grow straight, illustrating the moral of *Nitor in adversum*, "to press forward against circumstances" (see Rosemary Freeman, *English Emblem Books* [1948], pp. 77, 150–151). Thus these lines are not merely a description of Leonidas's double loss of crown and mistress or a complaint about these losses, but they carry in them a sense of heroic perseverance and growth. For a more direct use by Dryden of this emblem and a more elaborate discussion of its history, see *Heroique Stanzas*, ll. 57–58, in *Works*, I, 13, 199.

46 *Passengers*. Passersby, travelers (*OED*).

46 *grates*. Prison bars (*OED*).

131 *antique*. Used either in the sense of "ancient" or "antic"; Summers gives the latter. *NCD* defines "Anticks" as those who "dress themselves up with Ribbons, mismatch'd Colours, Feathers, etc. Zanies, Mountebanks, or Merry-Andrews."

134–136 *Masquerade . . . is Vizor-masque in debauch*. See note to prologue, l. 31 above.

148 *want*. In the sense of "lack," not "desire" (Saintsbury).

152 *I doubt*. I fear (*OED*).

176–177 *course . . . herd*. The analogy is to the hunting or coursing after game (Beaurline and Bowers).

182 *resty*. Sluggish, indolent (*OED*, citing this passage).

IV, ii

16 *Dark-lantern*. "A lantern with a slide or arrangement by which the light can be concealed" (*OED*). Here, more in the sense of a concealed source of light.

47–67 *Song.* The sexually explicit lyrics were possibly suggested by a French madrigal in *Recueil de quelques pieces nouvelles et galantes, tant en prose qu'en vers* (1664), pp. 188–189 (noted by Louis I. Bredvold and quoted in Allen, pp. 115–116n):

> Tirsis d'un excez de plaisir,
> Estoit sur le point de mourir
> Entre les bras de Filis qu'il adore,
> Quand Filis, que l'Amour range sous méme loy,
> Et que le mesme feu devore,
> Luy dit, ah! mon Tirsis, ah! ne meurs pas encore,
> Ie veux mourir avec toy.
> Tirsis alors suspend l'enuie;
> Qu'il avoit de perdre la vie;
> Mais par cette contrainte il se met aux abois,
> Et n'osant pas mourir il se meurt mille fois;
> Cependant lors qu'au sein de cette jeune Amante,
> Le Berger à longs traits boit l'Amoureux poison;
> Elle qui sent déja qu'il entre en pâmoison,
> D'un regard languissant, & d'une voix tremblante,
> Luy dit, mon unique soucy,
> Meurs, mon Tirsis; car ie me meurs aussi.
> Soudain ce Berger tout en flâme,
> Luy répond, comme toy ie me meurs, je me pâme.
> Ainsi dans les ravissemens
> Moururent ces heureux Amans;
> Mais d'une mort si douce & si digne d'envie,
> Que pour mourir encor ils reprirent la vie.

Chandler B. Beall ("A Quaint Conceit from Guarini to Dryden," *MLN*, LXIV [1949], 461–468) gives an extensive lineage for the song and the conceit of the *morte amorosa* in Italian, French, and English lyrics. It is Dryden's version that most urgently exploits the frustration of sexual mistiming. Nicholas Staggins' setting is typical of the popular song of the 1670's, a strophic triple-time air (see Spink, *English Song*, pp. 151–155 ff., 184 ff.). Staggins (1650?–1700), had earlier set the dialogue, "How unhappy a Lover am I," for Dryden's *1 Conquest of Granada.*

IV, iii

13–15 *Park-time . . . or two.* Doralice suggests two favorite activities of London gallants: hunting women in the park and visiting actresses backstage.

23 *dispatch here.* Eating houses were common places for sexual intrigue.

52–53 *Riddle, Read me, and take me.* Sutherland suggests a formula or cant phrase to be found in printed riddles, with a sexual pun on "Ride me and take me."

58 *I carry Steel.* The meaning is sexual as well as scientific.

64–65 *tell thee . . . tell you.* Noyes notes that Palamede uses the dismissive familiar singular pronoun and Doralice the more formal plural.

89 *I warrant you.* I guarantee that you will not be discovered *(OED).*

95 *bar'd the Dice.* Declared the cast void; barred it.

96 *nick'd him.* To nick is "to win at Dice, to hit the Mark" (*NCD*).

96 *Box.* The dice were shaken in a box and the boxkeeper directed the action of the game (see Charles Cotton, *The Compleat Gamester* [1674], pp. 1–5).

99 *Picture in the Hangings.* A wall-hung tapestry woven with figures on one side.

106 *Old Chios.* Wine from the Greek island of Chios (*Oxford Classical Dictionary*).

131–132 *with his mouth.* Openmouthed in admiration (Summers).

132 *Mon Monsieur.* Q1–3 (and Sutherland) read *Man Monsieur* which Sutherland glosses as "French serving-man," but the point is more likely that the Frenchified fop addresses his father impudently with a "my good man" in French (Beaurline and Bowers).

142–143 Melantha characteristically adopts the disdainful French attitude toward English spectators' desire for noise and gore. The differences in national theatrical tastes are vividly drawn by Dryden in the epilogue to *Aureng-Zebe* (1676):

> Bold Brittons, at a brave Bear-garden Fray,
> Are rouz'd: and, clatt'ring Sticks, cry, Play, play, play.
> Mean time, your filthy Forreigner will stare,
> And mutter to himself, Ha gens Barbare!

The tensions in dramatic art between showing and telling, spectacle and words, especially as they relate to French versus English or sophisticated versus unsophisticated audiences, are, of course, perennial topics of seventeenth-century critical debate and are discussed extensively by Dryden in *Of Dramatick Poesie* and *Of Heroique Playes*. Dryden's own management of military spectacle and violence is satirized in *The Rehearsal*. E. Nelson James provides an inventory of English "drum and trumpet" scenes of the 1670s ("Drums and Trumpets," in *Restoration and 18th Century Theatre Research*, IX [1970], 46–55; X [1971], 54–57).

187 *Good old Cause.* The common epithet for the Puritan revolution and program, here used satirically and with sexual innuendo. Summers notices the phrase used again by Dryden, more directly, in *Absalom and Achitophel*, ll. 79–82 (*Works*, II, 7–8):

> ... when to Sin our byast Nature leans,
> The carefull Devil is still at hand with means;
> And providently Pimps for ill desires:
> The Good old Cause reviv'd, a Plot requires.

IV, iv

123–126 The City of London was a stronghold of Puritan opposition to an alliance with the French (Noyes) against the Protestant and mercantile Dutch. Charles and his ministers, principally Arlington and Clifford, were secretly arranging just such an alliance (see, for example, "On the Prorogation" [1671] and "A Litany" [1672] in *Poems on Affairs of State*, I, ed. George deF. Lord [1963], 184, 190). For the City's opposition to Charles's policies and the growing suspicions of a royal arrangement with Louis XIV, see Ogg, pp. 343–371.

V, i

S.d. Straton. Palamede's father's servant is not listed in the *"Persons Represented."*

20 *Jocky.* Probably an ineffectual and younger version of the jockeys described in *NCD* as "rank Horse-Coursers, Race Riders; also Hucksters or Sellers of Horses, very slippery Fellows to deal with."

21 *crack of the field.* The favorite (Summers).

22–23 *the Court goes out of Town to a Horse-race.* Charles II was himself a passionate horseman and went often with members of his court to the races at Newmarket. He was there, for instance, at the end of March 1671 when news was sent to him of the death of the first Duchess of York (*Bulstrode Papers*, I, 179), and one week later, on the day after her funeral, it was "said his Ma^ty has some thoughts of going next weeke to New Markett againe, to be present at some horse races and other diversions of this season there" (*ibid.*, p. 181). He was certainly at Newmarket in late September (*ibid.*, pp. 201–202) and at the beginning of October with "all his traine . . . where it's said hee may stay about a fortnight" (*ibid.*, p. 206).

26 *mark.* The quarry of the hawk (*OED*, citing this line).

27 *bob'd.* "Cheated, Trick'd, Disappointed, or Baulk'd" (*NCD*).

27 *at retrieve.* Sutherland shows that Palamede is carrying on his hawking metaphor: though frequently on the point of satisfying his desires, he is disappointed every time.

30–76 For discussion of this exchange, see headnote, p. 473 above.

57 *Pieces.* Probably a gold guinea or twenty shillings of silver (see "JOBE, a Guinea, Twenty Shillings, or a Piece" in *NCD*), though the ratio of gold to silver fluctuated widely (see Steven B. Baxter, *William III* [1966], p. 335). The point here is the lavishness of Palamede's "tip" (roughly the equivalent of eighty best tickets to the theater!).

83 *let me die for the Parenthesis of all.* Melantha may use "Parenthesis" in the extended sense of "enclose" or "encompass," i.e., "let me get all my precious French words in." But the joke is then at least double: Melantha's rude insertion of herself into court society is truly a parenthesis or "digression" (*OED*), and "the disobedient word" that will "not come in" (l. 90) is "naiveté," the only word really appropriate to Melantha's lack of sensitivity to Palmyra's station and anxiety.

128 *long of.* Owing to, on account of (*OED*); "it's your fault."

150–159 This song is taken from the "Ballets des Nations" at the end of Molière's *Le Bourgeois Gentilhomme* (V, vi, Fifth Entry, First Minuet) which was originally performed at Chambord on 13 October 1670 and in Paris on 23 November 1670. The song is translated in an eighteenth-century bilingual edition (*Le Bourgeois Gentilhomme* / *The Cit Turn'd Gentleman* [1732]) as follows:

> What Pleasures in these Thickets dwell!
> How genial Phoebus chears the Day!

> *Another Man.*

> Whilst, in the Spray, sweet Philomel
> Alternate to the Echo tunes her Lay.

> This sweet Abode,
> This pleasant Grove,
> This sweet Abode,
> Invites to Love.

See also ll. 161–162n below. Neither song is included in Edward Ravenscroft's Restoration version of the Molière play, *The Citizen Turn'd Gentleman* (1672), which was first performed by the Duke's Company no later than 4 July 1672 (Van Lennep).

160 *humours*. Adapts to (*OED*).

161–162 The 1732 bilingual edition of Molière's *Le Bourgeois Gentilhomme* (Fifth Entry, Second Minuet), translates this song:

> See, my Clemene, see,
> Under yon spreading Tree,
> The am'rous Turtles coo and bill . . .

See also ll. 150–159n above.

176–177 *Chanson a boire . . . a moy*. A drinking song (unidentified).

212–213 *Strong-water*. Alcoholic spirits customarily offered to criminals as they were carted to the gallows (Summers).

262 *piecing*. Making-up, with word plays on "mending" and "making peace."

291 *glass*. The protective covering for young plants (Beaurline and Bowers).

297 *Indenture*. "Impression, with a play on sealing an agreement" (Beaurline and Bowers).

312 *Bilbo*. A sword; originally one from Bilbao, Spain (*OED*).

313 *Danger-field*. A conventional term for "a dramatic bully, whose sword and [Turkish] habit became proverbial" (Scott).

340 *delicate screw'd Gun*. A gun with a finely grooved bore (*OED*).

354 *standing Dish*. One that appears each day or at every meal (*OED*) and is therefore expected or boring. In its second use (l. 356), "standing" acquires a decidedly sexual meaning.

360 *propriety*. Property, but carrying with it a sense of what is suitable. See I, i, 76 and n, above.

370–371 *Fall on . . . enough*. A misremembering of Macbeth's challenge near the end of Act V: "Lay on Macduff, / And damn'd be him, that first cries hold, enough." These lines are omitted entirely from Sir William Davenant's popular and lavish Restoration adaptation, which was probably first performed in 1663 or 1664 but not printed until 1674 (*Macbeth, A Tragedy. With all the Alterations, Amendments, Additions, and New Songs. As it's now Acted at the Dukes Theatre*). The lines are included, however (p. 65), in *Macbeth: A Tragedy. Acted At the Dukes-Theatre* (1673), which was probably printed from the First Folio (with witches' songs from another source) to profit from the popularity of Davenant's adaptation. See Christopher Spencer, *Davenant's Macbeth from the Yale Manuscript* (1961), esp. pp. 2, 8, 16.

452+ *s.d. Enter Leonidas . . . Argaleon, disarm'd*. In *The Rehearsal*, II, iv ([1672], p. 18), Buckingham attacks the dramatic convenience and sentimental neatness of the bloodless coup that often ends a heroic drama:

> *Bayes*. There's now an odd surprise; the whole State's

> turn'd quite topsi-turvy, without any puther or stir in the
> whole world, I gad.
> *Johns.* A very silent change of a Government, truly, as
> ever I heard of.
> *Bayes.* It is so. And yet you shall see me bring 'em in
> again, by and by, in as odd a way every jot.
>   *[The Usurpers march out flourishing their swords.*
>   *Enter* Shirley.
> *Shir.* Hey ho, hey ho: what a change is here! Hey day,
> hey day! I know not what to do, nor what to say.   [Exit
> *Smi.* But, pray, Sir, how came they to depose the Kings
> so easily?

Buckingham may have had the end of the heroic action of *Marriage A-la-Mode* specifically in mind, and, indeed, *A Key to the Rehearsal* (1704, p. xvii) relates its sole note on a line in this passage to *Marriage A-la-Mode* and "such easy Turns of State." See headnote, pp. 463–464 above.

EPILOGUE

The epilogue, like the prologue, was first published in *Covent Garden Drollery* (1672), pp. 8–9, where it is assigned to "Mr. Moon," i.e., Michael Mohun, who played Rhodophil, Doralice's husband, in the early performances. As David M. Vieth points out ("The Art of the Prologue and Epilogue," *Genre*, V [1972], 277), Mohun speaks in character whereas Hart had spoken the prologue in his own person.

2 *Reformation.* The idea of reformation, an echo of *"reform'd"* from line 1 in the prologue, is mocked, as is Dryden himself, in the prologue and epilogue of Joseph Arrowsmith's *The Reformation* (1673), a play given by the Duke's Company which may have had its first performance as early as the spring of 1672.

3–6 *Not with dull Morals . . . confines of indifference.* Dryden here refers jestingly (as Kinsley notes) to the opening lines of Samuel Tuke's *The Adventures of Five Hours:*

> How happy are the Men of easie Phlegm,
> Born on the Confines of Indifference;
> Holding from Nature, the securest Tenure,
> The Peaceful Empire o'r themselves.

These lines begin a soliloquy that appears in the third edition (1671) of Tuke's play, but not in the earlier editions of 1663 and 1664. Dryden had already referred slightingly to this play in *Of Dramatick Poesie* (*Works*, XVII, 45, 378). For further commentary concerning Dryden's relationship to Tuke's play, see *Works*, VIII, 235–236, 243; X, 378, 443–444n.

4 *men of easie Phlegme.* Phlegm and phlegmatic carry the connotation of dull, sluggish (*OED*).

32 *the City.* The wives of the merchants of the City of London were proverbially considered fair game for the wits of court and town (Westminster); according to the epilogue to Congreve's *The Double-Dealer* (1694), "Cuckoldom, of Ancient Right, to Cits belongs."

The Assignation

Dryden wrote *The Assignation, or Love in a Nunnery*, first performed in
1672 or 1673, while in full career, some ten years after his first play, four
years after he succeeded Sir William Davenant as poet laureate, and before
his supremacy as comic dramatist had been challenged by Etherege and
Wycherley. Yet its first run was unsuccessful. Dryden acknowledged the
failure of the play in his dedicatory epistle for the first edition. Hostile
critics alluded scornfully to the reception it met: Edward Ravenscroft in
the prologue to *The Careless Lovers* and Elkanah Settle in the dedicatory
epistle for *The Empress of Morocco*, both plays acted and printed in 1673,
the year in which *The Assignation* was first printed. Many years later Gerard
Langbaine, perhaps Dryden's most severe censor, wrote bluntly that *The
Assignation* "was Damn'd on the Stage."[1]

The circumstances of the King's Company, for which Dryden wrote the
play, contributed to its cool reception and perhaps, because of the Company's urgent need for a new play by him, to limitations that are apparent
on the printed page. "It succeeded ill in the representation," Dryden wrote
in the dedicatory epistle to Sir Charles Sedley. "Whether the fault was in
the Play it self, or in the lameness of the Action, or in the number of its
Enemies, who came resolv'd to damn it for the Title, I will not now dispute," he added, suggesting with analytical accuracy categories of faults
of which the play stood accused. It is easy to imagine the competitive disadvantage and financial strain the King's Company experienced while acting in a renovated tennis court in Lincoln's Inn Fields in opposition to
the Duke's Company at its splendid Dorset Garden Theatre.[2] The King's
Company needed help from Dryden. The frequency with which he worked
variations on familiar character types and dramatic situations in *The Assignation* points to haste in composition. We may plausibly guess that the
"lameness of the Action" (i.e., "acting") resulted from haste in mounting
the play. The cast included experienced actors and actresses who had
proved their abilities.[3]

The date of the premiere is not known, though references to Dryden in
the prologues to plays acted at Dorset Garden establish as limiting dates
the early summer of 1672 and the first two months of 1673.[4] *The Assignation*
came after Ravenscroft's adaptation from Molière, *The Citizen Turn'd*

---

[1] Langbaine, p. 154.

[2] The Company's theater in Bridges Street, Drury Lane, burned on 25 January
1672. From the members' resumption of acting on 26 February 1672 until the com-
pletion of their new Theatre Royal, Drury Lane, in March 1674, they remained in
the improvised theater in Lincoln's Inn Fields. See Nicoll, I, 320–323.

[3] For the players and their roles, see section on the actors below.

[4] Van Lennep (p. 200) suggests November 1672. Judith Milhous and Robert D.
Hume, however, explain that "on the basis of publication data, *The Assignation*
could easily come half a year earlier; it is unlikely to be later than November
1672" ("Dating Play Premières from Publication Data," *HLB*, XXII [1974], 385).

Gentleman, which was acted, though not necessarily for the first time, on 4 July 1672.[5] Ravenscroft's prologue includes a derogatory reference to Dryden, and Dryden in his own prologue (spoken by Joseph Haines, who had the role of the egotistical and maladroit servant Benito) refers scornfully to Ravenscroft's play. Ravenscroft replied in kind in the prologue to his next play, *The Careless Lovers,* acted at Dorset Garden early in March 1673.[6] We know at least that *The Assignation* came between those two plays, and long enough before the second one for Ravenscroft to have written his retaliatory prologue, in which, addressing the audience, he made capital of the failure of Dryden's play:

> In fine, the whole by you so much was blam'd,
> To act their Parts, the Players were asham'd;
> Ah! how severe your Malice was that Day,
> To Damne at once, the Poet and his Play.

The date of publication of the English translation of Dryden's most important literary source, late 1671 or early 1672, would seem to be relevant to the date of the premiere. Yet we cannot know beyond doubt that Dryden did not go directly to the French original, first published in 1670.[7] The translation, *The Annals of Love,* bears the date 1672 on its title page, but it had been entered in the *Term Catalogues* in November 1671, a circumstance implying that it was about to be published or had already been published by that time. The close sequence of dates suggests that a reading of the translation led Dryden to write *The Assignation* during the first six to nine months of 1672.

The meager records of theatrical performances in the 1670s (after Pepys stopped writing his diary in 1669) reveal neither how thoroughly *The Assignation* was "damned" nor how many times it was acted during its first run. Yet despite its inauspicious beginning, its life on the stage was by no means terminated. John Downes lists it among the "most taking" plays of the King's Company.[8] In 1675 it was sufficiently well known to be the subject of satirical notice in the revised and lengthened third edition of *The Rehearsal.*[9] Later editions of Dryden's play suggest that it was revived during the seasons of 1677–78[10] and 1691–92.[11] The comprehensive theatrical records of the eighteenth century permit more complete knowledge of revivals, of which there were at least two, in 1716[12] and in 1743.[13] Drury Lane advertised the play in 1716 as "Not Acted these Twenty Years," implying that there had probably been a revival in the season 1695–96.[14] Such a record does not suggest that the play was an unqualified failure.

---

[5] Milhous and Hume, "Dating Play Premières," p. 385.

[6] *Ibid.*

[7] *Les Annales Galantes.* See Bruce Archer Morrissette, *The Life and Works of Marie-Catherine Desjardins* (1947), p. 90.

[8] Downes, pp. 12, 15.

[9] See below, pp. 538–539.

[10] Van Lennep, p. 262.

[11] *Ibid.,* p. 398.

[12] Avery, p. 408.

[13] Arthur H. Scouten, *The London Stage,* Pt. 3:1729–1747, pp. 1074–1075.

[14] Van Lennep, p. 450.

⟡⟐⟡

Although it survived its initial run, *The Assignation* has seemed to many
students anticlimactic, coming as it does just after *Marriage A-la-Mode*.[15] In
the earlier play Dryden had brought to the highest level of excellence he
was to reach the pattern of tragicomedy with which he had first succeeded
in *Secret Love* and about which he had written in *Of Dramatick Poesie*.
From 1667 to 1671 Dryden wrote or collaborated on seven plays: *Secret
Love, Sir Martin Mar-all*, an adaptation of *The Tempest* (with Davenant),
An Evening's Love, Tyrannick Love, The Conquest of Granada in ten acts,
and *Marriage A-la-Mode*. These included a farcical comedy retaining qualities of the *commedia dell'arte* present in its sources, four tragicomedies, and
two rhymed heroic plays. This is the record of a professional dramatist who
was at the height of his powers. All these plays have qualities that illumi-
nate our understanding of *The Assignation*, but the three original two-plot
tragicomedies—*Secret Love, An Evening's Love*, and *Marriage A-la-Mode*—
are most directly relevant to an interpretation and evaluation of it. *The
Assignation* presents a problem best stated as a question: How can it seemingly resemble the three earlier plays so closely and yet differ so markedly
from them in its impact upon audience or reader?

Two of Dryden's remarks about comedy provide help in answering this
question. In his preface to *Secret Love* Dryden alludes to criticism of the
play based on the assumption that decorum required a dramatist to accord
his characters the deference appropriate to persons of their rank in life:
"That which with more reason was objected as an indecorum, is the management of the last Scene of the Play, where *Celadon* and *Florimell* are treat-
ing too lightly of their marriage in the presence of the Queen, who likewise
seems to stand idle while the great action of the *Drama* is still depending."
Dryden insists, however, that he depicts the Queen as a character with
qualities appropriate to her supreme rank.[16]

In the preface to *An Evening's Love*, Dryden clarifies his conception of
decorum, writing comprehensively about what he regards as proper balance
and relationship among various dramatic elements:

> *I will not deny but that I approve most the mixt way of
> Comedy; that which is neither all wit, nor all humour,
> but the result of both: neither so little of humour as
> Fletcher shews, nor so little of love and wit, as Johnson:
> neither all cheat, with which the best Playes of the one
> are fill'd, nor all adventure, which is the common practice
> of the other. I would have the characters well chosen, and
> kept distant from interfaring with each other; which is*

---

[15] As already noted, the disparagement of *The Assignation* had its beginnings
soon after its first performance. It has often been restated in the intervening
years. But two recent critics have departed from tradition in praising the play for,
among other reasons, the thematic audacity it reveals: William Myers, *Dryden*
(1973), pp. 58–61; John A. Zamonski, "The Spiritual Nature of Carnal Love in
Dryden's *Assignation*," *Educational Theatre Journal*, XXV (1973), 189–192. Hume,
in his comprehensive study of Restoration drama (pp. 276–277), reverts to the
traditional disparagement of *The Assignation*.

[16] *Works*, IX, 117.

more than Fletcher *or* Shakespear *did: but I would have*
more of the Urbana, venusta, salsa, faceta *and the rest*
which Quintilian *reckons up as the ornaments of wit;*
and these are extremely wanting in Ben. Johnson. *As for*
repartie in particular; as it is the very soul of conversa-
tion, so it is the greatest grace of Comedy, where it is
proper to the Characters.[17]

The remarks in these prefaces describe accurately, if too programmatically,
principles that guided Dryden in writing *Secret Love, An Evening's Love,*
and *Marriage A-la-Mode.* He did not follow those principles in writing
The Assignation, and readers often come to the play with expectations that
it does not fulfill.

Most notable among Dryden's departures from his earlier practice is a
disregard, so extreme as to appear to be calculated, of decorum in characterization.[18] The Duke of Mantoua is a sovereign duke with an adult son
and heir. Yet, as victim of a lust inappropriate to his years, he suffers humiliation when he tries to seduce the youthful Lucretia. His humiliation
is deserved. The young woman wears the habit of a nun and resides in a
convent, although she has not taken vows of celibacy, a fact not known to
the Duke (or to spectator or reader until the fourth act [IV, iv]). To be sure,
Lucretia puts aside her habit and attends a masquerade in disguise, an
imprudent act that leads to the Duke's infatuation with and pursuit of her
and, when he learns her identity, to his misjudgment of her moral character. But the Duke exploits his rank to gain admission to the convent, dis-
simulating his motive for doing so; and when he discovers that his son is
his rival, he determines to send the son from Rome. In short, the Duke
emerges as a morally flawed as well as an undignified character.

The son, Prince Frederick, who assumes Lucretia to be a nun, is a reluctant lover. Yet after falling in love with Lucretia, he comports himself
with a lack of inhibition similar to that of Palamede and Rhodophil in
Marriage A-la-Mode rather than with the dignity of Leonidas, the character
of his own rank in that play. He once feigns a "most violent griping" so
that he may sit down upon, and thereby conceal from his father, Lucretia's
masking costume.[19] Frederick's farcical, even sordid, stratagem to deceive
his father distorts the subdued romantic idealism we are accustomed to
encounter even in the wittiest of Dryden's young lovers. It has been well
observed of Celadon and Florimell in *Secret Love* that, their freedom from
inhibition notwithstanding, they retain something of an "aura of the
ideal,"[20] and we could apply the remark to the witty lovers in *An Evening's
Love* and *Marriage A-la-Mode,* but scarcely to Prince Frederick.

In the egalitarian twentieth century, the seventeenth-century conception
of decorum in characterization, which was based on aristocratic assumptions
about the organization of society, can have little meaning except as an aid
to the interpretation of the drama of that era. We are disinclined to believe

---

17 *Ibid.,* X, 206.
18 Myers, *Dryden,* p. 59.
19 See pp. 538–539 below. Scott thought "the absurd and vulgar scene" might
have "had some share in occasioning the fall of the piece" (S-S, IV, 366).
20 John Harrington Smith, *The Gay Couple in Restoration Comedy* (1948), p. 58.

that a duke and a prince are necessarily superior beings who should be portrayed on stage as possessing an innate nobility. Yet the cynicism epitomized in the Duke's unconscionable exploitation of his rank emerges in the play as a dominant impression, one accentuated by the attitude Dryden assumes—following his French source—toward the celibacy of nuns and their isolation from worldly temptation.

In *The Assignation* more was involved than disrespect of Catholicism. In one of his earlier plays, *The Indian Emperour*, and in one of his later, *The Spanish Fryar*, Dryden depicts Catholic clergymen harshly. In *The Indian Emperour* a priest employs religious argument to rationalize a brutal effort to find yet more gold; in *The Spanish Fryar* the title character, whose physical appearance and easy conscience put us in mind of Sir John Falstaff, uses his priestly right of access to a young married woman to convey messages to her, at a price, from a young man intent on seduction. *The Indian Emperour* is more overtly anti-Catholic than *The Assignation*, and *The Spanish Fryar* is arguably so. Yet open hostility to the Catholic church can give less offense, at least to Protestants, than such lascivious innuendo as permeates the opening dialogue of the third act of *The Assignation* between Ascanio and Hippolita, the latter of whom, unlike Lucretia, is a "professed" nun. The revelation late in the play that Lucretia is free to marry may be interpreted as an equivocal evasion of a moral issue. Dryden exploits the titillation inherent in a forbidden love, repeatedly alluding to the celibacy of nuns in witty dialogue, before revealing that Lucretia has not taken her final vows. His ability to turn a clever phrase had not left him; but the occasional approach to blasphemy no doubt soured the repartee for some members of his first audiences.

The difference between *The Assignation* and Dryden's earlier tragicomedies of similar structure illustrates the importance of his literary sources in determining emotional impact. For both *Secret Love* and *Marriage A-la-Mode*, in which the serious plots turn on the fortunes of royal persons, he drew on the heroic romances of Madeleine de Scudéry.[21] For *An Evening's Love* he drew on several works and perhaps on their common ancestor, a comedy by Calderón. In his preface he refers to the literary ancestry of his play: *"It was first Spanish, and call'd El Astrologo fingido; then made French by the younger Corneille: and is now translated into English, and in print, under the name of the Feign'd Astrologer."* Thomas Corneille's French adaptation of Calderón was Dryden's principal literary source;[22] if the French play lacks the heroic ethos of Mlle de Scudéry's stories about royal persons, the Spanish grandees who appear in it possess the dignity for which their nation was famous. They appear even in cape-and-sword intrigue with a restraint consistent with seventeenth-century notions of propriety. In choosing the story on which he based much of *The Assignation*, Dryden departed radically from his earlier practices, with important consequences for the play.

---

[21] *Works*, IX, 117; see above, pp. 467–469.
[22] *Works*, X, 211, 434–443.

Langbaine first pointed out the major literary source, a story in the collection entitled *The Annals of Love*,[23] which, although Langbaine did not say so, was an anonymous translation of *Les Annales Galantes* (Paris, 1670) by Marie-Catherine Hortense Desjardins.[24] Dryden could of course have read the story in the original French; he may possibly, though by no means certainly, have taken a hint from another story in *Les Annales Galantes* when writing *Marriage A-la-Mode,* some months before the publication of *The Annals of Love.*[25] Yet whether he turned to the French or the English, he follows closely in his principal plot line Mlle Desjardins' "Frederic Barberouse, Henry son fils, et Constance," the fifth of the eighteen stories that comprise *Les Annales Galantes.*

Dryden took from the story not only the controversial subject of "Love in a Nunnery" and the Roman locale, but much of the action as well. The Prince's courtship of Lucretia, whom he assumes to be a nun; Lucretia's attendance at a masquerade given by the Prince's father; the father's sudden infatuation with her, not knowing her identity; the father's discovery of her identity, of an incriminating letter, and of the rivalry of his son; the father's determination to send his son away; the humiliation of the father by the "fair nun" and her confederates—all these elements Dryden found in the story. He made changes. In *The Assignation* the Prince, although he has the military strength to do so, declines to assume his father's position, preferring a filial submission which wins a paternal blessing on his planned marriage to Lucretia. Because in Dryden the young woman is not yet "professed," she is free to marry. In the story she has taken her vows, but the Pope gives her dispensation so that she can marry the Prince—or rather the Emperor, as he becomes when, with the support of the Pope, he deposes his father.

Mlle Desjardins' innovations in French prose fiction anticipated Dryden's innovations in this play. Her contribution to the establishment of historical fiction included departures from the pervasive "aristocratic bias of authorship in the seventeenth century" and the related conception of the "great man" as the controller of historical events. "In matters of love," according to Mlle Desjardins, "man's behavior is more or less stable throughout the ages."[26] She wrote fiction about historical sovereigns and princes of the past with an attention to the analysis of passion uninhibited by an assumption that individuals of royal or noble birth differ in emotional nature from common folk. Two of her three principal works had appeared before *The Assignation* reached the stage. The title of the third, published in 1675, describes the subjects to which she was drawn: *Les Désordres de l'amour.* Dryden in *The Assignation* writes about "the disorders of love," to which elderly men of high rank are not immune.[27]

---

[23] Langbaine, *Momus triumphans,* p. 6; *Account,* p. 155. See also Summers, III, 269–270; Allen, pp. 177–183.

[24] *Les Annales Galantes* was also published anonymously, although Mlle Desjardins acknowledged her authorship in 1671 (Morrissette, *Marie-Catherine Desjardins,* p. 90).

[25] See pp. 469–470 above.

[26] Morrissette, *Desjardins,* pp. 91–93.

[27] Moore (pp. 116–123) has argued that Dryden in *The Assignation* attempted

The Duke, in his attempt to enjoy Lucretia and in his cruelty to his son, is culpable. Yet he is driven by motives more complex than unseemly lust for a young woman. Lucretia's letter to his son, which he intercepts, mocks him bitterly. He would be a less credible character did he not respond vigorously to her taunts. Dryden's fidelity in representing passion led him to the depiction of episodes and relationships that intrude on perennial and widely felt inhibitions.

Whether the impulse for his innovations came from a reading of Mlle Desjardins (as seems likely) or from some other experience, he put aside theoretical formulations about dramatic characterization in an effort to achieve greater fidelity in the portrayal of persons of all ranks and professions, even to sovereigns and cloistered nuns. We may miss the harmonious world of *Marriage A-la-Mode*, in which the quality of a fairy tale is not absent; and we may find the Duke's misdeeds disturbing. Dryden perhaps did not succeed in reconciling the diverse plot lines and characters he brought together in *The Assignation*, but as an experiment in an honest portrayal of the passions of men and women, his play attracted attention to the end of the century and beyond.

In the early 1690s *The Assignation* attracted the attention of William Congreve, who made liberal use of it in writing *Incognita* (1692),[28] gracefully acknowledging his debt to Dryden by using four distinctive names of characters in *The Assignation* for characters in his novel. That Congreve chose Dryden's play as a literary source would suggest that it had some reputation at the time with discerning readers and theatergoers. In the short critical essay printed as a preface to *Incognita*, Congreve succinctly differentiates "novels" from "romances." Although he makes no reference to the drama—or to Dryden—his description of the two forms of prose fiction may be read as a commentary on the differences between *The Assignation*, based on a "novel," and *Marriage A-la-Mode*, based on a "romance." We recall Leonidas and Palmyra of the latter play as we read that "Romances are generally composed of the Constant Loves and invincible Courages of Hero's, Heroins, Kings and Queens, Mortals of the first Rank, and so forth." We can scarcely avoid thinking of *The Assignation*, as we read in the preface to a work partly based on it, that in contrast with romances

---

to write a form of comedy which Pierre Corneille would call "comédie héroïque." But the passage quoted by Moore from Corneille's "Discours de l'utilité et des parties du poëme dramatique" describing this form of comedy can scarcely be reconciled with *The Assignation*. Corneille wrote that royal persons are not inappropriate to heroic comedy "s'il ne s'y rencontre point de péril de vie, de pertes d'États, ou de bannissement" (*Oeuvres de P. Corneille*, ed. Ch. Marty-Laveaux [Paris, 1910], I, 23–25). The sovereign duke and his heir in *The Assignation* are certainly close to royal rank. Yet the Duke orders his son into banishment, and the son responds with a successful military rebellion against his father, who acknowledges that he is "Fit to be made prisoner first, and then depos'd" (V, iv, 138). Moore argues that, because neither the banishment nor the deposition is carried out, Dryden's plot meets the requirements of Corneille's formula. But the sequence of actions in Dryden's play is better explained by the convention in tragicomedy of calamity averted than by Corneille's remarks on heroic comedy.

[28] Montague Summers, ed., *The Complete Works of William Congreve* (1923), I, 4–5.

"Novels are of a more familiar nature."[29] Dryden drew on both forms of prose fiction for his tragicomedies of the early 1670s, with the result that the plays reveal a contrast between the heroic ethos of Mlle de Scudéry and the psychological realism of Mlle Desjardins.

The secondary plot of *The Assignation,* markedly different in tone from the story of the "fair nun," almost certainly derives from a play of Calderón de la Barca, *Con quien vengo, vengo.*[30] The parallels between Dryden and Calderón, with the exception of the final revelation, are confined to the first three-fifths of the plays, but in relevant scenes the resemblances are too detailed to be the result of coincidence. Conceivably, some as yet unidentified story or play, Spanish, French, or English, could have served Dryden as intermediary between his work and Calderón's. Yet the case for Dryden's use of *Con quien vengo, vengo* is strong, stronger than it is for his direct use of a Spanish play as source for any other work.[31] He seems to have had *Con quien vengo, vengo* before him as he wrote.

The "night-pieces" of the two young couples' courtship in enclosed gardens give a Spanish atmosphere to Dryden's play and to Calderón's, even though *The Assignation* is set in Rome and *Con quien vengo, vengo* is set in Verona. Also reminiscent of Spain is the force blocking the lovers' desires, the suspicious nature of a relative who is the sisters' guardian. Both pairs of sisters are confined to their houses and walled gardens: by a brother (Don Sancho, in Calderón), whose motive is the usual Spanish one of protection of family honor; by an uncle (Mario, in Dryden), whose motive, avarice, is typical of Restoration comedy.[32] It is the shared episodic detail of the two plays rather than the conventional situation of blocked young love which reveals that Dryden drew on Calderón.[33] Both plays present a young gallant, Camillo in *The Assignation* and Don Juan in *Con quien vengo, vengo,* attempting to court one of the closely guarded sisters, who encourages him despite the barrier imposed by the suspicious relative. In both plays the gallant arranges a nocturnal rendezvous by letter; in both the sister of the recipient, Laura in the English and Lisarda in the Spanish, intercepts the letter in the presence of the recipient, Violetta and Leonor respectively. After banter in a similar vein in both plays, the sister of the recipient determines to accompany her to the rendezvous in the guise of a maidservant. Meanwhile, a friend of each of the suitors decides to go along, pretending to be a servant. One difference marks the opening sequences of Calderón's play and Dryden's. Calderón begins with women and the scene

---

29 *Ibid.,* I, 111.

30 See James U. Rundle, "The Source of Dryden's 'Comic Plot' in *The Assignation,*" *MP,* XLV (1947), 104–111. For specific reference to parallel passages, see the notes to lines below.

31 At least three of Dryden's contemporaries accused him of plagiarizing Spanish authors: see the anonymous introductory epistle to *The Medal of John Bayes* (1682); Langbaine, pp. 149, 158; and Samuel Wesley, *An Epistle to a Friend concerning Poetry* (1700), pp. 17–18.

32 Cf. John Loftis, *The Spanish Plays of Neoclassical England* (1973), p. 114.

33 It is worth noting that Calderón and Dryden each use, though not in parallel situations, a proper name that is identical except for the final vowels, which are appropriate respectively to Spanish and Italian: "Ursino," an important character in Calderón; "Ursini," a family name mentioned casually in Dryden (III, ii).

between the sisters; Dryden, as usual in Restoration comedy, begins with men talking about women and the scene between the gallants. In the plays both couples meet by night on two occasions, one member of each couple assuming one of the other to be a servant. The result is emotional conflict between attraction to the wit and presence of the person met by night and repulsion arising from the assumption that he or she is of inferior rank.

In *Con quien vengo, vengo* as in *The Assignation* the young woman who pretends to be a servant sees by day the real servant of her sister's suitor, Celio in the Spanish and Benito in the English, finding it painfully difficult to reconcile her affection for the man she had met by night with the loutish appearance and manner of the servant she knows by day. Although the situation is parallel in the plays, Calderón and Dryden follow separate dramatic traditions in the delineation of the servants. Celio is a familiar character type of the *comedia*, the *gracioso*, a comical character of inferior rank (often, as here, a servant), sometimes a character of more perception than Celio, who like Sancho Panza of Cervantes' novel can assert the simple good sense of common humanity in opposition to the unworldly ideals of his betters.

Although not totally unlike the Spanish *gracioso*, Benito represents a character type of cosmopolitan ancestry, one with which Dryden earlier had scored in the title character of *Sir Martin Mar-all*, popular throughout his lifetime.[34] Sir Martin's apt surname describes comprehensively his role in the play: his obtuse bungling of the successive stratagems devised by his clever servant to help him win the woman he loves. Their difference in social position notwithstanding, Sir Martin and Benito have similar functions in the two plays: to interrupt cleverly conceived stratagems designed by other and more intelligent heads to overcome barriers to the courtship of young couples. A consequence for both *Sir Martin Mar-all* and *The Assignation* is a slowing down of consecutive action and, as a corollary, an intensified emphasis on ludicrous episodes, but this aspect is less apparent in *The Assignation* than in the earlier play. Benito's bunglings, though a principal comic resource of *The Assignation*, are on balance subordinate to two very busy plot lines. Sir Martin's, on the other hand, receive more attention than the slender threads of consecutive intrigue. The earlier play has, through French intermediaries, a source in the Italian *commedia dell'arte*, and in its dependence on farcical and disjunctive episodes it retains much which is distinctive of that form of improvised comedy.[35] Benito may owe something to the Italian tradition. But the strong narrative lines of *The Assignation* constitute a major difference between it and *Sir Martin Mar-all*.

Despite the success of *Sir Martin Mar-all* on stage, Dryden wrote harshly in the preface to *An Evening's Love* about the type of comedy it exemplifies, and some of his remarks are applicable to *The Assignation*. "*I am sometimes ready to imagine that my disgust of low Comedy,*" he writes,

> *proceeds not so much from my judgement as from my temper; which is the reason why I so seldom write it; and*

---

[34] Scott pointed out the resemblance between Sir Martin and Benito (S-S, IV, 366).

[35] *Works*, IX, 364–367.

that when I succeed in it, (I mean so far as to please the
Audience) yet I am nothing satisfi'd with what I have
done. . . .

The delight of audiences in low comedy, he adds,

confirms me in my opinion of slighting popular ap-
plause, and of contemning that approbation which those
very people give, equally with me, to the Zany of a
Mountebank.[36]

The reference to the *"Zany of a Mountebank"* implies that Dryden knew
the literary ancestry of such characters as Sir Martin Mar-all and Benito.[37]
Dryden wrote this passage the year before he wrote *The Assignation*. His
earlier—and highly successful—experiment with a character resembling a
"Zany," Sir Martin Mar-all, may be explained as a result of the participation
of his collaborator, the Duke of Newcastle, in writing the play. But why
Benito, in a comedy Dryden wrote independently and after his reputation
was firmly established? To be more precise, why is Benito given so much
time on stage as the focus of attention? The "comic plot" taken from *Con
quien vengo, vengo* required some such loutish servant as Calderón's Celio,
whose appearance and manner could occasion the emotional dilemma of
the young woman who had been captivated by the conversation of a man
she could not see in the darkness but whom she thought to be a servant. In
their adaptations from the *comedia* English dramatists of the Restoration
consistently reduced emphasis on, if they could not eliminate, characters
corresponding to the Spanish *graciosos*.[38] Dryden himself had alluded
scornfully in *Of Dramatick Poesie* to the character type.[39] Yet Benito is
more prominent in *The Assignation* than Celio is in Calderón's play.

We cannot follow the workings of Dryden's mind. But a tentative explanation for the prominence he gives Benito would turn on his awareness
of the perennial popularity of Sir Martin and on his need to write quickly
a comedy that would be financially successful. Dryden was a professional
dramatist who in the preface to *An Evening's Love* had affirmed the priority
of entertainment over instruction in comedy.[40]

The position in which Benito finds himself, a servant mistaken for his
master, resembles that of a character in Sir William Davenant's last play,
The Man's the Master, first performed in 1668, the year after the premiere
of *Sir Martin Mar-all*. Like Dryden in the latter play, Davenant drew on
French comedy, making such extensive use of his source, Paul Scarron's
Jodelet, ou le maître valet, that the English comedy may be considered a
free adaptation of the French.[41] Davenant departed from Scarron most
markedly in exaggerating the servant's egotistical absurdities as he took
advantage of his opportunity to play the gentleman and court a beautiful

---

[36] *Ibid.*, X, 202–203.
[37] *Ibid.*, p. 457.
[38] Loftis, *Spanish Plays of Neoclassical England*, esp. pp. 110–111, 115, 123.
[39] *Works*, XVII, 45, 377–378.
[40] *Ibid.*, X, 209.
[41] Loftis, *Spanish Plays of Neoclassical England*, pp. 91–95. Scarron's *Jodelet,
ou le maître valet* is in turn based on a Spanish play, Francisco de Rojas Zorrilla's
Donde hay agravios no hay celos.

woman, who, like Laura when she sees Benito by day, finds the servant re-
pulsive. In elaborating the role of Benito, Dryden followed a well-worn
path.[42]

◌◦◦✺◦◦◌

Dryden's departure from the conventions of dialogue he had followed in
his earlier tragicomedies appears, not necessarily to his disadvantage, in the
lines of verse spoken by the Duke. Several times when he is at his most
hypocritical, the Duke turns from prose to verse, and the sudden elevation
in diction gives emphasis to his treacherous abuse of the power that ac-
companies his rank. When, for example, the Abbess Sophronia intercepts
him in his pursuit of Lucretia (IV, iii), he addresses her deceitfully, offering
a bribe in the form of a promise of gifts to the convent:
> I had a Vision in the dead of night,
> Which show'd me this fair Virgin in my sleep,
> And told me, that from her I should be taught
> Where to bestow large Almes, and great Endowments,
> On some near Monastery.

The pious rhetoric succeeds, and the Abbess, not unmindful of worldly
gain, commands Lucretia to stay and leaves her alone with the lecherous
Duke: "The Holy Vision's will must be obey'd." Dryden's stylistic stratagem
resembles that of Ben Jonson, who employs rhetorical heightening in lines
spoken by hypocritical or affected characters.[43] The speeches in Jonson's
comedies that stay in our minds, such as Sir Epicure Mammon's fantasy of
the luxury his expected wealth will bring him, are spoken by villains or
their dupes. Honest men in Jonson's comedies, when they make their in-
frequent appearances, speak in unadorned prose.

The lyricism of young love, which in the earlier tragicomedies appears
in the serious or heroic action, finds muted expression in *The Assignation*
in exchanges between the couples of the "comic" plot. The emotional intensity of their conversation is occasionally signaled by passages of blank
verse, reserved in *Secret Love* and *Marriage A-la-Mode* for the serious characters of higher rank. Philocles and Candiope in the earlier play and
Leonidas and Palmyra in the later always speak in verse, but the witty
couples of both plays use prose to explore the vagaries of sexual passion
with a conversational honesty that provides the best-remembered passages
of all comedy in the first dozen years after the Restoration. Aurelian and
Camillo in *The Assignation*, as well as the sisters Laura and Violetta to

---

[42] Dryden probably took suggestions for episodes from a number of writers. The
trick used by Laura and Violetta to gain access to Frontona's house of rendezvous
(III, i) had been employed, with little variation except that required by context,
in a story by La Fontaine, *Contes*, Deuxième Partie, X (Langbaine, pp. 155–156;
Allen, p. 190). The episode in which Benito earns a beating from his master by
his singing (I, i) could have been suggested by the opening scene of Philippe
Quinault's *La Comedie sans Comedie* (Langbaine, p. 155; Allen, pp. 189–190),
though the occurrence is sufficiently commonplace to make gratuitous any effort
to find a source.

[43] Cf. Jonas Barish, *Ben Jonson and the Language of Prose Comedy* (1967), p. 2.

whom they make their addresses, share the emotional honesty—if not in full measure the wit—of the earlier characters of their social rank.

The third scene of Act II exemplifies the tone of romantic love suppressed by wit and interrupted by farce which is characteristic of the play. This scene is one of those derived from Calderón's *Con quien vengo, vengo;* and in its depiction of a nocturnal and hazardous rendezvous of young lovers in an enclosed garden it resembles many scenes in his intrigue plays, though with the difference that Calderón avoids the overt and emphatic erotic dimension of Dryden's dialogue. Here the maladroit Benito, who in singing as he "fums" on his guitar gives the alarm to the sisters' uncle and forces Aurelian and Camillo to an abrupt and dangerous departure, closely resembles the *gracioso* of the *comedia.*

The scene opens as the gallants, having climbed over the garden wall on a ladder, meet the waiting sisters. Camillo and Violetta, who know each other's identity, speak from the beginning in the idiom of romantic lovers, Violetta revealing none of the conventional reserve of the reluctant mistress until she takes alarm at the rapidity with which Camillo proceeds from the verbal expression of love to an effort to consummate it. At this critical moment their dialogue moves from metaphorical prose to verse. Violetta is speaking in reproach:

> At best, I see you would not love me long,
> For they who plunder do not mean to stay.
> *Cam.* I haste to take possession of my own.
> *Vio.* E're Heaven and holy vows have made it so?
> *Cam.* Then witness Heaven, and all these twinkling Stars——
> *Vio.* Hold, hold; you are distemper'd with your love:
> Time, place, and strong desires now swear, not you.
> *Cam.* Is not Love love without a Priest and Altars?
> The Temples are inanimate, and know not
> What Vows are made in them . . .

As the dialogue moves closer to instinctual and fleshly concerns, the language becomes more remote from conversational idiom, though Camillo's argument is the most commonplace one in the repertory of libertinism. Strange language this, to come from a witty couple in one of Dryden's tragicomedies. Presumably it is intended as mockery of self-serving romantic hypocrisy.

More familiar in tone, and yet more original in conception, is the exchange that follows between Aurelian and Laura, each thinking the other a servant. Dryden apparently took the situation from Calderón. Yet in the trial of wits we hear, if only briefly, the authentic note of the comedy of verbal encounter in which no one since Shakespeare had equaled Dryden. In *Of Dramatick Poesie* he had praised Beaumont and Fletcher's imitation of "the conversation of Gentlemen," preferring them in this respect to Shakespeare.[44] Yet it would be difficult to find a passage of dialogue in any of the plays written singly or in collaboration by Beaumont and Fletcher which could sustain comparison with Dryden's repartee when he is in top form, as he is in short stretches of conversation in this play.

---

44 *Works,* XVII, 56.

⟨⟩ⲱ⟨⟩

When Dryden came to publish *The Assignation* in the late spring of 1673, he had not only seen it fail on the stage. He probably knew that it had been sneeringly dismissed in the prologue of a Ravenscroft, and he certainly knew that it had been attacked in one of the Rota pamphlets.[45] Those same pamphlets had also attacked *The Conquest of Granada*, an evidently successful play, as well as *Annus Mirabilis* and various of Dryden's earlier works for the theater. The impulse for such attacks—it scarcely constituted an adequate occasion—seems to have been Dryden's imprudent examination of Jonson's grammatical errors in the *Defence of the Epilogue* appended to *The Conquest of Granada*,[46] so that the debate turned as much upon the social as upon the purely aesthetic aspects of letters. Dryden was judged an ill-bred parvenu as both dramatist and critic; he was judged, indeed, much as he had been satirized in *The Rehearsal* eighteen months before. The spring of 1673, then, witnessed a crisis in Dryden's career as public man of letters, a crisis that succeeded more than a year of ill fortune and ill judgment. Preparations for the third Dutch war had produced on 2 January 1672 a stop of the Exchequer, which denied Dryden his salary as historiographer and laureate, and this personal loss could only have been exacerbated by the burning of the Bridges Street Theatre three weeks later.[47]

Dryden had written *Marriage A-la-Mode* before his bad times began and could still declare himself pleased with the play when he came to publish it with *The Assignation*. *Marriage A-la-Mode* certainly reads as though written by a successful dramatist conscious of his powers. But, as far as we can tell from patchy records, *Marriage A-la-Mode* scarcely matched the success of such earlier plays as *Sir Martin Mar-all*, *Tyrannick Love*, and *The Conquest of Granada*, plays to which *Marriage A-la-Mode* is so obviously superior. Dryden followed *Marriage A-la-Mode* with *The Assignation*, a play evidently calculated to please a less sophisticated taste than that to which *Marriage A-la-Mode* appealed. But *The Assignation* failed, and by spring 1673 Dryden had written *Amboyna* and probably had seen it performed.[48] *Amboyna* obviously attempts to capitalize upon the chauvinism aroused by the third Dutch war, and, although *Amboyna* "succeeded on the Stage," Dryden admitted that it "will scarcely bear a serious perusal, it being contriv'd and written in a Moneth, the Subject barren, the Persons low, and the Writing not heightned with many laboured Scenes."[49] *The Assignation* and *Amboyna*, the two plays Dryden wrote for performance in Lincoln's Inn Fields, left him disillusioned with a theatrical career which seemingly had crested with *Marriage A-la-Mode*, the last play he wrote for performance in Bridges Street.

At this crisis in his career Dryden prepared to publish *The Assignation*.

[45] See below, pp. 526–531 *passim*.
[46] See above, 207:19ff.
[47] Ward, *Life*, p. 85.
[48] Macdonald, pp. 112–113; Van Lennep, p. 205.
[49] *Amboyna* (1673, sig. A4r–v; S-S, V, 8).

The Assignation was entered with *Marriage A-la-Mode* in the *Stationers'
Register* on 18 March 1673, advertised with *Marriage A-la-Mode* in the
London Gazette for 29 May–2 June, and listed, again with *Marriage A-la-
Mode,* in the term catalogue that was licensed on 16 June.[50] Between entry
of the play in the *Stationers' Register* and its publication Dryden read the
Rota pamphlets, the last two of which, defending him, were listed in the
term catalogue licensed on 6 May,[51] and he alluded to them when dedicating
the play to Sedley. The dedication, then, was given its final form within a
month or so before the play was advertised for sale.

Dryden uses the dedication to dissociate himself not only from his failed
play but also from the taste and pretensions of his opponents, who become
one with the fops banished from Sedley's table. As we read from dedication
into play, Dryden's opponents merge into the fools of the prologue who
serve as models for Haines's acting of Benito, until, in the opening scene,
they find themselves epitomized by Benito gazing clownishly at his reflection in a glass and talking complacently to himself. Theirs is the play; for
Dryden and Sedley, the "Genial Nights." Dryden certainly defends himself
against charges of blasphemy, atheism, licentiousness, and opposition to
learning.[52] But the charge that may well have stung him most—that of being
an ill-bred upstart—is answered, not openly, but by implication from the
whole strategy of the dedication, which places Dryden firmly within the
intimate circle of—his opponents would say—his social and intellectual
betters. Their "Genial Nights" together are socially, if not intellectually,
remote from "that memorable day" when Neander, the new man, found
himself in company with Eugenius, Lisideius, and Crites, whose "witt and
Quality have made [them] known to all the Town: and whom I have chose
to hide under these borrowed names, that they may not suffer by so ill a
relation as I am going to make of their discourse," a discourse that Neander
never presumes to interrupt and to which he must several times be per-
suaded to contribute.[53] To be sure, the deference of "that memorable day"
still shows in the account of those "Genial Nights" with Sedley. (The Dryden who knew the social decorums of the stage, however much he departed
from them in *The Assignation*, also knew the social decorums of the age.)
The old touches of self-deprecation are still there in Dryden's representing
himself as "the least amongst the Poets" and possessed of a "less [intel-
lectual] Estate" than Sedley. But that "least amongst the Poets" can also
claim in Sedley "the best Friend," and thus distinguish himself from the
Bayes who was covertly ridiculed by Smith and Johnson in *The Rehearsal*
and openly attacked by the Rota and a cabal of wits.

Those wits no doubt contributed in Dryden's mind to "the number of
its Enemies, who came resolv'd to damn" *The Assignation* at Lincoln's Inn
Fields. If so, they also helped swell the audience from whom Dryden turns
as ostentatiously in the dedication as he had in the prologue and the epilogue. Dryden had certainly rejected an audience before. In the preface to

---

[50] Macdonald, pp. 111, 112.
[51] *Ibid.,* pp. 201–204.
[52] For documentation of the charges see notes to dedication, below.
[53] *Works,* XVII, 8, 33, 44, 55, 64, 68.

An Evening's Love he remarked that *"a true Poet often misses of applause, because he cannot debase himself to write so ill as to please his Audience."* [54] But he could not bring himself to reject the audience wholeheartedly when he had a successful play on his hands.[55] *The Assignation's* failure required no qualification from him, and his total dismissal of the audience in prologue, epilogue, and dedication moves far indeed from that keen interest in how audiences respond to stage actions which he had expressed in *Of Dramatick Poesie*[56] and had reiterated in the preface to *The Conquest of Granada*.

Dryden's experience with *The Assignation* looks forward to the dedicatory dismissal of *Amboyna's* success, to his announced disillusionment with the heroic experiment in the prologue to *Aureng-Zebe*, to the making of *All for Love*, which, Dryden later confessed, he wrote for himself, not the people,[57] to the announcement when dedicating *The Spanish Fryar* that a play's value is properly and exclusively determined in the reading, not in the viewing, and to the lament in the preface to *Don Sebastian* that he was *"still condemn'd to dig in those exhausted Mines"* of the stage.[58] In the spring of 1673 three of Dryden's best plays—*Aureng-Zebe*, *All for Love*, *Don Sebastian*—still lay before him, and before him still lay in *The Spanish Fryar* his most durable stage success. But his theatrical career would never again seem as sunny as when, fresh from success with *The Conquest of Granada*, he turned to write *Marriage A-la-Mode*. Perhaps we should not single out for emphasis just one element from the cloud that gathered over Dryden between December 1671 and April 1673. But Dryden's failure with a play so evidently designed to satisfy a popular taste he had earlier chided must have left him disillusioned, a feeling anticipated in the epilogue and declared in the dedication. However small the consequences of *The Assignation's* initial failure for Dryden's later drama, it contributed greatly to the changed tone and attitudes of his subsequent criticism.

TITLE PAGE

Epigraph. *Aeneid*, XII, 914 (Loeb trans.: "the dread goddess denies fulfilment"; cf. Dryden's *Aeneis*, XII, 1321). The context of the quotation is an epic simile near the end of the *Aeneid*. Turnus, who has just been maddeningly tormented by a Fury sent by Jove, faces Aeneas, who brandishes his "fateful spear." In vain, the doomed Turnus hurls an enormous stone which misses Aeneas, and Virgil comments: "so to Turnus, howsoe'er by valour he sought to win his way, the dread goddess denies fulfilment." Given the grandeur and dignity of the two epic combatants and the magnitude of their struggle, Dryden's use of the phrase as an epigraph for his recent decidedly unsuccessful, maligned play suggests a mock-heroic response toward his detractors.

---

54 *Ibid.*, X, 204.

55 See *ibid.*, p. 202: *"let all men please themselves according to their several tastes: that which is not pleasant to me may be to others who judge better."*

56 See *ibid.*, XVII, 31–32.

57 *A Parallel betwixt Painting and Poetry* (1695), p. liv; Watson, II, 207) .

58 *Works*, XV, 66.

DEDICATION

P. 319 *Sir Charles Sedley, Baronet.* The second son of a Kentish baronet, Sir John Sedley, Charles Sedley (?1639–1701) inherited the baronetcy when his elder brother died in April 1656. A prominent court wit, he was perhaps honored by Dryden under the anagrammatic designation "Lisideius" in *Of Dramatick Poesie* (see *Works*, XVII, 355; see also commentary on *Notes and Observations* in XVII, 388).

319:2–4 *as common and unjust, as that of desiring Seconds in a Duel. 'Tis engaging our Friends* etc. For a similarly unsympathetic response to the development of the tradition of employing seconds in duels, first as witnesses and eventually as active participants, see John Cockburn, *The History and Examination of Duels* (1720), pp. 138–139.

319:12 *Action.* "Histrionic personation; acting of plays, performance" (*OED*).

319:12–13 *who came resolv'd to damn it for the Title.* Cf. epilogue, ll. 1–17.

320:5–8 *Horace and Ovid . . . took occasion to speak with honour of Virgil, Varius, Tibullus, and Propertius.* Of the four poets mentioned by Dryden, Horace praised Virgil most often. In *Satires*, I, vi, 54–55, for example, he called Virgil "that best of men" (Loeb trans.; see also *Satires*, I, x, 44–45; *Odes*, I, iii, 1–8; I, xxiv, 9–10; IV, xii, 13–16). In some instances Horace linked Virgil and Varius as men worthy of praise (*Satires*, I, v, 39–44; I, x, 78–83; *Epistles*, II, i, 245–247); in other places he singled Varius out for praise (*Odes*, I, vi, 1–2; *Satires*, I, x, 43–44).

Ovid praised Tibullus most often. He devoted an entire elegy (*Amores*, III, ix) to the death of the "refined Tibullus" (l. 66, Loeb trans.). As Horace with Virgil and Varius, Ovid tended to link Virgil and Tibullus (*Amores*, I, xv, 25–28) and Propertius and Tibullus (*Tristia*, II, 463–465). For additional praise of Tibullus, Virgil, and Propertius, see Ovid's *Remedia Amoris*, 395–396; *Amores*, III, xv, 7; *Tristia*, IV, x, 45–46, 49–55. For Varius, see *Epistulae Ex Ponto*, IV, xvi, 31.

320:14 *Exigencies of a War.* Dryden wrote this dedication during the third Dutch war (1672–1674).

320:15–16 *Lord Treasurer Clifford.* Thomas Clifford, a member of the famous Cabal, was created a baron with the title of Lord Clifford of Chudleigh on 22 April 1672. On 28 November of the same year he was made lord high treasurer and treasurer of the Exchequer (*DNB*). Later, a victim of the Test Act, he resigned the treasurership and left the Privy Council. Whether by natural causes or by his own hand, he died on 13 October 1673 (Evelyn, *Diary*, IV, 21n). Perhaps by Clifford's personal intervention, Dryden in 1671 began to receive his long-overdue salary for the post of poet laureate, and certainly by Clifford's order Dryden in June 1673 was repaid (with £60 interest) the £500 loan he had made the King in 1667 (see Ward, *Life*, pp. 52–53, 79–80, 99). Shortly thereafter, Dryden dedicated *Amboyna* to Clifford, beginning the dedication: "After so many *Favors*, and those so great, Conferr'd on me by Your Lordship these many yeares; which, I may call more properly one Continued Act of Your *Generosity* and *Goodness;*

I know not whether I should appear either more Ungrateful in my Silence, or more Extravagantly Vaine in my endeavours to acknowledge them" (*Amboyna* [1673], sig. A2; S-S, V, 4–5). When, nearly a quarter of a century later, Dryden dedicated his translation of Virgil's *Pastorals* to Clifford's son, he still remembered Clifford with feelings of real gratitude.

320:18–19 *I think him at least equal, if not superiour to Ovid in his Elegies.* The comparison of Tibullus and Ovid began with Quintilian (X, i, 93). In his preface to *Ovid's Epistles* (1680), Dryden later took a more cautious position on the relative merits of the elegies of Tibullus and Ovid (*Works*, I, 112–113). It was not until 1720 that a complete English translation of the elegies of Tibullus became available. In that year John Dart published *The Works of Tibullus, Containing his Four Books of Love-Elegies*. Included in Dart's edition was an essay on the elegy as a genre by G. Sewell, Dart's friend. In one section of his essay Sewell traces the history of the form in England from Chaucer to Sedley, stopping at one point to praise Waller and Sedley for their exclusive ability to write the "latter Species of Elegy, of a successful Love" (p. xi).

320:19–20 *he was . . . a Roman Knight.* Little is known of the life of Albius Tibullus, but, according to the brief vita transmitted in the manuscripts of his poems, he was of equestrian rank. He inherited an estate which was evidently confiscated in 41 B.C.

320:20 *as well as Ovid.* Cf. *Tristia*, IV, x, 7–8.

320:20 *Candour.* The primary meaning appears to be "Freedom from mental bias, openness of mind" (*OED*); but, given the general strategy of the dedication, Dryden might also have had in mind a second possible meaning: "Stainlessness of character" or "innocence" (*OED*).

320:24 *Non tu Corpus* etc. *Epistles*, I, iv, 6–11. Dryden's quotation contains two significant variants from the manuscripts of Horace's original: for *qui* (or the possible variants *quin* or *qun*) Dryden has substituted *quam* ("than"), and for *fama* he has substituted *forma* ("good looks" or "beautiful shape"). In the Loeb translation that follows, these variants are shown within brackets at the appropriate places: "Never were you a body without soul. The gods gave you beauty, the gods gave you wealth, and the art of enjoyment. For what more would a fond nurse pray for her sweet ward, if [than] he could think aright and utter his thoughts—if [than] favour, fame [good looks] and health fall to him richly, with a seemly living and a never failing purse?"

320:33–34 *which one of the Ancients called Eruditam voluptatem.* Although Quintilian (I, xii, 19) actually used the opposite phrase "ineruditis voluptatibus," Dryden's adaptation of it is true to the spirit of the phrase in its original context.

321:7–9 *the ignorant and ridiculous Descriptions which some Pedants have given of the Wits.* The most devastating attack on "the wits" to appear during the years just prior to the publication of *The Assignation* was part of a book published by John Eachard (*Some Observations Upon the Answer to an Enquiry into the Grounds & Occasions of the Contempt of the Clergy: With some Additions, In a Second Letter to R. L.* [1671]). Eachard begins his more than twenty-page attack on a series of "modish wits" with an account of the activities of a young man who has come up from the country to learn their ways, not the least of which was contempt for the clergy (pp. 169–170):

> But still, Sir, there be more contemners behind; for after these follows the young Gentleman, newly entred into the Modes and small accomplishments of the Town; who admiring himself in his Morning-gown, till about eleven of the clock, then it is time to think of setting the Muff; and if he chance to find out a new knot for fastning it, that day is very ingeniously spent: then he walks three or four turns in his Chamber, to make himself considerable; and looking in the glass, and finding it so to be, (having first turn'd down a new place onward in Littleton) he stretches forth, and in approbation of his own worth, tralos himself down the stairs: then at the gate, it is to be considered, where he shall eat; after that, which of the Houses he shall go to, and if he brings home a little of the Prologue, and learns but two or three of the Players names, his memory in the evening shall be commended, and his improvements acknowledg'd. And as for this Gentleman, he having nothing (poor heart) to say against the Clergie-man, he combs his Peruke at him; and (though the weather be temperate) he walks the room, and sweats very much against him; and by way of objection, now and then propounds three or four steps of a Corant; and if he be so far entred into prophane, as to tell him, that he has brought him a new Psalm from London, and then gives him in writing a baudy Song; he need not be witty again all the time that he stayes in the Countrey.

Eachard follows his picture of the neophyte wit with one of more advanced knowledge (p. 170), who, among his many accomplishments, knows his way around a handkerchief, a peruke, and a Dryden song (pp. 173–174):

> It is no such easie matter upon my word, to judge how much of the hankerchief shall hang out of the coat pocket, and how to poyse it exactly with the Tortoise-shell-comb on the other side; and if there be peruke to be order'd, where is the man of the Church that can tell when it is to be done to *Old Simon the King,* and when [to Dryden's] *After the pangs of a desperate Lover.* Heavens and Stars! It is such a task to be considerable, and of any moment in the World, that it would almost crack the brains of the most steady Clergieman, but to hear repeated all the accomplishments that are required, to make up a man of worth.

Some months later Dryden published his *Conquest of Granada,* prefixing thereto his *Of Heroique Playes: An Essay.* At one place in that essay he compares the sharp fancy of an excellent poet to the fancy of "a phlegmatick, heavy gown-man" (see 13:2 above). This characterization of divines probably offended many. Certainly it angered the anonymous author of *Remarques on the Humours and Conversations of the Town* (1673 [*T.C.*

21 November 1672]): "I find celebrated in a late Printed Discourse, the sufficiency of an excellent Poet, to instruct Mankind in the most important points they ought to believe, whilst at the same time, the Author mocks at the dullness of a heavy and Phlegmatick Gown-man" (p. 44). In his preface this writer observes that "vice and vanity walk bare-faced; and the Mode and humour of the times (how corrupted soever) passeth for the standard of Wit and good Company" (sig. *A*6). His assessment of the moral character of "the wits" is similar to that of Eachard: "Some there are who . . . having gotten great and admired names, become the Patrons, and Darlings of the Youth, who willingly sacrifice their early Vertue, their Interests, and the repose of their Family, to their mighty reputations; and think it enough to make them wear the Title of wits for ever, if they but be admitted to drink, and swear, with their glorious Masters" (pp. 64–65; cf. also pp. 41, 42, 79, 94). To the second edition of *Remarques*—"Corrected and Enlarged, in some further *Reflections* on *Marriage,* and the *Poetick Discipline*"—(1673 [*T.C.* 6 May 1673]), the author, in his appended "Reflections," added numerous negative remarks about Dryden and the wits (see sig. A8*v* and pp. 45–46, 50, 122–123, 144, 147–148), most to the present point one on *The Assignation:* "the Poetick fancy . . . whispered Intrigues through the Monastick Grate, and made assignations at the foot of an Altar: it coma'd amorous sentences with Beads; and vigourated a lascivious Song with the Airs of an Anthem" (pp. 175, 177–178).

321:10 *the People of Tartary.* Tartary (or Tartaria) seems to have fascinated the English in the seventeenth century. Peter Heylyn devoted twenty pages to that country in his *Cosmographie* (3d ed., "Corrected & Inlarged by the Author," 1667). Dryden's statement notwithstanding, Heylyn is self-confidently detailed about the people of Tartary (p. 161).

A few years later Elkanah Settle published his *Conquest of China by the Tartars* (1676) which, according to Langbaine (p. 440), was "founded on History. See Signior Palafax his History of China, translated in octavo; John Gonzales de Mendoza, Lewis de Guzman, &c."

321:10–11 *or the terra Australis.* Terra Australis ("the title given, from 16th c., to the supposed continent and islands lying in the Great Southern Ocean, for which Australia was at length substituted" [*OED*]) and its inhabitants were subjects of continued speculation during the seventeenth century.

321:11–13 *as we draw Giants and Anthropophagi in those vacancies of our Maps* etc. Although the practice of filling the terrae incognitae and cartouches of maps with fantastic peoples and beasts was most prevalent in the fifteenth and sixteenth centuries (see, e.g., A. F. van Langren's depiction [1595] of anthropophagi or cannibals dismembering a human body in Brazilia in Raymond Lister's *Antique Maps and Their Cartographers* [1970], pl. 11), when little was known about vast portions of the earth, it continued well into the eighteenth century in England.

321:14 *Atheism.* Eachard (*Some Observations,* p. 190) prayed that the wits "might plainly perceive, that this their childish way of Scoffing at God, and his immediate Servants, is so far from leading towards Wit, or Honour, that it is nothing else but dry, blunt, infacetious Atheisme." The author of *Remarques* (p. 69) repeated Eachard's charge, noting that poets were especially guilty: "The first great subject of their entertainments is Atheism."

This accusation, among others, shortly afterward (*T.C.* 7 February 1673) stimulated a reply by another anonymous writer (*Remarks upon Remarques: Or, A Vindication of the Conversations of the Town* [1673], pp. 58–59): "I hardly believe that he can instance in any one Modern Poet or other, that is in Judgment an Atheist. . . . I perceive Mr. Dryden has displeased your Tutor, Sir, and there is no more to be said, and so much for Atheism in Poets."

321:16–17 *a particular picque to some one amongst us.* Cf. *Raillerie a la Mode Consider'd: Or the Supercilious Detractor. A Joco-serious Discourse; shewing the open Impertinence and Degenerosity of Publishing Private Pecques and Controversies to the World* (1663 [1673]), p. 19.

321:30 *Trumperies.* "Worthless stuff, trash, rubbish" (*OED*). In the light of Dryden's reference to clothes in the preceding sentence, perhaps more specifically: "Showy but unsubstantial apparel; worthless finery" (*OED*).

321:32 *Blasphemy.* Eachard (*Some Observations*) had devoted pages (181–190) to the swearing and cursing of the wits and their imitators. In one place he writes: "And if these people would but a little examine themselves; and not count every Oath, Curse, abuse of Scripture, and the like, for Wit, Humour, Judgment, and every thing; they would find themselves not so wonderfully overstock'd with Ingenuity and Knowledge, as utterly to despair of receiving from the Pulpit any useful Advice, or Information" (p. 184). Cf. *Remarques* (p. 118): "they pride themselves in their amours to a Sempstress; and in swearing like those who keep company with the wits: nay you must take their oaths for their wit; for they believe their profuseness that way, a sufficient proof of their being furnished with that quality."

321:33 *applying Pigeons to the Soles of the Feet.* In his *History of Life and Death,* Bacon had traced the development of this kind of physic: "It is an old tradition that a bath made of infant's blood cures the leprosy, and restores the putrid flesh; and some kings have incurred popular dislike on this very ground." Similarly, he says, "The warm blood of kittens is used for erysipelas, and to restore the flesh and skin." It is common also "in extreme and desperate diseases to cut pigeons in two, and apply them one after another to the soles of the feet of the sick man. This sometimes gives wonderful relief, which is commonly imputed to their extracting the malignity of the disease. But in some way or other this treatment affects the head and comforts the animal spirits" (*The Works of Francis Bacon,* ed. James Spedding, Robert Leslie Ellis, Douglas Denon Heath [1870], V, 307; see also *Sylva Sylvarum,* II, 380). In spite of the rapid growth of experimental science, this practice continued well into the eighteenth century.

322:6–9 *They wou'd . . . come, like the Satyre, to warm themselves at that Fire, of which they were ignorantly afraid, when they stood at distance.* Summers considered this a reference "to a passage in Plutarch of which Dryden's memory does not appear to have been very exact." Plutarch uses the story of the satyr and the fire to illustrate Xenophon's assertion "that men of sense will even derive profit from those who are at variance with them":

> The Satyr, at his first sight of fire, wished to kiss and embrace it, but Prometheus said, "You, goat, will mourn your vanished beard, for fire burns him who touches it,

yet it furnishes light and heat, and is an instrument of
every craft for those who have learned to use it. So look at
your enemy, and see whether, in spite of his being in
most respects harmful and difficult to manage, he does not
in some way or other afford you means of getting hold of
him and of using him as you can use no one else, and so
can be of profit to you [*Moralia*, 86E-F, 87A; Loeb trans.].

322:9–10 *you have too great a Reputation.* Sedley's reputation as wit,
dramatist, and lyric poet was considerable during the Restoration period
(see, e.g., Langbaine, pp. 485–486).

322:10 *Censure.* During the Restoration period, Sedley was as notorious
for his moral lapses as he was famous for his wit and lyric power. His most
scandalous escapade took place in June 1663. In July, Pepys matter-of-
factly described "his debauchery a little while since at Oxford Kates;
coming in open day into the Balcone and showed his nakedness—acting all
the postures of lust and buggery that could be imagined, and abusing of
scripture and, as it were, from thence preaching a Mountebanke sermon
from that pulpitt, saying that there he hath to sell such a pouder as should
make all the cunts in town run after him————a thousand people standing
underneath to see and hear him." A number of years later, Anthony à
Wood's characterization of Sedley ("he lived mostly in the great City, became a Debauchee, set up for a satyrical Wit, a Comedian, Poet, and Courtier of Ladies, and I know not what" [*Athenae Oxonienses*, II (1721), 1099])
was doubtless heavily influenced by that escapade. Wood's own account
(p. 1100) of the incident placed more emphasis on the outraged response
of the people (especially the puritans) than did Pepys's.

322:13 *I have been us'd by my Critiques much more severely.* Although
Dryden at no place in the dedication says so, one of his detractors had
severely criticized the wit of *The Assignation* itself. In *The Friendly Vindication of Mr. Dryden from the Censure of the Rota by His Cabal of Wits*
(Cambridge, 1673), Dryden is portrayed as present at a round-table discussion, frequently quoting "ridiculous" lines from his own works in rebuttal
to an earlier attack (*The Censure of the Rota. On Mr Driden's Conquest of
Granada*, probably by Richard Leigh [Oxford, 1673]) by the Rota. Speaking to his assembled supporters (p. 6), Dryden

still implored the same favourable Aspects from them, and
that they would dare all Eyes which should observe or
read his Writings with any reflections on their faults:
though they may believe that it troubled not a little his
Conscience, that notwithstanding their assignation of favour to his late New Play called *Love in a Nunnery*, the
Town should conceive it Justice to condemn both his and
their Endeavours. Upon which, he more instantly desired them for the future to clap and bawl more exceed-
ingly for his sake, lest he sink by the Censure of the
World, as well as the Rota's: that whatsoever was his,
might be reverenced as a Play, and so voted, though without Intrigue or Wit.

Later in the pamphlet (p. 12), the anonymous author attacks the "bawdery"
of Dryden's recent comedies:

As for his Comedy, it was objected by some, that it was as great an offence to good Morality, as his Maximin was to Christianity. That his *Marriage a la Mode,* and his *Love in a Nunnery,* were most excellent Collections of Bawdery. But the wonder was, how Mr. Dryden came to conceive his fulsome Conceits to be refin'd Wit; as he had suggested to his Friends, since Bawdery had never that repute, before Mr. Dryden writ it.

322:15–18 *I am ridiculously enough accus'd to be a contemner of Universities* etc. In his *Life of Plutarch,* Dryden later (1683) acknowledged that the foundation of his learning was laid at Trinity College, Cambridge (*Works,* XVII, 269). But both before publication of *The Assignation* and after, he on a number of occasions spoke slightingly of the universities and their scholars. For example, in the *Defence of the Epilogue* he implies that the university scholar is impractical and ineffectual (215:11–15 above). And in a letter to Rochester in 1673 (Ward, *Letters,* p. 10) he wrote: "Because I deale not in Satyre, I have sent Your Lordship a prologue and epilogue which I made for our players when they went down to Oxford. I heare, since they have succeeded; And by the event your Lordship will judge how easy 'tis to passe any thing upon an University; and how grosse flattery the learned will endure."

322:18–19 *I am made a Detractor from my Predecessors.* In his *Mr. Dreyden Vindicated, in a Reply to the Friendly Vindication of Mr. Dreyden. With Reflections On the Rota* (1673 [*T.C.* 6 May 1673], pp. 9–10), Charles Blount defends Dryden against this charge.

322:20 *accusation of.* Indictment against.

322:21–23 *You find Horace complaining, that for taxing some Verses in Lucilius, he himself was blam'd by others.* Horace had begun his first satire with a short history of satiric writing, in which he allowed that Lucilius was "witty" but added that he was "wordy" and "harsh in framing his verse" (*Satires,* I, iv, 1–13; Loeb trans.). Evidently, this characterization of the verses of Lucilius led to a good deal of censure from other critics, for Horace begins his second poem (*Satires,* I, x) on the subjects of satire and excellence in writing with a defense of the positions he had taken in the first.

322:26 *Paginâ laudatur eâdem.* Horace's clause (*Satires,* I, x, 4) was actually *charta laudatur eadem* (Loeb trans.: "on the self-same page the self-same poet is praised"). In substituting *paginâ* for *charta,* Dryden would appear to be modernizing the original, since *charta* would not so readily have suggested "page" to Dryden's readers.

322:28–30 *I know I honour Ben Johnson more than my little Critiques* etc. In his *Defence of the Epilogue* appended to *The Conquest of Granada,* Dryden had, of course, much to say about Ben Jonson and the age in which he wrote. The "little Critiques" were not long in answering him. Leigh, in his *Censure of the Rota* (p. 4), lamely began the counterattack with an allusion to one of the passages (see 216:11–14 above) in the *Defence:*

But he [the speaker] was interrupted by a grave Gentleman *that us'd to sup in Apollo and could tell many Storys of Ben. Johnson,* who told them, that in his opinion Mr Dryden had given little proof of his Courage, since he

for the most part combated the dead; and the dead———
send no Challenges; nor indeed need they, since through
their sides he had wounded himselfe; for he ever play'd
the Critick so unluckely, as to discover only his own faults
in other men.

Another detractor, the author of *The Friendly Vindication*, ironically en-
dorsed Leigh's criticisms of Dryden's assessment of Jonson and added some
of his own (p. 12). In *Mr. Dreyden Vindicated*, however, Charles Blount
sided with Dryden against these detractors (pp. 9–10), and shortly thereafter the author of *A Description of the Academy of the Athenian Virtuosi*
(1673 [*T.C.* 6 May 1673], p. 31), declared: "And it is so unjust a calumny to
urge that he labours to pluck leaves from the Baies of Ben. Johnson, when
he adds to them by stiling him incomparable, one to be admir'd for many
excellencies."

322:30–31 *As for the Errors they pretend to find in me, I could easily
show them that the greatest part of them are Beauties.* This point had already cleverly been made by the anonymous author of *Description of the
Academy,* pp. 5–6.

322:31–33 *and for the rest, I could recriminate upon the best Poets of our
Nation.* With specific references to Cowley, the author of *Description of
the Academy* (pp. 24, 29–30) had already employed this strategy.

322:36–37 *two wretched Scriblers.* The author of *The Censure of the
Rota* and the anonymous author of *The Friendly Vindication*. According
to Macdonald (p. 203n), the Bodleian copy of the latter "has 'by Sʳ Robert
Howard' added in MS. on the title-page." Summers suggests, however, that
the author of that pamphlet was Edward Ravenscroft.

322:37 *who desire nothing more than to be Answer'd.* The end of *The
Friendly Vindication* reads: "FINIS or not FINIS As Mr. Dryden pleaseth"
(p. 17). The author of *Raillerie a la Mode Consider'd* (*T.C.* 24 November
1673) praises Dryden's prudent strategy of not answering and thereby denying the "scriblers" a new occasion for attack: "By this becoming scorn you
see how he prevents them from further undertaking against him, when
(like a Morose or Frumpish oddFellow, bob'd in the Street with a by-word)
had he turned again he would have had half the Town hooting at him"
(p. 28).

322:37–323:1 *I have not wanted Friends, even amongst Strangers.* The
authors of *Remarks upon Remarques, Mr. Dreyden Vindicated,* and *Description of the Academy* had all defended Dryden. The author of the last
of these claimed (p. 5) that he did not know Dryden personally ("I never
had the satisfaction of his acquaintance").

323:2–3 *than my contemptible Pedant cou'd attacque me. For the other.*
The author of *The Censure of the Rota* and the author of *The Friendly
Vindication*. Cf. *Raillerie a la Mode Consider'd,* which was published after
The Assignation (pp. 24–26):

Our Laureat himself cannot escape Calumny, (though I
must confess he too much dar'd it) that Reward of Wit
(Sacred to Poets) he finds could not defend him from the
blast of a Criticks Breath. In spight of Apollo's self they
will attaque him; some thinking to be reputed Wits for
only impudently daring to meddle with it.

Thus was he (for sooth) taken to Task, Post-poned, and there Lash'd on both sides by the two, too unkind Universities, Oxford first taking him up, while his Mother Cambridge Chastised him severely. In the first place, for forgetting his old Grammer Rules. So rigidly strict were they to keep him to the scrupulous Precepts of their (long since exploded) Pedantry.

323:3–5 *he is onely like Fungoso in the Play, who follows the Fashion . . . and adores the Fastidious Brisk* etc. Since both the author of *The Censure of the Rota* (p. 4) and the author of *The Friendly Vindication* (p. 12) had accused Dryden of being unfair to Ben Jonson, he must have taken considerable pleasure in turning to Jonson's *Every Man Out of his Humour* for this parallel. In that play, young Fungoso models his clothes on the dress of Fastidius Briske, an affected, swearing courtier. Unfortunately for Fungoso, Briske continually changes his clothes, and Fungoso can therefore never attain his goal of completely aping Briske.

323:6–7 *Mævius and Bavius.* Poetasters contemporary with Horace and Virgil. Horace devotes one of his epodes (*Epodes*, X) to an attack on Mævius, and Virgil scornfully refers to both in one of his pastorals (*Eclogues*, III, 90–91).

PROLOGUE

12 *grunt, like Hogs, about their Captive Swine.* Cf. Edward Topsell (*The History of Four-footed Beasts and Serpents*, "The whole Revised, Corrected, and Inlarged . . . by J. R." [1658], p. 522) on swine: "Their voice is called *Grunnitus* gruntling . . . which is a terrible voice to one that is not accustomed thereunto . . . especially when one of them is hurt or hanged fast, or bitten, then all the residue as it were in compassion condoling his misery, run to him and cry with him."

13 *split.* "Of a ship: to part or break by striking on a rock or shoal"; "Of persons: to suffer shipwreck" in this manner (*OED*). Dryden used the image similarly in the preface to *All for Love* (1678, sig. b2v; Watson, I, 226): "And this is the Rock on which they are daily splitting."

27 *lin'd.* Covered by a second layer of material (*OED*).

30 *Mamamouchi.* "The mock-Turkish title pretended to have been conferred by the Sultan upon M. Jourdain, in Molière's play *Le Bourgeois Gentilhomme*, IV, iii. Hence occas. used for: A pompous-sounding title; also, one assuming such a title; a ridiculous pretender to elevated dignity" (*OED*, citing this line as the earliest use in English). Actually, Dryden has in mind here not the M. Jourdain of Molière, but old Jorden, the parallel character in Edward Ravenscroft's *The Citizen Turn'd Gentleman* (1672), in part a translation of Molière's play. Dryden's attack (ll. 30–39) on Ravenscroft's play was probably motivated to a degree by some lines in its prologue which could have been taken to ridicule his *Conquest of Granada*. Ravenscroft had written (sig. A3v):

With plenty you are cloy'd, but when grown scarce
You will esteem 'em more; and then a Farce
Will entertain you for a Month at least;
Not what is good, but scarce does make a feast.

> Then shall the Knight that had a knock in's Cradle,
> Such as Sir Martin, or Sir Arthur Addle,
> Be flock'd unto, as the great Heroes now
> In Playes of Rhyme and Noyse with wond'rous show.
> Then shall the House (to see these Hectors kill and slay,)
> That bravely fight out the whole plot of th' Play,)
> Be for at least six months full ev'ry day.

Dryden made another slighting allusion to Ravenscroft's play in the epilogue ("Spoken by Mrs. Reeves") to *Secret Love*, l. 30 (see *Works*, IX, 203 and n). See also *Notes and Observations* (*Works*, XVII, 103).

30 *such a Fop.* Cf. Cureal to Jorden: "Y'are very modish and fine in this habit, you exceed all the young Gallants at Court" (*The Citizen Turn'd Gentleman*, p. 28).

31 *Monster in a Shop.* For other Dryden references to this kind of Restoration exhibition, see the note to *Don Sebastian*, I, i, 372, in *Works*, XV, 428.

32 *Hee'l fill your Pit and Boxes to the brim.* In his dedication to Prince Rupert (*The Citizen Turn'd Gentleman*, sig. A2), Ravenscroft says that the play had already been acted thirty times, and that Prince Rupert had attended most of those performances.

35 *Hullibabilah da, and Chu, chu, chu.* In *The Citizen Turn'd Gentleman* (V, i), Trickmore tells Jorden that the bogus Grand Turk wishes to marry Jorden's daughter, but that to be worthy enough to have the Grand Turk as his son-in-law, Jorden will have to be made "a Mamamouchi." The burlesque installation ceremony that follows includes nonsensical—but within their context, amusing—lines like *"Hula baba la chou, ba la baba la da"* and *"Chou, chou, chou."*

36–37 *Marabarah sahem* etc. In the fourth act of *The Citizen Turn'd Gentleman*, Jorden learns that in the "language" of the Grand Turk, "Marababa sahem" means "ah how much in love am I!"

38 *Grimace and habit sent you pleas'd away.* Cf. the similar complaint and phrasing in the preface to *An Evening's Love* (*Works*, X, 203:2–7).

39 *You damn'd the Poet, and cry'd up the Play.* Cf. Downes, p. 32:

> This Comedy was look[ed] upon by the Criticks for a
> Foolish Play; yet it continu'd Acting 9 Days with a full
> House; upon the Sixth the House being very full: The
> Poet added 2 more Lines to his Epilogue, viz.
> The Criticks come to Hiss, and Dam this Play,
> Yet spite of themselves they can't keep away.

41 *he hopes I'm Fool enough to please ye.* The failure of *The Assignation* did not go unnoticed by Ravenscroft. In the epistle to the reader in his next published play, he devoted a long, satiric opening paragraph to recent writers of "Epistles Dedicatory" and "long Prefaces." That he had Dryden in mind is obvious throughout. Among other things he suggests that he has been attacked because he is newly from the university (*The Careless Lovers* [1673], sigs. A2r-v). See the commentary on *Notes and Observations* in *Works*, XVII, 389–390.

In the second paragraph Ravenscroft comments on the prologue he is publishing before the play: "know it was Written in Requital to the Prologue, before the *Assignation, or Love in a Nunnery*, and not without Prov-

ocation, *Læsit prius"* (sig. A2v). The prologue itself begins by equating
Mamamouchi and Almanzor:

> They that observe the Humours of the Stage,
> Find Fools and Heroes best do please this Age,
> But both grown so extravagant, I scarce
> Can tell, if Fool or Hero makes the better Farce:
> As for Example, take our Mamamouchi,
> And then Almansor, that so much did touch ye.

A few lines farther along he turns to the unpopularity of *The Assignation:*

> An Author did to please you, let his Wit run
> Of late, much on a Serving-Man and Cittern,
> And yet you would not like the Cerenade,
> Nay, and you Damn'd his Nunns in Masquerade.
> You did his Spanish Sing-Song too abhor,
> *Ayeque locura con tanto rigor.*
> In fine, the whole by you so much was blam'd,
> To act their Parts, the Players were asham'd.

45 *Haynes.* Joseph Haines (1648–1701), who played the part of Benito
in *The Assignation* (see section on actors below). According to Downes (p.
32), Haines also acted the part of the "French Tutor and Singing Master" in
The Citizen Turn'd Gentleman.

PERSONS REPRESENTED

Mario Governor of Rome. In naming this character, Dryden may have
drawn from real life. After becoming pope, Alexander VII (1599–1667;
pope, 1655–1667) made his brother, Don Mario, the governor of Rome.
According to Lord Angelo Corraro, ambassador from the Republic of
Venice to Pope Alexander VII, the Pope loved Don Mario, who was five
years older than himself, better than any of his other kindred ("A Relation
of the State of the Court of Rome, Made in the Year 1661. at the Council
of Pregadi," trans. J. B., in *Rome Exactly Describ'd, As to the Present State
of it, Under Pope Alexandre the Seventh* [1664], pp. 14–15).

Torr' di Specchi. Tower of Mirrors. The convent Torr' di Specchi was
located near the Capitol.

I, i

12 *person.* The *OED* cites this usage of the word by Dryden, giving the
following definition: "A man or woman of distinction or importance; a
personage."

13 *Jack-Gentleman.* "Jack" has since the fourteenth century been "a
generic proper name for any representative of the common people" (*OED*).
The compound "Jack-Gentleman" is particularly appropriate for Benito;
he is a commoner who affects being a gentleman. Cf. the cluster of related
terms in this speech (ll. 8–13): "Sirrah," "Master," "man," "person."

40–41 *mirrour! there's a touch of his Poetry too, he could not call it a
Glass.* Cf. *An Evening's Love* (III, i, 86–92) in which the affected Aurelia
also avoids the more mundane word "glass" (*Works*, X, 250–251; see also
the note, p. 474).

44–45 *Guittar there, the younger brother of a Cittern.* The *OED* (*s.v.* "Cithara") notes that *"cither,"* *"cittern,"* and *"guitar"* are "all found in English as names of extant or obsolete instruments developed from the *cithara,"* an "ancient musical instrument of triangular shape with from seven to eleven strings, not unlike the lyre or phorminx."

46 *Tibert.* "The name of the cat in the apologue of Reynard the Fox; thence, used as a quasi-proper name for any cat" (the *OED* quotes this passage as an example).

66 *stickle.* Interpose between combatants or contending parties (*OED*).

76 *a Worm in's head.* Cf. Tilley, W907.

85–143 *you know their Uncle is suspicious* etc. This passage, in which Camillo dispatches Benito to Violetta with a letter, corresponds to the scene in *Con quien vengo, vengo* in which the servant Celio brings Leonor's letter to Don Juan, who has paid court to her secretly for two years in spite of her brother's opposition. Juan's friend Octavio takes the letter from Juan, commenting teasingly: "¡Grande extremo de amor!" The gallants then decide to go to the ladies with Octavio serving Juan "como vuestro criado" (Calderón, II, 1136b–1137b).

88 *Assignation.* The primary meaning here is, of course, "an appointment, tryst" (*OED*); but, given the eventual marriage of Camillo to Violetta (as well as of Aurelian to Laura) and the resultant shift of property thereby, a second meaning of the word becomes a possibility: "the action of legally transferring a right or property" (*OED*).

97 *take me with you.* A little earlier (l. 74) Camillo had said to Aurelian: "Now to our business: but we must first instruct *Benito.*" Camillo has barely begun to instruct the conceited Benito, however, when Benito cuts him off with: "I understand you already, Sir" (l. 94). Camillo responds: "Pray take me with you," probably meaning something like "Please wait for me to finish before you proceed." Camillo then goes on in the next twenty-five lines to explain the situation more fully to Benito. Cf. the similar phrasing and obvious sense of a line (V, iv) in Ben Jonson's *Every Man Out of his Humour:* "*Car.* Stay, take mee with you, George."

110 *Tickets.* Notes or billets (*OED*). Cf. the frequent use of the word in *The Annals of Love,* one of the sources for *The Assignation.*

144 *General of the Church.* "The General of the Holy Church is Constituted by the Pope's Breive, and his Staff, and Oath, being privately given him in the Chamber. In time of War he has Three Thousand Crowns a Month; and in time of Peace, but One Thousand; and of him about 500. Officers hold their place by Patent" (J. S., *The History of Monastical Conventions, and Military Institutions with a Survey of the Court of Rome* [1686], p. 125).

144–145 *the Duke of Mantoua, and the Prince his Son.* In Dryden's source, *The Annals of Love,* the father and son are the Emperor "Frederic sirnamed Barberossa" and Prince Henry (sig. A4).

150 *our Venetian Carnival.* In his *A New Voyage to Italy* (1699), I, 198, Maximilian Misson bitterly denounced Venetian carnivals:

> The Carnaval begins always the second Holiday in Christmas; that is, from that time People are permitted to wear Masks, and to open the Play-Houses and Gaming-Houses: Then they are not satisfied with the ordinary Libertinism,

they improve and refine all their Pleasures, and plunge
into them up to the Neck. The whole City is disguis'd,
Vice and Vertue are never so well counterfeited, and both
the Names and Use of 'em is absolutely chang'd. The place
of St. Mark is fill'd with a Thousand sorts of Jack-
Puddings. Strangers and Courtesans come in Shoals from
all parts of Europe: There is every where a general Motion and Confusion. You would swear, that all the World
were turn'd Fools in an Instant. It is true, that the Fury
of these Bacchanals does not rise presently to the height;
there is some moderation in the beginning. But when they
begin to be sensible of the dreaded approach of the fatal
Wednesday, which imposes an universal Silence, then it
is that they celebrate their great Feasts, and all without
reserve, revel on Shrove-Tuesday Masquerade.

152–242 *Let it go* etc. As in *The Assignation*, Lisarda in *Con quien vengo,
vengo* determines to accompany her sister by night in the guise of their
servant Nise ("En traje disimulado yo tu criada he de ser de noche"). The
banter and conversation of the two pairs of sisters in Calderón and Dryden
are similar in outline, but as always Calderón's language is more chaste,
more concerned with questions of honor, more theoretical in its conception
(Calderón, II, 1129a–1131a).

170 *Luted.* Closed or stopped with lute (a tenacious clay or cement), with
particular relevance to the orifice, cracks, or joints of a vessel (*OED*).

176 *keeping.* Protecting or preserving, but also with a pun on maintaining as a mistress (*OED*).

181 *twittering.* Primarily, trembling with eagerness (*OED*), but, in another sense (chirping), consistent with the bird imagery of lines 217–218,
232–234, 237.

237 *Baiting.* A term from falconry, meaning "beat[ing] the wings im-
patiently and flutter[ing] away from the fist or perch" (*OED*).

242 *fine.* "Of liquids: free from turbidity or impurity, clear" (*OED*).

II, i

20 *Rondaches.* Small, circular shields or bucklers. The *OED* cites this
passage.

23–24 *the old Almaine recreation; the Divine bottel.* The German love
of strong drink was by Dryden's day proverbial: *I Tedeschi, buoni Bevi-
tori* or "Germans, Stout Drinkers" (Giovanni Torriano, *Piazza Universale
di Proverbi Italiani* [1666]).

24–25 *the bounteous glass, that tun'd up old Horace to his Odes.* In
Horace's odes the pleasures and rewards of the cup are frequent themes.
See esp. *Odes*, I, xvii; I, xx; I, xxxi; II, xix; III, xix.

39–40 *as dangerous as cold Fruits without Wine.* This belief was commonplace during the Restoration. Torriano (*Piazza Universale di Proverbi
Italiani* included the following proverb in his collection: *Il frutto vuol il
vino in ultimo;* that is, "Fruit requires wine after it." Ultimately this idea
derives from the ancient theory that fruit is cold and moist, while wine is
hot and dry (cf. Hippocrates, *Regimen*, II, lii, and *The Art of Pruning
Fruit-Trees* [1685], p. 52). Since most men were believed to be "of a hot

and dry Complexion" and their stomachs therefore "weak and . . . tender through [a] natural distemperature," pure wine was prescribed as "the sole thing which opposes it self to the coldness, and humidity of . . . Fruit" (*Art of Pruning Fruit-Trees*, pp. 55, 68).

49 *where only Ladies of the best Quality are Profess'd.* Cf. *The Lives of the Fathers, Martyrs, and Other Principal Saints* (1756), p. 426: "Their abbey in Rome is filled with ladies of the first rank."

50 *Magpies.* Cf. the Italian proverb: "Italian women are Saints in the Church, Angels in the street, Devils in the house, Sirens at the windows, Magpyes at the door, and Goats in the Garden" (Torriano, *Piazza Universale di Proverbi Italiani*).

101–102 *of Royal blood, and Neece to his Holiness.* These details are from *The Annals of Love*, in which (p. 81) Prince Henry visited "a Monastery of Nuns where his Holiness had a Niece he loved most entirely: She was descended from the Blood Royal of Sicily."

120–121 *the name of Lucretia is the best excuse for my defeat.* An allusion to the legendary virtue of Lucrece, wife of Tarquinius Collatinus.

133 *Courts.* That is, court cards, or playing cards bearing the figure of a king, queen, or knave.

134 *Gentleman.* Summers: "As we should say, Dummy."

II, ii

1–10 *I'll proceed no farther, if Benito goes* etc. Whereas in *The Assignation* the gallants' plan is arrived at in two stages—Camillo's proposal (I, i, 141–143) and Aurelian's decision (which is motivated in part by fear that Benito's "folly will produce some mischief")—in *Con quien vengo, vengo* Octavio had decided immediately upon reading Leonor's letter to accompany Juan on his nocturnal visit, ordering Celio to exchange clothes—"capa, broquel y sombrero"—with him (Calderón, II, 1137a–b).

7 *patch'd breeding of a Valet de Chambre.* Clumsily made up of pieces, as in a patchwork. Cf. II, iii, 104–114 below.

28 *transitory.* The *OED* cites this passage and one other in Dryden (*Amboyna*, II, i) as the only instances of the word being used to mean "trifling, of little moment."

32 *pane.* "A section or length of a wall or fence"; for example, "the length between two angles, bastions, buttresses, posts, etc." The *OED* cites this passage.

II, iii

S.d. Night-piece. "A painting or picture representing a night-scene" (*OED*).

9–29 *Violetta, my Love* etc. In a corresponding meeting between Don Juan and Leonor in *Con quien vengo, vengo*, Juan pays elegant court to his love (Calderón, II, 1138a, 1139a–b).

30 *s.d.–122 Aur. stepping towards Lau.* etc. In *Con quien vengo, vengo* the witty lovemaking of the two disguised companions takes place as it does in *The Assignation* after the affectionate meeting of the other lovers (Calderón, II, 1138b–1140b). In Calderón, Octavio, showing his wit, declares in near Restoration terms that love ought to come without impediment: "el primero mandamiento de amor es, «no estorbarás»". In an aside, Juan

compliments Octavio on his imitation of Celio's bold, rhetorical style: "Bien el modo has imitado de Celio" (II, 1138a).

48–49 *applying the Plaister whilst the wound is green, 'twill heal the better.* Tilley gives the proverb, "A green Wound is soon healed" (W927) and lists a particularly relevant example: "1578 Lyly *Euph. Anat. Wit,* p. 249: Searche the wounde while it is greene, to late commeth the salve when the sore festereth."

53–54 *hainous malefactour, and is press'd by Law, because it will confess nothing.* In Dryden's day, *peine forte et dure* or pressing was the penalty for refusal to plead to a felony indictment. Because the property of those found guilty after indictment, plea, and trial devolved to the Crown, some prisoners chose to submit to this terrible punishment, thereby assuring the transference of their property to their chosen heirs.

Alleged malefactors were first warned of the painful consequences of their continued refusal to plead and then, if they remained obstinate, were taken to a low, dark room where, bound and pressed by weights, they suffered until a change of heart or death released them from their torture. As might be expected, such treatment usually brought about the desired plea. Occasionally, however, in spite of the stone or iron weights, a prisoner remained silent.

103 *your hand feels white.* Cf. *Don Sebastian* (I, i, 291; *Works,* XV, 90): "Blind Men say white feels smooth, and black feels rough."

133 *s.d. fums.* Plays with his fingers. The *OED* lists two occurrences of the word with this meaning, the present occurrence being the later of the two.

134 *Covert.* A hiding place (*OED*).

138–141 *Éveillez vous, Belles endormies* etc. Summers called this a "very popular old French song" and pointed out that it is referred to by Marie d'Aulnoy in the story "La Princesse Belle-Etoile et Le Prince Chéri," which is part of her novel *Le Gentilhomme Bourgeois.* An anonymous English translation ("The Story of the Princess Fair-Star and Prince Chery," in *A Collection of Novels and Tales, Written by That Celebrated Wit of France, the Countess D'Anois* [1721], II, 148) gives the following relevant passage: "At last, it being Moonlight, she discovered the Prince; upon which she retired, seeing a Gentleman, and not knowing who it might be: when he stopt under her Window, and the Apple sung an Air, the beginning of which words were, or something like it, *Awake, you sleeping Fair."* Cyrus L. Day has suggested that the four lines sung by Benito were "perhaps taken from a contemporary French song" (*The Songs of John Dryden* [1932], p. 156). The *Catalogue of Manuscript Music in the British Museum* (1908), II, 534, 535, 557, lists eighteenth-century manuscripts of the song under the titles "Réveillés-vous, belle endormie" and "Or écoutés la belle histoire."

159–160 *But still between kissing* etc. If this fragment was not written by Dryden for the occasion, its source has eluded the present editors.

III, i

3 *according to the Laws of Duel, the next thing is to strip.* In his chapter entitled "Code of Duelling Established in France," J. G. Millingen (*The History of Duelling* [1841], I, 281) lists as rule number 37: "The combatants will be requested to throw off their coats, and to lay bare their breasts, to

show that they do not wear any defence that could ward off a thrust. A refusal to submit to this proposal is to be considered a refusal to fight." Evidently this rule was not always enforced in England. In an entry for 19 August 1662, Pepys gives an account of a duel fought over the infamous Countess of Shrewsbury in which some of the participants evidently wore hidden armor.

11–12 *like flesh in Spain, 'tis delicate, because 'tis scarce.* A seventeenth-century commonplace. Cf. *An Evening's Love,* I, i, 36–43 and note (*Works,* X, 218, 467).

14–15 *as Milo did, by carrying a Calfe first, you may learn to carry an Oxe hereafter.* Proverbial (see Tilley, B711).

17 *worry.* Kiss vehemently.

40–45 *the narrowness of the Grate* etc. In his *Short History of Monastical Orders* (1693), Gabriel d'Emillianne comments on the immorality that, according to him, led to the first use of iron grates in nunneries (pp. 232–233). An equally harsh critic of the nuns and their subsequent behavior at the grates was the traveler Maximilian Misson: "In my former Letters I said nothing, or very little, concerning the Libertinism and Debauchery that reigns in the Monasteries, because I am not particularly acqainted with the Fashions of those places. I can only tell you what is generally known and acknowledg'd, That the Nuns receive Persons in Masquerade at the Grate; that they put themselves into all manner of Disguises, that they go *incognito* to see Plays, and elsewhere; that they joyn in publick Feasts, and have Tables made for that purpose, of which one half is within, and the other without the Grate; that they are concern'd in a thousand Intrigues, and are often the principal Actors in them" (*New Voyage to Italy,* I, 363–364).

63–95 *Now it comes into my head, the Duke of Mantoua makes an entertainment to night in Masquerade* etc. Cf. *The Annals of Love,* pp. 85–86: "He pitcht upon a night in which the Emperour gave an Entertainment in a Garden upon the Banks of the River Tiber: and Frederick having contrived a new way of Divertisement, resolved to appear in Masquerade, and no persons were to be admitted, but such as were in Disguise. Prince Henry caused Masquerade Cloaths to be made for Constance and her Camarades; he furnisht them with a Foreign Equipage, and (committing them to the Conduct of him who was Gallant to her which kept the Gates) took order for their entrance, and places in the Garden."

96–118 *But, Why thus melancholy* etc. In coordination with the order of the first scenes (see headnote, pp. 513–514), Calderón gives first the reaction of the ladies and Dryden that of the gallants. In *Con quien vengo, vengo* Leonor remarks sympathetically on Lisarda's "notable melancolía" whereas Camillo pellets his friend with jests. In Dryden the emphasis is on Aurelian's chagrin and Camillo's teasing, but in Calderón the focus is on Lisarda's humiliation, her "vergüenza." In a long soliloquy she bewails her shame at having fallen in love with the voice of a servant. She resolves to conquer her ignoble passion by seeing "Celio" again, hoping (or rationalizing) that the sight of him by day will check what the hearing of the night has awakened (Calderón, II, 1141a–1142b).

102 *Golls.* Hands.

114–115 *she has done you the courtesy to drive out Laura: and so one Poyson has expell'd the other.* Cf. the proverbs, "One Love drives out another" (Tilley, L538) and "One Poison expels another" (Tilley, P457). Dryden made effective use of this commonplace medical concept in *Don Sebastian*. In that play Benducar and the Mufti administer offsetting poisons to Dorax who later comments: "Thus, when Heaven pleases, double poysons cure" (IV, iii, 330; *Works*, XV, 180).

137 *tallent*. Two somewhat different meanings are possible: "mental power" or "inclination" (*OED*).

141 *Engine*. Plot.

164–219 *In my conscience this is he. Lord, what a Monster of a Man* etc. In *Con quien vengo, vengo* Lisarda sees the real Celio by daylight and (like Dryden's Laura) wonders how her affections could have been taken by him: "¿Que un hombre tal, con cuidado me tenga?" They part in confusion. Nevertheless, Lisarda perseveres in her resolve to see Celio again alone to cure herself thoroughly—"pues verle solo será remedio"—and calls him back to make a second rendezvous, even though she recognizes that she is "loca" (Calderón, II, 1142b–1145a).

202 *Bull-master-General*. That is, master of linguistic blunders. Cf. Tilley, B718; see esp. the quotation from *British Apollo*.

224 *copy of her countenance*. The *OED* interprets this not uncommon phrase as follows: "a mere outward show or sign of what [she] would do or be; hence, pretence."

265 *civil*. Refined or decent (*OED*).

267 *civil*. Public (*OED*).

276 *Fruit-woman*. "A woman who sells fruit; also, a bawd" (*OED*). A familiar example of this seventeenth-century type is the Orange-woman of the first act of Sir George Etherege's *Man of Mode* (1676). Cf. Thomas D'Urfey's *Collin's Walk Through London and Westminster* (1690), pp. 144–145.

286 *Il Diavolo e morto*. Cf. Tilley, D244.

287 *tickled it*. Ensured a satisfactory outcome. *OED* cites this line as an example.

III, ii

53 *fit*. Punish (*OED*).

74–103 *I am on fire till I discover her* etc. Cf. *The Annals of Love* (1672), p. 86: "But their conversation increasing insensibly, Constance (who understood the Emperours affairs better than he did hers) gave him so many pungent and ingenious answers, that augmented his desire of knowing who she was. He conjured her therefore to satisfie him in that point, but her reply was so ambiguous, he might believe she was of any good Family in Rome, and not know of which."

95 *when my Brother presented me to him at the Belvedere*. In the seventeenth century, almost all books by travelers to Italy contained sections on the marvels of "the Belvedere." The Courtile di Belvedere in the Vatican was designed by Bramante (1444–1514), and among its attractions were numerous statues available for viewing by "Persons of Quality," who were granted free admittance to the Pope's gardens.

127 *green*. By the word "green" the Duke means "vigorous," but Lucretia sarcastically misinterprets him in the following line, remembering that the word can also mean "simple, gullible" (*OED*).

III, iii

1 *Covent.* "The early form of CONVENT, . . . common down to 17th c., and surviving in some proper names, as in Covent Garden, London" (*OED*). In *The Annals of Love,* source for the Lucretia subplot, the spelling consistently employed is "Covent."

7–8 *you play the Brazen-head with me; you give me warning when Time's past.* Ascanio here alludes to the story of Friar Bacon and the brazen head, but his memory of the story seems inexact. The brazen head was not at fault. Friar Bacon's experiment failed because of the foolishness of his servant. (Cf. Robert Greene's *Friar Bacon and Friar Bungay,* acted 1594.)

10 *gust.* "The sense or faculty of taste." The *OED* lists this as the last occurrence of the word with precisely this meaning.

12–52 *Quick, Hippolita, where's the Key* etc. Although Dryden's version has Ascanio returning the key he had stolen for the purpose of making a "Print of it in Wax" (III, iii, 60), rather than Hippolita eventually finding it in a "fold of her sleeve," the incident is in other details quite similar to one in *The Annals of Love* (pp. 88–89):

> She of the Party which carried the Key, had been so much taken up with the contemplation of what she had seen, that she had forgot where she had laid it. She examined her Gallants Habit, and she examined her Religious, gropt up and down the Coach, turned over her Papers, but no Key: The hour they rise in the Monastery approached. The people which brought Commodities to the Market began to appear in the streets: and not one of the poor Sisters could imagine by what Miracle they should be conveyed out of the Coach where they were, into the Cells where they ought to have been. No wonder if they invoked their good Genius, and made millions of promises never to run themselves into the like errour again. There was not a Saint, nor Protectour belonging to their Covent, but they promised a Wax-candle, though by the tediousness of their delivery, they did not seem to be accepted: But at length their Destiny was merciful, and their Key found in the fold of her sleeve.

39 *swingingly.* The *OED* records this as the first use of the word in the sense of "very greatly . . . hugely, immensely."

52 *Ecce signum.* See Tilley, S443.

65–67 *Now will I have the headach, or the Meagrim, or some excuse, for I am resolv'd I'll not rise to Prayers.* In *The Annals of Love* (p. 89) the nuns found similar excuses to avoid early rising: "In the morning one was troubled with the Colick, another with the Headach, every one had her distemper, to excuse their lying in bed the next day."

66 *Meagrim.* Sick headache, or possibly, vertigo (*OED*).

IV, i

S.d.–53 *The Masking-habits of Lucretia and Hippolita laid in a Chair* etc. The third edition of *The Rehearsal* (1675) contains a passage (not in-

cluded in the first two editions) which effectively satirizes this section of
The Assignation (III, v; p. 35):

> *Bayes.* O, all in all Sir; they are these little things that
> mar, or set you off a Play: as I remember once, in a Play
> of mine, I set off a Scene I gad, beyond expectation, only
> with a Petticoat, and the Belly ake.
> *Smi.* Pray, how was that, Sir?
> *Bayes.* Why, Sir, I contriv'd a Petticoat to be brought
> in upon a Chair, (no body knew how) into a Prince's
> Chamber, whose Father was not to see it, that came in
> by chance.
> *Johns.* God's my life, that was a notable Contrivance
> indeed.
> *Smi.* I but, Mr. Bayes, how could you contrive the Belly-
> ake?
> *Bayes.* The easiest ith' World, I Gad: I'l tell you how,
> I made the Prince sit down upon the Petticoat, no more
> than so, and pretended to his Father that he had just
> then got the Bellyake: whereupon, his Father went out
> to call a Physician, and his man ran away with the Petti-
> coat.
> *Smi.* Well and what follow'd upon that?
> *Bayes.* Nothing, no Earthly thing, I vow to Gad.
> *Johns.* O, my word, Mr. Bayes, there you hit it.
> *Bayes.* Yes It gave a world of content. And then I paid
> 'em away besides, for I made 'em all talk baudy; ha, ha,
> ha; beastly, downright baudry upon the Stage, I gad; ha,
> ha, ha; [b]ut with an infinite deal of wit, that I must say.

6–14 *I'm glad however, you took the impression of the Key; but 'twas not
well to fright them* etc. No such ruse was necessary in *The Annals of Love*,
where (p. 84) the nun "that kept the Gates was so favourable, as to give
them the impression in Wax of all the Keys in the House: By these impressions the Prince caused new Keys to be made, and whilst the rigid old
Matron presuming upon her own providence, was sleeping quietly in her
bed, the Prince and his three Confidents past away whole nights with the
four Nuns in the Garden."

23+ *s.d. The Prince takes the Letter, and thinking to put it up hastily,
drops it.* Although in *The Annals of Love* (p. 92) the Prince is on horseback
(rather than in his dressing chamber) when he receives the letter, he loses
it in much the same manner: "The Prince was on Horse-back when he received it, and the Presence of the Emperour not allowing him time to read
it, he put it up (as he thought) safe in his Pocket. But whether the trouble
which was upon him, hindred him from putting it right in, or that it was
the inevitable Destiny of all Lovers to have their Secrets discovered by their
Letters; this from Constance fell down, and was observed by the Emperour."

58 *Troops drawn out, which I design for Milan.* In the seventeenth century Milan was an important military objective for any power intent on
subjugating Italy. First of all, it was of strategic importance because it

commanded the approach to a number of the most important Alpine passes
(cf. A. Lytton Sells, *The Paradise of Travellers* [1964], p. 30). Second, it
was a major source of food for many European states (cf. Sir Isaac Wake,
"A Discourse of the State of Italie," in *A Three fold Help to Political Observations Contained in three Discourses* [1655], pp. 71–72).

113–114 *to be . . . in Pension.* "To live as a boarder in lodgings, to board"
(*OED*, citing this passage). Cf. IV, ii, 32.

120–121 *Oranges in cold: to preserve them, they must be perpetually
hous'd.* The successful cultivation of orange trees in the northern climes
seems to have been a much admired feat. The Dutch appear to have been
the leaders among those who utilized greenhouses for the protection of
citrus trees. That the English were also intrigued by that science is apparent from their ready translation of Dutch books on the subject (for example, S. [i.e., Jan] Commelyn's *Belgick, or Netherlandish Hesperides. That
Is, The Management, Ordering, and Use of the Limon and Orange Trees,
Fitted to the Nature and Climate of the Netherlands* [1683]).

IV, ii

40 *play the fairest of our Game.* Play the game entirely according to rule
(*OED*).

IV, iii

26–29 *If that be my Beatrix with Laura, she's most confoundedly ugly*
etc. In *Con quien vengo, vengo* little is made of the appearance of the maid
Nise, Beatrix's Spanish counterpart. As in Dryden's play (where the real
Beatrix does not even speak), the male servant has the important role, but
the focus of the Spanish play remains on Lisarda's reaction to the real and
pretended Celios, not on the servants themselves or on Octavio.

28–29 *I had faln back from that face, like a Buck Rabbet in coupling.* Cf.
Topsell (*History of Four-footed Beasts*, p. 87) on the copulation of rabbits:
"They engender like Elephants, Tygres, and Linxes, that is, the male [or
buck] leapeth on the back of the female, their privie parts being so framed
to meet one another behind."

51–55 *I had a Vision . . . Where to bestow large Almes* etc. Cf. *The Annals
of Love* (p. 99): "He . . . declared himself a Benefactor to the Covent where
she was. There was not a night but he pretended some heavenly Revelation, which required him to enlarge both the Revenue, and Fabrick of that
Monastery. He designs a Dormitory in this place, a Chappel in that. The
Governess lookt upon him as the Tutelar Angel of her Order."

88–89 *I am bound by vow to stir no farther.* Actually, nuns under the
rule of St. Benedict were in general allowed more freedom to travel than
Lucretia here implies (cf. J. S., *History of Monastical Conventions*, p. 34).

93–104 *see if you know that hand* etc. Similarly, in *The Annals of Love*
(p. 97), "he shew her the Letter she interlined with the Princes, and swore
as heartily as she, he would shew it his Holiness, if she did not oblige him
to the contrary by an ingenuous confession. This Menace made poor Constance to tremble, she betook her self to her whimpering, and her tears, and
beseeched the Emperour that he would not ruine a Person of so Illustrious
Extraction, whose Reputation was entirely in his hands."

112–115 *For could I think my Son* etc. Cf. *The Annals of Love* (p. 97):

"Had you consummated your Intrigues with my Son, Madam, said the Emperour, I would dye a thousand deaths before I would propose any thing of that nature for my self; I am too good a Father to him, and not so impious inclined. But, Madam, the Amours and Gallantry betwixt you two having been so innocent, it cannot hinder you at all from granting me some favourable indulgence." At the time, of course, laws of "Affinity and Consanguinity" forbade the marriage of a man to his son's wife (see *The Parson's Vade Mecum* [1693], p. 81).

IV, iv

40 *Citizens of Bethlehem.* That is, of course, Bedlam.

72 *I am not yet profess'd.* In other words, she has not yet taken her vows. Constance, Lucretia's counterpart in *The Annals of Love*, had, however, "been four years a Nun" when she married the Prince (sig. A4).

113 *Victoria.* "The word employed as a shout of triumph" (*OED*).

IV, v

17 *Basta.* No more. Cf. the similar use of the word in *Marriage A-la-Mode*, II, i, 93.

36 *Love's a kind of warfare.* A variation on a proverb (cf. Tilley, L554, for example).

45–67 *My Ladies Woman, methinks you are very reserv'd to night* etc. In *Con quien vengo, vengo* Lisarda and Octavio—both still in disguise—meet a second time at night in Don Sancho's garden (not in Dryden's "Nunnery-Garden"), where they speak of the discrepancies between wit and appearance and between words and feelings; as Octavio explains proverbially: "en todas son la lengua y el corazón un reloj desconcertado" (Calderón, II, 1148a–1149a).

59 *sight of Owles.* See Tilley, O92.

71–98 *Curse on't, I have betray'd my self* etc. In *Con quien vengo, vengo* the mutual discovery of identities of the disguised couple does not follow immediately from their second night meeting as it does in Dryden; in Calderón the revelations are more complicated and extended. Octavio and Lisarda are interrupted by the arrival of Don Sancho crying perfidy—"¡Oh aleve, infame!"—and are accompanied by armed servants (Calderón, II, 1149b). The gallants try unsuccessfully to take their leave by scaling the garden wall. Challenges are issued and the code of honor "caballeresco"—"con quien vengo, vengo" (II, 1151b)—is invoked. Juan, Octavio, and Lisarda escape together, but Lisarda is mistaken for her sister, Leonor. Further romantic perturbations result from mistaken identities and the intricate code of obligations (see esp. II, 1155b) until Lisarda and Octavio discover (II, 1160a) their real identities: "tú eres aquel Celio, que entendidamente habla?" asks Lisarda, truth slowly dawning, and Octavio, no less relieved, replies with his own question, "eres tú aquella Nise de tan buen ingenio y gracia?" At the last moment the duels are stopped (II, 1165a–b), and the Governor of Verona agrees to stand "padrino de todos" in the rites of marriage, "los casamientos," and of friendship, "las amistades," which are to come.

91–93 *woo'd you by Proxy. . . . Sword betwixt us.* Summers noted that in 1477 "Mary, Duchess of Burgundy, was married by proxy to the Archduke

Maximilian" and that, according to "mediæval custom, the Duke of Bavaria, Maximilian's substitute, occupied the same bed as the Princess. They were both completely attired, separated by a naked sword, and attended by four armed officers of rank."

V, i

9 *our first Foundress.* St. Frances of Rome (1384–1440).

V, ii

16 *the Austin-Fryers.* Summers: "If any particular house is intended it is the Monastery of San Agostino, in the Piazza of the same name, which was begun by the architect Pintelli in 1480."

21 *Cappari.* "Gracious!" or "Watch out!" A clue to the derivation of the interjection is to be found in John Florio's dictionary: "Cappari, the shrub bearing caper. Also the capers themselves. Also an Adverbe importing take heed because the capers growing in Egypt are very venemous and dangerous where they touch, and therefore to be fled" (*Queen Anna's New World of Words* [1611]).

116 *I'll cut through that Wall with Vinegar.* The *OED* records a number of allusions to Hannibal's use of vinegar (acetic acid in a dilute form) in making his way through the Alps; cf. Francis Quarles (*Elegie*): "We cut our way Through these our Alpine griefes, and sadly rise With the sharp vinegre of suffused eyes."

119 *despair and dye.* Probably an allusion to Shakespeare's *Richard III* (V, iii, 118–120: "Ghost [*to Richard*]. Let me sit heavy on thy soul to-morrow! / Think how thou stab'st me in my prime of youth / At Tewkesbury: despair therefore and die!").

120–125 *All things go cross to men of sence* etc. Unlike Benito, his more ambitious and farcical English counterpart, Celio in *Con quien vengo, vengo* is mightily relieved by Octavio and Lisarda's mutual discovery of identity. Making the pun on his own name which the Spanish play frequently employs in pointing up the discrepancies between the "heavenly" and the earthbound, Celio gives homely thanks for happy endings: "¡Gracias al Cielo que ya llegamos a la posada!" (Calderón, II, 1160a).

160–164 *let the young Gallant storm to night* etc. Cf. *The Annals of Love* (p. 96): ". . . having a fair pretence to send him farther off; he gave Orders that night that he should prepare for a Journey into Germany within four and twenty hours."

V, iii

34 *there's Rhetorique in Gold.* Torriano lists two relevant Italian proverbs: *Dove l'oro abonda, manca la lingua faconda,* or "Where gold abounds, an eloquent tongue comes short"; *Dove parla l'oro, ogni lingua tace,* or "Where gold speaks, every tongue is silent" (*Piazza Universale di Proverbi Italiani*). Cf. Tilley, G285a.

V, iv

108–122 *this shall be the Seal of my affection* etc. Cf. *The Annals of Love* (p. 101):

> He pulled the Letter out of his Pocket, and gave it into
> her hands; but he was much surprised to see her run away

with the Paper, and to observe that at the very first step of her flight, he heard some body cry fire round about the Covent. This noise was made by her three Companions from their several Postes, they had agreed among themselves of this Stratagem before, and the Emperour suspecting nothing of it, was advancing towards the house to examine what might be the reason. But the Confusion was so great, and his Train which he had placed without, hearing the Name of Frederick, and Emperour, frequently reiterated in the Covent, they perswaded him . . . forcibly, that it was not safe for him to stay longer in the Garden. . . . had he followed the first motions of his Choler, he would have set fire to the Monastery indeed, and sacrificed Constance and all her Sisterhood to the justice of his resentment.

225–226 *Soveraign Princes bear a priviledge | Of entring when they please within our walls*. Summers, citing several authorities, says that "Kings as also queens regnant are permitted to enter the clausura ['enclosed space for religious retirement'], but actually on the very special occasions of such visits the monarch is attended by a retinue, which invariably includes prelates and superiors of the religious in the house."

EPILOGUE

3 *Zealous Rout*. Puritan mob.

3 *from Coleman-street did run*. Coleman Street seems to have been at one time a hotbed of sectarian activity. In his *Gangræna* (1646) Thomas Edwards wrote: "Upon the Ordinance of Parliament coming forth against mens Preaching who are not ordained Ministers, the last Lord Mayor having information of Mechanicks preaching in Colemanstreet, appointed some officers to go and see" (p. 94).

4 *the Story of the Fryer and Nun*. A traditional pornographic subject. Cf. *The Alchemist*, V, i.

6 *Vicar of Ten pounds a year*. Although it has been argued that the average value of London vicarages rose from approximately £20 to about £125 a year between 1535 and 1650 (see Paul S. Seaver, *The Puritan Lectureships: The Politics of Religious Dissent, 1560–1662* [1970], p. 147), a number of vicars, especially those outside London, were trying to scrape by on considerably less.

11 *Playing*. Sporting (with sexual implications; cf. *OED*).

11 *Content*. Satisfaction. The pun is obvious.

12 *the other side*. The Roman Catholics.

21 *behind our Scenes*. That is, "amidst the actors and stage-machinery." The *OED* quotes this passage as a seventeenth-century example of the phrase.

THE ACTORS

We do not know how the plays in this volume were first interpreted on the stages of Bridges Street and Lincoln's Inn Fields. But the survival of cast lists in first editions of the plays can help us to guess, however unreliably, at aspects of early interpretations. Something, indeed, can be gleaned from comparing the roles assigned to players in each of the three new dramas by Dryden in the seasons of 1670–1673.

The Company	The Conquest of Granada	Marriage A-la-Mode	The Assignation
Beeston, George[1]	Ozmyn		
Bell, Richard[2]	Duke of Arcos		
Boutell, Elizabeth	Benzayda	Melantha	Laura
Burt, Nicholas			Camillo
Cartwright, William	Abenamar	Hermogenes	Mario
Cox, Elizabeth		Palmyra	Violetta
Eastland, Mrs.	Halyma		
Gwyn, Nell	Almahide		
Haines, Joseph			Benito
Harris, William(?)[3]	Zulema		
Hart, Charles	Almanzor	Palamede	Aurelian
James, Elizabeth	Isabella	Amalthea	Sophronia
Knepp, Elizabeth			Hippolita
Kynaston, Edward	Boabdelin	Leonidas	Prince Frederick
Littlewood, John	King Ferdinand		
Lydall, Edward	Abdalla	Argaleon	
Marshall, Rebecca	Lyndaraxa	Doralice	Lucretia
Mohun, Michael	Abdelmelech	Rhodophil	Duke of Mantoua
Powell, Martin	Gomel		
Reeves, Anne	Esperanza	Philotis	Ascanio
Slade, Betty		Beliza	
Uphill, Susanna		Artemis	
Watson, Marmaduke	Hamet	Eubulus	
Wintershall, William	Selin	Polydamas	

[1] Highfill (I, 413–419) corrects Van Lennep in regard to Beeston's first name; it was George, not William, Jr.

[2] Richard Bell, an actor who played secondary roles, was killed in the fire that destroyed the Bridges Street Theatre on 25 January 1672. See Highfill, I, 1–2.

[3] Van Lennep lists a "William (?) Harris" as playing the role of Zulema in

We can see from the table that eight of the twenty-four actors named appeared in all three plays, four appeared in two, and twelve in only one. *The Conquest of Granada*'s cast list names twelve men and six women; the play also calls for messengers, guards, and attendants, as well as the unlisted role of Alabez and the listed but unassigned role of Don Alonzo d'Aguilar. *Marriage A-la-Mode* and *The Assignation* both list fourteen roles. *Marriage A-la-Mode* assigns seven parts to men, seven to women, and there is, additionally, the unlisted role of Straton. *The Assignation* lists eight parts for men, those of Fabio and Valerio being unassigned, and six parts for women, one of them, Anne Reeves's Ascanio, being a breeches role. The role of Frontona—"Lady Fruiterer"—is unlisted.

Certain inferences can be drawn from the statistics alone. The scope of each action—even the genre of each play—is declared by the size of the cast deployed and the ratio of male to female roles. The heroic dimension and military bearing of *The Conquest of Granada* obviously demand a fuller stage[4] and a more masculine one than does the romantic intimacy of *Marriage A-la-Mode,* whose comic poise requires that almost every Jack shall have his Jill or, at least, that the stage should offer a picture of sexual balance. Evidently, however, all three of these plays were designed for the size of the company that produced them,[5] and although there were surely walk-on parts and crowd scenes in the ceremonies and encounters of *The Conquest of Granada* and in the nocturnal Roman carnival of *The Assignation,* there is no evidence of the doubling of important roles which had been a feature of and a necessity for Shakespeare's company. Nevertheless, Shakespeare's playhouse shares with Killigrew's and Dryden's the intimate interrelationships of writing, business, and production as well as the sense that particular roles were conceived with particular performers in mind; moreover, both repertory companies provide systems of cross-references which extend our response to plays beyond their texts and to the craft of acting itself. Before inquiring, however, into possible significances of such combinations as Hart's Almanzor and Palamede, Mohun's Rhodophil and Mantoua, or Boutell's Benzayda and Melantha, we need to recall other specific conditions of Restoration companies which at times possibly, at other times evidently, influenced the creation and distribution of plays and roles.

Conquest of Granada. No Harris appears in the King's Company roster for the following 1671–72 season, but a Joseph Harris is listed in the King's Company in the 1672–73 roster. See Van Lennep, pp. 174, 177, 186, 198.

[4] The grandiose size of cast for heroic drama is satirized in *The Rehearsal* (1672; IV, i [p. 39]) in Bayes's (psychologically perceptive) belief that "Heroick Verse never sounds well, but when the Stage is full."

[5] In spite of the sketchiness of reporting and the vagaries of cast lists, the varying size of the King's Company during the three seasons under discussion may indicate something of the popular fortunes of Killigrew's company. In the season of 1670–71, the company roster as worked out in Van Lennep mostly from the cast lists of new plays gives the names of thirty-four actors. In the next season—the season interrupted by the Bridges Street fire as well as the first season of competition from the new Dorset Garden playhouse—there were only twenty-three listed acting members; in the season of 1672–73, there were twenty-six actors. See Van Lennep, pp. 173–174, 186, 198.

Each of the two patent companies instituted by Charles II held specified rights to old plays which stabilized their repertoires[6] and helped define their stylistic emphases. The system also helped stabilize the groups of actors.[7] A number of men in the King's Company were holdovers from pre-Restoration theater even after a decade of playing.[8] Some, like John Lacy, Charles Hart, and Michael Mohun, held shares in the company,[9] and, at least for the men, acting was a business as well as an art. The men's careers were longer and more stable than the women's. Charles Hart might conduct an affair with Lady Castlemaine, that woman for all seasons, but the men were not, as the women often were, in Downes's expressive phrase, "by force of Love . . . Erept the Stage."[10] When Pepys informed his diary of the liaison between Hart and Castlemaine (with Rebecca Marshall as go-between), he also noted that "the eldest Davenport [Frances] is it seems gone from this House [the King's] to be kept by somebody; which I am glad of, she being a very bad actor."[11] The sense of profession, at least of a single profession, may have been less strongly developed in the women, whose popularity with theatergoers may also have been more volatile than the men's. An actor's age was less important than that of an actress: Burt was near fifty when he played Camillo in *The Assignation;*[12] Mohun was near or past fifty[13] when he played such young or youngish gallants as Philocles in *Secret Love* and Rhodophil in *Marriage A-la-Mode.* Moreover, there were consistently fewer parts for women, and the proportion of eight female to three male roles in *Secret Love* was exceptional. These conditions obviously left the men with more influence in company operations than the women.

But within the system of shares and repertory there was evidently a star system, determined by talent, favor, and popularity, which influenced the

---

[6] The King, through the Lord Chancellor, assigned rights to old plays, the final disposition coming in 1668 and 1669. See Nicoll, pp. 352–354; Van Lennep, pp. cxliii, 151–152; John Freehafer, "The Formation of the London Patent Companies in 1660," *Theatre Notebook,* XX (1965), 6–30, esp. 24, 26–27.

[7] See Van Lennep, pp. ci–ciii; Freehafer, "Formation of the London Patent Companies," esp. p. 19.

[8] Burt, Cartwright, Hart, Mohun, Wintershall, and, just briefly, Kynaston all appear to have acted prior to the Restoration. Burt and Mohun were boy actors under Christopher Beeston (see Highfill, II, 432–434; Bentley, II, 511–512); Hart had been apprenticed to Robinson (Bentley, II, 463); Cartwright and Wintershall probably acted at the theater in Salisbury Court in pre-Restoration times (Highfill, III, 89–93; Bentley, II, 623); Kynaston played female roles for Rhodes in the Cockpit in Drury Lane immediately before the Restoration (Bentley, II, 546).

[9] Along with Dryden, each of these actors owned 1¼ shares; Killigrew held 2 shares, and Burt, Cartwright, Kynaston, Shatterell, and Wintershall held 1 each; the remaining ¾ share (of the 12¾ shares total) probably belonged to Robert Lewright. See Leslie Hotson, *The Commonwealth and Restoration Stage* (1928), pp. 243–245, 254–255; Ward, *Life,* p. 57.

[10] Downes, p. 35.

[11] See Pepys, *Diary,* 7 April 1668.

[12] Burt is believed to have been born about 1624. See Highfill, II, 432–434. Downes (p. 13) lists Burt in the role of Palamede, but it is probably a mistranscription for Hart or records a subsequent production.

[13] Mohun was an adult by 1637, when he was named in a restraining order. See Bentley, II, 512.

distribution of female as well as male roles. Nell Gwyn was notoriously such a star, celebrated as a comedienne, among other things. Her versatility, though, may not have extended to tragic roles. Pepys recorded his displeasure with her "acting of a serious part" in Howard's *The Surprisal*, "which she spoils."[14] Her casting in *The Conquest of Granada* may accordingly reflect her importance to the Company rather than her suitability to the role. One cannot but think that Nell Gwyn felt more comfortable prologizing in a broad-brimmed hat and waist belt than settling her conscience as the grave, veiled Almahide. Just so, she evidently caught the fancy more as that living "Slater'n" who rose to speak the epilogue to *Tyrannick Love* than as the suicidally devoted Valeria, who "dy'd a Princess acting in S. Cathar'n."[15] Valeria, of course, conceives a comprehensible, earthly passion for Porphyrius,[16] and the discrepancy between real Nell and represented Valeria, while marked, would have been less striking than when Nell as Almahide strove to console a frustrated Almanzor with a discourse on pure love and angelic appetite. At such a moment the always delicate balance of the heroic play must have threatened to tip.[17]

A role more obviously appropriate to Nell Gwyn's talent was that of Melantha in *Marriage A-la-Mode*, but when that play was cast and rehearsed, probably in fall 1671, Nell had left the Company to serve the King in her other capacity,[18] and whether or not Melantha's part was ever designed for Nell, it went to Elizabeth Boutell. With Benzayda in *The Conquest of Granada* to her credit, Boutell must already have seemed destined for parts like her Fidelia in *The Plain Dealer*, rather than her Cleopatra in *All for Love*.[19] She was, we are told, "low of Stature, had very agreeable Features, a good Complexion, but a Childish Look" and a weak though mellow voice.[20] She "generally acted the young Innocent Lady whom all the Heroes are mad in Love with,"[21] and her roles often maneuvered her into breeches, as they did in *The Conquest of Granada, Marriage A-la-Mode,* and *The Plain Dealer*. Her fair innocence obviously suited her admirably to the part of Benzayda, while her Laura in *The Assignation* may have been

---

14 See Pepys, *Diary*, 26 December 1667. Two other times in 1667 Pepys comments on Gwyn's charms and failings. In *The Indian Emperour*, which he saw on 11 November 1667, "Nell's ill speaking of a great part made me mad." On 28 December 1667 he "saw *The Mad Couple*, which is but an ordinary play; but only, Nells and Hearts mad parts are most excellently done, but especially hers; which makes it a miracle to me to think how ill she doth any serious part." Nell herself acknowledged her comic interest and talent in the epilogues to *The Duke of Lerma* and *Tyrannick Love*. See *Works*, X, 431–432.

15 See epilogue to *Tyrannick Love* (*Works*, X, 192–193).

16 Nature preceded art in this matter: Hart (who played Porphyrius) and Gwyn had been lovers, and he is reported to have brought her to the stage. See Wilson, p. 146; Pepys, *Diary*, 26 August 1667.

17 For a discussion of ironic response to the heroic play, see pp. 433–435 above.

18 Her second royal child was born Christmas Day, 1671.

19 See Van Lennep, pp. 253, 265. Among her other roles of innocence were Christina and Margery Pinchwife in Wycherley's *Love in a Wood* and *The Country Wife* (Van Lennep, pp. 181, 227).

20 Thomas Betterton (?), *The History of the English Stage* (1741), p. 21.

21 *Ibid.*

less sprightly in the playing than a reading suggests it could have been. But her role in *Marriage A-la-Mode* implies a stage Melantha more naive, more obviously helpless in her affectations, than she appears in a reading or than the character evidently appeared toward the century's end in the interpretation of Susanna Percival, later Mrs. Mountfort, later Mrs. Verbruggen. Percival, Cibber assures us, played Melantha without "the Sexe's decent Reserve," because "Modesty is the Virtue of a poor-soul'd Country Gentlewoman" and "she is too much a Court Lady to be under so vulgar a Confusion."[22] When Palamede delivers the letter to Percival's Melantha (II, i), she reads it "with a careless, dropping Lip and an erected Brow, humming it hastily over as if she were impatient to outgo her Father's Commands by making a compleat Conquest of him at once; and that the Letter might not embarrass her Attack, crack! she crumbles it at once into her Palm." Percival's Melantha then attacks her gallant with "a Flood of fine Language and Compliment, still playing her Chest forward in fifty Falls and Risings, like a Swan upon waving Water." Such a Melantha, "sinking under the conscious Load of her own Attractions," with a "dainty, diving Body" and a "whole Artillery of Airs, Eyes, and Motion,"[23] obviously gave to the part a centrality which a reading can support and which was confirmed in later adaptations by making Melantha's the title role—*The Frenchified Lady never in Paris*. But Boutell's Melantha in the original production must have been less dominant, less central, less swanlike.

Some lightness of emphasis here would certainly have been counterpointed by the casting of Rebecca Marshall as Doralice. Like her older sister, Ann, Rebecca Marshall was celebrated for her imperious beauty and was probably above average height, with dark hair and eyes.[24] With passionate roles her specialty, she clearly would have made a strong Berenice in *Tyrannick Love*, an admirably scornful Lyndaraxa in *The Conquest of Granada*, and she was aptly enough cast as Lucretia, the dominant female role in *The Assignation*. A powerful actress, with a spectacular offstage life,[25] she would have made a striking Doralice, especially in competition

---

[22] Cibber, I, 168–169. With notably less irony, the author of *The Art of Making Love* (1676) declares that true love should properly manifest itself in female confusion. This "amiable Constraint," according to him (p. 151), "is very different from the ordinary Affectation of those pert and impertinent Melantha's" which he finds "so tedious and ridiculous."

[23] Cibber, I, 168–169. According to Cibber (I, 167), Susanna Percival was also brilliant in male roles: "Her easy Air, Action, Mien, and Gesture quite chang'd from the Quoif to the cock'd Hat and Cavalier in fashion. People were so fond of seeing her a Man, that when the Part of Bays in *The Rehearsal* had for some time lain dormant, she was desired to take it up, which I have seen her act with all the true coxcombly Spirit and Humour that the Sufficiency of the Character required."

[24] See Wilson, p. 172. Pepys, *Diary*, 7 May 1668, called Marshall "mighty fine and pretty, and noble"; see also 11 September 1667.

[25] Pepys was fascinated by Marshall's sexual activities. On 26 October 1667 he reports that "Nelly and Beck Marshall falling out the other day, the latter called the other my Lord Buckhursts whore; Nell answered that 'I was but one [man's] whore, though I was brought up in a bawdy-house to fill strong water to the guest; and you are a whore to three or four, though a Presbyter's praying daugh-

with an understated Melantha from Boutell. Marshall's Doralice, indeed, could well have hinted at more than the bored sophisticate of Dryden's text, hinted, perhaps, at the provoked wives of later comedy.

The production emphases in *Marriage A-la-Mode* suggested by the casting of the principal comic roles for women are confirmed by the casting of the principal male roles. Obviously—and rightly, most readers would say—the Company's strength went to the comic rather than the heroic plot of the play. Mohun with a Maximin behind him, and Hart with an Almanzor, were evidently more prominent in the Company than Kynaston, and Kynaston played his Leonidas to the Palmyra of Elizabeth Cox, whose first recorded role came only in the preceding season.[26] Hart, indeed, was clearly the leading actor, playing most of the most glamorous roles. If the comic outweighed the heroic in the acting, then Hart's Palamede playing to Marshall's Doralice must have placed further weight upon one half of the comic quartet to a degree not demanded, though certainly not denied by the text. Indeed, the casting confirms the text in that Palamede and Doralice—beleaguered fiancé and disappointed wife—are the ones who most wittily and sexily pose and test the play's questions of passion and propriety.

If we can trust Richard Flecknoe's labored eulogy, Charles Hart's acting was remarkable for its versatility, for he "a delightful *Proteus* was, that cou'd / Transform himself into what shape he wou'd."[27] Hart, another Burbage, we are assured, "knew by Rules of the Dramatick Art, / To fit his Speech and Action to his Part."[28] Such versatility—he was later to play both Horner and Manly, and reach for an Othello after earlier disappointing Pepys as Cassio[29]—should caution us against speculating too confidently about his interpretation of Almanzor on the one hand, Palamede and Aurelian on the other. But even versatile actors have their own style and unmistakable presence. Hart played royalty so as to "Teach any King on Earth how to Comport himself"[30] (Lady Castlemaine evidently agreed, though finding a different sense for Downes's phrase, and Gwyn is said to have dubbed Hart "Charles the First"). We should expect, then, that Hart's Palamede and Aurelian laid hand to sword convincingly when a show of violence was needed to resolve the plots of *Marriage A-la-Mode* and *The Assignation*. We should expect that at least his Palamede implied the soldier in the gallant. But gallantry and elegance were also Hart's portion, for, as Flecknoe struggles to inform us, Hart "of an Excellent Orator had all / In voice and gesture, which we charming call," offering to audiences both "Beauty to th'Eye, and Musick to the Ear."[31] The Almanzor of such an actor could well have been more polished and supple than we can find

---

ter.' " Pepys thought this bit of behind-the-scenes repartee "very pretty." See also *Works*, X, 383.

26 Cox played Lydia in *Love in a Wood* (Van Lennep, p. 181).

27 "To Charles Hart," in Richard Flecknoe, *A Collection of the Choicest Epigrams and Characters* (1673), p. 46.

28 *Ibid.*

29 See Pepys, *Diary*, 6 February 1669.

30 Downes, p. 16.

31 Flecknoe, *Collection of Choicest Epigrams*, p. 46.

in a reading or deduce from Dryden's prefatory association of his hero with Achilles and Artaban.[32] Hart's Almanzor was evidently equipped to deliver heroic couplets, much trimmer than Flecknoe's, so as to realize their potential to exert civilized control over the heroic extravagance they conveyed.

When Hart's Palamede drew his sword for Leonidas, he was joined by Mohun's Rhodophil, and Major Mohun with a recent Abdelmelech to his credit, earlier a Montezuma and a Maximin,[33] could certainly have brought the proper military presence to a captain of guards. But Mohun, who according to Pepys a decade before was "said to be the best actor in the world,"[34] had turned fifty by the time *Marriage A-la-Mode* was first performed. This "little Man of Mettle"[35] obviously played Rhodophil as younger than himself, but we may yet suppose that his Rhodophil looked older in the acting—emphasizing authority—than it does in the reading. A different but equally intriguing ambiguity attaches to Mohun's possible interpretation of the Duke of Mantoua in *The Assignation*. The mere fact of casting—giving the part to a prominent actor rather than, say, to a specialist in older, supporting roles like William Cartwright—indicates a production emphasis upon the Duke and his scenes. As Maximin, Mohun had earlier played a sexually vigorous ruler with a grown son. But the generic mixture of *The Assignation* elicited from Dryden, as the heroics of *Tyrannick Love* did not, a comic emphasis upon the conflict between generations, upon the Duke's ancient folly in conflict with the Prince's youthfully attractive vigor. Mohun, in a climacteric of his life and career, had to speak both as an ultimately corrigible aberrant from the decorum of age and as a man practiced in authority who was "bred a Souldier" (IV, iii, 101).[36] We should expect so recent a Rhodophil as Mohun to give, at least until the final recantation, the Duke's view of himself as still "green at fifty" (III, ii, 127) rather than act the "Fop-gravity" of Lucretia's scornful phrase (IV, iii, 34).

Mohun's Rhodophil supported Kynaston's Leonidas; his Duke of Mantoua clashed with Kynaston's Prince Frederick. Of the leading actors in the King's Company, Kynaston has left fewest clues to his interpretation of roles in these three plays. He was not, to be sure, credited with the versatility of a Hart, nor are memorials of his acting more fragmentary than is usual from an age of imperfect theatrical records. The difficulty, the uncertain basis for speculation, derives from the seemingly contradictory nature of extant reports. Throughout a forty-year career Kynaston retained, in Drydenian phrase, a striking "masculine beauty."[37] This beauty was such that in the first season of the Restoration, when barely twenty,

---

[32] See 14:21–25 above.

[33] See *Works*, IX, 293; X, 381.

[34] Pepys, *Diary*, 20 November 1660.

[35] Downes, p. 17.

[36] Mohun had served as a captain in the King's army and afterward as a major in Flanders (Bentley, II, 512). Hart had been a lieutenant (Bentley, II, 463).

[37] Cibber (I, 121), who mightily admired Kynaston's beauty and dignity, reports that "to the last of him, his Handsomeness was very little abated; even at past Sixty his Teeth were all sound, white, and even, as one would wish to see in a

Kynaston acted a female role so as to make, said Pepys, "the loveliest lady that I ever saw in my life."[38] We might suppose, then, that Kynaston's Boabdelin was as weak and "contemptible" as Dryden found the character in "the History of *Granada*,"[39] that Kynaston's Leonidas suggested an easy metamorphosis into Prince Prettyman of *The Rehearsal*,[40] and that Kynaston's Frederick emphasized the scrupulously dutiful prince rather than the rival ruler. But by 1670 Kynaston was a decade from women's parts and a decade toward the "fierce, Lion-like Majesty in his Port and Utterance" which Cibber observed at the century's end and which "gave the Spectator a kind of trembling Admiration."[41] Cibber thought Kynaston excellent in heroic roles, which he played with "a quick imperious Vivacity in his Tone of Voice."[42] But others disagreed. Pepys in 1660 had thought Kynaston's "voice not very good";[43] much later, Edmund Bellchambers reported players' gossip which called it whining.[44] Even Cibber conceded that Kynaston sometimes conveyed indecision in a tyrant's role,[45] straining, perhaps, for more strength than he could command. The records, then, are somewhat contradictory, but from them emerges the Restoration equivalent of a matinee idol, lovely to look at, but without the great actor's presence and conviction. Kynaston was more likely to bring pathos than decision to the Boabdelin of Dryden's text, more likely in his Leonidas to stress the romantic at the expense of the heroic, and unlikely to challenge unequivocally a production emphasis on the comic plot of *Marriage A-la-Mode*. Then, too, the scenes in *The Assignation* between Mohun's Duke and Marshall's Lucretia could well have been stronger in the playing than those between Marshall's Lucretia and Kynaston's Prince.

The Assignation must in any event have proved a difficult challenge to the Company. Whether or not, as Ravenscroft thought, the players were

---

reigning Toast of Twenty. He had something of a formal Gravity in his Mien, which was attributed to the stately Step he had been so early confin'd to, in a female Decency."

38 Pepys, *Diary*, 18 August 1660. Cibber relates (I, 120–121) that Kynaston in petticoats "was so beautiful a Youth that the Ladies of Quality prided themselves in taking him with them in their Coaches to Hyde-Park in his Theatrical Habit, after the Play." And Pepys again, on 7 January 1661, praising *The Silent Woman*, remarks that Kynaston "the boy hath the good turn to appear in three shapes: 1, as a poor woman in ordinary clothes to please Morose; then in fine clothes as a gallant, and in them was clearly the prettiest woman in the whole house—and lastly, as a man; and then likewise did appear the handsomest man in the house."

39 See p. 416 above.

40 See p. 463 above. Actually, according to Bodleian MS Eng. poet. e4, Kynaston played Prettyman's alter ego, the indecisive Volscius who, torn between love and honor, hops offstage "with one Boot on, and the other off." See Montague Summers, *The Playhouse of Pepys* (1935), p. 193.

41 Cibber (I, 121) is here describing Kynaston's Morat in *Aureng-Zebe* and his Muley-Moluch in *Don Sebastian*.

42 Cibber, I, 121.

43 Pepys, *Diary*, 18 August 1660.

44 Quoted in Cibber, II, 340.

45 *Ibid.*, I, 124–125.

ashamed to act their parts, they could certainly be excused for failing to find a center, a production emphasis, in a play of such disparate styles that beside it, not just *The Conquest of Granada* but *Marriage A-la-Mode* as well, seems remarkable for unity of tone. *The Assignation* lifts its central comedy of young wit and courtship into the ambivalence and seriousness of the Duke's infatuation, and also lowers that comedy into the buffoonery of Benito.[46]

In any other season than that of 1672–73 we should expect Benito's part to fall to John Lacy, a shareholder and leading comedian of the Company, who specialized in the raucous farce so obviously demanded for the playing of Benito.[47] To be sure, there is no record of Lacy's taking part in a play by Dryden. But the only other play in which Dryden had a hand and which contained an obvious part for Lacy was *Sir Martin Mar-all,* and that play had been performed by the rival Duke's Company with the celebrated Nokes in the title role.[48] Similarly, we need not suppose any coolness between Dryden and Lacy simply because Lacy played Bayes in *The Rehearsal,* a part in which he was coached by Buckingham himself.[49] Most of the King's Company was no doubt involved in *The Rehearsal.* The play itself names Wintershall, Haines, and Cartwright, as well as Lacy;[50] a contemporary broadside added Littlewood and a contemporary manuscript added Kynaston;[51] later, *Key to The Rehearsal* (1704, p. 6), perhaps guessing from gossip rather than recording theatrical fact, gave the part of Amaryllis, Bayes's mistress, to Dryden's own reputed mistress, Anne Reeves, who certainly played minor roles, though some, like Philotis in *Marriage A-la-Mode*[52] and Ascanio in *The Assignation,* required of her more deftness in comedy than Amaryllis could have managed. Lacy's role in *The Rehearsal,* then, tells us no more about his relations with Dryden than is implied by the absence of a record of his acting in a Dryden play. He could have played Benito, except that, as far as we can tell (and again we may simply be confronted with imperfect records),[53] he was not listed in the King's Company for 1672–73, the season of *The Assignation*'s premiere, even though he was listed in the Company for preceding and succeeding seasons.

Benito's part, and with it the prologue, went to Joseph Haines, who was still early in a long career when he rejoined the Company in the preceding season[54] after being dismissed by Hart in 1668. There is a special piquancy to Haines's playing Benito to Hart's Aurelian, since Hart had dismissed Haines for provoking him on stage with clownish attempts at scene-

---

[46] See pp. 514–516 above.

[47] See Leo Hughes, *A Century of English Farce* (1956), pp. 157–159.

[48] For praise of Nokes in this role, see Downes, p. 28; Cibber, I, 142–144; *Works,* IX, 352–353.

[49] See Van Lennep, p. 190; Hume, p. 291.

[50] *The Rehearsal* (1672): Lacy (prologue); Wintershall (p. 13); Cartwright (pp. 10, 45); and Haines (p. 54).

[51] For Littlewood, see Van Lennep, p. 191; for Kynaston, see n.38 above.

[52] See pp. 473–474 above.

[53] See Van Lennep, p. 198.

[54] See *ibid.,* pp. 186, 191.

stealing,[55] much as Benito is made to provoke Aurelian by his clownish attempts to arrange intrigues and dominate encounters. Hart's Aurelian, we may suppose, kicked Haines's Benito with special zest. With his improvident life, his irrepressible self-advertisement both on stage and off, his specializing in prologues and epilogues[56]—when the player stands alone to droll with his audience—Haines emerges as a licensed clown of old courts who survived into the sophisticated skepticism of new courts. He was, then, rightly cast as Benito, who represents, after all, Dryden's attempt to graft old buffoonery upon new wit.

Haines later quipped with the Earl of Sunderland about the Virgin Mary;[57] Kynaston had already been beaten by hired thugs for impersonating Sedley on stage;[58] we have stories about Nell Gwyn, Becky Marshall, Betty Boutell; we have Charles Hart and Lady Castlemaine; and we inevitably recall some such stories when trying to reconstruct past performances. We do so not simply because theatrical historians love gossip, or simply because fragmentary stage records drive us backstage and beyond in order to fatten an otherwise lean discourse. We do so because we wish to stage past performances in the mind and, in the absence of full theatrical memoirs, must try to reconstruct the styles of players and envision those styles combined in the acting of a text. We know that a player's stage style can be wholly distinct from his life-style; something, no doubt, depends upon conventions of theatrical presentation, and much—very much—upon the place of theaters in society. But we also know that Restoration theaters were intimate with the society they addressed. Restoration records, patchy though they are, lead us from stage to pit and beyond as often as the text of plays and prologues themselves. We therefore use whatever we can from the records of life and stage in order to reconstruct personalities, styles, presences. We do so because we are interested in the acting potential of plays, especially those plays that have disappeared from the repertoire. We do so because our experience marches with Dryden's perception to force agreement that a play performed will differ, at times widely, from a play read, and that if we rest in a reading we leave much of our aesthetic work undone and much of our pleasure unexplored. We need not agree with

---

[55] See Wilson, p. 36.

[56] See Cibber, I, 273n; II, 314–318; Wilson, pp. 32–33. The assignment of prologues and epilogues—those charms of attention and applause—can reasonably be taken as one index to an actor's popularity and ability to work with an audience. This talent generally exerted itself in the direction of farce (as with a Jo Haines) or wit (as with a Charles Hart), taking the customary form of comment and, to paraphrase *The Rehearsal* (p. 7), of civility or censure. (Interestingly, no such assignments for Kynaston are listed in Van Lennep.) In the plays under consideration, Hart delivered one prologue (to *Marriage A-la-Mode*) and one epilogue (to *1 Conquest of Granada*) as did Mohun (to *2 Conquest of Granada* and to *Marriage A-la-Mode*); Gwyn gave the prologue to *1 Conquest of Granada* and Haines performed the prologue to *The Assignation*. The epilogists for *2 Conquest of Granada* and *The Assignation* are not known. For a more extensive anatomy of the genre itself, see David M. Vieth, "The Art of the Prologue and Epilogue: A New Approach Based on Dryden's Practice," *Genre*, V (September 1972), 271–292.

[57] See Cibber, I, 273.

[58] See Pepys, *Diary*, 1 February 1669.

Dryden that *"Beauties of the Stage"*—*"the Lights, the Scenes, the Habits, and, above all, the Grace of Action"*—are necessarily *"false"* and *"cast a mist upon"* the evaluative judgment of an audience, but those beauties are undeniably *"no more lasting than a Rainbow."*[59] Theatrical history seeks to paint yesterday's rainbows and so brings us closer than most scholarly endeavors to Rochester's view of the human condition by plunging us "into doubt's boundless sea." We can neither know nor hold from speculation.

---

[59] Dedication of *The Spanish Fryar* (1681, sig. A2v; Watson, I, 275).

TEXTUAL NOTES

Introduction

CHOICE OF THE COPY TEXT

The copy text is normally the first printing, on the theory that its accidentals are likely to be closest to the author's practice; but a manuscript or a subsequent printing may be chosen where there is reasonable evidence either that it represents more accurately the original manuscript as finally revised by the author or that the author revised the accidentals.

REPRODUCTION OF THE COPY TEXT

The copy text is normally reprinted *literatim,* but there are certain classes of exceptions. In the first place, apparently authoritative variants found in other texts are introduced as they occur, except that their purely accidental features are made to conform to the style of the copy text. These substitutions, but not their minor adjustments in accidentals, are recorded in footnotes as they occur. In the second place, the editors have introduced nonauthoritative emendations, whether found in earlier texts or not, where the sense seems to demand them. These emendations are also listed in the footnotes. In the third place, accidentals, speech headings, stage directions, scene headings, and so forth, are introduced or altered where it seems helpful to the reader. All such changes also are recorded in footnotes as they occur. In the fourth place, turned b, q, d, p, n, and u are accepted as q, b, p, d, u, and n, respectively, and if they result in spelling errors are corrected in the text and listed in the footnotes. The textual footnotes show the agreements among the texts only with respect to the precise variation of the present edition from the copy text; for example, in *Marriage A-la-Mode* at IV, iii, 155, the footnote "Hero] F; *Hero* Q1–4, D" has reference to the change from italics to romans; F actually reads "Heroe."

Certain purely mechanical details have been normalized without special mention. Long "s" has been changed to round "s," "VV" to "W"; swash italics have been represented by plain italics; head titles and any accompanying rules, act and scene headings, and display initials and any accompanying capitalization, have been made uniform with the style of the present edition; when a speech begins in the middle of a verse line, it has been appropriately indented; the position of speech headings and stage directions and their line division have been freely altered (braces in the speech tags have been omitted; those in the stage directions have been replaced by brackets; erratic uses of capitals in stage directions have been normalized); wrong font, and turned letters other than q, b, p, d, u, and n have been adjusted; medial apostrophes that failed to print have been restored; italicized plurals in -'s have been distinguished (by italic final "s") from possessives (roman final "s"); quotations have been marked with inverted commas at the beginning and end only and always; spacing between words and before and after punctuation has been normalized when no change in meaning results; the common contractions have been counted as single words, but otherwise words abbreviated by elision have been separated from those before and after if the apostrophe is present; if the elided syllable is written out as well as marked by an apostrophe, the words have been run together (*"speak'it"*).

TEXTUAL NOTES

The textual notes list the relevant manuscripts and printings, assign them sigla, and give references to the bibliographies where they are more fully described. Normally only the seventeenth-century manuscripts and the printed editions through Congreve's (1717)[1] are cited, since there is normally no likelihood that authoritative readings will be found in any later manuscripts or editions. The textual notes also outline the descent of the text through its various manuscripts and printings, indicate which are the authorized texts, and explain how the copy text was selected in each instance. A list of copies collated follows. If the differences between variant copies are sufficient to warrant a tabular view of them, it will follow the list of copies collated.

The sigla indicate the format of printed books (F = folio, Q = quarto, O = octavo, etc.) and the order of printing, if this is determinable, within the format group (F may have been printed after Q1 and before Q2). If order of printing is in doubt, the numbers are arbitrary, and they are normally arbitrary for the manuscripts (represented by M).

Finally the variants in the texts collated are given. The list is not exhaustive, but it records what seemed material, viz.:

All variants of the present edition from the copy text except in the mechanical details listed above.

All other substantive variants and variants in accidentals markedly affecting the sense. The insertion or removal of a period before a dash has sometimes been accepted as affecting the sense; other punctuational variants before dashes have been ignored. Failure of letters to print, in texts other than the copy text, has been noted only when the remaining letters form a different word or words, or when a word has disappeared entirely.

All errors of any kind repeated from one edition to another, except the use of -'s instead of -s for a plural.

Spelling variants where the new reading makes a new word (e.g., *then* and *than* being in Dryden's day alternate spellings of the conjunction, a change from *than* to *then* would be recorded, since the spelling *then* is now confined to the adverb, but a change from *then* to *than* would be ignored as a simple modernization).

In passages of verse, variants in elision of syllables normally pronounced (except that purely mechanical details, as *had'st, hadst,* are ignored). Thus *heaven, heav'n* is recorded, but not *denied, deny'd.*

Relining, except when passages printed as prose are reprinted as prose.

When texts generally agree in a fairly lengthy variation, but one or two

---

[1] How much Congreve had to do with this edition beyond writing the dedication, and how much the text represents Dryden's last thoughts, are questionable (see Macdonald, p. 151), but it has seemed wiser to include its variant readings always.

differ from the rest in a detail that would be cumbrous to represent in the usual way, the subvariations are indicated in parentheses in the list of sigla. For example:

Leonidas] Q₁–2 (~ .); *Leonidas* Q3–4, F, D (~ . D).

This means that D agrees with Q3–4 and F in all respects except that it adds a period; Q1–2 also add a period.

When variants in punctuation alone are recorded, the wavy dash is used in place of the identifying word before (and sometimes after) the variant punctuation. A caret indicates absence of punctuation.

As in the previous volumes, no reference is made to modern editions where the editor is satisfied that reasonable care on his part would have resulted in the same emendations, even if he collated these editions before beginning to emend.

The seventeenth-century printings were compared with the help of a computer and a Hinman collator.

The Conquest of Granada

The Conquest of Granada by the Spaniards: In Two Parts was first published in 1672 (Q1; Macd 76a) and was reprinted in 1673 (Q2; Macd 76b), 1678 (Q3; Macd 76c), 1687 (Q4; Macd 76d), and 1695 (Q5; Macd 76e). It was also reprinted in Dryden's *Comedies, Tragedies, and Operas* (1701), I, 379–468 (F; Macd 107ai–ii [two issues, the differences not affecting this play]), and in Congreve's edition of Dryden's *Dramatick Works* (1717), III, 5–175 and 17 unnumbered pages following (D; Macd 109ai–ii [two issues, the differences not affecting this play]). The separate edition of 1704 (Macd 76f–g [two issues]) is not noticed in the apparatus. Dryden revised Q1 during printing to add III, i, 45–107, and to adjust the preceding and following stage directions. The printer accommodated the change by replacing the original leaf C3 with a half sheet, C². In the apparatus the readings of C3 are distinguished as Q1a, those of C² as Q1b. Dryden also revised the text of Q2. Q3 was set from a copy of Q2, but Q4 was reprinted from a copy of Q1 with the cancel C², Q5 from a copy of Q4, F and the 1704 edition from copies of Q5, and D from a copy of the 1704 edition. Not only were Dryden's revisions in Q2 thus lost, but Q4 did not include Dryden's *Defence of the Epilogue* [to Part II]. *Or, An Essay on the Dramatique Poetry of the last Age.* The *Defence* was restored in D, where it was inserted on cancel sheets [1HI]⁶, [2HI]², with a note at the foot of [2HI]2v, "[*This must be plac'd immediately before* Marriage A-la Mode, VOL. III.]" (i.e., between H4v and H5). The text of the *Defence* in D was set from a copy of Q1, however, so that Dryden's revisions were still lost.

The songs in the play were published separately before the play itself appeared and often thereafter in the following collections: [B., L.], *The New Academy of Complements*, 1671 (Wing N530; Ds1), pp. 286–287 (= 296–297), Pt. I, Act IV; 306–307 (= 316–317), Pt. II, Act IV; *Westminster-Drollery*, 1671 (Wing W1457; Os1), pp. 31–33 and 116–117, Pt. I, Act III; 10–11, Pt. I, Act IV; 14–15, Pt. II, Act IV; anr. ed., 1671 (Wing W1458; Os2), pp. 31–33 and 116–117, Pt. I, Act III; 10–11, Pt. I, Act IV; 14–15, Pt.

II, Act IV [the two texts of the song in Pt. I, Act III, are distinguished in the apparatus as Os1a, Os2a, for the first text (pp. 31–33 in both editions) and Os1b, Os2b for the second (pp. 116–117 in both)]; anr. ed., 1671 (Wing W1459; Os3), pp. 33–34, Pt. I, Act III; 10–11, Pt. I, Act IV; 15–16, Pt. II, Act IV; anr. ed., 1672 (Wing W1460; Os4), pp. 31–33, Pt. I, Act III; 10–11, Pt. I, Act IV; 14–15, Pt. II, Act IV; *Windsor-Drollery*, 1672 (Wing W2980; Os5), pp. 5, Pt. I, Act III; 138–139 (= 162–163), Pt. I, Act IV; 1–2, Pt. II, Act IV; [Playford, John], *Choice Songs and Ayres for One Voyce . . . The First Book*, 1673 (Wing C3920 and P2465; Fs1), pp. 45, Pt. I, Act III; 37, Pt. I, Act IV; 38, Pt. II, Act IV; [Playford, John], *Choice Ayres, Songs, & Dialogues*, 2d ed. [of Fs1], 1675 (Wing P2462; Fs2), pp. 37, Pt. I, Act III; 29, Pt. I, Act IV; 32, Pt. II, Act IV; anr. ed., 1676 (Wing P2463; Fs3), paging as in 1675 ed.; [P., W.], *The Wits Academy*, 1677 (Wing P139; Ds2), pp. 122–123, Pt. I, Act IV; [B., L.], *The New Academy of Complements*, 1681 (Wing N531; Ds3), pp. 296–297, Pt. I, Act IV; 316–317, Pt. II, Act IV; anr. ed., 1698 (Ds4), pp. 296–297, Pt. I, Act IV; 316–317, Pt. II, Act IV; [P(layford), H(enry)], *Wit and Mirth: or, Pills to Purge Melancholy*, 1699 (Wing W3134A; Ds5), pp. 184–186, Pt. I, Act III; 180–181, Pt. I, Act IV; 182–183, Pt. II, Act IV. Wing lists another edition of *Choice Ayres*, 1684, in the British Library (P2464) but he appears to be in error; the volume in question is probably his P2461.

Fs1–3 and Ds5 give musical settings by John Bannister (Pt. I, Act III), Alphonso [*sic*] Marsh (Pt. I, Act IV), and Nicholas Staggins (Pt. II, Act IV).

The following contemporary manuscripts have been located: the songs in Folger MS V.a.226, pp. 29–30, 31–32, and 36–37 (M1); the songs in Act III of Pt. I and Act IV of Pt. II in Bodleian MS Rawl. poet. 65, fols. 37v and 38r (M2); the song in Act IV of Pt. I in Edinburgh University MS D.c.1, p. 108 (M3), and British Library MS Sloane 1487, fol. 4r-v (M4); the epilogue to Pt. I (wrongly said to belong to Pt. II) and the prologue to Pt. II in Bodleian MS Don. b.8, pp. 248–249 (M5); and the song in Act IV of Pt. II (with music) in British Library MS Add. 29,396, pp. 84–85 (M6). M1 was compiled by William Deedes from contemporary plays. When the volume is read in one direction, the selections deal with love; with the volume reversed the topics are miscellaneous. Besides the songs, which are in the series on love, Deedes takes many brief passages from both parts of the play (pp. 30–38; reversed, pp. 25–28); the variants are of no interest and except for the songs are not noted. M2 is a collection of poetry compiled by an Oxford man (St. John's College) in the last quarter of the seventeenth century. M3 is a tall thin folio of poems in several seventeenth-century hands. M4 is a volume of miscellaneous prose and verse in several seventeenth-century hands. The song is in a hand that a few pages farther on gives the date 1675 to extracts from Arthur Warwick's *Spare-minutes;* no 1675 edition of this popular work is recorded, so presumably the date is that of the manuscript. M5 is a collection of poetry and prose in the hand of Sir William Hayward, made about 1681–82. It annotates three couplets in the epilogue to Pt. I as "not spoke," and gives four lines in the prologue to Pt. II which were never printed. As with the additional lines to Dryden's epilogue to *The Man of Mode* in the same manuscript, the editors have concluded that the additional lines are not Dryden's (see *Works*, I, 397). M6 is a folio music manuscript mostly in the hand of Edward Lowe (d. 1682),

Purcell's predecessor as organist of the Chapel Royal. The song is in Lowe's hand.

The copy text for the present edition is one of the Clark copies of Q1 with uncanceled C3 (*PR3417.H1), emended according to Dryden's revisions in Q1b and Q2, and elsewhere by the present editor as shown in the footnotes; also, the use of romans and italics in *Of Heroique Plays. An Essay* has been reversed. The spelling "Benzayda" has been replaced by "Benzaida" when the metrics indicate four syllables.

The following copies of the various editions have also been examined: Q1: Clark (*PR3417.H1.1672), Huntington (D2256), Folger (D2256 bd. w. D2206h); Q2: Clark (*PR3417.H1.1673), Huntington (D2257), Folger (D2257 bd. w. D2291); Q3: Clark (*PR3417.H1.1678), Folger (D2258), Texas (Aj.D848.672cc); Q4: Clark (*PR3417.H1.1687 [cop. 1]; *PR3410. C93.v.1), Texas (Aj.D848.672cd); Q5: Clark (*PR3410.C91; *PR3410.C95; *PR3410.C95a); F: Clark (*fPR3412.1701 [2 cop.]; *fPR3412.1701a); D: Clark (*PR3412.1717 [2 cop.], *PR3412.1717a); Ds1: British Library (1076. e.29); Ds2: British Library (1078.c.1); Ds3: Huntington (86952); Ds4: British Library (C.136.aa.7); Ds5: British Library (Case 117.a.19); Os1: Bodleian (Univ. Microfilms, English Books, Reel 371); Os2: British Library (11621.a. 44); Os3: Harvard (*EC65.A100.671w); Os4: Folger (W1460); Os5: British Library (11626.aa.37); Fs1: British Library (K.7.i.20); Fs2: British Library (K.7.i.21); Fs3: British Library (K.7.i.19).

Press Variants by Form

Q1
Sheet A (inner form)
Folger cop. 2 has A3*v* signed A3.
Sheet C (outer form)
Uncorrected (?): Folger (2)
Corrected (?): Clark (2), Huntington
Sig. C2*v*
  Pt. I, II, i, 260 right.————] ~ ._
Sheet E (inner form)
Uncorrected: Clark cop. 2, Folger cop. 1, Huntington
Corrected: Clark cop. 1, Folger cop. 2
Sig. E1*v*
  Pt. I, III, i, 523 me.] ~ :
Sig. E2
  Pt. I, IV, i, 13 But] ~ ,
          21 and I] and
          36 I] ~ ,
          37 were] where
          39 Then'] ~ ,
Sig. E4
  Pt. I, IV, ii, 77 plain.] ~ :
          84 *Abdel.* What] What
Sheet L (outer form)
Uncorrected (?): Clark (2), Folger cop. 2, Huntington
Corrected (?): Folger cop. 1

Sig. L3
    Pt. II, II, i, 10+ *s.d. follow.*————] ∼————
                        Sheet Q (inner form)
    Uncorrected: Clark cop. 1, Folger (2), Huntington
    Corrected: Clark cop. 2
Sig. Q3
    Pt. II, IV, ii, 106 You've have] You've
                        Sheet R (inner form)
    Uncorrected: Clark cop. 1, Folger cop. 1
    Corrected: Clark cop. 2, Folger cop. 2, Huntington
Sig. R3*v*
    catchword My] *catchword* Your
                        Sheet S (inner form)
    Uncorrected: Folger cop. 1
    Corrected: Clark (2), Folger cop. 2, Huntington
Sig. S2
    Pt. II, IV, iii, 410 yidld] yield
                        Sheet T (inner form)
    Uncorrected: Huntington
    Corrected: Clark (2), Folger (2)
Sig. T4
    Pt. II, V, iii, 116 been] ∼ ,
            123 Take,]∼∧
            137 vain;] ∼ :
                        Sheet V (inner form)
    Uncorrected (?): Clark cop. 1, Folger cop. 2, Huntington
    Damaged (?): Clark cop. 2, Folger cop. 1
    Corrected (?): Folger cop. 1
Sig. V2
    Pt. II, V, iii, 232 And] ∼ , [correction?]
            238 ow'd:] ∼∧ [type battered?]
                        Sheet X (outer form)
    Uncorrected: Huntington
    Corrected: Clark (2), Folger (2)
Sig. X2*v*
    Defence, 207:20 Judicsous] Judicious
Sig. X3
    Defence, 207:23 faulrs] faults
                        Sheet X (inner form)
    Uncorrected: Clark (2), Folger cop. 1, Huntington
    Corrected: Folger cop. 2
Sig. X4
    Defence, 210:10 meaness] meanness

                        Q2
                    Sheet X (inner form)
    Uncorrected (?): Clark, Folger
    Corrected (?): Huntington

Sig. X4
    Defence, 211:6 re- / ,eiving] re- / ceiving
        211:29 Words:] ~ .

Q3
Sheet D (inner form)
Uncorrected (?): Folger
Corrected (?): Clark, Texas
Sig. D1*v*
    Pt. I, III, i, 263 *Heroe-like*] *Hero-like*

Q5
Sheet R (inner form)
Uncorrected: Clark cop. 2
Corrected: Clark copies 1, 3
Sig. R1*v*
    page number 111] 112
Sig. R2
    page number 112] 113
Sig. R3*v*
    page number 115] 116
Sig. R4
    page number 116]117

Conquest of Granada, Part I

Dedication: 3:3 Heroes] F, D; *Heroes* Q1–5. 3:3 *Æneids*] Q1–4, D; *Æneides* Q5, F. 3:8 guides] Q1, Q3–5, F, D; guids Q2. 3:19 taken] Q1–4, F, D; take Q5. 3:25–26 Highness.] Q1, Q3–5, F, D; ~∧ Q2. 4:1 The] Q2–5, F, D; the Q1. 4:8 e're] Q1–5, F; e'er D. 4:8 The] Q2–5, F, D; the Q1. 4:11 vertue.] Q1, Q3–5, F, D; ~ : Q2. 4:11 Your] Q3–5, F, D; your Q1–2. 4:17 arms:] Q1–2; ~ . Q3–5, F, D. 4:18 Conqueror:] Q1–2; ~. Q3–5, F, D. 4:22 *English*] Q2–5, F, D; English Q1. 4:23 victorious:] Q1–5; ~ . F; ~ , D. 5:1 injuries;] Q2–5, F, D; ~ . Q1. 5:2 yet a] Q1–4; a Q5, F, D. 5:3 expectations:] Q2–5, F, D; ~ . Q1. 5:7 acknowledg'd:] Q2–5, F, D; ~ . Q1. 5:8 *London;*] Q2–5, F, D; ~ . Q1. 5:14 original:] Q2–5, F; ~ . Q1; ~ ; D. 5:15 Or] Q2–5, F, D; or Q1. 5:19 if since] Q1–4; since Q5, F, D. 5:22 occasion.] Q1, Q3–5, F, D; ~ ; Q2. 5:22 The] Q3–5, F, D; the Q1–2. 5:25 You] Q2–5, F, D; you Q1. 5:27 Nation;] Q2–5, F, D; ~ . Q1. 5:31 till] Q1–5, F; 'till D. 5:31 vanquish'd.] Q1–4, F, D; ~∧ Q5. 5:33 did] Q1–4; have Q5, F, D. 5:34 till] Q1–5, F; 'till D. 6:2 Country:] Q2–5, F; ~∧ Q1; ~ ; D. 6:3 and] Q2–5, F, D; aud Q1. 6:14 perfect,] Q2–5, F, D; ~ : Q1. 6:14 courage:] Q2–5, F; ~ . Q1; ~ ; D. 6:15 Both] Q2–5, F, D; both Q1. 6:15 Greek] Q5, F, D; Greek Q1–4. 6:16 *Italian*] Q5, F, D; Italian Q1–4. 6:16–18 that . . . poem] *in italics in F, with an initial capital and preceding comma, as a quotation.* 6:18 poem;] Q2–5, F, D; ~ . Q1. 6:21 he is] Q3–5, F, D; he Q1–2. 6:22 frailties.] Q1; ~ , Q2; ~ ; Q3–5, D; ~ :

F.   6:22   Such] F; such Q1–5, D.   6:26   But] Q2–5, F, D; but Q1.
6:26   spirits;] Q2–5, F, D; ~ . Q1.   6:28   regular;] Q2–5, F, D; ~ . Q1.
6:32   an] Q1–4; and Q5, F, D.   7:11   already is] Q1–5, D; is already F.
7:13   Enemies] Q1–5, D; Enemie F.   7:13   friends.] Q1–5, F; ~ : D.
7:24   to all] Q1; all Q2–5, F, D.   7:31   J.] Q1–5, F; John D.
Of Heroique Playes: title   PLAYES.] Q1–5, D; ~ : F.   8:10   And]
Q2–5, F, D; and Q1.   8:17   field] Q1–4; *fields* Q5, F, D.   8:17   You]
Q2–5, F, D; *Yon* Q1.   8:21   erected:] ~ . Q1–5, F, D.   8:23   But]
Q2–5, F, D; but Q1.   8:28   it.] Q1–5, F; ~ : D.   8:28   They] Q2–5,
F, D; *they* Q1.   9:3   than] Q1, Q3–5, F, D; *then* Q2.   9:3   could
have] Q1–4; *have* Q5, F, D.   9:8   onely I have] Q1–4; *I have only* Q5, F,
D.   9:9–10   *English* Theatre] English Theatre Q1–5, F, D.   9:16   in
Recitative Musique] *in* Recitative Musique Q1–5, F, D.   9:17   his] Q1–
4; *this* Q5, F, D.   9:18   *Italian* Opera's] Italian Opera's Q1–5, F, D.
9:20   *French* Poets] F; French Poets Q1–5, D.   9:21   return:] ~ . Q1–5,
F, D (*recurn* Q1).   9:23   just Drama;] *just* Drama; Q1–5, F, D (Drama.
Q3–5, F, D).   9:28   stile:] ~ . Q1–5, F, D.   10:7   his] Q1–4; *the* Q5,
F, D.   10:9   was an] Q1–5, F; *was* D.   10:12   *I*] Q1–5, D; Il F.
10:12   *amori*,] Q1–4; ~ . Q5, F, D.   10:13   *audaci*] Q2–5, F, D; audace
Q1.   10:14   next] Q1–4; *first* Q5, F, D.   10:15   Heroick . . . Heroick]
Q1, Q4–5, F, D; *Horoick . . . Horoick* Q2; *Heroick . . . Horoick* Q3.   10:19
Promontories] Q1–4, D; *Promontaries* Q5, F.   10:19   out-lines] Q1–4,
D; *out-lies* Q5, F.   10:21   common Drama] *common* Drama Q1–5, F, D.
10:22   call'd] Q1–3, F; *call* D.   10:22   Action:] Q1–2; ~ . Q3–5, F, D.
11:1   write. His] F, D; *write. his* Q1; *write, his* Q2–5.   11:7   *Moderns:*]
Q1–2; ~ . Q3–5, F, D.   11:8   the Drama] *the* Drama Q1–5, F, D.   11:9
intended to divide] Q1–4; *to divide* Q5, F; *divides* D.   11:10   several
Canto's] *several* Canto's Q1–5, F, D (Canto's F, D).   11:13   Poem:] ~ .
Q1–5, D; ~ ; F.   11:15   latter] Q1–4, D; *later* Q5, F.   11:18   the
Latine] Q2–5, F, D; *the Latine* Q1.   11:22   *comprehendendæ*] Q2–5, F,
D; comprehendæ Q1.   11:23   *longè*] Q1–4, D; longæ Q5, F.   11:27
and in] Q1–3; *and* Q4–5, F, D.   12:3–4   what he] Q1–5, D; *what* F.
12:6   historian.] Q1–5, F; ~ : D.   12:6   The] Q2–5, F, D; *the* Q1.
12:11   Poems] Q1–4, F; *Poets* Q5, D.   12:14   And] Q2–5, F, D; and Q1.
12:19   And] Q2–5, F, D; and Q1.   12:23   may] Q1–4; *might* Q5, F, D.
12:24   representation] Q1–5, F; *Representations* D.   12:28   Spirits,]
Q1–5, D (~∧ Q2–5, D); *Spirit:* F.   13:4   notions] Q1–5, D; *Motions* F.
13:12   old Epique] Q3–5, F, D; *old* Epique Q1–2.   13:13   fayery-land]
Q2–5, F, D; *fayery land* Q1.   13:21   writing in] Q1–5, D; *writing* F.
13:23   the Drama] *the* Drama Q1–5, F, D.   13:30   the *English*] F, D;
the English Q1–5.   13:31   shows] Q1–5, D; *shows me* F.   13:31   *Catiline*] Q1–2, D; Cataline Q3–5, F.   13:34   the representations] Q1–3;
there presentations Q4; *their presentations* Q5, F, D.   14:1   an] Q1–5,
F; *on* D.   14:2   Play;] Q2–5, F, D; ~ . Q1.   14:3–4   the Theater]
the Theater Q1–5, F, D.   14:7   And] Q2–5, F, D; and Q1.   14:13
But] Q3–5, F, D; *but* Q1–2.   14:22   The first] Q2–5, F, D; *the first* Q1.
14:24   *Artaban* of] Q1, F, D; Artaban of Q2–5.   14:24–25   *Calprenede*]
Q1; Calpranede Q2–5, F, D.   14:25   The] Q3–5, F, D; *the* Q1–2.
14:32   the most] Q1, Q3–5, F, D; *the* Q2.   14:32   opprobrious] Q2, Q4–
5, F, D; approbrious Q1, Q3.   14:32   imagine.] Q1; ~ : Q2–5, F; ~ ; D.

15:1 They] *they* Q1–5, F, D. 15:3 Οἰνοβαρὲς] Οἰνοβαρὲ Q1–2; Οἰνοβαρὸς
Q3–5, F, D. 15:3 ἐλάφοιο, *Il. a. v. 225.*] Q3–5, F, D; ἐλάφοιο: Q1–2.
15:4 βασιλεύς,] D (~ ;); βασιλεὺς, Q1–2; βασιλεῦς, Q3–5, F. 15:4 *&c. Il. a.
v. 321.*] Q3–4; &c. Q1–2; Il. a. v. 321. Q5, F, D. 15:5 draw] Q2–5, F, D;
~ , Q1. 15:6 him.] Q1–5, F; ~ ; D. 15:7 Ἕλκετο] D; Ἕλκετο Q1–5,
F. 15:7 ξίφος. *Il. a. v. 194.*] Q3–5, F, D; ξίφος. Q1–2. 15:8 And, if]
F; *and, if* Q1–5, D. 15:10 it:] Q1–2; ~ . Q3–5, F, D. 15:11 *Nestor.*]
Q1–5, F; ~ ; D. 15:12 Ἀλλ'] D; Ἄλλ' Q1–5; Ἄλλ' F. 15:12 ὅδ'] Q3–
5, F, D; ὁδ' Q1; ὁδ' Q2. 15:12 πάντων] Q3–5, F, D; ~ . Q1–2. 15:12
ἔμμεναι] Q3–5, F, D; ἔμμέναι Q1; ἔμμέναι Q2. 15:12 ἄλλων,] Q1–3, D; ~ .
Q4–5, F. 15:13 πάντεσσι] Q3–5, D; πάντεσσι Q1–2; παντέσσι F. 15:13
ἀνάσσειν. *Il. a. v. 287, 288.*] Q3–5, F, D (287. Q3–4; *between ll. 12 and 13 in
Q3, on l. 12 in Q4–5, F, below l. 13 in D*); ἀνάσσειν. Q1–2. 15:14 And]
F; *and* Q1–5, D. 15:14–15 his *Art of Poetry*] his *Art of Poetry* Q1–5, F,
D. 16:2 him] Q2–5, F, D; *bim* Q1. 16:5 *e l'*] e' l' Q1; e'l' Q2–5, F;
e'l D. 16:5 *arme:*] Q1–3; ~ ᴀ Q4–5, F; ~ . D. 16:7 lor] Q1–4; los
Q5, F, D. 16:7 *diporto alle*] diporti a le Q1–5, F, D. 16:10 their
Hero's] D; *their* Hero's Q1–5, F. 16:11 frailties.] Q1; ~ : Q2–5, F; ~ ;
D. 16:11 They] F; *they* Q1–5, D. 16:12 contented] Q1; content
Q2–5, F, D. 16:13 not what] Q1–4, F, D; *not when* Q5. 16:14 ver-
tue.] Q1; ~ ; Q2–5, F, D. 16:14 For] *for* Q1–5, F, D. 16:16 than]
Q1, Q3–5, F, D; *then* Q2. 16:18 scruples.] Q1; ~ ; Q2, F, D; ~ : Q3–5.
16:19 Yet] yet Q1–5, F, D. 16:19 vertue] Q1–3; *vertues* Q4–5, F, D.
16:22 with] Q1–5, D; *with the* F. 16:24–25 He threatens] Q3–5, F,
D; *he threatens* Q1–2. 16:27 *Bulloign.* Q1, F, D; ~ ; Q2–5. 16:27
He] F, D; *he* Q1–5. 16:30 the Rhodomontades] *the* Rhodomontades
Q1–5, F, D. 17:1 execution.] Q1; ~ : Q2–5, F; ~ ; D. 17:1 For]
F; *for* Q1–5, D. 17:9 impossibilities.] Q1, F; ~ ; Q2–5, D. 17:9
They] F; *they* Q1–5, D. 17:11 Sovereign] Q4–5, F, D; *Soverign* Q1;
Soveraign Q2–3. 17:11 not.] Q1, F; ~ : Q2–5, D. 17:11 This] F,
D; *this* Q1–5. 17:14 us.] Q1–2; ~ ; Q3–5, F, D. 17:14 And] *and*
Q1–5, F, D. 17:18 before.] Q1; ~ : Q2–5; ~ ; F, D. 17:18 And]
and Q1–5, F, D. 17:19 him.] Q1; ~ ; Q2–5; ~ : F, D. 17:20 But]
F, D; *but* Q1–5. 17:27 him.] Q1; ~ : Q2–5, F; ~ ; D. 17:27 For]
F; *for* Q1–5, D. 18:3 their own] Q1–4; *their* Q5, F, D. 18:3 opin-
ions] Q1–5, D; *Opinion* F. 18:4 not:] Q1–4; ~ . Q5, F, D.

Prologue: 11 that.] Q3–5, F, D; ~ : Q1–2. 13 grew] Q1–4, F, D;
grow Q5. 15 language,] Q1, Q4–5, F, D; ~ᴀ Q2–3. 17 Mungrill-
wits] Q1; Mungril Wits Q2–5, F, D. 20 Stage.] Q1; ~ , Q2; ~ ; Q3–5,
F, D. 25 sence, dull sence] Q3–5, F, D; sence. -dull sence, Q1; sence,
dull sence, Q2. 28 Indians] Q5, F, D; *Indians* Q1–4. 30 grow;]
Q1–3; ~ᴀ Q4–5, F, D. 31 gath'ring] Q1–4; gathering Q5, F, D. 37,
38 French] Q5, F, D; *French* Q1–4. 39 English] Q5, F, D; *English*
Q1–4. 40 'ere] Q1; e're Q2–5, F; e'er D. 43 laugh.] Q1; ~ : Q2–3,
F, D; ~ ; Q4–5.

Dramatis Personae: Persons Represented] Q1–5, F; Dramatis Personae D.
MEN.] Q1, D; *omitted* Q2–5, F. By] Q1–4; *omitted* Q5, F, D. *Abencerrages*] D; Abencerrages Q1–5, F. *Zegrys*] D; Zegrys Q1–5, F (*and
similarly below with Zegry*). *Abencerrago*] D; Abencerago Q1–2; Abencerrago Q3–5, F (*and similarly below*). *Ozmyn,*] Q2–5, F, D; ~ᴀ Q1.

Abenamar.] Q2–5, F, D; ~∧ Q1.   *Spain*] Q2–5, F, D; Spain Q1.   *Alonzo d'Aguilar,*] Q3–5 (~ ~ ;), F, D; *Alonzo,* d'Aguilar; Q1–2.   *Spanish*] D; Spanish Q1–5, F.   WOMEN.] Q1, D; *omitted* Q2–5, F.   By] Q1; *omitted* Q2–5, F, D.   *Granada . . . Ellen*] Q2–5, F, D; Granada . . . ~ . Q1.   *Esperanza,*] Q2–5, F, D; ~∧ Q1.   *Isabel*] Isabella Q1–5, F, D.   *James*] Q2–5, F, D; *Jeames* Q1.

I, i

S.d. Boabdelin, Abenamar, Abdelmelech,] Q5, F; *Boabdelin, Abenamar, Abdelmelech.* Q1–4 (*Abdelmelech,* Q3–4); ACT I. SCENE I. *Enter* Boabdelin, Abenamar, Abdelmelech, *and* D.   4   and] Q2–5, F, D; & Q1.   5 *s.d.* Aben.] Q2–3, Q5, F, D; *Aben.* Q1, Q4.   13   new bends] Q1, Q4–5, F; new-bends Q2–3, D.   19   outdone] Q1, Q4; out done Q2–3, Q5, F; out-done D.   21   set] Q1–2, Q4–5, F, D; sets Q3.   23   'ere] Q1, Q4–5, F; e're Q2–3; e'er D.   24   Snuffing] Q1–4; snuffling Q5, F, D.   25   Champions] Q1, Q4; Champion Q2–3, Q5, F, D.   30   wore] Q1, Q3–5, F, D; ~ . Q2.   34   reverence] Q1–5, F; Rev'rence D.   37   till] Q1–5, F; 'till D.   40   Bulls] Q1, Q3–5, F, D; Pulls Q2.   40   arm,] Q1, Q4–5, F, D; ~ . Q2–3.   45   sped.] Q1, Q3–5, F, D; ~ , Q2.   48   man.] Q3, D; ~ : Q1–2, Q4–5, F.   49   began.] Q1, Q3–5, F, D; ~ : Q2.   52   awhile] Q1–5; a while F, D.   54   aloud] Q1–4, F, D; a loud Q5.   55   crowd] crow'd Q1; croud Q2–5, F, D.   56   Monarch-like] Q2–5, F, D; Monach-like Q1.   57   goar'd,] Q1, Q3–5, F, D; ~ . Q2.   58   *Moors*] Q2–3, D; Moors Q1, Q4–5, F.   61   every] Q1–5, F; ev'ry D.   62   *Mirador*] Mirador Q1–5, F, D.   69, 71   every] Q1–5, F; ev'ry D.   74   *s.d.* Abdel.] Q2–3, Q5, F, D; *Abdel.* Q1, Q4.   76   this] Q1–5, F; his D.   81   every] Q1–5, F; ev'ry D.   81   was] Q1–2, Q4–5, F, D; war Q3.   83   Beware, brave] D; beware, brave Q1–5, F.   96   bellowings] Q1–5, D; bellows F.   100   *Ataballes*] Ataballes Q1–5, F, D.   101   now!] Q1–5, F; ~ ? D.   101   alarms?] Q1–5, D; ~ : F.   101+   *s.d. To*] [~ Q1–5, F, D (*right justified*).   104   th' *Abencerrages*] Q2–3, D; the *Abencerrages* Q1, Q4–5, F.   104   fight,] Q1–2, Q4–5; ~ ; Q3, D; ~ . F.   107   th' *Abencerrages*] the *Bencerrages* Q1–5, D; the *Abencerrages* F.   112   King.] Q3, D; ~ : Q1–2, Q4–5, F.   112+   *s.d. [Exit*] Q4–5, F, D; ∧~ Q1–3.   112+   *s.d.* Boabdelin] Q2–3, Q5, F, D; *Boabdelin* Q1, Q4.   112+   *s.d.* Abencerrages,] Q1–5, D; ~ . F.   112+   *s.d.* Abenamar] Q2–3, D; Abenamat Q1, Q4–5, F.   114   every] Q1–5, F; ev'ry D.   117   retreat;] F, D; ~∧ Q1; ~ , Q2–5.   118   defeat:] Q1–5; ~ . F, D.   120   *Moorish*] D; Moorish Q1–5, F.   127+   *s.d. engage.*] Q1, Q4–5, F, D (~∧ Q5); *engage them.* Q2–3.   129   *s.d.* Abencerrages] Q5, F, D; *Abencerrages* Q1–4.   131   me] Q1–2, Q4–5, F, D; we Q3.   134   minds,] Q1–2, Q4; ~ ? Q3, Q5, F, D.   141   poor,] Q1, Q4–5, F, D; ~∧ Q2–3.   143   Enemy.] Q1–2, Q4–5, D; ~ ! Q3, F.   144   every] Q1–5, F; ev'ry D.   150   *Selin.*] Zulem. Q1–5, F, D.   153   th'] Q1–4, D; the Q5, F.   160   Coursers] Q1–5, D; Courser's F.   161   apart] Q1–4, F; a part Q5; a-part D.   162   steel-pointed] Q2–3, D; steel pointed Q1, Q4–5, F.   164   wanted] Q1–5, F; wanting D.   165   undefy'd.] Q2–3, F, D; ~ : Q1, Q4–5.   166   *Ozmyn.* Witness] Q2–3; [*Ozmyn showing his arm. /* Witness Q1, Q4–5; [*Ozmyn showing his Arm. / Osmyn.* Witness F; *Ozm.* [*showing his Arm.*] Witness D.   168   thee] Q1–4, F, D; the Q5.   170   villain blood] Q1–5, F; Villain-Blood D. 173 *Morocco*] Q2–5, F, D; *Marocco* Q1. 182 *Almanz.* Upon] F, D; Upon Q1–5. 182+ *s.d.* [*Advancing . . . sword.*] Almanzor, *advancing . . . sword.* Q1–5, F, D (*preceding l. 182 in Q1–5, F; run in with s.d. in l. 181 in D;* [Almanzor, . . . F). 184 nigher,] ∼. Q1–5, F; ∼ ; D. 186+ *s.d.* [Almanzor] F, D; ∧∼ Q1–5. 187 *Almanz.*] Q1–4, F, D; ∼ : Q5. 190 die] Q1, Q4–5, F, D; dye Q2–3. 190 live,] Q1–4; ∼∧ Q5; ∼ ; F, D. 197 neglect.] Q1–4, F, D; ∼∧ Q5. 201 giv'n] Q1–5, D; given F. 202 stroke.] Q2–5, F, D; ∼∧ Q1. 205 Soveraign] Q1–5, F; Sov'raign D. 208 'Ere] Q1, Q4–5, F; E're Q2–3; E'er D. 220 that] Q1–5, D; the F. 222 not] Q1–4, F, D; no not Q5. 222 Councel] Q1; Counsel Q3, F, D; Council Q2, Q4–5. 227 away:] Q1–3; ∼. Q4–5, F, D. 233+ *s.d. right justified* Q1–5, F, D (*with right bracket prefixed in Q2–4, F, D*). 233+ *s.d.* Abdalla] Q2–5, F, D; *Abdalla* Q1. 234 *Abdalla*] Q2–5, F, D; *Abdella* Q1. 234 Heav'n] Q1–2, Q4–5, F, D; Heav'ns Q3. 234 sake hold.] Q1–3; ∼ : Q4–5, F, D. 245 th'] Q1–4, D; the Q5, F. 246 *Xeriff*] Q1, Q4–5, F, D; *Zeriff* Q2–3. 249 Till] Q1–5, F; 'Till D. 250 own:] Q1–5; ∼. F, D. 252 fled;] Q1–2, Q4–5; ∼. Q3, D; ∼ : F. 257 unknown] Q2–5, F, D; unknwn Q1. 259 *Boabdelin.* Impute . . . ignorance; [*Coming to* Almanzor.] *Boabdelin coming to Almanzor. /* Impute . . . ignorance; Q1–5, F, D ([Boabdelin Q4–5, F, D; Almanzor. / *Boab.* Impute D). 264 *Almanzor.*] Q1–4, F, D; ∼∧ Q5. 264 to] Q4–5, F, D; too Q1–3. 268–269 *Boab.* Lay . . . cease / . . . [*To the Factions.*] *Boab.* to the Factions / Lay . . . cease Q1–5, F; *Boab* [*To the Factions*]. Lay . . . cease D. 270 Till] Q1–5, F; 'Till D. 270 slain.] Q3, F, D; ∼ : Q1–2, Q4–5. 273 armes.] F, D; ∼ : Q1–5. 275 regard?] Q3, F, D; ∼ : Q1–2, Q4–5. 276 heard.] F; ∼ : Q1–5, D. 277 now.] Q1–5, D; ∼ : F. 281 *Boabdelin!*] ∼ : Q1, Q4–5; ∼. Q2–3, F, D. 282 but hush'd] Q2–5, F, D; bu husht'd Q1. 283 now,] Q1–2, Q4; ∼ : Q3; ∼. Q5, F, D. 284 Crowd] Q1–4, F, D; Crow'd Q5. 284+ *s.d.* [*The*] Q2–5, F, D; ∧∼ Q1. 286 unmake, or make] Q1–5, F; make or unmake D. 287 Soul] Q1–3; ∼. Q4–5, F; ∼ ! D. 288 *s.d. Embracing*] Q2–5, F, D; *embracing* Q1. 288 controll!] Q1–5, F; ∼. D. 288+ *s.d.* [*A*] Q2–5, F, D; ∧∼ Q1. 288+ *s.d. Enter a Messenger.*] Q2–5, F, D; Enter a Messenger. Q1. 290 appear.] Q1–5, D; ∼ : F. 291 here.] Q1–4, F, D; ∼ : Q5. 291+ *s.d. Enter the Duke of* Arcos.] Q2–5, F, D; Enter the Duke of *Arcos.* Q1. 298 *Rodriques*] Q1–2, Q4–5, F, D; *Rodiques* Q3. 299 *Rodrique*] Q1–2, Q4–5, F, D; *Rodique* Q3. 310 *Moores*] Q2–3, F, D; Moores Q1, Q4–5. 317 gain your] Q1–3, D; gain you Q4–5, F. 318 resign'd;] ∼. Q1–5, F, D. 325 voyd.] F, D; ∼ : Q1–5. 326 Why] Q2–5, F, D; Whey Q1. 331 that,] Q1–4; ∼∧ Q5, F, D. 336 selves] Q1–4; self Q5, F, D. 338 Unthrifts] Q1–5, F; spendthrift's D. 341 your] Q2–5, F, D; you Q1. 342 Till] Q1–5, F; 'Till D. 350 What 'ere] Q1, Q4; What e're Q2–3; What e'er Q5, D; Whate'er F. 356 heavens] Q1–5, F (Heaven's Q2–3, F); Heav'n's D. 356 draws.] F, D; ∼ : Q1–5. 357 *Moors*] Q2–3, F, D; Moors Q1, Q4–5. 357+ *s.d.* [*Exit*] Q4–5, F, D; ∧∼ Q1–3. 357+ *s.d. Enter* Esperanza.] Q2–5, F, D; Enter Esperanza. Q1. 358 *Almahide*] Q3, F, D; ∼. Q1–2, Q4–5. 360 omen] D; *omen* Q1–5, F. 361 *Zambra*] Q1–4, D; *Zambray* Q5, F. 366 foe.] F, D; ∼ : Q1–5. 367 unto] Q3; to Q1–2; on to Q4–5, F, D. 370 should] Q2–5, F, D;

shoul Q1.   371   of] Q1–4; to Q5, F, D.   371   *s.d.* [*Exeunt*] Q4–5, F,
D; ∧~ Q1–3.

II, i

ACT] Q2–3, Q5, F, D; ~. Q1, Q4.   II.] Q1–5, F; II. SCENE I. D.   *s.d.*
Abdalla . . . *Sally.*] Q4–5, F, D (*Enter* Abdalla D); *romans and italics reversed
in Q1–3.*   8   *Moorish*] Q2–3, F, D; Moorish Q1, Q4; moorish Q5.   12,
13   *Lyndaraxa's*] Q2–3; Lindaraxa's Q1, Q4–5, F, D (*and similarly throughout the act, unless noted*).   19   by] Q1–4, F, D; to Q5.   21   All that
. . . do;] Q1–4, F, D (do: D); And that . . . do? Q5.   23   'ere] Q1, Q4; e're
Q2–3, D; e'er Q5; e'r F.   29   great] Q1, Q4–5, F, D; Gret Q2–3.   29+
s.d. right justified in Q1–5, F, D ([*To* Q4–5, F, D).   32   Ferdinand.] F, D;
~ : Q1–5 (Ferdinand Q1).   33–34   *Almanzor. Thus . . . find / . . . [To
the Duke of* Arcos.] *Almanzor to the Duke of Arcos. / Thus . . . find* Q1;
Almanzor *to the Duke of* Arcos. / Thus . . . find Q2–5, F ([Almanzor Q4–5,
F; *Almanz.* Thus F); *Almanz.* [*To the Duke of* Arcos.] Thus . . . find D.
38   French] Q2–5, F, D; French Q1.   43   *Duke of Arc.*] Duke of *Arc.*
Q1–5; *Duke of* Arc. F; D. *Arcos.* D.   44   You] Q2–5, F, D; Yout Q1.
47   'ere] Q1, Q4–5; e'r Q2–3; e're F; e'er D.   48   'ere] Q1, Q4–5; e're
Q2–3, F; e'er D.   54   Till] Q1–5, F; 'Till D.   56   morrow's] Q1, Q4–
5, F, D; morrows Q2–3.   56   dawn] Q2–5, F, D; daun Q1.   56   your]
Q1–5, F; the D.   62   Till conquering] Q1–5, F; 'Till conqu'ring D.
63   weak!] Q1–5, D; ~ ; F.   64   break.] Q1, Q4–5, F, D; ~ : Q2–3.
65   thee] Q1–4, F, D; the Q5.   72+   *s.d.* [*Exeunt*] Q4–5, F, D; ∧~ Q1–3.
78   brought:] ~ . Q1–5, F, D.   79   Till] Q1–5, F; 'Till D.   81+   *s.d.*
To] [~ Q1–5, F, D (*right justified*).   81+   *s.d.* Lyndaraxa.] Q2–3 (~ ,
Q2); *Lindaraxa.* Q1; Lindaraxa. Q4–5, F, D.   82   here.] D; ~ : Q1–5, F.
82+   *s.d.* [Zulema] Q4–5, F, D; ∧~ Q1–3.   82+   *s.d.* Lyndaraxa (*bis*)]
Q2–3; Lindaraxa Q1, Q4–5, F, D.   83 *s.d.,* 86 *s.d. Staying*] Q2–3, F, D;
staying Q1, Q4–5.   99   confidence:] Q1–5, F; ~ . D.   102   ere] Q1,
Q4–5; e're Q2–3, F; e'er D.   109   Till . . . be] Q1–5, F; 'Till . . . is D.
113   delay:] Q1–5, D; ~ . F.   127   till] Q1–5, F; 'till D.   130, 133, 137
Lyndar.] Q3; *Lindar.* Q1–2, Q4–5, F, D.   140   could] Q2–5, F, D; conld
Q1.   140   by.] ~ ; Q1–5, F; ~ , D (*Q1, Q4–5, F, D have an additional
line:* Because she is to be her Majesty.).   141   Queen?] D; ~ ! Q1–5, F.
145   not] Q1–5, F; but D.   153   *Lynd.*] Q3; *Lind.* Q1–2, Q4–5, F, D.
155   make] Q1–3, D; makes Q4–5, F.   157   seen.] Q1–5, D; ~ ; F.   160
Lynd.] Q3; *Lind.* Q1–2, Q4–5, F, D.   160+   *s.d.* [*He*] Q4–5, F, D; ∧~
Q1–3.   165+   *s.d.* [*Exit*] Q4–5, F, D; ∧~ Q1–3.   167   severe.] Q1–5,
F; ~ , D.   170   pleasure] Q1–3, Q5, F, D; pleasures Q4.   170   every]
Q1–5, F; ev'ry D.   172   pleasure,] F, D; ~∧ Q1–5.   188   flight;] Q2–5,
F; ~ . Q1; ~ , D.   198   Love but int'rest,] Q1–5; ~ , ~ ~∧ F; ~ ~ ~∧
D.   199–200   And wou'd, / Ev'n] *one line in Q1–5, F, D* (ev'n Q2–5, F,
D).   200   lie] Q1–5, F; lye D.   200   throne.] Q1, Q3–5, F, D; ~ : Q2.
207   vertue's] Q1, Q4–5, F, D; Vertues Q2–3.   212   Anchorit's] Q1–5, F;
Anch'rites D.   214   giv'n] Q1–5, F, D; given F.   214   will.] Q3, F, D; ~ :
Q1–2, Q4–5.   216   last;] Q4–5, F, D; ~ . Q1–2; ~ : Q3.   223   what
e're] Q2–3; what 're Q1, Q4; what e'r Q5; whate'er F; what e'er D.   247
an] Q1–5, D; of an F.   249   'ere] Q1; e're Q2–3, F, D; ere Q4–5.   259
they] Q1, Q3–5, F, D; thy Q2.   261   right.] Q1 (*some copies*), Q4–5, F, D;

~ .—— Q1 (*some copies*), Q2–3.　263　Court;] Q2–3; ~ . Q1, Q4–5, F;
~ , D.　269　of the] Q1–4; of his Q5, F, D.　272　advise.] Q1, Q4–5,
F, D; ~ : Q2–3.　274+　*s.d.* [*Exeunt*] Q4–5, F, D; ʌ~ Q1–3.

III, i

ACT] Q2, Q5, F, D; ~ . Q1, Q3–4.　III.] Q1–5, F; III. SCENE I. D.
s.d. Almanzor, Abdalla.] Q4–5; *Almanzor, Abdalla.* Q1–3, F; *Enter* Almanzor
and Abdalla. D.　2　fool] Q1a; Fool Q1b.　8　then] Q1a; than Q1b.
11　unfix't] Q1a; unfixt Q1b.　14　I'll] Q1–2, Q4–5, D; I'le Q3; Ill F.
14　heart] Q1a; Heart Q1b.　15　Vengeance] Q1a; Veng'ance Q1b.
18　sway.)] Q1, Q4–5, F, D; ~ʌ) Q2–3.　20　reign] Q1a; Reign Q1b.
22　friendship . . . right] Q1a; Friendship . . . Right Q1b.　24　friend-
ship] Q1a; Friendship Q1b.　25　Cause] Q1a; cause Q1b.　29　Op-
position] Q1a; opposition Q1b.　32　royal name] Q1a; Royal name Q1b.
34　too] Q1–2, Q4–5, F, D; to Q3.　36　loose] Q1, Q4–5, F, D; close Q2–
3.　37　'em] Q1–4; them Q5, F, D.　38　loose] Q1a; lose Q1b.　39
night:] Q1–4; ~ . Q5, F, D.　40　surprise] Q1a; surprize Q1b.　41　*Almanzor.* . . . will;] Q1a; *Almanz.* . . . Will, Q1b.　43　*Spaniards*] Q1a,
Q3–5, F, D; Spaniards Q1b, Q2.　43　assault] Q1a; Aslault Q1b.　44+
s.d.–107+ *s.d.* [Exit . . . / [*Exit* Abdalla.] Q1b, Q2–5, F, D (ʌExit (*bis*) Q1b,
Q2–3); *As they go out,* Abdelmelech *enters, leading* Lindaraxa: *she smiles
on* Abdalla. Q1a.　50　our] Q1b, Q4–5, F, D; your Q2–3.　51　foregoe.]
Q1b, Q3–5, F, D; ~ , Q2.　56　Councels] Q1b–2; Counsels Q3, F, D; Coun-
cils Q4–5.　59　Sence?] ~ ! Q1b–5, F, D.　63　sway.] Q1b, Q3–5, F, D;
~ , Q2.　65　consent.] Q3, F; ~ , Q1b–2, Q4–5; ~ : D.　71　every]
Q1b–5, F; ev'ry D.　73　lie] Q1b, Q4–5, F; lye Q2–3, D.　73　hand.] Q1b,
Q3–5, F, D; ~ , Q2.　76　I'm] Q2–3, Q5, F, D; ~ , Q1b, Q4.　77　bent.]
Q1b–3, D; ~ , Q4–5, F.　83, 85　till] Q1b–5, F; 'till D.　89　Howe're]
Q1b–2; How e're Q3; Howe'er Q4; Howe'r Q5, F; How e'er D.　93　am I]
Q1b–5, D; I am F.　94　*Circe's*] Q4–5, F, D; *Cyrce's* Q1b–3.　96+　*s.d.*
Stage] Q1b–5, D; *Stages* F.　98　'Ere] Q1b–3; Ere Q4–5; E'er F, D.　100
Abdalla.] Q1b; *Abdal.* Q2–5, D; *Abdal,* F.　101　till] Q1b–5, F; 'till D.
103　sake.] Q2–5, F, D; ~ , Q1b.　108　Smile] Q1a; smile Q1b.　109
You] Q1, Q3–5, F, D; Your Q2.　109　day.] Q1a, Q3; ~ , Q1b, Q2, Q4–5;
~ : F; ~ ; D.　113　heav'ns] Q1–3; heaven's Q4–5, F; Heav'n's D.　114
Lyndarax.] Lindarax. Q1a; *Lynd.* Q1b.　115　to] Q1a; of Q1b.　116
It] Q1, Q4–5, F, D; Its Q2–3.　117　But,] Q1a; ~ʌ Q1b.　117　grace.]
Q3, Q5, F, D; ~ : Q1–2, Q4.　118　*Lyndar.*] Q1a; *Lynd.* Q1b.　121
resign:] Q1–2, Q4–5, F, D; ~ . Q3.　124　*Lyndarax.*] Q2–5, F, D; *Lin-
darax.* Q1.　124　Civility,] Q1–3, Q5; ~ . Q4; ~ : F, D.　132　makes]
Q1–5, D; make F.　133　Sence:] Q1–2, Q4–5, F, D; ~ . Q3.　155
Love?] Q3, Q5, F, D; ~ . Q1–2, Q4.　156　Ah! . . . deserv'd?] Q5, F, D;
~ʌ . . . ~ , Q1–4.　158　Maid.] Q1–3; ~ ! Q4–5, F, D.　162　Brest,]
Q1, Q4–5, F, D; ~ ! Q2–3.　166　elsewhere.] Q1, Q3–5, F, D; ~ ; Q2.
172　had] Q1–2, Q4–5, F, D; hath Q3.　181　too short] Q1, Q4–5, F, D;
to short Q2–3.　185　both] Q1–5, D; we F.　186　swear?] Q1–2, Q5,
F; ~ : Q3–4; ~ ! D.　186+　*s.d. above l. 186 in Q1–5, F, D.*　187
Lynd.] Q2–5, F, D (~ʌ Q3); *Lind.* Q1.　190　cannot] Q2–5, F, D; canot
Q1.　192　till] Q1–5, F; 'till D.　193　love.] Q1, Q3–5, F, D; ~ , Q2.
195　War.] Q1–2, Q4–5, F, D; ~ ; Q3.　197+　*SONG.*] Q2–3, M1;

SONG. *Misplac'd. Sung at the dance, or* Zambra *in the third* Act. Q1 *(after the epilogue);* The Zambra Dance. SONG. Q4–5, F, D; *A Song at the Kings House.* Os1a, Os2a, Os3–4; *A Vision.* Os1b, Os2b; *Song 6.* Os5; *no title* Fs1–3, M2; *A SONG.* Ds5. 198–232 *romans and italics reversed from* Q1. *No stanza numbers in* Os1b, Os2b, M2; *no stanza division in* Os5. 199 *Love for none but]* Q1–5, F, D, Os1b, Os2b, Fs1–3, Ds5, M1–2 (*Jove for* Os1b, Os2b); none but Love for Os1a, Os2a, Os3–5. 199 *happy Lovers]* Q1–5, F, D, Os1–5, Fs1–3, M1–2; Lovers Ds5. 200 *straight]* Q1–5, F, D, Os1–2, Os4–5, Fs1–3, Ds5, M1–2; strait Os3. 201 *thought;]* Q1–5, Ds5, M1–2; ~ : F, D, Fs1–3; ~ . Os1a, Os2a, Os3–5; ~ , Os1b, Os2b. 202 *came]* Q1–5, F, D, Os1–5, Ds5, M1–2; comes Fs1–3. 203 *While]* Q1–5, F, D, M1–2; Whilst Os1–5, Fs1–3, Ds5. 203 *flow'rs]* Q1, Q3–5, F, D, Fs1–3, Ds5, M1–2; flowers Q2, Os1–5. 204 *Flow'rs, which so . . . became]* Q1–5, F, D, Os1–5, M1–2 (*Flowers, that* Os1–5); so . . . became, became Fs1–3, Ds5. 205 *Visions]* Q1–5, F, D, Os1b, Os2b, Fs1–3, Ds5, M1–2; Virgins Os1a, Os2a, Os3–5. 207 *temples]* Q1–5, F, D, Os5, Fs1–3, Ds5, M1–2; Temple Os1a, Os2a, Os3–4; shoulders Os1b, Os2b. 207 *shaded]* Q1–5, F, D, Os1b, Os2b, Fs1–3, Ds5, M1–2; shady Os1a, Os2a, Os3–5. 208 *not too]* Q1–5, F, D, Os1a, Os2a, Os3–5, Fs1–3, Ds5, M1–2; nor too Os1b, Os2b. 208 *nor fair:]* Q1–5, F, D, Os1–5, M1–2 (~ ~ . F; ~ ~ ; D); or fair: Fs1–3, Ds5. 210 *every]* Q1–5, F, Os1a, Os2a, Os3–4, M1–2; ev'ry D, Os1b, Os2b, Os5, Fs1–3, Ds5. 210 *grace]* Q1–5, F, D, Os1a, Os2a, Os3–5, Fs1–3, Ds5, M1–2; part Os1b, Os2b. 211 *which]* Q1–5, F, D, M1–2; *that* Os1–5, Fs1–3, Ds5. 211 *languish'd]* Q1–5, F, D, Os1b, Os2b, Fs1–3, Ds5, M1–2; languish Os1a, Os2a, Os3–5. 211 *desire.]* Q1–5, F, D, Os1–2, Os4–5, Fs1–3, Ds5, M1–2; ~ , Os3. 212 *fair]* Q1–5, F, D, Os1–4, Fs1–3, Ds5, M1–2; face Os5. 213 *can you]* Q1–5, F, D, Os1a, Os2a, Os4–5, Fs1–3, Ds5, M1–2; will you Os1b, Os2b; can Os3. 213 *bliss and yours]* Q1–5, F, D, Os1b, Os2–3, Os5, Fs1–3, Ds5, M1–2 (and you Os3); bliss Os1a, Os4. 213 *deny?]* Q1–5, F, D, Os1–2, Os4–5, M1–2; ~∧ Os3; ~ : Fs1–3, Ds5. 214 *love]* Q1–5, F, D, Os1a, Os2a, Os3–5, Fs1–3, Ds5, M1–2 (~ : Os3); Jove Os1b, Os2b. 214 *lonely]* Q1–5, D, M1–2; lovely F, Os1a, Os2a, Os3–5, Fs1–3, Ds5; lonesome Os1b, Os2b. 215 *suffring]* Q1–3, D, Os1b, Os2b, Fs1–3, Ds5, M1; suffering Q4–5, F, Os1a, Os2a, Os3–5, M2. 215 *made:]* Q1–2, Q4–5, Os1b, Os2b, M2; ~ . Q3, F, D, Os2a, Os3–5, Fs1–3, M1; ~∧ Os1a; ~ , Ds5. 216 *agree:]* Q1–5, F, D, Os1b, Os2–3, Os5, Fs1–3, Ds5, M1–2; ~ . Os1a; ~ , Os4. 218 *see.]* Q1–5, F, D, Os1a, Os2–5, Fs1–3, Ds5, M1–2; ~ , Os1b. 219 *No,]* Q1–5, F, D, Os1–4, Fs1–3, Ds5, M1–2; No, rather Os5. 220 *Rather than]* Q1–5, F, D, Os1–2, Os4, Fs1–3, Ds5, M1–2 (then Os4, M1–2); For rather then Os3; Than Os5. 220 *Maid:]* Q1–5, F, D, Os1b, Os2b, Os3, Fs2–3, M1; ~ . Os1a, Os2a, Os4, M2; ~ ; Os5, Fs1, Ds5. 221 *me thought she spoke]* Q1–5, F, D, Os1a, Os2a, Os3–5, M1–2; she spoke methought Os1b, Os2b, Fs1–3, Ds5. 222 *smile.]* Q1–5, F, D, Os1–4, Fs1–3, Ds5, M1–2; ~ ; Os5. 223 *I. She]* Q3, M1; ~ , she Q1–2, Q4–5, F, Os1–5, Fs1–3, Ds5, M2 (she's Q4–5); ~ : She D. 224 *is it thus,]* Q1–5, F, D, Os1b, Os2b, Os5, Fs3, Ds5, M1–2; it it thus? Fs1–2; yet, Os1a, Os2a, Os3–4. 224 *thus, thus she]* Q1–5, F, D, Os1, Os2b, Os3–4, Fs1–3, Ds5, M1–2; thus, she, Os2a, Os5. 224 *cry'd]* Q1–2, Q4–5; ~ , Q3, F, D, Os1–2, Os4–5, Ds5, M1–2; ~ . Os3. 225 *use]* Q1–5, F, D, Os1–5, Fs1, Fs3, Ds5, M1–2; us Fs2. 225 *Maid? And]* Os1b,

Os2b, Fs2–3, Ds5 (and); ~ , and Q1–5, F, D, Os1a, Os2a, Os3–5, Fs1, M2; ~ ; and M1. 225 *dy'd!*] Q1–5, F, D, M1; ~ . Os1–5, Fs1–3, Ds5, M2. 226 *straight*] Q1–5, F, D, Os1–2, Os4, Fs1–3, Ds5, M1–2; strait Os3, Os5. 227 *true:*] Q1–5, F, D, Os2a, Fs1–3, Ds5, M2; ~ . Os1a–b, Os2b, Os3–4; ~ , Os5; ~∧ M1. 228 *Fancy,*] Q1–5, F, D, Os5, M2; ~∧ Os1–4, Fs1–3, Ds5, M1. 228 *two,*] Q1–5, F, D, Os1b, Os2–3, Os5, Fs1–3, Ds5, M1–2; ~ . Os1a, Os4. 229 *Fancy*] Q1–5, F, D, Os1b, Os2b, Fs1–3, Ds5, M1–2; I fancy I Os1a, Os2a, Os3–4; I fancy'd love Os5. 229 *do!*] Q1–5, D, M1–2 (doe M2); ~ . F, Os1–2, Os4–5, Fs1–3; ~ : Os3; ~ , Ds5. 230 *disdain,*] Q1, Q4–5, D, M2, Os1–5, Fs1–3, Ds5; ~ . Q2–3, M1; ~ ; F. 231 *While*] Q1–5, F, D, Os1b, Os2b, Fs1–3, Ds5, M1–2; Whilst Os1a, Os2a, Os3–5. 231 *vain;*] Q1–3, Os4–5, M1–2; ~ ! Q4–5, D; ~ : F, Os1b, Os2b; ~ , Os1a, Os2a, Os3, Fs1–3, Ds5. 232 *Asleep*] Q1–5, F, D, Os1–4, Fs1–3, Ds5, M2; A sleep Os5, M1. 232 *you*] Q1–5, F, D, Os1b, Os2b, Os4, Fs1–3, Ds5, M1–2; I Os1a, Os2a, Os3, Os5. 232 *must*] Q1–5, F, D, Os1–5, Fs1–3, M1–2; most Ds5. 232 M2 has subscription: "Drydens Conquest of Granada. part .1." 232+ *The* Zambra *Dance.*] included in brace with the following s.d. in Q1–3; centered preceding the song in Q4–5, F, D. 235 dislodg'd;] Q1–4, D; ~ ? Q5, F. 236 *Zegry's*] Q2–3, F, D; Zegry's Q1, Q4–5. 238 King.] Q1, Q4–5, F, D; ~ , Q2–3. 241 Th'] Q1–5, D; The F. 242 thither] Q1–5, F; hither D. 245 care;] F, D; ~ . Q1–4; ~ , Q5. 248+ s.d. [*Exeunt*] Q5, F, D; ∧Exeunt Q1; ∧*Exeunt* Q2–3; [Exeunt Q4. 249 light?] Q3, D; ~ : Q1–2, Q4–5, F. 255 *Rubicon*] D; Rubicon Q1–5, F. 256+ s.d. [*A*] Q2–5, F, D; ∧~ Q1. 257 dies] Q1–2, Q4–5, F, D; dyes Q3. 260 faster,] Q1–2, Q4–5, F, D; ~∧ Q3. 262 below.] Q1–5, F; ~ : D. 264 Omen] D; *Omen* Q1–5, F. 264 I'le] Q1–5, F; will D. 265 appear:] Q1–2, Q4–5; ~∧ Q3; ~ , F, D. 267 Sphere.] Q1, F; ~ , Q2, Q4–5; ~∧ Q3; ~ : D. 269+ s.d. Zegrys;] D; Zegrys. Q1, Q4–5; Zegrys. Q2–3, F. 272+ s.d. Osmyn.] Q1–5, F; ~∧ D. 275 threatning] Q1, Q3–5, F, D; threatening Q2. 278 *Spaniard*] Q3, F, D; Spaniard Q1–2, Q4–5. 279 s.d. *Exit*] Q4–5, F, D; Exit. Q1; Exit. Q2–3. 279+ s.d. others.] Q2–5, F, D; ~∧ Q1. 281 his] Q1–2, Q4–5, F, D; is Q3. 282 Word] Q1–4, F, D; World Q5. 284+ s.d. [Almanzor] Q4–5, F, D; ∧~ Q1–3. 285–286 *Selin.* Now ... prepare: [*To* Ozmyn.] *Selin* to Ozmin. / Now ... prepare: Q1–5 (Ozmyn Q2–5); *Selin to Ozmyn.* Now ... prepare: F, D. 289 die] Q1, Q4–5, F, D; dye Q2–3. 291 pow'r.] Q1, Q4–5, F, D; ~ : Q2–3. 293 noblest] Q1–4; only Q5, F, D. 293 Fortitude,] Q1, Q3–5, F, D; ~∧ Q2. 294 remains] Q1–5, D; ~ ! F. 297 Heav'n] Q1–4, D; Heaven Q5, F. 301 Flatt'ry] Q1–4; flattery Q5, F, D. 301 Fate;] Q1–2, Q4–5, F, D; ~ . Q3. 303 live.] Q1, Q3–5, F, D; ~ , Q2. 304 terrible] Q1–5, F; terribly D. 307+ s.d. [Almanzor] Q4, F, D; ∧~ Q1–3, Q5. 307+ s.d. veyld.] Q1–4, F, D; ~∧ Q5. 308 way,] Q1–2, Q4–5, D; ~ ; Q3; ~ . F. 311 of th'] Q1, Q3–5, F, D; of the th' Q2. 318 s.d. Unveyling] Q2–5, F, D; unveyling Q1. 320 Till] Q1–5, F; 'Till D. 322 *Almanzor.* Well ... you: [*Looking fixedly on her.*] *Almanzor looking fixedly on her.* / Well ... you: Q1–5 ([Almanzor Q2–5); [Almanzor *looking fixedly on her.* / *Almanz.* Well ... you: F; *Almanz.* [*Looking fixedly on her.*] Well ... you: D. 324 word?] F, D; ~ , Q1–2, Q4–5; ~ ; Q3. 327 by?] ~ ! Q1–5, F; ~ . D. 336 numm'd] Q1–4, D; mum'd Q5, F. 338 every] Q1–5, F; ev'ry D. 339 Heart,]

Q1, Q4–5, F, D; ~ . Q2–3.   341 dispossest.] Q1–5, D (*some copies of Q5 lack period*); ~ ; F.   345 *s.d. Angrily*] Q2–3, D; *angrily* Q1; *Angerly* Q4–5, F.   345 Sir.] D; ~ : Q1–5, F.   347 *s.d. Aside*] Q4–5, F, D; *aside* Q1–3.   348 show:] Q1–2, Q4–5, F, D; ~ . Q3.   351 still.] Q1–4, F, D; ~ , Q5.   352 will,] Q1–2, Q4–5, ~ ; Q3; ~ . F, D.   353 heart.] Q1–5, F; ~ ; D.   363 *s.d. Softly*] Q2–3, F, D; *softly* Q1, Q4–5.   364 *s.d. Aside.*] F, D; *aside.* Q1–5 (~ , Q2–3; ~ ₐ Q5).   365 deni'd:] Q1–5, D; ~ . F.   369 Victory:] Q1–2, Q4–5, F, D; ~ . Q3.   377 him?] ~ ! Q1–5, F, D.   378 love too] Q1–3; loved too Q4–5, F, D.   389 knot's] Q2–3, Q5, F, D; knots Q1, Q4.   407 crowd] Q4–5, F, D; crow'd Q1–3.   407 on:] Q1–5, D; ~ . F.   412 'ore-powr's] Q1–3, D; 'ore-powers Q4–5, F.   412 bears] Q1–3; beats Q4–5, F, D.   420 a] Q1, Q4–5, F, D; an Q2–3.   424+ *s.d. [Exeunt]* Q4–5, F; ₐ~ Q1–3, D.   426 here.] Q1–3, Q5, F, D; ~ , Q4.   426+ *s.d. attended by* Hamet *and others.*] *attended.* Q1–5, F, D.   429 foe:] ~ . Q1–5, F; ~ , D.   431 own,] Q3, F, D; ~ ₐ Q1–2, Q4–5.   433 pay] Q1, Q4–5, F, D; ~ ; Q2–3.   437 *Albayzin*] Q3; *Albayzyn* Q1–2, Q4–5, F, D.   442 war.] Q1–4, F, D; ~ , Q5.   443 free.] Q1–3; ~ , Q4–5; ~ : F, D.   445 I'le] Q2–5, F, D; 'Ile Q1.   445 loose] Q1, Q5, F, D; lose Q2–4.   454 fills] Q2–5, F, D; fils Q1.   458 *Zulema.*] Q2–5, F, D; ~ , Q1.   459 own.] Q1, Q3–5, F, D; ~ , Q2.   461 *Almahida's*] Q1–5, F; *Almahide's* D.   469 know,] Q1–2, Q4–5, D; ~ ; Q3; ~ . F.   474 She] Q3–5, F, D; she Q1–2.   475 tittle] Q1–5, F; Title D.   480 divide.] Q1–4, F, D; ~ ₐ Q5.   497 they?] D; ~ ; Q1–5, F.   502 purge.] Q1, Q4–5, F, D; ~ , Q2–3.   508 from thy] Q1–4; from my Q5, F, D.   511 'ere] Q1, Q4; e're Q2–3; e'er Q5, D; e'r F.   518 kill.] D; ~ , Q1, Q4–5, F; ~ : Q2–3.   521 Farewell:] D; ~ , Q1–5, F.   523 me:] Q1 (*some copies*); ~ . Q1 (*some copies*), Q2–3; ~ : Q4–5; ~ ; F, D.   525+ *s.d. [Exit]* Q4–5, D; ₐ~ Q1–3, F.   527 too] Q1–5, D; to F.   527+ *s.d. [Zulema, Hamet and]* Q2–5, F, D; ₐ*Zulema, Hamet and* Q1.   529 shake.] Q1–3, F, D; ~ ; Q4–5.   533 *s.d. [Exeunt]* Q4–5, F, D; ₐ~ Q1–3.

IV, i

ACT] Q2–5, F, D; ~ . Q1.   IV.] Q1–5, F; IV. SCENE I. D.   *s.d. Boabdelin, Abenamar,*] Q4–5, F; *Boabdelin, Abenamar,* Q1–3; *Enter* Boabdelin, Abenamar, *and* D.   4 flow.] Q1–5, D; ~ , F.   9 in their first] Q1, Q4–5, F, D; in their Q2; that in their Q3.   12 every] Q1–5, F; ev'ry D.   13 But,] *some copies of Q1 lack the comma.*   17 While] Q1–4, F, D; Wile Q5.   17 *Almahide*] Q1–5, D; ~ . F.   21 and] Q1 (*some copies*), Q4–5, F, D; and I Q1 (*some copies*), Q2; I Q3.   21 dead.] Q1–3, Q5, F, D; ~ ₐ Q4.   31 defer:] Q1, Q4–5; ~ , Q2; ~ . Q3, D; ~ ; F.   32 too] Q1–5, D; to F.   36 I,] Q1 (*some copies*), Q3–5, F, D; ~ ₐ Q1 (*some copies*), Q2.   37 where] Q1 (*some copies*), Q3–4, F, D; were Q1 (*some copies*), Q2, Q5.   37 gold] Q1, Q4–5, F; ~ ; Q2; ~ , Q3, D.   38 poorer . . . Richer] Q1–4; poorest . . . richest Q5, F, D.   44 every] Q1–5, F; ev'ry D.   44 thought] Q1–3; though Q4–5; through F, D.   48 'Ere] Q1; E're Q2–3, F; Ere Q4–5; E'er D.   48 first] Q1–4; then Q5, F, D.   55 I'le] Q2–5, F, D; i'le Q1.   58 Since,] Q1–2, Q4–5, F, D; ~ ₐ Q3.   59 int'rest] Q1–5, D; Interest F.   62 *Boab.* That . . . desire [*Embracing him.*] D; *Boabdelin embracing him.* / That . . . desire Q1–5, F

([Boabdelin Q2-3, F). 66 sets to] Q1-3; sets Q4-5, F; sets a D. 68 'ere] Q1; e're Q2-3, D; ere Q4-5; e'r F. 70 *s.d. [Exeunt]* Q5, F, D; ˄~ Q1-4.

IV, ii

S.d. Lyndaraxa] Q2-5, F, D (*Enter* Lyndaraxa D); *Lindaraxa* Q1. 1 *Lynd.* O] F, D; O Q1-5 (Oh Q2-3). 3 ghess,] Q1, Q4-5, F, D; ~ . Q2; ~ ; Q3. 4 'em] Q1-4; them Q5, F, D. 7 Fortune] Q3, F, D; fortune Q1-2, Q4-5. 8+ *s.d.* Halyma] Q2-5, F; *Halyma* Q1, D. 11 *Lynd.*] Q2-5, F, D; *Lind.* Q1 (*and similarly below except as noted*). 11 appear.] Q1, Q3-5, F, D; ~˄ Q2. 11+ *s.d.* To] Q5, D; *in Q1-4, F, two line s.d. is preceded by a brace.* 11+ *s.d. Disguise.*] Q1-5, D; ~ ; F. 11+ *s.d. starts.*] Q2-5, F, D; ~ : Q1. 12 here.] Q1-5, F; ~ : D. 14 Guard] Q1-5, F; Guards D. 16 Eyes.] Q1, Q4-5, F, D; ~ : Q2-3. 23 *Abdel.*] Q3-5, F, D; *Abdal.* Q1-2. 29 bestow;] Q2-3, F, D; ~ . Q1; ~ , Q4-5. 36 late.] Q1, Q4-5, F, D; ~ : Q2-3. 38 easie;] Q3; ~ , Q1-2, Q4-5, F, D. 43 me:] Q1-5, D; ~˄ F. 44 see.] Q1-5, F; ~ , D. 48 die.] Q1, Q4-5, F, D (~ : D); dy. Q2; dye. Q3. 51 giv'n] Q1-5, D; given F. 52 th'] Q1-4, D; the Q5, F. 53 *s.d. [Is]* Q2-5, F, D; (*is* Q1. 54 *Lynd.*] *sic in Q1.* 54 Stay;] Q1-4; ~ . Q5; ~ , F, D. 62 *s.d. [Is . . . again.]* Q2-5, F, D; (*is . . . again.*) Q1. 63 *Lynd.*] *sic in Q1.* 63 dealing] Q1-3; dealings Q4-5, F, D. 63 tell:] D; ~ . Q1-4; ~˄ Q5; ~ ; F. 67-68 *Abdel.* Have . . . invent; / . . . *[Coming back.]* [Abdel. *coming back.* / Have . . invent Q1-5 (Abdel˄ Q2-3; invent, Q3); [Abdel. *coming back.* / *Abdel.* Have . . . invent F; *Abdelm. [coming back.]* Have . . . invent, D. 77 plain:] Q1 (*some copies*), Q4-5, F, D; ~ . Q1 (*some copies*), Q2-3. 79 tell,] Q1-5, F; ~ . D. 83 die] Q1, Q4-5, F, D; dye Q2-3. 83+ *s.d. [Leans]* Q4-5, F, D; (~ Q1-3. 83+ *s.d. Arm.*] Q4-5, F, D; ~ .) Q1-3. 84-85 *Abdel.* What . . . hear / . . . *[Weeping.]* D; [Abdelmelech *weeping.* / What . . . hear Q1-5, F (*some copies of Q1 have* "Abdel." *before* "What"). 85 Tear?] Q3; ~ ! Q1-2, Q4-5, F, D. 87 die] Q1, Q4-5, F, D; dye Q2-3. 97 show's] Q2-5, F, D; ~ , Q1. 100 before;] Q1-5, D; ~ . F. 111 here.] Q1, Q3-5, F, D; ~ : Q2. 112 goe:] Q1-5, F; ~ ! D. 114+ *s.d. [Exit]* Q4-5, F, D; ˄~ Q1-3. 115 *Lynd.*] *sic in Q1 and similarly hereafter.* 121 I] Q2-3, F, D; ~ , Q1, Q4-5. 121+ SONG.] Q1-5, F, D, M3; *Song* 302. Ds1, Ds3; SONG CXXXVI. Ds2; *Song* 303. Ds4; *A Song at the Kings House.* Os1-4; *Song* 261. Os5; *no title* Fs1-3, M1, M4; *A SONG.* Ds5. *No stanza division in Ds1, Ds3-4; no stanza numbers in Ds1-4, Os5, M1.* 122 and] Q1-5, F, D, Ds1-4, Os1-5, M1, M3; or Fs1-3, Ds5, M4. 123 Phillis is] Q1-5, F, D, Ds1-5, Os1-2, Os4-5, Fs1-3, M1, M3-4; *Phil s's* Os3. 124 to goe] Q1-5, F, D, Ds2-5, Os1-5, Fs1-3, M1, M3-4; go Ds1. 125 find:] Q1-2, Q4-5, F, D, Ds2; ~ . Q3, Ds3-4, Os1-4, Fs1-3, M1; ~ , Ds1; ~ ; Os5, Ds5; ~˄ M3-4. 126 Unknown . . . I am] Q1-5, F, D, Ds1-5, Os1-5, Fs1-3, M1, M4; unknowen . . . I'm M3. 126 her] Q1-5, F, D, Os1-5, Fs1-3, Ds5, M1; the Ds1-4, M3-4. 127 And when I would . . . I can] Q1-5, F, D, Ds1-5, Os1-5, Fs1-3, M1, M3; I meant for to . . . but could M4. 127 more,] Q1-5, F, D, Ds1, Os2, Os4, M1, M4; ~ : Ds2; ~ . Ds3-4, Os1, Os3, Fs1-3; ~˄ Os5, M3; ~ ; Ds5. 128 *line partially repeated in M4 (butt phillis); fully repeated in Ds1-5, Os1-4, Fs1-3.* 128 Than] Q1-5, F,

D, Ds1, Ds3–5, Os1–2, Os4–5; Then Ds2, Os3, Fs1–3, M1, M3 (*both times if line repeated*); But (*bis*) M4.　128　*too*] Q1–5, F, D, Ds1–5, Os1–5, Fs1–3, M1, M3; so M4.　128　*unkind!*] Q1–5, F, D; ∼ . Os5, M1, M3; ∼ , (*first time*) Ds1–4, Os3; ∼ . (*first time*) Os1–2, Os4; ∼ : (*first time*) Fs1–3, Ds5; ∼ . (*second time*) Ds1–5, Os1–4, Fs1–3; ∼ , M4.　129　*When*] Q1–5, F, D, Ds1–5, Os1–4, Fs1–3, M1, M3–4; When my Os5.　129　*bounds*] Q1–5, F, D, Os5, M1; burns Ds1–5, Os1–4, Fs1–3, M3; boyle M4.　130　*And the Love I would stifle is*] Q1–5, F, D, Ds1–5, Os1–5, Fs1–3, M1, M3; My Love it is openly M4.　131　*But asleep*] Q1–5, F, D, Os1–4, Fs1–3, Ds5, M1; Asleep Ds1–4, Os5, M3–4.　131　*awake*] Q1–5, F, D, Ds1–5, Os2–3, Os5, Fs1–3, M1, M3–4; wake Os1, Os4.　132　*my*] Q1–5, F, D, Ds1–4, Os5, M1, M3; mine Os1–4, Fs1–3, Ds5, M4.　132　*gone!*] Q1–5, M1; ∼ . F, Ds1, Os1–2, Os4, Fs1–3, Ds5; ∼ : D, Ds2; ∼ , Ds3–4, Os3, Os5, M4; ∼∧ M3.　133　*a sad*] Q1–5, F, D, M1; a sweet Ds1–5, Os1–5, Fs1–3, M3–4.　133　*Dream*] Q1–5, F, D, Ds1–5, Os1–5, Fs1–3, M1, M3; sleepe M4.　133　*does*] Q1–5, F, D, Ds1–4, Os1–4, M1, M3; doth Os5, Fs1–3, Ds5, M4.　133　*my sad*] Q1–5, F, D, Ds1–5, Os1–5, Fs1–3, M1, M4; my M3.　134　*alas, when*] Q1–5, F, D, M1; when Ds1–4, M3–4; alas∧ when Os1–4; alas! when Os5, Fs1–3, Ds5.　134　*wake and*] Q1–5, F, D, Os1–5, Fs1–3, Ds5, M1; awake Ds1, Ds3–4; awake and Ds2, M3–4.　135　*line partially repeated in Ds1, Ds3–4 (sigh, &c.), M4 (sigh to my all); fully repeated in Ds2, Os1–4, Fs1–3, Ds5.*　135　*How I*] Q1–5, F, D, Ds1–4, M1, M3 (*But I* Ds1 [*second time*]); *Then I* (*bis*) Os1–4, Fs1–3, Ds5; *I* Os5, M4.　135　*alone.*] Q2, Os5, M3; ∼ : Q1; ∼ ! Q3, Q5, F, D, Ds2, Fs1–3, Ds5, M1; ∼ ; Q4; ∼ , Ds1, Ds3–4, M4; ∼ , (*first time*), ∼ . (*second time*) Os1–4.　136　*be my*] Q1–5, F, D, Ds1–5, Os1–2, Os4–5, Fs1–3, M1, M3–4 (bee M4); being Os3.　136　*in . . . I*] Q1–5, F, D, Ds1–5, Os1–5, Fs1–3, M1, M3; yet . . . Ile M4.　137　*He should offer*] Q1–5, F, D, Ds1–5, Os1–5, Fs1–3, M1, M3; hee proffers M4.　137　*his*] Q1–5, F, D, Ds1–5, Os1–5, Fs1–3, M1, M4; her M3.　137　*Treasure*] Q1–5, F, D, Ds1–5, Os1–4, Fs1–3, M1, M3; Scepter Os5; treasures M4.　137　*vain:*] Q1–5, F, D, Fs1–3, M1; ∼ , Ds1, Ds3–4, Os1–2, Os4; ∼ ; Ds2, Ds5; ∼ . Os3, Os5; ∼∧ M3–4.　138　*O*] Q1–5, D, Os1–4, Fs1–3, Ds5, M1, M4; O! F; Oh! Ds1, Ds3–4; Oh∧ Ds2, Os5, M3.　138　*be*] Q1–5, F, D, Ds1–5, Os1–5, Fs1–3, M1, M3; bee M4.　139　*again:*] Q1–2, Q4–5, Ds2, Ds5, Os1–4; ∼ . Q3, F, Os5, Fs1–3, M1, M3; ∼ ! D; ∼ ; Ds1, Ds3–4; ∼∧ M4.　140　*be mine*] Q1–5, F, D, Ds1–5, Os1–5, Fs1–3, M1, M3; bee mine M4.　140　*for ever*] Q2–3, F, M1, M4; but ever Q1, Q4–5, D, Ds1–4, M3; ever Os1–5, Fs1–3, Ds5.　140　*be kind*] Q1–5, F, D, Ds1–5, Os1–5, Fs1–3, M1, M3; prove kind M4.　141　*could*] Q1–5, F, D, Os1–5, Fs1–3, Ds5, M1, M3–4; would Ds1–4.　141　*to . . . be*] Q1–5, F, D, Ds1–5, Os1–5, Fs1–3, M1, M3; in . . . bee M4.　142　*line partially repeated in Ds1, Ds3–4 (no, &c.); fully repeated in Ds2, Os1–4, Fs1–3, Ds5, M4.*　142　*And envy no*] Q1–5, F, D, Ds1–5, Os1–5, Fs1–3, M1, M3; Without Enuying any (*bis*) M4.　142　*Raign.*] Q1–5, F, D, Os5, Ds5, M1, M3; ∼ , (*first time*), ∼ . (*second time if line fully repeated*) Ds1–4, Os1, Os3–4; ∼ : (*first time*), ∼ . (*second time*) Fs1–3; ∼ , (*bis*) Os2; ∼∧ (*bis*) M4.　143　*Alas,*] Q1–5, F, D, Ds1, Ds3–4, M1; ∼∧ Ds2, Os5, M3; ∼ ! Os1–4, Fs1–3, Ds5; But alass∧ M4.　143　*too*] Q1–5, F, D, Ds1–5, Os1–4, Fs1–3, M1; to Os5, M3–4.　144　*she too*] Q1–5, F, D, Ds1–5, Os1–5, Fs1–3, M1, M3; phillis M4.　144　*power!*] Q1–4, M1; *pow'r!* Q5, F, D; pow'r, Ds1, Ds3–4; power: Ds2, Os2–3; power;

Os1, Os4–5; pow'r: Fs1–3, Ds5; pow'r∧ M3; power∧ M4.   145 *She* . . .
Martyrdom] Q1–5, F, D, Ds1–5, Os1–5, Fs1–3, M1, M3; Which . . . mortall
to M4.   146 *hour:*] Q1–5, D, M1; ∼. F, Os1–4, Fs1–3, Ds5; ∼, Ds1,
Ds3–4; ∼; Ds2, Os5; ∼∧ M3–4.   147 *her*] Q1, Q4–5, F, D, Ds1–5,
Os1–5, Fs1–3, M3–4; *me* Q2–3, M1.   147 *each minute*] Q1–5, F, D,
Ds1–5, Os1–5, Fs1–3, M1, M4; forever M3.   147 *poor*] Q1–5, F, D,
Ds1–5, Os1–4, Fs1–3, M1, M3; sad Os5, M4.   148 *I had*] Q1–5, F, D,
Ds1–5, Os1–5, Fs1–3, M1, M3; I'd M4.   148 *both False*] Q1–5, F, D,
Os1–4, Fs1–3, Ds5, M1, M3; though false Ds1–4, Os5; so faire M4.   148
Unkind,] Q1–5, F, D, Ds1–2, Os1–5, Fs1–3, Ds5, M1; ∼. Ds3–4; ∼∧ M3–4.
149 *line repeated in Ds1–5, Os1–5, Fs1–3, M4.*   149 *Pow'r.*] Q1–5, F,
D, M1, M3 (power M3); Power, (*first time*), Power. (*second time*) Ds1–4,
Os1–5 (Pow'r [*bis*] Ds1, Ds3); pow'r: (*first time*), pow'r. (*second time*) Fs1–3,
Ds5; power∧ (*first time*), power, (*second time*) M4.   149+ *s.d.* Abdalla
enters] Q1–5, F; *Enter* Abdalla D.   149+ *s.d. with* Selin] *with* Q1–5,
F, D.   151 Or] Q1, Q3–5, F, D; O Q2.   160 till] Q1–5, F; 'till D.
161 pow'r;] Q3; ∼. Q1–2, Q4–5, D; ∼: F.   168 your] Q2–5, F, D;
yonr Q1.   174 pray'rs] Q1–3, Q5, F, D; prayers Q4.   187 then]
Q1–4, F, D; than than Q5.   188 grown] Q1, Q3–5, F, D; ∼, Q2.   189
Who] Q2–3; That Q1, Q4–5, F, D.   194 Submit? . . . fault!] ∼! . . . ∼?
Q1–2, Q4–5; ∼! . . . ∼. Q3, F, D.   204 *s.d. Aside*] Q4–5, F, D; *aside*
Q1–3.   206 hand:] Q1–5, D; ∼. F.   210 choose] Q1, Q3–5, F, D;
chose Q2.   211 take.] Q5, F; ∼: Q1–4, D.   214+ *s.d.* [*Leads*] Q2–
5, F, D; ∧∼ Q1.   215 waite.] ∼: Q1–5, F, D.   217 'Ere] Q1; e're
Q2–3, F, D; ere Q4–5.   219 *Manes*] F; Manes Q1–5, D.   220+ *s.d.*
Gazul,] Q1–4, D; ∼. Q5; ∼: F.   220+ *s.d.* Reduan] Q1–4, D; Raduan
Q5, F.   221 *Selin.*] Q2–5, F, D; *Selyn.* Q1.   221 sent,] Q1, Q4, F,
D; ∼∧ Q2–3, Q5.   221 *Benzaida,*] Q1; ∼∧ Q2; *Benzayda*∧ Q3; *Benzayda,*
Q4–5, F, D.   222 rites] Q1–3; rights Q4–5, F, D.   223 th' accurst]
Q1, Q4; th' curst Q2; the curst Q3, Q5, F, D.   223 bind,] Q1–5, D; ∼. F.
223+ *s.d.* [*To* Gazul *and* Reduan.] Q2–5, F, D (Gazul. Q4); ∧*To* Gazul.
and Reduan. Q1.   224+ *s.d.* [*They*] Q2–5, F, D; ∧∼ Q1.   225 share,]
Q1–5, D; ∼? F.   226 prepare?] Q3–5, F, D; ∼. Q1–2.   236 thick
. . . breath,] Q1–2, Q4–5; ∼, . . . ∼∧ Q3; ∼∧ . . . ∼∧ F, D.   238 What,]
Q1–4, F, D; ∼∧ Q5.   240 innocence] Q1–4, D; insolence Q5, F.   244
die.] Q1–2, Q4–5, F, D (∼: D); dye. Q2–3.   246 thee:] Q1–2, Q4–5, D;
∼. Q3, F.   246+ *s.d.* [*Gives*] Q2–5, F, D; ∧∼ Q1.   248 his,] Q2–5,
F, D; ∼∧ Q1.   256 who 'ere] Q1–4, F, D; whoe'er Q5.   257 *Benz.*
Alas, . . . afford? [*To* Selin.] *Benz. to Selin.* / Alas . . . afford; Q1–5; *Benz.*
Alas, . . . afford? [Benzayda *to* Selin. F; *Benz. to Selin.* Alas, . . . afford? D.
258 sword.] F; ∼? Q1–5; ∼: D.   261 convay;] Q3, F, D; ∼∧ Q1–2,
Q4–5.   263 *Selin.* Waste . . . breath. [*To* Benz.] *Selin to Benz.* / Waste
. . . breath. Q1–5 (Wast Q5); [Selin *to* Benzayda. / *Selin.* Wast . . . Breath.
F; *Selin to Benz.* Waste . . . Breath. D.   264+ *s.d.* [*Giving*] Q2–5, F, D;
∧*giving* Q1.   266 in mine] Q1, Q3–5, F, D; is mine Q2.   266+ *s.d.*
Hamet] Q2–5, F, D; *Hamet* Q1.   268 attacque;] Q2–3; ∼. Q1, Q4–5;
∼: F, D.   271 *Selin.* Think . . . hence, [*To* Benz.] *Selin to Benz.* /
Think . . . hence, Q1–5; [Selin *to* Benz. / *Selin.* Think . . . hence, F; *Selin to
Benz.* Think . . . hence, D.   273 'Ere] Q1; E're Q2–3, F; Ere Q4–5; E'er
D.   274 *Ozmyn*] Q3–5, F, D; *Ozmin* Q1–2.   276 will.] Q1, Q3–5,

F, D; ~ , Q2.　276+　*s.d.* [*Exeunt*] Q4–5, F, D; ∧~ Q1–3.　276+　*s.d.*
[Benzayda] F, D; ∧~ Q1–5.　276+　*s.d. down;*] F; ~ . Q1–5, D (*drawn.*
Q3).　276+　*s.d. her.*] Q1–5, D; ~∧ F.　277　*Ozmyn*] Q4–5; *Ozmin*
Q1; *Ozm.* Q2–3, F, D.　277　*Benzaida*] Q2; *Benzaiida* Q1; *Benzayda* Q3–
5, F, D.　282　you.] Q1, Q3–5, F, D; ~∧ Q2.　290　die] Q1–2, Q4–5,
F, D; dye Q3.　291　th'] Q1–4, D; the Q5, F.　291　*Abencerrages*]
Q5, F, D; *Abencerrage's* Q1–4.　296　our] Q1–4, F, D; your Q5.　297
you.] Q1–2, Q4–5, F, D; ~ : Q3–5, F, D.　302　*Ozmyn.*] Q1, Q3–5, F, D; ~ , Q2.
311　joyn'd:] Q1–5, D; ~ . F.　313　your] Q2–3, Q5, F, D; yours Q1, Q4.
316　before . . . you make] Q2–3; when you . . . begin Q1, Q4–5, F, D.
317　I shall . . . take] Q2–3; will slide . . . in Q1, Q4–5, F, D.　319　e're]
Q1–4; ere Q5, D; e'r F.　327　die] Q1, Q4–5, F, D; dye Q2–3.　328
it.] Q1–2, Q4; ~ ? Q3, Q5, F, D.　328+　*s.d.* Gazul. Benzayda . . . *Sword.*]
~ .] [~ . . . ~ .] Q1, Q4; ~ ·∧ [~ . . . ~ ·∧ Q2–3, Q5, F, D.　329　*s.d. kills*]
Q3–5, F, D; *kils* Q1–2.　331　*Ozmyn.* Did . . . conspire [*Kneeling . . .
hand.*] [*Ozmyn kneeling . . . hand. /* Did . . . conspire Q1–5, F, D (*hand.*]
Q1; *kneels* D; *Ozm.* Did F, D).　338　every . . . our] Q1–5, F; ev'ry . . . the
D.　338　fly;] Q1–5, D; ~ . F.　341　amain.] Q1, Q4–5, F, D; ~ : Q2–
3.　343　pay;] Q1–3; ~ . Q4–5, F; ~ , D.　345–346　*Ozmyn.* . . . own
/ . . . [*Kneeling to his Father.*] D; Ozmyn, *kneeling to his Father. / Ozmyn.*
. . . own Q1–5, F (*to his Father.* Q1).　347–348　*Aben.* . . . age! / . . . [*Embracing him.*] D; [*Abenamar embracing him. / Aben.* . . . age! Q1–5, F.
348　rage?] ~ ! Q1–5, F, D.　349　Deliverance,] Q1–5, F; ~ ? D.　353
My Life, and . . . you] Q2–3; My Liberty and Life, / And . . . you're pleas'd
to Q1, Q4–5, F, D.　354　all.] Q1–3, F, D; ~ , Q4; ~ ; Q5.　355
Abenam. Instruct . . . Divinity, [*To her.*] D; [*Abenam. to her. /* Instruct . . .
Divinity, Q1–5, F (Abenam: Q1; / *Aben* Instruct F).　362　deliverer] Q1–
5, F; Deliv'rer D.　363　Joys] Q2–3; private Joys Q1, Q4–5, F, D.　363
s.d. [*Exeunt.*] Q4–5, F, D; ∧~ Q1–3.　363+　*s.d.* Almanzor, Almahide,
Esperanza.] Q2–5, F, D (*and* Esperanza. D); *Almanzor, Almahide, Esperanza.*
Q1.　367　oh] Q1–3; O Q4–5, F, D.　367　those.] Q1–2, Q4–5; ~ !
Q3, F, D.　372　every] Q1–5, F; ev'ry D.　374　difference] Q1–5, F;
diff'rence D.　377　die] Q1, Q4–5, F, D; dye Q2–3.　378　every] Q1–5,
F; ev'ry D.　389　Heaven's] Q1–5; Heav'ns F; Heav'n's D.　398
threatning] Q1, Q3–5, F, D; threatening Q2.　420　every] Q1, Q3–5, F;
ever Q2; ev'ry D.　421　Ear.] Q1–5, D; ~ : F.　429　e're] Q1–4; e'r
Q5, F; e'er D.　429　Sute.] Q1–2, Q4–5, F, D; ~ , Q3.　435　hope you
can] Q2–3; hope that you Q1, Q4–5, F, D.　444　'Tis but] Q2–3; It is
Q1, Q4–5, F, D.　452　Nor view the passage, but] Q2–3; Because they
onely view Q1, Q4–5, F, D.　454　success] Q2–3; event Q1, Q4–5, F, D.
458　right:] Q1–3; ~ . Q4–5, F, D.　461　miss.] Q1–5, D; ~∧ F.　467
sutes] Q1–3; suites Q4–5, D; suits F.　475　began:] Q1–2, Q4–5, F, D;
~ . Q3.　478　select,] Q2–5, F, D; ~ . Q1.　479+　*s.d.* [*Exeunt*] Q4–5,
F, D; ∧~ Q1–3.

V, i

ACT] Q2, Q5, F, D; ~ . Q1, Q3–4.　V.] Q1–5, F; V. SCENE I. D.　6+
s.d. Souldier] Q4–5; [~ Q1–3, F; *for* D *see next.*　7　*Sould.* Who] Who
Q1–5, F; *Sold. above.* Who D.　7　below? . . . demand?] Q1–2, Q4–5, F,
D; ~ : . . . ~ : Q3.　14+　*s.d.* Lyndaraxa] Q4–5; [~ Q1–3, F; *for* D *see*

next. 15 *Lynd.* What] What Q1–5, F; *Lyndar. above.* What D. 23
Why,] Q2–3, F; ~ʌ Q1, Q4–5, D. 29 oblige:] Q1–3, F; ~ . Q4–5, D.
30 siege.] Q1–5, F; ~ : D. 37 weep:] F; ~ , Q1–2, Q4–5; ~ . Q3, D.
42 command:] Q1–4; ~ . Q5, F, D. 46 Soveraignty] Q1–5, F; sov-
'raignty D. 52 'ere] Q1, Q4; e're Q2–3; e'r Q5, F; e'er D. 54 hate.]
Q1–5, D; ~ , F. 59+ *s.d.* [*Trampling*] Q2–5, F, D (*trampling* Q2–4);
ʌ *trampling* Q1. 61 *Lynd.*] Q2–5, F, D; *Lind.* Q1. 64 you:] Q1–4;
~ . Q5, F, D. 65 prosperous] Q1–5; prosp'rous F, D. 66 the] Q1,
Q4–5, F, D; th' Q2–3. 66+ *s.d.* [*Exit*] Q4–5, F, D; ʌ~ Q1–3. 68 I
hear] Q3, F, D; I fear Q1–2, Q4–5. 68 betrai'd:] Q1–4; ~ . Q5, F, D.
69 *Spanish*] Q4–5, F, D; Spanish Q1–3. 70 me.] Q1–4; ~ : Q5, F, D.
71+ *s.d.* [*Exit.*] Q4–5, F, D; ʌ~ . Q1–3 (~ : Q2). 71+ *s.d.* Ozmyn.
Benzayda. Abenamar.] Q2–5, F (~ , ~ , ~ . Q2–3, Q5, F); *Ozmyn. Benzayda.
Abenamar.* Q1; *Enter* Ozmyn, Benzayda *and* Abenamar. D. 72 I wish
(to merit this)] Q2–3; ——I wish / (To merit all these thanks) Q1, Q4–5,
F, D. 75 suffering] Q1–5, F; Suff'ring D. 79 *s.d.* [*To*] Q2–5, F,
D (*between 78 and 79* Q2–3); ʌ~ Q1 (*between 78 and 79*). 79 deliverer]
Q1–5, F; Deliv'rer D. 80 foe,] Q2–3, F, D; ~ . Q1, Q4–5. 81 death
by] Q1, Q3–5, F, D; death my Q2. 81 led,] Q1, Q4–5, D; ~ : Q2–3, F,
85 Ev'n] Q2–5, F, D; E'ven Q1. 93 generous] Q1–5; gen'rous D.
100 giv'st] Q1–3; gavest Q4–5; gav'st F, D. 105 kild'st] Q1–4, D; kill'st
Q5, F. 105 last:] Q1–5, D; ~ . F. 114 to] Q4–5, F, D; too Q1–3.
114 blame;] Q1, Q4–5; ~ ? Q2–3; ~ , F, D. 117 mind;] Q1–2, Q4;
~ ? Q3, Q5, F, D. 119 could] Q1–5, D; would F. 131 *s.d.* [*Exit*]
Q4–5, F, D; ʌ~ Q1–3. 137 'tis not so great an] Q2–3; it is much less
Q1, Q4–5, F, D (a much F, D). 138 as] Q2–3; than Q1, Q4–5, F, D.
138 will:] Q1–2, Q4–5, D; ~ . Q3, F. 140 A parent's] Q2–3; Your
fathers Q1, Q4–5, F, D. 146 mine.] Q1–2, Q4–5, F, D; ~ : Q3. 148
desire:] Q1–5, D; ~ . F. 154 every] Q1–5, F; ev'ry D. 156+ *s.d.*
Giving] Q4–5, F, D; *giving* Q1–3. 163 Each] Q1–3, D; Earth Q4–5, F.
165 foes] Q1–2, Q4; Foe's Q3, Q5, F, D. 168 permit] Q1–5, D; commit F. 169 *s.d.* [*Exeunt*] Q4–5, F, D; ʌ~ Q1–3. 169+ *s.d.* Abdelmelech,] Q2–3, Q5, F, D; ~ . Q1, Q4. 169+ *s.d.* Zulema,] Q1–2, Q4–5,
F, D; Zulema; Zulema, Q3. 170 *Lyndaraxa's*] Q2–3, Q5, F, D; *Lindraxa's* Q1; *Lyndraxa's* Q4. 178 haste] Q1–4, F, D; hast Q5. 178
night;] Q1–4; ~ ! Q5, F, D. 179+ *s.d.* [*Exeunt*] Q4–5, F, D; ʌ~ Q1–3.
179+ *s.d.* Hamet] Q1–5, F; *and* Hamet D. 181 conquering] Q1–4;
conqu'ring Q5, F, D. 182 That] Q1–3; The Q4–5, F, D. 183 desert?]
F; ~ ! Q1–5, D. 184 every] Q1–5, F; ev'ry D. 186 you] Q1–2, Q4–
5, F, D; your Q3. 196 *Spanish*] Q3, F; Spanish Q1–2, Q4–5, F. 202
Moor did never] Q2–3; never Moor did Q1, Q4–5, F, D (*Moor* D). 223
fly;] Q1–3; ~ʌ Q4–5, F, D. 225 war,] Q1, Q3–5, F, D; ~ . Q2. 226
are.] Q1–5, F; ~ , D. 227 *Almanz.* Emboldn'd . . . Prince [*Putting one
knee on the ground.*] D (*knee to*); *Almanz. putting one knee on the ground.*
/ Emboldn'd . . . Prince Q1–5 (*knee to* Q4–5); [*Almanz. putting one Knee
to the Ground.* / *Almanz.* Embolden'd . . . Prince, F. 229+ *s.d.* [*The*]
Q2–5, F, D; ʌ~ Q1. 230 ignorant] Q3–5, F, D; ~ . Q1; ~ , Q2. 232
Mistress.] F; ~ : Q1–5, D. 234 make *Almanzor*] Q2–3, F, D; ~ʌ ~ ,
Q1; ~ , ~ , Q4; ~ , ~ʌ Q5. 235 your] Q1–4, F, D; you Q5. 238
Almah. Almanzor, . . . request: [*Softly to him.*] *Almahide softly to him.* /

Almanzor, . . . request: Q1–5, F; *Almah. softly to him.* Almanzor, . . . Request: D.   241 *Almanz.* I . . . love. [*To her.*] *Almanzor to her.* / I . . . love. Q1–5; [Almanzor *to her.* / *Almanz.* I . . . Love. F; *Almanz. to her.* I . . . Love. D.   244 *s.d.* [*To*] Q2–5, F, D; ∧∼ Q1.   244 *s.d. King:*] ∼ . Q1–2, Q4–5, D; ∼ , Q3; ∼∧ F.   244+ *s.d. first line kneeling: second rising: and boldly.*] Q1–5, D ([First D); *kneeling.* [*Rising.* [*Boldly.* F (*on ll. 245, 246, 248*).   245 best.] Q1–4; ∼ ; Q5, F, D.   253 sale?] Q1–5, D; ∼ : F.   265 you] Q1–4, F, D; thou Q5.   267 'ere] Q1, Q4; e're Q2–3; e'er Q5, F, D.   268 thee] Q1–4, F, D; the Q5.   268 thankless,] Q1–2, Q4–5, F; ∼∧ Q3, D.   270 dost] Q1–3; doest Q4; do'st Q5, F, D.   273 know] Q1–4; now Q5, F, D;   277 thee:] Q1–5, D; ∼ . F.   279 *Almahide*] Q1, Q4–5, F, D; *Almadide* Q2–3.   281 thy] Q1–5, F; the D.   281+ *s.d.* [*Takes*] Q2–5, D; ∧∼ Q1.   282+ *s.d.* [*The Guards*] Q4, F, D; ∧∼ ∼ Q1–3, Q5.   282 poor,] Q1–2, Q4–5, F, D; ∼ ! Q3.   283+ *s.d.* [*Almahide*] Q4–5, F, D; ∧∼ Q1–3.   286+ *s.d.* [*Abenamar*] Q4–5, F, D; ∧∼ Q1–3.   287 a way,] Q1–2, Q4, D; away Q3, Q5 (∼ . Q5), F.   288 every] Q1–5, F; ev'ry D.   289 pleasure] Q2–3; leisure Q1, Q4–5, F, D.   295 *centered in Q1.*   297 thee] Q1–2, Q4–5, F, D; the Q3.   297+ *s.d.* [*He*] Q2–5, F, D; ∧∼ Q1.   298 *Boab.* As . . . opprest, [*To* Almahide.] D; *Boabdel. to Almahide.* / As . . . opprest, Q1–5, F.   300 Bends . . . almost dead] Q2–3; And, bending . . . dead Q1, Q4–5, F, D.   301 While the loud . . . sings . . . drooping head:] Q2–3 (Head. Q2); Hears from within, the . . . sing . . . head: Q1, Q4–5, F, D.   304+ *s.d.* [*Almahide*] Q4–5, F, D; ∧∼ Q1–3.   305 *Almah.* So] F, D; So Q1–5.   305 flow'rs] Q2–3, D; flowr's Q1; flower's Q4–5, F.   305+ *s.d. Turning*] Q4–5, F, D; *turning* Q1–3.   306 myst'ry] Q1–4, D; mystery Q5, F.   306 lies] Q1–2, Q4–5, F; lyes Q3, D.   311 thousand] Q2–5, F, D; thousaud Q1.   313 *Almahida*] Q1–5, F; *Almahide* D.   322 prefer,] Q1–5, D; ∼ ? F.   328–329 *Almah.* To . . . you; / . . . [*Smiling scornfully.*] D; *Almahide smiling scornfully.* / To . . . you; Q1–5, F (*Almah.* To F).   331 debas'd] Q1–3; debase Q4–5, F, D.   334 away.] Q1–3, Q5, F, D; ∼ , Q4.   339 *s.d. guards.*] Q1–5, F (∼∧ Q5); *Guard.* D.   345 do?] ∼ ! Q1–5, F, D.   356 agree.] Q1–3; ∼ : Q4–5, F, D.   366 almost wish] Q2–3; wish me in Q1, Q4–5, F, D.   366+ *s.d.* [*Exeunt*] Q4–5, F, D; ∧∼ Q1–3.   370 death:] ∼ . Q1–5, F, D.   372 rapid,] Q3, F, D; ∼ ; Q1–2; ∼∧ Q4–5.   374 *Boabdelin.*] Q1, Q4–5, F, D; ∼ : Q2–3.   376 blest.] Q1–4, F; ∼ : Q5, D.   379 Fav'rite] Q1, Q4–5, F, D; Favorite Q2–3.   380 know] Q1–5, F; knew D.   380 'ere] Q1, Q4; e're Q2–3; e'er Q5, F, D.   380 loose] Q1–4 (lose Q2–4); lost Q5, F, D.   382 *s.d.* [*Looking*] Q2–5, F, D; ∧*looking* Q1.   385–386 *Almah.* That . . . be: / . . . [*Unbinding him.*] D; *Almahide unbinding him.* / That . . . be: Q1–5; Almahide *unbinding him.* / *Almah.* That . . . be: F.   398 wish] Q2–3; have Q1, Q4–5, F, D.   405 *Almanz.*] *on a line by itself in Q1.*   405 betray?] Q1, Q3–5, F, D; ∼∧ Q2.   406 *s.d.* [*To*] Q4–5, F, D; ∧*to* Q1; ∧*To* Q2–3.   414 What] Q2–3; When all my joys are gone / What Q1, Q4–5, F, D.   417 still.] Q1–4; ∼ , Q5; ∼ : F, D.   419 once] D; ∼ , Q1–5, F.   421 you?] D; ∼ ! Q1–5, F.   422 way;] Q2–3; ∼ . Q1, Q4–5, F, D.   427 through] Q1–4, F, D; throw Q5.   427 no] Q1–5, D; to F.   431 Vision] Q1, Q3–5, F, D; Visions Q2.   432 pain;] Q2–3; ∼∧ Q1; ∼ : Q4–5, F, D.   434

buildings] Q1–4, D; building Q5, F.   436   none] Q1–5, D; non F.   437
Almah. Your Heart's,] Q2–3; *Almah.* It was your fault that fire seiz'd all
your brest, / You should have blown up some, to save the rest. / But tis, Q1,
Q4–5, F, D (rest: D).   438   falls] Q1–3; fall Q4–5, F, D.   445   con-
tribute] Q2–3, Q5, F, D; *Contribute* Q1, Q4.   447   may] Q1–5, D; my F.
448   love!] Q1, Q4–5, F, D; ~∧ Q2; ~ , Q3.   448   thing!] Q1–4; ~∧ Q5;
~ , F, D.   452   raptures] Q2–3; transports Q1, Q4–5, F, D.   465
dare.] Q3–5, F, D; ~ , Q1–2.   466   part;] Q2–3; ~∧ Q1; ~ , Q4–5, F, D.
474   for if] Q1–4; or if Q5, F, D.   476   *s.d. Veyles*] Q4–5, F, D; *veyles*
Q1–3.   479+   *s.d. She*] Q2–5, F, D; *she* Q1.   480   Farewell] Q2–5, F,
D; Farwell Q1.   480   sufferings] Q1–5, F; Suff'rings D.   482+   *s.d.*
She] Q2–5, F, D; *she* Q1.   489   wind.] Q2–5, F, D; ~∧ Q1.   489+
s.d. [Exit] Q4–5, F, D; ∧~ Q1–3.   489+   *s.d. As . . . saluting.*] *not cen-
tered in Q1–5, F, D.*   491+   *s.d. not centered in Q1–5, F.*   491+   *s.d.*
Abdelmelech] Q2–5, F, D; Abdemelech Q1.   492   *Abdelmelech*] Q2–5,
F, D; *Abdemelech* Q1.   493   *Abdel.*] Q1, Q3–5, F, D; ~ , Q2.   496
th'] Q1–4, F, D; the Q5.   497   *Lyndaraxa's*] Q2–5, F, D; *Lindaraxa's*
Q1.   498   force.] Q3, F, D; ~ : Q1–2, Q4–5.   501+   *s.d. One*] Q2–3;
[~ Q1, Q4–5, F, D *(right justified)*.   503   *Ozmyn*] Q2–5, F, D; *Ozmin*
Q1.   506   Till] Q1–5, F; 'Till D.   510   *Almahida's*] Q1–5, F; *Alma-*
hide's D.   516   a while] Q1, Q3–5, F, D; awhile Q2.   516+   *s.d.*
[Exeunt] Q4–5, F, D; ∧~ Q1–3.

Epilogue: Epilogue.] Q1–5, F, D; Epilogue to the second part of the
Seige of Granada. spoken by Hart. M5.   1   *than*] Q1–5, F, D; then M5.
2   *favours*] Q1, Q4–5, F, D, M5; *Favour's* Q2–3.   2   *past:*] Q1–2, Q4–5,
F, D; ~ ? Q3; ~ . M5.   7   *Misses*] M5; ~ , Q1–5, F, D.   8   *Jilt*] Q1–
5, F, D; Gilt M5.   8   *'em*] Q1–5, D; them F, M5.   12   *Fop*] Q1–5, F,
D; ~ , M5.   18   *yet,*] Q1, Q4–5, F, D; ~∧ Q2–3, M5.   19   *live*] Q1–5,
D; *lives* F, M5.   21   *be*] Q1–5, F, D; bee M5.   22   *Well*] Q1, Q4–5,
F, D, M5; ~ , Q2–3.   22   *he may*] Q1–5, F, D; may hee M5.   23–24
M5 has marginal note: not spoke.   23   *Till*] Q1–5, F, M5; 'Till D.   23
do] Q1–5, F, D; doe M5.   29   *Theatre!*] Q1–3; ~ ; Q4–5, F, D, M5.
30   *year!*] Q1–5, F, D; ~ , M5.   31–32   *M5 has marginal note:* not
spoke.   32   *are*] Q1–5, F, D; were M5.   35–36   *M5 has marginal*
note: not spoke.   35   *do*] Q1–5, F, D; doe M5.   36   *fell!*] Q1–2, Q4–
5, F, D; ~ . Q3, M5.   37   *much has*] Q1–5, F, D; has much M5.   38
Play:] Q1–5, F, D; ~ . M5.   39   *does*] Q1–5, F, D; may M5.

Conquest of Granada, Part II

Prologue: title Second] Q1–5, F, D; first M5.   *title* Granada.] Q1–5,
F, D; Granada. Spoken by Mohun. M5.   1   *They . . . they*] Q1–5, F, D;
Those, . . . those, M5.   2   *out*] Q1–5, F, D; now out M5.   2   *Spight:*]
Q1–5, D; ~ . F, M5.   3   *A Play-house*] *A* Play-house Q1–5, F, D; A play
house M5.   3   *'em*] Q1–5, F, D; them M5.   3   *starts*] Q1, Q3–5, F, D,
M5; start Q2.   4   *mean . . . Parts.*] Q1–5, F, D; meere . . . ~ : M5.   6

We take 'em] Q1–5, F, D; Wee take them M5.   6   *here.*)] Q1–5, D, M5;
~ₐ) F.   8   *those . . . Hate.*] Q1–5, F, D; ~ , . . . ~ : M5.   10   *Scriv-
'ners*] Q1–5, F, D; Scriveners M5.   10–11   *between these lines M5 has:*
      Some of them seeme indeed yᵉ poetts freinds;
      But 'tis, as France courts England, for her ends.
      They build up this Lampoone, & th' other Songe,
      And Court him, to lye still, while they grow stronge.
12   *Play.*] Q1–5, F, D; ~ : M5.   13   *Vizard Masque*] Q1–5, F; *Vizard-
Mask* D; Vizor-Maskes M5.   13   *appears in*] Q1–5, F, D; appeare ith'
M5.   14   *every*] Q1–5, F, M5; ev'ry D.   14   *who*] Q1–5, F, D; that
M5.   15   *Perks . . . his*] Q1–5, F, D; Ierkes . . . the M5.   16   *white*]
Q1, Q3–5, F, D, M5; *Whit* Q2.   17   *bears*] Q1–5, F, D; bares M5.   20
Damm'ee] Q1, Q4–5, F, D; Damm, ye Q2–3; damm mee M5.   20   *no:*]
Q1–2, Q4–5, F, D; ~ . Q3, M5.   21   *these*] Q1–5, F, D; the M5.   23
fill'd;] Q1–3, F; ~ . Q4–5; ~ , D, M5.   25   *Vizard Masques*] Q1–2, Q4–
5, F; *Vizard-Masques* Q3, D; Vizor Maskes M5.   25   *that*] Q1–5, F, D;
yᵉ M5.   28   *asking:*] Q1–5, F, D; ~ . M5.

I, i

ACT] Q3–5, F, D; ~ . Q1–2.   SCENE] Q1, Q3–5; ~ . Q2; ~ , F;
SCENE I. SCENE, D.   *s.d.* King] Q1–5, F; *Enter King* D.   *s.d.* Isabel;]
Q2–3; ~ . Q1, Q4–5 (Ysabel Q1); ~ , F, D (Isabella D).   *s.d.* d'Aguilar;]
D; ~ . Q1–2, Q4–5; ~ , Q3, F.   2   *Moorish*] Q2–3, D; Moorish Q1, Q4–
5, F.   6   o'resees] Q2–5, F, D; 'oresees Q1.   7   Till] Q1–5, F; 'Till D.
8   about:] Q1–5, D; ~ . F.   11   Till] Q1–5, F; 'Till D.   15   it] Q1–3,
Q5, F, D; is Q4.   17   *Qu. Isabel.*] D; Qu. *Ysabel.* Q1; Qu. *Isabel.* Q2–5,
F.   22   Ore] Q1, Q4–5, F, D; Oar Q2–3.   24   Misbelievers] Q1–5, F;
Misbeliever's D.   28   *K.*] D; K. Q1–5, F.   28   find,] Q1–5, F; ~ . D.
32   guide,] Q1–2, Q4–5, D; ~ ; Q3; ~ . F.   37   *Qu. Isabel.*] D; Qu.
Ysabel. Q1; Qu. *Isabel.* Q2–5, F.   37   *Moorish*] Q3, D; Moorish Q1–2,
Q4–5, F.   39   *Ferd.*] Q1–5, F; *K. Ferd.* D.   42   throne;] Q3, F, D; ~ .
Q1–2, Q4–5.   44   you:] F; ~ . Q1–5, D.   51   assures.] Q3–5, F, D;
~ ; Q1; ~ : Q2.   51+   *s.d. Gives*] Q2–5, F, D; *gives* Q1.   52, 53   *K.*]
D; K. Q1–5, F.   53   *tertia*] Q2–3; tertia Q1, Q4–5, F, D.   53   *Italians*]
Q2–3, D; Italians Q1, Q4–5, F.   55   *Arcos.*] Q1–5, F; *D. Arcos.* D.   56
hast,] Q1–5, D; ~ . F.   59   *Ferd.*] Q1–5, F; *K. Ferd.* D.   60   *Arcos.*]
Q1–5, F; *D. Arcos.* D.   62   *Moor*] Q2–3, D; Moor Q1, Q4–5, F.   63
K.] D; K. Q1–5, F.   66   *Arcos.*] Q1–5, F; *D. Arcos.* D.   68   Till] Q1–
5, F; 'Till D.   69   *Moors*] Q2–3, D; Moors Q1, Q4–5, F.   69   who,]
Q1, Q4–5, D; ~ₐ Q2–3; ~ . F.   70   of the] Q1–5, F; of a D.   72
breath,] Q2–3, F, D; ~ₐ Q1, Q4–5.   72   stay:] Q1–5, D; ~ . F.   78
Moor] Q2–3, D; Moor Q1, Q4–5, F.   79   'ere] Q1, Q4–5, F; e're Q2–3;
e'er D.   89   *Isabel.*] Q2–5, F, D; *Ysabel.* Q1.   92   hate:] Q1–5, D;
~ . F.   93   I with him] Q1–5, F; with him I D.   106   better] Q2–5,
F, D; betters Q1.   108   *s.d. To her*] Q2–5, F, D; *to her* Q1.   115   *s.d.*
To Benz.] Q2–5, F, D; *to Benz.* Q1.   120   every] Q1–5, F; ev'ry D.   125
me to my own care;] Q2–3; Me, the care of Me; Q1, Q4–5, F, D.   130
be:] Q2–3; ~ . Q1, Q4–5; ~ ; F; ~ , D.   136   blood.] Q1, Q3–5, F; ~ ,
Q2, D.   137   *Ferd.*] Q1–5, F; *K. Ferd.* D.   138   *Ferdinand.*] Q3, D;

~ : Q1-2, Q4-5, F.   141   Isab.] Q1-2, Q4-5, F; Qu. Isa. Q3, D.   143
Granada] Q1-5, D; Granda F.   144   Her best] Q1-5, D; Here best F.
145   a] Q1; an Q2-5, F, D.   146   degenerate] Q1-5, F; degen'rate D.

I, ii

s.d. Zulema] Q2-5, F, D; [~ Q1.   1   Zul. True] F; True Q1-5, D.   2
Foe?] ~ ! Q1-5, F, D.   12+   s.d. Enter King] Q1-5, F; Enter D.   12+
s.d. and] Q2-5, F, D; and Q1.   20   every] Q1-5, F; ev'ry D.   20+   s.d.
within.] Q2-5, F, D; ~∧ Q1.   23   they] Q2-5, F, D; thy Q1.   24
Alarm;] Q1-5, D; ~ . F.   25   under-ground] Q1-5, D; under gronnd F.
26   sound.] Q1-5, F; ~ : D.   36   discontent:] Q1-5, D; ~ . F.   43
not, . . . be;] Q3, Q5, F, D; ~ ; . . . ~ , Q1-2, Q4.   48   are.] Q3-5, F, D;
~ : Q1-2.   49   Boab.] Q1, Q3-5, F, D; ~ , Q2.   56   Conquerour.]
Q3; ~ .: Q1; ~ : Q2, Q4-5, F, D.   58+   s.d. To] Q4-5, D; [~ Q1-3, F.
59   dangerous] Q1-5, F; dang'rous D.   62   Councel] Q1; Council Q2,
F; Counsel Q3-5, D.   70   does] Q2-3, Q5, F, D; ~ , Q1, Q4.   74   pros-
perously] Q1-5, F; prosp'rously D.   76   Sec.] Q1-5, F; 2 D.   76
Haste] Q1-3, F, D; Hast Q4-5.   77   rage.] Q3-5, F, D; ~ : Q1-2.   78
Third] Q1-5, F; 3 D.   82   Go,] Q1-5, F; ~∧ D.   83+   s.d. [Exit] Q4-
5, F, D; ∧~ Q1-3.   83+   s.d. Abdelmelech.] Q2-5, F, D; ~ , Q1.   84
has] Q2-5, F, D; has Q1.   85   hate.] Q1, Q3-5, F, D; ~∧ Q2.   89+
s.d. Acclamation] Q2-3; Acclamation's Q1; Acclamations Q4-5, F, D.   94
E're] Q1-5, F; E'er D.   95   detain;] Q1-5, D; ~ . F.   96   heard, last
night] Q1-2, Q4-5, F; ~∧ ~ ~, Q3; ~ , ~ ~ , D.   98   K. Boab.] Q1-5,
F; Boab. D.   100   pray.] Q3, F, D; ~ : Q1-2, Q4-5.   100+   s.d. them
Qu.] Q1-5, F; them D.   104   K. Boab.] Q1-5, F; Boab. D.   108
think,] Q2-3; ~∧ Q1, Q4-5, F, D.   110   boast,] Q1-3; ~ ? Q4-5, F, D.
111   That,] Q1, Q4-5, F, D; ~∧ Q2-3.   111   lost?] ~ ! Q1-3; ~ : Q4-5,
F, D.   112   why] Q3-5, F, D; ~ , Q1-2.   113   last?] Q4-5, F, D; ~ !
Q1-3.   116   first:] Q3; ~ . Q1-2, Q4-5, F; ~ , D.   118   Q. Almah.]
Q1-2, Q4-5, F; Alma. Q3, D.   124   K. Boab.] Q1-2, Q4-5, F; Boab. Q3,
D.   126   rev'rence] Q1-5, D; Reverence F.   130   footnote added in
Q2-3.   131   murmures] Q1-3; murmur Q4-5, F, D.   131   Loves.]
Q1-5, D; ~ : F.   134   Boab. Since, . . . Wife, / [Taking . . . hand.] D;
[Boab. taking . . . hand. / Since, . . . Wife, Q1-5, F.   153   return:] Q1-5,
D; ~ . F.   163   prevent:] ~ . Q1-5, F, D.   166   K. Boab] Q1-2, Q4-
5, F; Boab. Q3, D.   170   Q. Almah.] Q1-2, Q4-5, F; Alma. Q3, D.
173   Wife!] Q1-5, D; ~ . F.   175   Boab. Curst . . . born! / [Letting
. . . up.] D; [Boab. letting . . . up. / Curst . . . born! Q1-5, F.   180   Q.
Almah.] Q1-2, Q4-5, F; Alma. Q3, D.   180   understand;] Q1-3; ~∧
Q4-5; ~ . F, D.   189   State:] Q1-5, D; ~ . F.   191   die] Q1, Q4-5,
F, D; dye Q2-3.   191   fear.] Q1-5, D; ~ ; F.   194   Boab.] Q1-5, D;
~∧ F.   196   innocence:] Q2-3, F; ~ . Q1, Q4-5, D.   201   mind.]
Q1-3; ~ ; Q4-5, F, D.   205   Throne!] Q1; ~ . Q2; ~ ; Q3; ~ , Q4-5,
F, D.   209   still!] Q1-5, D; ~ , F.   210+   s.d. [Exit] Q4-5, F, D; ∧~
Q1-3.   211   Almah. My] F; My Q1-5, D.   221   I'le imitate Alman-
zor, and will be] Q2-3 (be, Q2); I'le, like Almanzor, act; and dare to be Q1,
Q4-5, F, D.   223   meant?] Q4-5, F, D; ~ ! Q1-3.   225   Silk-worm-
like] Q1, Q4-5, F; Silk-worm like Q2-3, D.   226+   s.d. [Exit] Q4-5, F,
D; ∧~ Q1-3.   226+   s.d. Almahide.] Q1-4, F, D; ~∧ Q5.

II, i

ACT] Q2–5, F, D; ∼ . Q1.   SCENE] Q1–5, F; SCENE I. SCENE D.
s.d. Ozmyn *and* Benzayda.] Q2–5, F, D (*Enter* Ozmyn D; Benzayda∧ Q3);
Ozmyn and *Benzayda.* Q1.   2   in a] Q2–3; in the Q1, Q4–5, F, D.   2
Spanish] D; Spanish Q1–5, F.   6   Pow'r] Q1–5, D; Power F.   6
Spain.] Q1–2, Q4–5, F, D; ∼ : Q3.   8   flight.] Q3, F, D; ∼ : Q1–2, Q4–5.
9   *Ozm.*] Q1–5, D; *Oxmyn.* F.   10+   *s.d.* [*A . . . within,* Follow, follow,
follow————] *A . . . within follow, follow, follow———* Q1–5, F, D (*some
copies of Q1 have* follow.————; [*A* Q4–5, F, D; *within,* Q2–3, Q5, F, D;
Follow D).   13   save?] Q3; ∼ ; Q1–2, Q4–5, F; ∼ ! D.   14   dregs]
Q2–3, D; *dregs* Q1, Q4–5, F.   14   grave.] Q1–5, D; ∼ ! F.   14+   *s.d.*
Sits] Q2–5, F, D; *sits* Q1.   18   distrest.] Q3, F, D; ∼ : Q1–2, Q4–5.   19
opprest:] Q1–5, D; ∼ . F.   23+   *s.d.* [*Exit*] Q4–5, F, D; ∧∼ Q1–3.
23+   *s.d.* Moors.] Q1–5, F; ∼ , D.   28–29   *Ozmyn.* Who . . . me; / . . .
[*Shewing himself.*] *Ozmyn; shewing himself.* / Who . . . me; Q1–5, D (*one
line in D*); Ozmyn, *showing himself.* / *Ozm.* Who . . . me; F.   30   *s.d.*
[*Knows*] Q2–5, F, D (*s.d. on l. 29 in D*); ∧knows Q1.   33   Son.] Q1–5, F;
∼ , D.   35   *Roman*] Q2–3, D; Roman Q1, Q4–5, F.   41   Son:] Q1–2,
Q4–5, F; ∼ . Q3, D.   44–45   *Aben.* Yes; . . . thee. / . . . [*To a Sold.*] D;
Aben. to a Sold. / Yes; . . . thee: Q1–5; Aben. *to a Soldier.* / *Aben.* Yes, . . .
thee: F.   44   done, on him] Q1–2, Q4–5; ∼∧ ∼ ∼ , Q3; ∼∧ ∼ ∼ F, D.
53   own.] Q3, Q5, F, D; ∼ ; Q1–2, Q4.   55   *Ozmyn.* Then . . . dye. /
[*Putting . . . Selin.*] D; *Ozmyn putting himself before* Selin. / Then . . . dye.
Q1–5 (die∧ Q5); Ozmyn *putting himself before* Selin. / *Ozm.* Then, . . . die.
F.   58   have.] Q3, F, D; ∼ : Q1–2, Q4–5.   58+   *s.d.* [Aben.] Q4–5,
F, D; ∧∼ Q1–3.   58+   *s.d.* Spaniards.] Q1–5, D; ∼ , F.   59   save.]
Q1–3; ∼ ! Q4–5, F, D.   61–62   *Ozmyn.* Stay . . . here. / . . . [*Stops his
hand.* D ([*Stops Abdalla's Hand.* (*on l.* 62)); *Ozmyn stops his hand.* / Stay
. . . here. Q1–5; Ozmyn *stops his Hand.* / *Ozm.* Stay . . . here. F.   62
spoke] Q1–2, Q4; ∼ , Q3, F, D; ∼ . Q5.   64   *Arcos.* Depart, . . . Son. [*To
Aben.*] *Arcos to Aben.* / Depart, . . . Son: Q1–5, F, D (*D. Arcos* D; *same line*
F, D; Son. Q3–5, F, D).   66–67   *Ozm.* Heav'n . . . resign, / . . . [*To his
father.*] *Ozm. to his father.* / Heav'n . . . resign, Q1–5, F, D (*same line* F, D).
68   crime?] Q4–5, F, D; ∼ ! Q1–3.   71   haunt thee] Q1–5, D; haunt the
F.   71+   *s.d.* [*Exit*] Q4–5, F, D; ∧∼ Q1–3.   72–73   *Ozmyn.* Can . . .
degree / . . . [*Kneeling to* Selin.] F, D ([*Ozmyn kneeling* F); *Ozmyn kneeling
to* Selin. / Can . . . degree Q1–5.   76   separate th'] Q1–5, F; sep'rate the
D.   76   offence?] D; ∼ ! Q1–5, F.   78   *s.d.* [*Offers*] Q2–5, F, D; ∧∼
Q1.   79   fate] Q1–5, D; fat F.   85   care?] Q3; ∼ ! Q1–2, Q4–5, F, D.
89   Daughter] Q2–5, F, D; Daugher Q1.   90   *Benzaida*] Q1–2; *Benzayda* Q3–5, F, D.   91   *Ozmyn.* Blest . . . restore. / [*Embracing his knees.*]
D; *Ozmyn embracing his knees.* / Blest . . . restore. Q1–5 (restore∧ Q5);
[*Ozmyn embracing his knees.* (*on l.* 90) / *Oxm.* Blest . . . restore. F.   93
tenderness.] Q1–5, D; ∼ , F.   94   *Benzayda*] Q3–5, F, D; *Benzaida* Q1–2.
98   *s.d. To*] Q2–5, F, D; *to* Q1.   98   *s.d.* him.] Q1–5, D; ∼ , F.   101
you:] Q1–2, Q4–5, D; ∼ . Q3, F.   102   may] Q1–5, D; my F.   109
need:] Q1, Q4–5, D; ∼ . Q2–3, F.   114   And . . . fear,] Q3; ∼ , . . . ∼∧
Q1–2, Q4–5; ∼ , . . . ∼ , F, D.   117   news.] Q1–3, Q5, F, D; ∼ : Q4.
122   Since she refus'd] Q1–4; Since she refuse Q5; If she refuse F, D.   126

haste] Q1–4, F, D; hast Q5.   130 lies,] Q4–5, F, D; ~ . Q1–3 (lyes Q3).
131 may] Q1–5, D; my F.   131 supplies,] Q1–4, F, D; ~ . Q5.   132
Town.] Q3, F; ~ ; Q1–2, Q4–5, D.   133 renown;] Q1–5, D; ~ . F.
135+ *s.d. [Exit]* Q4–5, F, D; ∧~ Q1–3.   136 *Abdal.*] Q1–4, F, D;
Abdel. Q5.   136 *s.d. Aside*] Q4–5, F, D; *aside* Q1–3.   143+ *s.d.*
[Exit] Q4–5, F, D; ∧~ Q1–3.   148 till] Q1–5, F; 'till D.   152 your]
Q1, Q4–5, F, D; our Q2–3.   155 forsake.] Q1–4, F; ~ , Q5; ~ : D.
156 draw my] Q1–5, D; draw may F.   161 part.] Q1, Q3–5, F, D; ~∧
Q2.   162 attend] Q1, Q4–5, F; ~ ; Q2–3; ~ , D.   163 end.] Q1,
Q4–5, F, D; ~ : Q2–3.   165 Wind?] Q3, F, D; ~ . Q1–2, Q4–5.   170
Ozmyn. Then . . . be *[To her.]* D; Ozmyn *to her.* / Then . . . be Q1–5; [Oz-
myn *to her. (on l. 169)* / Ozm. Then . . . be, F.   171 your Father,] Q1–5,
D; ~ , ~ , F.   175 *[Exeunt.]* Q5, F, D; ∧~∧ Q1; ∧~ . Q2–4.

II, ii

SCENE II.] SCENE. Q1–5, F, D.   *s.d. An*] [~ Q1–5, F, D.   *s.d. Stage.*]
Q1–5, D; ~ , F.   3 every] Q1–5, F; ev'ry D.   8+ *s.d. affrighted*]
Q1–4; *frighted* Q5, F, D.   9 Go] Q1–5, F; ~ , D.   9 bring] Q1–4,
F, D; and bring Q5.   11 self,] Q2–3, D; ~∧ Q1, Q4–5, F.   13 wish'd]
Q1–4, F, D; wish Q5.   15 Woman] D; *Woman* Q1–5, F (~ , Q1).   17
Hyæna] *Hyæna* Q1–5, F, D.   21 overwise] Q1, Q4–5, F, D; otherwise
Q2–3.   25 Fame,] Q2–5, F, D; ~ . Q1.   30 Till] Q1–5, F; 'Till D.
31 lov'd?] Q4–5, F, D; ~ ! Q1–3.   33 Trust?] Q4–5, F, D; ~ ! Q1–3.
36 for] Q1–5, F; of D.   36 Enemy.] Q1–4, D; ~ ? Q5; ~∧ F.   37
true,] Q1, Q3–5, F, D; ~ . Q2.   37 Fortress] Q2–5, F, D; Fottress Q1.
41 indeed, . . . intent;] Q3, F; ~ ; . . . ~ , Q1–2, Q4–5, D.   42 th'] Q1–
4, D; the Q5, F.   43 *Lyndaraxa*] Q2–5, F, D; *Lindaraxa* Q1.   46
Grace:] Q1–5, D; ~ . F.   49 create;] Q3–5, F, D; ~ . Q1–2.   53 you]
Q2–3; we Q1, Q4–5, F, D.   59 *Alferez,*] Q1, Q3–5, F, D; ~ . Q2 (*indented, as a speech heading; still indented in Q3*).   59 *s.d. on l. 58 in*
Q1–2, Q4–5.   59 *s.d. Soldier.*] Q1–2, Q4–5, F, D; ~∧ Q3.   60 peace?]
Q3; ~ ! Q1–2, Q4–5, F, D.   59+ *s.d. [Exit]* Q4–5, F, D (*s.d. after l. 60*);
∧~ Q1–3 (*s.d. after l. 60*).   61 afford?] Q3, F, D; ~ ! Q1–2, Q4–5.   64
you are] Q2–5, F, D; your are Q1.   66 Heart?] ~ ! Q1–5, F, D.   68
you!] Q1–2, Q4–5, F, D; ~ . Q3.   69, 71 our] Q1–4; your Q5, F, D.
74 of] Q1–5, F; on D.   74 root.] Q1–4, F; ~ , Q5; ~ ; D.   78
again.] Q1–5, D; ~∧ F.   80 love.] Q1–4, D; ~∧ Q5, F.   82 confest.]
Q1–5, D; ~ : F.   89 show,] D; show, [*Alferez.* Q1–5, F (*on l. 90 in Q4–5,*
F).   90 Foe.] Q3, F, D; ~ , Q1–2, Q4–5.   91 move?] ~ ! Q1–5, F,
D.   94 live:] Q1–5, D; ~ . F.   96 rifle] Q2–5, F, D; riflle Q1.   98
seize.] Q2–5, F, D; ~ . Q1.   101 *Abdel.*] Q1–5, D; ~∧ F.   102 Conquerour?] ~ ! Q1–5, F, D (Conqu'rour Q2–3).   103 till] Q1–5, F; 'till D.
104 is] Q2–3; was Q1, Q4–5, F, D.   105 every] Q1–5, F; ev'ry D.   106
heart.] Q3, F; ~ : Q1–2, Q4–5, D.   107 *s.d. [To a Sold.]* Q3, F; *on line*
above in Q1–2, Q4–5, D.   107 *s.d. Sold.*] Q1–5, D; *Soldier*∧ F.   109+
s.d. [Exit] Q4–5, F, D; ∧~ Q1–3.   112 *Albazyin*] Q2–3; *Albazin* Q1;
Albazyn Q4–5, F; *Albayzyn* D.   113+ *s.d. [Trumpets]* Q2–5, F, D; ∧~
Q1.   115 *Lynd.*] Q2–5, F, D; *Lind.* Q1.   115 *s.d. Aside.*] Q4–5, F,
D (~∧ F); *aside.* Q1–3.   122 *s.d. [To her.]* *on l. 123 in F.*   122 *s.d.*
To] Q2–5, F, D; *to* Q1.   123 flatt'ries] Q1–4; flatteries Q5, F, D.   125

wary] Q1–4; weary Q5, F, D.   130   *Lynd.*] Q2–5, F, D; *Lind.* Q1.   130
obligements know] Q1–4; obligement knows Q5; Obligement know F, D.
133   *s.d.* [*Looking*] Q2–5, F, D (*looking* Q2–3); ∧*looking* Q1.   135   *omit-*
ted by F.   135+   *s.d.* [*He*] Q4–5, F, D; ∧~ Q1–3.   135+   *s.d.* cries]
Q1–4; cries out Q5, F, D.   135+   *s.d.* Help.] help: Q1–2; help. Q3–5, F;
Help. D.   135+   *s.d.* Spaniards] Q2–3, D; *Spaniards* Q1, Q4–5, F.
135+   *s.d.* Arcos,] Q3–4; ~ . Q1–2; ~∧ Q5, F, D.   135+   *s.d.* *Lyn-*
daraxa.] Q1–4, F, D; ~∧ Q5.   136   *Arcos*] Q1–5, F; D. Arcos D.   136
Spaniards] Q3, D; Spaniards Q1–2, Q4–5, F.   138–139   *Abdalla.* Your
. . . fire, / . . . [*To* Lyndar.] D; Abdalla *to* Lyndar. / Your . . . fire, Q1–5, F (*Ab-*
dalla to Lyndar. Q1).   140   had he] Q1–2, Q4–5, F, D; he had Q3.   142
Lynd.] Q2–5, F, D; *Lind.* Q1.   143   giv'n] Q1–3, Q5, F, D; given Q4.
144–145   *as in Q2–3; Q1, Q4–5, F, D have:*
> You see, Sir, with what hardship I have kept
> This precious gage which in my hands you left.

146   fight,] Q2–5, F, D; ~ . Q1.   147   right.] Q2–5, F, D; ~∧ Q1.   151
all.] Q1, Q4–5, F, D; ~ , Q2; ~ ; Q3.   156   *Abdal.*] Q1, Q4–5, F, D;
Abdel. Q2–3.   157   Soveraign] Q1–5, F; Sov'reign D.   159   lies.] Q1,
Q4–5, F; lies: Q2; lyes: Q3; lyes. D.   161   *Spaniards*] Q2–3, F, D; Span-
iards Q1, Q4–5.   161   Imperial] Q1–3, Q5, F, D; Imperil Q4.   162
Lyn.] Q2–5, F, D; *Lin.* Q1.   162   share:] Q1–5, D; ~ . F.   166+   *s.d.*
[*Exeunt:*] F; ∧*Exeunt.* Q1–5, D ([~ Q4–5, D).

II, iii

SCENE III.] SCENE, Q1–5, F, D (~∧ Q2–3, F, D; ~ . Q5).   *s.d.* Boab-
delin, Abenamar, Almahide;] Q2–4, F, D (Almahide, *and* D); *Boabdelin,*
Abenamar, Almahide; Q1.   4   threatning] Q1, Q3–5, F, D; threatening
Q2.   5   *Greek*] F, D; Greek Q1–5.   9   driv'n] Q1–4, D; driven Q5,
F.   10   Heav'n] Q1–4, D; Heaven Q5, F.   11   aid;] Q1–5; ~ , F; ~ !
D.   12   Not] Q2–5, F, D; No Q1.   12   *Almahida's*] Q1–5, F; *Alma-*
hide's D.   12   sake.] Q1–5, D; ~ ! F.   19   had not sent] Q1, Q4–5,
F, D; sent Q2; ever sent Q3.   20   Crown;] Q1–5, F; ~ ! D.   20   lost!]
Q1–2, Q4–5, F, D; ~ . Q3.   24   on] Q1–5, D; at F.   26   eyes.] Q1–5, F;
~ : D.   28+   *s.d.* [*Exit*] Q4–5, F, D; ∧~ Q1–3.   28+   *s.d.* Guards]
Q1–5, D; *Guard* F.   28+   *s.d.* seeing] Q2–5, F, D; *seing* Q1.   30   and]
Q2–3; or Q1, Q4–5, F, D.   30   would] Q1–5, D; should F.   32   yield-
ing] Q2–3; liquid Q1, Q4–5, F, D.   33   flies:] Q1–2, Q4–5, F, D; ~ . Q3.
34   every] Q1–5, F; ev'ry D.   37   *s.d.* [*To*] F, D; ∧~ Q1–5 (*after l. 36 in*
Q1–5, D).   38   goe:] Q1–5, F; ~ . D.   42   distrest.] Q1, Q3–5, F, D;
~ : Q2.   45   behold] Q1–3, D; ~ , Q4, F; ~ . Q5.   46   enjoy:] Q1–5,
F; ~ . D.   46   gold] Q4–5, F, D; ~ ; Q1–2; ~ , Q3.   51   please,] F;
~ . Q1–2, Q4–5; ~ : Q3, D.   55   view,] Q1–2, Q4–5, F, D; ~ . Q3.   56
new.] Q1–2, Q4–5, F, D; ~ , Q3.   70   sov'raign] Q1–4, D; soveraign Q5,
F.   74   Content:] Q1–5; ~ . F, D.   75–76   *omitted from Q5, F, D.*
77   *Almahide.*] Q2–5, F, D; ~ , Q1.   77   yields,] Q3–5, F, D; ~∧ Q1–2.
79   move?] ~ ! Q1–5, F, D.   81   the] Q1–4; a Q5, F, D.   82   Land,]
Q3, F, D; ~ . Q1–2, Q4–5.   83   Flow'ry] Q3–5, F, D; Flow'rs Q1–2.
85   Love's] Q1, Q4–5, F, D; Loves Q2–3.   88   see.] Q3–5, F, D; ~ : Q1–
2.   92   you] Q1–3; your Q4–5, F, D.   96   sake.] Q3; ~ , Q1–2; ~ :
Q4–5, F, D.   98   goe.] Q1, Q4–5, F, D; ~ ; Q2–3.   102   know] now

Q1–5, F, D.   106 *footnote added in Q2–3.*   109 worn.] Q3–5, F, D;
~ : Q1–2.   114 oh] Q1–3; O Q4–5, F, D.   115 denies.] Q1–2; ~ !
Q3–5, F, D.   115+ *s.d. [Exeunt]* Q4–5, F, D; ∧~ Q1–3.

III, i

ACT] Q2–5, F, D; ~ . Q1.   III.] Q1–5, F; III. SCENE I. D.   *s.d.*
Alhambra.] Q1–4, F, D; ~ , Q5.   *s.d.* Almahide *and* Esperanza.] D (*Enter*
Almahide); *Almahide, Esperanza.* Q1–5, F (*Almahide and* Q2–3).   7+
s.d. To] Q4–5, D; [~ Q1–3, F.   7+ *s.d. apart.*] Q2–5, F, D; ~ : Q1.
11 *Boab.* Marriage . . . Life, [*Aside.*] D; [Boabdelin *aside.* / Marriage . . .
Life, Q1–3; Marriage . . . Life, [Boab. *aside.* Q4–5, F.   15 please] Q2–5,
F, D; pleas Q1.   20 sowr] Q1, Q3–5, F, D; sower Q2.   23–24 *Alma-*
hide. Has . . . had? / . . . [*Walking to him.* D; [Almahide *walking to him.* /
Has . . . had? Q1–5 (∧Almahide Q4–5); [Almahide *walking to him.* (*on l.*
22) / *Almah.* Has . . . had? F.   25 You, nothing, . . . alone!] Q1–2, Q4–5,
F; ~ ! ~ , . . . ~ . Q5; ~ ! ~ : . . . ~ ! D.   26 till] Q1–5, F; 'till D.   26
known:] Q1–5, D; ~ . F.   27 relief.] Q3–5, F, D; ~ ; Q1–2.   33 more:]
Q1–5, D; ~ . F.   35 hand!] Q1–5, D; ~ . F.   36 withstand?] Q1–3;
~ ! Q4–5, F, D.   37 *Boab.* O . . . alone! / [*Sighing* . . . *her.*] D (Oh);
[Boab. *sighing* . . . *her.* / O . . . alone! Q1–5 (Boab∧ Q1; ∧Boab. Q2–3);
[*Boab. sighing* . . . *her.* / Boab. O . . . alone! F.   38 Hearts] Q1–4, F, D;
Heart Q5.   38 known?] ~ ! Q1–5, F, D.   43–44 *Almah.* Why . . .
croud / . . . [*Approaching him.*] D; [Almah. *approaching him.* / Why . . .
croud Q1–5 (∧Alma. Q2–3); [Almah *approaching him.* (*on l. 42*) / *Almah.*
Why . . . croud, F.   49 made!] Q1–5, D; ~——— F.   50 Guilt;]
Q1–5, F; ~ ! D.   52 conceal!] Q1–5, D; ~ . F.   54 so.] Q1, Q3–5,
F, D; ~ , Q2.   58 *s.d. She*] Q2–5, F, D; *she* Q1.   63 *Egypt*] D; Egypt
Q1–5, F.   70 lie] Q1, Q4; lye Q2–3, Q5, F, D.   76 Not] Q1–3, D;
Nor Q4–5, F.   76 Heav'n] Q1, Q3–5, F, D; Heaven Q2.   77 assign'd]
Q2–5, F, D; asign'd Q1.   79 wife.] Q1–2, Q4–5; ~ ! Q3, F, D.   81
given] Q1–2, Q4–5, F; giv'n Q3, D.   83+ *s.d. [Pointing]* Q4–5, F, D;
∧~ Q1–3.   83+ *s.d.* Almanzor's] Q2–5, F, D; Almonzor's Q1.   84
rare!] Q1–5, D; ~ . F.   85 Heav'ns,] Q1–4, D; Heavens, Q5, F (~ ! F).
85 despair?] F; ~ ! Q1–5, D.   88 *Almah.* You'r . . . jealousy, [*To Al-*
manz.] *Almah. to Almanz.* / You'r . . . jealousy, Q1–5, D (*on same line in D*);
Almahide *to Almanzor.* / *Almah.* You'r . . . Jealousie, F.   96 know,]
Q1–5, D; ~ . F.   100 dev'l] Q1–4; devil Q5, F, D.   101 Heaven]
Q1, Q4–5, F; Heav'n Q2–3, D.   102 Go,] Q1–2, Q4–5, F, D; ~∧ Q3.
102 *s.d. [To]* Q4–5, F, D; ∧~ Q1–3.   115 defend:] Q1–2, Q4–5, D; ~ .
Q3, F.   117 raign.] Q3–5, F, D. ~ , Q1–2.   118 place] Q5, F, D; ~ ;
Q1–4.   119 disgrace.] Q1–4, F; ~∧ Q5, D.   121 alone,] Q1, Q3–5,
F, D; ~ . Q2.   125 *Almah.* As . . . sent, [*To Boab.*] *Almahide to Boab-*
delin. / As . . . sent, Q1–5, F, D (*on same line in F, D*).   141 *Almanz.*
The . . . stand, / [*Pulling* . . . *her.*] D; *Almanz. pulling* . . . *her.* / The . . .
stand, Q1–5; [Almanzor *pulling* . . . *her.* / *Almanz.* The . . . stand, F.
142+ *s.d. it*] Q1–4; *it to* Q5, F, D.   144 *Turnus*] Q4–5, F, D; *Turnu's*
Q1–3.   148+ *s.d. [An]* Q2–5, F, D; ∧~ Q1.   151 unfortunate:] F;
~ . Q1–4; ~ , Q5, D.   153 *Spaniards*] Q2–3, D; Spaniards Q1, Q4–5, F.
155–156 *Abenam.* Why . . . Sir? . . . near: / . . . [*To Alman.*] *Abenam. to*
Alman. / Why . . . Sir, . . . near: Q1–5, F, D (Sir? Q3, D; near? Q5, F; *on*

same line in F, D).　157　sight.] Q1–4, F, D; ∼ , Q5.　159　lift] Q1–3,
Q5, F, D; left Q4.　159　an] Q1–5, F; my D.　160　Yet will I not re-
move . . . hence:] Q2–3; And yet I wonnot stir . . . ∼ . Q1, Q4–5, F, D.　163
s.d. on l. 162 in Q1–5, F.　163　*s.d.* To] Q2–5, F, D; *to* Q1.　165　owe:]
Q2–3; ∼ . Q1, Q4–5, F, D.　168+　*s.d. [Exeunt]* Q4–5, F, D; ∧∼ Q1–3.
168+　*s.d. within.*] Q1, Q4–5, F, D; ∼∧ Q2.　169　th'] Q1, Q3–5, F, D;
the Q2.　170　'ere] Q1, Q4; e're Q2–3, Q5, F; e'er D.　177　love?] ∼ !
Q1–5, F, D.　180+　*s.d. [Exeunt]* Q4–5, F, D; ∧∼ Q1–3.　181　O]
Q1–5, F; Oh D.　183　ev'n] Q1, Q4–5, F, D; even Q2–3.　187　tow'rs]
Q2–3, Q5, F, D; towr's Q1, Q4.　190　before:] Q1–2, Q4–5, D; ∼ . Q3, F.
194–196　*brace omitted from Q1, Q4–5.*　194　me;] Q1–5, D; ∼ . F.
196　fight,] Q1–5, D; ∼ . F.　200+　*s.d. [Exeunt. An Alarm within.]*
Q4–5, F, D ([*An*); *An Alarm within. Exeunt.* Q1–3.　201–202　*Alman.*
You . . . owe / . . . [*To* Abdal.] D; *Alman. to Abdal.* / You . . . owe Q1–5, F
(*on same line in F*).　202　respect] Q2–3; regard Q1, Q4–5, F, D.　211
ow] Q1–2, Q4–5, F, D; know Q3.　215　giv'n] Q1–4, D; given Q5, F.
216　Heav'n] Q1–4, D; Heaven Q5, F.　216+　*s.d. [Exeunt]* Q4–5, F, D;
∧∼ Q1–3.

III, ii

SCENE II.] SCENE Q1–5, F, D (∼ . Q2; ∼ , Q4–5, F).　5　*Ozmyn.*]
Q1–5, F; ∼ , D.　6　I withdrew] Q2–3; twice I drew Q1, Q4–5, F, D.　6
press.] Q1–5, F; ∼ : D.　9　gen'ral] Q1–4; general Q5, F, D.　10
loosening] Q1–2, Q4–5, F; loos'ning Q3, D.　10　crack,] Q3, Q5, F, D;
∼∧ Q1–2, Q4.　11　one,] Q3; ∼ ; Q1–2, Q4–5, F, D.　12　wind;] Q4–
5, F, D; ∼ , Q1–2, ∼ : Q3.　18　rul'st] Q1–4, D; rulest Q5, F.　18
here] Q2–3; there Q1, Q4–5, F, D.　19　Empyre's] Q1–4, F, D; Empires
Q5.　22　mak'st] Q1–4, D; makest Q5, F.　22+　*s.d.* Duke of Arcos,
Lyndaraxa,] Q2–3; Lyndaraxa, *Duke of* Arcos, Q1, Q4–5, F, D.　22+　*s.d.*
Guards] Q4–5, F, D; Guards Q1–3.　23　*Arcos.*] Q1–4, F, D; ∼ : Q5.
23　were] Q1–4, F; are Q5, D.　25　complain!] D; ∼ , Q1, Q4–5; ∼ .
Q2–3; ∼ ; F.　34　Cells:] ∼ . Q1–5, F, D.　36+　*s.d. [A]* Q4–5, F, D;
∧∼ Q1–3.　42　love] Q1–5, D; Life F.　42　gave.] Q3–5, F, D; ∼ :
Q1–2.　43　*Lynd.*] Q2–5, F, D; *Lind.* Q1.　44　*Abdelmelechs*] Q2–5,
F, D; *Adelmelechs* Q1.　45　hands.] Q4–5, F, D; ∼ : Q1–3; ∼ , D.　46
Lynd.] Q2–5, F, D; *Lind.* Q1.　46　bands,)] Q1–2, Q4–5, F, D; ∼ .) Q3.
48　*Arcos.*] Q1–5, F; D. Arcos. D.　54　*Lynd.*] Q2–5, F, D; *Lind.* Q1.
55　freed,] Q1–5; ∼ . F; ∼ ; D.　57　know;] Q1–4; ∼ , Q5, D; ∼ . F.
58　He's made] Q2–3; He is Q1, Q4–5, F, D.　58　Foe:] ∼ . Q1–5, F, D.
59　Kept,] Q1–5, D; ∼ . F.　59　Alhambra] Q2–3, Q5, F, D; *Almambra*
Q1, Q4.　59　Tour] Q1–3, D; Tower Q4–5, F.　66　e're] Q1–5, F;
e'er D.　66　to] Q1–2, Q4–5, F, D; too Q3.　67　E're] Q1–5, F; E'er
D.　68　Council] Q1–2; Counsel Q3–5, F, D.　70+　*s.d. [Exeunt]*
Q4–5, F, D; ∧∼ Q1–3.　76　Human] Q1, Q4–5, F, D; humane Q2–3.
78　obey.] Q2–5, F, D; ∼ , Q1.　80　forgot] Q1–4, F, D; forget Q5.　80
name:] ∼ . Q1–5, F, D.　84　do?] Q5, F, D; ∼ ! Q1–4.　85　does] Q1–
5, F; doe's D.　87　*Ozmyn,*] Q2–5, F, D; ∼ . Q1.　89　forsake:] Q4–5,
F, D; ∼ . Q1–3.　93　Foe? . . . fall?] ∼ ! . . . ∼ ! Q1–5, F, D.　94　He]
Q2–3; It Q1, Q4–5, F, D.　98　way:] Q1–5, D; ∼ . F.　104　again!]
Q1–4; ∼ . Q5, F, D.　107　These] Q1–5, F; Those D.　110　chains.]

Q1–5, F; ~ ! D.   116   grasps] Q1–4, F, D; grasp's Q5.   121   show?]
~ ; Q1–5, F, D.   122   Masculine] D; *Masculine* Q1–5, F.   124+   *s.d.*
[*Exit*] Q4–5, F, D; ‸~ Q1–3.   134   lie] Q1, Q4–5, F; lye Q2–3, D.

III, iii

SCENE III.] SCENE Q1–5, F, D (SCENE. Q4–5; SCENE, F).   *s.d. the
one*] Q1–4; *one* Q5, F, D.   *s.d.* Hamet:] ~ . Q1–5, F, D.   *s.d. and their
party*] Q2–5, F, D; and their party Q1.   *s.d. At the same*] *After which the
Barrs are opened; and at the same* Q1, Q4–5, F, D; *The same* Q2–3.   *s.d.
approaches,*] Q2–3; approaches the Barrs, Q1, Q4–5, F, D.   1   *Arc.*] Q1–
5, F; *D. Arcos.* D.   12   some] Q1–4, F, D; some some Q5.   13   *Arcos.*]
Q1–5, F; *D. Arcos.* D.   17   can,] Q3, F, D; ~ ; Q1–2, Q4–5.   19
would . . . valour] Q3–5, F, D; ~ , . . . ~ , Q1–2.   24   Sir, we should
value] Q2–3; we should esteem 'em Q1, Q4–5, F, D.   30–32   *brace omitted from Q1, Q4–5, F.*   33   *Arcos.*] Q1–5, F; *D. Arcos.* D.   45   *Arcos.
. . . one*] Q1–5, F; *D. Arcos. . . . a* D.   45   valour] Q1–4, D; value Q5, F.
46   you:] ~ . Q1–5, F, D.   47   beauteous] Q2–3, D; beaut'ous Q1, Q4–
5, F.   47   Queen] Q2–5, F, D; Qneen Q1.   49   be it] Q1, Q3–5, F, D;
it be Q2.   49+   *s.d. them.*] Q1–5, D; ~‸ F.   53   ———You] Q2–3;
‸~ Q1, Q4–5, F, D.   57   *Arcos.*] Q1–5, F; *D. Arcos.* D.   58   *s.d. retire*] Q2–5, F, D; *retire* Q1.   59   Heart!] Q1–5, D; ~ ? F.   60   Art:]
Q1–5, D; ~ . F.   62   Wooe.] Q1–5, F; ~ , D.   65   scape] Q1–5, F;
'scape D.   66   he, without, resistance] Q1, Q4–5, F, D; ~‸ ~‸ ~‸ Q2;
~‸ ~‸ ~ , Q3.   67   e're] Q1–5, F; e'er D.   68   You] F; *Lynd.* You
Q1–5, D.   68   remedy] Q1–5, D; ~ . F.   69   fly:] F; ~ . Q1–5, D.   90
self] Q4–5, F, D; ~ ; Q1–3.   91   possess:] Q2; ~ , Q1; ~ ! Q3; ~ . Q4–5,
F, D.   98   every] Q1–5, F; ev'ry D.   101   Ear:] Q1–5, D; ~ . F.   103
raise:] Q1–2, Q4–5, F, D; ~ . Q3.   105   Pride:] ~ . Q1–5, F, D.   112
before,] Q3–5, F, D; ~) Q1–2.   122   and] Q2–3; nor Q1, Q4–5, F, D.
124   desires,] F, D; ~ ; Q1–5.   131   till] Q1–5, F; 'till D.   133   Air.]
Q1–5, D; ~ : F.   139   than] Q1–5, D; then F.   146   reason's] Q1–5,
D; Reasons' F.   147   ground:] ~ . Q1–5, F, D.   168   the] F, D; th'
Q1–5.   172   *Almanz.*] Q2–5, F, D; ~ , Q1.   176   age,] Q3, D; ~ ;
Q1–2, Q4–5; ~‸ F.   184   Love?] ~ ! Q1–5, D; ~ . F.   185   E're] Q1–
5, F; E'er D.   186   off] Q1–5, F; up D.   187   sort,] Q1, Q3–5, F, D;
~ . Q2.

IV, i

ACT] Q2–5, F, D; ~ . Q1.   SCENE I.] Q4–5, F, D; SCENE Q1–3.
s.d. Abenamar, *and servants.*] Q2–5, F, D; *Abenamar,* and servants. Q1.   1
Pris'ner] Q1–2, Q4–5, F, D; Pris'ners Q3.   1+   *s.d.* [*Exit*] D; ‸Exit Q1–4;
[Exit Q5, F.   2   according] Q3, Q5, F, D; ~ , Q1–2, Q4.   2   *s.d. To
Selin*] Q2–5, F, D; *to Selin* Q1.   4   fear:] Q1–2, Q4–5, F, D; ~ . Q3.   8
live——— [*Drawing a Sword.*] Q2–3; live. Q1, Q4–5, F, D.   12   'ere] Q1,
Q4; e're Q2–3, Q5, F; e'er D.   12   Journey's] Q1–2, Q4, F, D; Journeys
Q3, Q5.   13   *Aben.* It . . . free: [*To Selin.*] *Aben. to Selin. / It . . . free:*
Q1–5; *Aben. to Selin*] It . . . free: F, D (*Selin.* D).   15   welcome] Q2–5,
F, D; welome Q1.   20+   *s.d. Enter a*] *Another* Q1–5, F; *Enter another*
D.   20+   *s.d. Souldier*] Q2–3; *Souldier or Servant* Q1, Q4–5, F, D.   21
outer] Q2–3, D; outter Q1, Q4–5, F.   24   *Benzaida*] *Benzayda* Q1–5, F,

D.   24+ *s.d. To*] D; [~ Q1–5, F.   26 *s.d. omitted from D.*   26 *To*]
Q2–5, F; *to* Q1.   29 friendship] Q2–5, F, D; frindship Q1.   37
here:] ~ . Q1–5, F, D.   40 Fortune] Q2–3, F, D; fortune Q1, Q4–5.
42 giv'st] Q1–5, F; gav'st D.   45 *Benzayda*] Q3–5, F, D; *Benzaida* Q1–
2.   46 *Aben.* Go . . . binde. [*To Sold.*] *Aben. to Sold.* / Go . . . binde.
Q1–5, F, D (binde∧ Q1; bind: F; *on same line in F, D; to a* D).   55 again.]
Q1–4, F, D; ~ , Q5.   56 *Benzayda*] Q2–5, F, D; *Benzaida* Q1.   58
Ozmyn, hold:] D; ~∧ ~∧ Q1–2, Q4–5; ~∧ ~ , Q3; ~∧ ~ ; F.   59 untold:] Q1–5, D; ~ . F.   65 *Benzayda*] Q2–5, F, D; *Benzaida.* Q1.   72
propose?] ~ ! Q1–5, F, D.   73 *Benzayda*] Q2–5, F, D; *Benzaida* Q1.
86 *Ozmyn's*] Q2–5, F, D; *Ozmin's* Q1.   88 *Benzayda*] Q2–5, F, D;
Benzaida Q1.   91 dy.] Q1–4, F; ~ , Q5, D.   93 stay;] Q1–2, Q4–5,
D; ~ . Q3, F.   94 father's] Q1–4, D; Fathers Q5, F.   96 strife:] F;
~ . Q1–3; ~ ; Q4–5, D.   98 *s.d. To* Aben.] Q2–5, F, D; *to* Aben. Q1.
108 fall?] Q3, F, D; ~ : Q1–2, Q4–5.   109 all:] Q1–2, Q4–5; ~ . Q3,
F, D.   110 *Ozmyn*] Q2–5, F, D; *Ozmin* Q1.   111 me.] Q1–2, F, D;
~ , Q3–5.   117 you!] Q1–3; ~ ? Q4–5, F, D.   120 her] Q1, Q4–5,
F, D; your Q2–3.   122 even] Q1–4; ev'n Q5, F, D.   123 pow'r] Q1–
4, D; power Q5, F.   125 denyes:] ~ . Q1–5, F, D.   126 which] Q2–
3; that Q1, Q4–5, F, D.   128 conflict's] Q1–3, F, D; conflicts Q4–5.
135+ *s.d. [Runs*] Q2–5, F, D; ∧~ Q1.   136 you!] Q1–4; ~ : Q5, F, D.
138 O] Q1–5, D; O my F.   138 name?] ~ ! Q1–5, F, D.   139
shame!] Q1–2, Q4–5, F; ~ . Q3, D.

IV, ii

SCENE II.] SCENE Q1–5, F, D (~ , Q4; ~ . Q5).   *s.d.* Almanzor, Ab-
delmelech,] Q4–5, F, D; *Almanzor, Abdelmelech,* Q1–3.   *s.d. Soldiers*]
Q1–5, D; *Slodier* F.   3 Brain,] Q1–4, D; ~ . Q5; ~ ; F.   6 War.]
Q1, Q3–5, F, D; ~ ; Q2.   7 *Spaniard*] Q2–3, D; Spaniard Q1, Q4–5, F
(Spaniards Q5).   7 lies] Q1–2, Q4–5, F, D; lyes Q3.   9 e're] Q1–4, D;
e'er Q5, F.   16 o're:] ~ . Q1–5, F, D.   18+ *s.d. Exeunt. An Alarm
within.*] Q4–5, F, D (*[An]*); *An Alarm within. Exeunt.* Q1–3.   20 men.]
Q3; ~∧ Q1; ~ : Q2, Q4–5, F; ~ ; D.   21 late.] Q3, D; ~ , Q1–2, Q4–5,
F.   27 o're-powr'd] Q1–4; o'er power'd Q5, F, D.   28 E're] Q1–3;
Ere Q4–5, F; E'er D.   28 will] Q2–3; shall Q1, Q4–5, F, D.   29
Spaniards] Q2–3, D; Spaniards Q1, Q4–5, F.   31+ *s.d. [Exit*] Q4–5, F,
D; ∧~ Q1–3.   35 enow] Q2–3; enough Q1, Q4–5, F, D.   40 *s.d.
after l. 39 in Q 1–3.*   52 and] Q1, Q3–5, F, D; and and Q2.   53 ev'n]
Q1–4; even Q5, F, D.   54 own,] Q1–4; ~ . Q5, F; ~ ; D.   57 wing,]
D; ~ . Q1–5, F.   61 *Abdelm.* No; . . . Sacrifice; [*Stopping her.*] *Abdel-
melech stopping her.* / No; . . . Sacrifice; Q1–5, F, D (*on same line in F*).
65 Accursed] Q1, Q3–5, F, D; Accused Q2.   71 *s.d. on l. 70 in Q1–3*
(*to Lynd.* Q1).   77 done.] Q1, Q3–5, F, D; ~ , Q2.   77 *s.d. on l. 76
in Q1–5, F* (∧*dyes* Q1–3).   77+ *s.d. She*] Q2–5, F, D; *she* Q1.   83
Lynd.] Q2–5, F, D; *Lind.* Q1.   85 knew:] Q1–4, F; ~ . Q5, D.   88
misfortunes] Q1–5, D; Misfortune F.   94 Love?] Q2; ~ ! Q1, Q4–5, F, D;
~ . Q3.   99 till] Q1–5, F; 'till D.   106 You've] *some copies of Q1
read* You've have.   110 more:] Q1–5, F; ~ . D.   111 and th'] Q1–4,
D; and the Q5, F.   112 adoe,] Q2–3, F, D; ~ ; Q1, Q4–5.   118 *Abdelm.*] Q1–3, Q5, F, D; ~ , Q4.   125 again!] Q1–3; ~ . Q4–5, F, D.   127

attend:] Q1–2, Q4–5, D; ~ . Q3, F.   135 will be] Q1–4, F, D; will Q5.
135 die] Q1, Q4–5, F, D; dye Q2–3.   138 awhile,] Q3, F, D (a while
Q3, D); ~ ; Q1–2, Q4–5 (a while Q5).   139 Till] Q1–4, F; 'Till Q5, D.
139 under; . . . fall,] Q3, F, D; ~ , . . . ~ ; Q1–2, Q4–5.   141+ *s.d.*
[*Exit*] Q4–5, F, D; ∧~ Q1–3.   145 *Spaniard*] Q2–3, F, D; Spaniard Q1,
Q4–5.   146 *Abdel.*] Q1–2, Q4–5, F, D; *Abel.* Q3.   148 stay.] Q3; ~ :
Q1–2, Q4–5, F, D.   149 *s.d. Aside*] Q3–5, F, D; *aside* Q1–2.   152+
s.d. [*Exit*] Q4–5, D; ∧~ Q1–3; *omitted from* F.

IV, iii

SCENE III.] Scene. Q1–5, F, D.   *s.d.* Zulema, Hamet.] Q4–5, F, D;
Zulema, Hamet. Q1–3.   9 love:] Q2–3; ~ :: Q1; ~ :——— Q4–5, F, D.
15 shou'd] Q2–3; must Q1, Q4–5, F, D.   15 haste] Q1–4, F, D; hast
Q5.   20 every] Q1–5, F; ev'ry D.   21 Evening] Q1–5, F; Ev'ning D.
22 Circle] Q2–5, F, D; Cercle Q1.   25 vain:] D; ~ . Q1–3; ~ ; Q4–5,
F.   28 favourite] Q1–5, F; fav'rite D.   28 Queen.] Q3, F; ~ : Q1–2,
Q4–5, D.   29 E're] Q1–4, F; E'er Q5, D.   29 unseen] Q2; ~ . Q1,
Q4–5; ~ , Q3; ~ ; F, D.   30 watch] Q1–4, F, D; watcht Q5.   30
agen.] Q3, F; ~∧ Q1, Q4; ~ , Q2; ~ : Q5, D.   32 *Spaniards*] Q2–3, F,
D; Spaniards Q1, Q4–5.   32+ *s.d.* [*Exeunt*] Q5, F, D; ∧~ Q1–4.   34+
Song, In two Parts.] Q1–5, F, D, M1; Song 318. Ds1, Ds3–4; *A SONG. A
Dialogue between two Friends.* Tune, *How severe is forgetful old age.* Os1–4
(*forgetful is old* Os3); SONG I. Os5; *no title* Fs1–3, M6; *A SONG.* Ds5; Song
in two Parts for Drydens Conq: of Gran: 2 pt M2.   *Stanzas not numbered
in* Ds1, Ds3–5, M1–2, M6. *Arranged in three ten-line stanzas in* Fs1–3, Ds5.
35 He.] Q1–5, F, D, M1–2 (~∧ M2); *Almanz.* Ds1, Ds3–4; *R.* Os1–4; *S.*
Os5; *omitted from* Fs1–3, Ds5, M6.   35 *I*] Q1–2, Q4–5, M2; ~ , Q3, D,
Ds1, Ds3–5, Os1–5, Fs1–3, M1, M6; ~ ? F.   36 *While*] Q1–5, F, D, Ds1,
Ds3–4, M1–2, M6; Whilst Os1–5, Fs1–3, Ds5.   39 *Who is*] Q1–5, F, D,
Ds1, Ds3–5, Os1–4, Fs1–3, M1–2; That is Os5; Who'se M6.   39 *while*]
Q1–5, F, D, Ds1, Ds3–4, M1–2, M6; whilst Os1–5, Fs1–3, Ds5.   39 *pain!*]
Q1–5, F, D, M1; ~ . Ds1, Ds3–4, Os1–5, Fs1–3, M2; ~ ; Ds5; ~∧ M6.   40
She.] Q1–5, F, D, M1–2 (~∧ M2); *Queen.* Ds1, Ds3–4; *W.* Os1–4; *H.* Os5;
omitted from Fs1–3, Ds5, M6.   40 *her Honour*] Q1–5, F, D, Ds1, Ds3,
Os1–5, Fs1–3, Ds5, M1–2, M6; hour Ds4.   40 *allows*] Q1–5, F, D, M1–2;
affords Ds1, Ds3–5, Os1–5, Fs1–3, M6.   41 *But*] Q1–5, F, D, Ds1, Ds3–5,
Fs1–3, M1–2, M6; As Os1–5.   41 *pains*] Q1–5, F, D, Ds1, Ds3–5, Os1–5,
Fs1–3, M1–2; paine M6.   41 *which*] Q1–5, F, D, Ds1, Ds3–5, Os1–4,
Fs1–3, M1–2, M6; that Os5.   42 *'Tis*] Q1–5, F, D, Ds1, Ds3–5, Os5, Fs1–3,
M1–2, M6; It's Os1–4.   43 *hopeless*] Q1–5, F, D, Ds1, Ds3–5, Fs1–3, M1–
2, M6; helpless Os1–5.   43 *Estate*] Q1–5, F, D, Ds1, Ds3–5, Os1, Os4–5,
Fs1–3, M1–2, M6; state Os2–3.   44 *o're, and*] Q1–5, F, D, Ds1, Ds3–5,
Fs1–3, M1–2, M6; over Os1–5.   44 *betimes*] Q1–5, F, D, Os1–5, Fs1–3,
Ds5, M1–2, M6; in time Ds1, Ds3–4.   45–64 *omitted from* M6.   45
He.] Q1–5, F, D, M1–2; *Al.* Ds1, Ds3–4; *R.* Os1–4; *S.* Os5; *omitted from*
Fs1–3, Ds5.   45 *Med'cine*] Q1–5, F, D, Os5, M1–2; medecine Ds1, Ds3–5,
Os1–4, Fs1–3.   46 *For*] Q1–5, F, D, Ds1, Ds3–4, M1–2; Yet Os1–5, Fs1–3,
Ds5.   46 *wish*] Q1–5, F, D, Ds1, Ds3–5, Fs1–3, M1–2; wisht Os1–5.   47
From] Q1–5, F, D, Ds1, Ds3, Os1–5, Fs1–3, Ds5, M1-2; For Ds4.   47 *de-
sire*] Q1–5, F, D, Ds1, Ds3–5, Os4, Fs1–3, M1–2; desires Os1–3, Os5.   48

Has . . . its] Q1–5, F, D, Ds1, Ds3–5, Os1–4, Fs1–3, M1–2; have . . . their Os5.
48 *Fire*]Q1–5, F, D, Ds1, Ds3–5, Os4, Fs1–3, M1–2; fires Os1–3, Os5.   49
But it] Q1–5, F, D, Os1–4, Fs1–3, Ds5, M1–2; But Ds1, Ds3–4; But they Os5.
49 *burns and consumes*] Q1–5, F, D, Ds1, Ds3–5, Os1–4, Fs1–3, M1–2; burn
and consume Os5.   49 *me within*] Q1–5, F, D, Ds1, Ds3, Os1–5, Fs1–3,
Ds5, M1–2; within Ds4.   50 *She.*] Q1–5, F, D, M1–2; *Queen.* Ds1, Ds3–
4; *W.* Os1–4; *H.* Os5; *omitted from* Fs1–3, Ds5.   50 *least*] Q1–5, F, D,
Fs1–3, Ds5, M1–2; last Ds1, Ds3–4; best Os1–4; worst Os5.   50 *'tis a*]
Q1–5, F, D, Ds1, Ds3, Os5, Fs1–3, Ds5, M1–2; a Ds4; it's a Os1–4.   50
pleasure] Q1–5, F, D, Ds1, Ds3–4, M1–2; comfort Os1–5, Fs1–3, Ds5.   53
wretched] Q2–3, F, D, Ds1, Ds3–5, Os1–5, Fs1–3, M1–2; *wretch'd* Q1, Q4–5.
53 *and*] Q1–5, F, D, M1–2; or Ds1, Ds3–5, Os1–5, Fs1–3.   54 *accounts*]
Q1–5, F, Ds1, Ds3, Os1–5, Fs1–3, Ds5, M1–2; *counts* D, Ds4.   54 *suff-
'rings*] Q1–5, F, D, Fs1–3, Ds5, M1–2; sufferings Ds1, Ds3–4, Os1–5.   55
He.] Q1–5, F, D, M1–2; *Al.* Ds1, Ds3–4; *R.* Os1–4; *S.* Os5; *omitted from*
Fs1–3, Ds5.   55 *ye*] Q1–5, F, D, Ds1, Ds3–4, M1–2; you Os1–5, Fs1–3,
Ds5.   55 *Gods,*] Q1–5, F, D, M1–2 (~ᴧ M2); Powers! Ds1, Ds3–4; Pow-
ersᴧ Os1–5; pow'rs! Fs1–3, Ds5.   56 *lye:*] Q1, Q4–5, F, D, F1–3, Ds5,
M2; ~ . Q2–3, M1; ~ , Ds1–4, Os1, Os3–5.   60 *She.*] Q1–5, F, D, M1–2;
Queen. Ds1, Ds3–4; *W.* Os1–4; *H.* Os5; *omitted from* Fs1–3, Ds5.   61 *In
her*] Q1–5, F, D, Ds1, Ds3–5, Os1–4, Fs1–3, M1–2; After Os5.   61 *to
your*] Q1–5, F, D, Ds1, Ds3–4, M1–2; to her Os1–5, Fs1–3, Ds5.   61
Love.] Q1–5, F, D, M1; ~ , Ds1, Ds3–4; ~ : Os1–5, Fs1–3, Ds5; ~ᴧ M2.
63 *Fate will*] Q1–5, F, D, Os1–5, Fs1–3, Ds5, M1–2; death shall Ds1, Ds3–4.
64 *For*] Q1–5, F, D, Ds1, Ds3–4, Os1–5, M1–2; When Fs1–3, Ds5.   64
to] Q1–5, F, D, Ds1, Ds3–4, M1–2; do Os1–5, Fs1–3, Ds5.   64 *closer*]
Q1–5, F, D, Ds1, Ds3–5, Fs1–3, M1–2; freely Os1–5.   65 *till*] Q1–5, F;
'till D.   66 *worthy*] Q1–4, F, D; worth Q5.   68+ *s.d.* [*Exit*] Q5,
F, D; ᴧ~ Q1–4.   68+ *s.d. Esperanza.*] Q2–5, F, D; ~ : Q1.   69 *A*]
D; *Solus. | A* Q1–5, F.   69 *through*] Q1–4, F, D; throw Q5.   70
shivering] Q1–4; shiv'ring Q5, F, D.   70 *o're.*] Q1–5, F; ~ : D.   72
delight!] Q1–5, D; ~ ; F.   73 *Tyrants,*] Q1–4, D; Tyrantsᴧ Q5; Tyrant'sᴧ F.   76+ *s.d.* [*He*] Q4–5, F, D; ᴧ~ Q1–3.   82 *pull thee*] Q1–
2, Q4–5, F, D; ~ the Q3.   82 *by thy*] Q1–3; ~ the Q4–5, F, D.   85
gone?] ~ ! Q1–5, F, D.   92 *door was*] Q1–5, D; Door is F.   92 *but
this*] Q1–4, D; and this Q5, F.   92 *Heav'ns*] Q1, Q4–5, F, D; Heaven's
Q2–3.   93 *speak!*] ~ . Q1–5, F, D.   94 *Spirit;*] Q1–3, ~ , Q4–5, F;
~ ? D.   95 *Ghost.*] Q4–5, F, D; ~ ! Q1–3.   95 *gave thee*] Q1–3, Q5,
F, D; gave the Q4.   95 *birth,*] ~ : Q1–5, F, D.   102 *above;*] Q1–4,
D; ~ . Q5, F.   103 *th'*] Q1–4, D; the Q5, F.   103 *steepy*] Q1–4;
steeply Q5, F, D.   106 *from*] Q1–5, D; from from F.   106 *Heav'nly*]
Q1–4, F, D; Heavenly Q5.   107 *An Angel gave me charge to*] Q2–3; A
Watchman Angel bid me Q1, Q4–5, F, D.   110 *e're*] Q1–4, F; e'er Q5,
D.   112 *Almanz. Speak, . . . on:* [*Bowing.*] D (*bowing*); [Almanzor *bow-
ing. | Speak, . . . on:* Q1–5 (ᴧAlmanzor Q2–5); [Almanzor *bowing. | Almanz.
Speak, . . . on:* F.   112 *Parent form*] Q1–5, F; Parent-form D.   115
oh] Q1–3; O Q4–5, F, D.   115 *Heav'nly*] Q1–4, D; Heavenly Q5, F.
116 *care,*] Q1; ~ᴧ Q2–3, F, D; ~ .) Q4–5.   117 *names!* Q1–5, F; ~ :
D.   122 *Ghost.*] Q1, Q3–5, F, D; ~ : Q2.   128 *stock*] Q2–3; flock
Q1, Q3–5, F, D.   128 *destroy.*] Q1, Q3–5, F, D; ~ : Q2.   130 *would*]

Q1–5, F; should D.   130   learn.] Q1–5, D; ~ₐ F.   131   Heav'n] Q1–
4, D; Heaven Q5, F.   133   dost] Q1–4, F, D; does Q5.   137   thee,]
Q2–3; ~ : Q1, Q4–5, D; ~ ; F.   137   when] Q1–5, F; Then D.   137
done:] ~ , Q1–4; ~ ; Q5; ~ . F, D.   139   Heav'n] Q1–4, D; Heaven Q5,
F.   140   Flowers] Q1–5, F; Flow'rs D.   141   Blest] Q1–4, F, D; lest
Q5.   142   Heav'n] Q1–4, D; Heaven Q5, F.   142+   *s.d. [Exit]* Q4–5,
F, D; ₐ~ Q1–3.   143   Heav'n] Q1–4, D; Heaven Q5, F.   146   or-
dain:] Q1–5, F; ~ . D.   149   (while . . . draws;)] Q2–3; ₐ~ . . . ~ ;ₐ Q1,
Q4–5, F, D.   149   Heav'n] Q1–4, F, D; Heaven Q5.   152   Slave:]
Q1–2; ~ . Q3–5, F, D.   155   talk.———] D; ~ ;——— Q1–5, F.   157
dy,] Q1–2, Q4, F, D; ~ ; Q3; ~ . Q5.   158   on] Q1, Q3–5, F, D; one Q2.
160   giv'n] Q1–4, D; given Q5, F.   160   day;] Q1, Q4–5, F; ~ .; Q2; ~ .
Q3; ~ : D.   172   Necessity.] Q3–5, F, D; ~ : Q1–2.   174   give?———]
D; ~ .——— Q1–4; ~ₐ——— Q5, F.   182   should] Q1–4, F; shall Q5,
D.   183   remove:] Q4, F; ~ . Q1–3; ~ , Q5; ~ ; D.   184   love!] Q1–
3; ~ . Q4–5, F, D.   192   done:] Q1–4; ~ . Q5; ~ , F; ~ ; D.   193
desires] Q1–4; desire Q5, F, D.   197   Love's] Q2–5, F, D; Lov's Q1.
206   *s.d. Kneels]* Q4–5, F, D; *kneels* Q1–3.   207   die] Q1, Q4–5, F, D;
dye Q2–3.   209   self,] Q2–3, F, D; ~ₐ Q1, Q4–5.   210   nigh] Q1–4;
high Q5, F, D.   218   half-yielding] Q2–3; half yielding Q1, Q4–5, F, D.
222   have] Q2–3, D; had Q1, Q4–5, F.   225   Away!] ~ : Q1–3; ~ . Q4–
5, F, D (A way Q4–5).   233   lie] Q1, Q4–5, F; lye Q2–3, D.   256   to
be] Q1–5, D; to F.   263   Heav'n] Q1–4, D; Heaven Q5, F.   266   dye.]
Q1–4; ~ , Q5, F, D.   268   attone.] Q1–4, F, D; ~ : Q5.   274   gen-
'rous] Q1–4, D; generous Q5, F.   275   loose] Q1, Q4–5, F; lose Q2–3, D.
275   higher.] Q1, Q3–5, F, D; ~ₐ Q2.   280   gone!] Q1–2, Q4–5, F, D;
~ ; Q3.   281   yet:] Q1–2, Q4–5, F, D; ~ ! Q3.   282   forget:] F; ~ .
Q1–5, D.   284+   *s.d. [Exeunt]* Q4–5, F, D; ₐ~ Q1–3.   284+   *s.d. he
is]* Q1, Q3–5, F, D; *is* Q2.   286   further] Q1–4; farther Q5, F, D.   286
disgrace.] Q1, Q3–5, F, D; ~ₐ Q2.   288   Queen.] Q3, Q5, F, D; ~ : Q1–
2, Q4.   291   vain:] Q3; ~ . Q1–2, Q4; ~ ; Q5, F, D.   292   now are]
Q1–4; are now Q5, F, D.   293   oh] Q1–3; O Q4–5, F, D.   293   heav'n]
Q1–4, D; Heaven Q5, F.   293   some help!] Q5, F, D; ~ ~ . Q1, Q3–4;
~ ~ : Q2.   293   haste] Q1–4, F, D; hast Q5.   294   door.] Q3, Q5, F,
D; ~ : Q1–2, Q4.   295   here?] ~ ! Q1–5, F, D.   296   heav'n] Q1–4,
D; Heaven Q5, F.   296+   *s.d. [As]* Q4–5, F, D; ₐ~ Q1–3.   299+   *s.d.
[They]* Q4–5, F, D; ₐ~ Q1–3.   299+   *s.d.* Abdelmelech] Q2–5, F, D; Ab-
demelech Q1.   301   He is] Q3; He Q1–2, Q4–5, F, D.   301   escap'd.]
Q5, F, D; ~ : Q1–4.   302   they,] Q5; ~ . Q1–4, F; ~ : D.   303   say:]
Q1–4; ~ . Q5, F, D.   304   here,] Q5; ~ . Q1–4; ~ ; F, D.   306   Help]
D; help Q1–5, F.   306+   *s.d. [Zulema]* Q4–5, F, D; ₐ~ Q1–3.   306+
s.d. and within] Q1–5, D; *and* F.   306+   *s.d. cry,* Help] D *(Help); cry
help* Q1–5, F.   306+   *s.d. attending* Boabdelin.] Q1, Q4–5, F, D; *at-
tending.* Q2–3.   312   Queen?] ~ ! Q1–5, F, D.   313   speak.] Q5, F;
~ : Q1–4; ~ , D.   313   seen?] ~ ! Q1–5, F, D.   316   Pow'r] Q2–3;
Mouth Q1, Q4–5, F, D.   323   hear:] Q1–4; ~ . Q5, F, D.   325   Till]
Q1–5, F; 'Till D.   328   Heav'n] Q1–4, D; Heaven Q5, F.   328   hear?]
~ , Q1–5; ~ ! F, D.   328   *Almanz.*———] F *(without the rule); (Almanz.)*
Q1–5, D *(on same line as preceding speech; no parens in D).*   333   *Zu-
lema.* I . . . Confident; *[At the door.]* D; [*Zulema, at the door.* / I . . . Con-

fident; Q1–5, F (*on same line in F*). 338 expose!] Q1–2, Q4–5, F, D; ~ . Q3. 340 us he was so] Q1–5, D; he was our friend F. 344 Ear:] Q1–4; ~ . Q5; ~ ; F, D. 350 doubt:] *some copies of Q1 lack the colon.* 353 tell:] Q1–4, D; ~ ; Q5; ~ . F. 355 hearts] Q1, Q4–5, F, D; heart's Q2–3. 356 break:] Q1–4; ~ ; Q5, F; ~ . D. 358 scap'd] Q1–5, F; 'scap'd D. 359 stay.] Q3–5, F, D; ~ : Q1–2. 360 haste] Q1–4, F, D; hast Q5. 362 womankind] Q1–2, Q4–5, F, D; Woman kind Q3. 366 curse?] Q3, D; ~ ! Q1–2, Q4–5, F. 367 Dull] Q3–5, F, D; ~ , Q1–2. 368 be?] ~ ! Q1–5, F, D. 375 haste] Q1–4, F, D; hast Q5. 381 Heav'n] Q1–4, D; Heaven Q5, F. 381 three.] Q1–4, F, D; ~‸ Q5. 382 Sir;] Q1–3; ~ , Q4–5, D; ~ . F. 383 draw:] Q1–5, D; ~ . F. 384 to] Q1–5, D; do F. 384 die] Q1, Q4–5, F, D; dye Q2–3. 387 Prerogative?] Q3; ~ . Q1–2, Q4–5, F, D. 398 you,] Q1–4, F, D; ~ ? Q5. 402 *Ozm.*] Q1, Q3–5, F, D; ~ , Q2. 403 lies] Q1–2, Q4–5, F, D; lyes Q3. 407 th'] Q1–4, D; the Q5, F. 409 Champions] Q5, F, D; Champion's Q1–2, Q4; Champion Q3. 409 th'] Q1, Q4, D; the Q2–3, Q5, F. 410 yield.] Q3, F, D; ~ : Q1–2, Q4–5 (*some copies of Q1 have* yidld). 411 Field:] Q3, D; ~ , Q1–2, Q4–5; ~ . F. 412 strife;] Q1–3; ~ , Q4, F, D; ~ . Q5. 413 th'] Q1–4, D; the Q5, F. 416+ s.d. [*Exeunt.*] Q4–5, F, D; ‸~ Q1–3.

V, i

ACT V.] Q1–5, F; ACT V. SCENE I. D. 2 beside.] Q3, F, D; ~ , Q1–2, Q4–5. 5 find?] Q3, D; ~ ; Q1–2, Q4; ~ , Q5; ~ ! F. 6 Woman-kind:] Q1–2, Q4–5; ~ . Q3, F, D. 12 ill;] Q1–2, Q4–5; ~ . Q3, F, D. 14+ s.d. To] Q2–5, F, D; [~ Q1. 14+ s.d. guarded.] Q1–5, D; ~‸ F. 15 nor are] Q1–4, D; nor is Q5, F. 15 Deities:] F; ~ . Q1–5, D. 17 dethron'd,] Q1–3, D; ~ . Q4–5; ~ : F. 18 own'd.] Q1–3, Q5, F, D; ~ , Q4. 20 thee?] D; ~ ! Q1–5, F. 21 debarr'd?] D; ~ ! Q1–5, F. 22 Guard:] Q1–2, Q4–5, D; ~ . Q3, F. 27 free.] Q2–3, D; ~ , Q1, Q4–5; ~‸ F. 28 thee.] Q1–5, F; ~ : D. 29 late! ———] Q1–5, D; ~‸——— F. 34 Wou'd fall] Q2–3; Would sowze Q1, Q4–5, F, D (W'ould Q1). 37 Dar'd,] Q1, Q4–5, F, D; ~ . Q2; ~‸ Q3. 40 victory.] Q1–5, D; ~ ., F. 43 shall] Q1–5, F; must D. 44+ s.d. [*Exeunt*] Q4–5, F, D; ‸~ Q1–3.

V, ii

SCENE II. / *The*] The Q1–5, F, D. s.d. fill'd] Q2–5, F, D; fil'd Q1. 3 peal] Q2–3; peals Q1, Q4–5, F, D. 4 over fighting] Q1, Q3–5, F, D; over-fighting Q2. 5 Innocence;] Q2–3; ~ . Q1, Q4–5; ~ , F, D. 6 defence;] Q1–2, Q4–5, F; ~ . Q3, D. 11 power] Q1–5, F; Pow'r D. 17 thy] Q1–5, D; the F. 20+ s.d. guarded:] ~ . Q1–5, F, D. 22 Th'] Q3, D; The Q1–2, Q4–5, F. 25 look,] Q1–2, Q4–5, F, D; ~ ? Q3. 25 word?] Q3, D; ~ ; Q1–2, Q4–5; ~ ! F. 35 s.d. Aside.] Q4–5, F, D; aside Q1; aside. Q2–3. 36 s.d. Goes] Q4–5, F, D; goes Q1–3. 36+ s.d. Moors] D; *Moors* Q1–5, F (*Mores* Q1). 37 appear:] Q3, Q5, F, D; ~ ? Q1–2, Q4. 39 Zegrys] D; Zegry's Q1–5, F. 48+ s.d. Alcoran] Q2–3, Q5, F, D; Alcoran Q1, Q4. 48+ s.d. Moors] D; *Moors* Q1–5, F. 48+ s.d. bare] Q1–5, D; naked F. 49 appear:] Q1–3, Q5, F, D; ~ ?

Q4.   52 fame.] Q3, Q5, F, D; ~ : Q1-2, Q4.   53 *Zegrys*] Q1-3, D;
Zegry's Q4-5, F.   53 Traitors] Q2, F, D; Trators Q1, Q4; Traytors Q3,
Q5.   55-56 *Selin.* Madam, . . . two; / . . . [*To* Almahide.] *Selin.* to *Al-
mahide.* / Madam, . . . two; Q1-5, F, D (Selin‸ Q2-3, Q5; *on same line in F,
D;* [*Selin to* Almahide.] F; *Selin to* Almahide. D).   55 two;] Q1-4, D;
~ ? Q5; ~ , F.   56 dye?] Q3-5, F, D; ~ ; Q1-2.   58+ *s.d.* Alcoran.]
Q2-3, F, D; *Alcoran.* Q1, Q4-5 (~‸ Q5).   59 *Lynd.*] Q2-3, Q5, F, D;
Lind. Q1, Q4.   59 'em] Q1-4; them Q5, F, D.   60 th'] Q3, D; the
Q1-2, Q4-5, F.   60 give.] Q1-3, F; ~ ; Q4; ~ : Q5, D.   61 fight]
Q2-5, F, D; sight Q1.   62 me.] Q1-5, D; ~ , F.   62+ *s.d. She*] Q2-
5, F, D; *she* Q1.   62+ *s.d.* Benzayda] Q3-5, F, D; *Benzaida* Q1; Ben-
zaida Q2.   67 every] Q1-5, F; ev'ry D.   68 Victors] Q1-5, F; Victor's D.   68+ *s.d.* [*The Trumpets*] D; ‸~ ~ Q1-5, F.   68+ *s.d.*
Hamet:] Q1-5; ~ . F; ~ ; D.   68+ *s.d.* Zegrys] D; Zegry's Q1-5, F.
68+ *s.d. advantage:*] Q1-5; ~ . F; ~ ; D.   68+ *s.d. till*] Q1-5, F;
'till D.   68+ *s.d. he looks*] Q1-2, Q4-5, F, D; *looks* Q3.   69 *Ham.
to Ozmyn.* Our . . . be. / [*Thrusting.*] *Ham.* to *Ozmyn thrusting.* / Our . . . be.
Q1-5, F, D (be: Q1-3; *on same line in F;* [Hamet . . . thrusting.] F; *thrust-
ing,* D).   69 difference] Q1-5, F; Diff'rence D.   70 *Alman.*] Q1-5,
D; *Almah.* F.   70+ *s.d.* [*Hamet leaves*] D; ‸~ ~ Q1-5, F.   70+ *s.d.*
Hamet, *advancing first,*] Q1, Q4-5, D; ~‸ ~ ~ , Q2-3, F.   71 *Lynd.*]
Q2-5, F, D; *Lind* Q1.   71 haste] Q1-4, F, D; hast Q5.   72+ *s.d.*
[*Almanzor looks*] D; ‸~ ~ Q1-5, F.   72+ *s.d.* Zegrys] Q1, D; Zegry's
Q2-5, F.   72+ *s.d.* Queens trumpets sound.] Q1-4, F, D; ~ ~ ~ , Q5.
73+ *s.d. Stabbing*] Q4-5, F, D; *stabbing* Q1-3.   74 dye] Q1-2; ~ : Q3;
~ . Q4-5, F, D.   80 oh] Q1-2; oh! Q3; O Q4-5, F; O! D.   83 of
――] Q3-5, F, D; ~ .―― Q1-2.   83 *s.d. Dies.*] Q4-5, F, D; *dies*
Q1; *dies.* Q2; *dyes.* Q3.   83 *Almah.* . . . offence!] *omitted from* Q2-3,
except for Alma. in catchword in Q2.   84-85 *Almanzor.* If . . . cause, /
. . . [*To the Judges.*] [*Almanzor to the Judges.* / If . . . cause, Q1-5, F, D (*on
same line in F, D;* *Almanzor* Q4-5, D; *Judges.*] F).   84 remains] Q1-5,
D; remain F.   88+ *s.d.* [*The Judges*] D; ‸~ ~ Q1-5, F.   88+ *s.d.*
Abdelmelech] Q2, Q5, F, D; *Abdelmelech* Q1, Q3-4.   93 *Benzayda.*
That . . . tear: / [*Running to* Ozmyn.] F (Benzayda *running*); [Benzayda
running to Ozmyn. / That . . . tear: Q1-5, D (‸Benzayda Q4-5, D; *on same
line in D*).   96+ *s.d.* [*Exit*] Q4-5, F, D; ‸~ Q1-3.   97 slain:] Q1-2,
Q4-5, D; ~ ; Q3; ~ . F.   102 *s.d. Aside*] Q4-5, F, D; *aside* Q1-3.   103
Zegry's] Q1, D (Zegrys D); Zegry's Q2-5, F.   104+ *s.d.* [*Exit*] Q4-5, F, D;
‸~ Q1-3.   104+ *s.d.* Alabez.] Q1, Q4; ~ ; Q2-3, Q5, F, D.   104+
s.d. The] *the* Q1-5, F, D.   104+ *s.d.* Esperanza] Q1-5, F; *and* Esperanza
D.   106 you:] Q1-5, D; ~ . F.   113 till] Q1-5, F; 'till D.   115
shoot] Q1-4, D; shout Q5, F.   116+ *s.d.* [*Exit*] Q4-5, F, D; ‸~ Q1-3.
117 *s.d. Aside.*] Q4-5, F, D; *aside‸* Q1; *aside.* Q2-3.   118 have?] ~ !
Q1-5, F, D.   120 brow.] Q3; ~ : Q1-2, Q4-5, F, D.   120+ *s.d.* [*He*]
Q3, F; ‸~ Q1-2, Q4-5, D.   125 I will] Q1-4; will I Q5, F, D.   127
hear] Q1, Q3-5, F, D; here Q2.   135 by] Q1-4; in Q5, F, D.   138
mind?] ~ ! Q1-5, F, D.   142 show?] ~ ! Q1-5, F, D.   143 ev'n]
Q1-2, Q4-5, F, D; even Q3.   147 Pray'rs to Heav'n] Q1-4, F; Prayers
to them Q5, D (Pray'rs D).   148 in War] Q1-4, F; with War Q5, D.

149 Bed:] ~ . Q1–5, F, D.   151 dies] Q1–2, Q4–5, F, D; dyes Q3.
152+ *s.d.* [*Exit*] Q3–5, F, D ([~ . Q4); ∧~ Q1–2.   160+ *s.d.* [*Exit*]
Q4–5, F, D; ∧~ Q1–3.

V, iii

SCENE III. / *Enter*] Enter Q1–5, F, D.   2 know.] Q1, Q4–5, F, D;
~ , Q2; ~ ; Q3.   3 e're] Q1–4; e'er Q5, F, D.   15 *Almanzor. I must
confess,* [*Starting back.*] D; [Almanzor *starting back. / I must confess,* Q1–
5, F (∧Almanzor Q2–5, F; *on same line in F*).   17 side:] Q1–5, D; ~ . F.
21 shew you knew where] Q2–3; shew / You knew where deepest Q1, Q4–
5, F, D.   25 Bed:] Q2–5, F, D; ~ , Q1.   30 Love] Q1–5, D; Lore F.
33 *Almah.*] Q2–5, F, D; ~∧ Q1.   33 down?] Q1, Q4–5, F, D; ~ . Q2–3.
44 long.] Q1–4, F, D; ~ , Q5.   54 kill?] D; ~ ! Q1–5, F.   62 ayd:]
Q1–2, Q4–5; ~ . Q3, F, D.   63 giv'n] Q1–4, D; given Q5, F.   65
Vestals] Q1–5, D; Vassals F.   72 man] Q1–4, F, D; ~ . Q5.   74
spies;] Q1–4, D; ~ , Q5; ~ . F.   76+ *s.d. follows l. 77 in Q1–5, D; on
l. 77* ([Boabdelin) *in* F.   76+ *s.d.* Boabdelin] Q2–5, F, D; *Boabdelin*
Q1.   77 *Almah.*] Q1, Q3–5, F, D; ~ , Q2.   81 love?] Q3; ~ ! Q1–2,
Q4–5, F, D.   85 *s.d. Descends.*] Q4–5, F, D (~∧ Q5); *descends.* Q1–3
(~∧ Q1).   89+ *s.d. Betwixt*] Q2–5, F, D; *betwixt* Q1.   90 every]
Q1–5, F; ev'ry D.   90+ *s.d. She*] Q2–5, F, D; *she* Q1.   93 heav'n]
Q1–4, D; heaven Q5, F.   93 joy,] Q1–4, D; ~ . Q5; ~ , F.   95 *King
Boab.*] Q1–5, F; *Boab.* D.   97 vain:] ~ . Q1–5, F, D.   98 haste] Q1–
4, F, D; hast Q5.   98 ordain.] Q1–5, D; ~ , F.   98 *s.d. To*] Q2–5, F,
D; *to* Q1.   98 Guards] Q1–5, F; *the* Guards D.   100, 101 every] Q1–
5, F; ev'ry D.   101 *Almanzors*] Q1–5, D; *Almanzor's* F.   101+ *s.d.*
[*He*] Q2–4, F, D; ∧~ Q1, Q5.   102–103 *Abdelm. What . . . spight,* [. . .
To the King.] D; *Abdelm. to the King. / What . . .* spight, Q1–5, F (*King*∧
Q5; *on same line in F*).   103 right?] D; ~ ! Q1–5, F.   103+ *s.d.
turns, and*] Q1–5, F; *turns,* D.   105 at th'] Q2–3, D; at the Q1, Q4–5, F.
105 *Elvira*] Q2–3, F, D; *Elvira* Q1, Q4–5.   106 has] Q2–3, Q5, F, D;
'has Q1, Q4.   107 *Zegrys*] Q3, D; *Zegry's* Q1–2, Q4–5, F (*in Q1 apostro-
phe worked up into line above before* has).   107 *Spanyards*] Q2–3, D;
Spanyards Q1, Q4–5, F.   116 been,] Q1 (*some copies*), Q4–5, F, D; ~∧
Q1 (*some copies*), Q2–3.   123 Take] *some copies of Q1 add a comma.*
129+ *s.d.* [*Exeunt*] Q4–5, F, D; ∧~ Q1–3.   129+ *s.d.* Isabel] Q1–5,
F; Isabella] D.   129+ *s.d.* Spaniards] D; *Spaniards* Q1–5, F.   130
Ferd.] Q2–5, F, D (*K. Ferd.* D); ~∧ Q1.   131 maintain'd.] F, D; ~; Q1–
5.   134 *Ferd.*] Q2–5, F, D (*K. Ferd.* D); ~∧ Q1.   134 *Moores*] Q2–3,
D; Moores Q1, Q4–5, F.   134 fight;] Q2–3, F, D; ~ . Q1, Q4–5.   137
Moorish] D; Moorish Q1–5, F.   137 vain:] *some copies of Q1 have a
semicolon.*   140 *K.*] D; K. Q1–5, F.   141 sought:] Q1–2, Q4–5; ~ .
Q3, F, D.   143 fame.] Q1–5, D; ~ , F.   143+ *s.d.* [*Exeunt*] Q4–5,
F, D; ∧~ Q1–3.   143+ *s.d.* Isabel] Isabella Q1–5, F, D.   144 *Zegry*]
Q2–3, D; Zegry Q1, Q4–5, F.   152 *Moors and Spaniards*] Q2–3, D;
Moors and Spaniards Q1, Q4–5, F.   153 yet:] ~ . Q1–5, F, D.   156
Castilian] Q2–3, D; Castilian Q1, Q4–5, F.   156+ *s.d. heard,* Victoria,
Victoria.] D; *heard. Victoria, Victoria.* Q1–5, F (*heard,* F).   157 presage.]
Q3, F, D; ~ : Q1–2, Q4–5.   158 *D. of*] Q1–5, F; *D.* D.   158 *Gra-
nada*] Q2–5, F, D; Granada Q1.   159 *Moors*] Q2–3, D; Moors Q1, Q4–5,

F. 162 several] Q1-5, F; sev'ral D. 162 *Moors*] Q2-3, D; Moors
Q1, Q4-5, F. 165 Till] Q1-5, F; 'Till D. 171 hand.)] F, D; ~ :)
Q1-5. 172 withstand?] Q4-5, F, D; ~ ! Q1-3. 173 *D. of*] Q1-5,
F; *D.* D. 173 *Moorish*] Q2-3, D; Moorish Q1, Q4-5, F. 175 crowd]
crow'd Q1; croud Q2-5, F, D. 176 till] Q1-5, F; 'till D. 178 'ere
scarce] Q1-4 (e're Q2-3); e're Q5; before F; kills e'er D. 185 *D. of*]
Q1-5, F; *D.* D. 185 *Arcos*] Q1-4, F, D; *Arces* Q5. 185 did] Q1,
Q3-5, F, D; bid Q2. 198 vain,] Q3, D; ~ . Q1, Q4-5; ~ ; Q2, F. 205
fall.] Q1, Q3-5, F, D; ~ , Q2. 206 *Arcos*] Q1-5, F; *D. Arcos* D. 206
Moors] Q2-3, D; Moors Q1, Q4-5, F. 209 stood.] Q1-2; ~ ; Q3; ~ ,
Q4-5, D; ~ : F. 213 prove] Q1-4; proves Q5, F, D. 217 my] Q1-4,
D; his Q5, F. 217 love.)] Q1-4, F, D; ~∧) Q5. 223 'ere] Q1, Q4;
e're Q2-3, Q5, F; e'er D. 227+ *s.d.* Isabel] Q1-5, F; Isabella D.
227+ *s.d. Ladies:*] ~ , Q1-5, F, D. 227+ *s.d.* Moors *and* Spaniards]
D; *Moors and Spaniards* Q1-5, F. 227+ *s.d. Guards:*] ~ . Q1-5, F, D.
227+ *s.d.* Abenamar,] Q1-4, F, D; ~ . Q5. 228-229 *K. Ferdinand.*
All . . . tell, / . . . [*Embracing Qu.* Isabel.] *K. Ferdinand embracing Qu.*
Isabel. / All . . . tell, Q1-5, D (*Qu∧* Q1; *on same line in D*); *K. Ferd.* All . . .
tell, [*King* Ferdinand *embracing Queen* Isabel. F. 232 And] *some*
copies of Q1 add a comma. 238 ow'd:] *some copies of Q1 omit colon.*
240 *s.d. To*] Q2-5, F, D; *to* Q1. 240 *s.d.* Abdelm.] Q3-5, F, D; *Abdelm.* Q1-2. 244 *Abdelm.* This . . . heart. / [*Stabbing . . . Ponyard.*]
F; *Abdelm. stabbing . . . Ponyard.* / This . . . heart. Q1-5, D (*Abdelm∧* Q1;
[Abdelm. Q4-5; *on same line in D*). 244 *Lynd.*] Q2-5, F, D; *Lind.* Q1.
244 Oh] Q1-3; O Q4-5, F, D. 246 Lady.———] Q1-5, F; ~ ,
D. 246 Murderer] Q2-5, F, D; Murdere Q1. 247 *Abdelmelech.*
I'le . . . her. / [*Stabbing himself.*] F; *Abdelmelech, stabbing himself.* / I'le
. . . her. Q1-5, D (*on same line in D; I . . . D*). 248 *s.d.* [*To* Lynd.] Q2-
5, F, D; ∧*To Lynd.* Q1. 253 *s.d.* Dyes] Q4-5, F, D; *dyes* Q1-3. 260
line.] Q1-3, F, D; ~ , Q4-5. 263 *s.d.* [*To*] Q2-5, F, D; ∧~ Q1. 263
s.d. Moors] Q2-3, D; *Moors* Q1, Q4-5, F. 264 *s.d. They*] Q2-5, F, D;
they Q1. 265 'ere] Q1, Q4; e're Q2-3, Q5, F; e'er D. 265 *s.d.* Dyes]
Q4-5, F, D; *dyes* Q1-3. 268 Ferd.] Q1-5, F; *K. Ferd.* D. 269 fu-
neral] Q1-2, Q4-5, F; fun'ral Q3, D. 269+ *s.d.* [*The*] Q2-5, F, D; ∧~
Q1. 269+ *s.d.* Bodies] Q1-3, Q5, F, D; *Body's* Q4. 269+ *s.d.* Benzayda:] ~ . Q1-5, D; ~ ; F. 269+ *s.d.* Isabel] Q1-5, F; Isabella D.
269+ *s.d. show.*] Q1-5, D; ~ , F. 270 *Duke of Arcos.* See . . . mine; /
[*Presenting . . . King.*] F; *Duke of* Arcos *presenting . . . King.* / See . . . mine;
Q1-5, D (*D. Arcos* D; *on same line in D*). 272 *K.*] Q2, D; K. Q1, Q3-5,
F. 272 secure] Q1, Q4, F; ~ , Q2-3, Q5, D. 273 pow'r] Q1-3, D;
power Q4-5, F. 275 friend.] Q3, F, D; ~ , Q1-2, Q4-5. 276 *s.d.*
To Almanz.] Q2-5, F, D (Almanzor: Q4); *to Almanz.* Q1. 278 bring:]
Q1-5, D; ~ . F. 279 Streams] Q2-5, F, D; Sreams Q1. 279 Spring:]
Q1-2, Q4-5, F, D; ~ . Q3. 286 it] Q1-5, F; its D. 292 day!———]
Q2-3; ~ ;∧ Q1, Q4-5, F; ~ ,∧ D. 294 *Q.*] Q2, D; Q. Q1, Q3-5, F. 296
Almah.] Q3, D; *Qu. Almah.* Q1-2, Q4-5, F. 300-301 *Qu. Isabel.* That
. . . me; / . . . [*Embracing her.*] *Qu. Isabel embracing her.* / That . . . me; Q1-
5, F, D (*Q∧* Q2; / *Q. Isab.* That F; *on same line in D*). 304 reverence]
Q1-5, F; Rev'rence D. 306-307 *K. Ferd.* You, . . . gain, / . . . [*To* Alma-
hide.] *K. Ferd. to Almahide.* / You, . . . gain, Q1-5, F, D (*on same line in F,*

D). 309 *Qu. Isabel.* May . . . blest. / [*To* Almahide.] *Qu. Isabel to Al-mahide.* / May . . . blest. Q1-5, F, D (*on same line in F, D*). 310 *Alma-hide.*] Q3, D; *Qu. Almahide.* Q1, Q4-5, F; Q∧ *Alma,* Q2. 314 I'me] Q2-3, Q5, F, D; 'Ime Q1, Q4. 324 climb] Q1-4, D; clime Q5, F. 332 pow'r] Q1-4, D; power Q5, F. 334 her hand.] Q1-4, F, D; ~ ~∧ Q5. 334+ *s.d. Gives*] Q2-5, F, D; *gives* Q1. 336 Conquerour:] ~ . Q1-5, F, D. 338 Commands] Q1-5, F; Command D. 342 *Moors*] Q2-3, D; Moors Q1, Q4-5, F. 347 Live] Q3-5, F, D; live Q1-2. 348 Spain] Q2-5, F, D; Spain Q1. 348+ *s.d. omitted from Q1-5, F.*

Epilogue: EPILOGUE to the Second Part of GRANADA.] Q1-5; EPI-LOGUE, F, D. 9 *Play:*] ~ . Q1-5, F; ~ , D. 11 *Fame*] Q2-3; Fame Q1, Q4-5, F, D. 11 *then*] Q1-4, F, D; *thin* Q5. 12 dead.] Q1-4, F, D; ~ : Q5. 15 Jonson, . . . *height*] Q1-2, Q4; ~∧ . . . ~ , Q3, F, D; ~∧ . . . ~∧ Q5. 23 *now*] Q1-5, D; *new* F. 30 *than*] Q1, Q3-5, F, D; *then* Q2. 33 hath] Q2-3; has Q1, Q4-5, F, D.

Defence of the Epilogue: Defence of the Epilogue is entirely omitted from Q4-5, F. 203:1 will] Q2-3, D; wil! Q1. 203:6 Postscript] Q2-3, D; Preface Q1. 203:8 *English*] Q3, D; English Q1-2. 203:9 Epi-logue] *Epilogue* Q1-3, D. 203:21 trust:] Q2-3; ~ . Q1; ~ , D. 204:4 *lutulentum*] Q2-3; *luculentum* Q1, D. 204:10 *recideret*] Q2-3; *re-cederet* Q1, D. 204:17 And] Q2-3, D; and Q1. 204:26 *Conversa-tion:*] D; ~ . Q1-3. 204:28 Language] *Language* Q1-3, D. 205:5 *English*] D; English Q1-3. 205:25 self.] Q1-2, D; ~ : Q3. 205:26 failings:] Q2, D; ~ . Q1, Q3. 205:26 them:] D; ~ . Q1-3. 205:32 *English*] D; English Q1-3. 205:34 Solecism] *Solecism* Q1-3, D. 206:4 *coronam:*] Q1-3; ~ . D. 206:11 *of*] of Q1-3, D. 206:12 *Shakespear:*] ~ . Q1-3, D. 206:21 his *Humorous Lieutenant,* his] Q2-3, D; *his Hu-morous Lieutenant, his* Q1. 206:22 *Shepheardess*] Q2-3, D; Shepheard-ess Q1. 206:23 them:] Q2-3, D; ~ . Q1. 206:29 *Leoncius*] Q1-3; *Leontius* D. 206:30 *Lieutenant*] *Lieutenant* Q1-3, D. 206:32 Shepheard] *Shepheard* Q1-3, D. 207:1 Women:] Q2-3, D; ~ . Q1. 207:3 theirs:] Q2-3; ~ . Q1, D. 207:5 converse:] Q2-3, D; ~ . Q1. 207:12 them:] Q2-3, D; ~ . Q1. 207:13 Wit:] Q2-3, D; ~ . Q1. 207:17 Language;] D; ~ . Q1-3. 207:19 *Jonson*] Johnson Q1-3, D. 207:20 Judicious] *some copies of Q1 have* Judicsous. 207:23 faults] *some copies of Q1 have* faulrs. 207:26 *Cædimus*] Q3; *Cædimus* Q1-2, D. 207:26 *crura*] Q2-3; *cura* Q1, D. 207:27-210:21 *the bracketed passage was deleted by Dryden from Q2-3.* 207:28 first] Q1; last D. 207:28 *Jonson*] Johnson Q1, D. 208:5 horrour:] D; ~ . Q1. 208:17 Oratory.] Q1; ~ : D. 209:7 twice. To] D; ~ . to Q1. 209:7-8 *give fire at face of a full cloud*] give fire at face of a full cloud Q1, D. 209:8 *and stand his*] and stand his Q1, D. 209:9 *his*] His Q1, D. 209:17 not] Q1; nor D. 209:17 after,] D; ~ . Q1. 209:24-25 *unfear'd . . . unaffraid:*] Unfear'd . . . Unaffraid. Q1, D (Unaffraid: D). 210:2 *ports . . . gates*] Ports . . . Gates Q1, D. 210:7 *Jonson*] Johnson Q1, D. 210:7 these,] D; ~∧ Q1. 210:8-9 *as prose in Q1, D* (*&c.* Q1). 210:10 *some copies of Q1 read* meaness. 210:12 Poetry,] D; ~ . Q1. 210:18 there] D; *there* Q1. 210:23 *Jonson*] Johnson Q1-3, D. 211:1-5 *the bracketed passage was deleted by Dryden from Q2-3.* 211:5

Jonson] *Johnson* Q1, D.   211:7   on] Q1-2, D; upon Q3.   211:17   us,] Q1, D; ~ . Q2-3.   211:29   Words:] Q1, Q2 *(some copies)*, D; ~ . Q2 *(some copies)*; ~ ; Q3.   211:30   may ... *colligere;*] Q2-3; ~ .... ~ . Q1; ~ , ... ~ . D.   211:31   amongst] Q2-3, D; a- / amongst Q1.   211:32   they themselves] Q1-2, D; themselves Q3.   212:1   yet another way] Q1-2, D; another way yet Q3.   212:3   Signification,] D; ~ . Q1-3.   212: 4-5   Expositors:] Q1-3; ~ ? D.   212:11   thought,] Q2-3, D; ~ . Q1.   212:15   Tongue.] Q1-3; ~ ; D.   212:20   fore-mention'd] Q2-3, D; fore mention'd Q1.   212:20   *Jonson*] *Johnson* Q1-3, D.   212:21   admire:] Q2-3; ~ . Q1; ~ ; D.   212:23   them;] Q3; ~ . Q1; ~ , Q2, ~ : D.   212:26   my dead] Q1-2, D; my Q3.   212:29   this.] Q1, Q3, D; ~ : Q2.   212:30   language.] Q1-2, D; ~ , Q3.   213:1   below the] D; below—the Q1-3.   213:1   Writer] Q1-2; Writers Q3, D.   213:12   fourth, and] Q2-3, D; ~∧~ , Q1.   213:14   *Jonson*] *Johnson* Q1-3, D.   213:15   not] Q1-2, D; nor Q3.   213:16   Wit:] ~ . Q1-3, D.   213:26   either to] Q1-2, D; to Q3.   213:30   full:] Q2-3; ~ . Q1; ~ , D.   213:31   Drama] *Drama* Q1-3, D.   213:34   fool)] Q3, D; ~ .) Q1-2.   213:35   thus,] Q2-3; ~ . Q1; ~ : D.   214:6   after,] Q3; ~∧ Q1-2, D.   214:10   stamp?] Q1-2, D; ~ . Q3.   214:21   *Jonson's*:] *Johnson's*: Q1-3, D (~ . Q1; ~ ; D).   214:25   Clergy;] Q2-3, D; ~ . Q1.   215:1   Tongue] Q2-3; *Tongue* Q1, D.   215:11   Master-piece,] Q2-3, D; ~ . Q1.   215: 14   Books,] Q2; ~ . Q1; ~ ; Q3; ~ : D.   215:16   *Mercutio*] Q1, D; *Mercurio* Q2-3.   216:2   genius] *genius* Q1-3, D.   216:3   it:] Q2-3; ~ . Q1, D.   216:7   Comedies] *Comedies* Q1-3, D.   216:8   them:] Q2-3; ~ . Q1, D.   216:12   Wits:] Q2-3; ~ . Q1, D.   216:30   impression] Q2-3; impressions Q1, D.   216:32   Rebellion:] Q2-3; ~ . Q1, D.   216: 34   The desire] Q2-3, D; the desire Q1.   217:5   *English*] Q2-3, D; English Q1.   217:21   characters] Q1-3; Character D.   217:22   Let] Q2-3, D; let Q1.   217:25   so much] Q2-3, D; so- / much Q1.   217:30   end:] Q2-3; ~ . Q1, D.   217:32   Comedies] Q2-3; *Comedies* Q1, D.   217:33   Playes:] Q2-3, D; ~ . Q1.   218:4   Theatre] Q2-3; *Theatre* Q1, D.

Marriage A-la-Mode

Marriage A-la-Mode was first published in 1673 (Q1; Macd 77a) and was reprinted in 1684 (Q2; Macd 77b), 1691 (Q3; Macd 77c), and 1698 (Q4; Macd 77d). It was also reprinted in Dryden's *Comedies, Tragedies, and Operas* (1701), I, 469–514 (F; Macd 107ai–ii [two issues, the differences not affecting this play]), and in Congreve's edition of Dryden's *Dramatick Works* (1717) III, 177–269 (D; Macd 109ai–ii [two issues, the differences not affecting this play]). Q2, F, and D were all set from copies of Q1, Q3 from a copy of Q2, and Q4 from a copy of Q3. Since there is no evidence that Dryden revised the text, the copy text for the present edition is the Clark copy of Q1 (*PR3418.C1), emended as shown in the footnotes.

The songs in the play were published separately before the play itself appeared and often thereafter in the following collections: V[eel], R[obert], Gent., *New Court-Songs, and Poems,* 1672 (Macd 53; Os1), p. 72, Act I; p.

77, Act IV; *Covent Garden Drolery*, 1672 (Macd 54a–b [two issues, the differences not affecting this song]; Os2), p. 62, Act IV; anr. ed., 1672 (Macd 54c; Os3), p. 62, Act IV; *Westminster Drollery, The Second Part*, 1672 (Wing W1462; Os4), pp. 119–120, Act IV; anr. ed., 1672 (Wing W1463; Os5), pp. 119–120, Act IV; [Playford, John], *Choice Songs and Ayres for One Voyce . . . The First Book*, 1673 (Wing C3920 and P2465; Fs1), p. 39, Act I; p. 27, Act IV; [Head, Richard], *The Canting Academy*, 1673 (Wing H1243; Ds1), p. 174, Act IV; 2d ed., 1674 (Wing H1243A; Ds2), p. 128, Act IV; [Playford, John], *Choice Ayres, Songs, & Dialogues*, 2d ed., 1675 (Wing P2462; Fs2), p. 35, Act I; pp. 22–23, Act IV; anr. ed., 1676 (Wing P2463; Fs3), paging as in 1675 ed.; [P., W.], *The Wits Academy*, 1677 (Wing P139; Ds3), p. 72, Act IV. Wing lists another edition of *Choice Ayres*, 1684, in the British Library (P2464), but he appears to be in error; the volume in question is probably his P2461. Fs1–3 give musical settings by Robert Smith (Act I) and Nicholas Staggins (Act IV).

The prologue and epilogue were also printed in Os2–3, pp. 6–8. In Os2, sig. B4, which is a cancel in the second issue, contains the prologue from l. 20 to the end and the epilogue through l. 24. In the apparatus, variants in the cancel are distinguished by the siglum Os2b. Macdonald has numbered the variants in reverse order, apparently: his 54a, in which the title page lists the collector as R. B., has the cancel B4; his 54b, in which the title page lists the corrector as A. B., has the uncanceled B4. Elsewhere in the present edition, Macdonald's ordering has been accepted by oversight. In the prologue, Os2 has two additional lines after line 6; in Os3 they replace the usual lines 3–6. This may indicate that Os3 preceded Os2 and that Os2 conflates Os3 and the usual text.

The prologue and epilogue are also to be found in Bodleian MS Top. Oxon. 3.202, pp. 121–122 (M1); and the song in Act IV, in Edinburgh University Library MS Dc.1.3, p. 108 (M2) and British Library MS Lansdowne 740, fol. 170*v* (M3). M1 is a collection of prose and verse in a single hand; the dated pieces belong to the 1660s and 1670s. M2 is a tall thin folio of poems in several seventeenth-century hands. M3 is a quarto half sheet in a seventeenth-century hand bound in a miscellaneous collection; the first part of the sheet gives rules for extracting square roots. M1 has a triplet in the prologue after l. 19 which was never printed.

The additional lines in the prologue in Os2–3 and M1 do not appear to the present editors to be Dryden's, but Christie (p. 415) and Saintsbury (IV, 258) thought otherwise about the couplet in Os2–3.

The following copies of the various editions have also been examined: Q1: Clark (*PR3418.C1. cop. 2), Huntington (122840), Texas (Aj.D848. 673m), Folger (D2306); Q2: Clark (*PR3418.C1.1684 [2 cop.]), Huntington (D122841); Q3: Clark (*PR3418.C1.1691; *PR3418.C93; *PR3418.C94); Q4: Clark (*PR3418.C1.1698 [2 cop.]; *PR3410.C95a); F: Clark (*fPR3412.1701 [2 cop.]; *fPR3412.1701a); D: Clark (*PR3412.1717 [2 cop.]; *PR3412. 1717a); Os1: British Library (11631.aa.39); Os2, *first issue*: Clark (*PR1213. C87); Os2, *second issue*: Harvard (11445.1*); Os3: Folger (C6624B); Os4: British Library (11621.a.45); Os5: Harvard (*EC65.A100.672wa); Ds1: Huntington (82254); Ds2: Clark (*PR3506.H972.1674); Ds3: British Library (1078.c.1); Fs1: British Library (K.7.i.20); Fs2: British Library (K.7.i.21); Fs3: British Library (K.7.i.19).

Dedication: 221:5 e're] Q1–2, F, D; e'er Q3–4. 221:10 Theatre]
Theatre Q1–4, F, D. 221:16 Lordship's] Q1–2, Q4, F, D; Lordships
Q3. 222:27 than] Q1–3, F, D; then Q4. 222:20 have] F, D; having
Q1–4. 222:31 Lordship's] Q1–2, Q4, F, D; Lordships Q3. 222:36
censures.] Q2–4, F, D; ∼∧ Q1. 222:26 never can] Q1–4, D; can never
F. 223:13 you,] Q1–3, F, D; ∼ . Q4. 223:14 Lordship's] Q1–2, Q4,
F, D; Lordships Q3. 223:32 Poesie] Q1, Q4, F, D; Posie Q2–3. 224:2
and] Q1–3, F, D; add Q4. 224:5 King] Q2–4, F, D; *King* Q1. 224:7
already,] Q1–3, F, D; ∼ . Q4.
Prologue: PROLOGUE.] Q1–4, F, D; *A Prologue to Marriage* Al la mode,
by Mr. Heart. Os2–3 (Hart Os3); Prologue to Marriage Alla mode. 1672 By
Mr Driden M1. 1 *we are*] Q1–4, F, D; are we Os2–3, M1 (wee M1).
6 *after this line Os2 has:*
> Those that durst fight are gone to get renown,
> And those that durst not, blush to stand in Town.

In Os3 the foregoing lines replace ll. 3–6. 4 *White-Wig*] Q1–4, F, D,
M1; While Wig Os2. 4 *make*] Q1–4, F, D; Masks Os2; Masque M1.
4 *jar.*] Q1–4, F, D, Os2; ∼ , M1. 5 *have*] Q1–4, F, D, M1; hath Os2.
6 *we . . . hear.*] Q1–4, F, D; we . . . ∼ ; Os2; wee . . . ∼ , M1. 7 *march'd*]
Q1–4, F, D, M1; went Os2–3. 9 *Tireing-room.*] Q1–4, F, D, Os2–3; ∼∧
M1. 10 *Adieu,*] Q1–4, F, D, Os2, M1; ∼ . Os3. 11 *true;*] Q1–4, F,
D; ∼ . Os2–3, M1. 12 *e're*] Q1–4, F, D, M1; ere Os2–3. 13 *cannot*]
Q1–4, F, D, Os2–3; could not M1. 14 *bloud.*] Q1–4, F, D, Os2–3; ∼∧
M1. 16 *they*] Q1–4, F, D, M1; the Os2–3. 17 *maintain.*] Q1–4, F,
D, Os2–3; ∼———— M1. 19 *appear.*] Q1–4, F, D, Os2–3; ∼ , M1. 19
after this line M1 has:
> All noise is husht within our Empty walls   ⎞
> The Old Cat-fac't Critick now noe longer Brawles ⎬
> But vents his treadbare jests in Hospitalls   ⎠

20 *ere*] Q1–4, F, D, Os2b, M1; are Os2a, Os3. 20 *Plays*] Q1–4, F, D,
Os2–3; Play M1. 21 *venture*] Q1–4, F, D, Os2b, Os3, M1 (venter Os2b);
veture Os2a. 21 *in:*] Q1–4, F, D; ∼ . Os2–3; ∼ , M1. 22 *her last*]
Q1–4, F, D, M1; her Os2–3. 23 *the . . . Air.*] Q1–4, F, D, Os2–3; th' . . .
∼ , M1. 24 *come*] Q1–4, F, D; roam Os2–3, M1. 26 *Shows*] Q1–4,
F, D, Os2–3; Scenes M1. 26 *and*] Q1–4, F, D, M1; with Os2–3. 26
Scenes] Q1–4, F, D, Os2–3; Shewes M1. 26 *elsewhere*] Q1–4, F, D, Os2b,
Os3, M1; else where Os2a. 27 *we*] Q1–4, F, D; 'tis Os2–3; wee M1.
27 *presume*] Q1–4, F, D, M1; presum'd Os2–3. 27 *hear.*] Q1–4, F, D;
∼ : Os2–3; ∼ , M1. 29 Moorcraft] Os2–3 (∼ ,); *Moorcraft,* Q1–4, F,
D, M1 (∼∧ M1). 29 *Masquerade.*] Q1–4, F, D, Os2–3; ∼ , M1. 30
There's] Q1–4, F, D, M1; Here's Os2–3. 30 *hope . . . we*] Q1–4, F, D,
Os2–3; hopes . . . wee M1. 30 *to day*] Q1–4, F, D, Os2b, Os3, M1; to do
Os2a. 31 *Play:*] Q1–4, F, D; ∼ . Os2–3; ∼ , M1. 33 *We . . . come
behind*] Q1–4, F, D, Os2–3; Wee . . . bee outdone M1. 35 *'em*] Q1–4,
F, D, Os2–3; you M1. 35 *Couch*] Q1–3, F, D, Os2–3, M1; *Coach* Q4.
35 *within:*] Q1, D, Os2–3; ∼ . Q2–4, F; ∼ , M1. 36 *how e're*] Q1–4,
F, D, Os2a, Os3, M1; how ere Os2b. 36 *fall*] Q1–4, F, D, M1; falls Os2–
3. 37 *T'*] Q1, F, D; *To* Q2–4, Os2–3, M1.
Dramatis Personae: Persons Represented] Q1–4, F; Dramatis Personae D.
MEN. By] Q1–4, F; MEN. D. *Polydamas*] Q1–2, F, D; *Polydamus* Q3–4.

Polydamas] Q1–3, F, D; *Polydamus* Q4.　　WOMEN. By] Q1–4, F; WOM-
EN. D.　　*Beliza*] D; *Belisa* Q1–4, F.

I, i

2+　*s.d.* [*They*] F, D; ∧~ Q1–4.　8　*Till*] Q1–4, F; 'Till D.　15–18
*in Q1–4, F, D all lines are equally indented; except in F, they are preceded
by a line space and divided and capitalized as follows:* 'Tis . . . | Should . . . |
Or . . . | For . . . | Is . . . | When . . . .　16　another:] Q1, F, D; ~ ? Q2–4.
18+　*s.d.* Beliza.] Q1, Q3–4, F, D; ~ , Q2.　22　my self] Q1–2, Q4, F, D;
my Q3.　29　me?] Q1–2, Q4, F, D; ~ . Q3.　43　till] Q1–4, F; 'till D.
43　is,] Q1–3, F, D; ~∧ Q4.　56　self.] Q1–4, F; ~∧ D.　61　Fortune]
Fortune Q1–4, F, D.　67　marry'd;] Q1–3, F, D; ~ ? Q4.　67　Woman?] Q1, F, D; ~ ! Q2–4.　71　Fortune] *Fortune* Q1–4, F, D.　73
days:] F; ~ . Q1–4, D.　77　till] Q1–4, F; 'till D.　80　*s.d.* (*Aside . . .
Lady*)] ∧~ . . . ~ . Q1–4, F, D.　87+　*s.d.* [*Exit*] Q2–4, F, D; ∧~ Q1.
95　*s.d.* [*Sees* Palamede] Q2–4, D (∧~ Q2–4); [Sees *Palamede* Q1, F (∧~ Q1).
103　him?] Q1–2, F, D; ~ . Q3–4.　106　another] Q1–3, F, D; an other
Q4.　111　till] Q1–4, F; 'till D.　116　years] Q2–4; ~ , Q1, F, D.
122　me.] Q1–3, F, D; ~ ! Q4.　136　say?] Q1–2, F, D; ~ : Q3–4.　136
that best] Q1–4, D; best that F.　140　*Palamede*,] Q1–4, D; ~ ; F.　145
memory;] Q1–4, D; ~ . F.　150　fashion] Q2–4; ~ , Q1, F, D.　151
at that] Q1–3, F, D; at the Q4.　160　*Rhodophil:*] Q1–4, D; ~ . F.　170
but] Q2–4, F, D; ~ , Q1.　172　*Pala.*] Q2–4, F, D; ~ , Q1.　183　seen
there] Q1–4, D; seen F.　194　another] Q1–3, F, D; an other Q4.　197
French Word] Q2–4, D (French Q2–4); French-word Q1; *French*-Word F.
212　haste] Q1–3, F, D; hast Q4.　220　and as proud] Q1–3, F, D; as
proud Q4.　223　vices] Q1–4, D; Voices F.　228　*Rho.*] Q1–3, F, D;
~ ! Q4.　233　*speech omitted from Q2–4.*　234　*s.d.* (*To . . . whisper.*)]
D; ∧~ . . . ~ .∧ Q1–4, F.　234　friend?] Q1–2, F, D; ~ : Q3–4.　236
kiss'd] Q2–4, F, D; kis'd Q1.　237+　*s.d.* [*Exeunt*] F, D; ∧~ Q1–4.　239
Amal.] Q1–4, D; ~∧ F.　249　*Polydamas*] Q1–2, F, D; *Polydamus* Q3–4.
255　*Theagenes;*] Q1–4, D; ~ . F.　256　*Polydamas*] Q1–2, F, D; *Polydamus* Q3–4.　259　*Polydamas*] Q1–2, F, D; *Polydamus* Q3–4.　264
o'rcome] Q1–2, ov'rcome Q3–4; o'ercome D.　269　*Polydamas*] Q1–2, F,
D; *Polydamus* Q3–4.　270　father's] Q1–2, Q4, F, D; Fathers Q3.　293
He] Q2–4, D; he Q1, F.　296+　*s.d.* Guards] Guard Q1–4, F, D.　296+
s.d. Attendants.] Q1–3, F, D; ~ , Q4.　302　*s.d.* Aside.] D; aside. Q1–4, F
(~ , Q2).　306　make] Q1, F, D; makes Q2–4.　316　Lord] Q1, F, D;
the Lord Q2–4.　317+　*s.d.* [Palamede] F, D; ∧~ Q1–4.　317　You're]
Q1–4, F; You are D.　319　fellow-soldiers] Q1, F, D; ~ . Q2; ~ , Q3–4.
324　your] Q1–2, Q4, F, D; you Q3.　329+　*s.d.* Exeunt] Q2–4, F, D
(*Exit.* Q3–4); ~ . Q1.　330　miracles!] Q1, F, D; ~∧ Q2–4.　333
Daughter,] Q1, F, D; ~ . Q2–4.　336　but] Q1–4, D; but but F.　342
Poly.] Q1–3, F, D; ~ , Q4.　343　*s.d. To*] Q3–4, F, D; *to* Q1–2.　344
Sir:] Q1–2, F, D; ~ . Q3–4.　347–348　*one line in Q1–4, F, D* (a Virgin).
357+　*s.d.* Guards] Q2–4; Guard Q1, F, D.　357+　*s.d. off.*] Q1–4, F;
~∧ D.　360, 365　Eudocia] Eudoxia Q1–4, F, D.　367+　*s.d.* Palm.]
Q1–4, D; ~∧ F.　368　Eudocia] Eudoxia Q1–4, F, D.　378　Queen,]
Q3–4; ~ . Q1–2, D; ~ ; F.　378　Again.] Q1–2, F, D; ~ , Q3–4.　380
Sir.] Q1–3, F, D; ~ , Q4.　383　to] Q1–3, F, D; on Q4.　392　with

the] Q1–3, F, D; with Q4.   398 Heaven] Q1–4, F; Heav'n D.   401
thee] Q1–2, Q4, F, D; the Q3.   402 Sun] Q1–2, F, D; Son Q3–4.   405
further] Q1–4, D; farther F.   407 *s.d. Kneeling*] F, D; *kneeling* Q1–4.
433 forbid] Q1–3, F, D; ~ . Q4.   444 it.] Q1–4, D; ~ , F.   445 *indented in Q1 as if a new speech*.   454+ *s.d.* Palmyra.] Q1–3, F, D; ~ ∧
Q4.   458 Courtiers,] Q1, F, D; ~ . Q2–4.   462 wrong,] Q1–3, F, D;
~ . Q4.

II, i

7 *étourdy*] *etourdy* Q1–4, F, D.   8 he] Q1–4, D; we F.   12 *Phil.*]
Q1–3, F, D; ~ , Q4.   20+ *s.d. Letter.*] Q1–3, F, D; ~ ∧ Q4.   27 Let-
ter] Q1–4, F; ~ . D.   28 O] Q1–2, F, D; Oh Q3–4.   28 sent me!]
Q1–4, D; ~ ! ~ ∧ F.   29 *homme*)] Q1–3, F, D; ~ .) Q4.   30 *neighbour*:] Q1–3, F, D; ~ . Q4.   45 any] Q1–4, F; a D.   56 you?] F; ~ !
Q1–4, D.   56 Jigs] F, D; *Jigs* Q1–4.   57 *fade*] fad Q1; sad Q2–4, F,
D.   76 by the] Q1–3, F, D; the Q4.   80 *obligeant, charmant, ravis-
sant,*] obligeant, charmant, ravissant, Q1–4, F, D.   84 the] Q1–3, F, D;
thee Q4.   89 nay, and] Q1–4, F; and D.   103 other] Q1–3, F, D;
old Q4.   106 out] Q1–3, F, D; out the Q4.   113 loves] Q1–4, F;
Lovers D.   115 ever] Q1–4, F; over D.   118 Navigation?] Q1–2, D;
~ . Q3–4, F.   119 life,] Q1–2, F, D; ~ . Q3–4.   121 'tis.] Q1–4, F;
~ : D.   134 fellow!] Q1, F, D; ~ , Q2–3; ~ . Q4.   134 *s.d. him*]
Q1, Q3–4, F, D; ~ . Q2.   134 *s.d. forward* Q1–3, F, D; *forwards* Q4.
135+ *s.d. Looking*] F, D; *looking* Q1–4.   140–141 *printed as verse
(. . . / To . . .) in Q1–4, F*.   146 where?] Q1–2, F, D; ~ ! Q3–4.   147
There.] Q1–4, D; ~ , F.   147+ *s.d. after l. 146 in Q1–4, D*.   148
printed as verse (. . . / O . . .) in Q1–4, F.   149–150 *printed as verse
(. . . / I have . . .) in Q1–4, F*.   151 *s.d. Aside*)] Q3–4, D; ~ .) Q1–2, F.
153 *s.d. Aside*)] Q1, Q4, F; ~ .) Q2–3, D.   159 *s.d. Aside*)] Q4; ~ .)
Q1–3, F, D.   172+ *s.d. and*] Q1–3, F, D; *ands* Q4.   186 *s.d.* [*Whispers*] Q3–4, F, D; ∧~ Q1–2.   187 *Rho.*] Q2–4, F, D; *Rho*∧ Q1.   187
Woman.] Q1–3, F, D; ~ , Q4.   187, 188+ *s.d.* [*Aside*] Q3–4, F, D; ∧~
Q1–2.   189 *s.d.* (*Raising her Voice*)] ∧~ ~ ~ . Q1–4, D; [~ ~ ~ .] F.
194 *s.d.* [*Aside*] Q3–4, F, D; ∧~ Q1–2.   197 *a la*] D; *al a* Q1–4, F.
198 *en*] in Q1–4, F, D.   198 Gallanteries] Gallanteries Q1–2; Gallantries Q3–4, F, D.   206 *enjoué*] *enjouué* Q1–4, F, D.   207 *a d'autre,
a d'autre*] ad autre, ad autre Q1–4, F, D.   209 *s.d.* (*To* Artemis)] *To*
Artemis. Q1–4 (*Aretemis* Q1); [*To Artemis.*] F; [*To* Artemis.] D.   223
Rhodophil] Q2–4, D; *Rodophil* Q1, F.   224 All.] Q1–3, F, D; ~ ∧ Q4.
224 *s.d.* [*Exit*] Q3–4, F, D; ∧~ Q1–2.   225 *Rhodophil*] Q2–4, D; *Rodophil* Q1, F.   225 *s.d.* [*Whispers*] Q3–4, F, D; ∧~ Q1–2.   226 *Dor.*
(*To* Pala.)] *Dor. to Pala.* Q1–4, D (*To* Q2–4); [*Dor. to Pala.*] F.   227
her?] Q1–2, F, D; ~ ! Q3–4.   229 all] Q1–3, F, D; to Q4.   230
hope?] Q1, F, D; ~ . Q2–4.   231 be so] Q1–3, F, D; be Q4.   260
night. [*Exit.*] Q1, F, D; night. Q2–4.   261 *s.d. To*] Q2–4; *to* Q1, F, D.
271 ignorance,] Q1–2, F, D; ~ . Q3–4.   283 you.] Q1–3, F, D; ~ ! Q4.
285 forc'd.] Q1–2, F, D; ~ , Q3–4.   299 T'] Q1–3, F, D; 'T Q4.   304
hearts?] Q1–4, D; ~ ∧ F.   314 *Leon.*] Q1–3, F, D; ~ , Q4.   316 *s.d.
Aside.*] Q2–4, F, D; ~ ∧ Q1.   320 with [*To him.*] with Q1–4, F, D.
325 pow'r] ~ , Q1–4, F, D.   336 vow] F; ~ , Q1–4, D.   341 than]

Q1–3, F, D; then Q4.   341 you:] Q1–3, D; ~ , Q4; ~ . F.   350 *s.d.*
Kneeling.] F (~ʌ), D; *kneeling.* Q1–4.   355 Prince his] Q1–4, F; Prince's
D.   366 would] Q1, F, D; will Q2–4.   369 ere] Q1–2; e're Q3–4, D;
e'er F.   373 by that] Q1–3, F, D; that Q4.   382 interest] Q1–3, F,
D; intrest Q4.   400 King's] Q1–3, F, D; Kings Q4.   403 mutter,]
Q1–4, D; ~ . F.   403 *s.d.* [*Going.*] Q3, F, D; (~ . Q1–2; [~ʌ Q4.   404
s.d. Going] Q3–4, F, D; *going* Q1–2.   405 *s.d. Softly*] Q1–2; ~ . Q3–4,
F, D.   421 *Palm.*] Q2–4, F, D; ~ʌ Q1.   434 stay:] Q1–4, D; ~ . F.
446 my very] Q1–3, F, D; my Q4.   461 Prince his] Q1–4, F; Prince's
D.   465 Heav'n] Q2–4, F, D; Heav'en Q1.   502 *s.d. Exeunt.*] Q1–4,
D; ~ʌ F.

III, i

1 heart!] Q1–4, F; ~ ; D.   9 have fail'd] Q1–4, D; fail F.   9 *s.d.*
Kissing] Q1–4, F; *Kisses* D.   12 you?] Q1–3, F, D; ~ ! Q4.   17 imag-
in'd] Q4; ~ , Q1–3, F, D.   32 *s.d. Aside*] Q1–2, Q4, F; ~ . Q3, D.   32
I am] Q1–2, F, D; I'm Q3–4.   34 gone?] Q1, F, D; ~ ; Q2–4.   36
time.] Q2–4, F, D; ~ʌ Q1.   40 own] Q1–3, F, D; one Q4.   43 *Dor.*]
Q1–4, D; ~ʌ F.   44 provok'd.] Q2–4, F, D; ~ , Q1.   52 it was I]
Q1–3, F, D; I Q4.   61 thy] Q1–2, F, D; the Q3–4.   62 in] Q1–3, F,
D; in the Q4.   65 be but] Q1, F, D; be Q2–4.   66 ha?] Q1–2, F, D;
~ ! Q3–4.   72 What] Q1–2, F, D; Why Q3–4.   75 to] Q1–3, F, D;
to the Q4.   78 or a] Q1–3, F, D; or but a Q4.   79 taken] Q1–4, D;
take F.   81 out.] Q1–2, F, D; ~ : Q3–4.   82 jaded.] Q1, Q3–4, F,
D; ~ʌ Q2.   83 thee] Q1–2, F, D; the Q3–4.   90 us.] Q1–2, F, D; ~ :
Q3–4.   91 we] Q1–3, F, D; wee Q4.   93 to] Q4; too Q1–3, F, D.
96 *chagrin*] chagrin Q1–4, F, D.   107 Town-Lady.] Q1, Q3–4, F, D;
~ʌ Q2.   123 upon the] Q1–3, F, D; upon Q4.   128 Carriers-day]
Q1, D; Carrier's day Q2–4, F.   136 *Dor.*] Q2–4, F, D; *Dor*ʌ Q1.   140
sing,] Q1–3, F, D; ~ . Q4.   141 &c.] Q3–4, F, D; *&c.* Q1–2.   149
I'm] Q1–3; I am Q4, F, D.   151 Countrey-acquaintance] Q1–2, F; Coun-
try Acquaintance Q3–4, D.   153 'em] Q1–4, F; them D.   155 Town-
Lady,] Q3–4; ~ ; Q1, F, D; ~ʌ Q2.   160–161 Countrey-house] Q1–2, F;
Country House Q3–4, D.   161 there] Q1, Q4, F, D; their Q2–3.   174
tendre] tender Q1–4, F, D.   182 do] Q1–3, F, D; to do Q4.   183
Spirituellé] Q1–2, F, D; *Spirituellée* Q3–4.   187 *risque*] risque Q1–4,
F, D.   189 & *usé*] *& use* Q1; *& usè* Q2–3, D; *& usé* Q4, F.   194 ex-
pences] Q1–4, F; Expence D.   195 *Drain'd?*] Drain'd? Q1–4, F, D (~ !
Q3–4).   195 there!] Q1–2, F, D; ~? Q3–4.   195 *Épuisée*] Epuisée
Q1–4, F, D.   197 *s.d. Shows*] Q1–2, Q4, F, D; *Shew* Q3.   199 till]
Q1–4, F; 'till D.   200 words] works Q1–4, F, D.   200 'em] Q1–3, F,
D; them Q4.   204 to me] Q1–4, D; me F.   206 a *figure*] a figure Q1–
4, F, D.   207 *Naiveté*] Q3–4, F, D; *Naivetè* Q1–2.   211 *naiveté*] Q2–
3, F, D; *naivetè* Q1, Q4.   214 *Équivoque*] Equivoque Q1–4, F, D.   214
Éclaircissement] Esclaircissement Q1–4, F; *Eclaircissement* D.   214
Suitte] F; *Suittè* Q1–2, D; *Suitté* Q3–4.   214 *Bévue*] Beveue Q1–4, F, D.
214 *Façon*] Facòn Q1–4, D; Facon F.   215 *étourdy*] etourdy Q1–4, F,
D.   220 How] Q1–4, D; *Mel.* How F.   222 *Sovereignly!*] Q1–4, F;
~ ? D.   224 Point Gorget] Q1–2, F, D; Point-Gorget Q3–4.   230

Indian-Gown] D; *Indian-Gown* Q1-4, F. 231 *s.d. again.*] Q3-4, F, D;
~ : Q1-2. 240 *s.d. Letter*] Q1-2, F; ~ . Q3-4, D. 240-241 you
———] Q2-4, F; ~ .——— Q1, D. 243 there's] Q1-4, F; there is D.
255 rude.] Q1-2; ~ , Q3-4, F, D. 257 Madam———] Q1-4, D; ~ .
——— F. 258 ah, ah, ah.] Q1, F, D; ha, ha, ha. Q2-4. 258+ *s.d.*
Polydamas] Q1, F, D; Polydamus Q2-4. 264 love] Q1-4, D; lov'd F.
264 the] Q1-3, F, D; this Q4. 265 title] Q1-4, D; Tittle F. 265+
s.d. guarded.] Q1, Q3-4, F, D; ~∧ Q2. 273 lie.] Q1-2, F, D; lye Q3-4.
289 and the] Q1, F, D; and Q2-4. 295 Prince his] Q1-4, F; Prince's
D. 298 ere] Q1-4, F; e'er D. 313 ———Look] ∧~ Q1-4, F, D.
313-314 Piety; / And] Piety; and Q1-4, F, D. 330 please,] Q1-3, F,
D; ~∧ Q4. 341+ *s.d. knees.*] Q1-3, F, D; ~∧ Q4. 356+ *s.d. as in*
D; *after l. 357 in Q1-4; on l. 357 in* F. 367 has once] Q1-3, F, D; once
has Q4. 375 but that] Q1-4, D; that that F. 381 this] Q1, F, D;
the Q2-4. 389 their] Q1-3, F, D; there Q4. 402 Sir;] Q1, F, D;
~ , Q2-4. 402 King,] Q1-2, F, D; ~ . Q3-4. 403 lie] Q1-2, F, D;
Lye Q3-4. 408 forget] Q1, F, D; forgot Q2-4. 414+ *s.d. Kneels*]
Q3-4, F, D; *kneels* Q1-2. 443 your] Q1-2, F, D; you Q3-4. 445
you] Q1-2, Q4, F, D; your Q3. 446 regard] Q1, Q3-4, F, D; reguard
Q2. 470 alone] Q1, Q4, F, D; lone Q2-3. 471 ere] Q1-4; e'r F;
e'er D. 472 Nature.] Q1, F, D; ~ , Q2-4. 474 fate.] Q1, F, D; ~ ,
Q2-3; ~ ; Q4. 477 Scene] Q1, F, D; seen Q2-4.

III, ii

S.d. at] Q1-4, F; *at the* D. *s.d. him.*] Q1-3, F, D; ~∧ Q4. 6 them.]
Q1-4, D; ~∧ F. 24 your] Q1-2, Q4, F, D; you Q3. 26 nothing.]
Q1, Q3-4, F, D; ~∧ Q2. 29 ere] Q1-4; e'r F; e're D. 30 Animal,]
Q1-2, F, D; ~ ! Q3-4. 32 *Pala.*] Q1-4, D; ~∧ F. 50 your] Q1-3,
F, D; you Q4. 63 further] Q1-4, D; farther F. 69 *s.d. Within*]
Q1-2; ~ . Q3-4, F, D. 72 me] Q1-2, F, D; of me Q3-4. 72+ *s.d.*
He] Q4, F; [~ Q1-3, D (*s.d. flush right in Q1-4, run into speech in* D).
72+ *s.d. Melantha.*] Q1-3, F, D; ~∧ Q4. 73 How!] Q1, F, D; ~∧ Q2;
~ , Q3-4. 74 *Surprenant*] Q1-2, F, D; *Suprenant* Q3-4. 78 com-
pany?] Q1, Q3-4, F, D; ~ . Q2. 90 so very] Q1-3, F, D; so Q4. 92
alone.] Q1, Q3-4, F, D; ~∧ Q2. 93 mistaking:] Q1-4, F; ~ . D. 93
me, I] Q1-3, F, D; I Q4. 94 us.] Q1, Q3-4, F, D; ~∧ Q2. 95 *s.d.*
Within.] Q1-4, D; ~∧ F. 96 voice. Who's] voice? who's Q1-4, F, D.
96 there] Q1, Q3-4, F, D; their Q2. 98 the] Q1-3, F, D; that Q4.
99 *Palamede, Palamede,*] Q1-3, F, D; ~ . ~ , Q4. 106 for you now.]
Q1-2, D; for you. Q3-4; now. F. 107 thunder-struck] Q1-3, F, D; ~ .
Q4. 110 Spouse?] Q1-4, D; ~ : F. 113 *s.d. husband*] Q1-2; ~ .
Q3-4, F, D. 114 i'faith?] ~ ! Q1-4, F, D. 114 you?] ~ ! Q1-4, F,
D. 116-117 *printed as verse in Q1-4,* F (Spouse! / Prethee). 119
these] Q1-3, F, D; this Q4. 123 hither on] Q1-3, F, D; hither on the
Q4. 131 *Palamede, Palamede,*] Q1, Q3-4, F, D; ~ . ~ , Q2. 133
avow] Q1, F, D; vow Q2-4. 133 apparence] Q1-2; appearance Q3-4,
F, D. 137 none] Q1-4, F; n'own D. 139 *s.d. Aside*] Q1-2; ~ . Q3-
4, F, D. 139 am I] Q1-2, F, D; I am Q3-4. 148 one.] Q1-4, D; ~ ,
F. 148+ *s.d. one another*] Q1, F, D; *each other* Q2-4.

IV, i

5 lov'd,] ~‿ Q1–4, F, D.   6 greatness.] Q1–3, F, D; ~‿ Q4.   12 perhaps, too] Q1–2, F, D; ~‿ ~ , Q3–4.   16 one] Q1, Q3–4, F, D; on Q2.   18 *Amal.*] Q1, Q3–4, F, D; ~ , Q2.   19 mistaken, [*To him*] mistaken, Q1–4, F, D.   30 speak. [*Aside.*] speak. Q1–4, F, D.   31 Sir, [*To him.*] Sir, Q1, F, D; Sir. Q2–4.   34 griefs] Q1–4, D; Grief's F.   46 careless] Q1–3, F, D; carless Q4.   56 you] Q1–3, F, D; your Q4.   62 failings,] Q3–4; failing, Q1–2; failing‿ F, D.   64 I?] Q1–2, Q4, F, D; ~ ! Q3.   64 never. 'Tis] ~ : 'tis Q1–4, F, D ('Tis Q3–4, D).   66 come] Q1, F, D; came Q2–4.   88 Masquerade] F, D; *Masquerade* Q1–4.   93 thunder,] Q1, F, D; ~ . Q2–4.   99 *Leon.*] F, D; *Leonidas.* Q1–4.   101 bred] Q1, Q4, F, D; bread Q2–3.   103 Foster-Father] Q4, F; Foster, Father Q1–3; Foster Father D.   103 *s.d.* *Kneeling.*] Q1, Q3–4, F, D; ~ , Q2.   113 know] Q1–2, F, D; now Q3–4.   125 servant,] Q1–3, F, D; ~ . Q4.   130 going] Q1–2, F, D; go Q3–4.   131 with] Q1–3, F, D; without Q4.   132 know you?] Q1–4, D; ~ ~ ; F.   142 Salvages] *Salvages* Q1–4, F, D.   153 Woman] Q1–3, F, D; women Q4.   155–156 absence.] Q1, Q3–4, F, D; ~‿ Q2.   163 *s.d.* *Aside*] Q1–2, F; ~ . Q3–4, D.   164 was a] Q1–4, D; was F.   164 for] Q1–3, F, D; for a Q4.   184 with the] Q1–4, D; with he F.   187 the] Q1–4, D; the the F.   187 I] Q2–4, F, D; ~ , Q1.   194 Youth.] Q1–4, D; ~‿ F.   197 sober.] Q1–3, F, D; ~‿ Q4.   203 *s.d.* *Aside*] Q1–2, F; ~ . Q3–4, D.   206 the] Q1–3, F, D; this Q4.   209 *s.d.* Rhodophil] Q2–4, F (~ . Q3–4); *Rhodophil* Q1, D (~ . D).

IV, ii

s.d. Polydamas] Q1–2, F, D; Polydamus Q3–4.   2 what,] Q1–3, F, D; ~‿ Q4.   3 of high] Q1–3, F, D; high of Q4.   9 *s.d.* Leonidas] Q3–4 (~ .); *Leonidas* Q1–2, F, D (~ . D).   10 ere] Q1–2, F; e're Q3; e'er Q4, D.   14+ *s.d.* Palmyra.] Q1–3, F, D; ~‿ Q4.   19 this] Q1–3, F, D; the Q4.   21 sake:] Q1–4, F; ~ . D.   25 *Leon.*] Q1–4, D; ~‿ F.   35 known.] Q1, F, D; ~ , Q2–4.   42 hand.] Q1–3, F, D; ~ ; Q4.   46 tormented. [*Exit.*] Q1–4, D; tormented. F.   46+ *s.d.* SONG.] Q1–4, F, D, Os1; *A SONG.* Os2–3; A New SONG. *Marriage All a Mode.* Os4–5; *A Lover dying with delight.* Ds1–2; SONG LXXXVII. Ds3; *The Lover's Trance.* M2; *no title* Fs1–3, M3.   *Four-line stanzas in Os1, Ds1–3 (no spacing between stanzas in Ds1–2), Fs1–3; five-line stanzas in M2–3. Stanzas not numbered in Os1, Ds1–3, M3.*   47 *Whil'st*] Q1–4, F, D, Os2–5, Ds1–3, Fs1–3, M3; While Os1, M2.   47 Alexis] Q1–4, F, D, Os1, Ds1–3, Fs1–3, M2–3; *Alixis* Os2–5 (*and so throughout*).   49 *hands*] Q1–4, F, D, Os1–5, Ds1–3, M2–3; hand Fs1–3.   50 breast,] Q1–4, F, D, Os1, Ds1–2; ~ . Os2–5; ~ ; Ds3; ~ : Fs1–3; ~‿ M2–3.   51 *fierce pleasure*] Q1–4, F, D, Os1–5, Ds3, Fs1–3, M2–3; first pleasures Ds1–2.   51 *too hasty to stay*] Q1–4, F, D, Os1–5, Fs1–3, M2; too stay Ds1; to stay Ds2; too hasty M3.   52 *the*] Q1–4, F, D, Os1–5, Ds1–3, M2–3; a Fs1–3.   52 *just*] Q1–4, F, D, Os1–5, Ds3, Fs1–3, M2–3; was Ds1–2.   52 away.] Q1–4, F, D, Os1–5, Ds1–3, Fs1–3, M2; ~‿ M3.   53–62 omitted from M3.   55 Oh] Q1–4, F, D, Os1–5, Ds1–3, M2; O Fs1–3, M3.   55 dear,] Q1–4, F, D, Os2–5, M2; ~ ! Os1, Ds1–2, Fs1–3; ~‿ Ds3.   55 *I am*] Q1–4, F, D, Os1–5, Ds1,

Ds3, M2; am I Ds2; I'm Fs1–3.   55   *robb'd*] Q1–4, F, D, Os1, Ds3, Fs1–3,
M2; rob'd Os2–5, Ds1; rob'b Ds2.   55   *bliss;*] Q1–4, F, D, Os1–5, Ds3,
Fs1–3; ~ , Ds1; ~ ? Ds2; ~ₐ M2.   56   *'Tis*] Q1–4, F, D, Os1–5, Ds3,
Fs1–3, M2; 'Twas Ds1–2.   57   *die*] Q1–4, F, D, Os1, Ds1–3; dye Os2–5,
Fs1–3; doe M2.   57   *alone.*] Q1–3, F, D, Os1–5, Ds1–3, Fs1–3, M2; ~ₐ
Q4.   58   *haste*] Q1–4, F, D, Os1, Ds2, M2; hast Os2–5, Ds1, Ds3, Fs1–3.
60   *while*] Q1–4, F, D, Os1, M2; whilst Os2–5, Ds1–3, Fs1–3.   61   *Till*]
Q1–4, F, Os1–3, Ds1–3, M2; 'Till D, Os4–5, Fs1–3.   61   *dear*] Q1–4, F,
D, Os1–5, Ds3, Fs1–3, M2; Love Ds1–2.   61   *let us*] Q1–4, F, D, Os1–5,
Ds1, Ds3, M2; let me Ds2; Lets Fs1–3 (*in Fs1–3 l. 62 begins here.*)   61
go] Q1–4, F, D, Os1–5, Ds1–3, Fs1–3; do M2.   62   *Now die*] Q1–4, F, D,
Os1, Ds1–3; Now dye Os2–5, Fs1–3; Now do M2.   62   *will die*] Q1–4,
F, D, Os1, Os4–5, Ds1–3; will dye Os2–3, Fs1–3; will do M2.   63   *in-
tranc'd*] Q1–4, F, D, Os1, Os4–5, Ds1–3, Fs1–3, M2–3; in tranc'd Os2–3.
63   *they*] Q1–4, F, D, Os1–5, Ds1–3, M2; she Fs1–3; he M3.   63   *lie*]
Q1–4, F, D, Os1, Ds1–3; lye Os2–5, Fs1–3, M2–3.   64   *Till*] Q1–4, F,
Os1–3, Ds1–3, M3; 'Till D, Os4–5; while Fs1–3, M2.   65   *To*] Q1–4, F,
D, Os1–5, Ds1–3, Fs1–3, M3; Too M2.   65   *new*] Q1–4, F, D, Os1–5,
Ds3, Fs1–3, M2–3; more Ds1–2.   65   *die:*] Q1–4, F, D, Ds2; die. Os1;
dye, Os2–3, Ds1; dye; Os4–5; die; Ds3; dye: Fs1–3; dyeₐ M2–3.   66
Then] Q1–4, F, D, Os1–5, Ds3, Fs1–3, M2–3; Thus Ds1–2.   66   *di'd*]
Q1–4, F, D, Ds1–2, M3; dy'd Os1, Ds3, Fs1–3, M2; did Os2–5.   66   *but*]
Q1–4, F, D, Os1–5, Ds3, Fs1–3, M2–3; oh! Ds1–2.   67   *di'd*] Q1–4, F, D,
Ds1–2, Fs2; dy'd Os1, Ds3, Fs1, Fs3, M2–3; did Os2–5.   67   *slow.*] Q1–4,
F, D, Os1–5, Ds1–3, Fs1, Fs3, M3; ~ₐ Fs2, M2.   68   return? [*To Arga.*]
Q1–3, F, D; return? Q4.   77   are you] Q1–4, D; are yon F.   78   *Arga.*]
Q1, Q3–4, F, D; ~ₐ Q2.   78   is] *the s did not print in some copies of Q2.*

IV, iii

s.d. Palamede;] Q1–2, F, D; ~ₐ Q3–4.   1   *s.d. Aside*] Q1–2, F; ~ .
Q3–4, D.   5   understands] D; understand Q1–4, F.   9   smile, . . .
briskly,] Q1, Q3, F, D; ~ , . . . ~ₐ Q2; ~ₐ . . . ~ , Q4.   12   think] Q1–2,
Q4, F, D; thing Q3.   15   Mistris's] Q1–4, D; Mistrises F.   19   not]
Q1–4, D; no F.   26   hast] Q1–2, F, D; has Q3–4.   35   further] Q1–2,
D; farther Q3–4, F.   37   angry. [*Aside.*]] angry. Q1–4, F, D.   40
onely?] Q1–2, Q4, F, D; ~ . Q3.   55–56   something in her] Q1–4, F;
something D.   58   Steel] Q1–3, F, D; a Steel Q4.   63   self. [*Aside.*]]
self. Q1–4, F, D.   64   thee] Q1–3, F, D; the Q4.   67   Boy's] Q1–3, F,
D; Boy is Q4.   67   word. [*Aside.*]] word. Q1–4, F, D.   76   ha?] Q1–2,
F, D; ~ ! Q3–4.   77   has] Q1–2, F, D; hath Q3–4.   78   therefore]
Q1–3, F, D; the for Q4.   78+   *s.d.* Rhodophil;] Q1–4, D; ~ₐ F.   80
Boy?] Q1–2, F, D; ~ , Q3–4.   81   side.] Q1–2, F, D; ~ , Q3–4.   85
you] Q1–2, Q4, F, D; your Q3.   87   *a-la-derobbée*] Q3–4; al-a derobbée
Q1–2, D; a-la derobbée F.   94   *s.d.* Doralice] Q1–2, Q4; ~ . Q3, F, D.
98   *printed as verse* (. . . me? / Am . . .) *in Q1–4, F.*   107   Mistresses;]
Q4; ~ , Q1–3, F, D.   111   is] Q1–2, F, D; ~ , Q3–4.   117   invention.]
Q1, Q3–4, F, D; ~ , Q2.   118   dispute.———] Q1–3, F; ~ₐ——— Q4;
~ ,——— D.   122   *s.d.* Melantha] Q2–4, D (~ . Q3–4, D); *Melantha.*
Q1, F.   124   Sir.] Q1–4, D; ~ ? F.   125   *O, Monsieur,*] O, Monsieur,
Q1–4, F, D.   125   *vot'*] vot Q1–4, F; *votre* D.   125   *humble.*] Q1–3,

F, D; ~∧ Q4.   126 *Votre*] *Votrè* Q1–3, F; *Votré* Q4, D.   130 new-
lac'd] Q1, D; new lac'd Q2–4, F.   132 *Mon*] Q4; *Man* Q1–3, F, D.
133 thee] Q1–3, F, D; the Q4.   137 ere] Q1–4; e'er F; e're D.   140
s.d. *Embracing*] Q3–4; *embracing* Q1–2, F, D.   144 Boy?] Q1–2, F, D;
~ ! Q3–4.   144 thee] Q1–3, F, D; the Q4.   147–148 mouth and
gapes,] Q1, F; ~ , ~ ~∧ Q2–4; ~∧ ~ ~∧ D.   154 s.d. *To* Melantha]
Q4; *to* Melantha. Q1–3, D (*To* Q3); *to* Melantha. F.   155 Hero] F;
Hero Q1–4, D.   168, 170 till] Q1–4, F; 'till D.   172 them] Q1, F, D;
'em Q2–4.   172 till] Q1–4, F; 'till D.   175 Boy.] Q1–3, F, D; ~ , Q4.
183 s.d. *Aside*.] Q1–2, Q4, F, D; ~ : Q3.   185 *Pala.*] Q1, F, D; *Pal.*
Q2–3; *Palm.* Q4.

IV, iv

s.d. Eubulus,] Q1–4, F; Eubulus, *and* D.   9 long] Q1–4, D; org F.
12 Letters] Q1–4, D; Letter F.   14 he] Q1–3, F, D; that he Q4.   17
Till] Q1–4, F; 'Till D.   18 true] Q1–4, D; rue F.   19 Prince's] Q1–
3, F, D; Princes Q4.   21 I] Q1–2, F, D; we Q3–4.   34 Till] Q1–2,
F; 'Till Q3–4, D.   34 own.] Q1–3, F, D; ~ , Q4.   38 doubt?] Q1,
F, D; ~ ; Q2; ~ ! Q3–4.   43 few:] ~ . Q1–4, F, D.   54 *Leon.*] Q2–4,
F, D; ~∧ Q1.   55 Who] Q1–2, Q4, F, D; Why Q3.   56 *Leon.*] Q2–
4, F, D; ~∧ Q1.   60 *Palmyra's*] Q1, Q4, F, D; *Palmira's* Q2–3.   62
much] Q1–2, Q4, F, D; much as Q3.   76 there.] Q1–2, Q4, F, D; ~ , Q3.
82 dang'rous] Q1–2, D; dangerous Q3–4, F.   89 your] Q1–2, Q4, F,
D; you Q3.   90 more your] Q1, Q3–4, F, D; more you Q2.   99 their]
Q1–3, F, D; the Q4.   105 I'll] Q1–2, F, D; I will Q3–4.   106 Within
there] Q1–2, F, D; (*Within there* Q3–4.   110 s.d. *Kneeling*] Q3, F, D;
kneeling Q1–2, Q4.   111 bonds] Q1–2, D; Bands Q3–4, F.   115 s.d.
Within] Q2–4, F (~ . F); *within* Q1, D (~ . D).   119 *Poly.* What] Q1–3,
F, D; What Q4.   119 these] F, D; this Q1–4.   119 midnight-
consultations] Q1–2, F, D; Midnight Consultations Q3–4.   122 good.]
Q1–2, F, D; ~ , Q3–4.   128 their] Q1, Q3–4, F, D; there Q2.   131
s.d. *Kneeling*] Q3–4, F, D; *kneeling* Q1–2.   132 lie] Q1–2, F, D; Lye
Q3–4.   132 hear] Q1, Q4, F, D; here Q2–3.   133 thy] Q1–4, D; they
F.   138 *Leon.* O] F; O Q1–4, D (Oh D).   138 w' not] Q1, F; wo'nt
Q2–4; wo'not D.   144 shall] Q1–3, F, D; all Q4.

V, i

1 thou?] Q1–4, D; ~ , F.   2 Yes,] Q1–3, D; ~ . Q4, F.   3 Gentlemen ride] Q1–2; Gentleman rid Q3–4.   5 'em] Q1–3, F, D; them Q4.
33 Father] Q2–4, F, D; Fathet Q1.   67 be the] Q1–3, F, D; be a Q4.
71 What,] Q1–4, D; ~∧ F.   71 ungrateful?———But] D; ungrateful?
——— / ———But Q1–4, F.   79 follow] Q2–4, F, D; follôw Q1.   80
Now] *starts a new line in Q1–4, F.*   83 *naiveté*] *naivete* Q1–4, F, D.
83 let me die] Q4, F, D; let me die Q1–3.   84 s.d. *Aside*] Q2–4, D (~ .
Q3–4, D); *aside* Q1, F.   86 Madam] Q2–4, F; ~ , Q1, D.   87 *figure*]
figure Q1–4, F, D.   89 *Naiveté*] *Naivete* Q1–4, F, D.   94 s.d. *To*
Melantha] *to Melantha* Q1–4, F, D (*To* Q4, D; ~ . Q3–4, D).   94 die]
Q1–4, F; dye D.   98 *figure*] figure Q1–4, F, D.   100 to the] Q1–3,
F, D; the Q4.   103 s.d. *Princess*] Q1–2, F, D; ~ . Q3–4.   104 *Bévue*]
Beveue Q1–4, F, D.   105 *Éclaircissement*] *Eclaircissement* Q1–4, F, D.

109 *tendre*] tender Q1-4, F, D. 113 you.)] Q3-4; ~ʌ) Q1-2, F, D. 114+ *s.d. led*] Q1, Q4, F, D; *lead* Q2-3. 116 *figure*] figure Q1-4, F, D. 117 *étourdy*] etourdy Q1-4, F, D. 118-119 *Palm. . . . Leonidas!*] one line in Q*1-4*, F, D. 119 *Leon.*——] ~ .ʌ Q1-4, F, D. 122 Oh] Q1-4, D; O! F. 126 *s.d. Holding*] Q2-4, D; *holding* Q1, F. 126 *s.d. her*] Q1-2, F; ~ . Q3-4, D. 128 *s.d. Turning*] Q2-4, D; *turning* Q1, F. 128 *s.d. angrily*] Q1-2, F; ~ . Q3-4, D. 134 *désespéré*] desesperé Q1-4, F, D. 141 *J'enrage!*] l'enrage Q1, F, D (~ . F); 'enrage! Q2; l'enrage! Q3-4. 142 *êtes*] étes Q1, F, D; ètes Q2-4. 145 *A d'autres, a d'autres*] Ad' autres, ad' autres Q1-4, F, D (ad . . . ad F). 146 *s.d. Cries.*] D; cries! Q1, F; Cries! Q2-4. 148 *qu'il*] Q1-3, F, D; qu'el Q4. 149 Pursue] F; pursue Q1-4, D. 152 *minouet*] minouét Q1-4, F, D. 154 him:] Q1-3, D; ~ . Q4, F. 157, 158, 159 *séjours*] sejours (Sejours l. 158 Q1-2) Q1-5, F, D. 160, 163 Let] *does not begin a new line in Q1-4, F, D.* 168 *Cabarets*] Q1, F, D; Caberets Q2-4. 169 *éveillé*] eveille Q1-4, F, D. 170 *tendre*] tender Q1-4, F, D. 171+ *s.d. speaks.*] Q1-3, F, D; ~ʌ Q4. 174 that——] ——that Q1-4, F, D. 180 *gayeté*] Q1-3, F, D; gayetè Q4. 180 *esprit*] Q1-2, F, D; esperit Q3-4. 187 *s.d. hat*)] Q1-2, F; ~ .) Q3-4, D. 200 from] Q1, Q3-4, F, D; form Q2. 203 henceforward] Q1, Q3-4, F, D; hence forward Q2. 209 room] ~ , Q1-4, F, D. 212 in] Q1-3, F, D; into Q4. 215 *Dor.*] Q1-3, F, D; ~ʌ Q4. 221 comes——] ~ . Q1-4, F, D. 226 Love] F, D; love Q1-4. 233 wear] Q1, Q3-4, F, D; were Q2. 233 Husband.] Q1-4, F; ~ , D. 234 wear] Q1, Q3-4, F, D; were Q2. 235 them] Q1-4, D; 'em F. 238 is the] Q1-2, F, D; is a Q3-4. 240 if that] Q1-3, F, D; if it Q4. 263 one] Q1, Q3-4, F, D; on Q2. 266 together;] ~ , Q1-4, F, D. 272 grapes] Q1-4, F; ~ ; D. 272 line;] F; ~ , Q1-4, F, D. 281 fair] Q1, F, D; fare Q2; far Q3-4. 282 her,] Q1, Q3-4, F, D; ~ʌ Q2. 289 come and catch] Q1-4, D; catch F. 289 taking] Q1-3, F, D; a taking Q2-4. 290 *s.d. Aside*)] Q1-2, F; ~ .) Q3-4, D. 291 an] Q1-3, D; and Q4; en F. 291 ere] Q1-4, F; e'er D. 291 further.] D; further. [*Aside.* Q1-4, F. 292 *s.d. Doralice*] *Doralice* Q1-4, F, D (~ . Q3-4, D). 292 Cry you] Q1-3, F, D; Cry your Q4. 313 *Danger-field*] F; Danger-field Q1-4, D. 315 fools,] Q1-3, F, D; ~ . Q4. 320-321 that I] Q1-3, F, D; I Q4. 322 *Dor.*] Q1-2, F, D; *Pal.* Q3-4. 323 there's] Q1-3, F, D; there is Q4. 324 in ye] Q1-3, F, D; in you Q4. 326 discover'd.] Q1-4, D; ~ , F. 331 *s.d. To Rhod.*] *to Rhod.* Q1-4, F, D (*To* Q2-4). 333 *Rhodophil.*] Q1, Q3-4, F, D; ~ , Q2. 336 are] Q1-2, Q4, F, D; art Q3. 345 shooting.] Q1-3, F, D; ~ , Q4. 350 so?] Q2-4; ~ . Q1, F, D. 358 both be] Q1-2, F, D; be both Q3-4. 358 cut.] F; out? Q1-4, D (~ . Q2-4, D). 360 propriety.] Q1-2, F, D (~ : Q2); Property. Q3-4. 363 as by] Q1-4, D; as F. 364 but one] Q1-3, F, D; one Q4. 369 *Palam.*] Q1; *Palm.* Q2; *Pal.* Q3-4; *Pala.* F, D. 370 *Macduff*] D; *Machduff* Q1-4, F. 373 hear] Q1, Q3-4, F, D; here Q2. 373 more.] Q1-3, F, D; ~ʌ Q4. 376 begg'd.] Q1, Q3-4, F, D; ~ , Q2. 381 thy] Q1, F, D; the Q2-4. 390 *s.d. off,*] Q1-4, D; ~ . F. 391 innocence?] ~ ! Q1-4, F, D. 395 seek?] ~ ! Q1-4, F, D. 396 vengeance!] Q1, F, D; ~ . Q2-4. 401 'em?] Q1-3, F, D; ~ : Q4. 409 you.] Q1, Q3-4, F, D; ~ʌ Q2. 410 *s.d. Aside.*] Q2-4, F, D; ~ʌ Q1. 411 true.] Q1-4, D; ~ʌ F. 411

s.d. as in Q4, F, D; *centered on a separate line, with final bracket, in Q1–2;*
flush right but with final bracket in Q3.   412 Hear] Q1, Q3–4, F, D;
Here Q2.   421 Nay, then] Q1, F, D; ~ˌ ~ˌ Q2; ~ˌ ~ , Q3–4.   424
say] Q1–2, F, D; ~ , Q3–4.   425+ s.d. off.] Q1–4, D; ~ ; F.   434
cure.] Q1–4, D; ~ , F.   434 *Arte.——*] ~ ·ˌ Q1–4, F, D.   435–436
may have / More] may / Have more Q1–4, F, D.   436 s.d. follows] Q1–
2, F, D; *follow* Q3–4.   436+ s.d. swords.] Q1–4, D; ~ , F.   443 moment;] Q1–4, D; ~ ? F.   444 But,] Q1–3, F, D; ~ˌ Q4.   452+ s.d.
victorious;] ~ . Q1–4, F, D.   455 Heav'n] Q1–4, D; Heaven F.   467
This] Q1–3, F, D; This is Q4.   476 injury's] injuries Q1–4, F, D.   477
O] Q1–4, D; Oh F.   479 before.] Q1–4, D; ~ ! F.   483 cheeks,]
Q1, F, D; ~ . Q2–3; ~ˌ Q4.   485 blushes.—] Q1, F, D; ~ˌ— Q2–4.
486 were] Q1–3, F, D; are Q4.   488 and] Q1–3, F, D; and, and Q4.
489 prayers] Q1–4, D; Pray'rs F.   493–494 *printed partly as verse*
(. . . his / Majesty . . . Royalty / Becomes . . .) *in Q1–4, F.*   495 nothing.]
Q1, Q3–4, F, D; ~ : Q2.   497 was such] Q1–3, F, D; was Q4.   497,
499, 500 *figure*] figure Q1–4, F, D.   505 affected. [*Aside.*] affected. Q1–
4, F, D.   506 s.d. To] Q3–4; *to* Q1–2, F, D.   506 s.d. Rhodophil]
Q1–4; ~ . F, D.   508 s.d. To Amalthea)] Q1–3; ~ ~ .) Q4, F, D.   510
desert,] Q1–4, D; ~ˌ F.   510 we give] Q1, F, D; give Q2–3; I give Q4.
511 Brother's] Q1–3, F, D; Brothers Q4.   512 Till] Q1–4, F; 'Till D.
516 repair'd,] Q1–2, F, D; ~ . Q3–4.   521 all I hope] Q1–3, F, D; all
hope Q4.   527 not] Q1–3, F, D; no Q4.   528 you] your Q1–4, F, D.
528 trouble.] Q1, F, D; ~ , Q2–4.   529 s.d. Aside.] Q1–3, F, D; ~ˌ Q4.
530 fairest,] Q1, D; ~ . Q2–4; ~ˌ F.

Epilogue: Epilogue.] Q1–4, F, D; *Epilogue to Mr.* Moon. Os2–3 (*by Mr.*
Os2b; Mohun Os3); Epilogue to yᵉ Same M1.   2 *Reformation:*] Os2–3;
~ . Q1–4, F, D; ~ , M1.   4 *compose;*] ~ . Q1–4, Os2–3; ~ : F, D; ~ ,
M1.   5 *Poets*] F, D, Os2–3, M1; Poet's Q1–4.   6 *indifference:*] ~ .
Q1–4, F, D; ~ ; Os2–3; ~ , M1.   7 *examples*] Q1–4, F, D, M1; example
Os2–3.   7 *drawn*] Q1–4, F, D, Os2–3; borne M1.   8 *hear, and see*]
Q1–4, F, D; see and hear Os2–3, M1.   8 *the*] Q1–4, F, D, Os2–3; our M1.
9 Rhodophils] Q1–4, F, D, M1; *Rhodophis* Os2–3.   9 *Theatre,*] Q1–3,
F, D, Os2–3; ~ . Q4; ~ˌ M1.   10 fear.] Q1–4, F, D, Os2b; ~ : Os2a,
Os3; ~—— M1.   11 *too*] Q1–4, F, D, Os2–3; to M1.   12 done.]
Q1–4, F, D; ~ : Os2–3; ~ , M1.   13 would] Q1–4, F, D, Os2a, Os3, M1;
wood Os2b.   13 *Women's*] M1; Woman's Q1–4, F, D; Women Os2–3.
13 *frailty*] Q1–4, F, D; faulty Os2–3; frailties M1.   14 *stript*] Q1–3, F,
D, Os2–3, M1; strip Q4.   14 *there.*] Q1–3, F, D, Os2–3; ~ , Q4, M1.
15 *are*] Q1–4, F, D, M1; were Os2–3.   16 one.] Q1–4, F, D, Os2a, Os3;
~ ; Os2b; ~ , M1.   17 *Wits*] Q1–4, F, D, Os2–3; Witt M1.   17 *bent*]
Q1–4, F, D, Os2a, Os3, M1; lent Os2b.   18 *treat*] Q1–4, F, D, M1; fret
Os2–3.   18 complement:] Q1–4, F, D; ~ . Os2–3; ~ˌ M1.   19 *Hus-*
bands] Q1–4, F, D, M1; Husband Os2–3.   20 Mell,] F; Mell, Q1–4, D,
Os2–3, M1 (~ . M1).   21 *each of*] Q1–4, F, D, M1; of Os2–3.   22
Gallant.] Q1–4, F, D, Os2a, Os3; ~ : Os2b; ~ˌ M1.   24 *off*] Q1–4, F,
D, Os2–3; out M1.   24 *stuff:*] Q1–4, F, D; ~ . Os2–3; ~ , M1.   25
not,] Q1, F, D, M1; ~ . Q2; ~ ; Q3–4, Os3; ~ˌ Os2.   26 were] Q1–4,
F, D, M1; are Os2–3.   26 *Plot:*] Q1–4, F, D; ~ . Os2–3; ~ , M1.   28
when] Q1–4, F, D, Os2–3; as M1.   28 short.] Q1–3, F, D, Os2–3; ~ ,

Q4, M1.   30 *friend.*] Q1–4, F, D, Os2; ~ , Os3, M1.   31 *Court*] Q1–
4, F, D, M1; Town Os2–3.   31 *and*] Q1–4, F, D; nor Os2–3, M1.   31
Town] Q1–4, F, D, M1; Court Os2–3.   32 *I*] Q1–4, F, D, Os3, M1; O
Os2.

The Assignation

The Assignation: or, Love in a Nunnery was first published in 1673 (Q1;
Macd 78a) and was reprinted in 1678 (Q2; Macd 78b) and in 1692 (Q3;
Macd 78c). It was also reprinted in Dryden's *Comedies, Tragedies, and
Operas* (1701), I, 515–554 (F; Macd 107ai–ii [two issues, the differences not
affecting this play]), and in Congreve's edition of Dryden's *Dramatick
Works* (1717), III, 271–357 (D; Macd 109ai–ii [two issues, the differences
not affecting this play]). Both Q2 and Q3 were set from copies of Q1, F and
D from copies of Q2. Since there is no evidence that Dryden revised the
text, the copy text for the present edition is the Clark copy of Q1 (*PR3417.
E1), emended as shown in the footnotes.

The song in Act III was separately printed as follows: H., V., *London
Drollery*, 1673 (Wing H147; Os1), p. 2; *Methinks the Poor Town has been
troubled too long*, 1673 (Wing M1939; Os2), p. 12; 2d ed., 1673 (Wing
M1940; Os3), pp. 34–35; [Playford, John], *Choice Songs and Ayres for One
Voyce . . . The First Book*, 1673 (Wing C3920 and P2465; Fs1), p. 59; [Play-
ford, John], *Choice Ayres, Songs, & Dialogues*, 2d ed., 1675 (Wing P2462;
Fs2), p. 50; anr. ed., 1676 (Wing P2463; Fs3), p. 50. Wing lists another edition of *Choice Ayres*, 1684, in the British Library (P2464), but he appears
to be in error; the volume in question is probably his P2461. Fs1–3 give a
musical setting by Robert Smith.

The following copies of the various editions have also been examined:
Q1: Texas (Aj.D848.673n2; Aj.D848.673a2a), Yale (Plays 326.Ij.D848.690D),
Folger (D2241); Q2: Clark (*PR3412.E1.1678), Yale (Ij.D848.673Asb), Fol-
ger (D2242 bd. w. D2327c3); Q3: Clark (*PR3417.E1.1692; *PR3410.C93;
*PR3410.C94); F: Clark (*fPR3412.1701 [2 cop.]; *fPR3412.1701a); D: Clark
(*PR3412.1717 [2 cop.], *PR3412.1717a); Os1: Clark (*PR1209.L84); Os2:
British Library (11633.de.39); Os3: Harvard (25252.9*); Fs1: British Library
(K.7.i.20); Fs2: British Library (K.7.i.21); Fs3: British Library (K.7.i.19).

Press Variants by Form

Q1
Sheet B (inner form)
Uncorrected: Folger, Yale
Corrected: Clark, Texas (2)
Sig. B2
I, i, 81   h'll] he'll

Sheet H (outer form)
Uncorrected: Texas (cop. 1; cop. 2 lacks leaf), Yale
Corrected: Clark, Folger

Sig. H3
    IV, iv, 131 hast dealt] has dealt
                                        Sheet L (inner form)
    Uncorrected: Clark
    Corrected: Folger, Yale, Texas (2)
Sig. L1*v*
    V, iv, 238 it,]~ .

                                Q2
                        Sheet A (inner form)
    Uncorrected: Clark
    Corrected: Yale, Folger
Sig. A2
    Dedication, 319:2 Playes] Plays
                        319:10 it e're it,] ~ , ~ ~∧
Sig. A4
    Dedication, 321:34 despetate] desperate
                322:1 orhers] others

                                Q3
                        Sheet G (inner form)
    Uncorrected: Clark (cop. 1)
    Corrected: Clark (cop. 2, 3)
Sig. G3*v*
    V, ii, 74–75 and discover to you that *Lucretia* and I have no resemblance,
                but only in our Misfortunes] I will hide my Face, and not look
                upon you, to convince you that I know you

Dedication: 319.2 Dedicating Playes] *Dedicating Playes* Q1–3, F, D.
319:2 Duel] *Duel* Q1–3, F, D.   319:8 Comedy] *Comedy* Q1–3, F, D.
319:13 it] Q1, Q3, F, D; in Q2.   319:17 Fortune] F, D; fortune Q1–3.
319:27 will] Q1, Q3, F, D; well Q2.   320:3 Epistle] *Epistle* Q1–3, F,
D.   320:14 War,)] Q1, Q3; ~ .) Q2, D; ~∧) F.   320:27 fari] Q1–3,
F; *fariut* D.   320:32 an innocent] Q1–2, F, D; innocent Q3.   321:3
such] Q1–2, F, D; on such Q3.   321:7 or of] Q1–3, D; or F.   321:11
Giants] Q3; *Giants* Q1–2, F, D.   321:12 vacancies] Q3, F, D; vacances
Q1–2.   321:12 Maps] *Maps* Q1–3, F, D.   321:31 Bankrupt] Q3, F,
D; Bancrupt Q1–2.   322:5 of] Q1–3, D; of being F.   322:6 Proselites.
They wou'd] Q1–3, D; Proselytes; F.   322:6 much good] Q1–3, F; much
D.   322:9 at] Q1–3, D; at a F.   322:12 till] Q1–3, F; 'till D.   322:
13 been] Q2–3, F, D; ~ , Q1.   322:14 for a] Q1–2, F, D; for Q3.
322:21 Latine] Q3, D; Latine Q1–2, F.   322:30 better.] Q1, Q3, F, D;
~∧ Q2.   322:33 if] Q1, Q3, F, D; it Q2.   323:4 Fastidious] *Fastidius*
Q1–3, F, D.
    Prologue: 26 Poet] Q1–2, F, D; Poets Q3.   30 Mamamouchi] D;
Mamamouchi, Q1–3, F.   35 Hullibabilah da] F, D (de F); *hullibabilah
da* Q1–3 (*de* Q2).   35 Chu, chu, chu] F, D; *Chu, chu, chu* Q1–3.   36
Marabarah sahem] F, D; *Marabarah sahem* Q1–3.   36 ye] you Q1–3, F,
D.   37 Oh how we love the Mamamouchi!] *Oh how we love the Mama-
mouchi!* Q1–3, F, D (Mamamouchi F, D).

Dramatis Personae: Persons Represented] Q1–3, F; Dramatis Personae
D.   By] Q1–3; MEN. By F; MEN. D.   *D inserts* WOMEN *above
names of actresses.*   *Mario–*] Q1–2; ~ . Q3; ~— and F (and *between the
actresses' names*); ~ˬ D.

I, i

S.d. a Room.] D; *ROME.* Q1–3, F.   7 *Aurelian*] Q1–2, F; *Aurelia*
Q3; *Aur.* D.   15 Glass sayes] Q2–3, F, D; Class sayes Q1.   18 *Aurelian*] F; *Aurelia* Q1–3; *Aur.* D.   19 I . . . have?] *set as a line of verse
in Q1–3, F.*   20+ s.d. *[He]* F, D; ˬ~ Q1–3.   23 I!] ~ ? Q1–3, F, D.
37 send] F; sent Q1–3, D.   41 Rogue] Q1, Q3, F, D; Rouge Q2.   53
hear . . . sing.] Q1, Q3, F; here . . . ~ , Q2; here . . . ~ . D.   53+ s.d. *[He]*
F, D; ˬ~ Q1–3.   56 ye] Q1–2, F, D; you Q3.   61+ s.d. *[He]* Q3, F,
D; ˬ~ Q1–2.   65 time] Q1–3, F; Tune D.   65+ s.d. *[As]* F, D; ˬ~
Q1–3.   66 then] Q1, Q3, F, D; than Q2.   81 he'll] *some copies of
Q1 have* h'll.   81 you.] Q1, Q3; ~ : Q2, F, D.   94 him.] Q3, D; ~ ,
Q1–2; ~ˬ F.   106 Society] Q2–3, F, D; Socitey Q1.   108 Sisters]
Q3, F, D; *Sisters* Q1–2.   110 it,] Q1, Q3; ~ ; Q2, F, D.   126 be
gone] Q1–2, F, D; begone Q3.   127 *Jupiter.*] Q1–2, F, D; ~ , Q3.
148 from] Q1, Q3, F, D; form Q2.   150 Carnival] Q1, Q3; Carnivals
Q2, F, D.   151+ s.d. *[Exeunt]* F, D; ˬ~ Q1–3.   152 say.] F, D; ~ :
Q1–3.   156 I'll] Q1–3, D; to F.   167 be trusted] Q1–2, F, D; stbe
trued Q3.   167 much as] Q3, F, D; much Q1–2.   173 *there's*] Q1,
Q3; *there* Q2, F, D.   177 are] Q1–2, F, D; ars Q3.   184–185 now
am] Q1–2, F, D; am now Q3.   190 of the] Q1–2, F, D; of all Q3.   196
understood] Q1–2, F, D; understand Q3.   199 aware?] ~ ! Q1–3, F, D.
201 s.d. *[Aside]* F, D; ˬ~ Q1–3 (*no space preceding; followed by next
sentence on same line in Q1–3, F*).   210 seen him lately] Q1–2, F, D;
lately seen him Q3.   215 hearsay] D; heresay Q1–3, F.   242 sweet-
est] Q1–3, D; sweeter F.   242 s.d. *[Exeunt]* F, D; ˬ~ Q1–3.

II, i

ACT] Q3, F, D; ~ . Q1–2.   s.d. Princes Page] *Princes Page* Q1–3, F,
D.   1 Father's] Q3, F, D; Fathers' Q1; Fathers Q2.   23 *Almaine*]
Q3, D; Almaine Q1–2, F.   24 tun'd] Q1–2, F, D; turn'd Q3.   36
Courtship] Q1, Q3, F, D; Court ship Q2.   37+ s.d. *Nunnery.*] Q3, F,
D; ~ˬ Q1–2.   45 chatting] Q1–3, D; Cheating F.   47 Nunnery?]
~ . Q1–3, F, D.   48 *Torr'*] *Torre* Q1–3, F, D.   49+ s.d. *right justi-
fied in Q1–3, F, D (with bracket preceding in F, D).*   50 you,] Q3; ~ˬ
Q1–2, F, D.   52 be but] Q1–3, F; be D.   52 when you] Q1, Q3, F,
D; when yon Q2.   55 never yet] Q1–3, F; never D.   58+ s.d.
[Exeunt] F, D; ˬ~ Q1–3.   58+ s.d. *The . . . approach.*] *centered on sep-
arate line in Q1–3, F, D.*   59 to] D; to Q1–3, F.   68 till] Q1–3, F;
'till D.   73 But,] Q1, Q3; ~ˬ Q2, F, D.   81 *Luc.*] Q1, Q3, F, D;
Duc. Q2.   82 s.d. *[The]* F, D; ˬ~ Q1–3.   84 Page] *Page* Q1–3, F, D.
86 *Asca.*] Q1, Q3, F, D; ~ˬ Q2.   95 Your] Q2, F, D; You Q1, Q3.
111 *Hip.*] Q1, Q3, F, D; ~ , Q2.   118+ s.d. *[They]* F, D; ˬ~ Q1–3.
157 s.d. *[Bell]* Q3, F, D; ˬ~ Q1–2.   160 Prayers] Q2–3, F, D; Prayets
Q1.   164+ s.d. *[Exeunt* Women] ˬ*Exeunt Women* Q1–3, F, D ([~ F,
D; *Woman* Q2).   177 s.d. *[Exeunt]* F, D; ˬ~ Q1–3.

II, ii

5 objection is] Q1, Q3; objection's Q2, F, D. 9 *Aur.*] Q1, Q3, F, D; ~ , Q2. 20 till] Q1–3, F; 'till D. 27 scape] Q1–2, F, D; 'scape Q3. 30 *s.d. [Exit]* F, D; ∧~ Q1–3. 32 *s.d. [Exeunt.]* D; ∧~ . Q1, Q3; ∧~∧ Q2; *omitted from F.*

II, iii

11 O speak] Q1, Q3; Speak Q2, F, D. 12 made] Q1–2, F, D; make Q3. 14 then.] Q1, Q3; ~ , Q2, D; ~ ; F. 30 Damsel] Q1–2, F, D; Damosel Q3. 46 one] Q1, Q3, F, D; on Q2. 49 *s.d. by the*] Q1–3, F; *by her* D. 57 yet] Q2–3, F, D; yer Q1. 61+ *s.d. [They]* F, D; ∧~ Q1–3. 62–74 *Vio. . . . joyes.*] *as prose in Q1–3, F, D* (will . . . a thousand . . . too . . . forbear . . . and all . . . that . . . from). 71 hours] Q1–3, F; Hour D. 80 E're] Q1, Q3, D; E'er Q2, F. 97 both?] Q2, F, D; ~∧ Q1; ~ . Q2. 97+ *s.d. again.*] Q1–2, F, D; ~∧ Q3. 99 it were] Q1, Q3; 't were Q2, F, D. 100 fingers] Q1, Q3; finger's Q2, F. 102 tho' it] Q3, F, D; th' it Q1; tho i' Q2. 131 thy] Q1–3, D; they F. 138, 139 *Éveillez*] Eveillez Q1–3, F, D. 140 *la tete*] Q1–3, D; *le tete* F. 146+ *s.d.* Women] *Women* Q1–3, F, D. 147 This way, this way.] Q1–3, D; This way. F. 150 till Q1–3, F; 'till D. 174 *[Playes]* Q3, D; ∧~ Q1–2, F (*s.d. centered on separate line*). 175 *Benito:*] Q1–2, D; ~ . Q3, F. 176 *la*] Q1, Q3; *le* Q2, F, D. 178+ *s.d. right justified in Q1–3, F, D* (*bracket preceding in F, D*). 180 'em.] F, D; ~ : Q1–3. 198+ *s.d. [Exeunt]* F, D; ∧~ Q1–3.

III, i

ACT] Q3, F, D; ~ . Q1–2. *s.d. The Front*] Q1–3, F; SCENE *The Front* D. *s.d.* Ascanio,] Q1–2, D; ~∧ Q3, F. 1 Brother.] Q3, F, D; ~ , Q1–2. 14 did,] Q1, Q3; ~ ; Q2, F, D. 18 could] Q2–3, F, D; Could Q1. 22 *Hip.*] Q1, Q3, F, D; ~ , Q2. 22 *Lucretia* is] Q1, Q3; *Lucretia's* Q2, F, D. 24 *s.d. [Ascanio]* F, D; ∧~ Q1–3. 34 scape] Q1–2, F, D; 'scape Q3. 47 defiance] Q3, F, D; defyance Q1–2. 53–54 actions.] *period missing in some copies of Q1.* 68–69 *last sentence on a separate line in Q1–3, F.* 72 die] Q1–2, F, D; dye Q3. 88 *jusqu'au*] *jusqu'a* Q1–3, F, D. 90 How will] F, D; How, Will Q1–3. 92 Page] *Page* Q1–3, F, D. 101 at] Q1–3, D; at the F. 103 abaters] F; abettors Q1–3, D. 104 it] Q1, Q3, F, D; is Q2. 105 who is] Q1, Q3; who's Q2, F, D. 105 Weapon] Q1–3, D; Weapons F. 108 she is] Q3; she Q1; she's Q2, F, D. 114 courtesy] Q2–3, F, D; courtisy Q1. 115 the other] Q1, Q3, D; th' other Q2, F. 128 *Cam.*] Q1, Q3, F, D; ~ , Q2. 158 from] Q1, Q3, F, D; form Q2. 165 Workiday rough-hewn] Q2, F, D; Workiday-rough-hewn Q1; Workiday-rough hewn Q3. 171 See,] Q1–2, F, D; ~∧ Q3. 187 honour,] Q1–2, F, D; ~∧ Q3. 201 Dreaming!] Q1, Q3; ~ ? Q2, F, D. 210 hours.] Q1–2, F, D; ~∧ Q3. 219+ *s.d. Manet*] F, D; Manet Q1–3. 226+ *s.d. within.*] Q1, Q3, F, D; ~ , Q2. 227 *her Cloaths.*] Q2–3, F, D; ~ ~ , Q1. 228 I] Q1–3, F; and D. 232 Sir.] Q1, Q3, F, D; ~∧ Q2. 267 *Ben.*] Q1, Q3, F, D; ~ , Q2.

270 *Fron.*] Q1, Q3, F, D; ~ , Q2. 274 are a] Q1–3; are F, D. 295+
s.d. [He] Q3, D; ∧~ Q1–2, F (*s.d. centered*). 307 rapt] Q1–2, F, D;
wrapt Q3. 308 go] Q1–2, F, D; grow Q3. 324 Frontona.]] ~ .
Q1, Q3; ~ ,] Q2, F; ~ .] D. 340 further] Q1–2, D; farther Q3, F.
341 henceforward] Q1, Q3, F, D; hence forward Q2. 348 *Cam.*] Q1,
Q3, F, D; ~∧ Q2. 349 on,] Q1–2, F, D; ~∧ Q3. 355 I'll] Q2–3,
F, D; I'lll Q1. 357 *s.d. [Exit]* D; ∧~ Q1–3, F. 359 alwayes] Q1,
Q3, F, D; aways Q2. 362 fortune.] Q1, Q3, F, D; ~∧ Q2. 362+
s.d. [Exeunt.] F (*without bracket*); *omitted from Q1–3, D.*

III, ii

SCENE] Q2–3, F, D; ~ . Q1. *s.d.* Hippolita] Q1–2, F, D; Hippolito
Q3. 7 Singing.] Q1, Q3, D; ~ , Q2, F. 10–11 are. / At] are: at
Q1–3, F, D. 11 *s.d. [Aside.]* D; ∧~ Q1–3, F (~∧ Q3). 17+ *s.d.*
SONG *and* DANCE.] Q1–3, F, D; *A New Song.* Os1; *Song in Love in a
Nunnery.* Os2–3; *no title* Fs1–3. *Stanzas not numbered in Os2–3.* 18
Love] Q1–3, F, D, Os1; *hope* Os2–3, Fs1–3. 19 *consented*] Q1–3, F,
D, Os1, Os3, Fs1–3; *lamented* Os2. 20 *that*] Q1–3, F, D, Os2–3, Fs1–3;
the Os1. 20 *discover,*] Q1–3, F, D, Os2–3, Fs1–3; ~ . Os1. 23
Shamefac'd] Q1–3, F, D, Os2–3, Fs1–3; shameface Os1. 24 *from*] Q1,
Q3, F, D, Os1–3, Fs1–3; *form* Q2. 25 *Ice I am,*] Q1–3, F, D, Os2–3,
Fs1–3; I see, I am Os1. 26 *my own*] Q1–3, F, D, Os2–3, Fs1–3; mine
own Os1. 27 *and let*] Q1–3, F, D; *and bid* Os1–3, Fs1–3. 27 *her:*]
Q1–2, F, D; ~ . Q3, Os1; ~ , Os2–3; ~ ; Fs1–3. 28 *Powers*] Q1–3, F,
D, Os1–3; pow'rs Fs1–3. 29 *to*] Q1–3, F, D, Os2–3, Fs1–3; *of* Os1.
30 *when*] Q1–3, F, D, Os1–3, Fs2–3; whom Fs1. 31 *Bid 'em*] Q1–3,
F, D; Let 'em Os1; *Let them* Os2–3, Fs1–3. 32 *it is*] Q1–3, F, D, Os1–3,
Fs1–2; is it Fs3. 33 *That Fire which burns*] Q1–3, F, D, Os1; *Those
flames that burn* Os2–3, Fs1–3. 33 *Heart*] Q1–3, F, D; Soul Os1–3,
Fs1–3. 35 *But if*] Q1–3, F, D; *If that* Os1–3, Fs1–3, 35 *this Night
he*] Q1–3, F, D, Os2–3, Fs1–3; then he might Os1. 37 *ere*] Q1–2; e're
Q3, F, Os1–2, Fs1–3; e'er D; e'r Os3. 38 *I'me*] Q1–3, F, D, Os2–3, Fs1–
3; I am Os1. 39 *After*] Q1–3, D; *Duke, after* F. 39 I must] Q1–3,
D; must F. 51+ *s.d. [Duke]* ∧~ Q1–3, F, D (*s.d. centered in Q1–3, D;*
Duke Q1–2, F, D). 52 you.] Q1, Q3, F, D; ~ , Q2. 57 there] Q1,
Q3, F, D; their Q2. 74 aside.] Q1–2, D; ~ , Q3; *omitted from* F. 74
till] Q1–3, F; 'till D. 76 *Colonne?*] Q2, F, D; ~ ; Q1, Q3. 77 have
seen] Q1–2, F, D; have Q3. 84 *Duke.*] Q1–2, F, D; *Duc.* Q3. 84 not
she] Q1–3, D; not F. 86–87 enter'd. Her] Q1–2, F, D; enter'd her Q3.
100 *Roman*] Q3, D; Roman Q1–2, F. 100 *Dutch*-woman] D; Dutch-
woman Q1–3, F. 111 *Duke.*] Q1, Q3, F, D; ~ , Q2. 116 speak.]
Q1, D; ~∧ Q2–3, F. 117–118 *second sentence begins on same line as
first in Q1–3, F, D.* 123 it in] Q1–3, D; in F. 143 her.] Q1, Q3,
F, D; ~ , Q2. 144+ *s.d.* Hippolita.] Q1, Q3, F, D; ~ : Q2. 146
ere] Q1–2; e're Q3, F; e'er D. 147 she?] Q1–2, F, D; ~ , Q3. 163 it]
in some copies of Q1 the i *is in the line above.* 166 must] Q3; must
must Q1; must, must Q2, F, D. 166 *s.d. [Exit]* Q3, F, D; ∧~ Q1–2.
170 *Fred.*] Q2–3, F, D; ~∧ Q1. 171 to] Q2–3, F, D; too Q1. 171
s.d. [Exeunt] Q3, F, D; ∧~ Q1–2.

III, iii

III.] Q1, Q3, F, D; .3 Q2.   *s.d.* Lucretia] Q1–3, F; *Enter* Lucretia D.
5   wide World] Q1–2, F, D; wide Wide Q3.   8   opportunity] Q2–3, F,
D; opportun y Q1.   10   my] Q1–3, D; a F.   22+   *s.d. [Here . . . away.
Exit.*] F; *Here . . . away. [Exit.* Q1–3 *(first sentence centered)*; *[Here . . . away.*
D.   26   *s.d. [Clock]* F, D; ∧∼ Q1–3.   26   *s.d.* strikes.] Q1, Q3, F, D;
∼∧ Q2.   40   wicked;] Q1, Q3, D; ∼ ? Q2, F.   56   hasty,] Q1, Q3, F,
D; ∼ . Q2.   61   for,] Q1, Q3; ∼∧ Q2, F, D.   72   make] Q1–2, F, D;
makes Q3.

IV, i

ACT] Q3, F, D; ∼ . Q1–2.   *s.d. A*] Q1–3, F; SCENE *A* D.   *s.d.* Fred.]
Q1–3, F; *Enter* Frederick D.   10   *s.d. [Gives]* F, D; ∧∼ Q1–3.   16
has] Q1–2, F, D; hath Q3.   22   me.] Q3, F, D; ∼ , Q1–2.   23+   *s.d.*
[The] Q3, F, D; ∧∼ Q1–2.   23+   *s.d.* Prince] Q2–3, F, D; prince Q1.
36   it to] Q1–2, F, D; to Q3.   39   Now, now] Q1–2, F, D; ∼ . ∼ Q3.   41
Robe] Q1–2, F, D; Rob Q3.   42+   *s.d. [Frederick running . . . down.]*
∧*Fred. Running . . . down.* Q1–3, F *(Frederick* Q3; *centered in all);* ∧*Fred.*
[Running . . . down.] D.   43   *Fred.* Sir] Sir Q1–3, F, D.   53+   *s.d.*
[Ascanio] F, D; ∧∼ Q1–3.   54   *Duke*] Q1, Q3; ∼ . Q2, D; ∼ , F.   55
Fred.] Q3, F, D; *Fre.* Q1–2.   55   better,] Q2–3, F, D; ∼ . Q1.   57
perhaps,] Q1, Q3, F, D; ∼ . Q2.   58   *Milan*] Q3; *Millan* Q1–2, F, D.
61   *s.d. on line below in Q1–3, F, D.*   70   *Duke*,] Q1; ∼∧ Q2, F; ∼ .
Q3, D.   72   *s.d. [Opens]* F, D; ∧∼ Q1–3.   73   *nights*] Q1, Q3, F, D;
night Q2.   99   remember] Q1–2, F, D; ∼ , Q3.   104   from] Q1–3,
D; of F.   108   inclos'd.] Q1–2, F, D; ∼ , Q3.   108   *s.d.* Duke] *Duke*
Q1–3, F, D.   123   *s.d. Exeunt.*] Q2, Q3 *(some copies)*, D; ∼∧ Q1, Q3
(some copies); omitted from F.

IV, ii

S.d. Camillo, Aurelian] Q3 (Camillo *and* Aurelian); *Camillo, Aurelian*
Q1–2, F, D.   4   sake, then,] Q1, Q3, F; ∼ , ∼∧ Q2; ∼∧ ∼∧ D.   11   be
a] Q1–2, F, D; a Q3.   24   Sir, no Plot;] Q1, Q3; ∼ : ∼ ∼ , Q2; ∼ , ∼ ∼ ,
F; ∼ ; ∼ ∼ , D.   24   you?] Q1, Q3; ∼ . Q2, F, D.   34   miserable.]
Q1, Q3, F, D; ∼∧ Q2.

IV, iii

S.d. Valerio] Q1, Q3, F, D; Valeria Q2.   *s.d. Musick, in*] ∼ . *In* Q1–3,
F, D.   1   *Valerio*] F, D; *Valeria* Q1–3.   3   Miracle.] Q2–3, F, D; ∼ ,
Q1.   18   *Mar.*] Q1, Q3, F, D; ∼∧ Q2.   19   *s.d.* Sophronia.] Q2–3, F,
D; ∼ , Q1.   21   Cloysteral] Q1–2, F, D; Cloysterial Q3.   25   *Cam.*]
Q2–3, F, D; ∼∧ Q1.   26   *Aur.*] Q1–3, D; ∼ , F.   37+   *s.d.* Sophronia]
Q3, F, D; Sophonia Q1–2.   39   *s.d. Screaking*] screaking Q1–3, F; Shreik-
ing D.   48   permitted,] Q1, Q3, F, D; ∼ . Q2.   55   Monastery] Q1–2,
F, D; Monastry Q3 *(Q3 uses this spelling for both prose and verse).*   57
aside] Q1, Q3, F, D; side Q2.   60   habit:] ∼ . Q1–3, F, D.   65   it,]
Q1; ∼ : Q2, D; ∼ . Q3, F.   66   wishes.] Q1, Q3; ∼ : Q2, F, D.   67–68
that's / All my Converse] D; that's all my / Converse Q1–3, F.   98–100
two lines in Q1–3, F, D (noble / To Q1–3; Noble / to F; to / Destroy D).

104 Luc.———] ~ .ᴧ Q1–3, F, D.   106 hope] Q1–2, F, D; ~ ; Q3.
111 *Duke.*———] ~ .ᴧ Q1–3, F, D.   112 e're] Q1, Q3; e'er Q2, F, D.
115–117 *Luc.... Chastity.*] *two lines in Q1–3, F, D* (ᴧYou ask ... / Nor ...
you know ...).   124 hope;] Q1–2, F, D; ~ . Q3.   130–133 *as prose
in Q1–3, F* (when ... of all ... betray ... and I).   129 me?] ~ ! Q1–3,
F, D.   130 base,] ~ . Q1, Q3; ~ ? Q2, F, D.   132 fame?] F; ~ : Q1–
3, D.   136 till] Q1–3, F; 'till D.   140–141 *as verse in Q1–3, F, D*
(little. / I ... Letter / I).   141 *Hippolita;*] Q1, Q3; ~ ! Q2, F, D.   142
know it,] Q1–2, D; ~ , ~ᴧ Q3; ~ᴧ ~ᴧ F.   150 *s.d. Exit.*] *Exeunt.* Q1–3,
F, D (~ᴧ Q2, F).

IV, iv

9 selves.] Q3, F, D; ~ , Q1–2.   10 one, how] F; ~ . How Q1–3, D.
12 inclin'd.] Q1–2, F, D; ~ , Q3.   29 negligence.] Q1, Q3, F, D; ~ ,
Q2.   33 mischief?] Q2, F, D; ~ . Q1, Q3.   41 Madness] Q2–3, F,
D; Maddess Q1.   61 him———] Q1, Q3; ~ ?——— Q2, F, D.   65
your] Q1–2, F, D; you Q3.   65–66 *sentences not on separate lines in
Q1–3, F, D.*   66 *s.d. Aside.*] Q1, Q3, F, D; ~ᴧ Q2.   78 Madam?]
Q1, Q3; ~ , Q2; ~ ; F; ~ ! D.   79 do.] Q3, F, D; ~ , Q1–2.   85–86
agreeable] Q1–3, D; suitable F.   87 out!] Q1, Q3; ~ . Q2, F, D.   90
Luc.] Q1, Q3, F, D; *Duc.* Q2.   90–91 *sentences on separate lines in Q1–3,
F.*   95 to't] Q1–2, F, D; too't Q3.   110 she is] Q1–3, D; she's F.
131 has dealt] *some copies of Q1 have* hast dealt.   141 House.] Q1–2,
F, D; ~ , Q3.   142 Madam.] Q1, Q3, F, D; ~ᴧ Q2.

IV, v

SCENE] Q2–3, F, D; ~ . Q1.   5–7 *I ... Tiber*] F; *all romans Q1–3;
romans and italics reversed in D.*   8 see.)] Q1–2, F, D; ~ᴧ) Q3.   9–10
Bring ... Violetta] F; *romans and italics reversed in Q1–3, D* (Violetta D).
11 you hear that] Q1, Q3; your hear Q2, D; you hear F.   24+ *s.d.
[Exit]* F, D; ᴧ~ Q1–3.   39–40 Quintessence] Q2, F, D; Quintesence
Q1, Q3.   56 faces.] Q1, Q3, F; ~ , Q2; ~ ; D.   57 am I ... fool?]
Q1–2, F, D; I am ... ~ ! Q3.   63 you not] Q1–2, F, D; you Q3.   66
to be so] Q1, Q3, F, D; bto eso Q2.   71 *aside.*] Q1, Q3, F, D; ~ , Q2.
92 contented] Q1–3, D; content F.

IV, vi

12+ *s.d. [Aur.]* F, D; ᴧ~ Q1–3.   12+ *s.d.* Women] *Women* Q1–3,
F, D.   15 voice.] F, D; ~ , Q1–3.   18+ *s.d. [All go off. A]* Q1–3, D
(ᴧ*All* Q1–3); [*Exeunt omnes.* / [*A* F.   18+ *s.d. After ... re-enter*] *part
of the preceding stage direction in F.*   21 escape?] Q2, F, D; ~ , Q1,
Q3.   25 where] Q1–3, D; when F.   31–32 be / Caught in] D; be
caught / In Q1–3, F.   33+ *s.d. [Exeunt]* F, D; ᴧ~ Q1–3.

V, i

ACT] Q3, F, D; ~ . Q1–2.   19 knit———] ~ . Q1–3, F, D.   19
your] Q1, Q3, F; our Q2, D.   42 heaven] Q1–3; Heav'n F, D.   51
commerce.] Q1, Q3; ~ ; Q2, D; ~ : F.   61 *Camillo*] Q1 (*text*); ~ , Q1
(*catchword*), Q2–3, F, D.   72–73 *one line in Q1–3, F, D* (make).   73+
s.d. [Kisses] D; ᴧ~ Q1–3, F.   73+ *s.d.* Lau. and Vio.] Q3, F, D; *Lau.*

and Vio. Q1–2.   80–81   *prose in Q1–3, F, D* (ᴧIn . . . will).   81   *s.d.*
[*Exit*] F, D; ᴧ~ Q1–3.   89   *s.d.* [*Exit*] F, D; ᴧ~ Q1–3.   93+   *s.d.*
[*Exit*] F, D; ᴧ~ Q1–3.

V, ii

S.d. all] Q1–3, F; *And all* D.   5   for,] Q1, Q3; ~ᴧ Q2, F, D.   7   die
of] Q1–3, D; die with F.   13   makes a] Q1–3, F; makes D.   16   *Austin-
Fryers*] *Austin-Fryers* Q1–3, F, D.   21   Now] *starts a new line in Q1–3, F.*
21   *Benito,*] Q1, Q3, F, D; ~ . Q2.   26   Sister] Q1–3, F; Sister's D.
29–30   those . . . Thieves] Q1, Q3, F, D; thoses . . . Thieve Q2.   34+
s.d. Guards] *Guards* Q1–3, F, D.   34+   *s.d.* Torches.] Q1, Q3, F, D; ~ :
Q2.   36+   *s.d.* [Aurelian . . . Dukes Guards . . . Servants] ᴧ~ . . . *Dukes
Guards . . . Servants* Q1–3, F, D.   40   Carnival] *Carnival* Q1–3, F, D.
48+   *s.d.* [Duke] F, D; ᴧ~ Q1–3.   52   'em?] Q1–2, F, D; ~ : Q3.   68
set as a line of verse in Q1–3, F.   74–75   I will hide my Face, and not look
upon you, to convince you that I know you] *uncorrected copies of Q3 have*
and discover to you that *Lucretia* and I have no resemblance, but only in
our Misfortunes (*cf. ll. 71–72*).   75+   *s.d.* Benito] Q2–3, F, D; *Benito*
Q1.   77–78   deliver'd.] Q1, Q3, F, D; ~ , Q2.   85   *Mar.*] Q1, Q3, F,
D; ~ , Q2.   96   I] *failed to print in Q3.*   101   our] Q1–2, F, D; your
Q3.   107+   *s.d.* [*As*] Q3, D; ᴧ~ Q1–2, F (*line centered*).   109+   *s.d.*
[*Runs*] Q3, F, D; ᴧ~ Q1–2.   109+   *s.d.* Duke] *Duke* Q1–3, F, D.   111
for] Q1 (catchword), Q2–3, F, D; ~ , Q1 (text).   119+   *s.d.* [Aurelian]
F, D; ᴧ~ Q1–3.   131   which] Q1–2, F, D; that Q3.   142   alone.] Q2,
F, D; ~ , Q1, Q3.   143–147   *as verse in Q1–3, F, D* (. . . / She spoke . . . /
She demur'd . . . / And somewhat . . . / Engagement . . . / I).   143   Assig-
nation,] Q1, Q3, F, D; ~ . Q2.   167   *s.d. at end of preceding sentence in
Q1–3.*   167   *s.d.* Guards] *Guards* Q1–3, F, D.

V, iii

9–10   *one line in Q1–3, F, D.*   9   Fred.] Q1, Q3, F, D; ~ , Q2.   9
Heaven] Q1–3, F; Heav'n D.   22   attended?] Q1–2, F, D; ~ ! Q3.   33
me.] Q1, Q3, F, D; ~ , Q2.   36   question.] Q1, Q3, F, D; ~ᴧ Q2.   37
s.d. Souldiers] *Souldiers* Q1–3, F, D.   46   thanks] Q1–3, D; Thank F.

V, iv

S.d. Lucretia] Q1–3, F; *and* Lucretia D.   16–17   noble / Dealing from]
noble dealing / From Q1–3, F, D.   20   trust your] Q1–2, F, D; trust you
Q3.   22   Duke.] Q1–2, F, D; ~ , Q3.   27   *Duke.*] Q2–3, F, D; ~ᴧ Q1.
41   Lion's] Q1–2, F, D; Lion' Q3.   42–43   *one line in Q1–3, F, D* (a
tender).   54   Duke.] Q1–2, F, D; ~ , Q3.   55   you.] Q2, F, D; ~ , Q1,
Q3.   67   stoln] Q1, Q3; stolen Q2, F, D.   70   throbbing] F, D; throbing Q1–3.   77   ask me,] Q1–3, D; ask, F.   80   Keep] Q1–3, F; Keep
still D.   94   Virgin-honour] Q1, Q3; Virgin honor Q2, F, D.   96
tryal,] Q2–3, F, D; ~ . Q1.   107   I wonnot,] Q1, Q3, F, D; ~ ~ . Q2.
115+   *s.d.* in] Q1–3, F; at D.   116–117   *as prose in Q1–3, F, D* (they).
118+   *s.d.* Valerio.] Q1, Q3, F, D; ~ , Q2.   119–121   *as prose in Q1–3,
F, D* (and . . . away).   122   Monastery] Q1–2, F, D; Monastry Q3.
123–124   *as prose in Q1–3, F, D* (to).   125–130   *as prose in Q1–3, F, D*
(to be . . . and cowardise . . . were . . . o're).   135–138   *as prose in Q1–3,*

F, D (fit).   142 th'] Q1–3, D; the F.   143 Rival?] F, D; ~ : Q1–3.
145 And] Q1, Q3; ~ , Q2, F, D.   155 ———I] ∧~ Q1–3, F, D.   164
ev'n . . . hurry'd] Q1–2, F, D; even . . . hurr'd Q3.   178 Sacrifice.] Q1, Q3;
~ : Q2, F, D.   199–200 *Duke*. . . . difficulty;] *on one line in Q1–3, F, D*
(∧You . . . to help).   208 come, . . . blessings,] Q1–2, D; ~∧ . . . ~ , Q3;
~∧ . . . ~∧ F.   211 duty] ~ . Q1–3, F, D.   212 Father.] D; ~ ? Q1–
3, F.   220 *s.d. [Exeunt]* F, D; ∧~ Q1–3.   222 pardon,] Q2–3, F, D;
~ . Q1.   230 *Aur.*] Q1, Q3, D; *Aul.* Q2, F.   238 it.] *some copies of
Q1 have comma.*   239 it] Q1, Q3, F, D; is Q2.   246 Musick] Q3,
F, D; *Musick* Q1–2.   246 the one] Q1–2, F; one Q3, D.   246 other.]
Q1–2, F, D; ~∧ Q3.   251 Musick] Q3, F, D; *Musick* Q1–2.   256
e'en] Q2–3, F, D; een Q1.   259 Nunnery] F, D; *Nunnery* Q1–3.   264
Lucretia.] Q3, F; ~ : Q1–2, D.   275+ *s.d. [Exeunt.] omitted from Q1–3,
F, D.*

Epilogue: 14 Play] *Play* Q1–3, F, D.   14 *to*] Q1, Q3, D; *too* Q2, F.
15 *but yet*] Q1–2, F, D; *but* Q3.

APPENDIX

Vaughan's Commendatory Poem

[John, Lord Vaughan (1640–1713), later 3d Earl of Carberry, was reported by Pepys (16 November 1667) to have been "one of the lewdest fellows of the age, worse than Sir Charles Sidley." Dryden later dedicated *Limberham, or The Kind Keeper* to him.]

On Mr. Dryden's Play, The Conquest of Granada

TH' applause I gave among the foolish Croud,
Was not distinguish'd, though I clap'd aloud:
Or, if it had, my judgment had been hid:
I clap'd for Company as others did:
Thence may be told the fortune of your Play,
It's goodness must be try'd another way:
Let's judge it then, and, if we've any skill,
Commend what's good, though we commend it ill:
There will be Praise enough: yet not so much,
As if the world had never any such:
Ben Johnson, Beaumont, Fletcher, Shakespear, are
As well as you, to have a Poets share.
You who write after, have besides, this Curse,
You must write better, or, you else write worse:
To equal only what was writ before,
Seems stoln or borrow'd from the former store:
Though blind as *Homer* all the Antients be,
'Tis on their shoulders like the Lame we see.
Then, not to flatter th' Age, nor flatter you,
(Praises though less, are greater when they'r true)
You'r equal to the best, outdone by you;
Who had outdone themselves, had they liv'd now.

Vaughan.

INDEX TO THE COMMENTARY